A HISTORY
OF
THE ROMAN PEOPLE

second edition

Fritz M. Heichelheim,
Cedric A. Yeo, Allen M. Ward

Eastern Kentucky University   *University of Connecticut*

PRENTICE–HALL, INC., ENGLEWOOD CLIFFS, NEW JERSEY 07632

Library of Congress Cataloging in Publication Data

HEICHELHEIM, FRITZ M. (Fritz Moritz), 1901–1968.
 A history of the Roman people.

 Bibliography: p. 526
 Includes index.
 1. Rome—History. I. Yeo, Cedric A. II. Ward,
Allen Mason   III. Title.
DG209.H5 1984   937   83–13880
ISBN 0-13-392118-2

Editorial supervision and interior design: Serena Hoffman
Cover design: George Cornell
Manufacturing buyer: Ron Chapman

ISBN 0-13-392118-2

PRENTICE-HALL INTERNATIONAL, INC., *London*
PRENTICE-HALL OF AUSTRALIA PTY. LIMITED, *Sydney*
EDITORA PRENTICE-HALL DO BRASIL, LTDA., *Rio de Janiero*
PRENTICE-HALL CANADA INC., *Toronto*
PRENTICE-HALL OF INDIA PRIVATE LIMITED, *New Delhi*
PRENTICE-HALL OF JAPAN, INC., *Tokyo*
PRENTICE-HALL OF SOUTHEAST ASIA PTE. LTD., *Singapore*
WHITEHALL BOOKS LIMITED, *Wellington, New Zealand*

Contents

Part Two
The High Point of the Roman Republic

Part Three
The Late Roman Republic

XIV THE GRACCHI AND THE STRUGGLE OVER LAND REFORM, 133 TO 121 B.C. 155

XV THE BREAKDOWN OF THE SYSTEM, 121 TO 88 B.C. 167

XVI MARIUS AND SULLA: CIVIL WAR AND REACTION, 88 TO 78 B.C. 181

XVII PERSONAL AMBITIONS AND PUBLIC CRISES, 78 TO 60 B.C. 190

XVIII THE RISE OF CAESAR, 60 TO 52 B.C. 209

XIX CAESAR WINS AND IS LOST, MID-50s TO 44 B.C. 218

XX THE LAST DAYS OF THE REPUBLIC, 44 TO 30 B.C. 232

XXI LIFE AND CULTURE IN THE LATE ROMAN REPUBLIC, CA. 100 TO CA. 30 B.C. 249

Part Four
The Early Roman Empire

XXVII CLAUDIUS, NERO, AND THE END OF THE JULIO-CLAUDIANS, A.D. 41–68 327

XXVIII THE CRISIS OF THE PRINCIPATE AND RECOVERY UNDER THE FLAVIANS, A.D. 69–96 340

XXIX THE FIVE "GOOD" EMPERORS, A.D. 96–180 352

Part Five
The Transformation and Dissolution
of the Roman Empire

Preface

Fritz M. Heichelheim, who originally conceived this book, died only six years after it first appeared. The fact that it has remained in print for over twenty years speaks for itself. We could offer no finer tribute to the man who inspired it. During the past twenty years, however, the study of ancient Rome has been one of the most dynamic fields in the disciplines of classics and history. New facts have been discovered, different interpretations of the data have been advanced, and shifts in emphasis within the classroom have occurred. Therefore, a revised edition is needed to keep *A History of the Roman People* abreast of the times.

One of the previous edition's great virtues was a style comprehensible to the average American undergraduate without a sacrifice in substance. We have kept that feature throughout. The chapters, however, have been broken down into smaller units that will not overwhelm the student's ability to absorb new material and that instructors can easily incorporate into daily assignments. We have also given greater emphasis to interpretive themes both within and among the individual chapters. By so doing, we hope to give students a deeper understanding of the reasons for the changes and developments that took place over the long period of time that Roman history embraces and to provide a firmer basis for further discussions in the classroom. Nevertheless, we have maintained, and even underscored, the book's chronological organization because most undergraduates are not familiar enough with the basic data of Roman history to avoid being confused by a purely topical approach.

Within this framework, we have included much more material on social and cultural history, along with the political and economic matters that dominated the previous edition. Some may still lament the lack of excerpts from the works of Roman authors in the discussions of literature, but passages taken out of context from larger works seldom make sense to students unfamiliar with them. Therefore, it seemed much more practical to present an adequate interpretive background against which to view relevant works.

Unfortunately, the requirements of space and economy have necessitated a reduction in the total number of illustrations. This is particularly regretable in the discussions of art and architecture, but the text should give students a grasp of basic principles that will enhance the value of classroom slides or illustrations in other assignments. On the other hand, we have significantly increased the number of maps to make the geographical context of historical events more comprehensible to students unfamiliar with the ancient world. Finally, we have extended the coverage of events to include the more than two-hundred years between the deaths of Constantine the Great and Justinian, for not until well after Constantine does the Roman Empire begin its final dissolution, and not until Justinian's failure to restore the Empire to its former borders in the West does the permanence of the breakup become clear.

We should like to take this opportunity to thank all who have taught us in the past, and also our own students and colleagues, who have been sounding boards for our ideas over the years. Special thanks are owed to Professor Sarah B. Pomeroy of Hunter College and to Professor Kurt A. Raaflaub of Brown University, who carefully read over our manuscript and offered valuable suggestions for improvement throughout. Finally, we are deeply grateful for the patience, cooperation and support of the staff at Prentice-Hall, particularly editors Steven Dalphin and Serena Hoffman.

Cedric A. Yeo
Allen M. Ward

I

The Foundations
of Early Rome and Italy

Most people remember Rome chiefly for its great empire, whose culture and ultimate disintegration immensely affected the development of modern western European nations and the civilization that they founded. To understand how the Roman Empire and its culture were created, however, it is necessary first to understand the geographic, demographic, and ethnic conditions that shaped the development of Rome from a primitive village in prehistoric Italy to the urban republic whose confederacy embraced all the peoples of Italy. That accomplishment gave the Romans the resources and outlook that helped them to conquer the greater part of western Europe, much of the Ancient Near East, and most of North Africa and unite them into a single political and cultural entity.

Geography Around 750 B.C., when archaeological evidence shows that the nucleus of the later city was forming on the site of Rome, advanced civilization was only just beginning in Italy. To the east, Greece, Crete, and the Aegean islands had already had a brilliant period of high civilization from roughly 2000 to 1200 B.C. under the Minoans and Mycenaeans, who had been located closer to the earlier centers of civilization in the Ancient Near East and Egypt. It simply took longer for the influence of civilization to spread west to Italy. Nevertheless, despite this initial geographic disadvantage, Italy was geographically favored to dominate the Mediterranean Sea and the older centers of civilization around its eastern basin.

First, Italy juts out like a giant pier from the continental mass of Europe southeastward 750 miles into the middle of the Mediterranean. Therefore, it and its geological extension, the island of Sicily, separated from it only by the narrow strait of Messana (Messena, Messina) and from North Africa by a mere ninety miles of water, naturally dominate the sea lanes that link the eastern and western Mediterranean basins and the lands around them. Accordingly, before the rise of greater powers to the north and west, strategically and economically the power that controlled Italy was in an ideal position for dominating the whole Mediterranean world.

Second, Italy enjoyed internal geographic advantages that made it possible for a single city to unite it and become strong enough to use its great strategic and economic advantages overseas. Although the Apennine mountains cut through Italy in a great arc swinging

Italy
in the 6th Century B.C.

Areas dominated by

Greeks

Etruscans

out from the northwest southeastward along the Adriatic coast and then back to the southwest coast along the Tyrrhenian Sea, they are not a serious barrier to internal unity. On the average they are 4000 to 6000 feet high and are pierced by numerous easy passes. Moreover, the plains of Italy and Sicily were among the largest and best agricultural areas in the Mediterranean world.

Bounded by the Alps on the north and northwest and by the Apennines on the south, the northern or continental part of Italy is a vast alluvial plain watered by the Po and Adige rivers. On the west coast, between the Apennines and the Tyrrhenian Sea are the wide lowland plains of Etruria, Latium, and Campania, fertilized by a layer of volcanic ash and weathered lava ejected by the many volcanoes that had been active in earlier geologic times. These plains are watered by the Arno, the Tiber, the Liris, and the Volturnus, which were easily navigated by small ships in ancient times and provided convenient communication between the coast and the interior. These fertile plains supported dense populations that made Italy, in Vergil's words, the "mother of men,'' the main source of ancient military might.

Wood and Mineral Resources   The physical geography of Italy also made available other valuable resources. Although ancient Italy was not rich by modern standards, it was for its time. Until they were over cut in the late first millennium B.C., extensive forests provided abundant wood for fuel and timber for ships and buildings. The most abundant mineral resources were stone building materials— granite, sandstone, marble, basalt, limestone in the form of tufa, and volcanic pozzolana for making cement. Etruria not only possessed these resources but also was the area richest in metals important for the ancient economy. It produced lead, zinc, mercury, copper and tin and controlled most of ancient Italy's iron ore on the island of Elba.

The Site of Rome   Geographically, Rome was ideally situated to unite Italy and take full advantage of her resources and strategic position. It was centrally located on the naturally favored west coast fifteen miles up its largest river, the Tiber, on the northern edge of Latium. Here the Tiber is slowed somewhat by an island in midstream, which provides the first convenient bridgehead nearest the river's mouth. Also at this point seven hills ranging from two to three-hundred feet above sea level rise above the river's east bank and make the site easily defensible. The hills nearest the Tiber are the Capitoline, the Palatine, and the Aventine, separated from each other by intervening valleys. Further to the east and enclosing them in a kind of arc stand the other four: the Quirinal, Viminal, Esquiline, and Caelian. On these seven hills stood the later city of Rome. Two other hills across the river, the Janiculum and Vatican, were ultimately incorporated too.

The ancient Romans are said to have given much of the credit for the greatness of the city to the Tiber River (Livy 5.45.5). Although the importance attributed to the Tiber alone can be exaggerated, it was significant. In early times the Tiber and its valley were important routes for bringing salt from the coast into central Italy. Eventually Rome became Italy's largest river port, although sandbars at the Tiber's mouth prevented the city from being a major ocean port. On the other hand, Rome was safe from naval attack, and the river served as a barrier against attacks from the north, while its valley gave Roman armies easy access to central Italy.

Rome also possessed ''a site uniquely adapted to the growth of a city,'' as Livy remarked. There were excellent building materials nearby: tufa, peperino, and travertine, all easily quarried and shaped with the simplest tools, as well as selce for paving streets and pozzolana for making cement. As already noted, Rome possessed in Tiber's midchannel an island that afforded the most convenient locality for a bridge to span the river. Her central geographic position in Italy made her the focal point of the main routes of communication running up, down, and across the peninsula—communications which permitted her armies, with minimum expenditure of effort, to strike in almost any direction at will. The seven hills made possible the observation of enemy movements, and the proximity of the hills to one another facilitated the fusion of several village communities into a single state, ultimately the largest in area and population in all Italy. As a river port, bridge town, road center, and magnet of trade and population, Rome was thus favored by nature to be the capital of a unified Italy and, given Italy's central location and large population, seat of a Mediterranean empire.*

The Peoples of Pre-Roman Italy
Population is another factor that cannot be ignored as a source of political and cultural strength. The population of Italy by the beginning of the Roman Republic (ca. 500 B.C.) was the product of a diverse ethnic and cultural heritage that stretched back thousands of years. The Romans recognized part of this diversity in their own early legends, which, for

* See Cary, *Geographical Background of Greek and Roman History*, pp. 132–133.

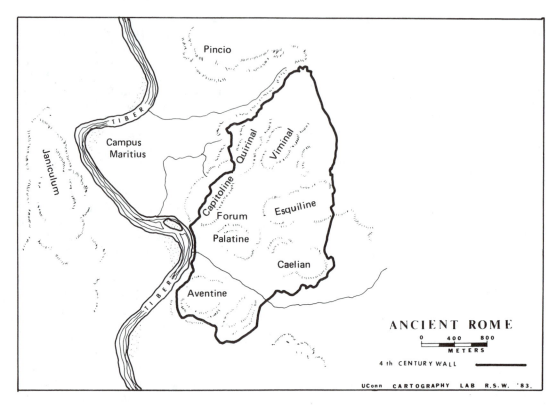

ANCIENT ROME

0   400   800
METERS

4 th CENTURY WALL

UConn CARTOGRAPHY LAB R.S.W. '83.

example, told how Romulus attracted settlers to Rome by establishing a place of asylum for exiles and outcasts from all over Italy; how these men stole their first wives from the neighboring Sabines; how an Etruscan immigrant named Tarquin rose to become the fifth king of Rome; or how the powerful Sabine Attus Claudius and his whole clan of four thousand relatives and dependents added their strength to Rome's in return for citizenship.* This recognition of their own heterogeneous origins, as opposed to the highly exclusive attitude of the ancient Greek city-states, allowed the Romans to assimilate other people and unite Italy into a strong federation based on an unusual degree of equality and fairness for ancient times.

*Livy (2.16.4) gives his name as Attius Clausus, but Attus and Claudius are both early Sabine names as revealed by ancient inscriptions and are probably the correct names of the founder of the Claudian *gens* at Rome. Among his descendents the name Attus was Latinized to Appius.

Neolithic and Bronze-Age Peoples, 3000 to 1000 B.C.   Immigrants had been bringing the basic elements necessary for advanced civilization into Italy since sometime around 3000 B.C., when Neolithic farmers seem to have crossed the Adriatic and settled on the southeastern shore, where they introduced the cultivation of wheat and barley and the breeding of cattle and sheep. By 1800 B.C. immigrants from central Europe had arrived in the Po River Valley and introduced the Bronze Age in Italy by bringing with them the technique of mixing melted copper with tin to produce bronze, an alloy used to make sharper and harder tools and weapons than could be made from stone and copper.

The best known and most interesting people of the Italian Bronze Age migrated from what is now Hungary to northern Italy around 1700 B.C. They are called Terramaricoli, from *terramara* (black earth), which the modern peasants of the region used to dig up from the mounds of decayed refuse that marked the sites of their villages. The Terramaricoli brought significant skills and cultural features that gave them distinct advantages over the other peoples of northern and central Italy: superiority in the production of field crops (flax, beans, and two varieties of wheat); breeding of livestock (cattle, sheep, pigs, and horses); skill and ingenuity in making pottery; and superiority in the craft of bronze casting and the manufacture of bronze tools and weapons such as sickles, axes, chisels, daggers, and swords. Finally, they introduced into Italy the custom of cremation and perhaps an Indo-European language.*

Eventually, the Terramaricoli were joined by the people of the Apennine culture, semi-nomadic herdsmen who entered Italy in small bands on the west and southeast coasts by way of the Ionian Sea. They too probably spoke an Indo-European language, one that became the ancestor of those spoken by the Apennine tribes of historical times. They established close commercial and cultural relations with the Terramaricoli and helped to spread their influence south.

Early Iron-Age Peoples, 1000 to 750 B.C.
The Villanovans provided the transition from the Bronze Age to the Iron Age in Italy between 1000 and 800 B.C. The Villanovan culture takes its name from Villanova, a small hamlet five miles northeast of Bologna, where it was discovered in its most typical form. The Villanovans built curved-sided huts, cremated their dead, and put the ashes into tall biconical urns first of earthenware and later of bronze. The earthenware urns were handmade, smoke-blackened vases decorated with incised geometrical patterns—meanders, rows of chevrons, and swastikas. Covered with inverted basins or bowls, they were placed in round holes or rectangular stone-lined tombs.

* The term Indo-European is a purely linguistic one used to identify the family of related languages that include Sanskrit in India, Persian, Armenian, the Slavic tongues, Greek, the Celtic dialects, the Germanic languages, English, Latin, and all the Latin-derived Romance languages.

Various tools and weapons and small ornaments such as brooches, bracelets, and razors were placed inside and around the tomb. These objects are the chief sources of information on the date and origin of the Villanovans.

Unfortunately, the evidence is inconclusive. Where the Villanovans actually came from is still undetermined. Some archaeologists assume that they were descendants of the Terramaricoli because of the similarity of burial rites; others believe that they came over the Alps, swept through the Po Valley without leaving a trace of their passage, and finally settled around Bologna. Against both opinions stands the fact that the first and oldest Villanovans lived not near Bologna, but in southern

A typical biconical cinerary urn for cremation burials in the Villanovan period.   (Courtesy Fratelli Alinari, Florence)

Etruria and northern Latium, including the site of Rome. This group was the Southern Villanovans. Some of them probably spread northward at a later date.

The Southern Villanovans used two kinds of funeral urns: (1) the standard biconical urn covered either with an inverted bowl as at Bologna or with a crested helmet of bronze or pottery, and (2) a hut-urn, a miniature imitation of their small, curved-sided houses. The shape and decoration of their vases, brooches, swords, and razors have led recent archaeologists to believe that the early Villanovans were an Indo-European-speaking people who made their way over the Adriatic Sea from the Balkans, later crossed the Apennines, and finally settled in Latium and Etruria sometime during the ninth century B.C.. The evidence, however, is very ambiguous, and many questions remain to be answered.

In southern Etruria and northern Latium, the Villanovans were neighbors of the Fossa People, an Indo-European-speaking people probably also of Balkan origin, who stretched along the west coast from Etruria south to Calabria. Those living right next to the Villanovans used the same or adjacent cemeteries but did not cremate their dead. Instead, they buried the dead in long rectangular pits or trenches, *fossae* (sing. *fossa*), lined with stones. Hence, archaeologists call them the Fossa People. Their culture, a blend of many elements—Balkan, Sicilian, Greek, and native Italic—was quite dynamic in its influence upon the southern Villanovans. Their water jug was probably a prototype of the Villanovan burial urn, and the geometric signs with which they decorated their pottery and scabbards—meanders, zigzag lines, swastikas, false spirals, and concentric circles—were freely used by both the Southern and Northern Villanovans.

The Ethnic Makeup of Italy ca. 500 B.C.

By the end of the sixth century B.C. the various prehistoric groups known only from archaeology had evolved or been transformed by the immigration of newer settlers like the Greeks into a number of different peoples identified in the written sources of Roman history. These inhabitants are the ones with whom the Romans interacted and who helped to shape the course of later Roman history. Their names will occur often in the next few chapters, and it will be helpful to review them.

Ligurians (Ligures) The Ligurians inhabited the northwest corner of Italy between the Alps, the Ticinus River, and the western flank of the Apennines down to the Arno River. They were largely descended from the early Neolithic inhabitants of the area but had received an admixture of Indo-European-speaking immigrants whose language caused Ligurian to develop into an Indo-European dialect. Their chief town was Genoa, but they never reached a high state of development and were often convenient targets for Roman commanders looking for easy triumphs in the second century B.C.

Veneti In the northeast, bounded by the Adige River, the Alps, and the Adriatic eastward to Histria (Istria) were the Veneti. They were descended from the people of an early Iron Age culture known as the Atestines. They were excellent metalworkers and spoke an Indo-European dialect closely related to Latin but written in a different alphabet.

Raeti The Raeti lived west of the Veneti in the mountains and in the valley of the Adige. Apparently they too spoke an Indo-European dialect. They were forced to keep to the mountainous districts by the aggressive Etruscans, who were pushing northwards.

Etruscans The Etruscans inhabited Etruria (Tuscany) between the Tiber and the Arno. By 500 they had also crossed the Apennines and occupied the valley of the Po from the Rubicon to Lake Maggiore. They were a non-Indo-European-speaking people and had developed a rich, powerful urban culture. Their impact on Rome and Italy was very great, and they will be treated more fully in the next chapter.

Piceni (Picentes) The Piceni inhabited Picenum in central Italy, on the east coast near Ancona. Descended in large part from Indo-European-speaking invaders from Illyria, they were a warlike and independent people. A number of the leading men of Picenum became important at Rome in the second and first centuries B.C., the most important of whom was Pompey the Great.

Latins On the west coast of central Italy south of the Tiber lies the fertile, well-watered plain of Latium, home of the Latins. They were another Indo-European-speaking group that had evolved out of the general spread of such speakers throughout most of Italy in the late Bronze and early Iron Age. Their dialect was one of the Italic group that predominated in the central Apennine region. The foothills of the Apennines in the east and the rolling central plain were ideal for herding and the cultivation of grain. The west was well forested and provided an abundant supply of wood for building and fuel. Accordingly, the Latins had grown in numbers and had developed many prosperous towns—Alba Longa (destroyed ca. 600 B.C.), Antium, Ardea, Aricia, Cora, Lanuvium, Lavinium, Pometia, Praeneste, Rome, Tibur, and Tusculum. Eventually, Rome would unite them all, and through Rome their Italic dialect would become one of the most important languages in the world.

Umbro-Sabellians Throughout the central Apennines, from the Rubicon in the north, where the mountains come close to the Adriatic at Ariminum (Rimini), and down to Campania, dwelt a group of tribes speaking related Italian dialects called Umbro-Sabellian. Among these tribes were the Umbrians, Vestini, Frentani, Sabines, Aequi, Marsi, Volsci, and Samnites. Though their family of Italic dialects was Indo-European, these dialects retained a large element of the non-Indo-European language spoken by earlier inhabitants of the region. The Umbro-Sabellians were primarily pastoralists and peasant farmers, whose constant need for more land to support their growing populations brought them into frequent and bitter conflict with the wealthier, more urbanized peoples of the neighboring plains, especially Latium and Campania, who also often sought to expand their own territories. The external history of Rome during the early Republic (509 to 264 B.C.) revolves primarily around wars with these neighboring tribes, particularly the Aequi, Marsi, Volsci, and Samnites.

Oscans and Iapygians Speakers of Oscan dwelt in Lucania and around Campania. They were largely descendants of an earlier non-Indo-European-speaking people. Nevertheless, even before the Samnites gradually moved into their territory and superimposed their Italic dialect, the Oscans may already have been influenced by earlier Indo-European-speaking migrants. Across the Apennines, along the lower Adriatic and around the Gulf of Tarentum, were several tribes known collectively as Iapygians. One of these tribes was the Massapii, who have given their name to the language of the Iapygians, Massapian. It too was Indo-European but was not part of the Italic dialect group.

Greeks All around the coast of southern Italy from the Bay of Naples to Tarentum, Greeks had established important colonies since the end of the ninth century. Several were prosperous trading centers and exercised significant cultural and economic influence upon the other peoples in Italy. They will be discussed further in the next chapter.

All these various peoples of diverse ethnic and geographic origins and having distinctive cultural heritages made up the population of Italy around 500 B.C. At this time, therefore, Italy was fragmented and disunified. But, as the descendants of these various peoples were absorbed into the Roman state through peaceful alliance or, most often, violent conquest, they merged into the Roman People (*Populus Romanus*).

II

Etruscans and Greeks
in Pre-Roman Italy

Most peoples of prehistoric Italy in the early centuries of the first millennium B.C. remained relatively primitive and underdeveloped. Two groups, however, began to exert a profound influence on the growth of complex civilization in Italy. These influences were especially important in Latium, particularly at Rome—the city that eventually united all of the peoples of Italy under its control. One group was the Etruscans, who inhabited Etruria across the Tiber from Latium; the other was the Greek colonists who began to settle south of Latium by the middle of the eighth century B.C. in Campania and along the rest of the southern Italian coast around to Tarentum. In fact, so many Greeks settled in southern Italy and Sicily that the area became known as *Magna Graecia* (Great Greece).

Etruria Etruria is bounded by the Arno River on the north, the Tiber River to the east and south, and the Tyrrhenian Sea on the west. Geographically it falls roughly into northern and southern halves. In the north there are fertile river valleys, plains, and rolling sandstone or limestone hills. The southern part is wilder and rougher, shaped by the actions of volcanoes, wind, and water. The soft,

volcanic stone called tufa has been carved into deep valleys or gullies surmounted by peaks or small mesas on which many of the earliest Etruscan cities are found.

At a time when village life predominated in the largest part of Italy, except in *Magna Graecia,* the centers of Etruria had already become towns, and some of the towns were becoming cities. These cities were often built on Villanovan sites, sometimes on the coast or a river near it—Caere (Cerveteri), Tarquinii, Vulci, and Populonia—and sometimes inland —Volsinii, Orvieto, Clusium (Chiusi), Perugia, Arretium, and Faesulae. Ancient sources say that at their height the Etruscan people were leagued in a federation of twelve city-states, but to list their twelve cities is not easy since the various sources do not agree on the names. In addition to the towns just mentioned (which found a place in written history by fighting against the Romans), archaeology is constantly finding others.

Sources for Etruscan History Most modern knowledge of the Etruscans is derived from the ruins of their cities and, more particularly, their tombs. Tombs of all sizes, shapes, and types—the well and trench tombs of Villanovan times, the *tumuli,* those great mushroom-shaped, grass-covered mounds with bases of hewn stone, the circular stone vaults built into hillsides, and the corridor tombs cut out of rock—all these, whether containing pottery, metal wares, furniture, jewelry, or wall paintings, help to reveal the cultural life of the Etruscan people.

Roman writers from the first century B.C. and the first century A.D. preserve important information on late Etruscan religion, but there are none for earlier periods. Nearly ten thousand Etruscan inscriptions (some dating back to the seventh century B.C., others as late as the age of Augustus) have been found. Many can be translated with a fair degree of confidence, although the Etruscan language is not fully understood. They have not yet shed much light on early Etruscan political history because only about a dozen contain more than thirty words, and nearly all contain only long lists of proper names, religious formulae, dedications, and epitaphs. Nevertheless, useful social, religious, and cultural inferences can be made from their stylistic and statistical patterns.

The sounds of Etruscan words are known because they are written in a Greek alphabet apparently borrowed from the Greek colony of Cumae near Naples. Not enough different words and sentences occur, however, to link Etruscan positively with any other language. Most scholars agree that it is neither Indo-European nor Semitic, but no one knows what it is.

Little can be learned from ancient Greek and Latin sources either. The Greeks have little to say, other than to accuse the Etruscans of being scandalously fond of luxury. Cicero made some comments on their religious life, and Livy concentrated only on their wars with Rome.

Etruscan Origins The question of where the Etruscans originated has been generating speculation and controversy for at least twenty-five hundred years. According to the Greek historian Herodotus (ca. 460 B.C.), the earliest Etruscans were immigrants—Lydians from the west coast of Asia Minor—who sailed west to find a new homeland when their own

Etruscan tumuli at Caere (Cerveteri). (New York Public Library Picture Collection)

was suffering from famine (Book I.94). About 450 years later, another Greek historian, Dionysius of Halicarnassus (Herodotus' birthplace), took the opposite view in his *Roman Antiquities* (Book I.25–30) and claimed that the Etruscans were native to Italy.

Some modern historians have argued that the Etruscans migrated from central Europe before 1000 B.C. and settled in the Po valley and later in Etruria. This view has been largely rejected. On the other hand, there is much to support both those who favor Dionysius and say that the Villanovans developed into the Etruscans after contact with outsiders, and those who favor Herodotus and say that a small but significant number of advanced immigrants from the eastern Mediterranean led or drove the development of Etruscan civilization.

The archaeological record shows no abrupt invasion of any large group to account for Etruscan origins. Most Etruscan towns appear on or near earlier Villanovan sites without a radical break in the archaeological record that would indicate an invasion of new people. For example, as at Tarquinii (Tarquinia), one of the earliest Etruscan cities, different styles of burial and the kinds of objects found in graves appear as a progressive development from early Villanovan cremation and burial in simple urns to either cremation and burial or inhumation (burial of the whole body) in trench graves, with more luxurious grave goods in each case, and finally to the general practice of inhumation in elaborately decorated and furnished rock-cut chamber tombs, which are an outstanding feature of high Etruscan civilization.

On the other hand, the development of the urban culture that produced these rock-cut chamber tombs occurred so rapidly in southern Etruria that many think it not likely to have been brought about by the Villanovans alone. Contemporary Villanovan sites elsewhere in Italy show no such development. Therefore, it is entirely possible that about 750 B.C. a small but significant number of immigrants from the more culturally advanced eastern Mediterranean arrived in Etruria. Then,

through their possession of advanced weapons, superior administrative skills, and higher technology, they could have quickly achieved power and leadership among the local Villanovans, who would have soon adopted and modified their ways to create a new civilization.

The Etruscan Economy Whatever the ultimate answer to the question of Etruscan origins may be, Etruscan civilization could not have existed without the natural wealth of Etruria itself. The fertility of the soil and the mineral resources of the region were sources of great wealth. The Etruscans exploited these sources of wealth on a large scale through agriculture, mining, manufacturing, lumbering, and commerce.

The alluvial river valleys produced grain for domestic use and export and flax for linen cloth and sails. Less fertile soils provided pasture for cattle, sheep, and horses, while the hillsides supported vines and olive trees. As the population expanded, an ingenious system of drainage tunnels (*cuniculi*) and dams won new land by draining swamps or protected the old by checking erosion.

The Etruscans energetically exploited the rich iron mines on the coastal island of Elba and the copper and tin deposits on the mainland. At Populonium (Populonia) the iron ore from Elba was smelted into pig iron. The mining and refining of copper was carried on around Volaterrae (Volterra) and Vetulonium (Vetulonia). Many Etruscan cities exported finished iron and bronze wares, such as helmets, weapons, chariots, urns, candelabra, mirrors, and statues in return for other raw materials and luxury goods. They also made linen and woolen clothing, leather goods, fine gold jewelry, and pottery. Virgin forests of beech, oak, fir, and pine fueled the fires of Etruscan smelters, supplied wood for fine temples, houses, and furniture, and provided timbers for the ships of war and commerce.

Trade with Carthage, Sicily, Corcyra, Athens, Phoenicia, and Egypt kept Etruscan Italy in close contact with the advanced urban cultures of the Mediterranean world. It led ultimately to the introduction of a money economy in Italy and a standard coinage. The earliest coins found in Etruria were minted by Greek cities in Asia Minor. After 480 B.C. Etruscan cities began to issue their own silver, bronze, and gold coins.

Etruscan foreign trade was mainly in luxury goods and high-priced wares. It enriched the trading and industrial classes and stimulated among the upper class a taste for elegance and splendor. Accordingly, the Etruscans earned a reputation for excessive luxury among contemporary Greeks.

Etruscan Cities and Sociopolitical Organization The Etruscans developed several strong states, each centered on a rich and powerful city. For economic reasons, they built cities in fertile valleys or near navigable streams; for military reasons, they built on hilltops whose cliffs made them easily defensible. At first they fortified their cities by wooden palisades or earthen ramparts and then with walls of masonry, often banked with earth.

Inside the walls, the Etruscans seem to have laid out some of their cities on a regular grid plan, as the Greeks had begun to do. In some cases they appear to have centered the plan on two main streets intersecting at right angles like the *cardo* and *decumanus* of the later Roman military camp. The first buildings to go up were temples for the gods and palaces for the king. Then, as the population increased, side streets were paved, drains dug, and places built for public entertainment. These cities, as in Greece, were the political, military, religious, economic, and cultural centers of the various states that sprang up between the Tiber and the Arno before the seventh century B.C. Along the coast were Caere (Cerveteri), Tarquinii (Tarquinia), Vulci, Vetulonium (Vetulonia), Rusellae, and Populonium (Populonia); those were the oldest. With the possible exception of Veii to the south, such inland cities as Volsinii (Bolsena), Clusium (Chiusi), Perusia (Perugia), Cortona, and Arretium (Arezzo) were founded later and illustrate the growth and expansion of Etruscan civilization.

A dozen of the leading Etruscan cities formed a league primarily for the joint celebration of religious festivals. The jealousy of the member cities and their insistence on rights of sovereignty prevented the formation of a federal union which might have acted to repel aggression that later threatened to destroy them one by one. When events at last forced the cities to unite, it was too late.

During the early period, the executive power of the Etruscan city-states was in the hands of kings elected and assisted by councils of aristocratic chiefs, of whom they were colleagues. The king was the symbol of the state, commander-in-chief of the army, high priest of the state religion, and judge of his people. He wore purple robes and possibly a golden crown, and he rode in a chariot inlaid with ivory. As he passed through the streets, heralds preceded him and lictors accompanied him with the fasces and double-bitted ax—symbols of justice and religion. Yet he was neither a hereditary monarch nor an absolute ruler. Sometime during the sixth or fifth century B.C., the nobles stripped him of his political, military, and judicial powers, and set up republics governed by aristocratic senates and headed, as in Rome, by annually elected magistrates. The real power in the state was at all times in the hands of a small circle of landowning families who, having acquired or seized large tracts of the best land, became the landed aristocracy and enjoyed all the privileges of a warrior aristocracy and priestly class. In some cities they were later forced to share the government with a small group of wealthy outsiders who had won wealth and social standing through mining, craftsmanship, or commerce. The middle and lower classes consisted of small landowners, shopkeepers, petty traders, artisans, foreign immigrants, and the serfs or slaves of the wealthy.

Etruscan Family Life The most striking feature of early Etruscan society was a highly developed family life and the more or less equal status of women. Etruscan family life seems different from that of many cultures in the ancient world and almost unparalleled in Europe till the twentieth century. It was more comradely and integrated than the Greek, less patriarchal and authoritarian than the Roman, and not so inhibiting and ascetic as the early Christian. It was based on greater legal and social equality of father and mother, on comradeship and mutual respect between husband and wife.

The Etruscan woman was not a chattel or household drudge confined to her part of the house or denied her husband's company or respect. Nor was she idealized or placed on a pedestal, as in the romantic tradition of medieval chivalry or the cavalier tradition of the aristocracy of England and the Virginia Tidewater. The Etruscan wife, on the contrary, was accepted as a person in her own right. She was her husband's equal, his partner and companion. Children bore the names of both parents. The wife's tomb was often more splendid than the husband's; on covers of sarcophagi (coffins) her portrait statue was sculptured beside his, the one not inferior to the other in dignity and self-assurance.

The Etruscan woman often appeared in public with her husband. She went to religious festivals with him; unlike her Greek counterpart, she reclined beside him at public banquets. The common practice of decorating women's hand mirrors with words indicates a high degree of literacy among those who could afford these expensive items. Many Etruscan women also took a keen interest in sports, either as active participants or as spectators. Their presence at public games, where male athletes sometimes contended in the nude, made them appear worse than immodest to the Greeks, who usually forbade their women to witness such exhibitions. The Greeks probably also disapproved of the wearing of elaborate dresses by Etruscan women in public and their use of cosmetics, fine clothes, and jewelry to make themselves more alluring.

This respect and freedom accorded to Etruscan women may have had an impact on the development of the Roman family, where women also had a much higher standing than among many of the ancient Greeks.

Etruscan Culture and Religion   Although Etruscan as a spoken language persisted as late as the second century A.D. and

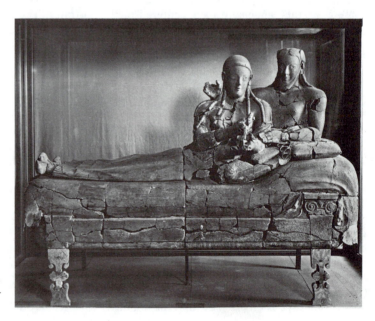

Clay sarcophagus from Caere ca. 500 B.C. (New York Public Library Picture Collection)

enough written materials survived till the first century to enable the Emperor Claudius I (41–54 A.D.) to write twenty books on Etruscan history, all the Etruscan literary works are lost. There were probably many works on religion and the science of divination and, perhaps, annals of families and cities. There were also some rustic songs and liturgical chants. If the Etruscans composed dramas or works on philosophy or science, no trace of them has been preserved or recovered.

If there was an intellectual vacuum in their society, the Etruscans redeemed themselves partially by their passion for music. They had a predilection for the flute, whose shrill strains accompanied all the activities of life—banquets, hunting expeditions, athletic events, sacrifices, funerals, and even the flogging of slaves. As flutists, trumpeters, and lyre players, they were renowned in Rome and throughout Greece. Dancing was also a major element of their culture. They danced at banquets, at religious festivals, and funerals. No matter what the occasion, they danced with ecstasy and abandon and with an almost orgiastic physical exuberance.

Sports The tomb paintings show that outdoor sports assumed an important place in Etruscan life. Because of their association with religion and rites for the dead, sports were serious affairs, and to neglect them was considered a sacrilege. There were also sociological reasons for the popularity of games. The growth of cities, the expansion of industry and commerce, and the rise of a wealthy leisured class gave the time, opportunity, and money for indulgence in sports of all kinds. Hunting and fishing, which for prehistoric people had been a labor of necessity, became a form of recreation for the Etruscan rich. Next to hunting, riding and chariot racing were favorite sports. Organized athletic competitions, such as were common in Greece, were especially popular. They gave the upper-class youth a chance to display their skill and prowess; they served also as a source of entertainment for the masses. Most illuminating in this regard is the great frieze in the *Tomb of the Chariots* at Tar-

quinii, which shows a vast stadium and a large number of spectators of both sexes applauding and cheering the charioteers, the runners, the boxers, the wrestlers, and acrobats. Several paintings reveal the popularity of the equivalent of the Roman gladiator contest. This deadly sport, thought to have been a relic of the primitive custom of human sacrifice, formed part of the funeral games and originally was intended to supply blood to sustain the spirit of the deceased.

Religion Most modern writers assert that the religion of the early Etruscans was pervaded with fear and gloom and dominated by a superstitious and authoritarian priesthood. This view seems inconsistent with the evidence from the wall paintings of the tombs, which reveal the early Etruscans as a joyous, life-accepting people. They believed that the ruling powers of the universe—vague, impersonal, nameless, and incomprehensible—manifested themselves in every living thing: in human beings, in trees, in every flash of lightning, in lakes and streams, in the mountains and the sea. To penetrate their mystery, to make these powers speak, to wrest from them their secret, called for elaborate ritual. Once discovered, the will of the deity must be obeyed and executed with meticulous care. As time went on, Etruscan religion became more and more formal, theological, and legalistic, a vested interest of the priesthood, in whose hands lay the spiritual life of the people.

Under Greek influence the gods of the Etruscans became personalized and anthropomorphic. First among them was Tinia, later the Roman Jupiter, who spoke in thunder and hurled his lightning bolts across the sky. He executed the decrees of destiny. With him were associated the two originally Italic goddesses, Uni (or Juno) and Minerva. Together they formed a celestial triad whose temple (*kilth*) stood in every Etruscan city and on the Capitoline Hill at Rome. With nine other deities they formed the council of the Twelve Gods, six male and six female. The Etruscans believed that an infernal triad ruled over the lower world: Mantus (Hades), Mania (Persephone), and Tekum (Ceres), the goddess of the harvest.

Minor Etruscan deities included Vertumnus, the god of vines and gardens, and several other gods peculiar to certain cities and sacred places. In addition, there were the inferior deities or demons, of whom the most horrid was Charun, whose Greek namesake was Charon, the conductor of the dead to the underworld. He was represented in Etruscan art with a big nose, pointed ears, bluish skin, and snakes crawling over his head and shoulders.

The most striking aspect of Etruscan religion was the so-called *disciplina*. It was an elaborate set of rules that aided the priests in their study and interpretation of natural phe-

nomena to forecast the future, to know the will of the gods above, and to turn away the wrath of the malignant spirits beyond the grave. There were several kinds of divination, but the most important was the inspection of the livers of sheep and other animals slaughtered for sacrifice by special priests *(haruspices)*. Thunder, lightning, and numerous other omens were also studied as tokens of the divine will. The flight of birds, which the Romans studied with scrupulous care before battles, elections, or other affairs of state, was for the Etruscans of secondary importance.

Etruscan Art and Architecture   The art of the Etruscans was their most remarkable

A banquet scene from the "Tomb of the Leopards" at Tarquinii ca. 525 B.C.   (Courtesy Fratelli Alinari, Florence)

and enduring achievement. Religion gave it occasion and impulse. As in Greece, Etruscan temples and precincts were lavishly decorated with ornamental reliefs and paintings. Believing, like the Egyptians, in the survival of life after death, the Etruscans provided elaborate tombs for the dead, some of gigantic size, such as the tumulus of Regolini-Galassi (about 158 feet in diameter) at Caere (Cerveteri), and they spared no expense in their construction and decoration. In his grave the Etruscan noble or merchant prince had his chariot and hunting gear, his jewels and favorite Greek vases, his wines, his wife decked out in her costly robes and finery, and beautiful pictures that magically brought to life pleasant hours at home, in the country, and at the seaside.

In these tombs are preserved many masterpieces of both Greek and Etruscan art —black-figured vases imported from Athens, sarcophagi (coffins) with sculptured lids, statues, silver goblets, gold and silver jewelry, engraved gems, and wall paintings. The desire to perpetuate the personality of the dead gave rise to the tradition of the sculptured portrait (later to develop among the Romans into the portrait busts that have preserved for us the likenesses of many illustrious Romans).

Origin, Development, and General Features   Three currents swelled the main stream of Etruscan art. The first was the native Villanovan, whose simple geometric designs persisted, especially at Clusium (Chiusi) and other inland centers. Second was the eastern Mediterranean. Contacts with eastern Mediterranean culture brought an influx of what historians of this subject call Oriental motifs—Assyrian, Hittite, Persian, and Egyptian. Of these the earliest and most notable were Assyrian hunting scenes, stylized horses, double-headed birds, long-necked water fowls, sphinxes, lions, and bulls. Even before this Orientalizing trend had reached its height (near 650 to 600 B.C.), there began to flow from Greece the third great current of influence upon Etruscan art, first from Corinth, then from Ionia, and later from Athens. Throughout the sixth century B.C. Greece ex-

erted a powerful influence upon the art of Etruria and the entire Mediterranean world. Attic black- and later red-figured vases were imported in tremendous quantities and were much admired and imitated by the Etruscans. Numerous Greek artists and craftsmen appeared in the harbors and cities of southern Etruria. But the Hellenic influence was somewhat diluted by the multiplicity of local schools and traditions in Etruria and by the conservative tendencies of native artists, who, during the sixth and early fifth centuries, worked with considerable originality and creative freedom.

The next century (450 to 340 B.C.) witnessed both a weakening of Hellenic influence and a decline in the quality of Etruscan art production. The regression in art coincided with a political, social, and economic crisis probably brought on by wars with Rome, the Gauls, and the Greeks. There was also a psychological reaction against classical Greek art. The Etruscans preferred action to abstract thinking and the concrete and specific to the general and the ideal. They found it difficult to understand or appreciate the idealism, restraint, perfection, and austere beauty of Athenian art in the age of Pericles, and they continued to reproduce the styles and motifs worked out in the preceding period.

During the next century (340 to 230 B.C.), there occurred a renaissance of Etruscan art—inspired, perhaps, by peace with Rome and a general improvement in the social and political situation of the period. Cultural relations with the Greek world improved, particularly with Athens and southern Italy. This renaissance in Etruria was preceded by changes in Greek art itself.

Even before Alexander's time, Greek art had begun to lose some of the old ideals of perfection. As it became less restrained and austere and more freely expressive of sentiment and emotion, it more readily evoked appreciation by the Etruscans and invited imitation. From Etruria it passed to Rome.

Houses and Temples   The earliest architecture of Italy was Etruscan, and it greatly influenced Roman styles. The Etruscan style of house served as a model for the Roman with its *atrium,* an unroofed central court around which the living rooms were arranged. Roman temples show the extensive influence of Etruscan temple design, which was quite different from the Greek. Compared with the Greek temple, the Etruscan temple was a rather low, squat, top-heavy building. Often set on a hill, it was also raised up on a stone base mounted in front by a broad flight of walled-in steps. The walls of the temple itself were built of brick, and the roof and columns of wood. Columns were used only for a deep porch in front. The solid walls of the cella (main chamber) were directly behind it. The cella itself, almost square in shape, was subdivided into three smaller chambers, one for each of a triad of gods. Each chamber had its own door at the front of the temple. Topping the whole structure was a long, low-pitched wooden roof.

The brick and woodwork were sheathed with terra-cotta tiles brightly painted or decorated with sculptured Greek motifs like leaf moldings and acanthus scrolls. The pediment and gable were adorned with terra-cotta friezes and statuary of gods and mythical scenes. The overall effect was somewhat jarring because the highly ornamented pediment and gable clashed with the plain columns below. The Romans, whose taste was later influenced by the Greeks, eventually produced a very harmonious integration of Etruscan and Greek temple styles.

The Arch Etruscan architects were famous for their use of arches and vaults. Early Etruscan builders formed arches and vaults by corbeling, projecting out each course of stones in stepped pattern until everything met at the top to form a solid whole. In the third century B.C., however, the Etruscans borrowed the familiar round arch made from bricks or voussoirs, stones cut into truncated wedges to fit the desired curve. They then applied it to the construction of city gates, sewers, bridges, and tombs. Adopted by the Romans, the arch and the vault permitted many of the great engineering and architectural accomplishments associated with Roman civilization.

Sculpture Etruscan sculpture is truly outstanding, and though influenced at first by Near Eastern and later by Greek sculpture, it developed into a genuinely national art—vital and true to nature.

Clay, not marble, was the medium used by the early Etruscan sculptors in some of their best work. Their skill in handling this soft, flexible material is evident in numerous sofa-shaped sarcophagi with complicated reliefs sculptured on the sides and figures of married couples on the covers. Solemn or gay, attractive or ugly, the faces of the men and women reclining on these elaborate terra cotta sofas belong to real people. The realism exhibited in this portrait sculpture and carried at times to the extreme of caricatured violence is as alien to Greek taste as is the naked physical strength and vigor of motion displayed in the celebrated *Apollo* of Veii. Except for the smile, typical of Greek archaic statues, the naturalism of the *Apollo* is apparent from the vigor of the god's stride and the tenseness of his powerful leg muscles as he advances boldly upon his enemy. It was from Veii, according to tradition, that Tarquin the Proud summoned Vulca to Rome to make a statue of Jupiter for the temple on the Capitoline.

The special forte of later Etruscan sculptors was bronze. In this medium were created several masterpieces, such as the celebrated *Capitoline Wolf* (sixth century B.C.) and the equally famous *Chimaera* of Arretium (Arezzo) (fifth century B.C.). Because of their merit, they were once thought to have been of Greek workmanship, but though traces of Greek influence are there, the defiant wolf is undoubtedly Etruscan. And so is the *Chimaera*. Its realism is such that one can almost hear the roar of pain torn from the brute when he was hit by the deadly darts of Bellerophon. Two other genuine Etruscan works are the so-called *Capitoline Brutus* (a bronze head of the second century B.C.) and the famous statue *Orator* (second century B.C.). The orator, with his stern

The Capitoline Wolf, *sixth-century Etruscan bronze. (National Gallery of Art Picture Collection, Washington, D.C.)*

The Chimaera, *fifth-century Etruscan bronze.* *(Courtesy, Fratelli Alinari, Florence)*

features and commanding personality, has all the dignity of an Appius Claudius or Cato the Elder.

Painting Painting, although perhaps not the greatest of the Etruscan arts, is the best preserved. It is preserved in the tombs, especially those of Tarquinii and Caere, which surpass even the tombs of ancient Egypt as repositories of ancient painting. Although the Greeks probably excelled in painting as they did in sculpture and architecture, their paintings (except those preserved on pottery) have been lost, dispersed, or destroyed with the buildings that housed them. The Etruscan works are therefore of particular historic importance, for they furnish the sole link between the lost Greek and later Roman paintings.

The drawings are bold and incisive; the colors are bright and achieve fine effects through juxtaposition and contrast. The themes, usually taken from life, are developed with direct and uncompromising realism and are often brutally frank. In the Tomb of the Augurs at Tarquinii (sixth century B.C.) one painting shows two wrestlers locked together in struggle. Another painting in the same tomb depicts a sport as brutal as the gladiatorial contests of the later Roman arena; a burly, thick-set man, his head covered by a sack, is trying to knock down a savage dog whose leash is held by an opponent. If the man wins, he has his adversary at his mercy; if he loses, he will be left to the dog.

The festive side of life is a favorite theme in tomb paintings. In the *Tomb of the Lionesses* may be seen men and women reclining at a banquet, a massive bowl wreathed with ivy, and musicians playing. Everybody is in high spirits. A dancing girl has just thrown off her wraps and, with passion and abandon, is performing a lively and voluptuous dance. One of the male spectators, carried away with the excitement, leaps to his feet and takes up the rhythmic movements of the girl. Scenes of this kind are very commonly depicted in tomb paintings and, taken together, provide an interesting commentary on Etruscan social and religious life.

The Rise and Fall of Etruscan Power

Etruscan Expansion in Italy   By the middle of the seventh century B.C. the Etruscans had firmly established themselves in Etruria proper and were prepared to expand. This expansion does not seem to have been carried on by any cooperative public effort, however. Rather, the main impetus probably came from freebooters and entrepreneurs using private

armies to seize greater wealth and opportunity than they could find at home.

First, they crossed the Tiber and seized many Latin towns on the lucrative trade route to Campania. By the end of the seventh century, an Etruscan dynasty had even gained control of Rome. Early in the sixth century they broke into Campania, where they founded Capua and several smaller towns. In 540 B.C., with the help of the Carthaginians, they won a naval victory over the Phocaean Greeks near Corsica and forced them to withdraw to Massilia (Marseille), a powerful Phocaean Greek colony on the southeast coast of what is now France. Doubtless, encouraged by that victory, in 525 they attacked Cumae in order to break the Greek hold on the Campanian coastal region. They failed.

During the latter part of the sixth century B.C., the Etruscans also began to expand at the expense of tribes to the north. By the end of the sixth century, the power of the Etruscans was at its height, their influence extending from the Alps to Salernum (Salerno) and from the east to west coasts. Their ships sailed both seas and disputed with the navies of Greece and Carthage for mastery of the western Mediterranean.

The success of the Etruscans against the less advanced peoples of Italy was assured by their superior weaponry and tactics. With their convenient sources of metals and their skill in metalworking, they had earlier adopted the Greek hoplite style of warfare, in which soldiers wore metal helmets, breastplates, and greaves (shinguards) and fought in ranks instead of as individual "heroes." After the Romans had acquired this style of warfare from their Etruscan kings, they too were poised for rapid expansion against their neighbors.

Decline of Etruscan Power   Despite the speed and vigor of their expansion, their wealth, and their brilliant culture, the Etruscans were unable to prevent armed uprisings by rebellious subjects or to defend their conquests against the Romans, the Greeks, the

Samnites, or the Gauls. The basic weakness lay in their inability to establish a stable political organization and a unified military command. In the first place, Etruscan conquests stemmed not from the concerted drive of an expanding national state, but from the uncoordinated efforts of individual war chiefs or conquistadores in whom love of adventure, desire for fortune, or dissatisfaction with domestic politics had generated a drive for conquest. The separate colonies that they established were bound together by commercial, cultural, and religious ties rather than by a centralized political authority or firm alliance. They were unable to hold their easy conquests or to resist the attacks that brought their empire tumbling to ruins.

In 474 B.C. the Etruscans suffered a naval disaster at the hands of Hieron I of Syracuse, who later deposited a still-existing Etruscan helmet at Delphi as thanks for victory. That disaster broke Etruscan seapower and exposed Corsica, Elba, and Etruria itself to Greek attack. In the early fifth century, the Romans, not content with merely the expulsion of their Etruscan dynasty, passed to the offensive with an assault upon Veii. Finally, in 438 B.C. the Samnites took Capua and liquidated all Etruscan influence in Campania. At the beginning of the fourth century B.C., the Gauls burst into the Po valley, seized Felsina (near Bologna), and marched south against Clusium (Chiusi) in Etruria. After 350 B.C. the Etruscans, their conquests lost, fought a losing battle for survival with the Romans, whom they had taught so much, and the destiny of Italy passed forever out of their hands.

The Greeks in Italy The Greek influence on early Italy and Rome was profound. Sometimes it was direct, through trade and settlement; sometimes it was indirect, especially through the Etruscans, who traded extensively with the Greeks, adopted much of their art and culture, and carried them to other parts of Italy.

At first Greek contact with Italy was through traders looking for supplies of metal like copper and iron. Beginning in the eighth century, traders familiar with Italy and Sicily pointed the way for permanent settlers from Greek cities wishing to gain strategic commercial outposts and find relief from a growing shortage of agricultural land that was beginning to cause social and political problems. Although it may have maintained sentimental, religious, and commercial ties with its mother city, each new settlement became a completely independent political entity, just like the individual city-states in the Greek homeland.

Greek Colonies in Italy It is significant that the chief sponsor of the first major Greek settlement in Italy at this time (ca. 750 B.C.) was Chalcis on the island of Euboea, just off the east coast of central Greece. Chalcis, whose name means copper in Greek, was a center of metalworking and fought a famous war with its neighbor Eretria in the eighth century for the rich Lelantine plain, which lay between them. The need for copper and land brought settlers from Chalcis to Italy, which was relatively well endowed with both.

Along with the Chalcidians came some people from Eretria and two other neighboring towns, Cumae and Graia. They settled first about 750 B.C. on the island of Pithecusae just off the northern tip of the Bay of Naples. As they expanded, they moved across to the mainland and established Cumae, named for Cumae in Euboea. Later, a little farther east on the bay, they founded a separate port town, and when they outgrew those two places, they established another city, Naples ("New City"), to handle the overflow.

All of these towns left their marks on the Romans. It was probably from Cumae, either directly or through Etruscan intermediaries, that the Romans derived the Latin alphabet, in which these words are written. Through Cumae many Greek gods were adopted by neighboring Italic tribes—Heracles (Hercules), Apollo, Castor and Polyduces (Pollux), for example. The oracle of the Sibyl at Cumae won great renown, and a collection of her sup-

Greek Colonial World

Areas of Greek settlement

posed sayings, the *Sibylline Books,* was consulted for guidance at numerous crises in Roman history.

Although the Greeks called themselves Hellenes, the Romans called them Greeks because of the Graians (Graei), whom they first met in settlements around the Bay of Naples. The port for Cumae became Puteoli (Pozzuoli), the most important trading port in Italy through most of Roman history. Naples became the most populous city in the rich district of Campania and opposed Roman expansion there for many years. After the Romans took control of it, however, wealthy Romans built sumptuous seaside villas all around its bay, and many, like Vergil, learned Greek literature and philosophy from Naples' poets and philosophers.

Numerous other Greek settlers soon followed the founders of Cumae. Attracted by fertile soil, Achaean Greeks settled on the western shore of the Gulf of Tarentum at Sybaris around 720 and Croton around 700. They in turn founded others on the opposite coast of Italy: Sybaris sponsoring Posidonia (Paestum), Scidros, and Laos; Croton setting up Terina and Temesa. Sybaris became so

famous for its wealth and luxurious pleasures that such things are still referred to as sybaritic, and people who indulge in them are called sybarites. Sybaris was eventually destroyed by its rival Croton, which is renowned as the seat of Pythagoras and his community of philosophers. The Romans even believed (quite wrongly) that one of their early kings, Numa Pompilius, was a disciple of Pythagoras.

To the north of Croton and Sybaris, the Spartans founded Taras (Tarentum, Taranto) also about 700 B.C. It became a great manufacturing center and gave its name to the whole gulf by which sailors seeking its wares reached it. A captive slave, Lucius Livius Andronicus (see pp. 147–148), from Tarentum in the mid-third century B.C. first adapted Greek epic, tragedy, and comedy to Latin and laid the foundations of serious Roman literature.

Two hundred and fifty years after the settlement of Tarentum, Athenians founded Thurii near the site once occupied by Sybaris. Eventually, jealousy and suspicion between Tarentum and Thurii involved Rome and led Tarentum to call in King Pyrrhus of Epirus against the Romans. That fateful move led to the final Roman takeover of all the Greek cities in southern Italy.

Sicily   Across from Italy on the fertile island of Sicily, the Greeks founded even more cities than in Italy proper. There they were the rivals of the Phoenicians, who held onto Panormus (Palermo), Solus, and Motya in the west while the Greeks eventually occupied most of the rest of the island at the expense of the older Sicel, Sican, and Elymian inhabitants. The oldest of the Greek cities here, as in Italy proper, was founded under the leadership of Chalcis. Founded about 730, it was named Naxos for some fellow settlers from the island of Naxos and was located at the base of Mt. Aetna, where it guarded the strait of Messana between Sicily and Italy. Within the next few years, the Chalcidians also founded Catanae, Leontini, and Zancle (later called Messana) on Sicily and Rhegium across the strait on the toe of Italy.

Dorian Greek cities predominated on the southeast and southern coast of Sicily at places like Selinus, Gela, Acragas (Agrigentum), and Syracuse. Of them, Syracuse, founded by settlers from the island of Corcyra off the northwest coast of Greece around 730, was the most important. Growing even larger than Athens, it rivalled her in wealth, power, and culture. Hieron, one of Syracuse's early fifth-century

tyrants, led the Greeks of the west to victory over the Etruscans in the naval battle of Cumae in 474. The Etruscans' defeat marked the start of their long decline. Dionysius I briefly gained ascendancy in southern Italy and Sicily at the beginning of the fourth century but could not sustain it. In 264, the rivalry between Carthage and Syracuse over the city of Messana contributed to Roman intervention and the First Punic War, which ended with the Romans in control of Sicily.

Decline of the Greek Cities in Italy and Sicily   As was the case with the Etruscans, the Greek city-states founded in Italy and Sicily, though starting from a higher level of prosperity, culture, and political sophistication, ultimately failed to stop the Roman conquest of Italy in the fourth and third centuries B.C. The individual Italian and Sicilian Greek cities were unable to find a middle ground between uncooperative independence and predatory imperialism. Rather, they perpetuated the fierce independence and predatory rivalries of Greek city-states everywhere. Therefore, their alliances were weak and their empires unstable. The Romans ended their independence one by one while borrowing heavily from their artists, writers, and philosophers.

III

Early Rome, 750 to 500 B.C.

At the time when Villanovan villages were becoming Etruscan cities in Etruria and the Greeks were founding cities in southern Italy and Sicily, the site of Rome boasted only a few collections of crude huts inhabited by herdsmen and simple agriculturalists who had no idea that they would later be considered the founders of the most powerful city in the ancient world. The date that later Romans widely accepted as the date of Rome's founding was, in modern Western terms, April 21, 753 B.C. It was established by the Roman antiquarian Marcus Terentius Varro in the late first century B.C. He arrived at it without any scientific proof by studying the myths and legends about Rome's earlier days. Modern historians cannot pretend to be so precise as Varro, but archaeological excavations confirm that although there were some settlements there in Neolithic times and again around 1500 B.C., uninterrupted habitation of the site does go back to around 750 B.C.

Sources for the History of Early Rome (ca. 750 – ca. 500 B.C.) The ancient historical tradition about early Rome is a confused mass of truth and fiction, of legend and patriotic invention. The oldest extant literary

sources for early Rome are the first book of Livy's 142-book history of Rome, *Ab Urbe Condita,* the first three books of the *Roman Antiquities* by the Greek historian Dionysius of Halicarnassus, and fragments of Books Seven to Nine of the world history of Diodorus Siculus, a Greek from Sicily. All three wrote under the Emperor Augustus at the end of the first century B.C. (see p. 311), and had to rely on the work of earlier writers who had established the basic historical tradition for early Rome. They often perpetuated previous errors and added more of their own in trying to emphasize new themes or produce more dramatic and entertaining narratives. Plutarch's biographies of the early Roman kings Romulus and Numa Pompilius, which were written in the late first or early second century A.D., merely continued the process. The same can be said for the fragmentarily preserved first three books of the *Roman History* of Cassius Dio, a Bithynian Greek who was a high Roman official in the late second and early third centuries A.D. For all of Rome's history, from its founding to the time of Augustus, there are numerous brief summaries based extensively on Livy in the works of the fourth- and fifth-century A.D. writers Florus, Aurelius Victor, Eutropius, Festus, Orosius, and Julius

22

Obsequens. From the same period come summaries of each of the books of Livy, except 136 and 137, in the *Periochae*.

The earliest written accounts of Rome's history were set down in the late third and early second centuries B.C. by a group of historians called annalists, who narrated events on a year-by-year basis, and by patriotic epic poets, who also tried to present coherent versions of early Roman history (see pp. 148–151). These accounts are all lost, but they established the basic outline on which all later authors ultimately depended. Unfortunately, their accounts were written hundreds of years after the events that they described, and there were few reliable records for them to use. Both annalists and poets had to rely on legends and folktales and such written records as had survived the Gallic sack of Rome around 390 B.C.

Even before the sack, however, written records were not very extensive, although writing had existed at Rome since at least the mid-sixth century B.C. There had been some tombs and monuments with inscriptions containing some information about early people and events. Inscribed dedications on temples may have given some chronological as well as religious information, and early treaties and laws were inscribed on stone and bronze. Some of the important priesthoods maintained written records, but they were little more than brief notations of yearly magistrates and the occurrence of significant religious or secular events, such as festivals, floods, fires, famines, plagues, and earthquakes.

How much of this material survived the Gallic sack is not known, but clearly some of it did. The Lapis Niger or Black Stone inscription, named for the black stone under which it was found in the Roman Forum, goes back to the late sixth or early fifth century B.C. (see p. 28). Also, inscriptions of several treaties in very old Latin were still extant in Augustus' day. The annalists probably had access to an accurate and complete text of Rome's earliest law code, the Twelve Tables, which was compiled in the mid-fifth century B.C. and preserved some of the customs and unwritten laws

of earlier centuries (see pp. 57–58). It was still being memorized by schoolchildren in the late first century B.C.

For the period from roughly 750 to 500 B.C., however, there never could have existed many public written documents. For this period the main sources were popular legends and folktales. Sometimes the early poets and annalists could supplement them by the traditions of the great noble families who preserved wax masks (*imagines*) and busts of their ancestors, whose accomplishments were inscribed on funeral monuments and whose memories were kept fresh in funeral speeches for their latest descendants. Family pride, however, often led to unhistorical exaggeration and the twisting of facts. Sometimes Greco-Sicilian historians like Timaeus (ca. 356 to 260 B.C.) and Philinus (ca. 250 B.C.) also preserved some useful information from the traditions of the cities of *Magna Graecia,* which had had contacts with early Rome.

Nevertheless, although the annalistic tradition of early Roman history rests on very little hard, documentary data, it still preserves much usable information. Legends and folklore reflect the conditions experienced by the people who created them. They preserve the general social, economic, political, and cultural context of early Roman history even though specific names, dates, and events are highly questionable. Moreover, this general picture can be further illuminated by the work of anthropologists who have studied societies with similar conditions and by archaeologists who have excavated the site of early Rome and contemporary settlements in Latium and Etruria.

Comparative anthropology, for example, sheds much light on early Roman religion (see pp. 40–45). To archaeologists, the foundations of primitive huts and artifacts from graves have revealed the simple way of life that characterized Roman society at its earliest stage (see pp. 25–27). Similarly, the excavated remains of public buildings and temples, like the Capitoline temple of Jupiter, indicate that the sources have correctly represented Rome under the kings of the sixth cen-

tury B.C. as one of the richest and most powerful cities of Italy (see pp. 27–28).

Legends of Rome's Founding According to the standard tale of Rome's beginning, it all started with the Trojan hero Aeneas, who escaped the fall of Troy and after many years of wandering landed in Latium. There he met King Latinus, won the hand of Latinus' daughter Lavinia after a war with her native suitor, and founded a city in his new wife's honor, Lavinium. Aeneas's son, Ascanius (Iulus), subsequently founded Alba Longa. Numitor, the twelfth Alban king after Ascanius, had a daughter, Ilia (Rhea Silvia), who became pregnant by the god Mars and bore two sons, Romulus and Remus, who were set adrift on the Tiber and washed up on shore near the site of Rome. There a she-wolf found them and suckled them. They were discovered by a shepherd, Faustulus, who raised them. Subsequently, they each founded a settlement near the site of their miraculous rescue, but Romulus soon killed Remus in an argument. Finally, lacking wives, Romulus and his men carried off the women of a nearby Sabine village and thereby ensured the perpetuation of their city.

This account did not take its basic shape until the end of the third century B.C. after poets and historians had creatively combined, confused, rejected, and reconciled many separate tales of Latin, Greek, and Etruscan origin. The story that Romulus and Remus came from Alba Longa and founded Rome is part of the earliest Latin tradition. In the early period, Alba Longa was Rome's chief rival for leadership of the other Latin towns, and the story would have been useful propaganda to bolster Alba's claim to leadership. Archaeological evidence does show close connections between early Rome and Alba but cannot be used to prove any Alban origin for Rome.

The characters Romulus and Remus look like two slightly different versions of the typical eponymous (giving one's name to) hero whose name is actually derived from that of the city which he is supposed to have founded. The

Latins at Rome would have been familiar with such stories from the Greek settlers in southern Italy. In fact, one Greek legend claims that Rome was founded by Romus, the son of Odysseus and Circe.

Greek settlers in Italy and Sicily were naturally anxious to link their area with the glorious epic traditions of their native land. The wanderings of Odysseus in the *Odyssey* already provided one link, and in the sixth century the Sicilian Greek poet Stesichorus added another by having the Trojan hero Aeneas migrate to the west in a similar series of adventures. Significantly, Aeneas quickly became associated with the Etruscans, who were the great foes of the Greeks in Italy, as the Trojans had been of the earlier Greeks in the Homeric epics.

The Etruscans eagerly adopted Aeneas as their own. Through him they could have a past as ancient and glorious as their Greek rivals. Sixth-century votive statues of Aeneas carrying his father, Anchises, have been found at Veii, and the same scene appears on seventeen vases found in Etruscan tombs of the late sixth and early fifth centuries. Probably the Etruscans popularized the story of Aeneas when Etruscan kings ruled Rome during the sixth century.

The Etruscans may have added the story of the she-wolf to the legend of Rome's founding. The great bronze she-wolf that still adorns the Capitol is an Etruscan work of about 500 B.C. The twin babes were not added until the Renaissance, but there is an Etruscan relief sculpture of about 600 B.C. that shows a wolf suckling a baby boy.

One of the last elements to become part of the standard legend was the list of Alban kings. As Greek scholars and historians became more skilled, they became concerned with establishing precise chronologies. In the early part of the third century B.C., the Sicilian Greek historian Timaeus, the first comprehensive writer on the western Greeks and events relevant to them, equated the foundation date of Rome with that of Carthage, supposedly 814 B.C. About fifty years later another Greek, Eratosthenes, established the standard

CENTRAL ITALY

date in antiquity for the fall of Troy, 1184 B.C. Clearly, Aeneas could not have wandered 370 years before getting to Italy, and a large gap existed between his son's founding of Alba Longa and Romulus' founding of Rome. The Alban king list was handy for bridging this gap, and its tradition was flexible enough to be adapted to fit changes in the accepted date for Rome's foundation as the ancient equivalents of 748 and finally 753 B.C. gained favor.

Latium and Early Rome Since the legendary account of Rome's origin is an almost completely unhistorical construction, what is known about earliest Rome must be inferred from the physical evidence of geography and a few archaeological artifacts.

By the eighth century B.C., Latium was being settled by the Latins. They spoke an Indo-European dialect and apparently lived by farming and raising livestock. They wore coarse, homespun clothing and made crude pottery by hand. Except for some jewelry and bronze or iron tools, they seem to have imported few foreign goods. Their houses were

round or elliptical wooden huts with thatched walls and roof held together by beams or poles. Smoke from the fireplace escaped through a hole in the roof, and a single large doorway served for lighting and ventilation. Foundations of just such houses have been found on the Palatine Hill at Rome.

The farms, though small, fostered the growth of many villages, which later developed into towns or cities. In the north was Tibur by the Anio and the fortress town of Fidenae overlooking the Tiber. Inland, lofty Praeneste guarded the road from Etruria to Campania and there was also Tusculum. Perhaps the oldest of all was Alba Longa, the religious center of Latium and legendary mother city of Rome. By the sea lay Lavinium with Ardea close by. East of these stood Aricia, Lanuvium, and Velitrae. In the south, particularly in the rich Pontine district, there were clusters of towns such as Setia, Cora, Pometia, Suessa, Satricum, and Norba.

By 750 B.C. three or four rural villages like those elsewhere in Latium occupied some of the hills that later Rome made famous. Each early hill-top village probably had different dialects and customs. Of these primitive settlements, the one on the Palatine Hill may have been the original Rome. Others were located on the Esquiline and Quirinal hills and probably the Caelian as well. They all used the slopes and interconnecting valleys as cemeteries. The people of the Palatine practiced cremation, those of the Esquiline inhumation in trench graves. Burial practices on the Quirinal changed from cremation burials in urns to inhumation in trenches, as happened at Villanovan sites in Etruria. Eventually the villages needed more burial space and set up a common cemetery beneath the Palatine on the site of the future Roman Forum. Such cooperation probably preceded the eventual amalgamation of the separate villages into a single entity.

The Early Roman Economy   Flocks and herds were undoubtedly the main source of livelihood of the early Romans. This fact is correctly inferred from their myths, religious customs, and language. Rome's legendary eponymous founder and his twin brother, Remus, allegedly were raised in a sheepherder's cottage; the festival of the *Palilia* on April 21st, the day on which Romulus supposedly founded Rome, celebrated cleanup day of stalls and stables; in honor of *Tellus*, or Mother Earth, the primitive goddess of fruitfulness of animals as well as of crops, the early Romans twice annually celebrated the festival of the *Fordicidia*, at which they sacrificed a pregnant cow in the spring and a pregnant sow in early winter.

Because of this pastoral tradition, the Romans, like the Jews of the Old Testament, sacrificed animals to their gods: to Juno a goat, to Mars a bull, to Jupiter a white bullock. Traces of the same background is evident in the name given to one of their city gates, the "Mooing Gate" *(Porta Mugonia),* as well as in the words *egregius* (meaning out of the flock, and therefore excellent) and *pecunia* (meaning wealth in flocks but later money in general).

Even so, pasturage could not be pursued on a very large scale until the Romans had conquered wider grazing lands and seized command of the roads to summer pastures in the Apennines. Their battle for the trails with the Sabine mountaineers ended with a coexistence pact that gave to the Romans access to summer pastures in the mountains, to the Sabines winter pastures in the Lower Tiber Valley, and rights of intermarriage to both.

Meanwhile, the Romans had other sources of livelihood. They fished, raised pigs and chickens, and planted gardens of turnips, peas, beans, lettuce, and cabbage. In small plots of land adjacent to their houses they cultivated *spelt,* a hard kind of emmer wheat, which, like durum, was more suitable for making porridge than bread. They probably also gathered wild grapes and figs, which they either ate as fruit or brewed into wine.

A change in the primitive life of the Romans was not slow in coming. In the eighth century B.C. the Mediterranean world was then astir with commercial activity in which the Romans were soon to take part. To the shores of Latium came the Phoenicians and the Greeks. The Etruscans were crossing the Tiber and occupying Satricum and Praeneste as way stations along the road to Campania.

Changes in ancient trading patterns encouraged people to take advantage of Rome's location. Long before Rome was settled, people from the hill country of the central Apennines had been beating a path along both sides of the Tiber to and from the salt beds near the river's mouth. (Salt was a valuable commodity in Europe even as late as the French Revolution. It was the special treasure of the lower Tiber.) While it was relatively simple to get down the river by raft, the strong current made it next to impossible to get back up again, so that trails along the banks were used instead. The trail along the west bank was less broken and irregular and led to the best and most easily worked beds. When this trail came under the control of Etruscan Veii, independent salt miners and merchants had to use the Old Salt Road *(Via Salaria)* which ran along the east bank. When the Etruscans later crossed the river and seized the fortress of Fidenae in the mid-seventh century, the salt men lost the use of this road. To save their lives or escape the tolls, they had to bypass Fidenae by a wide detour inland via Nomentum on the Allia. Returning to the river at Antemnae, they followed the Old Salt Road to Rome. The vicinity of Rome provided the only safe and convenient place to cross the Tiber, both because it was beyond Veii's range of control and because Tiber Island facilitated the building of bridges. The earliest was the Sublician Bridge *(Pons Sublicius)*, built of wood in the late seventh century. Once built and guarded from the Capitoline citadel, it attracted many roads and helped the early city to grow.

Growth of the City The growth of separate villages into a significant town during the seventh century B.C. can be traced in the archaeological record and in some of the archaic Roman religious practices that survived into historical times. Archaeology shows an increase of standardized, professionally crafted products, which suggests greater commercial interaction and greater overall level of wealth. One of the mid-seventh-century trench graves on the Esquiline, for example, contained a suit of armor and a chariot; imports of expensive Etruscan metalware and pottery increased greatly after about 625 B.C.

The religious festival of the Septimontium (Seven Hills or Enclosed Hills) seems to have originated in the establishment of a common religious festival by the communities on the Palatine, Esquiline, and Caelian Hills, which actually embrace seven separate heights: the Oppius, Cispius, and Fagutal on the Esquiline; the Cermalus, Palatinus, and Velia on the Palatine; and the Caelian itself. Religious association seems to have led to political union under the Palatine community prior to the later incorporation of the Quirinal.

Two ancient priesthoods, the Salii and the Luperci, were each divided into two groups representing the Palatine and the Quirinal. This practice indicates that the priesthoods originally were common to two independent communities. According to Livy (2.13), the combination of the Palatine and Quirinal com-

munities resulted in what is known as Rome of the Four Regions: the Palatine, Esquiline, Caelian, and Quirinal Hills. These four regions also fall generally within the ancient sacred boundary of the city of Rome.

Archaeologically, it is clear that by the end of the sixth century B.C. the cemetery in the Forum had been closed, the area drained, and substantial houses built there. The Forum was not yet paved, but the houses had tiled roofs and sizable timbers. Rome seems to have been experiencing the same accelerated growth that other Latin towns were experiencing under Etruscan influence at this time.

Etruscan Influence The first Etruscan settlers in Latium were probably not military adventurers but enterprising merchants who were interested in Latium mainly because roads ran through it to the rich markets of Campania. The communities first to be Etruscanized lay along the two main routes between Etruria and Campania. The one followed the coast from Ostia to Ardea and Satricum; the other skirted the foothills of the Apennines. The more important inland route from Caere or Veii led across the Tiber at Fidenae to Tibur and Praeneste. Easily guarded from these strong points, it offered merchants a safer commercial route to Campania than was permitted by the storms, piracy, and enemy attacks likely on coastal trips.

Before the Etruscans established military and political control over Latium, their commercial activity had revolutionized its cultural life. They may have introduced the use of the alphabet, which they had learned from the Greeks of Cumae a few generations earlier. Craftsmen following close upon the heels of the merchants introduced at Praeneste and other sites, the latest techniques in working with metals, clay, leather, and wool. The Etruscans turned the Iron Age hilltop villages of the Latins into *oppida,* walled towns or cities with fortified citadels. They taught the Latins to build timber-frame houses. They built temples and decorated them in the Etruscan style, made religion an organized institution, and founded regular city-states. Thus, by 600 B.C. the institutions, industries, and fine arts of Etruria were transplanted to Latium. The princely tombs of Praeneste—with their hand-hammered cauldrons of bronze, their silver bowls, delicately carved ivories, and their exquisite gold ornaments—were almost exact replicas of the famous Regolini-Galassi tomb at Caere. The temples at Satricum, Lanuvium, and Velitrae, with their colored terracotta ornaments, were scarcely distinguishable from those built in Etruria.

There soon developed in Latium the class distinctions of Etruria. The Etruscan merchants and warlords and perhaps some well-to-do Latin families constituted an aristocracy of wealth that dominated the economic and social life of many Latin cities. Profit from trade or piracy not only enabled them to acquire large estates at the expense of small but formerly independent farmers, who were compelled to remain on the land as slaves, tenants, or serfs, but made it possible for them to live in princely splendor and adorn themselves and their homes with articles imported from Etruria, Greece, Egypt, and even the Baltic.

Agriculture continued as the chief occupation and main support of the population, and Latium was well cultivated during the period of Etruscan domination. The Etruscans cleared forests and bushland, drained swamps, and introduced better made iron plowshares and superior methods of cultivation as well as improved varieties of wheat, vines, and fruit trees. Better agriculture stimulated population growth, which in turn stimulated more agricultural development.

As the population of the region increased, it became necessary to clear and plow more and more land, first the hillsides and eventually even the slopes of the mountains. Rains beating down upon those thin-soiled, denuded slopes soon peeled off the topsoil and carried it down, along with gravel and other debris, to the lower plains. Rivers clogged with silt went on the rampage, flooded their banks, and left a mass of weeded, debris-tangled muck over once-fertile fields as they receded. To save both the lowland and hillside farms,

intelligent landowners with large capital and numerous tenants constructed an elaborate network of *cuniculi,* rock-cut drainage channels approximately five feet high and two feet wide. This remarkable drainage system, which must have required much engineering skill, an enormous expenditure of labor, and a numerous and well-disciplined population, preserved the agriculture of the Latin Campagna for many generations. The *emissaria,* drainage canals, of the same period opened up several hundred acres of fertile agricultural land for new settlements on the shores of the Alban Lake and of Lake Nemi by lowering the level of their waters.

The Early Roman State   According to tradition, from its founding to about 500 B.C. Rome was ruled by seven kings. The first four were Latin and Sabine: Romulus, Numa Pompilius, Tullus Hostilius, and Ancus Marcius. The last three were Etruscan: Tarquinius Priscus (Tarquin the Elder), Servius Tullius (Mastarna), and Tarquinius Superbus (Tarquin the Proud). Therefore, the period from ca. 750 to ca. 500 B.C. is often called the Monarchy, or Regal Period. It is a reasonable assumption that early Rome was ruled by kings. So, too, were Aricia, Tusculum, Lanuvium, and probably other city-states in Latium and Etruria. Moreover, the existence of a large amount of Etruscan material in the archaeological remains of sixth-century Rome corroborates the general view that Rome's last kings were Etruscan.

That kings ruled Rome during the sixth century B.C. is supported by the word RECEI, a form of the word *rex* (king), clearly inscribed on a mutilated stone pyramid found beneath the Lapis Niger (Black Stone), the oldest monument in the Roman Forum (early fifth century B.C.). The existence of kings is attested also by the survival in Republican times of the term *interregnum* (period between reigns) and of the titles of *interrex* (Acting King) and the priestly *rex sacrorum* (the King of Sacrifices). The *Regia,* or King's House, which served in Republican times as the official residence of the Pontifex Maximus, may have been originally the palace of the kings.

In all of her history, Rome never had a written constitution but, as in Great Britain today, only a constantly growing and changing mixture of custom, precedent, and legislation that determined what the "constitution" was at any historical moment. The constitution of the Regal Period was not complex. The basic outline was still preserved in the Republic that followed, and much can be inferred from what is known about similar monarchies in early Greece.

The King The living symbol of the unity, power, and authority of the early Roman state was the king. Though he held his office for life, he acquired it neither wholly by direct inheritance nor by popular election. Some writers today, notably Italian, insist that he was nominated by his predecessor. The ancient opinion, influenced, no doubt, by the machinery set up in the Republic for the election of consuls, was that on the death of each king the right of *auspicium,* determining the will of the gods by taking *auspices,* which bestowed upon royal authority its divine sanction, reverted automatically to the senate, an advisory body of the community's leading men. Thereupon, the senate chose one of its members to serve for five days as *interrex.* He in turn appointed another senator to hold office for five days, and so on, until a ruler pleasing to both the gods and the senate could be selected. Then, the last to act as *interrex* presented the nomination to an assembly of adult male citizens (the Popular Assembly, or *comitia curiata*) for confirmation. The function of this assembly was simply to attend and witness the last taking of the *auspices,* to express approval of the new king by acclamation, and, upon his assumption of the royal command *(imperium),* to pledge him loyalty and obedience. This formal investiture of the king gave him almost unlimited sovereignty or "the power of life and death."

In the Etruscan period, the king's power was probably almost total, embracing three broad areas of function: command of the army, the administration of justice, and the priesthood. As chief of state and supreme commander of the army, he had the power to make peace and war, direct foreign affairs, and conclude treaties with other states; to enforce military discipline, draft citizens into the army, and levy taxes in time of war; and to distribute booty among his soldiers or land among citizens in repayment of wartime loans. As director of internal affairs and administrator of justice, the king probably possessed both law-making and law-enforcement powers and issued edicts deemed necessary for the security and government of the state. Nevertheless, he had little to do with the formulation of private or civil law, since in early Rome that seems to have been created neither by royal decree nor by statute, but evolved out of use and custom and the social conscience of the community. He promulgated the so-called "royal laws" in his capacity of high priest, for at that time law, not divorced from religion and custom, was regulated by priests.

The king possessed extensive powers for carrying out his many duties as chief of state, commander-in-chief, chief justice, and high priest. He enforced the laws, whether based on custom or decree, through the agency of his lictors. Against violators of these laws he had various remedies, such as corporal punishment, imprisonment, fines, and the seizure of movable property. He imposed the death penalty only upon those guilty of serious crimes against the gods or the state—treason, parricide, and sacrilege. He seldom intervened in private disputes unless called upon, and even then limited himself to enunciating the general principle, leaving particular cases to be determined by regular judges or special arbiters.

The king's most important functions were religious, for religion was the foundation of royal power, and with it was entwined the destiny of the state. As supreme head of the state religion, the king's person was inviolable and sacrosanct. His duties were to represent the people in their relations to the gods of the state, to perform in person certain public sacrifices, to take the *auspices* and so learn the will of the gods, to appoint the priests and supervise their activities, to draw up the calendar, and to proclaim the feasts acceptable to each of the gods. The gods had to be consulted before every important act of state—the election of rulers, the calling of the people to assembly, and the departure of armies for battle.

The king entrusted the details of administration to his officials: to the prefect of the city, who governed when the king was absent; to the judges, who tried cases of treason and other public crimes; to the pontiffs, who supervised the sacrifices, fixed the calendar, and interpreted the civil law; to the augurs, who ascertained and interpreted the will of the gods; and to the Vestal Virgins, who kept aglow the city's sacred fires.

The Senate   The second branch of the early Roman government was the senate, a council of leading elders who advised the king. Probably the earliest senate was a congress of clan leaders, one of whom later became the king. The king must soon have become a permanent part of the government and, as his powers increased, he made the senate a purely advisory council. He added new members, after the clans *(gentes)* had broken up into a larger number of rich and powerful families. Sometime between 575 and 450 B.C. the senate came to consist of three hundred members, a constitutional number that remained fixed till the first century B.C. the time of Sulla (ca. 85 to 80 B.C.).

Powers and Functions of the Senate   The senate could not legislate and could give advice only when consulted by the king. This advice was not always accepted, although it was not politically "wise" for a king habitually to ignore or reject it, especially on major issues, since he was bound sooner or later to incur the enmity of the leading families and might, like the last Tarquin, even lose his throne.

As noted above, the *auspices* seem to have reverted to the senate on the death of the king until the senators could agree on a new king. The senate possessed still another ancient source of authority, summed up in the phase *auctoritas patrum,* which gave it the power to ratify resolutions of the popular assembly before enactment.

The Popular Assembly (comitia curiata)   The third organ of the government was the Popular Assembly, traditionally known as the *comitia curiata*. Its origins are obscure and the functions usually attributed to it were probably based on reconstructions of later times. It was the oldest known assembly, as old, perhaps, as the unified Roman community itself, and was composed of all citizens capable of bearing arms. This assembly met only on summons by the king to transact business put before them by him. Marshalled in primitive times by heralds, but during the Etruscan period by lictors, the eligible citizens assembled regularly in the Forum, though occasionally for religious ceremonies on Capitoline Hill. They lined up in groups called *curiae,* to which the assembly as a whole owed the name of *curiata.* Each *curia* seems to have been a group of related families living in a given area and organized as a unit for religious, military, and political purposes, as well as for taxation and voting. Ten *curiae* are said to have made up each of the three tribes —Ramnes, Tities, and Luceres—into which the Roman people are said to have been divided originally. Voting in the *comitia curiata* was by units, each *curia* having one vote, which was determined by the majority vote of its members.

Functions of the Comitia Curiata   The role of the *comitia curiata* in government during the Monarchy seems to have been a passive one. Legislation in primitive societies was rare (the law of custom seldom required modification or change), and the people were summoned by the king not to speak but to listen. Though they are said to have possessed even then ultimate sovereign power *(maiestas),* that power was latent, theoretical, still in a state of development. Nevertheless, the king was wise not to ignore it, if only to win the people's cooperation and consent to major changes in law and policy. They participated in public religious functions celebrated by the king. They were present at his inauguration to witness the final *auspices* and to swear the formal oath of loyalty and obedience to him when he assumed the *imperium*. They heard proclamations concerning peace and war and other important matters of state. Besides these public functions, the assembly witnessed, if not authorized, wills and adoptions, and dealt with other matters connected with private law.

This primitive assembly became politically obsolete during the early Republic, if not before the end of the Monarchy. It was superseded by another assembly of the people in arms, known as the *comitia centuriata*. The only remaining political function of the *comitia curiata*, which was reduced to thirty lictors, one for each *curia*, was to confer the power of command, *imperium*, upon the magistrates elected by the *comitia centuriata*.

The new assembly may have owed its rise to a reform of the army and to the introduction of new equipment and tactics in the time of the Etruscan kings, as will be discussed later.

Achievements under the Kings The names of the kings after Romulus (though too few to account for the whole period from ca. 750 to ca. 500 B.C.) and some of the deeds traditionally ascribed to them may well be based on a core of historical facts. According to tradition, Numa was a priest-king who introduced the arts of peace to Rome after Romulus, the warrior-king. Such a scheme is obviously too pat, and all of the institutions attributed to Numa—cults, priesthoods (for example, flamens, pontiffs, Salians, Vestal Virgins), the twelve-month solar calendar —would have taken more than a single reign to develop. It may well be, however, that a king named Numa played a crucial role in the process of uniting several small villages into a single state and earned a permanent place in the folk traditions of the Romans.

Tullus Hostilius stands out in more detail. The family of the Hostilii did not

become prominent at Rome until after the list of kings had long been set. This fact indicates that his name was not a later pious fiction to please some powerful people, as often appears the case with many names in traditional accounts of early Rome. That he led a counterattack against Alba Longa in the mid-seventh century B.C. and destroyed it receives support from the disappearance of Alba about 650 B.C. Even the name given to the opposing Alban commander, Mettius Fufetius, adds weight to the story because "Mettius" is Latin for the Oscan *meddix*, a kind of magistrate; the "mistake" of turning an unfamiliar foreign title into a proper name, as the tradition was handed down through the years, actually supports its authenticity.

Like Tullus Hostilius, Ancus Marcius, the fourth traditional king, seems authentic because there were no other prominent Marcii at Rome until long after the list of kings had been fixed in tradition. There is no archaeological evidence to support the story that, during his reign at the end of the seventh century B.C., Ostia was founded at the mouth of the Tiber; but it was at this time that the Romans were taking an active interest in the salt pans at the Tiber's mouth. Therefore, the view that Ancus Marcius built the wooden *Pons Sublicius* across the Tiber to connect with the salt route may well be genuine. Perhaps he also established the venerable priesthood of the pontiffs *(pontifices)*, whose name means bridgebuilders.

An apparently independent Etruscan tradition antedating the earliest Roman historical speculations corroborates the existence of the Tarquins. A fourth century wall painting in the François tomb near Vulci bears, among others, the name of Gneve Tarchu Rumach (Gnaeus Tarquinius of Rome). Macstrna (Mastarna), also named in this painting, cannot with absolute certainty be identified with King Servius Tullius, to whom some ascribe the Etruscan name Mastarna, although the name Caelius Vibenna (Caile Vipinas), the legendary friend of the Roman king, also appears here. Other Etruscan inscriptions prove that the Tarchna (Tarquins) were Etruscan nobles. An inscription at Vulci mentions the name of Tanaquil, the legendary wife of Tarquin the First and guardian of Servius Tullius.

Under Etruscan rule (from ca. 575 to 508 B.C., or later) Rome rapidly developed economically, culturally, and politically. Her territory expanded from approximately 58 square miles to 350 or more; her total population in the city and surrounding outstripped that of any of her Latin neighbors. The city itself was laid out as the *Roma Quadrata* (Rome of the Four Regions), ascribed to Servius Tullius by an extant papyrus fragment of an unknown Latin author, possibly Cato the Censor, and it was surrounded by a ritually plowed furrow (the so-called *pomerium*). Laid out also with *cardo* and *decumanus* intersecting, according to Etruscan city planning, at right angles, the city contained numerous public buildings, a forum, drainage works, the grand circus, and the great Capitoline temple of Jupiter, which covered almost an acre of ground, was constructed and decorated by the finest architects and artists of Etruria, and, according to the Greek historian Polybius, was dedicated in 509 or 508/7 B.C. to the triad of Jupiter, Juno, and Minerva—old Italic deities whose worship the Etruscans introduced into Rome.

The Etruscan kings themselves probably did much to promote the economic development of Rome. Their building projects not only served to beautify the city, but created a reservoir of skilled labor. Besides encouraging the immigration of traders and craftsmen, they made living quarters available to foreign merchants on the Aventine, to which annual fairs held in the precincts of the temple of Diana attracted people from all over Latium for both worship and trade. Also, the text of a treaty signed with Carthage, as preserved in translation by Polybius, may, if authentic, reveal the extension of Roman trade outside of Italy toward the close of Etruscan rule.

Under the Etruscan kings the simple monarchy of the past became a powerful institution. It was dignified by an elaborate state ceremonial and arrayed with awe-inspiring symbols of kingly power that became perma-

nent parts of Roman public life forever after: lictors armed with *fasces* (rods bound around a double-bitted ax), the ivory eagle-headed scepter and golden wreath, the purple embroidered toga, the curule chair (movable seat of office), and the triumphal four-horse chariot. The Etruscan kings used their powerful positions to reform Roman military practices and thereby turn Rome into the most powerful state in Latium.

The Early Roman Army   Among the early Romans were men no doubt as brave as Agamemnon or Ulysses, but no Homer sang of their arms or deeds in war. The lack of such a contemporary witness is not sufficiently made up for by archaeology to enable modern scholars to reconstruct the story of early Roman warfare in detail, but a reasonable sketch can be made.

Before the close of the seventh century there seems to have been little organized fighting by masses of armed men. Like the heroes of the *Iliad,* the clan chiefs rode to battle in chariots, got off, and met their opponents in individual combat. Their arms were spears, swords or battle-axes, and large oblong shields protected their bodies from neck to knee. Behind each chief there followed on foot a crowd of retainers, who backed him up more by cheering than by fighting. Warfare came into being only with the rise of the state.

In the sixth century, the period of the Etruscan kings, there occurred a syndrome of changes—economic, social, military, and constitutional—more revolutionary in their impact on world history than the fall of the Monarchy and the birth of the Republic at the end of this century: the growth of Rome as a road center and trading post; its increase in area, population, and wealth; the rise of private property and the individual family; the decay of the clans as political and military units; and the incorporation of all such primitive organizations into a single city-state. These important developments dictated a radical change in military tactics and in the composition of the army. The new army was a citizen army; its strength lay in the heavily armed infantry, which moved as a massive expression of the unity of the newborn state.

A similar pattern had earlier occurred in Greece. The rise of the city-states had rendered the Homeric style of individual warfare obsolete. In its place came new arms and tactics, the most important of which was a battle formation, the hoplite phalanx, in which heavily armed infantry troops advanced to the attack in tight ranks from eight to twelve lines deep. Each soldier now carried a long thrusting spear. He was protected by a small round shield fastened to the left arm, and by a helmet, corselets, and greaves all made of metal. First employed with increasing efficiency by the Lydians of the early seventh century B.C. and perfected by the Spartans, the phalanx soon developed into a machine of great striking power. Introduced into Italy by the Greeks during the last decades of the seventh century B.C., it gradually spread among the Italic tribes, and during the sixth century, as shown by a decorated ostrich egg found at Vulci, near Tarqunii, was adopted by the Etruscans who passed it on to the Romans.

The first formal Roman army seems to have been based on the three tribes, with each of the ten *curiae* in a tribe providing a quota of ten cavalry and one hundred infantry. The one thousand infantry of each tribe were commanded by a tribune of the soldiers, *tribunus militum,* and the one hundred cavalry by a tribune of the cavalry, *tribunus celerum.* Tradition ascribes a complete military reform to King Servius Tullius (mid-sixth century B.C.), and there is good reason to accept the basic outline recorded, although all of the changes probably were not introduced by one king, but happened gradually during at least the last half of the sixth century B.C. This reorganization enabled Rome to meet her increasing military commitments.

To replace battle losses and field a larger army required a larger body of citizens, who alone were eligible for the draft. As it happened, Etruscan Rome was filled with immigrants willing to endure military service in return for citizenship. To give it to them, it was necessary to free citizenship from the kinship groups of tribe and clan and give it a civil basis. Therefore, although the so-called Servian reorganization arose out of military necessity, it became more than a simple reform of the army, for it transformed the state as well and had revolutionary political implications, although many of them probably were not worked out until the fifth and fourth centuries B.C. Its outcome was a city-state based no longer on the ancient clans but on the citizen as a member of both the community and the army.

For military purposes, according to tradition, Servius Tullius assigned the free population to new territorial tribes, four urban and sixteen rural, based strictly on residence. The new tribes served as census districts for the registration of citizens and the assessment of their property for the purposes of taxation and military recruitment.

The assessment of property was very important, because a man's wealth determined the kind of equipment that he could supply, since the state did not supply any for him. If not at first, at least eventually there were five census classifications, *classes* (sing. *classis*), based on the possession of a minimum amount of land—probably 20, 15, 10, 5, and 2½ or 2 *iugera* respectively (one *iugerum* equals about two-thirds of an acre). In later times, the minimum requirements were based on monetary evaluations. Each class was also divided into juniors, *iuniores,* men between the ages of seventeen and forty-six eligible for front line duty, and seniors, *seniores,* men from forty-seven to sixty who could be used for garrison duty and guarding the city's walls.

Furthermore, members of each census class were assigned to units called centuries, *centuriae* or "hundreds." Even the original centuries probably were not groups of precisely one hundred each but were groups responsible for supplying the army with one hundred men from their numbers. The officer in charge of the one hundred from each group naturally became known as a *centurion.* Since the cavalry and the heavily armed legionary troops comprised the biggest part of the army and required the most expensive equipment, the men of the higher census classes were spread over more centuries, while the men of the lower classifications, who supplied light-armed auxilliaries, skirmishers, carpenters, smiths, trumpeters, and other support personnel, were concentrated in fewer centuries.

The precise numerical impact of the original reform on the size of the Roman legion is not known and is not so important as the eventual political organization of the citizen body that resulted. By the mid-fifth century B.C. a new popular assembly, the *comitia centuriata,* based on the organization of the citizens by centuries, had become firmly established (see pp. 52–53).

During the Regal Period, therefore, Rome had grown from a collection of separate little agricultural villages huddled on neighboring hilltops to a unified city-state covering 350 square miles along the lower Tiber and embracing the largest population in Latium. Especially in the Etruscan period it had become an important commercial crossroad with a thriving urban center around the Forum, although agriculture remained the primary basis of its wealth. It had acquired a relatively sophisticated political and military system that made it a significant force in Latium and southern Etruria. Although the Etruscan kings would soon be overthrown and a republic created, their legacy would endure.

IV

Early Roman Social Structure, Religion, and Values

To understand Roman history, it is necessary to understand the nature of Roman personal and social relations and the religious and ethical frameworks within which they operated. At the center was the Roman family. It was the basis of the early state, which was simply a community organized to protect the interests of its constituent families and controlled by the families' heads, *patres*. What concerned the families as a group was the state, the *res publica* (literally the common wealth or common thing). Its close connection with the *patres* of the families is confirmed by the Latin word for country, *patria,* which comes from the adjective *patrius,* "belonging to the father." Roman religion and law are basically extensions of the religious and ethical practices of the families and *patres* who made up and controlled the community.

The predominance of the family over the state never completely disappeared in Roman history, as can be seen in the dynastic ambitions of Roman emperors right up to the end. The family was a living thing, as the state was not. Citizens could be motivated to benefit the state not so much for the state's sake as for the honor and prestige that could be gained for themselves and their families. The approval of one's ancestors, whose presence was always felt in the traditions handed down from generation to generation and in the death masks and busts that adorned the Roman home, and the chance to perpetuate oneself in the memory of future generations, were powerful incentives to civic action. On the other hand, where the interests of the family seemed to be at variance with those of the state, there was always a great temptation to sacrifice the state's interests if the two could not be reconciled. Therefore, the state could easily become the battleground of competing interests among the powerful families that controlled it.

Historical Development of the Roman Family The English word *family* is used to translate the Latin word *familia,* from which it is derived, but the two words are not exact equivalents. The early Roman family was not primarily a genealogical concept. Though later writings often use the word *familia* in the sense of an association of blood relations, it was not simply a group of persons connected by ties of blood or marriage. It was rather an association of housemates—blood relatives, adopted members, slaves, and former slaves who had been freed. Moreover, it included the spirits of deceased members, whose presence

Junius Brutus, a Roman noble, with busts of his ancestors; lifesize marble, first century A.D. *(New York Public Library Picture Collection)*

and subject to the absolute control of the head of the household, called the *pater familias.*

Under the guidance, control, and management of the *pater familias,* the Roman family was not only a community of work and property, but a system of defense, law, and government—a miniature state. In the earliest Roman law it was recognized as a closed, self-sufficient, self-contained association, an economic unit operating under self-given rules within the larger framework of the economic system then prevailing and completely free from interference by the state. It was also a religious organization, a community of worship centered around the cult of the hearth and the cult of the dead.

Genealogically, the early Roman family was probably a single extended unit with several generations living and working together in one household. Linguistic evidence supports this view; comparative law and folklore justify it; and survivals of it down to historic times seem to confirm it. Plutarch says that in the early first century B.C. Marcus Crassus lived with his two married brothers in his father's little house and all had their meals together at the same table. Similarly, Aemilius Paullus, from the previous century, was part of a family of sixteen grown men who with their wives and many children all lived together in one small house and worked a small farm near Veii. These instances are evidently the latest survivals of an earlier form of Roman family life.

In early Rome the cultivation of tough soil with crude tools, the herding of livestock, and the absence of large numbers of slaves made the extended family an economic necessity. As the economy and population expanded, however, the Roman family usually became too large for all members to live in a single household. Brothers and sons set up new households, which remained united as one family under a single patriarchal head so long as their *pater familias* was alive or mentally competent.

The Gens   Originally, the Roman family had been subordinate to the *gens.* The Latin

was felt and who were believed to take an active interest in the family's welfare and activities.

The Roman family also consisted of objects as well as persons, as is clear from the origin of the word *familia,* which is thought to have meant first dwelling-place or house, then the house-community. Therefore, it came to mean in a legal sense the house-property. Both persons and property were at the disposal of word *gens,* whose plural form is *gentes,* is etymologically connected with Greek *genos* and with the English word *kin,* and is commonly translated *clan.* It is usually considered a group of families united by a common name and by the belief of common descent from a single male ancestor (divine, human, or animal).

In early times every Roman had two names, a personal or given name *(praenomen)* and the name of his gens *(nomen);* later, as the *gens* became larger and was subdivided into families, a third or family name *(cognomen)* was added. Thus, for example, Gaius Julius Caesar had three names—Gaius the given name, Julius the name of his *gens,* and Caesar the name of his family within the Julian *gens.* The word *gens,* therefore, meant to the Romans an association of families united by ties of blood, a social organization which has analogies in practically all Indo-European-speaking peoples of antiquity. The importance of the *gens* itself may have emerged as earlier even large tribal groups lost coherence.

Some modern writers hold, and perhaps rightly, that the region around Rome was originally settled by three tribes—the Tities, Ramnes, and Luceres of Roman tradition. As these tribes disintegrated, their settled territory was broken into small rural administrative units known as *pagi.* Henceforth, the Romans were divided into rural *pagani* and urban *montani* (inhabitants of the seven hills). Within each *pagus* lived a *gens.* It exercised jurisdiction and censure over its members, and within its own territory or *pagus* it fostered a spirit of solidarity and mutual assistance. After the formation of the city-state, the *gens* sent its leader into the senate, the advisory council of the king.

In primitive times, the *gens* had its own army, isolated survivals of which persisted even as late as the early first century B.C. Territory seized from an enemy was not assigned to individual families, but was declared public land and reserved for occupation by the *gentes;* the residents of the conquered territory were reduced to dependents called clients *(clientes).*

Later, during the fifth century B.C., as the state took over the functions of defense,

police, and law enforcement, the *gens* ceased to exist as a true political and economic organization. Its influence lived on mainly as a religious community and as a bond of sentiment among families of the same name. The heads of the individual families, seeing its usefulness gone, tended to regard it as more of a nuisance than a source of protection. The family, however, remained of paramount importance.

It may be concluded that by the middle of the fifth century, if not before, three major developments had occurred or were already in progress: (1) the decay of the *gens* as a political and economic organization; (2) the expansion of families into several households; and (3) the development of private ownership of landed property and its concentration in the hands of the all-powerful *pater familias.*

The Pater Familias   The *pater familias* was not necessarily a begetter of children. The phrase meant simply "master of the household." He might have no children of his own; he might even be a bachelor. The only qualification was that he be subject to no authority save that of the state, that he be legally independent and self-sufficient in dealing with other families and the state. In a legal sense he was the family, and without him there was no family or household.

His power within the family was absolute, unlimited by the state or by any other social agency, and subject only to such moral and economic conditions as temporarily prevailed. Accordingly, he was the source of law within the family, and there his orders were recognized by the community as having the force of law. His authority was based on ancestral custom, of which he was sole judge and interpreter. He was the judge of the household, and his rulings could not be set aside by any external authority, even though he might kill, mutilate, expel, or give into bondage his sons or housemates, and though he might break or dispose of the household property.

The father's absolute power, the *patria potestas,* was seldom despotic or tyrannical. He had a duty to consult other members of the family, especially the adult males and his wife, the *mater familias*. His function was to promote the welfare of the entire family, not destroy it by abuse. An important part of that function, therefore, was to ensure the favor of the unseen powers who might work for good or for ill. Each morning and evening, with the *pater familias* as priest, the entire family, including the slaves, offered prayers and sacrifices to the dead. An essential element in Roman ancestor worship was the cult of the *genius* of the living *pater familias,* in whom was incarnated the unity and perpetuity of the family. The *genius* was more than a personification of his power of procreation. It was his guiding spirit, his inseparable companion, the source of his authority and strength, and the tie that bound him to his ancestors. He offered daily sacrifices to his departed ancestors at the family hearth, whose ever-burning fire symbolized the unity and continuity of the family.

Children born to him in wedlock as well as those adopted into the family were subject to his will, regardless of their age and status. His sons were not absolved from his authority even after they had married and set up households of their own, unless he formally freed them. Similarly, a daughter remained under her father's *potestas* unless he permitted her to enter a form of marriage that transferred her to her husband's possession *(conventio in manum)*. In the male line of descent, a *pater familias* retained this authority not only over his children but also over succeeding generations so long as he lived or remained mentally competent. The authority of a *pater familias,* however, did not take precedence over their rights and duties as citizens, as voters in the tribal lists, or as soldiers. Sons under his *potestas* could also contract legal marriages and acquire property, though in the eyes of early Roman law they could not fully own this property, enter into contracts binding upon the family estate, or withhold for their own use any income accruing from their work.

Such was the power wielded by the *pater familias* in a society where law was based on custom and not enforced by any agency of the state. Respect for and obedience to tradition implanted by religious precept usually rendered his exercise of authority not a brutal display of force, but a recognized distribution of the only justice that could be secured until the "moral imperative" was replaced later by the "legal imperative" established by the state.

The state, moreover, benefitted from the patriarchal, authoritarian nature of the Roman family. Family life fostered obedience to authority and the willingness to do one's duty. On the civic level, the king and later the Republic's magistrates stood in a position of authority similar to that of the *pater familias.* They exercised the same duties between members of different families as did the *pater familias* within the family. They could expect the same kind of obedience from subordinates. As commanders in war, they had the right to execute anyone who refused to obey, just as the *pater familias* had the right to do with anyone under his authority. Under normal circumstances, the obedience to authority fostered by the Roman family therefore helped hold in check the centrifugal forces that also existed within the state from the pursuit of family interests.

Clientage   Another social institution of great significance to the state was *clientage,* the relationship between patron and client. It was much like that between a medieval feudal lord and his vassals. In early and primitive Rome, however, clients may not have been at first dependents of individual *patroni* or small single families, but rather of the *gens* as a whole.

The origin of clients was varied. Some were non-Roman inhabitants of conquered territory; some were Romans unable to make a living as free men or to defend their lives and property; some were emancipated slaves; some were strangers who voluntarily sought admission into the *gens* so as to be able to reside permanently on Roman soil and eventually to acquire Roman citizenship. This arrangement was advantageous to both *gens* and client. In return for a grant of land, for political and financial support, for protection in the courts, and for the privilege of sharing in the religious life of the *gens,* the client was expected to be loyal and cooperative, to render military service, to do field work, and to assist in other ways when called upon. In this way the client gained security, and the *gens* workers and soldiers.

As the *gens* declined in importance, clients were no longer its dependents, but those of the rich and powerful families that had become independent of their *gentes*. Such families eagerly sought clients not only for economic reasons, but for social and political ones. It was a mark of prestige to have as many dependents as possible. Moreover, in elections for political office, clients customarily campaigned and voted for their patrons or for candidates whom their patrons favored.

The relationship between patron and client was strengthened by the religiously sanctioned concept of *fides,* faithfulness in performing one's obligations. It was an offense against the gods for either a patron or a client, once having accepted their mutual relationship, to shirk the duties imposed. This view was accepted even in Rome's earliest law code, the Twelve Tables: "Cursed be the patron who has done his client wrong."

The attitudes behind the patron-client relationship also affected dealings between Rome and other states. It was always Roman policy to grant a treaty to others only from a position of strength, and not accept one forced upon Rome. Therefore, Rome assumed the superior position of a patron, not the inferior one of a client, or even one of an equal partner. *Fides* obligated the Romans to abide by any treaty and look out for the interests of the other party. On the other hand, the other party was expected to be a faithful client to its Roman patron in ways that usually were not spelled out in a written treaty. An ally failing to understand this Roman attitude and thinking itself not obligated beyond the letter of a treaty could quickly find itself the object of unexpected Roman anger.

Patricians and Plebeians   Although it is not exactly clear when or how, at some point before the end of the Monarchy and the beginning of the Republic (ca. 500 B.C.)

the Roman people became divided into two distinct social and political classes, the patricians and the plebeians, nobles and nonnobles, as was typical of ancient city-states. Both classes enjoyed the basic rights of citizenship but differed from each other in social and political privileges. The patricians monopolized the senate, filled the priestly colleges, and held high positions like that of *interrex*. Social convention divided them into greater and lesser *gentes (patres maiorum gentium* and *patres minorum gentium),* but the distinction was not very significant.

As citizens the plebeians had the right to make commercial contracts, own real property, contract valid marriages, sue or be sued in court, and vote in the popular assemblies. They were not, however, usually allowed to become members of the senate, be public priests, or hold offices of state, and the patricians generally did not intermarry with them. Moreover, these distinctions widened over time and tended to become more formal in the late sixth and early fifth centuries B.C.

The distinction between the two classes cannot be explained simply in terms of wealth. Many plebeians were as wealthy as patricians, although the great majority were not. Neither did the origin of the two classes have any particular ethnic basis, for both the patricians and the plebeians were a mixture of Latin, Sabine, and Etruscan elements. Nor did the plebeians seem to have originated solely as clients of the *gentes,* for the earliest plebeians were themselves divided into *gentes.* It is, however, possible that the founders of some plebeian *gentes* were fortunate or enterprising clients who had managed to prosper and establish their own independent but socially inferior *gentes.* Conversely, some formerly wealthy and powerful *gentes* may have been less successful than others in agriculture, warfare, and business, so that they sank to a lower social and economic position incompatible with patrician status. Finally, in the period of the Etruscan kings, the number of plebeians was swollen by immigrant merchants, traders, artisans, and laborers, and the inhabitants of outlying villages conquered and absorbed by Rome. Many of the newcomers were also not of inferior economic status but would not have been accepted by Roman patricians as their social equals.

Early Roman Religion Religion played an important role in both the private and political life of Rome. A religion of home, farm, and pasture, it was concerned with present rather than with past or future needs. It inculcated the virtues of hard work, discipline, duty, courage, and loyalty. When the religion of the home became the religion of the state, it cemented the people together in a single community and gave the state an internal strength and cohesion that endured for centuries. Despite class struggles, changes of government, and foreign wars, it provided a common bond between rich and poor, patrician and plebeian, farmer and city dweller, and enabled the Roman state to face the world with unity and strength.

Like other Italic peoples, the Romans had a varied religious inheritance from the past: from the various prehistoric inhabitants of Italy, from the Indo-European-speaking immigrants of Central and Balkan Europe, from the Etruscans in the north and the Greek colonists of the south. As a result, the Roman heritage contained elements of almost every known religious experience: totemism, magic, taboo, dynamism, animism, polytheism, and anthropomorphism. There are traces of totemism in the cults of the *gens*. Magic and taboo, though barred from the state religion, persisted among the common people throughout all Roman history.

Magic and Taboo   Magic, the mechanical use of certain materials, rites, formulae, or spells designed to force Nature, spirits, or other people to do one's will, survived during the classical period. An example of sympathetic magic was the ceremony of the "Dripping Stone" *(lapis manalis):* a wet stone kept near the Temple of Mars outside the Porta Capena was brought into the city to produce rain during droughts. Another was the *Luper-*

calia, which Shakespeare popularized in *Julius Caesar.* Two bands of youths with their brows smeared with the blood of a slaughtered goat and wearing goat skins around their thighs raced around the Palatine striking all the women they met with leather whips. The purpose of this rite was to dispel the curse of sterility. Charms and spells were commonly employed to drive away diseases, plagues, and foul weather, to fix broken bones, and to bring good crops and even success in war.

Allied to magic was another primitive survival usually known by its Polynesian name of *taboo.* In general it is a prohibition against persons, things, or acts regarded as dangerous to individuals or to the community. It was taboo for a woman to take part in the worship of Hercules, for a man to witness the female-administered rites of the Bona Dea (Good Goddess), or for a horse to enter the sacred grove of Diana. A whole set of inexplicable ancient taboos fenced in the life and office of Jupiter's high priest, the *Flamen Dialis.* He might not see an army in battle gear nor do any kind of common work; never ride or touch a horse, a she-goat, or a dog; never cut his hair or nails with an iron knife; never wear an unbroken ring or have knots tied in his clothing; and never eat, among other things, wheat bread, raw meat, or beans. He could not be unmarried, and he had to be united with his wife, the *Flamenica Dialis,* by the most ancient form of marriage, *Confarreatio.* The *flamenica* performed an equal role in administering Jupiter's cult and was bound by similar taboos.

Dynamism and Animism   The native religion of the early Romans is called *animism* by some scholars and *dynamism* by others. Dynamism, a term derived from the Greek word *dynamis* ("power"), is the belief that supernatural powers are synonymous with certain objects, places, and natural processes; living beings are inhabited by and indeed synonymous with supernatural spirits, which are conceived of as impersonal, immanent, and pervasive. Animism, on the other hand, being derived from *anima,* the Latin word for "soul" or "spirit," regards these same objects as inhabited by a discrete spirit which has a personal will, although it never attains the personality of a god of human form (anthropomorphic). Though dynamism is often regarded as a more primitive form of animism, actually both phases of belief existed side by side and were closely related.

The earliest form of animism was probably a vague belief in collective and undefined spirits, usually thought of as hostile or malignant powers haunting persons, objects, and places like thick woods, dark caves, volcanoes, or old forest trees struck by lightning. These spirits aroused fear and had to be propitiated with offerings and prayers. As farm and family life became more settled and secure, certain spirits came to be regarded as friendly and helpful beings, if properly placated. They had their abode in such familiar objects in the house and on the farm as the house door (Janus), the fireplace (Vesta), and the boundary stones that marked off one farm from another (Termini), and over all was Jupiter or the sky, the region of light, cloud, and storm.

The later animism recognized, in addition to the spirits of particular things and places, spirits presiding over definite human activities, especially the ones having to do with the making and storage of farm crops. Of these the most individualized and universal in their worship were Ceres, the spirit of grain crops; Consus, of the stored harvest; Saturn, of planting; Robigus, of rust or mildew; Flora, of flowers; and Pomona, of fruits.

As religion became more highly organized, each separate operation of farm work had a special spirit (plowing, harrowing, sowing, weeding, harvesting, and storing). Each of these many functional spirits received offerings at the proper season of the year. When certain spirits were observed to be operating at the same time in many places and for many families, they tended to become more real, more personal, and more human in form and personality. They gradually acquired names, had special priesthoods and rituals attached to their worship, and eventually attained the status of gods.

Numen or Mana   The supernatural powers dwelling in certain sacred objects and places, in natural processes, in human activities, and in gods were thought of as possessing a mysterious invisible force or influence, which Latin writers of the late first century B.C. and early first century A.D. called *numen* (plural *numina*), but modern anthropologists identify by the Melanesian name of *mana*. *Numen* was both a particular and a general concept. A spirit was a *numen* and its life-force was *numen* in general. To the early Romans nothing exists except by virtue of its particular *numen,* and without it no act can be performed. It is not the cobra that strikes, but the *numen* within the cobra; it is not the spear that kills, but the *numen* within the spear. Jupiter is the sky as well as the *numen* of the sky, Janus both the door and the spirit within the door. Like *mana, numen* connotes the triple idea of Power, Life, Will. As Power it brings about effects beyond human capability; as Life, it possesses a living consciousness; as Will, it can act for good or evil, if it wills.

Sacrifice and Prayer   It was this mysterious Power-Life-Will association that evoked the feeling of religion *(religio)* in its primary sense of fear or anxiety and in its secondary sense of a desire to establish right relations with the various *numina* by propitiation, prayer, sacrifice, and other rituals. A Roman sacrifice was made in the conviction that it was good for the spirits as well as for the worshipper, and the accompanying prayer *"Macte esto"* ("Be thou increased") reflects the belief that the offering increased the spirits' power to perform their special function for his benefit. Sacrifice replenished the store of vital force consumed by the spirit. To restore the vital force taken from Mother Earth by growing crops, the Romans held the annual spring festival of the *Fordicidia,* at which they killed a pregnant cow and made a burnt sacrifice of her aborted calf, in order to "transfer" to the earth the fertility of a cow in calf. Sacrifice was also a means of infusing *numen* into objects not possessing it before. To consecrate a new boundary stone between farms, the Romans used to make offerings of incense, grain, honey, and wine together with the blood of a lamb or sow. To restore the *numen* of all boundary stones each spring, they performed similar rites at the festival of *Terminalia*.

If by sacrifice the *numen* or *mana* of a spirit could be increased, renewed, strengthened, or conferred, it was by prayer that worshippers expressed their desire as to the use and direction of that increased power. To make sure that their desires and petitions were clearly and fully understood, they worded their prayers in exact and unambiguous language. Any slip of the tongue made it necessary to start all over again. Having correctly and reverently performed the two chief acts of worship—sacrifice and prayer—the worshippers had done their part. The rest lay with the will of the unseen powers.

Gods of the House and Fields   The cults and festivals of house and field were the oldest and the most vital; they preceded the founding of Rome and outlived her fall. In the time of her greatness some found expression in the wall paintings of Pompeii; many in the poetry of Vergil, Horace, Ovid, and Tibullus. Greek and oriental cults did not completely supplant them; Christianity did not utterly destroy them. Under various names and disguises, they have survived to modern times among the peasants of Italy and Spain.

The spirits of the house were few, but all illustrated the various phases of animism previously outlined. They were partly local, partly functional in character. There was Janus, the spirit of the door, who represented the home in its insecure relation to the outside world. He faced both in and out, letting in friends and shutting out enemies. Family life began with Janus. At weddings it was the custom for the bride to smear his doorposts with wolf's fat and to be lifted over his threshold. At the birth of a child the threshold was struck with an ax, a pestle, and a broom to repulse wild spirits from the outside. When someone died in the house, the corpse was carried out feet first for fear that the ghost might find its way back in.

Inside the house was Vesta, the spirit of the fireplace, whose fire gave warmth and cooked the daily meals. She was pure spirit, the *numen* of the living flame. Of her no image or statue was made in early times. Yet she was the center of family life and worship. To her the head of the house presented his bride or newborn child. Before her hearth stood the dining table, also a sacred object. The salt dish was on it and the sacred salt cake baked by the daughters of the house. At dinner the head of the family ceremoniously threw part of the cake into the fire. As Janus began, so Vesta ended the roll of deities invoked in family prayer.

Not far from the fireplace was the pantry. Here dwelt a vague group of nameless spirits collectively known as the Penates. With Vesta they shared the offerings made at the fireplace because they guarded the food that Vesta cooked. In Latin literature they were a synonym for home. So were the Lares.

Originally the Lares were probably not gods of the house but of the fields. As spirits of the fields, the Lares were worshipped at the Feast of the Crossroads *(Compitalia)*, a thanksgiving festival in which even slaves took part. The plows were hung up as a sign that the season's work was done, and everybody joined in the feasting and fun. Still more picturesque was the festival of the *Ambarvalia*, held toward the end of May to secure divine favor for the growing and ripening crops. The farmer and his family, dressed in white with olive wreaths around their heads, solemnly drove a pig, a sheep, and a bull *(suovetaurilia)* three times around the farm. The three animals were then killed, opened, examined for omens, and burned upon the altar fire. There followed a long prayer for good weather and good crops to Mars, originally the god of agriculture.

Besides the *Fordicidia* and *Terminalia* already described, there took place in spring the *Liberalia*, for Liber (the god of wine), the *Cerealia*, for Ceres (the goddess of grain), and the *Robigalia*, at which a red dog was sacrificed to avert mildew or rust, which attacked wheat. Shepherds had their spring festivals too. The

Palilia, or Feast of Pales, spirit of flocks and herds, took place in April just before the annual trek to summer pastures. At dawn the herdsmen sprinkled the animals with water, swept out the stalls, and decorated the barns with green branches. Then they lit a bonfire of straw, brush, and other stuff, through which both the flocks were driven and the shepherds leaped. After an offering of milk and cakes to Pales and a prayer for the health, safety, and increase of the flocks, they spent the rest of the day in sports, eating, and drinking.

Two festivals held in late summer or early fall are noteworthy because they are coupled with the names of Jupiter and Mars, whose association with agriculture was, in later times, largely forgotten. The first was the Feast of Wine *(Vinalia Rustica)* held on August 19th in honor of Jupiter, whose high priest after the sacrifice of a ewe-lamb solemnly inaugurated the grape-picking season by cutting the first bunch of grapes. The other was the festival of the October Horse in honor of Mars, in his dual capacity as god of war and god of farming. A chariot race was held. The near horse of the winning team and a spear were sacrificed to Mars. The horse's tail, a phallic symbol, was rushed over to the King's House, where its blood, still warm, dribbled upon the hearth—the seat of vitality in the house, to which the strength and virility of the horse were thus transferred. The horse's head, cut off and decked with cakes, was fought over by the men of two adjacent wards in Rome, the winners being allowed to hang it up as a trophy in their ward.

Jupiter and Mars Unlike most of the numerous spirits animating the world of the early Roman farmer, Jupiter and Mars entered history fully anthropomorphic, endowed with human personality and form. Conceived originally as the sky and the spirit immanent in the sky, as the source and giver of light, and the unseen force in lightning, storm, and rain, Jupiter had long ago become a spirit of the vine as well, and was associated with Venus, the primitive Italic spirit of vines and gardens.

With the growth of political and urban life among the Latins and the Romans, Jupiter lost status as a farmer's god but came into his own as a god of cities and towns. He was the tribal deity of the Latins and the guardian of many Latin towns. In Rome he was the greatest of all gods, the symbol of the Roman state, the giver of victory, and the spirit of law and justice.

Rome similarly exalted Mars. Once an Italic spirit of the forest, he became the protector of the farmer's crops and herds, but later, as god of war, the defender of the Roman state against its enemies. Thus, with the rise of Rome as a city and a state, Jupiter and Mars lost all connection with agriculture, save the memory preserved in the rustic festivals just described.

Other Roman gods had undergone similar changes. The Italian and Etruscan gods, long before their introduction at Rome, had come under the anthropomorphizing influence of the Greeks living in south Italy. The outward signs of this influence were temples and statues. Unlike the old native spirits, the new anthropomorphic gods had to have houses to dwell in and statues to embody them.

Italic Cults After Rome had become a bridge town, a road center, and a trading post, she came into close contact with the cults of Latium and southern Etruria. She adopted as her own those which best filled newly felt needs. The most prominent and widespread of these cults was that of Juno, who was worshipped all over Italy and was a special favorite in Latium and southern Etruria. The growing popularity of her worship in Rome indicates that the city was becoming the cultural capital of the two districts lying on opposite sides of the Tiber.

From Falerii, a semi-Etruscan town higher up on the north side of the Tiber, came the cult of Minerva, an old Italian goddess of arts and crafts but worshipped under the name of Menvra in many Etruscan towns. Her worship in Rome, perhaps introduced by immigrant Faliscan workmen skilled in the pottery and metal trades, is clearly in line with the archaeological evidence of close commercial and industrial ties between Rome and south Etruria. The expansion of Roman commercial contacts is likewise pointed up by the erection in the Cattle Market *(Forum Boarium)* of an altar to Hercules, the patron god of the Greek and Italian traveling salesmen. Politically, the transfer of the worship of Diana from Aricia to the Aventine highlights Roman aspirations to leadership over the Latin League. So too does the coming to Rome of two other Latin goddesses destined to have a great future: Fortuna imported from Anzio and later identified with Tyche, the Greek goddess of luck or chance, and Venus, formerly worshipped at Ardea as a goddess of gardens and orchards, but later identified with Aphrodite, the Greek goddess of love and beauty.

Of the deities just named, all, except Hercules, had belonged originally to the spirit world of old Italy but had, before their adoption in Rome, been transformed through Greek influence into gods of human personality and form. Even Ceres, the most earthy and the most native of Italic spirits, did not escape the effects of this transforming influence. Identified with Demeter, the Greek goddess of cereals, she had a cult more foreign than that of Hercules in the Cattle Market. Her temple on the Aventine was not only the Grain Exchange but, during the early Republic, the church of the dispossessed and the political rendezvous of the plebs, who at that time were excluded from the religious and political life of the state.

Etruscan Influence   Contact with the Etruscans gave an even stronger impetus to the influx of Greek anthropomorphic ideas among the Romans. Of the gods worshipped by the Etruscans, Uni and Menvra were the Italic Juno and Minerva. Tinia, a truly Etruscan deity, was early identified with Jupiter. The temple that the Tarquins built on the Capitoline to that triad of deities must have been something new to the Romans, who had hitherto never set up for their gods anything more elaborate or permanent than a rude altar of stones or sods. The elevation of its site,

its massive appearance, and the beauty of its Greco-Etruscan ornaments provided the proper home for Rome's greatest deity. The Capitoline temple, together with the two temples of Diana and Minerva on the Aventine, firmly established temple building as a permanent feature of Roman religious life and powerfully reinforced the current trend from animism to the Greek anthropomorphic conception of deity.

Of even greater significance for Rome was the introduction of the Etruscan Discipline, *Disciplina Etrusca,* which prescribed religious rituals and the interpretation of omens through such things as thunder and lightning, the flights of birds, and the entrails of sacrificial animals, especially by inspecting their livers *(hepatoscopy).* Roman nobles, who served as priests, often sent their sons to Etruscan cities to learn this valuable lore. The Etruscan priests who interpreted these signs were called *hauruspices,* and on critical occasions the Romans would summon *hauruspices* from Etruria when they wanted extra assurance that they understood the divine will.

Greek Cults   The introduction of Greek anthropomorphic ideas and cults through Etruscan and Italian contacts was followed before and after the fall of the Monarchy by more direct contacts with the southern Italian Greeks. From Cumae, the nearest and oldest Greek settlement, came the worship of Apollo, the god of healing and prophecy, not long after 500 B.C. Despite his unlatinized name, Apollo became in later times one of the greatest gods of the Roman pantheon.

Cumae was also the home of the Sibyl, Apollo's inspired priestess, whose oracle must have been known in Etruscan Rome, though the story of Tarquin's purchase of the *Sibylline Books* is probably pure legend. The earliest collection of Sibylline oracles seems to have been made around 500 B.C. at the beginning of the Republic. Kept in the temple of Jupiter and guarded in strictest secrecy by a special college of two priests, the oracles were consulted only by command of the senate in time of war, disaster, plague, or famine. Consulted in times of stress, the *Sibylline Books* played a decisive role throughout the Republic in replacing the native animism of the past with a new Greco-Roman anthropomorphism.

Consultation usually resulted in the introduction of some new Greek deity or form of worship. For example, during the famine of ca. 496 B.C., a temple on the Aventine was promised and three years later dedicated to Ceres, Liber, and Libera, a triad of farm gods identical in almost everything but name with Demeter, Dionysus, and Persephone. The following year also saw the dedication on the Aventine of a temple to another Greek god, Hermes, under the name of Mercury. Like Hercules, he was a god of traders and especially of the grain merchants in both Etruria and Greek Italy. His temple was a grain market as well as a rendezvous of merchants and traders.

Seaborne imports from southern Italy seem to account for the early reception of Poseidon, the Greek god of the great open sea. He was identified with Neptune, though the latter was originally not a sea god but the spirit of springs and ponds and other small waters. Neptune quickly received the trident and sea horses of Poseidon and all of the mythology associated with him.

In addition to introducing new gods, the *Sibylline Books* prescribed new forms of worship, some exceedingly spectacular and emotional and all quite foreign to the pious, sober spirit of the early Roman religion. These innovations, both numerous and of great variety, consisted of funeral and secular games, stage plays and other dramatic performances, ritual dances, religious parades, and banquets of the gods (*lectisternia*) at which images of the gods grouped in pairs of the opposite sex were publicly displayed reclining on couches before tables spread with food and drinks.

The Roman State Religion The foreign cults just described were not the only factors involved in the changing religious life of the Roman people. Equally important changes occurred when the primitive religion of house and fields became organized as the religion of the state.

The state itself was essentially a religious institution. It embraced and incorporated all the older and smaller social and religious communities such as the family, the clan, and the tribe. According to the legend, it had been inaugurated, with religious ceremonies, by Romulus. The *pomerium,* which enclosed the city, was a sacred boundary. As the city grew and expanded, it was the responsibility of the state to provide for the common religious life of all the people on behalf of the whole community.

Household cults had great appeal because family life was very much the same in town and country. The most popular and successful were those of Janus and Vesta. Janus, the spirit of the house door, became the god of the Sacred Gateway at the northeast corner of the Forum. As the early armies probably marched through this gate on their way to war, it was kept closed only in peacetime. Another of the household deities to find a place in the state religion was Vesta, the Sacred Hearth, whose holy fire, relit only on March 1, the New Year's Day of the state, was kept burning by the Vestal Virgins. Unlike many of the old field cults and festivals listed in the state calendar, the worship of Janus and Vesta aroused genuine religious feeling among the citizens because it fostered a sense of belonging to one great national family. The cults that roused the strongest feelings of pride and love of Rome were those of Jupiter and Mars. Mars was the god of her triumphant armies, his altar the symbol of her military power. Jupiter Optimus Maximus (Best and Greatest) sent down upon Rome "the continual dew of his divine favor."

The Values of Early Roman Society

People act within a framework of commonly held values and moral assumptions. If one wants to understand how and why people behave as they do, it is, therefore, necessary to understand the ethical framework within which they operate. The early Romans developed a deeply held set of values that affected not only their own history but later ages as well. It is significant that most modern European names of moral concepts stem from Latin, and some of them still retain their original meaning. The English words *virtue, prudence, temperance, fortitude, justice, piety, fidelity, constancy,* and *perseverance* stem from Latin roots. Of these words, *virtue* alone has a distinctly different meaning from that which it had in ancient Rome. All of the corresponding Latin concepts were a vital part of early Roman life. They were enshrined in the *mos maiorum* (ancestral custom) and were consciously fostered by men and women through education and example in private and public life.

Virtue (Virtus)   The word *virtus*, which is derived from *vir* (man, a male) included everything that made up the true man and a useful member of society. It is virtue, says the poet Lucilius (ca. 180 to 103 B.C.), for a man to know what is good, what evil, what useless, shameful, and dishonorable; to be an enemy of bad men and customs, to be a friend and protector of those that are good; to place first one's country's good, next that of one's parents, and last that of one's self.

Virtue also meant a strong and healthy body, the ability to provide for one's family, interest in and devotion to the state, and heroism in war. If heroism was the greatest of these, it was not the individual heroism of Achilles or Hector; it was virtue only when used for the good and safety of the state. The ideal Roman hero was one whose courage and wisdom saved his country in time of peril. The virtues cited as examples in the moral education of the youths were drawn not from heroic poetry, as in Greece, but from history. Young men were taught that it was glorious to die for their country, as did the heroes of the past. So important was *virtus* as an element of early Roman values and character that it has become the generic term for all kinds of human excellence in many modern languages.

Piety (Pietas)   Four virtues were distinctively Roman and of great historic significance; piety, faith, gravity, and constancy.

The first, piety *(pietas)*, was a family virtue. It implied devotion and loyalty by men and women to the family group and a willing acceptance of parental authority, which gave unity and strength to the family. It further meant reverence and devotion to the gods as members of the family, as shown in action by the exact performance of all required religious rites and ceremonies. Piety toward the state connoted obedience to the laws, faithful service, and patriotism consistent with justice, law, and the constitution. In this virtue patriotic writers saw the prime reason for Rome's greatness.

Faith (Fides)   Another virtue the Romans took pride in was faith, which was called the "foundation of justice," and the "supreme guarantee of human happiness." It had special importance within social units larger than the family—the *gens* and the state. It meant being true to one's word, the paying of one's debts, the keeping of sworn oaths, and the performance of obligations assumed by agreement. Based on religion and law, it was the foundation of public and private life. Violation of it was an offense against both the gods and the community. A patron who broke faith with his client by unjust abuse of his power was placed under a curse. A magistrate who broke faith by acts of injustice and oppression against the people gave the latter the right to rebel. Faith rooted in the social conscience was stronger than written law or statute as a force for holding all parts of the society together in a common bond of relationship.

Gravity (Gravitas) and Constancy (Constantia)   Faith had to be supplemented by two other Roman virtues: gravity and constancy. The first meant absolute self-control—a dignified, serious, and unperturbed attitude toward both good and bad fortune. To cite some extreme examples, no Roman was supposed to dance in public nor were husbands and wives supposed to kiss each other outside of their own homes. The second virtue was constancy or perseverance, even under the most trying circumstances, in doing what seemed necessary and right until success was won. Of this virtue Rome herself was the greatest exponent, for in her long history she suffered many disastrous defeats. That she never broke under those defeats and often turned them into victories is no small tribute to Roman education.

Dignitas and Auctoritas Those who exhibited the qualities discussed above, especially in public life, acquired *dignitas* (reputation for worth, honor, esteem) and *auctoritas* (prestige, respect). They were highly prized by Roman aristocrats because they confirmed their leading role in society. Those who demonstrated virtue by successfully defending the community in warfare and who promoted the public welfare by faithfully performing their duties as patrons, priests, magistrates, and senators acquired the honor and prestige that set them apart from others and gave them the power to continue to lead, which in turn gave them the opportunity to earn more *dignitas* and *auctoritas* and thereby enhance their status in the community in competition with their aristocratic peers.

By 500 B.C., Rome's characteristic social structure that centered on the patriarchal family and that was dominated by an aristocratic elite had become fixed for many centuries to come. The complex amalgam of native animism, Etruscan divination, and Greco-Etruscan anthropomorphism and the various rituals associated with them had assumed its form for the future. Along with these social and religious developments had evolved the system of values that defined the Romans' view of themselves as individuals and as a people.

The ultimate effect of these develop-ments was conservative. Roman family life, religion, and morality fostered a conservative type of human being. The authoritarian, patriarchal family and the attitude of dependency inherent in clientage produced an obedience to authority that greatly benefitted the aristocrats who controlled the state. The reverence for ancestors and their customs enshrined in the words *mos maiorum* worked against attempts at radical innovation among all classes, as did the sobriety and piety of the Roman ethical tradition. Furthermore, since established customs had already been sanctioned by the gods, it was an offense against them to change those customs. The resultant abhorrence of innovation is signified by the Roman term for revolution, *res novae* (new things). Therefore, many archaic and obsolete practices, institutions, and offices continued to exist at Rome long after they had ceased to have a useful function.

New things had to be justified by finding precedents in the past, a practice at which the Romans became particularly adept as they were forced to adapt to new circumstances. In religion, therefore, the ancient *Sibylline Books,* with their convenient ambiguities and even opportune forgeries, justified the introduction of new cults and rituals from time to time, while priests skilled in the interpretation of divine will could adduce new meanings from old words. Even in politics, in a society where the vagaries of oral tradition predominated over written records, ''ancestral precedents'' might be of as recent origin as an orator's latest speech. Therefore, Roman conservatism was saved from being stultifying, and change could occur, while a deep sense of continuity, one of Rome's greatest strengths, was maintained.

V

The Rise
of the Roman Republic,
509 to 287 B.C.

The period of Roman history known as the Republic extended from about 500 (traditionally 509, B.C.) until 27 B.C., the beginning of the principate of Augustus, which marks the beginning of the Roman Empire. The term *republic (res publica)* has come to mean a form of government, not necessarily democratic, but essentially different from that which exists under a king or emperor. To the Romans the words *res publica* (common wealth, public thing) originally referred to common property and public affairs, as opposed to private property and affairs. To those looking back from the time when Rome was ruled by an emperor of almost unlimited power, so that he had assumed essentially private control over what had formerly been common and public, *res publica* came to be associated with the form of government that had essentially evolved in the fifth and fourth centuries B.C., a form that was far from democratic, but one in which the conduct of public affairs was shared equally among the members of an aristocratic class working through laws and institutions that limited the arbitrary exercise of power. The creation of that system is not always well documented, but a reasonable outline of the process can be drawn.

Sources of Information for Early Republican History   For this and the following chapter, the two chief literary sources are Livy (Books 2–5) and Dionysius of Halicarnassus (*Roman Antiquities,* Books 4–20). Their information was still largely derived from the early annalists and must be used with caution. The other major representative of the annalistic tradition is Cassius Dio, whose *Roman History* is preserved in extensive fragments for this period (Books 4–10). Two important brief sources are Polybius, a mid-second-century Greek historian, who treats the theory and development of the Roman constitution in Book 6 of his universal history of the Mediterranean world, and Cicero, the famous Roman orator and political figure of the mid-first century B.C., who contributed thirteen short chapters (25–37) in Book 2 of his *De Re Publica.* Plutarch's biography of Pyrrhus is also valuable for the period of the Pyrrhic War (280 to 275 B.C.). A few facts, some important and some not, are included in Plutarch's life of Camillus and Books 10 to 14 (11–14 fully preserved) of Diodorus' world history. The latter's most important contribution is his list of Roman consuls (chief yearly magistrates) beginning with approximately 486 B.C.

Temple Dedications Temple dedications also furnish fairly important data for fixing the chronology of this period. The dedication date of the Capitoline temple, inscriptionally established as 507 B.C., has been pronounced by one of our most skeptical critics as the oldest datable event of Roman history, the cornerstone of Roman chronology. Although the chief priests (pontiffs) took pains in accurately recording such important events as temple dedications, the dates of some have been established independently of pontifical recording. For example, the year 431 B.C. has been verified by Greek sources as the dedication date of the temple of Apollo on the Flaminian Meadows.

The Fasti In ancient states, calendar years were not numbered in chronological sequence but named after one or more of the chief annual magistrates: in Athens after the head archon, in Sparta after the chief ephor, in Rome after the consuls. All such officials are known as eponymous (naming) magistrates. Such a system made phenomenal demands upon the memory unless lists were handy for business, legal, and official purposes. During the fifth and fourth centuries of the Roman Republic, many such lists must have been available to public officials, priests, and private individuals.

The oldest, perhaps, and certainly the most famous list of Roman magistrates was that kept by the pontiffs from the earliest years of the Republic. At the beginning of each year the head pontiff had a white-washed tablet set up in his office. Across the top of the tablet were written the names of the consuls, the other important magistrates, and the priests. Then followed a list of the feast or holy days (*nefasti*) and the regular days (*fasti*) on which it was right to do business or hold court. Opposite each day space was left for noting unusual events such as eclipses, earthquakes, plagues, prodigies, temple dedications, wars and triumphs, and the like. At the end of the year the tablet was stored away in the archives for future reference. It was probably from this primitive ''card index'' that lists of magistrates were compiled for public and private use.

The question of how this information and how much of it was ultimately passed on to later times is greatly debated, but it was eventually published after the pontiffs stopped setting up the yearly boards in 130 B.C. and became known as the *Annales Maximi*. It recorded the names of the magistrates, the triumphs, and temple dedications from the beginning of the Republic. This was probably the chief source of the numerous *Fasti* compiled by various Roman historians. The *Fasti* all together account for the names of 1074 consecutive eponymous Roman magistrates from the Elder Brutus in 509 B.C. to Basilius Junior of A.D. 565.

The Capitoline Fasti Another source of information are inscriptions. Of some thirty-five consular lists of varying completeness found on inscriptions at Rome, Ostia, Anzio (Antium), and other places, the most official and extensive is that commonly called the *Capitoline Fasti,* incised on marble (probably around 18 B.C.) upon the Arch of Augustus in the Forum. Besides the list of consuls and other eponymous magistrates from the beginning of the Republic to Augustus, the *Capitoline Fasti* contained a list of all who won military triumphs since Romulus. The consular list, half complete, has fragments of no year earlier than 483 B.C. Though of capital importance, this list is not superior in reliability or authority to those of Livy or Diodorus. It is based upon the common stock of source material available in the last century B.C.

The Reliability of the Roman Historical Tradition It is upon the soundness of the *Fasti* that the entire structure of historical tradition for the early Republic must rest. Within the span of 185 years from 486 B.C., when Diodorus begins his list, to 302 B.C., Livy and Diodorus, though using entirely different sources, agree in 97 percent of the consular names. The same consistency exists between Diodorus and the *Capitoline Fasti* within the same period.

Nevertheless, scholars who believe that only patricians could hold high office in the early Republic reject up to sixty-five plebeian names that appear in the *Fasti* from 509 to 400 B.C. On the other hand, it is probably anachronistic to see an absolute exclusion of plebeians from high office in those years of transition from Monarchy to Republic, so that it is unwise to reject a name just because it is plebeian. Some tampering and mistakes probably did occur in the transmission of so many names, but the incidence of such occurrences does not seem great. Used with reasonable care, the *Fasti* can provide a reasonable outline for reconstructing the history of the early Republic.

From Kingship to Republic The transition from kingship to republic is one of the most disputed questions of Roman history because of the unreliability of the literary sources and the scarcity of archaeological material. According to ancient tradition, the Romans overthrew Tarquin the Proud because of his tyrannical government and his son's rape of Lucretia, the noble wife of Tarquinius Collatinus. It is said that her suicide, prompted by the shame of defilement, set off a violent revolution that resulted in the expulsion of the Tarquins, the abolition of kingship, and the establishment of the Republic with fully developed institutions of government.

The traditional account contains many improbabilities and gives rise to difficulties almost impossible to solve: the character of the revolution that brought about the change of government, the time of its occurrence, and the nature of the executive authority that replaced the kingship.

Many scholars would reject the tradition of a sudden overthrow of the Monarchy. It is more probable that the final passage from Monarchy to Republic was only the climax of a slow evolutionary process that may be called revolutionary only from the standpoint of its ultimate result. Another part of the tradition

that must be rejected is the sudden appearance of a fully developed executive to replace the kings. The consulship, with its equal division of powers, collegiality, and veto, evolved probably only after a long period of experimentation and development.

It is agreed that the collapse of the Monarchy resulted from social, economic, and political deterioration climaxed, perhaps, by military reverses; it is the date of the climax that is disputed. Many scholars still accept the traditional dating of the *Fasti* (509 to 507 B.C.). Some recent scholars have argued for a much later date (from 474 until 450 B.C.), but their arguments rest on archaeological evidence that is difficult to interpret and does not necessarily negate the traditional dating.

According to independent Greek chronology, while attempting to seize the Campanian city of Cumae ca. 525 B.C., the Etruscans suffered a decisive defeat that resulted in a Latin revolt against domination by Etruscan Rome and the severance of land communications between Etruria and Campania. This situation, together with a simultaneous invasion of Latium by the Sabines and other mountain tribes, may have provoked an economic and political crisis in Rome and contributed to the eventual breakdown of the Tarquin regime, which probably had gradually lost its control over the army and its power to prevent some of the more powerful aristocratic families from seizing control of the state.

The crisis that provoked the fall of the Tarquin monarchy could also have occurred after 474 B.C., when the Etruscans incurred a decisive naval defeat at the hands of Hiero I of Syracuse that led to their final loss of Latium. Support for this thesis has come from Swedish archaeologists digging in the Roman Forum. Their finds reveal continued strong Etruscan cultural influence until the period from about 475 to 450 B.C. That, however, does not necessarily indicate the continued presence of an Etruscan monarchy at Rome during this period. Despite a loss of political control, continued strong cultural influence would not be surprising while Etruscans were still powerful in the rest of Latium.

Development of the Consulship Even more disputed is the nature of the executive that replaced the king. Some scholars conjecture that it was a dictatorship, some a triple praetorship, others an embryonic form of praetor-consulship.* None of these conjectures, except perhaps the last, is free from objection, whether it be conflict with the *Fasti,* ancient tradition, or inherent probability. Whatever its initial form or name, however, the chief magistracy of the Republic had become known as the consulship probably by the mid-fifth century B.C. On it was bestowed the earlier kings' power to command *(imperium).* It was held jointly by two men elected for a single year. To prevent either from abusing his power, each had the full power to veto the other. Besides commanding the legions, the consuls acted as judges, summoned meetings of the *comitia centuriata,* and placed legislative proposals before it.

The consuls were surrounded with much of the old royal paraphernalia. Although they wore the purple toga of the old kings only at festivals, a purple hem distinguished their daily clothes. They sat on a portable ivory throne *(sella curulis),* and each was attended by twelve lictors carrying *fasces,* the double-headed axe in a bundle of rods that symbolized the power of execution and punishment.

The consuls, however, did not retain the religious functions of the kings, which were transferred to a lifetime official, the *Rex Sacrorum,* King of Sacrifices. Since he retained only the most archaic religious functions, the *Rex Sacrorum* steadily lost importance in comparison with various other priesthoods (see pp. 53–55).

The Senate At the dawn of the Republic the consuls were probably, in fact as well as in law, more powerful than the senate, which acted, as it had for the kings, merely as an ad-

* It is usual to refer to the chief magistrates of the early Republic by their later, better-known title of consuls, but their original name was probably praetors. That is confusing because later on the title praetor was revived for new magistrates who were given the judicial functions originally performed by the chief magistrates.

visory council. The power and influence of the senate increased, however, as the constitution developed, so that the consuls and other magistrates were obligated in practice, if not by law, to seek its advice on all major foreign and internal policies. They could safely neither oppose nor ignore this advice.

Several facts account for the growth of the senate's power. Unlike the kings, the consuls were annual officials who at the end of their term of office might have to explain to the people any mistakes they might have made while going against the advice of the senate. Their political career might end in dishonor or find its reward in a lifetime seat in the senate. The senate, on the other hand, was a permanent organ of government. It was made up of experienced ex-magistrates, who were members for life. They numbered about 300 during much of the Republic and 600 in the first century B.C. Finally, only to the senate belonged the dignity of an antique tradition, unbroken from the earliest beginnings of the Roman state. Of the public assemblies, the *comitia centuriata* was of comparatively recent origin and had not even yet attained full maturity, while the *comitia curiata* was a decrepit body whose functions had atrophied into empty formalism.

Authority (Auctoritas) The source of the senate's power was its so-called *auctoritas,* a concept that had both religious and constitutional connotations. In practice the term meant the prestige and esteem that the senate possessed because of the dignity and outstanding qualities of its members. Constitutionally, before 339 B.C. it was the power to ratify laws passed by the popular assemblies and to approve the election of magistrates. Without that ratification, no bill passed by the popular assemblies could become law. Behind this authority lay the religious idea that all laws and resolutions must be pleasing to the gods. According to Cicero, some of the senators, who traced an ancestry reaching back to the dawn of history, pretended to possess an uncanny knowledge of divine will. Strange as it may seem to a different age, such a claim was widely accepted among the Roman people, whose religious outlook did not include a wide gulf between gods and men.

Control over Finances   The senate had complete control over finances except, perhaps, for funds expended at the command of the consuls. Even though first the consuls and later the censors held the keys to the treasury, it was actually the senate in both law and custom that decided what funds were to be earmarked for war and public works. A soldier could not get his pay nor a victorious general his triumph unless funds for the purpose were made available by the senate. This control over finances gave the senate practical control over the government.

Advice-Giving Function   The ultimate basis of senatorial control over internal and foreign affairs, the army, the treasury, and the government lay in its right to give official advice to the magistrates on all laws that they wished to propose to the popular assembly. As long as the Republic endured, the senate never lost this advice-giving function, based not on statute law but on custom.

The advice given by the senate consisted of two parts: (1) opinions *(sententiae),* which individual senators expressed about the matter on which the magistrate sought advice; and (2) the decree of the senate *(senatus consultum),* or the final form of the solution adopted in answer to the problem the magistrate laid before them. The *senatus consultum* was not a unilateral act of the senate, but the joint act of the senate and the presiding magistrate. The latter alone made it legal; he alone could enforce it, modify it, or revoke it altogether. It was strictly limited in its effect and time of enforcement. If revoked by a magistrate or vetoed by a plebeian tribune, it was then registered as a *senatus auctoritas,* as an expression of the authoritative opinion of the senate that such and such a course of action would be in the best interests of the state. The senate thereby absolved itself of responsibility for the consequences. If something then went wrong, the magistrate who had ignored the advice would have to face the wrath of the people. Though not above the

law, the senate could in times of crisis take extralegal measures to ensure the safety of the state.

The Comitia Centuriata   As previously explained (see p. 34), the military reorganization ascribed to Servius Tullius had resulted in the creation of a new popular assembly, the *comitia centuriata,* which became the primary assembly of the early Republic. Even after military recruitment and organization were no longer based on them, the centuries in the Centuriate Assembly continued to be classified into cavalry, infantry, and technical ranks according to people's ability to afford the appropriate equipment. The Centuriate Assembly was still summoned by a trumpet on orders of a magistrate with the power of command, *imperium,* and it met at dawn on the Campus Martius (Mars' Field), in a military formation outside the sacred boundary *(pomerium).* During its meetings red flags flew on top of the Capitoline and Janiculum hills. The lowering of one of these flags would stop all proceedings, because such action originally warned that enemies were approaching and signalled the assembly to march off to face the foe.

Functions of the Comitia Centuriata   The powers of the Centuriate Assembly encompassed electoral, legislative, and judicial functions. It elected the higher magistrates upon nomination by their predecessors. As the constitution evolved, these magistrates included not only the yearly consuls and occasional dictators, but also the censors and praetors, who will be discussed below. The higher magistrates, particularly the consuls, also convened the centuries to accept or reject legislative proposals, accept declarations concerning war or peace, and ratify treaties. Cases of murder and high treason were tried before the Centuriate Assembly, and early in the Republic it became a court of appeal from coercive acts or capital punishment by a magistrate exercising authority within the city.

Upper-Class Bias of the Comitia Centuriata   In its fully developed form the *comitia cen-*

turiata comprised eighteen centuries of *equites* (men of the first census class who were designated as cavalry); eighty infantry centuries (forty senior and forty junior) also of the first census class; twenty each (half senior and half junior) for classes two through four; thirty (half senior and half junior) for the fifth class; and five centuries for people below the minimum property assessment (two for craftsmen, two for trumpeters, and one for the proletarians). The total, therefore, was one hundred and ninety-three centuries. They voted as units, a majority of each century determining its vote, and proceeded in order down from the eighteen equestrian centuries until a majority of ninety-seven votes was reached, whereupon the voting stopped. It was very unlikely that centuries below the fourth class, though containing the largest number of citizens, would ever be called upon to vote, and it was possible for the first class alone to dominate the voting since its ninety-eight centuries constituted a majority.

Accordingly, the system was far from democratic. The rich, with their ninety-eight centuries, could always outvote the lower census classes. The old could always outvote the young, since the seniors, though numerically fewer, had as many centuries as the juniors. Moreover, close votes within some centuries might mean that the total unit vote was different from that of the majority who voted, just as in the Electoral College system for electing presidents of the United States, in which it is possible for a candidate to lose the popular vote but win a majority of the Electoral College. Thus, the organization of this assembly, theoretically representing all classes and citizens in arms, was actually dominated by the conservative landowning aristocracy in the highest centuries.

The Priesthood and the Priestly Colleges During the Republic official priesthoods, known as colleges, organized for the correct performance of public worship, played a larger and more independent role than they had under the kings, who were both rulers and chief priests. All priests and pontiffs then owed their appointments to the king and acted as his assistants and advisers. After the fall of the monarchy, elected magistrates took over his political and military powers, his religious functions being divided between the King of Sacrifices *(Rex Sacrorum)* and the Supreme Pontiff *(Pontifex Maximus)*. In later times, as the powers of the former declined, those of the latter greatly increased. For the chief pontiff had acquired jurisdiction not only over the powerful college of pontiffs, but over the Vestal Virgins and the special priests *(flamines)* assigned to the worship of Jupiter, Mars, and Quirinus, and of twelve lesser deities. Even the King of Sacrifices, though the nominal successor of the overthrown priest-kings and in the early Republic a personage of great dignity and prestige, was in actual fact subject to the jurisdiction of the Supreme Pontiff.

The members of the priestly colleges or associations were more important to the organized religion of the state than any of the individual priests or priesthoods. They were priests, but not necessarily men of exceptional piety or endowed with special psychic or clairvoyant powers. They were, rather, men of learning, political experience, and high social rank who did not form any professional priestly class. Their wealth enabled them to perform their priestly duties without financial reward. Some had been magistrates before becoming priests; some were priests and magistrates simultaneously; and many were members of the senate. The chief qualification for membership in a priestly college was an exact knowledge of religious tradition, of divine law, and of correct ritual and ceremonial procedure.

There were two main colleges, that of the augurs and that of the pontiffs. The college of augurs, consisting of three life members (later increased to five and eventually to fifteen or sixteen), assisted the magistrates to take the *auspices* and thereby learn the will of the gods before undertaking any important public business, such as the election of the higher magistrates and meetings of the popular assemblies.

As the magistrate scanned the skies and reported to the blindfolded augur what he saw, the augur applied his expert knowledge of signs to determine and interpret the will of the gods. The signs were derived from thunder and lightning, the flight and cries of birds, the feeding of sacred chickens, and the behavior of certain animals and snakes. If the omens, especially those unsolicited, were pronounced as unfavorable, it was the duty of the magistrate to postpone the proposed action until the omens were right. In this way the augurs were in a position to exert considerable influence on politics during the Republic.

Still more important was the college of pontiffs. Originally the pontiff *(pontifex)* was a magician whose incantations were believed to give permanence to the flimsy bridges in early Latium. Though its function under the kings was purely advisory, the college assumed, from the birth of the Republic, a constantly growing, all-pervading control over every aspect of the state religion except augury. The original three members were later increased to six, in 300 B.C. to nine, and in 82 B.C. to fifteen. They held office for life, their functions were many, and their influence great.

The pontiffs were the custodians and interpreters of the sacred law governing both the religious and legal relations of the community to the gods. They alone knew the exact formulae applicable in all legal transactions and the proper forms employed in the making of vows. They were the sole keepers of the temple archives and prescribed the various rituals, prayers, chants, and litanies for use in public worship. They also supervised the dedication and the consecration of temples and altars, the burial of the dead, and the declaration of war and the making of treaties. It was they who organized the calendar that fixed the dates of festivals and the days on which the magistrate might not sit in court. The president of their college, judge and arbiter of things human and divine, had the power to convene and the right to preside over the Curiate Assembly. Since this assembly passed laws on adoptions and wills, the pontiffs exercised through it a dominant influence on the law of wills.

Equally important was the influence of the pontiffs on the law of claims. As claims

brought before the courts had to follow the precise meaning of the law on which they depended, they would best stand if drafted with the advice and assistance of the pontiffs, who held a monopoly of jurisprudence throughout the first two centuries of the Republic (500 to 300 B.C.).

Role of Pontiffs in Roman Law   The pontiffs' superintendence of the state religion was overshadowed by their contribution to the field of early Roman law, which became, in the form finally given to it in the Justinian Code, the basis of European law and a prime element in the formation of modern Western civilization. This contribution to the development of law and legal science was not the result of their political activities (many of them had seats in the senate and acted as members of standing committees on religious and legal affairs), nor of their judicial function for, though magistrates frequently referred cases to them for judicial review, the pontiffs were not judges nor regularly practicing lawyers. Their contribution arose from their functions as consultants and interpreters of the law during the early Republic.

Since it is impossible for even the wisest and the most gifted of lawmakers to foresee all the possible needs of the future, as cases arise that are not covered by existing law, judges and interpreters must determine not only the exact meaning but the spirit of the law and be able to expand its details or to apply new meanings to old. The pontiffs based their interpretations on precedents, of which they alone had knowledge and whose mystery the publication of Rome's first law code, the Twelve Tables, around 450 B.C. (see pp. 57–58) did not entirely dispel. To precedents based on ancestral custom *(mos maiorum),* they added interpretations or commentaries on the Twelve Tables and formulae or instructions for the performance of legal acts, especially opinions *(responsa)* on the legality of acts both contemplated and already performed. In step with the needs of the Roman state, the pontiffs gradually began the buildup of a body of jurisprudence that was based upon the principles of ancient unwritten customs and the Twelve Tables. Their achievement was not unlike that of English and American judges in the creation of the common law, or that of the Supreme Court in the development of the constitutional law of the United States.

The virtual monopoly of legal science by the college of pontiffs until the late fourth century B.C. and thereafter arose from the original lack of differentiation between Roman religion and Roman law. Criminal law was based on the principle that an offense against the community was an offense against the gods. In private lawsuits both parties swore oaths which, if violated, would provoke the wrath of the gods. The first Roman jurists of sacred, private, or public law came from the college of pontiffs, each assisted by a staff of secretaries, copyists, and recorders. Magistrates consulted the entire college on matters of religious and constitutional law; private disputes were referred to the pontiff appointed by the college to deal with such cases. This authority was not challenged until the later fourth or third centuries B.C., when knowledge of the law passed gradually into the hands of a wide circle of laymen.

Struggle of the Orders (Classes) One fiction created by the annalistic tradition is that of the absolute and exclusive domination of the state by the patrician minority after the fall of the Tarquins. Such absolute domination is highly improbable in a period of war and uprising in Latium, internal unrest, and confusion, with Sabine and Volscan tribesmen moving in to fill the power vacuum left by the Etruscans while the Tarquins struggled to restore the Monarchy. It would have been practically impossible under these conditions for the patricians to maintain their control of the government without the support, cooperation, and partnership of some of the rich and powerful families of the plebeian class.* That

is the most likely reason why there are some plebeian names in the early consular *Fasti*.

It is probable that the patrician leaders sought the military and political support of the plebeian upper classes until they had consolidated their power and dispelled the danger of a restoration of the Monarchy. When the crisis had passed and the support of the plebeians was no longer needed, the patricians apparently proceeded to establish a monopoly of office for themselves and become a closed social and political cast from which they excluded families of the plebeian upper class.

One method that the patricians could well have employed to exclude the plebeians from public office or military commands was the refusal to present candidates, even those elected by the early Centuriate Assembly, to the Curiate Assembly for formal conferment of the *imperium,* without which no elected consul could take office. The reaction finally culminated in the prohibition of intermarriage between patrician and plebeian families.

Under the leadership of well-to-do plebeians who felt the patrician attempts to exclude them from the senate and high offices most keenly, a broad plebeian movement confronted the patricians with the threat of secession and the creation of a new and separate state. The organization of such a movement was probably not too difficult because the demands of the poorer plebeians for economic reforms must have been no less urgent than those of the plebeian leaders for admission to office. This struggle for political, social, and economic reform was to dominate the internal history of the Roman Republic for the next

---

*Although the term *plebeian* has come to connote the masses of the underprivileged poor, it appears unlikely that a society as culturally and politically advanced as

Etruscan Rome could have been composed solely of two rigidly defined classes: a small exclusive patrician minority at the top and a large, undifferentiated plebeian mass below. The plebeian class (p. 39) contained several classes differing in wealth, occupation, and social status: the rural and urban poor, clients of the rich, merchants and craftsmen, and some rich and powerful landowning families with clients of their own. The Servian centuriate reform (see Chap. 3, p. 33) seems to have given recognition to this class by the division of classes on the basis of wealth and the admission of the plebeian rich into the military and, perhaps, political life of the state.

two centuries. Its outcome was the evolution of the Roman constitution itself as later shaped by the great legislative acts of ca. 367 and 287 B.C.

The collapse of Etruscan domination in Rome and Latium undoubtedly disrupted commerce and industry and precipitated an economic depression resulting in hardships for artisans, merchants, and their families within the city. The small plebeian farmers were also in difficulties. Their farms, probably not more than an acre and a half in area, were too small to support their families. Worse still, they did not receive a fair share of the public lands that they often helped to conquer. Forced to serve in the army, they had to neglect their farms and sometimes came back to find them looted by the enemy. They were also victims of the harsh debtor laws. In cases of default, money lenders could without legal action seize farms, sell farmers into slavery, or even put them to death.

Secession of the Plebs   In answer to stubborn patrician resistance to the demand for political, economic, and social justice, the plebeians took the revolutionary step of seceding from the state. It was largely a nonviolent movement but was exceedingly dangerous to military security at a time when Rome was frequently subject to attacks by the Etruscans and surrounding hill tribes like the Aequi and Volsci.

After one of these attacks, according to tradition (though not a very reliable one), the victorious Roman army had just reached the gates of the city. Hearing that their demands for reform had just been rejected by the senate, the plebeian soldiers deserted their patrician general and headed for the Sacred Mount about three miles from the Anio. Knowing that without their help Rome was unable to fight any battles, they waited for the patricians to make the next move. They set up their own temporary organization headed by two tribunes and took an oath to a constitution known as the Sacred Law *(lex sacrata)*. The *lex sacrata* was a military oath well known in Italy, especially among the Sabines and Samnites; in

this case it was used to declare the plebeian tribunes to be sacrosanct or inviolate. Anyone laying violent hands on a tribune would be placed under a curse and could be killed with impunity. These actions are supposed to have taken place in 494 B.C., certainly too early a date.

The first secession of the plebeians may actually have occurred around 471 B.C. on the Aventine, where they took the oath to the *lex sacrata*, organized an assembly known as the Plebeian Tribal Council *(concilium plebis tributum)* or simply Council of the Plebs, and appointed a tribune for each of the four urban tribes. The historical number of plebeian tribunes was fixed at ten a few decades later, never to be changed again. The earliest tribunes were probably not elected, but rose to the top of the revolutionary heap through their power of leadership and were afterwards confirmed by acclamation. After the Aventine secession, all tribunes as well as their assistants, the *aediles,* were elected by the Council of the Plebs. To be eligible for election, a tribune had to belong to a plebeian family.

The Powers and Duties of a Plebeian Tribune   The duty and function of a plebeian tribune was to protect the life, person, and interests of all plebeians who called upon him for help against the arbitrary power of a magistrate. Always on call, he had to keep his house open day and night and never go outside the city limits. In order that he might perform his duties without fear, his person was declared inviolate or sacrosanct. Anyone laying violent hands upon him or willfully interfering in the performance of his duties was laid under curse or pain of death.

The tribunes also had the power of intercession or veto over any bill passed by the popular assemblies, any decree of the senate, and any act of a magistrate (except a dictator) that was considered harmful to plebeian interests. This power was effective only inside Rome and one mile beyond city limits, and could not be employed to protect plebeians guilty of serious crimes. Though not based on specific constitutional law, the veto became accepted by custom and politically effective. Even the senate later recognized its effectiveness and encouraged the tribunes to employ it against trouble-making consuls.

Aediles The auxiliaries of the tribunes as protectors of the common people were the two plebeian *aediles,* who were originally caretakers of the temple of Ceres on the Aventine, which was not only a marketplace and trading post, but a center of early plebeian political agitation. Their functions became numerous and varied. They were custodians of the plebeian treasury and archives and, according to Livy (Book 3:55), of the decrees of the senate from ca. 449 B.C. onward. In later times they acted as police and supervised marketplaces, weights and measures, public works, food and water supplies, and public games.

The Plebeian Tribal Council (Concilium Plebis Tributum) The tribunes and aediles were elected by the Plebeian Tribal Council (Council of the Plebs), which was usually convened and presided over by tribunes but occasionally also by aediles. Only plebeian members of the ''tribes'' (eventually four urban and thirty-one rural) into which all Roman citizens were divided could vote. Each ''tribe'' had one vote determined by a simple majority of those voting. Plebeian resolutions *(plebiscita)* were not binding upon the whole state unless ratified by the *comitia centuriata,* and perhaps not even then without the express approval of the senate. Only after the *lex Hortensia* of 287 B.C. did *plebiscita* have the force of law by themselves.

The Plebeian Battle for Social Justice Having proved themselves indispensable to Roman military defense, the plebeians became a power within the body of the state. They had their own public assembly and their own leaders and champions, to whom the patricians could do no violence. Their battle for social justice contributed in the development of the Roman constitution, to the ultimate benefit of the patrician class itself.

One source of discontent was the lack of laws not subject to the bias of patrician oral tradition. Around 452 B.C., after some unsuccessful attempts to obtain written laws, the tribunes suggested to the senate that a committee be chosen (representing both parties) to frame just and equitable laws. The senate turned down the suggestion of plebeian participation but did agree to set up a commission of ten men, *decem viri,* to codify the existing laws. Probably, however, the story that a group of senators went to Athens to study the laws of Solon first is apocryphal.

During the two years prior to the decemviral commission, two laws seem to have been passed under plebeian pressure. The first was the *lex Icilia,* setting aside land on the Aventine for plebeians. The other was the *lex Aternia-Tarpeia,* limiting the fine that a consul could impose to thirty cattle and two sheep. Moderate consuls also seem to have returned to power. If the official Roman *Fasti* are correct, there may also have been three plebeian consuls, namely Spurius Tarpeius and Aulus Aternius of the year 454 and Titus Genucius of the year 451 B.C. All three were connected at one time or another with the plebeian tribuneship.

The Decemviral Commission The tradition surrounding the work of the decemvirs is confused and contradictory. Supposedly, at the end of 452 the regular consulship and tribunate were suspended, and during 451 the decemviral commission—ten patricians chaired by Appius Claudius—ran the government and codified the laws. Apparently, at the end of the year they had not finished their task to everyone's satisfaction, and a second decemvirate—half patrician and half plebeian but still chaired by Appius Claudius—was appointed to complete the project.

Appius Claudius supposedly now forced the addition of unfair laws, such as the prohibition against marriages between patricians and plebeians, and acted like a tyrant. For example, he was said to have claimed falsely the beautiful Verginia as his slave to satisfy his lust, so that in desperation her father killed her to save her from dishonor. In protest to Appius and the decemvirs, the plebeians are said to have seceded again, so that the commission resigned and ten tribunes and two consuls friendly to the plebs were elected for 449.

While the makeup of the revised decemviral commission may be historical, much of this account seems fanciful. Appius probably was arrogant and high handed, but it is difficult to see how he could have forced the plebeian members to adopt a ban on patricioplebeian marriages, and the story of Verginia, which looks like a traditional moralizing tale, was probably attached to him because of his prominence and arrogance. The one solid fact is that the decemvirs did produce a codification of existing early Roman public and private laws, which were set up eventually, if not originally, on twelve bronze tablets in the Forum. This code was henceforth known as the Law of the Twelve Tables.

The Twelve Tables The Law of the Twelve Tables, while not among the most sublime achievements of the human intellect, was the seed from which Roman civil law grew to maturity and from which the system of Roman jurisprudence evolved through the interpretative applications of the pontiffs and later of the professional jurists. Livy declared that it was the fountain of all private and public law, and Cicero, that it was the body of the entire Roman law. As the basis and source of law, it may well be compared with the Constitution of the United States.

Style and Content of the Twelve Tables About one-third of the text of the Twelve Tables is preserved in quotations by later authors. The style is archaic, simple, brief, harsh, but legally clear and exact, as in Table I, "If he calls him to court, go he shall; if he doesn't, plaintiff will call witness, then will take him"; or Table VII, "They will keep road repaired, if they don't cobble it, man may drive team where he wants to"; or Table VIII, "If burglary be done at night, if (owner) kills him, he shall be killed by law, if by day, not, unless burglar defends himself with weapon."

The Code of the Twelve Tables was neither a constitution nor a comprehensive code of laws. Though its main source was the old law of custom, it did not entirely replace primitive unwritten law. It served the more limited purpose of clearly formulating existing law and custom, which had previously been subject to the vagaries of oral tradition and pontifical lore. The law of the Twelve Tables, designed to maintain peace, harmony, and justice within the state, codified the preexisting law of custom but was also capable through interpretation of meeting future needs. It elevated the position of women by allowing a wife who had not been married with *conventio in manum* freedom from her husband's authority if she stayed away three days and nights a year from home. It reduced powers of the *pater familias* not required for the maintenance of family unity, guaranteed the right to property and testament, provided for the intervention of the state in civil disputes, abolished family revenge, and permitted the referral of capital cases to the *comitia centuriata*. It also abolished torture as a means of obtaining evidence from free men.

In short, the basic importance of the Twelve Tables was that they established in principle some equality in law between patrician and plebeian and, more or less, the equality of all free citizens before the law. Nevertheless, since they primarily codified existing practice, they did not really get at the roots of plebeian discontent.

Post-Decemviral Developments The annalists have obscured the realities of the situation, but apparently some significant steps, known as the Valerio-Horatian laws, were taken in 449 on behalf of the plebeians by the new consuls, L. Valerius Potitus and M. Horatius Barbatus. They included regulations concerning the right of appeal from a magistrate, legal recognition of the sacrosanctity of plebeian tribunes, and provision that bills passed in assemblies voting by tribes would become law if ratified by the senate.

The Comitia Tributa (Tribal Assembly)
Not only did the *concilium plebis* vote by tribes, but also another assembly that had come into being about this time or a little earlier, the *comitia tributa,* or Tribal Assembly, an assembly of all citizens voting by tribes instead of in the more cumbersome centuriate organization. The *comitia tributa* was more convenient, and since it also followed the custom of voting by units, it still gave more weight to the votes of conservative landowners in the more numerous rural tribes. It was summoned by a magistrate with *imperium,* and besides having the right to vote on proposals placed before it and to hear appeals, it elected the *quaestors* and the *curule aediles* (who will be discussed below).

Plebeian Triumphs About 445 B.C. two facts served to help the plebeians in the seesaw conflict with the patricians. The most important was the critical military situation, which, as the patricians clearly saw, could not be met without plebeian good will and cooperation. The second was that one of the consuls of that year was M. Genucius, a plebeian. It was probably through Genucius that the plebeians were able to rescind the law against mixed marriages. The *lex Canuleia* rescinding the older law was first proposed by the tribune C. Canuleius and passed by the Plebeian Council but could not have become a public law unless presented to the *comitia centuriata* by a consul.

A compromise in the class struggle was the formal admission of plebeians to the supreme magistracy, not as consuls but as military tribunes with consular power. This was evidently a shrewd maneuver by the patricians, because it still guaranteed their control of the consulship and at the same time secured military unity by giving plebeians a share in the government. Though the *Fasti* indicate that plebeians occasionally had held consulships before 445, the decision to substitute military tribunes with consular power for the following year marks the first time, according to annalistic tradition, that the supreme office of the state was officially open to both classes (Livy 4.6.8).

Military Tribunes with Consular Power
For the next seventy-eight years of the *Fasti,* between 445 and 367 B.C., consular tribunes held the highest office fifty times and consuls twenty-eight, the senate apparently deciding between the two. The number of consular tribunes varied from three to nine, at first usually three, sometimes four, later six. They had exactly the same military and executive powers as consuls. Eleven dictatorships occurred during their years of office. Had they not possessed the consular *imperium,* they would not have been constitutionally able to delegate powers that they themselves did not possess. Yet they differed from consuls in that they did not have the right to a triumph nor to the rank of ex-consul with a seat in the senate after their term of office. Nor did they have the privilege of being buried in the royal purple toga.

Each member of this college could participate in all the activities belonging to the office. Each had the power of veto, though the magistracy as a whole may have operated in theory on the principle of unanimity. In practice there was a division of responsibility: one remained in the city for the administration of justice and other executive functions; the others conducted the necessary military operations.

Though military command was one of their more important functions, no correlation can be proved between years of war and their years of office. Just as many wars occurred when consuls were in office as consular tribunes. After 400 B.C. of the *Fasti,* fifteen plebeian names occur; in the years 399 and 396 B.C., five out of six consular tribunes were plebeian; in 379, five out of eight. The years 399 and 396 were years of war with Veii, and it may well have been that in war years the plebeians were especially successful in breaking into the consular tribunate. To reject all these names as interpolated is to reject solid and reliable parts of the Roman historical tradition.

Growth of the Magistracies

The Censors   The year 443 of the *Fasti,* immediately following the establishment of the first consular tribuneship, saw the rise of another important magistracy, the censorship, which maintained itself with ever-increasing power to the time of Sulla, if not the Principate. The alleged purpose of the new office was the assumption of duties formerly performed by the consuls, especially the compilation of the census, which was the official list of Roman citizens for purposes of voting, taxation, and military service. To carry out these duties two censors were elected by the *comitia centuriata* every four or five years; but by a law passed in 434 of the *Fasti,* they could serve only for eighteen months.

At first the censors may have been rather unimportant people, not much better than clerks or secretaries. They did not have the *imperium* or the right to the *fasces,* could not call the people or the senate to assembly, nor even nominate their own successors. Later their job of registering citizens and their property, of assessing their liability to taxes and military service, and of assigning them to tribes and centuries for voting eventually made their office, even without the *imperium* and the *fasces,* more feared and respected than the consulship itself. So eminent was the magistracy of a censor that when he died he was accorded the honor of burial in the full purple toga of royalty.

Their Powers and Functions   In addition to the job of making up the tax registers, the military registers, and the lists of voters, censors acquired after 312/10 B.C. the power of appointing senators and of removing them from the senate if their moral life did not meet the standards of the Roman moral code. By putting a black mark opposite a man's name, the censor could remove a citizen from his tribe, demote him from a rural tribe to a city tribe, or take away his civil rights altogether for at least five years.

The censors were also concerned with the spending of funds appropriated by the senate or released by the consul. They drew up contracts for major public works such as roads, bridges, aqueducts, and public buildings. Control of the tax registers and of the state revenues gave them the knowledge required for making up the annual budget. They granted contracts for collecting such revenue, leased public lands, mines, salt works, and fishing rights, and arranged for the collection by speculators or publicans of port dues and of taxes owed by squatters on public land. The only kind of revenue with which they had nothing to do was that obtained from war booty.

The Quaestors   The origin of these minor but not unimportant officials is obscure. Most ancient sources carry them back to the Monarchy, perhaps rightly so, though modern writers have seen their first appearance in the early Republic. In the early years of the Republic they may have been appointed by the consuls as assistants, but after 287 B.C. they were elected by the Tribal Assembly. At first two, and both patrician, their number was increased to four in 421 of the *Fasti,* when the office was first thrown open to the plebeians, though it was not until the year 409 of the *Fasti* that plebian quaestors were actually appointed. Though their original function was to investigate murders, minor crimes against property also came under their jurisdiction.

Two of the four quaestors accompanied the consuls to the battlefield, where they served as quartermasters in charge of supplies and the payment of troops. The other two remained in the city to serve as keepers of the public treasury and prosecutors of tax delinquents. Since the state treasury was in the temple of Saturn, they were also in charge of the state records and documents kept in that building. A large staff of copyists and secretaries assisted in the discharge of these important duties.

Temporary Halt in Plebeian Gains   The expansion of plebeian rights and privileges was interrupted by the strenuous war against the Etruscan city of Veii and the disastrous invasion of the Gauls at the beginning of the fourth century B.C., which culminated in the sack of

Rome around 390 B.C. (pp. 69–72). These difficult times turned people's attention from internal disputes to preserving the state as a whole. Class conflicts and political rivalries are luxuries that a group fighting for its life cannot afford.

Further Reform on Behalf of the Plebeians About 376 B.C., in a period of lessened immediate danger, two plebeian tribunes, C. Licinius Stolo and L. Sextius Lateranus—both very able and dynamic examples of the new plebeian leaders whose wealth, social position, and marriage to women of the ancient patrician aristocracy gave them the power to break down the bars of exclusion from the highest political office—introduced before the Plebeian Council three proposals: (1) that interest already paid on debts be deducted from the principal, and the remainder of the debt, if any, be paid within three years in equal installments; (2) that no one be allowed to have more than 300 acres of public land; and (3) that the consular tribuneship be abolished and only consuls be elected, of whom one must be a plebeian. In 367 B.C. these proposals supposedly were enacted into law.

Although there are many problems with details in the existing account of the Licinio-Sextian laws, there is no reason to reject the core of the tradition. That these laws abolished the military tribunes with consular power seems certain, since no more appear after 367. They probably specified, however, only that one of the restored consulships each year *could* be held by a plebeian. That one *must* be held by a plebeian was probably not specified until a law of L. Genucius in 342 B.C. Some kind of restriction on the growing monopolization of public land, *ager publicus,* by large landowners also seems reasonable, although the limit of 500 *iugera* may be an interpolation by annalists from later legislation. Soon large tracts of public land were acquired through Roman conquests in central Italy, and many thousands of small holdings were created for impoverished peasants. Accordingly, one of the major economic grievances of the poor plebeians was alleviated for over a century.

The Licinio-Sextian legislation on debt poses no problems and seems to be another attempt to alleviate a major source of discontent, especially among those who had few assets and were threatened with debt slavery. The process continued as regulations restricted interest rates to probably 8⅔ percent a year in 357 and 4¹⁄₆ percent in 347. In 342 Genucius tried to abolish giving loans at interest completely, but this impractical law soon became a dead letter. A much more practical move was the creation in 352 B.C. of a special governmental board of five, *quinqueviri mensarii,* who helped debtors in trouble by assuming mortgages that could be adequately secured—in many cases probably by the new allotments of land that were now being distributed. Finally, the *lex Poetilia* of either 326 or 313 B.C. so severely limited the circumstances whereby a person could be enslaved for debt that the practice soon disappeared.

The Creation of a New Nobility and Further Changes in the Magistracies The Licinio-Sextian legislation of 367 effectively opened up the consulship to the wealthy plebeians, whose circumstances permitted a career of unpaid public service. Such a moment was bound to come anyway, because the old patrician families that had dominated the early Republic were inexorably dying out. The universal tendency of upper classes to have small families, the patrician refusal to intermarry with plebeians even after the *lex Canuleia* of 445 B.C., and deaths in battle during the numerous wars with Rome's neighbors had severely reduced their ranks. For example, only twenty-nine of fifty-three patrician *gentes* recorded for the fifth century appear in the fourth. With plebeians frequently (regularly after 342 B.C.) holding the consulship, a new, patricio-plebeian consular nobility replaced the old, exclusively patrican nobility. It was made up of those families who had a member that had held the office of consul. A man who was the first of his family to reach the consulship was a *novus homo,* new man. He thereby ennobled his family and enjoyed the undying gratitude of succeeding generations.

The New Praetorship   Still, the old patricians did not immediately surrender all of their control. The growing complexity of public business made it desirable to split off the vital judicial functions of the consuls and give them to a separate magistracy. The patrician-dominated senate, therefore, revived the ancient title of *praetor* and gave the consuls' judicial functions to the new office of praetor, which was restricted to patricians. The consuls could now give their undivided attention to military and foreign affairs, and the patricians could still maintain internal control through domination of the legal system.

Originally there was only one praetor, and he was a junior colleague of the consuls. His full title was *praetor urbanus*. He was entrusted with the administration of justice within the city and was later made responsible for the loyalty and the maintenance of law and order in other cities as they came under Roman control. Like the consuls, he was elected annually by the Centuriate Assembly. As a junior colleague of the consuls, he possessed the *imperium* and could, if necessary, assume command of an army. Although he ordinarily convened and presided only over the minor assemblies, he could, in the absence of the consuls or if deputized by them, summon meetings of the Centuriate Assembly or the senate and perform all the executive functions of a consul. He had the *fasces* and six lictors, the purple-bordered toga, the curule chair, and all the other insignia of a higher magistrate. Eventually, when the praetor's duties dealing with other cities had become burdensome after more than a century of Roman expansion in Italy, those duties were given to a second praetor, the *praetor peregrinus*. Thenceforth, the praetorship took on the character of a separate magistracy independent of the consulship, and members were added to it as the administrative needs of the state increased.

The Curule Aedileship   Another office, the curule aedileship, was created at this time to assume some of the functions of an expanding municipal administration. The curule aedileship was so called because the two new aediles had the right to the curule chair. The first curule aediles were patricians, but plebeians were later eligible in alternate years. Their functions were the same as those of the plebeian aediles previously described (p. 57). The increase in the number of aediles from two to four is evidence of the expanding functions of municipal administration.

The Cursus Honorum   The course of offices, *cursus honorum*, that marked an aristocratic political career for centuries was now all in place: quaestor, aedile, praetor, consul, and censor, in ascending order. Because they were officers of the plebs only, not magistrates of the whole state, the tribunes of the plebs stood outside of this *cursus*. So too did the office of dictator, which was an emergency creation and not an expected part of a regular career.

After 367 B.C. offices not open to plebeians soon yielded to their pressure. In 356 the distinguished plebeian C. Marcius Rutilius became a dictator, and in 351 he was the first to reach the censorship. Then, in 339 another plebeian dictator established the rule that one censor had to be a plebeian. Finally, plebeians gained access to the praetorship in 337. Also, to prevent any one person from monopolizing high offices, it was made illegal for a magistrate to hold more than one curule office (one which allowed the holder a curule chair: curule aedile, praetor, consul, censor) in any one year or the same office twice within ten years.

Promagistracies   As Roman affairs became more complicated, the yearly magistrates were not numerous enough to handle all of the administrative and military tasks required. In order to create officers with the requisite authority, therefore, the senate resorted to the creation of acting magistrates called promagistrates. The first use of this new device was at the siege of Naples in 327 at the start of the Second Samnite War (see p. 76), when it seemed advisable to maintain the consul who started the siege in command after his normal year of office. Therefore, the senate voted to make him an acting consul, *pro consule*.

A magistrate who had his power extended in this way was said to have been prorogued. While prorogation was used sparingly at first, its use was gradually extended to other magistrates, and promagistrates became quite common, especially proconsuls and propraetors.

Admission of Plebeians to Religious Offices Another legislative reform was the admission of plebeians to a share in the responsibility of looking after and interpreting the Books of the Sibyl. This had hitherto been an exclusive prerogative of the patricians, who made use of it to block plebeian proposals for social, political, and economic reform. A new commission of ten men, five of whom had to be plebeian, was set up to take charge of these books.

One of the last patrician bulwarks was the priesthood. In the year 300 B.C. the *lex Ogulnia* increased the number of the pontiffs to eight and of the augurs to nine, of whom four pontiffs and five augurs must be plebeian. The only priestly offices still reserved to the patricians were the King of Sacrifices, the special priesthoods *(flaminatus)* of Jupiter, Mars, and Quirinus, and the college of the Salii, or Leaping Priests.

Concord of the Orders The main grievances of the plebeians were now satisfied. As a symbol of harmony, a temple of Concord was vowed and dedicated. Yet there still remained a few constitutional reforms that completed the process begun in 367 B.C.

In 339 B.C. the *lex Publilia* abolished the senate's right to veto legislation after passage in the Centuriate or Tribal assemblies, although it specified that magistrates had to obtain approval of proposals by the senate before presentation to an assembly. Appius Claudius, (not the decemvir, but the famous blind censor of 312, who built the Appian Way) tried to help the urban plebs by distributing people who owned no land through the twenty-seven then-existing rural tribes, instead of just the four urban ones. There were fewer people in the rural tribes, so that an individual's vote

carried more weight in them. In 304, however, the censors reduced the value of freedmen's votes by restricting all freedmen to registration in the four urban tribes.

Nevertheless, liberal changes continued. In 304 Cn. Flavius, the son of a freedman, published a useful handbook of procedures and legal formulae to give the average citizen better access to the courts. In 300 the consul M. Valerius Maximus obtained a law that guaranteed the right of appeal, *provocatio,* from a magistrate's sentence of death or whipping within the city. About 290 another law abolished the senatorial veto over the election of magistrates and required that the senate ratify the results of elections in advance.

Finally, in 287 B.C. the aftermath of the long, tedious Samnite Wars (see pp. 73–77) brought another crisis over debts, and the plebs seceded to the Janiculum Hill across the Tiber. The consuls appointed the plebeian Q. Hortensius as a dictator to deal with the situation. He obtained a law, the *lex Hortensia,* that gave resolutions of the *concilium plebis, plebiscita,* the full force of law. In this way, the plebeians now had the right to legislate for the whole state.

The Realities of the Roman Constitution As should now be clear, the constitution of the Roman Republic was not worked out all at once according to some set of theoretical principles and enshrined in a single document. Like the British constitution, it evolved over a period of centuries through a combination of custom, precedent, and specific legislation. It is not easy therefore to define the result. With the passage of the *lex Hortensia* in 287 B.C., many have seen the emergence of a truly democratic constitution at Rome. Others, like the second-century B.C. Greek historian Polybius, have called it a mixed constitution, a blend of the three "good" types of constitution defined by Aristotle: monarchy, represented by the magistrates; aristocracy, represented by the senate; and democracy, represented by the tribunes of the plebs and the popular assemblies. According to this theory, each branch balanced the other, so that no one could become more powerful at the expense of the other two. Both views are wrong. The Republic was controlled by a powerful oligarchy.

Roman society was extremely conscious of rank and prestige, as expressed in the importance placed on such words as *dignitas* and *auctoritas*. Modern egalitarian ideals did not exist; it was naturally assumed that some men were better than others. Business in the senate, for example, was conducted along strict lines of seniority in rank. At each census the censors designated one of the prestigious ex-consuls as the *Princeps Senatus,* First Man of the Senate. This man gave his opinions first in debate. Then followed, usually on strict lines of seniority, the censors-elect and censors (when there were such), ex-censors, the consuls-elect (if elections that year were over), the consuls and ex-consuls, praetors-elect, praetors, ex-praetors, and so on down the ranks. Debate seldom went beyond the ranks of the ex-praetors before the topic was exhausted, whereupon the membership signified its vote by moving to one side of the room or the other. The men of the lower ranks were called *pedarii* because the only way that they usually had to express themselves was with their feet, *pedes,* as they walked across the room.

Under this system, then, it is clear that senatorial debate would be framed by the consular nobility and would proceed along lines laid down by the early speakers. That is especially true since most of the men of lower rank had been elected to their magistracies through the help of powerful ex-consuls and looked to their continued patronage for election to higher office. Therefore, they were most likely to side with their consular patrons on a particular issue to avoid giving offense.

For the same reason, magistrates during their brief year of office were not really independent of the noble-dominated senate. Not only were they dependent for advice on the collective wisdom of the ex-magistrates who comprised the senate, but they themselves were looking to become senators if they were not already, and those who already were senators hoped to advance in rank. Even the consuls were dependent on the senate for funds and for appointment to prestigious or lucrative military commands and, after the acquisition of an overseas empire, provincial governorships. Accordingly, there was great pressure to conform to the wishes of the powerful consulars in the senate, who formed a virtual oligarchy.

Even the tribunes of the plebs, who started out as protectors of the common citizens, became co-opted by this oligarchy. As the number of plebeian families who had held high office and joined the senate grew, many of the new tribunes tended to be young men from their ranks who were starting out on political careers. Naturally, most of them desired to cooperate with the consular nobles, who controlled the senate, and were willing to exercise their vetoes over fellow tribunes in the interest of powerful nobles. Eventually, the tribunes seemed to be so tamed that they too were admitted to the ranks of senators, even though they were not strictly part of the *cursus honorum.*

Finally, the various popular assemblies were dominated by the interests of the land-owning senatorial aristocracy and its consular nobility. During most of the Republic, of course, the *comitia curiata* was merely a *pro forma* carry-over from the past, so that there was little need to influence it one way or another. The *comitia centuriata, comitia tributa,* and *concilium plebis* were different, however. They had exclusive rights to elect magistrates and pass legislation, and they had important judicial functions. As already explained, because of the unit-voting procedure, the one hundred and ninety-three centuries of the *comitia centuriata* were dominated by the ninety-eight centuries belonging to men of the wealthiest census class (pp. 52–53). That class was made up of the largest landowners, who shared the outlook of the wealthy senators and magistrates. The situation was hardly changed by a slight reform, probably after 241 B.C., that necessitated voting by the second highest census class before a majority could be reached.

The unit-vote rule also stifled the vote of the ordinary citizen in the *comitia tributa* and *concilium plebis.* In both of these assemblies voting was done by tribes. After 241 B.C. the number of tribes in which all Roman citizens were enrolled became fixed at four urban and thirty-one rural. Obviously, the large number of landless urban dwellers, who had only four votes, were outweighed by the thirty-one votes of the rural tribes. Furthermore, since all voting had to be done at Rome, the small landowners in the rural tribes were at a great disadvantage, compared with the wealthy aristocratic landowners and their friends, who maintained houses in Rome or could afford to go to Rome to vote. Even if a small landowner did get to Rome to vote, he was probably a client of the aristocrat whose estate was in his neighborhood and would vote as his patron wished. Thus, the votes of many rural tribes were controlled by a handful of nobles, the same ones who dominated the *comitia centuriata,* the senate, and the magistracies.

The Struggle of the Orders had lasted with varying degrees of intensity for about two hundred years. During that time, the Republic had evolved the laws, institutions, and practices that would be its hallmarks for two hundred and fifty more years. The ordinary plebeian had made some gains: removal of the threat of enslavement for debt, protection from the arbitrary use of magisterial power, a more open legal system, and some successful attempts to obtain land for those without it. Those who gained the most, however, were the wealthy plebeian landowners, who, after obtaining political equality with the old patrician aristocracy, combined with the latter to create an exclusive patricio-plebeian oligarchy hardly different from that which had existed at the start of the Republic.

From the ordinary Roman's point of view, there was nothing inherently wrong with that. So long as his modest needs were fairly met, he was content to be ruled by his betters. For him that was the natural state of affairs. All he asked was not to be abused by those in power. If he did feel abused, he rioted and looked for an aristocratic patron who promised to alleviate the grievance.

VI

The Roman Conquest of Italy, 509 to 264 B.C.

Although the previous chapter has treated them separately, the episodes in the struggle between the patricians and the plebeians and the development of the Republican constitution took place during a seemingly endless series of wars between the Romans and the other peoples of peninsular Italy. It was the need for plebeian cooperation in fighting these wars that forced the patrician minority slowly, often grudgingly, to yield to the plebeian leaders' demands, and it was the need for unity in the face of enemies that prevented either side from going to the extreme of civil war.

Conflicts with Immediate Neighbors The wars of the fifth century B.C. make up a large part of Livy's narrative from the beginning of the second to well past the middle of his fifth book. As Livy described them, many are probably fictitious rhetorical exaggerations found in his sources, which he embellished further. A large number are probably glorified plundering raids or border skirmishes over the possession of small amounts of land. Such fights often occurred between Rome and her close neighbors: the Latins, Sabines, Hernici, Aequi, Volsci, and Etruscans. Patriotic Roman historians, of course,

claimed that Rome fought others only in self-defense. Hardly any nation ever believes that it is the aggressor, and even fewer admit it. The Romans were as often to blame as their neighbors, and for the same reasons.

The Romans and other peoples of Italy were basically subsistence farmers and pastoralists. In primitive agrarian societies such as theirs, shortage of land was chronic as populations expanded. At Rome, for example, one of the poor plebeians' constant grievances during the Struggle of the Orders was lack of land. Moreover, since wealth and status in such societies were based on land, wealthy leaders always wanted more too. The only way to obtain more for everyone in any community was to take it from another.

Plunder and prestige were often objects of warfare too. The peasant soldier of modest resources found it attractive to increase his wealth by taking someone else's. His aristocratic leaders also looked forward to a large share of war's spoils. Even more, however, leaders sought the prestige that would accrue for conducting a successful armed exploit, which counted heavily in the heroic, aristocratic code of antiquity.

There were some serious wars during the fifth century B.C., especially with the

Etruscans and Latins, that had major consequences for the future power of Rome. Right at the beginning of the Republic, Lars Porsenna from the Etruscan city of Clusium sought to reestablish an Etruscan monarchy at Rome. Despite the heroic legend of Horatius preventing Rome's fall by defending the *Pons Sublicius* until it could be destroyed, Porsenna actually seems to have captured Rome and held it for a while. About 506 B.C., however, other Latin cities, strongly supported by Aristodemus, the tyrant of Cumae, came to Rome's rescue. They defeated Porsenna's son Arruns at Aricia. Rome was freed, and Etruscan power was weakened because the Latins now blocked vital Etruscan communications with Campania.

Ironically, Rome soon came into conflict with the other Latins. Rome was not a member of the Latin League that had helped rescue her. The leaders of the Republic, moreover, sought to regain the leadership in Latium that Rome had enjoyed under the Etruscan kings. The result was a battle at Lake Regillus between the Romans and the Latin League, which was probably led by Tusculum. Despite patriotic Roman claims of victory through the divine aid of Castor and Pollux, the battle seems to have been a draw and merely invited the neighboring hill peoples, such as the Aequi and Volsci, to encroach on Latium during the conflict. It also encouraged the plebeians to press for more rights at Rome.

In 493, the Romans and the Latin League decided to settle their differences with a treaty, the *foedus Cassianum,* which was negotiated by the plebeian leader Spurius Cassius and was still on view in the Forum four hundred years later. This treaty was of great significance to the expansion of Roman power in Latium because in it Rome's position was equal to that of the Latin League as a whole. The Romans were to contribute half the forces used for common defense, and the League the other half. Whichever side summoned such an army was to command it, and any spoils were to be split evenly—half to Rome and half to the members of the League. Clearly, Roman power was bound to increase at the Latins' expense. Rome alone could decide to summon the common army, while the League would have to have a reason satisfactory to individual members before it could do so; thus, the single city of Rome enriched itself with half of any spoils, while the other half was split among several.

Skillful Roman diplomacy also gained another advantage. The territory of the Aequi and Volsci were separated by that of the Hernici, who feared these tribes more than they feared Rome. The Romans made a defensive alliance with the Hernici around 485 B.C. that isolated the Aequi and the Volsci from each other and thereby made it easier to defeat them in the long run. The principle evident here, divide and rule (*divide et impera*), aided Roman expansion for centuries. Indeed, the Romans had successfully used it earlier when, in 504 B.C. according to tradition, the patricians had given patrician status to the Sabine chieftan Attus Claudius and all of his clan, who were granted land north of the Anio River on the Sabine border in return for defending the area from other Sabines. Attus Claudius' Roman name became Appius Claudius and was borne by numerous important descendants throughout the Republic.

The Aequi and Volsci   The Aequi and Volsci were Rome's most persistent enemies during the fifth century B.C. Early on the Aequi had seized the strategic height of Mount Algidus near Tusculum southeast of Rome, and it was difficult to dislodge them. In 458 according to the *Fasti* a Roman army is reported to have been trapped by the Aequi in the valley below Mount Algidus and would probably have been annihilated had not five horsemen broken out just in time to bring news of the disaster to Rome. According to tradition, the situation was so alarming that a delegation from the senate went out to see Cincinnatus, who was plowing at the time on his four-acre farm. At their insistence he accepted the offered dictatorship and administered a shattering defeat to the Aequi, after which he resigned his dictatorship, went back home, and yoked

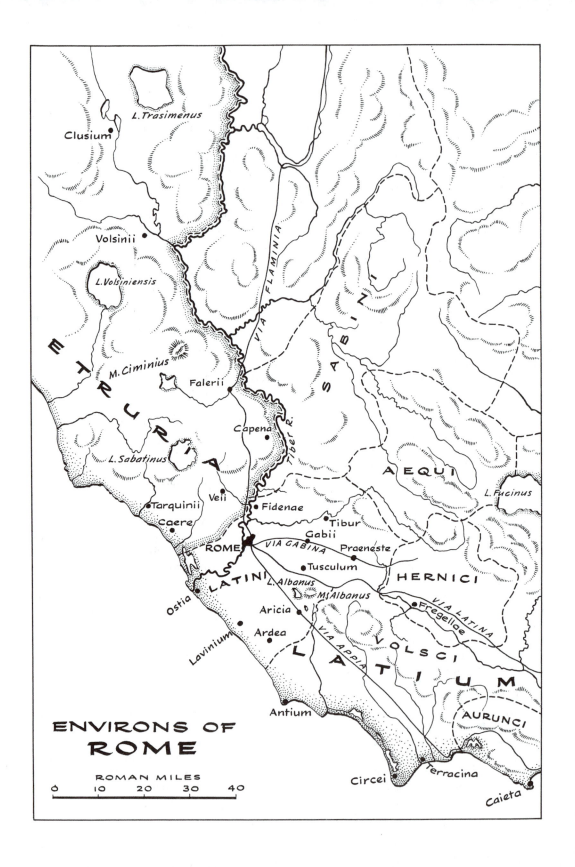

L. Trasimenus

Clusium

Volsinii

L. Volsiniensis

ETRURIA

M. Ciminius

Falerii

Capena

L. Sabatinus

Tarquinii

Veii

Caere

Fidenae

Tiber R.

VIA FLAMINIA

SABINI

AEQUI

L. Fucinus

Tibur

Gabii

ROME

VIA GABINA

Praeneste

Tusculum

HERNICI

L. Albanus

LATINI

Mt Albanus

VIA LATINA

Ostia

Aricia

Fregellae

Lavinium

Ardea

VIA APPIA

VOLSCI

LATIUM

Antium

AURUNCI

ENVIRONS OF
ROME

Circei

Terracina

Caieta

ROMAN MILES

0   10   20   30   40

up his ox. Still, Cincinnatus' victory was not complete. The Romans did not drive the Aequi off Mount Algidus until 431 B.C.

The Volsci were even more difficult. They constantly raided Latium from the southeast and seized several Latin towns along the coast. According to Roman legend, at one point a Roman patrician named Coriolanus, exiled through plebeian hostility, led a Volscian attack against Rome in 491 until his brave mother and wife, Veturia and Volumnia, persuaded him to turn back. Whatever the truth of the story, the Volsci did penetrate as far north as the Alban Mount, and it was not until the end of the century that Rome and the Latin allies pushed the Volsci out of Latium and secured the border with a series of colonies.

The War with Veii   Roman aggression during the fifth century was directed particularly against the Etruscan city of Veii, fifteen miles north on the other side of the Tiber. It was large, rich, well fortified, and Rome's chief rival for control of the lower Tiber valley. The only Etruscan stronghold left in Latium in the mid-fifth century was the bridgehead of Fidenae, across the river from Veii, where the latter kept a garrison. In 479 the Romans had unsuccessfully tried to take Fidenae. At a battle on the Cremera River, just across the Tiber from Fidenae, the Roman clan of the Fabii, who apparently were still fighting in the old heroic style, was practically annihilated. About 426, however, under the command of A. Cornelius Cossus, who killed the king of Veii in combat, the Romans succeeded in capturing Fidenae.

After twenty years, the Romans renewed the conflict by besieging Veii itself. Livy describes the siege as a ten-year epic struggle comparable to the Trojan War of Homeric fame. It was not that grand, but it was the greatest military operation that Rome had yet mounted. The Romans finally won by tunneling under Veii's wall—not so picturesque a maneuver as the Trojan Horse, but an apt illustration of the Roman use of engineering skills in warfare, which often proved more successful than a legionary assault.

The Romans subsequently destroyed Veii, sold its inhabitants as slaves, and annexed its territory, which almost doubled the area of the *ager Romanus* (Roman territory). The dictator Camillus, the victor of Veii, his face and hands painted red like the statue of Jupiter, rode in triumph in a four-horse chariot through the streets of Rome, which was quite unaware of the war clouds even then gathering in the north.

The Gallic Sack of Rome   While Camillus was celebrating his triumph over Veii, the Gauls were pouring over the Alps. Within a few short years they would be roaring down the peninsula and leaving death and havoc wherever they passed. Rome, directly in the path of their advance, would not escape.

The new invaders, whom the Romans called *Galli* (Gauls), were part of the large Indo-European-speaking group of peoples known as Celts. They were particularly skilled as metal workers, and for several centuries had been settled in central Europe from the Rhine to the middle Danube. They had developed rapidly after 700 B.C. through trade with the Greeks and Etruscans. By 500 B.C., population growth and pressure from migrating Germanic tribes were forcing them outward. Although Celtic tribes seeking to settle in Greece were repulsed, in the early third century B.C. one, the Galati, was deflected to Asia Minor and settled in the territory that came to be known from their name as Galatia. Many other Celtic groups migrated to northern Italy, the British Isles, most of France, and many parts of Spain. Their descendants are still found in Brittany (Bretagne), Ireland, Wales, and the Scottish Highlands.

The Celtic Invasion of Northern Italy   Perhaps as early as 500 B.C., Gauls began to cross the Alps into northern Italy, which was dominated by the Etruscans. In successive waves, five great tribes with their women and children, flocks and herds, chariots, wagons, and pack animals fanned out over the plains. The Etruscans were able to put up little resistance in the open country. Although Bologna held out till 350 B.C. and Marzabotto was not taken without a long and bitter struggle, the rest of the country was occupied without much difficulty. Many of the invaders finally settled down and became good farmers—peaceful, contented, hard-working, and prosperous. The entire country from Como to Ancona, from Milan to Verona, was one continuously populated Celtic territory and became known to the Romans as Cisalpine Gaul (Gaul on this side of the Alps).

The Senones, who arrived with the last wave of invaders, found the best land already taken in the north, marched southward, and about 390 B.C. descended upon the Etruscan town of Clusium (Chiusi). The uneasy Romans sent envoys up there to negotiate, but one of the envoys became involved in a fight with a Gallic chief and the negotiations broke down. All hope for peace was gone.

The Allia   Since Rome was not well fortified, the Romans marched out to intercept the Gauls. They made contact with the Gauls near the Allia, a small stream flowing northward into the Tiber about eleven miles from Rome. The Gallic iron-shod cavalry and infantry armed with long, well-tempered swords struck the stiff, slow-moving Roman phalanx of spearmen. Their lines broken, the panic-stricken Romans swam across the Tiber to Veii. The road to Rome was open.*

Hearing of the disaster at the Allia, some Romans fled across the river to Caere, and others hastily fortified the Capitol. The Gauls marched into the open city and burned everything except the Capitol, which was reportedly saved by the alarm raised by the cackling of Juno's sacred geese and the valor of Marcus Manlius.

---

* The Romans were so affected by this disaster that they observed its anniversary every year. They recorded the date as July 18. Livy gives the year corresponding to 390. Polybius, whose years begin in July and end in June, gives the equivalent of 387/86, and Didorus Siculus gives the equivalent of 386.

After besieging the Capitol for seven months, the Gauls learned that the Veneti had invaded their lands in the Po valley. Eager to go back home, they readily accepted a ransom of a thousand pounds of gold and marched away.

Up from the Ashes   Rome was badly damaged, her defenses smashed, the wealth of her citizens exhausted, and her prestige in Latium at a low ebb.

When the Romans returned to rebuild their ruined city, they recognized the need for strong defenses. Having learned how impregnable to direct assault were the walls of Veii, they decided to build similar walls of the same grayish yellow tufa quarried at Grotta Obscura near Veii. This stone was superior to any previously used, and they continued to use it in all squared-stone masonry until the end of the second century B.C. It was cut into rectangular blocks of uneven dimensions and laid down so that rows of headers alternated with stretchers,—that is, the long axis of the stones in one course was at a right angle to that of the stones in the other. In this way was built the so-called ''Servian Wall,'' about twelve feet thick, twenty-four feet high, which extended around the entire city, including the Aventine, a distance of five and a half miles.

After the Gauls had departed from Roman territory, some Latin cities, especially Tibur, Velitrae, Praeneste, Antium, and Satricum, began to assert their independence and even to show hostility to Rome. The rest seem to have remained loyal to the alliance of the *foedus Cassianum*. To make matters worse, the Etruscans, Aequi, Hernici, and Volsci, all of whom Rome is supposed previously to have conquered, invaded what was left of Roman territory. Camillus beat back their attacks with tremendous success, so it is reported, but it is useless to repeat the details because the tradition, with its confused chronology, its duplications, and inventions, is obviously unsound. Nevertheless, it is probable that Rome succeeded in stabilizing the situation in Latium at this time.

ITALY
ABOUT 265 B.C.

ROMAN TERRITORY
ALLIED TERRITORY
☐ ROMAN CITIZEN COLONIES
■ *Latin Colonies*
● <u>Greek Cities</u>

•Mediolanum
Cremona•
•Verona
•Patavium
Placentia
•Mantua
•Aquileia
P O
•Parma
Mutina•
L L I A   C I S A L P I N A
•Genua
Bononia•

•Luna

A R N O
Faesulae•
Luca•
•Florentia
•Ariminium
U M B R I A
☐SENA
GALLICA

E T R U R I A
Arretium•
Firmum•
T I B E R
Perusia•
Volsinii•
Narnia
Asculum
•CASTRUM NOVUM
ELBA
Falerii
Hadria
Cosa
Tarquinii•
N E R A
Sutrium
Alba
Fucens
VESTINI MARRU-
CINIUM
Caere■
Arsioli
Corfinium
Rome
Tibur
PAELIGNI
FRENTANI
A D R I A T I C   S E A
Praeneste
MARSI
Ostia
Signia
Fregellae
•Aesernia
•Luceria
•Cannae
Ardea
Norba
Suessa
S A M N I U M
Asculum
ANTIUM
Setia
Cales
Saticula
•Barium
Circeii
TERRACINA
Beneventum HIRPINI
A P U L I A
MINTURNAE
SINUESSA
Capua☐
•Venusia
C A L A B R I A
Pontia
Cumae
•Neapolis
Paestum
(Posidonia)
Tarentum
•Brundisium
L U C A N I A
G U L F
O F
Heraclea
•Sybaris
T Y R R H E N I A N
Thurii
T A R E N T U M

S E A
•Croton

A L E R I A
C O R S I C A

•Aleria

D I N I A

•Carales

B R U T T I U M
•Caulonia
•Locri

•Panormus
Drepanum•
•Segesta
Messana
•Rhegium
AEGATES IS.
Himera
Lilybaeum■
S I C .
Tauromenium
Henna•

More real, perhaps, than the danger from invasion was the fear of dictatorship. Under similar circumstances a Greek state might easily have succumbed to the appeal of a strong-man government as the most efficient way of getting things done in a hurry, especially in a time of emergency. Not so with Rome. The Republican tradition of liberty seems to have been too firmly set against it.

There was no lack of candidates; among them was no less a figure than Camillus himself, the hero of many battles and the chairman of the committee in charge of rebuilding the city walls. In spite of his splendid record of achievement and his immense personal prestige, he was driven into exile. Two other top military and political leaders with similar ambitions were executed, and reforms were made without the efforts of an all-powerful leader.

Initial Conquests in Central Italy   It may be granted that the reorganization of the government begun about 367 B.C. permitted greater efficiency in administration and at the same time removed friction between the ancient patrician families and the new but powerful plebeian nobility. Foreign problems were among the most compelling reasons for governmental reorganization and political equalization of the two social classes. But to say that the reform movement was expressly designed for the future conquest of Italy would be an extreme exaggeration. The Romans were only trying to meet an immediate crisis. Nevertheless, once Rome had correctly appraised and met the crises of the fourth century B.C., conditions were created that helped to make possible the conquest not only of Italy, but of the Mediterranean world.

Besides Rome, the chief military powers in Italy in 350 were the Gauls, the Etruscans, and the Samnites. Of these, the Etruscans and the Gauls were the least to be feared.

The Etruscans were a moribund league of cities unable to do anything really effective, though still capable of making trouble. By 474 B.C. they had lost Campania to the Greeks and Samnites; by about 400, the north to the on-slaught of the Gauls. Now they were squeezed in a vise between the Gauls from the north and the waxing might of Rome in the south.

The Gauls had never been able to repeat their performance of the Allia. Walled cities were proof against their attacks, though later raids into Latium and Apulia revived old memories of their wild terror. When they came back about 349 B.C., the Romans easily routed them. Their earlier attacks had actually helped rather than hindered the Romans, for they had revealed Rome's lack of defense against attack and her need for governmental reform. They had helped to eliminate the Etruscan threat and, by the savagery of their attack, their indiscriminate killing, and wholesale plundering, had driven many Italian communities to look to Rome for leadership and protection. Finally, because of their spasmodic, uncoordinated, and ineffectual operations, they had left the fate of Italy to be decided between the Romans and the Samnites, an Umbro-Sabellian group from the south-central Apennines that had been extending its territory at the expense of the Oscans in Campania and Lucania (see p. 7).

The Samnites and Rome   Probably out of mutual fear of the Gauls, the Romans and Samnites signed a treaty of alliance around 354 B.C., but that was a forced marriage that could not last. For a long time, population pressure and the lack of resources in the Samnites' homeland had been forcing them to expand their territory at their neighbors' expense. Their constant pressure behind the Volscans had long been forcing the latter to invade Latium and wage endless wars with the Romans. To the Greeks of south Italy they had been a constant and unnerving menace.

Around 350 B.C. the Samnites seemed much stronger than the Romans. They held more than three and a half times as much territory (8300 as opposed to 2300 square miles) and had more than double the population (perhaps 650,000 as opposed to probably 317,400). Even these figures do not convey the initial weakness of the Romans because they include territories and populations already unreliable and hostile, which ten years later were at war with Rome. Nevertheless, before the end of the century Rome owed her victory over the Samnites to the superiority that she gradually acquired in manpower and resources. With each succeeding decade Rome expanded and gained in strength.

On the other hand, Samnite expansion into Campania and Lucania did not increase Samnite war-making power. Many of the original Samnite settlers had become rich and had risen to a position of leadership among the local aristocracy. As they did not want the status quo upset by a mass invasion of their have-not kinsmen, they were inclined to line up behind the Romans. Similarly, the Lucanian Samnites, or at least the dominant faction, had turned their backs on their northern kinsmen and wanted to play a big role in the world of the Greek city-states. From time to time they made alliances with the Romans against their own people.

Even more serious and dangerous were the relations of the Samnites with the people of their own background living on their northern borders: the Marsi, Paeligni, and Marrucini. When the Romans made alliances with the latter they were able to march right into the heart of Samnium. Though the Samnites were brave fighters and passionately devoted to the defense of their mountain homeland, they were too clannish to cooperate with people outside their immediate neighborhood.

The Samnite homeland itself was divided into four main tribes forming, in time of war, a loose confederacy liable to come apart when unity and cohesion were most required. The confederacy lacked a national assembly, which might have enabled the Samnites to formulate a clear, long-range war policy. Their most brilliant victories failed to produce any permanent results.

The Samnites could and did give the Romans many painful lessons in mountain fighting. From their many encounters with the Greeks the Samnites had learned that the hoplite phalanx, though irresistible on level ground, was a distinct liability in mountainous terrain. After a while the Romans mastered the secret of mountain fighting, but the Samnite slowness to copy Roman political and diplomatic methods spelled the difference between final victory and defeat in the long series of wars that the two people eventually fought with each other.

The First Samnite War, 343 to 341 B.C. About 343 the Samnites attacked the Sidicini, an insignificant state north of Capua. Capua appealed to Rome for help, which the Romans readily gave because it made them allies of Italy's second biggest city and gave them a foothold in Campania. The war itself was not a serious one, and the battles recorded are undoubtedly fictitious. Some scholars would reject this war altogether, but without it, it seems hard to explain the presence of the Romans in Campania and some of the events that followed.

Capua was saved. But the Roman soldiers, failing to understand why they had to fight so far from home, mutinied. The Romans were glad to make peace and so were the Samnites, who feared Archidamus, the Spartan king who had landed in Italy in 343/42 B.C. in response to an appeal for help from the Greek city of Tarentum. The peace terms of 341 B.C. acknowledged the Samnite right to occupy the Sidicini's territory and the Roman alliance with Capua.

The Latin War of 340 to 338 B.C. The Latin and Campanian allies of Rome regarded the treaty of 341 as a shameful betrayal of the Sidicini, and when the Samnite occupation of that small state began about 340, they took up arms in its defense, contrary to the wishes and advice of Rome. For years the Latins had been chafing against their Roman alliance, which seemed to them another form of domination. As the Gauls were no longer a menace after 349, they saw in the Samnite occupation a chance to make their bid for freedom and independence. The Latins were already at war with Samnium and their insubordination brought them also into a war with Rome. The war gave the Romans a chance to settle the Latin problem (with the help of the now-friendly Samnites) before they got involved in any major conflict.

By 338 B.C., according to the *Fasti,* the bitter conflict was over. The Campanians had already accepted the generous terms offered them and had deserted their allies. The Latins and the Volscans were soon afterward crushed, never to rise up again, and the Old Latin League was dissolved. From now on the future of the Latins would be determined at Rome's pleasure.

The Roman System of Alliances   The Old Latin League, dissolved around 338 B.C., had had a long history. It had grown out of one of the ancient religious leagues formed for the joint celebration of common festivals. It acquired a political and juridical status by the treaty concluded by Spurius Cassius (see pp. 67, 70) between the early Roman Republic and perhaps thirty Latin cities. It had been renewed about 358 B.C., with some added provisions tightening Roman control.

In the original treaty ascribed to Spurius Cassius, which established an offensive and defensive alliance, Rome had formally renounced all claims to domination over Latium. The terms were that peace should exist between the two parts forever, that the enemies of the one be the enemies of the other, that both contribute equal numbers of troops for war, and that booty taken in wars fought in common be divided equally. There were also provisions relating to the private rights of citizens, known as *Latin Rights.* They were specially important.

The rights, which Roman citizens were to enjoy in each of the allied Latin cities and Latin citizens in Rome and in each of the other Latin cities, were intermarriage *(conubium),* the right to do business and make legally binding contracts *(commercium),* and the right to change residence *(migratio).* The children of a Roman husband or wife married to a Latin inherited Roman citizenship and both their parents' property. Latin citizens doing business in Rome could sue or be sued in Roman courts and could enjoy the benefits of the Roman law of sale and of succession. All contracts could be enforced only in the courts of the place where originally drawn up. In early times Latin citizens had the mutual right of changing residence and afterwards of acquiring citizenship. A Latin moving to Rome would vote in a tribe that he had drawn by lot.

Latin Rights after 338 B.C.   When the Romans scrapped the Old Latin League, they did not leave a vacuum for underground hostility or sullen resentment to fill. At least six Latin cities or municipalities *(municipia),* on losing their old independence, were incorporated into the Roman state with full rights of citizenship, including the right to vote and hold office. Local government in these cities still continued to function. The colonies founded by the League received the same rights. The rest of the Latin cities and some trusted Etruscan allies received limited Roman citizenship without the right to vote *(civitas sine suffragio),* but with the obligation to furnish troops for the Roman army when called upon. They were allowed the right to local government, but might not formulate an independent foreign policy or form leagues among themselves. They were also prohibited from the rights of intermarriage and of making contracts among themselves; those they could enjoy only with Rome.

They were now fully protected against foreign attack and were assured the full benefits of Roman civil law in all their business enterprises. In addition, they could still enjoy the privileges of local government. Many of them were no doubt grateful for the benefits already given and hoped to prove themselves worthy, by loyal cooperation with Rome, of admission later to the privileges of full citizenship.

Thus did Rome bind to herself with ties of loyalty and hope all her defeated Latin enemies. The wisdom and success of this policy was vindicated, for they remained faithful even in the darkest hours of defeat against all the allurements of the Samnites and future enemies like Pyrrhus and Hannibal.

Extension of Latin Rights to Italian Communities   The settlement of the year 338 was not only epoch making in the history of citizenship in general and of working relationships between conquered communities and the center of power, but it set the pattern for the conquest first of Italy and later of the Mediterranean world. It was a stroke of political genius unique in the ancient world and, as a weapon of conquest, was worth more than many legions. Prior to 338 a conquered city was usually either completely destroyed, as Veii had been by the Romans themselves, or left to smolder in discontent, ready to burst into rebellion the moment the conqueror had relaxed his grip. The Romans instead devised the municipal system of government within the Roman superstate.

Municipia Municipia (municipalities) were cities and towns in Latium, Etruria, and Campania, whose inhabitants had the full burdens *(munera)* of Roman citizens without the rights of voting and acquiring property in Rome. They were required to furnish troops or money contributions for war and were prohibited from making war against or concluding treaties with other states. Otherwise they could conduct their local affairs as they had done in the past, according to their own constitutions, laws, and traditions. Because they enjoyed the Latin rights of intermarriage and the benefits of Roman civil law, their status may be said to have been halfway between complete independence and full Roman citizenship.

Colonies   Another Roman device was the planting of colonies at strategic points throughout Italy. The idea was not a new one, for the planting of colonies was one of the joint activities of the Old Latin League, the purpose of which was to hold down conquered territory and at the same time serve as an outlet for surplus population. Two such colonies were founded in southern Etruria on land conquered from Veii. A number of other colonies were established on conquered Volscan territory. Nine such colonies were in existence at the time of the breakup of the League.

It was not until after 338 that the planting of colonies became established Roman policy. During the next fifty years colonies were founded at Ostia, Antium, Terracina, Sinuessa, and Minturnae to guard harbors and waterways or defend the coasts of Latium (Rome then had no permanent fleet). Other colonists were sent to Campania and Apulia to occupy key points and forge a ring of fortresses around Samnium, and to Umbria and other points north to keep the Gauls in check.

There were two kinds of colonies: Roman citizen colonies and Latin colonies. Latin colonies were by far the more numerous. Up until the First Punic War (264 to 241 B.C.), twenty-one Latin colonies were founded, but only nine Roman citizen colonies. The two types differed not in the colonists, since both Latins and Romans could be accepted for either, but in the size of population and constitutional status. Until 194 B.C. or later, Roman citizen colonies were limited to 300 families, while Latin colonies varied between 2500 and 6000 families. It is said that one at Venusia, thirty miles north of Tarentum, consisted of 20,000. Roman citizen colonies were too small to form a state, and the colonists never ceased to be full Roman citizens. Latin colonies had the status of Latin allies or ordinary *municipia;* they had the right of local self-government with their own laws, elected magistrates, census, and coinage. If a Latin colonist moved to Rome, he could become a Roman citizen, provided he left in his place a son of military age.

Roman citizen colonies were simply small garrisons sent to places that were of strategic importance, but unattractive and incapable of economic or community growth. The Latin colonies often became, especially in north Italy, the first foundations of some very large cities.

Defensive Alliances   The Romans also made a number of defensive alliances with Greek and Italian city-states who felt threatened by the Samnites and other neighboring tribes. Rome signed treaties with them that differed according to mutual need, dependence, and the gravity of the military situation. All allied states were commonly required to place their military forces at Rome's disposal and agree to leave the conduct of foreign affairs in her hands. In return she agreed not to impose taxes upon them and to allow each allied city to raise, equip, and command its own troops, who would fight under the command of a Roman general. Rome would also provide the allied troops with food and subsistence pay at her own expense, and would share the spoils of war with them. Furthermore, all allied cities could enjoy the Latin Rights of Roman civil law and intermarriage. At the same time they would be permitted local self-government under their own laws and political institutions.

The Final Conquest of Central Italy

The Second (Great) Samnite War, 327 to 304/3 B.C.   Though not really intended to provoke hostilities with the Samnites, Rome's system of colonies and alliances effectively cut off their chance for expanding westward and were bound to cause friction. Samnite sensibilities were further offended in 334, when the Romans made a move to the east of them by signing a treaty with Tarentum (Taranto), who was fighting neighboring Oscan tribes. Hostilities between the Romans and Samnites finally broke out in 327, when the Samnites, backing one side in an internal dispute at Naples, garrisoned the city. The Romans backed the other faction, besieged Naples, and won control of the city. Full-scale war with the Samnites followed.

The military history of this war is obscure. Most of the battles that the annalists record are unimportant even if they did take place, except the battle of the Caudine Forks, which took place in 321 according to the *Fasti.* The Romans, attempting to march from Campania across the Apennines to Apulia, were misled by false information into a trap at a pass called the Caudine Forks, where they were compelled to surrender, give hostages, and

agree not to renew the war. Stripped down to single garments, they were ignominiously driven under a yoke that consisted of two spears stuck in the ground and united at the top by a third. To pass under the yoke was a token of complete defeat and unconditional surrender.

New Military Tactics   The battle of the Caudine Forks made clear to the Romans that they needed to learn about mountain fighting. They used the peace to good advantage by reorganizing the legion so as to form three lines separately trained, differently armed, and able to maneuver independently. The new formations could operate better in mountainous terrain, and some troops were armed with Samnite javelins instead of phalanx spears. Now able to put four legions into battle instead of two, and to fight as well on the plains as the Greeks, and as well in the mountains as the Samnites, the Romans found an excuse in 316 for repudiating the peace treaty and renewing the war.

Despite their military reorganization, the Romans still had a difficult task against the rugged Samnites. The very next year the Romans suffered another serious defeat at Lautulae near Terracina, a coastal town in southern Latium. This reverse almost caused the Campanian allies to run out of their alliance, but strong pressure soon brought them back into line. The Latins stood firm, partly because the Samnites were getting too close to home and partly because the Romans had dealt with them so fairly after 338 B.C.

After stabilizing the situation on the Campanian front both by recovering lost ground and setting up colonial bases at key points, the Romans shifted their attention to the Apulian front, where they had earlier established a big base at Luceria. At the same time they continued their policy of Samnite encirclement. They concluded military alliances with the Lucanians in the south and with the Marsi, Marrucini, Paeligni, and Frentani in the north, all close kinsfolk of the Samnites.

This offensive strategy in the north came none too soon, for the Samnites began to copy

Roman diplomatic tactics and persuaded some southern Etruscan cities, whose treaties with Rome were about to expire, to create a second front against Rome. There was also a danger that they might induce the Gauls to effect a junction with their army. The Gauls made no move, and the Romans continued to create a broad buffer zone across central Italy from which they were able to make devastating raids into the heart of Samnium. By this show of force they also compelled the Etruscans to renew and observe their treaties.

The man who is thought to have masterminded this astute military and diplomatic strategy was the old censor of 312/10 B.C., Appius Claudius the Blind. A shrewd politician, he built Rome's first great aqueduct and promoted numerous reforms to gain popular support. It was also his idea to run a highway from Rome to Capua over which troops could be swiftly moved in any kind of weather. That was the famous Appian Way.

In spite of the brilliance of their strategy and their constancy and doggedness in danger and defeat, the Romans did not easily win the Second Samnite War. Both sides were still fairly evenly matched in territory and population. Each side had unreliable allies. Some Roman allies considered defecting to the Samnite side when they saw Rome becoming too strong for their own future security. The war was long and bloody, and the victory was by no means absolute, as the peace of 304/3 B.C. clearly shows. The Samnites lost none of their original territory, none of their independence, and none of their capacity to fight again.

The Third Samnite War, 298 to 290 B.C. Nevertheless, the balance of power had gradually been shifting steadily in favor of Rome. After 304/3 B.C., she controlled an area of 9242.77 square miles and a population of some 927,000, as compared with 5676.13 square miles and 498,000 population of the Samnites. The danger of the growing disparity had become clear to the Sabines, the Etruscans, the Umbrians, and even the Gauls, who all joined forces with the Samnites in 295 B.C. in the hope of stopping Rome. They fought the Romans at

Sentinum in Umbria. The consul Decius Mus inspired the Romans to valor by devoting himself to the gods and purposely exposing himself to death at enemy hands. The Romans won the fight for central Italy. In 290 B.C. the Samnites, knowing that all hope was gone, surrendered and sued for peace. Their lands were annexed, and they accepted the status of Roman allies.

Etruscans and Gauls   The Etruscans and Gauls fought on, however, and lost a major battle at Lake Vadimo in 283 B.C. After another defeat in the following year, the Gauls asked for peace. The Etruscans continued to resist for a number of years but finally surrendered under moderate terms. The only Etruscan city to lose territory was Rome's former friend Caere. It was annexed, probably in 273, and its citizens were granted Roman citizenship without the right to vote, *civitas sine suffragio.*

The Pyrrhic Wars and the Conquest of Southern Italy   The Etruscans had fought on after 282, and the Romans eventually granted them moderate peace terms because Rome was now faced with another serious crisis. Victory against the Samnites in central Italy had removed a powerful buffer between Rome and the most powerful Greek city-state in southern Italy, Tarentum. From their side of the Apennines, the Tarentines had also been fighting the Samnites, as well as Bruttians and Lucanians, and been trying to push them back. In so doing, they had called in a number of Greek military adventurers from across the Adriatic to help them. The first had been King Archidamus of Sparta, from 343/42 to 338 B.C.; next was Alexander of Epirus, the uncle of Alexander the Great, from 334 to 331/30; then another Spartan king, Cleonymus in 303/2; and after him Agathocles of Syracuse, 298 to 289 B.C. Not one had succeeded either in making Tarentum a strong power or in carving out an empire for himself.

The Tarentines had even become so distrustful of Alexander of Epirus that they withdrew their support, and he was killed in a battle with the Lucanians. Nevertheless, he left them an important legacy. While he was attacking the Samnites in 334, he had negotiated a treaty with the Romans. They had agreed not to come to the aid of the Samnites, who had temporarily become Rome's allies after the First Samnite War. Part of that treaty was a Roman promise not to send ships into the Gulf of Tarentum. With Alexander's death, the Roman's considered the treaty dead too, but the Tarentines thought differently.

They were already upset because Rome had rejected their attempt to mediate between the two sides in the Second Samnite War and had established the colony of Venusia on their Apulian border after the Third Samnite War. Then in 285 Thurii, a Greek city not far from the western shore of the Gulf of Tarentum under attack by the Lucanians, appealed to Rome for help rather than to her ally, Tarentum. Perhaps the Thurians believed that Rome was stronger than Tarentum and more reliable, as well as less dangerous. With some misgivings the Romans answered the appeal, defeated the Lucanians, and stationed a small garrison in Thurii. Rhegium, Locri, and probably Croton also asked for and received Roman protection.

Roman interference in the internal affairs of Greek Italy further aroused the suspicion and enmity of Tarentum. Therefore in 282, when a Roman naval squadron of ten ships was cruising about in the Gulf of Tarentum in violation of the treaty of 334, the Tarentines attacked without warning, sank four ships, and killed the admiral. Then the Tarentines fitted out an expedition, marched to Thurii, drove out the Roman garrison, and sacked the town. When ambassadors from Rome came to seek redress and reparations, they were publicly insulted, ridiculed for their bad Greek, and refused a hearing. The Tarentines might have been more disposed to listen and make amends had they not called in another Greek adventurer, King Pyrrhus.

Pyrrhus was king of Epirus, a small mountainous country in northwestern Greece.

The ambitious Pyrrhus, educated in Egypt, had married a Ptolemaic princess and had for some years been subsidized by Ptolemy II. He had been king of half of Macedonia from 288 to 285 B.C. and had delusions of being another Alexander the Great. The invitation from Tarentum presented a real opportunity to establish the empire that he craved.

In the spring of 280 B.C. he arrived in Italy with twenty-five thousand mercenaries. Pyrrhus had hired twenty thousand heavily armed phalanx men, and purchased twenty Indian war elephants. Shortly after landing, he met the Roman army at Heraclea. He found to his surprise that his hoplite phalanx was unable to make a break through the Roman legions, which were equipped and drilled in Samnite style and always able, after giving ground here and there, to close their ranks. For the first time since Marathon, the phalanx had met its match.

Nevertheless, Pyrrhus was able to use his elephants to good advantage. Instead of using his elephants like modern tanks to make a break through the center of the Roman lines, which might have let the elephants through and then closed before the infantry could follow, he adopted the unorthodox tactic of attacking both flanks with elephants and cavalry. The encircled Romans lost seven thousand men and were forced to retreat. But Pyrrhus himself lost four thousand men and won only a tactical victory. (Such an outcome has since been known as a "Pyrrhic victory.")

He was aided, however, by the Oscan and Samnite tribes, who had revolted again in 283. Therefore, with most of southern Italy under his control, Pyrrhus next tried to force a decision by a lightning attack on Rome. He marched as far as Praeneste, within forty miles of the capital, but he found to his surprise that Rome's other allies, upon whose help he had depended, did not flock to his colors. He then tried a peace offensive, and when that also failed he was forced to get ready for another battle.

He met the Romans in battle at Asculum in Apulia. The first day the Romans fought on rough ground, where the Pyrrhic phalanx was ineffective; the next day Pyrrhus feigned a retreat to more level ground. The Romans followed. His elephants broke through the Roman center lines. This victory too was costly: a loss of four thousand men. It was then that Pyrrhus is said to have declared: ''Another such victory and I am lost!''

Pyrrhus' Sicilian Venture, 278 to 275 B.C. His costly victories over the Romans dissuaded Pyrrhus from further attempts to establish an empire in Italy. Besides, opportunities had opened up elsewhere. The Celts had invaded Macedonia in 279 B.C. and killed the king. Pyrrhus, if he was strong enough, might go there as champion of the Greek world and win back the Macedonian throne. Sicily, about to be conquered by the Carthaginians, offered still another possibility. Hard-pressed Syracuse sent envoys begging for his help. He decided, perhaps after some prodding from Egypt, to try out his luck in Sicily. Peace talks were begun with the Romans and would have gone smoothly for him had not Mago, the admiral of a large Carthaginian fleet anchored off Ostia, suddenly appeared offering to supply Rome with ships, money, or anything reasonable that she might want, if she would keep Pyrrhus occupied in Italy. Finally, Pyrrhus was obliged to leave half of his army in Tarentum to defend his allies and set sail for Sicily in the fall of 278 B.C. without any definite commitment from Rome.

His successes in Sicily were immediate and colossal. He had driven the Carthaginians off the main island and was besieging their last stronghold, the small island of Lilybaeum, when Carthage sued for peace. There loomed before Pyrrhus the possibility of making a lightning attack on defenseless Carthage and of conquering Egypt with the aid of traitors from within. These dreams never materialized. In some mysterious way the Sicilian city-states suddenly found the encouragement to declare themselves neutral. Only Syracuse remained faithful to him, and even she was divided by civil strife. The Sicilian venture had

failed. There was nothing else to do but to return to Italy.

Pyrrhus lost part of his fleet in a naval battle with the Carthaginians during his attempt to get back to Italy in 276 B.C. Later in Italy he captured a few Greek towns, plundered the treasures of the temple of Persephone at Locri, and made his way to Tarentum. Regrouping his forces, he marched northward into Samnium. He lost several of his prize elephants during an indecisive battle with the Romans near Beneventum, and finally withdrew to Tarentum to avoid getting caught between two consular armies.

Though he had never lost a land battle, his entire Italian campaign had been a failure. He returned to Greece in 275 B.C. and again became king of Macedonia in 274. Two years later he lost his life in an attack on Argos, when some woman dropped a pot on his head from a second story window. Pyrrhus gone, all Italy from Pisa and Ariminum (Rimini) in the north to Brundisium (Brindisi), Tarentum, and the straits of Messana in the south came under the undisputed domination of Rome.

Reasons for Roman Success in Italy
Many scholars have sought some particular reason for Rome's success in defeating her numerous hostile neighbors and conquering peninsular Italy in the fifth, fourth, and early third centuries B.C. There is, of course, no single cause sufficient to explain it. Rome had a unique combination of advantages that accounts for her victories. Various of these advantages were, to be sure, shared by one or another of her enemies. The crucial point is that no one shared Rome's combination.

Part of the reason for Rome's success was the reorganization of the government around 367 B.C., which secured greater unity in the face of external danger. Her success was also due in part to her usual willingness and ability to fulfill her treaty obligations and to the statesmanlike quality of her leaders in building strategic alliances. Her strong but generous policy toward her Latin allies had secured their loyalty in the long run. Also, most other Italian communities found their alliances with Rome fair and regarded the Samnites in the south and the Gauls in the north as greater menaces to their security than the Romans.

The strategic advantages of Rome's central geographic location in Italy had allowed Roman armies to move quickly against attacks on more than one front and prevent enemies from combining forces easily. The fertility and population of both their immediate territory and that of their staunchest allies gave the Romans the resources and manpower to recover from initial defeats and eventually wear down their opponents. The Etruscan kings had also given the Roman army superior organization and tactics, which the Romans continued to improve, compared with those of the less-developed tribes who often encroached on Roman territory. Moreover, the authoritarian and aristocratic social structure produced well-disciplined soldiers who obeyed a leadership determined to preserve and increase its honor.

Finally, the irrational factor of sheer luck cannot be ignored. The Romans were lucky that their potentially strongest enemies, the highly developed Etruscan and Greek city-states, were both rent by jealousies and rivalries that prevented either group from mounting any unified opposition. It was fortunate that the brilliant military adventurers from Greece who sought Italian empires were poor diplomats. How fortunate for the Romans that the Gauls who sacked Rome around 390 were not in a position to occupy their conquest permanently and left before the Roman people had lost heart.

With this combination of advantages, the Romans had united all of peninsular Italy under their control through a strong and flexible system of alliances and had created a durable confederacy that made Rome by 264 B.C. one of the major powers in the Mediterranean world. Thereupon, Rome became locked in a titanic struggle with the nearest of the other major powers, Carthage, for control of the western half of that world. The strength and durable nature of Rome's Italian confederacy were major factors in her ultimate victory in that struggle.

VII

The Beginning of
Roman Imperialism and the
First Punic War, 264 to 241 B.C.

Between 264 and 133 B.C. the Roman Republic was at its height in many ways. By 264 the Struggle of the Orders that had caused much internal agitation had abated. To preserve unity in the face of hostile neighbors, the patricians had gradually yielded to the wealthy plebeians' demands for equal access to the social and political levers of power. The acquisition of booty and territory from conquered neighbors had helped to alleviate the economic distress of the poor plebs. Therefore, between 264 and 133 B.C. the Roman political system remained basically stable under the control of the new patricio-plebeian aristocracy in the senate. Many changes were taking place on other fronts, however, and they will be the subjects of this and the next six chapters.

Beginning with the First Punic War, this period also saw the Roman Republic steadily acquire a Mediterranean-wide empire. Yearly warfare had practically become a way of life during the early Republic. Citizens of all classes had become accustomed to the profits of war, and aristocratic leaders craved military glory and benefitted politically from the popularity won in victorious campaigns. Imperialism was an appetite that grew with feeding as Rome swallowed Sicily, Sardinia,

Corsica, Spain, Macedonia, Greece, and large parts of North Africa and Asia Minor. Despite sometimes staggering defeats, the Republic's military strength seemed inexhaustible as all opposition was inevitably and often brutally crushed. The Republic's imperial success, however, created the very problems that led to its destruction in the period of turmoil after 133.

Along with Rome's acquisition of an overseas empire, there was an acceleration of the integration of Roman culture and Hellenistic Greek civilization, which in 264 B.C. still dominated the political, economic, and cultural life of the world from the Himalayan Mountains in the East to the Atlantic coast of Spain in the West. (The term *Hellenistic* is used to designate the distinctive phase of Greek civilization that flourished after Alexander the Great [d. 323 B.C.], when many non-Greek peoples adopted numerous elements of classical Greek civilization.) After 264, Roman culture rapidly matured under the influence of the Hellenistic Greeks, whose poetry, drama, history, rhetoric, philosophy, and art provided the models for Romans to produce a distinctive Greco-Roman civilization that characterized the Mediterranean world until the fall of the Roman Empire.

Sources for Roman History from 264 to 133 B.C.   At this point in Roman history there are, for the first time, fairly reliable literary sources of information. The early annalistic writers used by Polybius, Livy, and others were contemporaries of this period and had either personally witnessed the events of which they wrote or learned of them directly from those who had. Polybius himself had come to Rome just a century after the outbreak of the First Punic War in 264 B.C. His brief account of that war and his detailed description of the Second and of Rome's subsequent conquest of the Mediterranean world are quite reliable. Unfortunately, his work is intact only to the year 216 B.C. (Books 1–6) and preserved only in fragments to its end with the events of 145/44 B.C. (Books 7–40). Livy, however, who used Polybius extensively along with Roman annalists, is complete for the years 219 to 167 (Books 21–45). After that he is represented by the summaries of the *Periochae* (46–56) and epitomes of the late Empire (see pp. 515–516).

From 167 to 133, Velleius Paterculus, who wrote in the early first century A.D., provides a brief narrative in his compendium of Roman history (Books 1–2.1), about whose sources there is considerable question. Cassius Dio used Polybius and the Roman annalists heavily, and extensive fragments of the relevant books of his *Roman History* are preserved (11–23). The work of early annalists and Polybius are also preserved in the fragments of Books 23 to 32 of Diodorus Siculus, as well as in Books 6 to 9 and Book 11 of the *Roman History* of Appian, a Greek from Alexandria who wrote in the second century A.D. Although the difficult question of their sources poses problems of reliability, the biographies of the Carthaginian generals Hamilcar and Hannibal by Cornelius Nepos (late first century B.C.) and Plutarch's lives of Cato the Elder, Flamininus, and Aemilius Paullus help to flesh out some of the main characters of the period. The late-first-century B.C. geographer Strabo also preserves some useful facts, and Book 7 of the *Description of Greece* by the mid-second-century A.D. traveller Pau-

sanias has important information on Roman activities in 146 B.C.

Moreover, for the first time there are contemporary works of literature, like the plays of Plautus and Terence and fragments of numerous other works, that help to illuminate the life and culture of the period (see pp. 148–151). Contemporary coins now begin to supply abundant numismatic evidence that shows not only economic history but reveals much about the officials who issued them and the places, events, and concepts depicted on them. Inscriptions are also more numerous and important, preserving the texts of treaties and laws and the epitaphs that help to reconstruct the political relationships and careers of famous people and the daily lives of ordinary people. Finally, extensive archaeological excavations at Rome, Carthage, and hundreds of other sites reveal much about social, economic, political, and cultural trends.

Carthage   The expansion of Rome to the "toe" of the Italian peninsula by 264 B.C. had brought Roman power to the Straits of Messana, within only three miles of Sicily. There the powerful North African city of Carthage had long been vying with Greek colonists for control. By this time Carthage had become a major Hellenistic power. Although never conquered by Alexander nor an inheritor of any part of his conquests, Carthage had been extensively influenced by the Greeks through constant commercial contact and rivalry in Sicily and the western Mediterranean. The upper classes had adopted Greek methods of government, farming, manufacture, architecture, dress, jewelry, art, metalwares, and even language. Soon Carthage and Rome, who was rapidly rising in the same Hellenistic world, would become locked in a titanic struggle that would make Rome the dominant power in the western Mediterranean.

Carthage was situated on Cape Bon, a small tongue of land jutting out from North Africa into the Gulf of Tunis and had been founded by Phoenicians, who were famous as traders and merchants long before the Greeks. (The adjective *Punic* is derived from the Latin word for Phoenician, and that is why Rome's wars with the Phoenician colony Carthage are called the Punic Wars.) The story of Carthage's founding, like that of Rome's, is encrusted with legends. Archaeological discoveries, however, show that it too should be dated to around 750 B.C. and not between 860 and 814 as formerly conjectured. In a strategically advantageous position at the narrowest part of the Mediterranean and with access to either end, Carthage was in an ideal location for a maritime power. After she had occupied the island of Malta (Melita) between Sicily and North Africa, she was practically able to exclude the Greeks, her toughest commercial and colonial rivals, from the western half of the sea.

For several decades Carthage remained an obedient daughter of Tyre, but during the seventh century the mother city became subject to Assyria and afterward to Babylon and Persia. Tyre now was unable either to control or protect the Phoenician colonies to the west. Therefore, to protect and expand their mercantile interests, the favorably situated Carthaginians created a navy second to none in the Mediterranean and eventually built up an empire of former Phoenician colonies and other peoples from Bengazi in the east to Gibraltar and Portugal in the west that included Sardinia, Corsica, parts of Sicily, and the Balearic Islands.

Instead of making the other Phoenician settlements and native peoples loyal and cooperative allies, as the Romans had done with the peoples of Italy, the Carthaginian leaders forced them to become tribute-paying subjects. The only people who received moderately good treatment from Carthage were the Sicilians, because she was competing for their loyalty first with Syracuse and later with Rome. As a result of her short-sighted imperialistic policy, Carthage failed to win friends and, during her struggle with Rome, was forced to stamp out numerous revolts among her Spanish and North African sub-jects, a distraction that seriously hampered her during the war. As events later proved, Carthage could ill afford such policies in spite of her enormous wealth and overwhelming naval power.

Carthaginian Wealth and Trade   Carthage controlled by far the richest mining resources of the Mediterranean basin. Sardinia had relatively small resources of mineral wealth, but of remarkable variety—lead, zinc, copper, iron, and silver. The mines of Spain were richer, and even after two and a half milennia of continuous working, Spanish mines still produce millions of tons of iron ore, as well as lead, zinc, mercury, copper, gold, and silver. Leaving Gades (Cadiz) in Spain, the Carthaginians would sail north to Cornwall, as the Phoenicians probably had done long ago, and load their ships with valuable cargoes of tin. From the same port, other expeditions passed along the west coast of Africa as far south as the Gold Coast, the Cameroons, and even Gabon, from which they brought back gold, ivory, slaves, and war elephants.

Not all the mineral cargoes carried in Carthaginian ships were utilized by the metal foundries of Carthage. Many of them were rerouted to the Hellenistic East. For several centuries prior to the First Punic War, the carrying trade from West to East was virtually a Carthaginian monopoly since Greek, Etruscan, or Roman shipping was excluded from almost half of the western Mediterranean by treaty or by naval force. Any Greek ship caught in western waters was usually sunk. This policy enabled Carthaginian merchants to sell within that area cheaply manufactured goods at monopolistic prices. The only Carthaginian manufactures that might have competed in a free market were textiles, especially the purple-dyed fabrics that enjoyed a good reputation in all parts of the Mediterranean world.

Agriculture   The contribution that the Carthaginians made to scientific agriculture and especially to the development of the slave-worked plantation is usually ignored. It was they who taught the Romans the technique of organizing large masses of slave labor on agricultural estates or plantations for the production of single marketable crops or staples. Although the slave trade and the limited use of slaves as farm hands and shop workers were known in Greece and other ancient countries, slave labor was never able to compete with native free labor in Greece, in the Seleucid Empire, or in Ptolemaic Egypt. It remained for the Carthaginians, while relying on Greek and Hellenistic treatises for the scientific cultivation of specific farm crops, to work out a system of plantation management involving the large-scale use of slave labor.*

Carthaginian Government   As described by Aristotle, the Carthaginian form of government was an oligarchic republic apparently consisting of four branches: an executive of two annually elected *shophetim* (judges), a senate of three hundred members, a popular assembly, and a supreme court of one hundred and four members. With the possible exception of the popular assembly, which did not have much actual power, the government was made up of a small group of rich businessmen, merchants, and landowners who constituted a powerful oligarchy. The two judges and all the generals, though elected by the assembly, were invariably men of substantial wealth and belonged to the inner circle of this exclusive oligarchy.

The real power of government lay in the hands of two bodies: the supreme court and a council of thirty men chosen by the assembly to act as a committee of the senate. The council, of which the two judges were members ex of-

ficio, prepared the agenda for the deliberations of the senate. The members of the supreme court were also members of the senate, but unlike the council were selected not by the assembly, but by a cabinet of five executive heads dealing with finance, the army, and the navy, whom Aristotle called *Pentarchs*. The supreme court, though originally intended to check dictatorial tendencies, gradually became itself one of the most dreaded bodies in the state and, working together with the Pentarchs, the most greedy and corrupt. Such was the government of Carthage until its reformation by Hannibal after the Second Punic War.

The Navy and Army   Before the First Punic War the pride of Carthage was her large navy, needed to guard her monopoly of western Mediterranean trade, enforce embargoes, protect her colonies, and prevent piracy. Taking no chances with disloyal and half-hearted crews, she manned her ships with her own citizens commanded by naval experts. The army, on the other hand, contained few citizen troops and was composed largely of conscripted natives of Libya, Sardinia, and Spain, troops hired from the allied but independent chiefs of Algeria and Morocco, and mercenaries picked up in every part of the Mediterranean. It was difficult to maintain the loyalty of so heterogeneous a group in times when Carthaginian prestige or funds were low. Moreover, a general's task was not only difficult but dangerous: if he won too many battles, he might be accused of dictatorial ambitions and be hauled up before the supreme court; but if he lost too many, he might be nailed up on the cross. This situation sometimes led to a loss of experienced leadership at critical times.

---

*Shortly after the destruction of Carthage in 146, the senate expressly ordered, no doubt for the use of rich landowners in Italy, a translation of Mago's classic work of thirty-two volumes on Carthaginian agriculture—perhaps the only part of Punic literature that they thought worthy of preservation and study. The influence of this work on later Roman writers about agriculture can scarcely be overestimated. Nor did its influence die with them. It was transmitted indirectly to the Moors of medieval Spain and probably to the Spaniards, who established slave-worked plantations in the New World.

Outbreak of the First Punic War in 264 B.C.

In Sicily the two great republics of the western Mediterranean, Rome and Carthage—one strong on land, the other at sea—began a long struggle that the citizens of neither had wanted. Until 264 B.C. neither power had done anything to antagonize the other; their relations had been diplomatically correct, if not friendly. In 348 B.C. they had concluded a treaty that may have renewed an earlier one dating from the first year of the Roman Republic. The Carthaginians agreed not to seek any permanent territory in Latium and not to attack or interfere with any Latin town that was leagued with Rome. For their part, the Romans agreed to a Carthaginian monopoly of western Mediterranean trade. Only Sicily and Carthage itself were to be open to Roman merchants. Obviously, commercial interests were not yet strong at Rome. Even in 306, according to Livy, the Romans willingly renewed the treaty once more. A generation later, in 279, the Romans and Carthaginians concluded a modest mutual defense pact in the face of Pyrrhus' military adventures. Therefore, that the Romans and Carthaginians went to war against each other only fifteen years later seems surprising, especially since many Roman senators sought to avoid giving offense to Carthage over the incident that eventually sparked the conflict.

Roman Intervention in Sicily, 264 B.C. The critical incident involved the Mamertines, a group of Campanian mercenaries who named themselves after Mamers, or Mars, the god of war. They had been hired by Syracuse, but in 289 B.C. they deserted and seized the strategic town of Messana in the northeastern corner of Sicily quite close to the straits that bear its name. The Mamertines killed off all the men of Messana, took their wives, and made plundering raids on Syracusan territory. To exterminate this menace, Hiero II, the young and able king of Syracuse, attacked Messana in 265 B.C. and was on the point of capturing it when the Mamertines appealed for help to the admiral of a nearby Carthaginian fleet, who came ashore with a strong force to prevent the Syracusans from getting control of so strategic a location. Frustrated, Hiero abandoned the siege and went home.

The Mamertines, though grateful to the admiral for his assistance, feared that the Carthaginians, who had sought control of all Sicily before, intended to remain in Messana permanently. They appealed to the Roman senate for military aid and an alliance with Rome, which was more distant and therefore appeared less threatening to their independence. The Roman senators were divided. The conservative majority in the senate feared that an alliance with the Mamertines might mean war, which they particularly wanted to avoid because victorious generals in the past were often able to acquire political advantage over their fellow senators, and because Rome, without a navy, was unprepared to wage war against the strongest naval power of the Mediterranean. They also argued that it was beneath the dignity of Rome to ally herself with the Mamertines, a lawless gang of deserters, cutthroats, and thieves like those Roman soldiers who had recently been punished for privately seizing Rhegium, (Reggio), just across the straits from Messana. Faced with this difficult decision, the senate decided to do nothing.

Appius Claudius Caudex, one of the Roman consuls and grandson of the famous censor, and his friends, who were favorable toward the Mamertine request, were unwilling to let the matter drop so easily. They brought it up before the people who, though sick of war, were persuaded to accept the alliance, with all of its dangers to peace. The practice of willingly taking on an entangling alliance that was bound to create serious problems with third parties was one that the Romans would often adopt during their imperial expansion.

Two legions under the command of Appius Claudius marched down to Rhegium in 264 and prepared to relieve Messana. He sent across the straits an advance guard, which met only token opposition from the Carthaginian fleet at Messana. The Mamertines had meanwhile requested that the Carthaginian general withdraw his garrison from the town. He foolishly complied and let the Romans march in unhindered, an error for which he later suffered crucifixion.

The loss of Messana stung the Carthaginian government to action. They sent an army over to reoccupy it and persuaded Hiero II of Syracuse to make an alliance with them. The allies now joined forces to attack and blockade the town. Appius Claudius managed to sneak his main force across the straits under cover of darkness. When the Carthaginians rejected his demand that they raise the siege, he attacked first the Syracusans and then the Carthaginians, both of whom he easily defeated. His action saved Messana but resulted in war with both Carthage and Syracuse.

Causes of the War   Although some people tried to avoid hostilities with Carthage, there were a number of underlying factors that helped to cause the First Punic War. One of the most important was that by 264 B.C. Rome had extended her system of alliances to include all of the Greek city-states in southern Italy. Many of these states, such as Tarentum, Thurii, and Rhegium, were heavily involved in commerce and competed with Carthage. It had been a long-standing policy of Carthage to hinder their commercial activity. In keeping with that policy, one of her major goals was to gain control of Sicily and the vital straits of Messana. Success would have given the Carthaginians a stranglehold on the shipping of the southern Italian Greek merchants.

Within their system of alliances, the Romans looked upon themselves as patrons and their allies as clients whose interests they were bound by *fides* to protect. Although they had little direct interest in overseas commerce, many Romans believed that as ally and patron of the southern Italian Greek cities, Rome had to protect their commercial interests and prevent Messana from falling into Carthaginian hands. They argued that if the Romans did not act, their position and credibility as patrons of their allies would be undermined and their hard-won position as leaders of all peninsular Italy jeopardized.

Another important factor leading to war was the traditional Roman fear of powerful neighbors—fear that had become almost paranoid after centuries of struggle with neighboring peoples like the Etruscans and Samnites. Now that the Romans had expanded their power all the way to the "toe" of the Italian

"boot," they suddenly found themselves face to face with the powerful Carthaginians on Sicily across the straits. The war with Pyrrhus had taught them the danger to be expected from anyone who controlled Sicily, which could be used to invade Italy. Therefore, many Romans probably saw an advantage in preventing Carthage from further consolidating her position in Sicily.

A third factor that contributed to the willingness of some Romans to provoke a war with Carthage was the desire for military glory among ambitious aristocrats. Many of the well-established senators had opposed the Mamertine alliance precisely because they feared that it would lead to a major war that would give opportunities for lesser men to move ahead or for rivals to gain an advantage. Appius Claudius Caudex was one of those eager for an important command and the chance of securing a coveted triumph, and that is why he brought the issue directly to the voters, whom he was able to persuade to accept the Mamertine alliance. It is hardly coincidental that he was the consul put in charge of the force sent to aid the Mamertines.

That many Roman citizens were persuaded by Appius Claudius Caudex's arguments points up a fourth factor in the outbreak of the First Punic War. After long years of constant warfare involved in establishing Roman control over peninsular Italy, many Roman citizens had become accustomed to supplementing their incomes with booty taken from defeated foes. Sicily, rich and prosperous, offered prospects of easy pickings for Roman soldiers—a fact that, according to Livy, Appius Claudius did not fail to stress in his speech to the assembled people. This combination of factors overwhelmed opposition to the Mamertines' request for aid and led Rome to take the unprecedented step of claiming an interest in affairs beyond the Italian mainland, with momentous consequences for the history of Rome, Carthage, and the whole Mediterranean world.

From the Carthaginians' point of view, although they were not prepared for a major war, they had to reject Appius Claudius' demands and accept the risk of fighting. The Romans clearly appeared as the aggressors since they had had no previous interests in Sicily, while the Carthaginians had long been one of the dominant powers there. To have tolerated Roman interference would have jeopardized centuries of effort in Sicily because the Carthaginians would have appeared weak and unwilling to protect their interests in a situation where justice seemed to be on their side. Moreover, to have negotiated and agreed to the Roman claims of a protectorate over the Mamertines would have left the Mamertines free to cause trouble on Sicily under the umbrella of Roman power. From the Carthaginian perspective, therefore, the Romans had to be opposed.

Expansion of the War   The Carthaginians were at a serious disadvantage, however. Most of their warships had been lying in the docks ever since the Pyrrhic War; ships had to be outfitted, while crews had to be hired and trained, a matter requiring considerable time. Even with only the few ships available in 264, however, the Carthaginian admirals should have easily been able to prevent Appius Claudius from slipping across the straits. Their failure to do so angered Hiero II and helped to break up his alliance with Carthage. When the Romans attacked Syracuse in 263 with an army of forty thousand men, Hiero, becoming alarmed at Carthaginian lack of support, capitulated, made an alliance with Rome for fifteen years, and agreed to help finance the war against Carthage. In 262, with the help of Hiero II, the Romans attacked and besieged Agrigentum (Acragas in Greek, modern Girgenti), Syracuse's old rival and the second largest Sicilian city, where the Carthaginians had a strong garrison. After the defeat of a Carthaginian relief army, the city was captured, and its inhabitants were enslaved.

After the fall of Agrigentum, the Romans saw the possibility of driving the Car-

thaginians out of Sicily altogether. The obstacle was the Carthaginian fleet, which was now fully ready for action. Such a fleet could cut communications with Italy and starve the Roman army into submission and surrender. It could also raid the Italian coastal cities without hindrance. Rome realized that she must build a navy at all costs or else get out of the war.

Rome Builds a New Fleet, 261 B.C. The Romans' first attempt to create a navy was in 311 B.C., when they built twenty *triremes*. (The trireme was so named because it had three banks of oars. One man pulled each oar. Such a vessel was light and fast, but not very seaworthy.) Even this puny navy was allowed to lapse into decay after 278. Rome depended entirely on her allies in south Italy who, although they had nothing better than a trireme available, supplied the ships that enabled Appius Claudius in 264 B.C. to put his army across the straits. Perhaps it was just as well that Rome had had no navy in 264 B.C. She might have been tempted to use the trireme, which Hellenistic navies had abandoned in favor of heavier ships for warfare on the high seas.

The pride of the Carthaginian navy was the *quinquereme,* now believed to have been a one-deck ship of from fifty to sixty oars, five *(quinque)* men to an oar. The quinquereme was heavier and slower than the trireme, but more seaworthy. What counted most was its weight, because in the absence of guns ancient naval warfare consisted mainly of ramming or boarding. In order to sink enemy ships by ramming, weight was essential—a fact that rendered the light trireme obsolete.

The Romans had no ships like the quinquereme until they captured one as Appius crossed over to Sicily. Using it as a model and with the help of shipbuilders from allied Greek cities, they built one hundred quinqueremes and twenty triremes in about sixty days. Building ships was not so hard a problem as finding crews to man them. Most of the trained oarsmen had to be recruited from the Greek seaports of south Italy and there were never enough of them. While the building of ships was in progress, the Romans had set up wooden stages on land in order to train raw recruits to row. It was indeed fortunate for the Romans that the trireme had become obsolete, because every rower on board a trireme had to be a skilled oarsman. But on a quinquereme, where there were five men to an oar, only one or two of them had to be skilled, while the others followed their lead.

There was another reason why the quinquereme was well suited to Roman needs. Since they were better soldiers than sailors, the Romans took advantage of the quinquereme's size to convert sea fights into land battles. They installed in their new quinqueremes a device that the Athenians had invented in the Peloponnesian War during their ill-fated Sicilian expedition but had failed to use successfully. It was a movable bridge or gangway with a heavy grappling spike at the end. From this spike or beak came its Roman name *corvus* —crow or raven. This bridge was fastened to the mast by a rope running through a pulley and could be raised upright or allowed to fall flat upon the deck of an enemy ship, which was held fast as the spike embedded itself deeply into the planks. The Romans then rushed over the bridge and fought just as on land. As the Athenians had found, such a device was impractical on a light ship such as the trireme, and it rendered even heavy ships like the quinquereme much less seaworthy.

With this brand new fleet, the Roman consul Duilius put to sea in 260 B.C. and met the Carthaginians off Mylae not far from Messana. The Punic admiral, anticipating an easy victory, launched a reckless frontal ramming attack, but many of his best ships were grappled by the *corvus,* boarded by the Roman marines, and captured. He broke off the engagement and escaped. Duilius celebrated his triumph in Rome, where in his honor a column ornamented with the rams of the ships that he captured was erected in the Forum. After failing to modify his tactics and losing another sea fight near Sardinia in 258 B.C.,

the incompetent Carthaginian admiral was promptly crucified.

The Roman Invasion of Africa, 256 to 255 B.C.

After their unexpected victories at sea, the Romans decided to end the war quickly by an invasion of Africa. In 256 the consuls, Regulus and Vulso, set sail with two hundred and fifty warships, eighty transports, and about fifteen thousand troops. They engaged the Carthaginian fleet off Cape Ecnomus on the east coast of Sicily. Hasdrubal, the Punic admiral, feigned retreat in the center of his line to draw in the Romans, while the rest of his ships, dispersed in echelon formation, were to turn around and attack from behind. This plan might have worked had it been understood, accepted, and carried out by his two rear admirals. Instead, the Romans won a third victory. Though Carthaginian seapower was temporarily broken and Carthage herself was open to invasion, the Romans knew that Hasdrubal had found the answer to the *corvus,* and after 255 B.C. they never made use of it again.

Regulus landed in Africa in the fall of 256 B.C. He inflicted a minor defeat on the Carthaginians and, thinking that they were just about ready to give up, offered them terms of peace so harsh that they were rejected. Though winter would have been the best season for African fighting, he decided to wait until spring. Meanwhile, Carthage had not been idle. She had engaged the services of Xanthippus, a Spartan strategist skilled in the use of the Macedonian phalanx and war elephants. New mercenary troops were hired, and many citizens of Carthage volunteered for service. All that winter the work of preparation and training continued unabated.

In the spring of 255 B.C., Regulus decided to begin the Battle of Carthage. He advanced into the valley of the Bagradas but found the enemy already waiting for him. Here Xanthippus had drawn up his phalanx—elephants in front and cavalry on the wings. In vain Regulus strengthened his center; the elephants broke through anyway and trampled the massed legionnaires to death as the Punic cavalry outflanked and encircled them. The entire Roman army was destroyed, except for a remnant of two thousand men who escaped to the coast to be rescued by the navy. Regulus himself was taken prisoner. Thus, the Romans suffered as severe a defeat on land as the Carthaginians had at sea.

Rome Loses the Naval Advantage   In 255 B.C. luck began to run against the Romans at sea, although an armada of two hundred and fifty ships sent for the blockade of Carthage met and defeated a Carthaginian fleet of two hundred ships off Cape Hermaea. After taking on board the remnants of Regulus' army, they put out to sea again. As they were approaching the shores of Sicily, a sudden squall caught them, and all but eighty vessels were lost. Two years later another fleet, returning from a raid on Libya, was wrecked off the northern shores of Sicily. These unexpected catastrophes temporarily ended Roman naval superiority in the Mediterranean.

The War in Sicily, 254 to 241 B.C. From 254 to the end of the war, Sicily and its surrounding waters remained the sole theater of military operations. After capturing Panormus (Palermo) in 254, the Romans drove the Carthaginians almost out of the island except for two strongholds at the western tip— Lilybaeum and the naval base of Drepana —both of which they blockaded by land and sea. For a moment the Carthaginians seemed content merely to hold their naval bases in Sicily and meanwhile concentrated their main effort on expanding their empire in Africa and stamping out native revolts in order to secure their resources at home. In 249, however, they regained the initiative.

Carthaginian Successes at Sea, 249 to 247 B.C. Though the Romans had rebuilt their navy after the disasters of 255 and 253 B.C., they had lost the advantage at sea. Since 255 they had been forced to abandon their best of-

fensive weapon, the *corvus,* partly because the Carthaginians had devised successful defensive tactics against it and partly because its weight made their ships very vulnerable to storms at sea. Moreover, the admirals now in command of the Roman fleet were not in the same class with Duilius, the victor of Mylae, nor even with Regulus of Ecnomus.

In 249 the poor tactics of the consul Publius Claudius Pulcher resulted in the loss of ninety-three out of one-hundred and twenty Roman ships off Drepana (Trapani). Supposedly, when the sacred chickens had refused to eat before the battle, a very bad omen and disconcerting to the crews, he exploded, "Throw the damn chickens into the sea; if they won't eat, let them drink!" A second Roman defeat followed soon after Claudius' debacle. The other consul sailed out from Syracuse with eight hundred transports escorted by one hundred twenty warships. This enormous fleet was completely destroyed, partly by Carthaginian attack and partly by storm. For the next few years the Carthaginians had undisputed mastery of the sea. They were now able to break the Roman blockade of Lilybaeum, cut communications between Rome and Sicily, and make raids upon the Italian coast itself.

Hamilcar Barca and Carthaginian Failure, 247 to 241 B.C. Never had the war picture looked brighter for Carthage, especially after she had sent to Sicily in 247 B.C. the young Hamilcar Barca, the most brilliant general of the war, whose lightning moves behind Roman lines and daring raids upon the Italian coast made him the terror of Rome. Well did he merit the name of *Barca,* which in Punic meant blitz or lightning.

Despite the brilliance of Hamilcar Barca and the amazing successes of the Carthaginian navy, Carthage lost the war, chiefly because of her inability to deliver the final blow when Rome was staggering in defeat. Rome's ultimate victory was not wholly due to doggedness, perseverance, or moral qualities, as has often been suggested, but to the weakness of the Carthaginian state itself—a result of the internal division and fatal conflict of interest between the commercial magnates and the powerful landowning nobility.

At the very moment when the Carthaginian navy and the generalship of Hamilcar Barca seemed about to win the war, a landowning group headed by the so-called Hanno the Great, which had prospered with the conquest of territory in North Africa, came into control of the Carthaginian government. To them the conquest of vast territories of great agricultural productivity in Africa was more important than Sicily, the navy, and the war against Rome. That the dominant faction in the Carthaginian government was not interested in winning the war is clearly evident from the fact that in 244 B.C. the entire Carthaginian navy was laid up, demobilized, and its crews, oarsmen, and marines transferred from the navy to the army of African conquest.

Meanwhile, Rome saw that her only chance for survival lay in the recovery of her naval power. She persuaded her wealthiest citizens to advance money for the construction of a navy by promising to repay them after victory. In 242 a fleet of two hundred Roman ships of the latest type appeared in Sicilian waters. In the following year on a stormy morning near the Aegates Islands, it encountered a Carthaginian fleet of untrained crews and ships undermanned and weighted down with cargoes of grain and other supplies for the garrison at Lilybaeum. The result was a disaster that cost Carthage the war. The garrison at Lilybaeum could no longer be supplied and would soon be starved into surrender. There was no alternative but to sue for peace.

Roman Peace Terms, 241 B.C.   The Carthaginian government empowered Hamil-

car Barca to negotiate peace terms with the consul Lutatius Catulus, the victor of the recent naval battle. Both sides were exhausted and weary from the long, continuous, and bitter struggle. The Roman negotiators, well aware of the slim margin of victory, were disposed to make the terms relatively light. Carthage was to evacuate Lilybaeum, abandon all Sicily, return all prisoners, and pay an indemnity of 2200 talents in twenty years.* These terms seemed too lenient to the Roman voters, who had to ratify the treaty in the *comitia centuriata*. They increased the indemnity to 3200 talents to be paid in ten years. The Carthaginians were also required to surrender all islands between Sicily and Italy, to keep their ships out of Italian waters, and to discontinue recruiting mercenaries in Italy.

As in all major wars, the victors and vanquished both were profoundly affected and underwent significant changes. First of all, the war had exacted enormous tolls in men and material on both sides. Although casualty figures are often grossly inflated by ancient sources, Rome and Carthage each had lost hundreds of ships and tens of thousands of men. The sea power of Carthage was broken and her control of the western Mediterranean was ended for all time. Rome, on the other hand, had become a major naval and overseas power irrevocably involved in the affairs of the wider Mediterranean world. This change not only altered the way in which Rome dealt with foreign powers but also caused major internal changes, as will be seen in the following chapters.

* For the value of Roman monetary units see p. 145.

VIII

Between the Wars,
241 to 218 B.C.

One of the effects of the First Punic War was to make many Romans profoundly suspicious of Carthage and ready to weaken her further to prevent any attempt on her part to even the score. Others had tasted the seductive fruits of overseas conquest and wanted more. At Carthage there were those who deeply resented the humiliation that Rome had inflicted and hoped someday to restore Carthaginian prestige abroad, while others decided to concentrate on the intensive agricultural development of the territory around Carthage. More immediately, however, Carthage suffered a major crisis because of her inability to pay the mercenary troops that made up the bulk of her army. The temptation to take advantage of this situation at Carthage's expense eventually proved too great for a number of Romans to resist, quite contrary to the reputation for fair dealing on which the Romans prided themselves.

The Truceless War and Roman Trickery, 241 to 238 B.C. No sooner had Carthage made peace with Rome at the end of the First Punic War than she had to fight with her own mercenaries a war of the utmost cruelty and barbarity. Upon their return from Sicily, the mercenaries, twenty thousand of them, demanded from the government their accumulated pay and rewards promised to them in Sicily by Hamilcar Barca. These reasonable demands were rejected by the Carthaginian government, which was then dominated by reactionary landlords such as Hanno the Great. The mercenaries mutinied and were joined by the oppressed natives of Libya, the Libyphoenicians from the east and the Numidians of the west. The deadly revolt flared up everywhere. The mercenaries became masters of the open country, from which Carthage was isolated. It was a war without truce and, therefore, is known as the Truceless War. A similar revolt subsequently broke out in Sardinia.

For the first time in their lives, the citizens of Carthage really had to fight. Hanno assumed command of the army, but his "greatness" failed to achieve any military success. The situation deteriorated until Hamilcar Barca took command. After three years of the bloodiest fighting, during which all manner of atrocities, crucifixions, and inhumanities were committed on both sides, Hamilcar finally stamped out the revolt.

In her terrific struggle for survival, Carthage received the unexpected sympathy and help of Rome, who furnished her with supplies while denying them to her enemies, and permitted her to trade with Italy and even recruit troops there. Rome also rejected appeals for alliance from the rebels of Utica and Sardinia.

After the revolt against Carthage had been stamped out in Africa, however, a faction unsympathetic to Carthage gained the upper hand in the Roman senate. As Hamilcar was moving to reoccupy Sardinia in 238 B.C., this group persuaded the senate to listen to the appeal of the Sardinian rebels, declare war on Carthage, and rob Carthage of both Sardinia and Corsica, while demanding an additional indemnity of 1200 talents. Rome was able to commit this act of international piracy with impunity because Carthage had no fleet and could not fight back, though the natives of Sardinia fought ferociously against Roman occupation, which was not fully completed until 225 B.C. The two islands were grouped together as the second Roman province.

Carthaginian Recovery Shortly after the loss of Sardinia and Corsica, Carthage made a strong recovery mainly because of the genius and energy of Hamilcar Barca, who defeated the mercenaries and reinstated Carthage as a great Mediterranean power. Under his leadership, the loss of the two islands was more than offset by the reconquest of Spain. During the First Punic War and later the Truceless War, Carthage had lost most of her Spanish possessions except Gades to native rebellions and most of her trade to the Greek colony of Massilia, her chief commercial rival in the western Mediterranean. Hamilcar recovered those possessions and much more besides. Landing at Gades in 237 B.C., he conquered all of southern Spain, and by a judicious mixture of war and diplomacy founded a bigger and richer empire than Carthage had ever possessed.

Hamilcar Barca was unfortunately drowned in 229 B.C., but his son-in-law, Hasdrubal, continued the work of empire building. He founded New Carthage, now called Cartagena, which became the capital, the navy

and army base, and the arsenal of the Carthaginian empire in Spain. All the important mining districts were now brought back under Carthaginian control.

For several years many Romans had been watching these developments with growing suspicion and alarm. What chiefly stirred their apprehension was the knowledge that the Barca family, which had been so successful against Rome in the First Punic War, had under their control a vast empire in Spain, a small but modern navy, and a fine army composed of Carthaginian citizens and the flower of the manhood of North Africa and Spain, who were well equipped and undergoing intensive training in constant warfare against the Spanish tribes. In addition, the mines of Spain furnished them an annual revenue of between two and three thousand talents. This enormous revenue enabled the Barca family to wield almost kingly power in both Spain and Carthage.

Nevertheless, the Carthaginian expansion in Spain did not affect the economic interests of Rome so directly as it did those of Massilia. Massilia, long bound to Rome by ties of friendship and probably through a formal alliance by this time, complained to the Romans of the Carthaginian threat to her Spanish colonies and especially to her trade, which she had expanded at the expense of Carthage during the First Punic War. About 231 B.C. the Romans sent emissaries to Spain to investigate, but they came back apparently satisfied with Hamilcar's explanation that he was only trying to explore new sources of revenue to enable Carthage to pay her indemnity to Rome.

The Ebro Treaty Nevertheless, the continued Carthaginian expansion in Spain evoked ever louder complaints from Massilia. At last the Romans in 226 B.C. negotiated with Hasdrubal the famous Ebro Treaty, which prohibited him from crossing the Ebro River with warlike intent, but allowed him a free hand south of the river. Since the Ebro flows eastward into the Mediterranean across the northern part of Spain, this treaty gave him control over almost seven-eighths of the entire peninsula. Massilia was probably less satisfied, although she was guaranteed the security of her two coastal colonies lying between the Ebro and the Pyrenees and was not excluded from peaceful trade with Carthaginian Spain.

Roman Problems after 241 B.C.   Between the First and Second Punic Wars, Rome's most pressing problems were: (1) the administration of her two newly acquired provinces of Sicily and Sardinia plus Corsica; (2) the reform of her government to satisfy the claims of the middle-class farmer, who had shouldered the heaviest burdens of the war; (3) the conquest of northern Italy to secure her frontiers against future Gallic attack and at the same time to open up more lands for farm settlement; (4) the suppression of piracy on the Adriatic Sea; and (5) the limitation of Carthaginian expansion in Spain.

The conquest of Sicily presented Rome with the entirely new problem of governing a country outside of Italy. She naturally first tried out her old Italian policy of making the newly conquered cities her allies by giving them local self-government in return for military and naval assistance in time of war. As a matter of course, she entered into alliances with Syracuse and Messana and later with two other cities. Subsequently, she discovered that it was impossible to apply this policy to that part of the island which the Carthaginians had formerly controlled.

The Sicilians had never been used to the Roman form of government; their traditions had been entirely different. Military help would be given unwillingly, small in any case, and probably quite useless. Rather than be called upon to fight, they preferred to pay tribute in the form of money or farm products, as they had always done, and be left alone. This policy, though foreign to her own traditions, was the one Rome decided to adopt. It seemed expedient for the first time in her

history to fall in line with a policy long practiced in the East by the Hellenistic monarchies and later adopted in the West by Carthage and Syracuse.

From time immemorial Egypt and other states of the ancient Near East had held the theory that all land belonged to the deity and, therefore, to his or her earthly representative, the king. A farmer no more "owned" a piece of land than a person living in a hotel owns a room. He was allowed the use of it, provided he paid his tithe: one-tenth of the harvest. This theory had been adopted by Alexander the Great, all the Hellenistic kings after him, and later Carthage and Hiero II of Syracuse.

This ancient Near-Eastern theory of state ownership of land was alien to the Romans, who believed in private ownership of land, with the exception of public land *(ager publicus)* confiscated by the state from an enemy. After their conquest of Sicily they adopted the Near-Eastern practice there, but regarded the revenue collected from farm land in Sicily not as rent but as a tax levied to defray the expenses of administration and defense, which was later called *tribute* (the name of the property tax collected from Roman citizens in time of war).

Those parts of Sicily which had formerly been under the rule of Carthage or Syracuse had very much the same system of taxation and planned economy as Hellenistic Egypt had. The Romans applied the Syracusan system to the other parts of the island, with the difference that they permitted the farmers to plant whatever crops they pleased, whereas under Hiero II, just as in Ptolemaic Egypt, they had been told just what crops they had to plant each year. The *lex Hieronica,* a revised Latin translation of the laws of Hiero II, was used by the Romans not for crop planning but for taxation purposes only.

The Taxation of Roman Sicily   In an agricultural province such as Sicily, the principal source of provincial revenue was the tithe (one-tenth of such harvested crops as wheat or barley and one-fifth of garden produce and fruits). Until the year 212 B.C. only about half of Sicily was required to tithe to the Roman provincial administration. The rest of the province was exempt; the five cities of Centuripae, Halaesa, Segesta, Halicyae, and Panormus were rewarded for their help during the war by being left free and independent; the four other cities of Messana, Syracuse, Tauromenium, and Leontini, as allies of Rome, were obliged to furnish military or naval assistance at Rome's request.

After 212 B.C. Syracuse, together with the cities dependent upon her, lost the privileged status of a nontaxpaying ally as a result of an unsuccessful revolt against Rome and became subject to the tithe. In addition, some of the land controlled by these rebellious communities was confiscated and declared public land *(ager publicus),* which was rented out either to former owners or to others at an annual rental of one-third of the harvested crops.

The system of tithe collection, which Carthage and Syracuse had both used in the past and which Hiero II of Syracuse had worked out in the *lex Hieronica,* was adopted by the Romans. Each year the magistrates of Sicilian cities subject to the tithe took a census of all the farmers in their surrounding territory, both owners and renters, recording the size of the farms, the acreage under cultivation, and the amount of seed sown. The records, signed under oath, were filed in the records office of local administrative centers and were open to inspection by contractors, *publicani* (either private individuals or agents of tax-collecting firms), preparing to make their bids for the collection of the annual tithe. On the basis of these census returns, they would complete their estimates of the crop prospects and would appear before the Roman *quaestor,* the provincial treasurer, on the day appointed for the auctioning of contracts and make their bids, which were based on 10.4 percent of the estimated crop, of which 10 percent went to the treasury, the remaining fraction to the contractor. The highest bidder, after receiving the contract and after paying the treasury in ad-

vance, would go to the farmers and draw up signed agreements specifying both the amount of the tithe and the date of its delivery at the public warehouses. These agreements would be filed in the offices of the local magistrates, who were held responsible both for their enforcement and for the delivery of the tithe to the provincial treasury.

The other sources of provincial revenue were: custom dues *(portoria),* levied at the rate of 5 percent on all imported and exported goods; the *scriptura,* paid in cash on each head of grazing stock on pasture land; rentals on public lands of one-third of the annual crop; and royalties on mines and quarries.

Provincial Governors   The Romans first attempted to govern Sicily directly from Rome by quaestors responsible to the magistrates of the city. Fourteen years of experience taught them that Rome was too far away for direct administration and that a magistrate with full executive powers was required in the province to deal with such problems of defense and the maintenance of law and order as arose. A quaestor did not have sufficient authority; only a magistrate possessing the *imperium,* such as a consul or a praetor, would do. Accordingly, after 227 B.C. the Roman assembly annually elected two additional praetors, one as governor of Sicily, the other for the combined province of Sardinia and Corsica.

The Provincial Edict   Though the Roman Senate laid down the general principles governing provincial administration, it left the details to be filled in by the praetor as governor of the province. Each newly elected praetor on taking office would publish an edict similar to that of the city praetor and setting forth the rules and regulations that he intended to follow during his year of office. The edict would specifically state the rules of procedure that he would apply in his administration of justice. These edicts varied little from year to year and were changed only under special conditions.

Duties and Powers The provincial praetor was assisted in administration by one or more quaestors, who served as treasurers and receivers of revenues derived from taxes. Three *legates*—lieutenants—of senatorial rank, who were nominated by him and appointed by the senate, acted not only as liaison officers between the praetor and the senate, but as his advisors and often as his deputies. He also had with him a number of comrades or young family friends, who, as members of his staff, might gain an insight into the workings of provincial administration. In addition, he had a staff of clerks and secretaries as well as numerous household servants. The functions of the provincial praetor were many. He commanded the armed forces within the province, supervised the quaestors in their financial administration, and was responsible for the administration of justice in all civil and criminal cases involving Roman citizens and for the arbitration of disputes arising between the subject communities.

Inside the province the powers of the praetor were practically absolute. There was no colleague of equal rank to oppose his decisions or acts, no plebeian tribune to interpose his veto in defense of private individuals, no senate as in Rome to exercise by its higher authority a moral restraint over his abuse of arbitrary power, and no popular assembly to pass laws that he had to obey. As subjects of a foreign power, the people of the province had neither the right of appeal nor legal guarantees of the rights of life, liberty, and property. Although some cities had charters granted them by the Roman senate and guaranteeing local liberties, they could easily be circumvented by unscrupulous governors. Although his term of office was theoretically limited to one year, it was sometimes longer than that because of the failure through neglect or corrupt influence to elect a successor. Theoretically, too, the provincials had the right to bring charges against the praetor for misgovernment and extortion, but they were rarely known to have done so until the time of Cicero (70 B.C.), and then only under the most unusual circumstances and for the most flagrant crimes of extortion and tyranny. In time, the practically unlimited power of Roman provincial governors was dangerous to Rome's republican form of government, which depended upon the willingness of individual members of the ruling aristocracy to respect the equal authority of their colleagues in time of conflict and disagreement. Men accustomed to almost royal independence abroad became impatient with republican restrictions at home.

The Praetor Peregrinus That praetors rather than consuls should be elected to govern provinces seemed to be a logical consequence of the step taken in 242 B.C. of adding another praetor, the *praetor peregrinus,* to deal with the legal disputes, too numerous for the city praetor to handle, arising among the foreign merchants and immigrants entering Rome in large numbers. Since Roman law did not necessarily apply to all the points at issue, it was necessary to supplement the Roman civil law *(ius civile)* with models and precedents from the laws of other people and develop rules of procedure based on common concepts of equity.

An International System of Law Provincial governors in framing their edicts and, apparently, the city praetor in dealing with disputes between Roman citizens and foreigners, followed the same practice as the *praetor peregrinus.* In this way there was gradually built up a system of international law or law of nations *(ius gentium)* that overlaid the narrow civil law of Rome as the Romans became more and more involved in the wider world. In time this system was vastly expanded and was not only incorporated in the Justinian Code and in the Code Napoléon, but has become the basis of modern international law. The best authorities on international law today are found in France, Holland, Switzerland, Italy, and especially the Latin American countries, whose civil law is based largely on that of Rome.

Gaius Flaminius and the Problems of Reform

The period after the First Punic War was an age not only of imperial expansion but of reform—social, economic, constitutional, and legal. This reform movement arose as a result of the growing tension between the small and less affluent landowners, on the one hand, and the aristocracy of large landowners who had profited most from the First Punic War through loans to the government, which were frequently paid off by grants of public land, on the other. Those who tilled small farms around Rome and in Latium were particularly dissatisfied with their lot. Subject to the draft and forced to fight long campaigns far from home, they had to neglect their crops —their major means of livelihood. During the war many of them had fallen into debt and later were unable to raise the money to pay back their loans, since the price of wheat was falling as a result of competition with wheat imported from Sicily. Another cause of grievance was the lack of newly conquered land suitable for distribution and settlement, since the new provinces of Sicily and Sardinia offered no opportunity for colonization. These and perhaps other grievances led to political agitation and the demand for reform.

The leader of the reform movement was Gaius Flaminius. As plebeian tribune in 232 B.C., he forced through the Tribal Assembly, without previous consultation with the senate and in spite of its violent opposition, a plebiscite requiring that the *ager Gallicus*—public lands confiscated south of Ariminum (Rimini) a half century before from the Gauls—be cut up into small farms and distributed among plebeian families. His unorthodox disregard of senatorial authority and privilege set a precedent followed by other champions of popular causes a century later (see p. 168).

The Gallic Wars and Conquest of Northern Italy, 225 to 222 B.C.

An aristocratically biased tradition (preserved by Polybius) alleges that the land distributions after 232 B.C. alarmed the Gauls of northern Italy, who had been peaceful farmers ever since 283 B.C., and provoked them to invade central Italy. While that may well have been a contributing factor, it certainly cannot be the sole explanation for Gallic unrest, which had begun as early as 236 B.C., when the Boii made an abortive attack upon Ariminum. Periodically the Gallic tribes in northern Italy had sought to accommodate their expanding populations by conquering new territories to the south, and in 236 the return of now-unemployed Gallic mercenaries, who had served Carthage during the Truceless War, may have caused further unrest.

After 236 the Romans were preoccupied with problems in the Adriatic, and the Gallic tribes prepared more thoroughly to challenge Rome. In 225 B.C. a coalition army of Gauls, estimated at seventy thousand men, crossed the Apennines, pushed down into Etruria, and plundered as they went. Faced with this menace, the Romans took a census of their available manpower in central and southern Italy. The census, according to Polybius (Book 2.24), showed roughly 700,000 infantry and 70,000 cavalry, of which 250,000 infantry and 23,000 cavalry were Roman. From this large reserve of manpower they raised two powerful consular armies, which converged upon the Gauls near Cape Telamon on the central coast of Etruria and almost annihilated them.

After this victory, the Romans resolved to end the Gallic menace for good by the conquest of northern Italy. During his consulship of 223 B.C., Gaius Flaminius subdued the Insubrian Gauls by a decisive victory, which led by 220 B.C. to the submission of all the Gauls (except the Taurini of the Piedmont and a few other sub-Alpine tribes). During his censorship in 220 B.C., he arranged for the construction of the great military highway, the Flaminian Way, which ran northeast from Rome to Ariminum on the Adriatic and was the predecessor of one of the most important rail lines and motor roads in modern Italy. In the same year (or slightly later) he founded Latin colonies at Cremona and Placentia (Piacenza) both to control crossings of the middle Po and to provide outlets for land-starved Roman farmers.

The Reform of the Centuriate Assembly During the career of Gaius Flaminius, probably in his censorship of 220 B.C., there took place a reform of great constitutional importance—the reorganization of the Centuriate Assembly, which had long since become the stronghold of entrenched wealth. In 241 B.C. two new voting tribes had been added to the Roman citizen body, which brought the number of tribes to a final total of thirty-five. As a result of the reorganization the tribes became purely administrative divisions to which newly enfranchised citizens were assigned, regardless of place of residence. The Centuriate Assembly was reorganized with reference to the new tribal organization in order to make voting in that assembly somewhat more equitable.

Previously, the richest people controlled the majority of votes in the Centuriate Assembly. Eighteen centuries had been assigned to the cavalry or equestrian class and eighty to the first of the five property classes; the other four had only twenty, twenty, twenty, and thirty centuries respectively, with five for the *proletarii*. As a result of the unit voting rule, the wealthiest class had ninety-eight votes compared with ninety-five for the rest of the citizens. After the reform the cavalry retained its eighteen centuries and the proletariat its five, but the five property classes were each assigned seventy centuries divided equally between juniors and seniors (men over forty-five years old), to make a total of 373 centuries (350 plus 23).

To keep the traditional total of 193 votes in the Centuriate Assembly, however, the 280 centuries of the four lower property classes cast their ballots together in groups of two and three centuries each to produce one hundred unit votes. In this way, the wealthiest citizens could not alone determine the outcome of the voting, since they controlled only 88 votes (the 18 equestrian centuries plus the 70 centuries of

the first class), compared with the 105 controlled by the other citizens (the 5 of the *proletarii* plus the 100 votes controlled by the 280 centuries of the other four property classes). Voting would now have to go down to at least the second census class before a majority of the unit votes could be achieved in the *comitia centuriata*.

This reform shows the growing influence of those citizens who met the financial qualifications of the second census class, perhaps including merchants as well as landowners. The difference in wealth between the first and second census classes was not so great, however, as to cause frequent, significant differences in interests, and it was not a great threat to the large landowners to increase the value of the votes controlled by the second property class.

One other change in procedure was the transfer of the right of casting the first vote from an equestrian century to one of the junior centuries of the first class, which was chosen by lot each time.

Other Reforms of the Period In the attempt to build up their political support, various politicians promoted other reforms. In 218 B.C. the tribune Quintus Claudius, probably at the instigation of Gaius Flaminius, obtained passage of the *lex Claudia* that made it illegal for a senator to own or operate ships large enough for overseas trade. Since Flaminius supposedly was the only senator to support this bill, it may be assumed that a significant number of senators had become involved in overseas trade. On the other hand, if the bill's expressed intent really had been to prevent senators from becoming involved in commercial affairs, it is likely that at least some principled or jealous senators would have supported it. It is much more likely that by limiting senatorial competitors Flaminius and Claudius were seeking the favor of numerous wealthy non-senators who had also helped to fill the vacuum in overseas commerce after the defeat of Carthage in the First Punic War.

Earlier, following the trend set by Appius Claudius the Blind, the censor of 312/310

B.C., and by Gnaeus Flavius, the aedile of 304/3 B.C., Tiberius Coruncanius, who was the first plebeian ever to hold the office of Pontifex Maximus (254 B.C.), had announced that he was prepared to give free legal advice to any person. In the age of Gaius Flaminius, the learned jurist Sextus Aelius Paetus Catus began work on his famous commentaries on the Twelve Tables together with the legal interpretations handed down by the pontiffs. After the publication of this work in 204 B.C., anyone, poor or rich, could inform himself about Roman laws.

The Illyrian Wars, 229 to 228 and 220 to 219 B.C.

In between threats from the Gauls in northern Italy and just prior to the outbreak of the Second Punic War in 218 B.C., the Romans were occupied with the two Illyrian wars, the first wars fought by the Romans in the eastern half of the Mediterranean. They were easily won police actions rather than wars of defense or imperial expansion.

During the First Punic War, Agron, the ruler of Illyria, which embraced most of the coastal regions of Yugoslavia as well as Albania, had greatly expanded his kingdom by warring with his neighbors to the south. After his death, his wife, Queen Teuta, continued the aggressions, conquered Epirus, and extended her conquests to the Corinthian Gulf. But it was not the aggressions of Queen Teuta that caused the Romans to interfere. Rather it was her inability or unwillingness to curb the piracy in which the Illyrians had been engaged since time immemorial. And no wonder, for the rugged, broken, and deeply indented coast of Illyria with its myriads of small islands seemed intended by nature just for the pursuit of this profitable business. The light and speedy crafts of the Illyrian pirates would waylay many a passing merchant ship. With the Greeks grown weak, they roved the seas at will, attacked not only Greek but Italian ships, and captured or killed their crews. Growing ever bolder, they ransacked towns along the Adriatic shores of southern Italy. Since many of the pirates' victims were Roman allies, Rome was compelled to act.

In 230 B.C. two Roman envoys arrived in the Illyrian capital of Scodra (Scutari, Skadar) to lodge complaints, but Teuta was busy waging war at the moment and had no time to listen to silly complaints about what her subjects claimed a natural right to do. The protests were insolently rejected and the envoys haughtily dismissed. On the way back, one of the envoys was killed.

Rome was not slow to respond. In the summer of 229 B.C., a fleet of two hundred ships appeared off the island of Corcyra (Corfu). Demetrius of Pharos, whom Teuta had charged with the defense of the island, betrayed her and surrendered to the Romans without a fight. The fleet then sailed north to support a Roman army of twenty-two thousand men engaged in attacking the towns of Apollonia and Dyrrhachium (Durazzo). Teuta, unable to resist, was compelled to sue for peace. She was permitted to retain her crown on condition that she renounce her conquests in Greece, abandon all claims to islands and coastal towns captured by the Romans, and agree not to let more than two Illyrian ships at a time sail past Lissus, the modern Albanian town of Alessio. As a reward for his treachery, Demetrius was granted control of his native island of Pharos, as well as some mainland towns.

Now Demetrius could not be true to anyone, not even to the Romans. Conspiring with Antigonus Doson, the acting king of Macedonia, who looked askance upon Roman interference in Balkan affairs, he stealthily extended his kingdom over all Illyria after Teuta's death, invaded Roman protectorates, attacked Greek cities further south, and made piratical raids far into the Aegean.

The Romans could not overlook these activities, and in a speedy campaign they conquered the Albanian kingdom of Demetrius, who fled for refuge to the court of the youthful Philip V, now king of Macedonia. All the while whispering plots of revenge into the young king's ear, he remained there for several years. The Romans could not further pursue their Illyrian campaign, for at that moment ominous news began to come in from the western end of the Mediterranean.

After Hamilcar Barca died, Hasdrubal, his son-in-law, had brought under Carthaginian control almost all of the Spanish peninsula south of the Ebro River. Hasdrubal, assassinated as the result of a personal quarrel with a Celtic subordinate in 221 B.C., was succeeded by Hannibal, the eldest son of Hamilcar Barca.

Hannibal and Developments in Spain
Not much is known about Hannibal's character. Polybius tells the romantic story, perhaps true, that Hamilcar consented to take the nine-year-old Hannibal with him to Spain only on condition that he go to the altar and swear never to be friends to Rome.* From then on Hannibal spent his entire life in the army. Even after he had become a general, he ate with his men and dressed like them; he slept on the same hard ground between the sentries and the outposts and was covered only with a cloak. His power of leadership must have been exceptional, for he commanded for fifteen unbroken years an army composed of Africans, Spaniards, Gauls, Phoenicians, and

many other ethnic groups, and never once in all those years were they known to mutiny or rebel, though he led them on long, fatiguing marches, across wide rivers, through swamps, and over the snow-capped Alps.

After two years of preparation, Hannibal advanced northwest from the Carthaginian capital of Spain, New Carthage (Cartagena), toward what is now Salamanca and conquered several tribes of the Upper Tagus and the Douro rivers. Now all of Spain south of the Ebro, except Saguntum (Sagunto), was formally claimed by Carthage. Saguntum, a town perched on a rocky plateau overlooking the central eastern coast, was a trading partner of Massilia and had become an ally of Rome sometime between 230 and 219 B.C.†

In 219 B.C. Hannibal besieged Saguntum because of what he termed its unprovoked attacks on neighboring tribes subject to Carthage. After a desperate siege of eight months the town fell. With its fall began the Second Punic War, which made Rome the strongest power in the Mediterranean world and set in motion the events that led to her conquest of the Hellenistic kingdoms of the Greek East.

---

* Later, Roman authors say that Hannibal swore eternal hatred of Rome, which implies a more active hostility to Rome than the Polybian version and is, perhaps, a Roman attempt to put all blame for the war on Hannibal and his family.

† Saguntum and its principal trading partner, Massilia, had both adjusted the weights of their silver coins to that of the Roman Victory coin *(victoriatus)*, which was first introduced from Illyria around 231. Since no mention was made of Saguntum in the Ebro Treaty of 226, Saguntum possibly became allied with Rome sometime after 226, no doubt at the insistence of Massilia.

IX

The Second Punic War,
218 to 201 B.C.

Causes of the Second Punic War
Neither side had actively sought the Second
Punic War. The simplistic view that Hannibal
and the Barcid family had been planning to attack Rome for a long time out of a bitter desire
for revenge was a convenient fiction for both
sides. It was favored by the Romans because it
absolved them of any blame, and it was later
accepted by many Carthaginians because it
allowed them to make the Barcids alone their
scapegoats in dealing with the Roman victors.

Between 238 and 219 B.C. both the Carthaginians and the Romans adhered to the
provisions of the treaty that had ended the
First Punic War and the Ebro treaty, which
had been negotiated with Hasdrubal. The Romans' acceptance of friendship with the city
of Saguntum, south of the Ebro, broached
neither treaty. It was a step taken primarily
to keep the good will of Rome's valuable
ally Massilia and indicated no official Roman hostility toward Carthaginian activity in
Spain, although some Roman senators may
well have thought that should any conflict arise
in the future, Saguntum could provide a strategic base from which to operate. At the time,
Hannibal apparently took no exception to the
fact that Rome had ruled against a pro-

Carthaginian faction in arbitrating a civil
dispute at Saguntum, and he was careful not to
provoke Saguntum in order to avoid angering
the Romans.

There were a number of factors, however, that led to mutual fear and misunder-
standing that forced both sides into a corner
and made them willing to accept and support
the declaration of war when an impasse in their
relationship was reached. First of all Saguntum, encouraged by Carthage's commercial
rival in Spain, Massilia, constantly complained to the Roman senate about Hannibal
as he tried to advance his control over all other
territory up to the Ebro. In 220, probably to
appease Saguntum and Massilia as well as to
check up on Carthaginian intentions, the
senate sent ambassadors to investigate the situation. They pointed out to Hannibal that
Saguntum enjoyed *fides* with Rome and
reminded him of the Ebro treaty. To Hannibal, this action must have seemed like gratu-
itous Roman interference. Probably he also
feared that the Romans were now trying to use
the Saguntines against Carthage, just as they
had previously used the Mamertines on Sicily
and the rebellious mercenaries on Sardinia.
He immediately sent his assessment of the

situation to the Carthaginian senate and asked for instructions. The Carthaginian senate apparently agreed with his interpretation, for his next act was to besiege Saguntum in early 219.

That the Romans had no immediate plans to use the Saguntine situation as a pretext for war against Carthage in Spain is clear. They were in the process of sending two consular armies in the opposite direction, to Illyria. When news of Hannibal's attack on Saguntum reached Rome, the senate did not think that the situation was serious enough to take any action. The fall of Saguntum in early 218 placed matters in a different light, however. It must have stirred up public opinion against Carthage in Rome. Roman prestige was badly damaged by the destruction of a city that had fruitlessly claimed the protection of Roman *fides*. Despite earlier reluctance, the senate now had to take serious action against Hannibal. An embassy of leading senators and the two consuls was sent to Carthage to demand the surrender of Hannibal unless the Carthaginians wanted war.

The majority of Carthaginian senators could not tolerate the humiliation of abandoning a commander whom they had supported. On top of the resentment that must already have existed over the way in which the Romans at the end of the First Punic War had imposed a treaty harsher than the one originally negotiated and had later robbed Carthage of Sardinia and Corsica, that would have been too much to bear. The Carthaginian senate chose war.

There are a number of reasons why many Romans were also in favor of war. There was probably a genuine fear, eagerly encouraged by Massilia, that the Carthaginians in Spain and the Celtic tribes in southern Gaul would eventually join forces to attack Rome. Also, as the *lex Claudia* of 218 reveals, there was now a significant group of Romans engaged in overseas trade. With the revival of Carthage through expansion in Spain, Roman merchants and traders would have feared stronger competition and would have wanted to weaken Carthage once more. Finally, there were always ambitious aristocrats who sought to increase their prestige and power through successful military commands. Such men were the two consuls of 218, Publius Cornelius Scipio and Tiberius Sempronius Longus, whose families had previously helped to engineer the perfidious Roman seizure of Sardinia and Corsica. Therefore, both sides accepted the challenge of war for a second time.

Hannibal's War Strategy Hannibal had command of a splendid army—loyal, well trained, and equipped with the best Spanish swords and spears—but no navy to complement and assist it. Roman naval superiority was so great that Carthage could neither safely transport and supply large armies by sea nor prevent the Romans from establishing beachheads wherever they chose. Their seapower permitted them to wage war on several fronts simultaneously, to invade Africa and Spain, and to land several armies in both countries at the same time.

Since Hannibal's only strong base and source of manpower and supplies was Spain, and since he had only one really well-trained and reliable army, his sole chance of success lay in establishing a single front, preferably in Italy; for so long as Rome was in danger, the Romans would be compelled to concentrate the bulk of their forces in Italy. Only an invasion of Italy would enable him to seize the initiative. Only an invasion of Italy would render useless the great Roman navy.

An even stronger reason behind Hannibal's decision to invade Italy lay in his hope of cutting at the roots of Roman military power, which was potentially six or seven times that of Carthage. Only by wrecking Rome's system of alliance and her Italian confederation could he hope to paralyze and destroy that enormous war potential. He knew that the Gauls of northern Italy were already at war with Rome and would rally around him, and he also hoped that her confederate allies in central and southern Italy would break away from their confederation and join him as their liberator.

Roman War Plans The Romans planned to wage an offensive war. Their unchallenged naval superiority would enable them to seize and hold the initiative at once and to choose the theater of military operations. One army under the consul Publius Cornelius Scipio actually landed at Massilia for the invasion of Spain; another assembled in Sicily for an invasion of Africa. The decision to land at Massilia was theoretically good strategy since it offered alternate objectives: an invasion of Spain or the interception of Hannibal in France, should he decide to invade northern Italy. It also permitted the possibility of using the fleet of Massilia for operations in Spanish waters. The Romans partially achieved only two of these objectives since they landed at Massilia too late to intercept Hannibal. He was already on his way to the Alps.

The March to the Alps Around the first of May in 218 B.C., Hannibal set out from New Carthage with about forty thousand infantry, six thousand cavalry, and some sixty elephants. He crossed the Ebro, passed over the Pyrenees, and in the middle of August reached the Rhone, which he crossed before Scipio was able to intercept him. When Scipio discovered that he had arrived too late, he ordered his brother to lead the army into Spain while he himself sailed back to Italy in order to lead the two legions in Cisalpine Gaul against Hannibal as he came down the Alps.

Hannibal's route is not known. The two most probable routes into the Alps would have been up the valleys of the Durance or the Isere rivers and into Italy by one of the passes in either the Mont Cenis or Mont Genevre groups. None of the many brilliant victories that he won afterward has stirred the imagination as did this crossing of the Alps. The way was not easy. He suffered great losses because of the dangerous passes, the deep snows and biting frost of late autumn, and most of all the treacherous attacks of the mountain tribes. By the time he reached the level plains of northern Italy, he had only about twenty-six thou-

sand infantry, four thousand cavalry, and twenty elephants left. The Insubres and the Boii, already at war with Rome, eagerly joined his army and made up for the loss of men. The elephants, of course, could not be replaced. After a short rest his army met the Romans at the Ticinus River.

The Battle of the Ticinus, 218 B.C. The battle of the Ticinus was a minor cavalry engagement in which Hannibal's Numidian cavalry encircled and defeated Scipio's cavalry, which was inferior in speed, equipment, and training. The consul himself was wounded and would have been taken prisoner had he not been rescued by his own seventeen-year-old son, also named Publius Cornelius Scipio, the future Africanus, conqueror of Carthage and victor over Hannibal. The Romans were forced to retire south of the Po.

Even this minor defeat was serious enough to compel Rome to abandon the planned invasion of Africa and to transfer the other consul, Titus Sempronius Longus, and his army to northern Italy. Before their transfer to Italy, the Romans had been able to seize Malta, which controlled communications between Africa and Sicily, but Hannibal's attempt to maintain a single front was already succeeding.

The Battle at the Trebia, 218 B.C. The two consuls, Scipio and Sempronius, with a combined force of over forty thousand men, held a strong position on the eastern or right bank of the Trebia, a small southern tributary of the Po. On a bitterly cold December morning, Hannibal sent over the river a cavalry detachment weak enough to be easily defeated and compelled to retreat. Encouraged by their easy victory, the Romans waded in pursuit across the rain-swollen river to the other side; there they were at once attacked and encircled by Hannibal's men, who had lain concealed in heavy underbrush. Only ten thousand Romans succeeded in breaking out of the encirclement and in reaching Placentia (Piacenza). The entire Po valley fell into Hannibal's hands.

The loss of northern Italy infuriated those who had promoted the conquest and settlement of that region. They helped to elect as consul for 217 B.C. Gaius Flaminius, who in his consulship in 223 B.C. had subdued the Insubres and placed the Cisalpina under Roman control. Gnaeus Servilius was the other consul. New legions were called into service, and the new consuls were instructed to hold the line and, if possible, recover northern Italy.

The Battle of Lake Trasimene, 217 B.C.

Servilius took the road to Ariminum, and Gaius Flaminius went to Arretium (Arezzo) in Etruria in order to block Hannibal's invasion of central Italy. Hannibal did move down into Etruria, but by an unexpected route—a pass which was most difficult and which, therefore, had been left unguarded. After leading his army through terrain flooded by the Arno and losing many men and horses on the way, he reached Etruria, where Flaminius began to follow him closely. He tried to coax the Romans into battle by exposing his flank as he marched past. Flaminius refused to bait but continued to follow closely in his tracks. When widespread looting and the burning of peaceful homes also failed to bring on a battle, Hannibal adopted an ingenious ruse. He made it appear as if he were going to march against Rome itself. Suddenly veering eastward toward Perugia, he passed along the north shore of Lake Trasimene, where a ridge of fairly steep hills descends almost to the water's edge to leave a narrow road or passage way along the shore, except where it retreats to form a small plain about five miles long. He concealed his men in the hills above the plain and waited. Into this plain early one foggy morning Flaminius marched with his army of thirty-six thousand men. Suddenly Hannibal's men came thundering down the hillsides. In the ensuing two-hour battle, most of the Romans were either killed or captured, and Flaminius himself was killed. The same fate afterward befell four thousand cavalrymen whom Servilius had sent down the Flaminian Way, perhaps to support the legions wiped out at Trasimene.

The news of Trasimene filled Rome with fear of imminent siege. The fear was groundless because Hannibal knew that the siege of a large fortified city without siege engines and a strong supply base would have been foolhardy. Also, the Romans still had field armies capable of intervening. Hannibal had another plan.

This brilliant battle tactician was also a politician and a master of grand strategy. He had invaded Italy in the hope that he might find chinks in the Roman alliance system that he might pry open, widen, and exploit. Victorious battles were only means to this end, but since they had so far produced satisfactory results only in the north and not in Etruria or central Italy, he decided to see what could be accomplished further south.

Fabius Maximus Cunctator, 217 B.C.

The defeat at Trasimene, the fear of a siege, the daily meetings of the senate, the death of Flaminius, the people's idol, the eclipse of his faction in the senate, and the return of more conservative senators to control all served to revive the dictatorship—an office defunct for thirty years—and to introduce the strange, enigmatic figure of Quintus Fabius Maximus of illustrious lineage and decidedly conservative views on politics and war. His elevation to office was most unusual and, to him in particular, most unsatisfactory.

It was the ancient custom in times of crisis for the consuls to transfer, for six months, their lictors, their military commands (*imperia*), and executive powers to a dictator who would then appoint his own master of the cavalry. Now that one consul was dead and the other cut off from Rome, Fabius owed his appointment to the Centuriate Assembly. It also appointed his master of the cavalry, M. Minucius Rufus, a rash, impulsive, headstrong person who was always in disagreement with Fabius over the conduct of the war.

Fabius worked out and adopted an original but somewhat negative strategy, which did not consist of any new battle tactics—he avoided battles because the Roman cavalry was much inferior to Hannibal's—but was rather a kind of psychological warfare based on attrition and exhaustion. It called for the avoidance of all pitched battles until Hannibal should inadvertently work himself into an impasse and be forced to fight under highly unfavorable conditions. Meanwhile, Fabius kept his army always on hilly terrain, where Hannibal could not use his superior cavalry to advantage, and attempted to wear him down by constantly dogging his heels, hampering his movements, and preventing him from acquiring allies, feeding his army, or establishing bases. By this frustrating strategy Fabius hoped to prevent Hannibal from achieving the chief objective of his campaign—the destruction of the Roman system of alliance.

This cautious strategy of Fabius is to this day known as "Fabian," and in his own time it earned for him the title of Cunctator, or Delayer. Minucius hated his tactics and so did many others whose minds were incapable of grasping their military significance. Naturally the strategy of attrition is a double-edged weapon and puts as hard a strain on the user as on the enemy.

In 217 B.C. Minucius appeared before the assembly convened to elect new consuls and in a ringing speech declared that Rome had not yet brought her full force to bear against Hannibal and urged the election of men who would seek a speedy end of the war. The newly elected consuls, Terentius Varro and Lucius Aemilius Paullus, were expected to make short work of Hannibal.

The Battle of Cannae, 216 B.C.   The two consuls, with an army of eighty thousand men, set out to reach Hannibal in Apulia in the vicinity of Cannae, a small fortress but an important supply base near the Aufidus River. They placed their infantry in the center in three lines, closer together than usual. The right wing cavalry, commanded by Paulus,

stood between the infantry and the Aufidus; the left wing, under Varro, stood out on the open plain.

Except for the cavalry on the wings, Hannibal arranged his troops in a less conventional manner than the Romans. His front line, composed mainly of Gauls and Spaniards, bulged forward. Behind them in an echelon formation he posted his heavily armed African veterans.

Under a blazing morning sun, the Roman infantry advanced against Hannibal's front line, which for some time resisted stubbornly but was slowly forced by the weight and pressure of the Roman attack to give ground and sag inward. Still they did not permit a breakthrough. The African troops on the wings stood firm. The more deeply the Romans pressed into this slowly sagging pocket, the more closely they became packed together.

All this time a cavalry battle was in progress. The Punic left wing attacked and easily destroyed the Roman right wing, which was somewhat cramped for space between the legions and the river. Wheeling around, the victorious cavalry wing attacked the rear of Varro's left wing, now engaged by Hannibal's right, and completed its destruction. With both wings of the Roman cavalry gone, the Punic cavalry was free to attack the rear of the Roman infantry.

The Roman infantry soldiers had already wedged into so tight a pocket that they were no longer able to use their weapons—a helpless mass unable to prevent the horrible massacre that followed. When the battle ended, seventy thousand Romans, including numerous senators and nobles and the consul Aemilius Paulus, were left dead on the field. Among those who managed to escape were the consul Varro and two others, Marcellus and the young Publius Cornelius Scipio, who lived to fight Hannibal again. Hannibal's victorious tide had now reached its crest.

Hannibal's victory at Cannae remains a classic example of battle tactics, for it depended not only on an unorthodox disposition of troops, but on timing and coordination. If his crescent-shaped front line had retreated too fast or had permitted a Roman breakthrough, his army would have been cut into two easily defeated segments. If his cavalry had not completed the destruction of the Roman cavalry in time to strike at the rear of the Roman infantry, the results of the battle might have been entirely different.

The Aftermath   The effect of this bloodiest of all Roman defeats was more serious than that of Lake Trasimene. The Romans were so fearful of a march on Rome that they made feverish preparations for defense, enrolled all citizens above the age of sixteen, and even organized two slave legions.

More serious still was the fact that Hannibal almost achieved his war aims. The Roman allies were exhausted; some began to waver in their loyalty. Several towns in Apulia and most of Lucania and Bruttium went over to Hannibal. The big cities of Capua in Campania and Syracuse in Sicily revolted against their alliance with Rome and opened their gates to him. He captured Tarentum. Even some of the Latin towns and colonies began to complain about taxes and the terrific drain on their manpower and economy. More serious still, Philip V of Macedon, who was eager to drive the Romans from their bridgeheads in Illyria, concluded a mutual assistance pact with Hannibal in 215 B.C.

Never did the war picture look brighter for Carthage than in the years between 216 and 212 B.C. After Cannae, the Romans returned to the Fabian strategy of attrition and the avoidance of battles such as Cannae. They now began to concentrate on keeping their Italian allies loyal and winning back the cities that had gone over to Hannibal in order to prevent Hannibal from provisioning his army in Italy or obtaining reinforcements from Carthage. Meanwhile, they prosecuted with vigor the war in Sicily, Illyria, and Spain. These tasks required the expenditure of enormous sums of money and manpower, for a fleet of at least two hundred ships had to be maintained, and twenty-five legions at home and abroad fed and supplied.

Because of their enormous manpower and resources, the Romans were able not only to check Hannibal, but to reconquer the disloyal cities. Without reinforcement from Carthage or Spain, Hannibal could not protect his Italian allies and, at the same time, keep his army intact. He was forced to stand helplessly by and watch the Romans reconquer his new allies one by one. His helplessness neither increased his prestige nor encouraged other cities to revolt against Rome.

The Romans won back the Apulian cities, then laid siege to Capua. Hannibal could neither supply Capua with arms and food nor defend it by attacking the Romans. At last he tried to relieve Capua and force the Romans to abandon the siege by a pretended attack upon Rome. When the ruse failed, he had to leave Capua to its fate. The fall of Capua in 211 B.C. restored all Campania to Roman control. Two years later the Cunctator occupied Tarentum, which Hannibal had captured in 213 B.C.

The Siege of Syracuse   The year before Capua's defeat, Syracuse fell after a long siege led by the famous Roman general, Marcellus. Ever since the year of her revolt from Rome (214 B.C.), Syracuse had been able to defend herself by means of artillery and other devices invented by the mathematician and physicist, Archimedes. During the siege, Carthage gave Syracuse little effective support except a feeble attempt to lend naval assistance. The city was finally betrayed by a Spanish army captain. It was looted after its capture, its art treasures shipped to Rome, and its independence destroyed for all time. After the fall of Agrigentum in 210 B.C., all Sicily fell under the Roman yoke once more.

The First Macedonian War, 215 to 205 B.C.   After his alliance with Hannibal, Philip V of Macedon attempted to open a second front against Rome in Greece and the Balkans. In 214 he attacked Roman protectorates and naval bases in Illyria and hoped, with the help of a Carthaginian fleet, to invade Italy and assist Hannibal. The expected Carthaginian fleet did not arrive, but a Roman flotilla of fifty ships did. The Romans easily recaptured the naval bases and some of their former protectorates. In order to prevent Philip's intended invasion of Italy, they created an anti-Macedonian coalition in Greece by an offensive alliance with the Aetolian League and with other Greek states. Though Philip conducted four brilliant campaigns against the Greek coalition, the Greek war served Rome's purpose well by keeping Philip occupied so that he was unable to give Hannibal any effective assistance in Italy. Thus, in both Italy and the Balkans, a balance of power was established that prevented for a time a definite conclusion of the war.

The War in Spain, 218 to 207 B.C. It was in Spain that Hannibal lost the first round of the war. His opponent was the consul of 218 B.C., Publius Cornelius Scipio, who, though not a good battle tactician, understood the meaning of grand strategy. Unable to prevent Hannibal's crossing of the Rhone, he had sent his brother Gnaeus to Spain, where he joined him after the defeat of his own army at the Trebia. The purpose of this Spanish campaign was to deprive Hannibal of his main base and source of manpower and supplies, and to prevent Hannibal's brother Hasdrubal from bringing reinforcements to Italy.

The success of the Spanish campaign hinged on Roman naval supremacy in the Spanish coastal waters. That was established by a naval encounter in 217 B.C. and by the help of Massilia. In 215 B.C. the two Scipios met Hasdrubal in battle near Ibera on the Ebro. Though Hasdrubal employed exactly the same tactics as Hannibal had at Cannae, he lost the battle because his center was too weak to prevent a Roman breakthrough before the wings could close in and complete the encirclement. His army was split into two segments, each easily destroyed, and the Scipios followed up their success by the capture of Saguntum in 211 B.C. The Carthaginian position in Spain was further weakened by the recall of Hasdrubal to North Africa to suppress the revolt of Syphax, a treacherous and unprincipled king of the Numidians.

After Hasdrubal's defeat, many Spanish tribes went over to the Romans, but after Hasdrubal's return the Scipios later learned how treacherous and unreliable their Spanish allies could be. During 211 B.C. many Spaniards deserted, the Roman army was destroyed, and the Scipios were slain. Thus died the Scipios, who with meager forces had powerfully contributed to the final victory of Rome.

Scipio Africanus The future Scipio Africanus, son and nephew of the slain Scipios, who had rescued his father at the battle of the Ticinus, had also been at the battle of Cannae. After that disaster he persuaded the remnants of the Roman army to keep fighting. In 210 B.C., after the death of his father in Spain, he was appointed by the Centuriate Assembly at his own request as commander of the Roman forces in Spain. Though a private person, having held no rank higher than that of a curule aedile, he was granted the *imperium* and the rank of proconsul, an unprecedented occurrence.

Scipio had had a good Greek education, was more individualistic than most Roman aristocrats, and had a better sense of humor. While he showed an unusual degree of kindness and clemency to defeated enemies, he could also be unscrupulous and deceitful. As a general, he possessed courage, resourcefulness, self-confidence, and the power to inspire confidence in his men.

In Spain, Scipio replaced the short Italian sword (useful only for stabbing) with a longer Spanish one, which with its well-tempered steel point could be used either for stabbing or slashing. It is probable, though not absolutely certain, that he also introduced the Spanish javelin (*pilum*). He broke away from the close order of the old Roman legion, which was drawn up in three lines, each composed of ten maniples. So heavy a formation could advance with terrific force, but could not easily wheel or turn, and so might be readily outflanked, as at Cannae. Also, it tended to act as a whole and did not permit the individual soldier to fight separately or in smaller units. Scipio adopted a new formation similar to that used by Hannibal at Cannae, one capable of expanding or contracting quickly, if required to do so. These innovations required much more drill and training than ever given to Roman armies in the past. The new Roman soldier soon became an efficient instrument of conquest.

Conquest of Spain After training his troops, Scipio boldly marched through enemy territory in 209 and captured the stronghold of New Carthage by taking advantage of an unusual opportunity. The defenders had neglected the walls of the seaward side of the city, where the water usually was deep. A strong north wind, however, had pushed the water back enough for Roman soldiers to wade through and scale the walls. This piece of luck convinced Scipio's soldiers that he was divinely inspired, a belief that he eagerly encouraged, and from then on they carried out his orders with blind faith.

The capture of New Carthage gave Scipio a fine base, access to local silver mines, a number of ships, and immense quantities of booty, money, and weapons along with ten thousand Spaniards whom the Carthaginians had held hostage to ensure the loyalty of their compatriots. Scipio generously allowed the hostages to return home with a share of the booty. That act earned him much valuable goodwill among the Spanish tribes.

Hasdrubal was able to escape with most of his army after being defeated by Scipio in 208, and he marched away to join Hannibal in Italy. With Hasdrubal gone, however, it was easier for Scipio to defeat the other Carthaginian generals in Spain, especially since they did not get on well with each other. Carthaginian power finally collapsed after the battle of Ilipa in 207 B.C., in which Scipio proved himself a master of encircling tactics. Soon the whole of Spain was in Roman hands, and even the ancient Phoenician colonies of Gades (Cadiz) and Malaga voluntarily became Roman allies.

The Battle at the Metaurus and Death of Hasdrubal, 207 B.C. The years just before Hasdrubal's crossing of the Alps had not been good for Rome. With so many farmers in the army, agricultural production had declined, many fertile districts had been repeatedly devastated, and famine was widespread. Had Rome not succeeded in obtaining some wheat from Egypt, the food problem would have been acute. Some of the Italian and Latin allies were so exhausted by the war that they refused to supply Rome with any more men or money.

Had Hasdrubal succeeded in effecting a junction with Hannibal's army, Rome might have lost the war, but Hannibal did not attempt to join his brother in northern Italy for fear of losing Bruttium, his only good base in Italy. He did advance as far north as Apulia but found his way barred by four Roman legions commanded by one of the consuls, Gaius Claudius Nero.

Moreover, Hasdrubal's message to his brother asking him to march into Umbria and meet him near Rome was intercepted. The Romans now knew exactly where he was. Four Roman legions were waiting for him in the north. Then Claudius Nero, leaving a small part of his army behind to watch Hannibal, quietly set out for the north and six days later reached the Metaurus River. Suddenly and unexpectedly Hasdrubal found himself matched against the superior strength of two Roman armies. He tried to retreat over the river but it was too late. His splendid army was destroyed and he himself was killed. Several days later his severed head was thrown into Hannibal's camp. Hannibal knew then that he had lost the war and sadly withdrew to Bruttium.

Two other misfortunes followed swiftly. In 205 B.C. a Punic fleet bringing reinforcements and supplies was lost in a storm. That same year Hannibal's brother Mago, who had landed at Genoa with an army, was defeated, wounded, and compelled to withdraw again to Genoa, where he received orders from Carthage to set sail for home. During the voyage, he died.

The End Approaches   In 206 B.C., Scipio returned to Rome and was elected to the consulship. The senate debated how to end the war. Scipio, who had already made a deal with two petty kings of Numidia, Massinissa and Syphax, wanted to invade Africa. Fabius, leader of the senate, who did not like the young upstart, his Greek ideas, his air of superiority, and his reckless strategy, vigorously opposed the African venture.

Finally Scipio obtained the senate's reluctant permission to go to Africa, but not to raise troops. He appealed directly to the people for volunteers for the African expedition, and about seven thousand enlisted. They, together with the two legions already in Sicily, made up the African Expeditionary Force. Fabius' certainty that the expedition would fail did not take into account Scipio's extraordinary boldness, cunning, and charismatic leadership. Nor were these traits appreciated by the conservative-minded M. Porcius Cato (Cato the Elder), who was a quaestor in 204 and was assigned to Scipio in Sicily.*

In 204 B.C. Scipio landed near Utica in Tunisia and immediately became involved in the quarrels of two Numidian kings, Syphax and Massinissa, both of whom were in love with Sophonisba, the beautiful daughter of Hasdrubal Gisco, the Carthaginian governor of Numidia. Syphax, the stronger of the two petty kings, won the hand of Sophonisba, deposed his rival, and allied himself with Carthage. Massinissa, now a king without love, land, or throne, found refuge in Scipio's camp.

---

* Some scholars date Cato's quaestorship to 205, but that is probably too early, and the story that Cato and Scipio quarrelled openly in 204 is probably an anachronistic reflection of their later public hostility.

Scipio had perfidiously entered into peace negotiations with Carthage and Syphax for the sole purpose of lulling their suspicions and learning the nature and disposition of their camps. Having learned what he wanted to know, one night he surrounded Syphax's camp, which was constructed of osiers and reeds, and set it on fire. The Carthaginians, thinking that the fire was accidental, rushed out to help, and both armies were attacked and destroyed. Scipio had now proved himself the master of Syphax and Massinissa in guile and treachery. He would soon be Hannibal's master in battle.

Massinissa then captured Syphax, married Sophonisba, and returned to Numidia in triumph after winning back all that he had lost. In exchange for benefits received from Scipio, Massinissa was requested to provide the Roman army with cavalry. Later Scipio began to fear that Sophonisba might charm her husband into an alliance with Carthage. By conferring upon Massinissa a curule chair and certain other hollow honors and benefits, he persuaded him to get rid of Sophonisba by adding a little poison to her wine.

The Carthaginians, imitating Scipio's guile, perfidy, and treachery, opened peace negotiations with him and at the same time recalled Hannibal from Italy. Before leaving Italy, Hannibal inscribed on a bronze tablet a chronicle of all his deeds since crossing the Alps, and he deposited it in the temple of Hera Lacinia near Croton. (Polybius maintains that he read it.) After Hannibal's arrival in Africa, the peace talks suddenly ceased. The war continued until Scipio and Hannibal fought at Naraggara, which was a three-day march west of Zama, although Zama is the name conventionally given to the battle.

The Battle of Zama (Naraggara), 202 B.C.   Weak in cavalry, Hannibal was forced to adopt innovative tactics. After the standard procedure of posting what cavalry he had to protect both flanks of the infantry, he arranged his center in an unusual way. First came elephants, next the light infantry units, then a screen of heavy infantry units, then an empty space, then another screen of heavy infantry. Finally, placed back some distance in the rear stood his veterans from Italy as a fighting reserve. The first three lines of infantry were to be sacrificed in the absorption of the initial Roman attack and used later to attack the Roman rear.

The Roman battle order also consisted of two cavalry wings. As he had learned to do in Spain, however, Scipio subdivided the legions into small units with spaces between for the elephants to run through without breaking up the formations. Therefore Hannibal's elephants had little effect on the Roman lines but did a great deal of damage when they stampeded to his own cavalry wings, which, weak to begin with, were soon put out of action by Massinissa's cavalry.

Hannibal's first line, consisting of some twelve thousand mercenaries—Ligurians, Celts, and Moors—resisted the initial Roman attack long and valiantly, but when the second line of Libyans and Carthaginians did not come to their support as quickly as expected, they thought themselves deserted and retreated in panic, only to be cut down by the second advancing line. Hannibal was therefore forced to bring his reserve units forward earlier than he had planned in order to stabilize the front lines. After initial surprise, the well-disciplined Romans regrouped. Then, Hannibal's reserve units were hit in the rear by a strong cavalry attack. Unable to resist the second phase of the Roman offensive, the Carthaginians were crushed. The weakness in cavalry, which Scipio's treacherous actions against Syphax had created, had been Hannibal's undoing. Most of the Carthaginians were killed, but Hannibal managed to escape.

Peace Terms   It was Hannibal himself who advised Carthage to ask for peace, even though he knew that the terms would be hard. In 201 B.C., Carthage was compelled to surrender all territories outside of Africa, to recognize the independence of Numidia and Massinissa's alliance with Rome, to agree not to wage war outside of Africa and not even within Africa without Roman permission, to reduce her fleet to ten light triremes or coast-guard vessels, and to pay an indemnity of ten thousand talents, payable in fifty years. The power of Carthage as a state was broken forever. Peace declared, Scipio returned to Rome to celebrate a magnificent triumph, which his rivals in the senate had petulantly tried to deny him, and to have conferred upon him the proud title of Africanus.

Reasons for Roman Success   Even if Hannibal had won the battle of Zama, Carthage would still have lost the war, for its outcome had been determined in Italy by Hannibal's failure, despite his victories at Trasimene and Cannae, to wreck the Roman confederate alliance, the destruction of which was the main objective of his total war strategy and his sole hope of ultimate victory. The prime mover and chief architect of Roman victory was not Scipio Africanus, the victor at Zama, but Fabius Maximus Cunctator, whose favorite tactics of attrition and exhaustion had frustrated Hannibal's main design and afforded time for the mobilization of Rome's enormous war potential. By delaying he saved the state *(cunctando restituit rem)*.

While there were, no doubt, rival factions within the Carthaginian government, Hannibal's efforts were not negated by political problems at home. Carthage supported Hannibal and the war consistently to the best of its ability. It was the strength of the Romans' system of alliances, founded on a remarkable degree of justice and mutual benefit for its day, that gave them an overwhelming superiority in human and material resources, which, when coupled with the Roman will to use them despite all adversity, ensured Hannibal's defeat.

The Fate of Hannibal   Like Julius Caesar and Napoleon of later history, Hannibal revealed unusual talents as an administrator during his postwar career. After the war, the Carthaginian aristocracy tried to protect its wealth by corruption and by forcing the burden of paying the war indemnity onto the lower classes. The people turned to Hannibal, the popular war hero remembered for his fairness and good treatment of ordinary soldiers, and elected him *shophet,* or judge, in 196 B.C.

Hannibal established a system of taxation based on income and ability to pay and made the government accountable to the people for its expenditures. The financial administration was so efficient that in 191 B.C., only ten years after Zama, Carthage offered immediate payment of the forty remaining installments of her war indemnity. Rome refused the offer. Commerce and industry re-

vived as never before, and Carthage again became one of the busiest ports of the Mediterranean. Nevertheless, Carthage soon lost the benefits of efficient administration. Rome became alarmed at the remarkable recovery of Carthage and, acting upon his political enemies' accusation of planning another war, demanded the surrender of Hannibal as a war criminal. To save his life, Hannibal escaped from Carthage and took refuge in the East. Unfortunately, the Romans' attention now turned in that direction too. Eventually they hounded him to death in 183 B.C. as they added that part of the world to their growing empire (see p. 119).

X

War and Imperialism in the Hellenistic East, 200 to 133 B.C.

No sooner had Rome conquered Carthage and won dominion over the western Mediterranean than she began to assert herself in the eastern half too, so that the Republic's overseas empire continued to expand. The Romans had no consistent policy or program for expansion, but their motives follow a complex pattern similar to that which has been traced through their rise in Italy and their first two wars with Carthage. No one factor can explain it. Several factors operated at once, with sometimes one and sometimes another being more prominent, and all interacting to reinforce each other.

The Background of Roman Expansion in the East   The empire created by the military genius of Alexander had originally embraced Macedonia, Greece, most of Asia Minor, Egypt, and the entire Middle East, extending from the Mediterranean to central Asia and northern India. After his death in 323 B.C., that empire had fallen apart in the struggle for power among his generals, not one of whom was able to establish himself as sole ruler and preserve its unity. Before 275 B.C. three dynasties, descended from three of his generals, had established powerful kingdoms: the

Antigonids, descended from Antigonus the One-eyed, ruled over Macedonia and from time to time over large parts of Greece; the Ptolemies over Egypt, Cyrene, bridgeheads along the Red Sea and East Africa, Phoenicia, several islands in the Aegean, and some cities along the coast of Asia Minor and the Gallipoli penninsula; the Seleucids over most of the old Persian empire embracing the western and southern parts of Asia Minor, northern Syria, Mesopotamia, Persia, and at one time also northwestern India, Afghanistan, and Turkestan in central Asia.

Among the minor Hellenistic states was Pergamum, in the northwest corner of Asia Minor. Under Attalus I and his successors in the second half of the third century B.C., Pergamum, enriched by agriculture and a flourishing foreign trade, blossomed into a center of art and literature and a champion of Hellenism. Another important small state was the island republic of Rhodes, which lay off the southwestern tip of Asia Minor. Like Pergamum, it too was a brilliant cultural center, but it owed its material prosperity solely to seaborne trade, which it guarded with a small but efficient navy.

In Greece the once-powerful city-states of Thebes, Athens, and Sparta still maintained

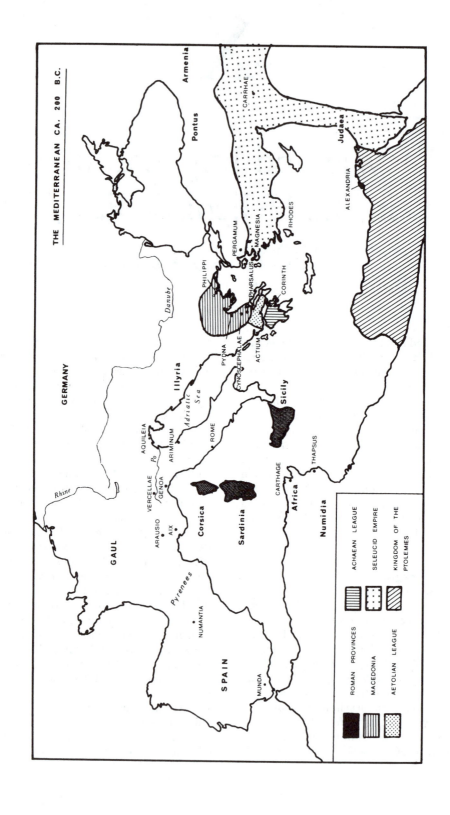

THE MEDITERRANEAN CA. 200 B.C.

Armenia

Pontus

CARRHAE

Judaea

RHODES

ALEXANDRIA

PERGAMUM

MAGNESIA

PHILIPPI

PHARSALUS

CORINTH

Danube

PYDNA

CYNOSCEPHALAE

ACTIUM

GERMANY

Illyria

Adriatic Sea

Sicily

AQUILEIA

ARIMINUM

Po

ROME

VERCELLAE

GENOA

Corsica

Sardinia

CARTHAGE

THAPSUS

Africa

Rhine

ARAUSIO

AIX

Numidia

GAUL

Pyrenees

NUMANTIA

SPAIN

MUNDA

ROMAN PROVINCES

MACEDONIA

AETOLIAN LEAGUE

ACHAEAN LEAGUE

SELEUCID EMPIRE

KINGDOM OF THE
PTOLEMIES

a precarious independence. There were also two political and military federations. One was the Aetolian League of small townships and rural communities, which by 250 B.C. embraced most of central Greece north of the Gulf of Corinth. The other was the rival Achaean League, which included many minor cities of the Peloponnesus but not Sparta, Elis, and Messenia.

The existence of the small Hellenistic states depended upon the balance of power established between 277 and 225 B.C. among the three major powers of Egypt, Syria, and Macedon. If one of the major powers succeeded in expanding its influence and territory, the other two combined against it. Though not one of the three liked this balance of power, it was the salvation of the kingdom of Pergamum, the republic of Rhodes, the Achaean and Aetolian Leagues of Greece, and toward the end of the century, of Egypt itself. When it was finally disturbed, Pergamum, Rhodes, the Greek Leagues, and Egypt all made repeated appeals to Rome to help restore the balance. They never dreamt that eventually all, both great and small, would become subject to Roman domination.

Antiochus III of Syria and Philip V of Macedon While the Second Punic War was raging in the West, the balance of power was being disturbed in the East by the ambitions and warlike activities of two young monarchs, Antiochus III of Syria and Philip V of Macedon. In 223 B.C. when Antiochus became king as a youth of eighteen, the Seleucid empire had already crumbled into almost total disruption. By 205, however, he had completed the conquest of large areas of Asia Minor, reconquered Armenia and northern Iran, and crossed the Hindu Kush mountains into the valley of the Indus, where he received one hundred and fifty valuable war elephants as tribute. On his way back to Antioch, he assumed the title of Antiochus the Great, and his exploits were hailed throughout the Greek world as second only to those of Alexander.

In Macedon, Philip V was understand-

ably apprehensive about the Roman attitude toward him at the end of the First Macedonian War (205 B.C.). To strengthen his position on the Adriatic court vis à vis the Roman protectorates, he apparently acquired some additional Illyrian territory shortly after the war. In the winter of 203/2 B.C., however, Philip turned his attention eastward to an opportunity to restore Macedonian control over the Aegean. That had always been a major object of Antigonid ambitions in competition with the Ptolemies of Egypt, which had enjoyed *amicitia* (friendship) with Rome since 273 B.C., and was now badly governed under the rule of the child-king Ptolemy V, who was at the mercy of corrupt and worthless advisors.

In 203/2 B.C. Philip sought to acquire naval power by supporting the raids of an Aetolian pirate, Dicaearchus, in return for a share of the profits. Philip then used these profits to build a fleet of his own. On the Greek mainland he boldly strengthened his position wherever he could and reneged on his agreement to restore certain territories to the Aetolian League. The Aetolians asked the Romans to intervene in Greece again, but they refused because they were still occupied with Carthage. Also, many Roman senators were resentful that the Aetolians had made a separate peace with Philip in 206 B.C.

Having acquired a fleet, however, Philip overplayed his hand in 201. Instead of being content with attacking Egyptian possessions in the Aegean, he attacked many free Greek cities, enslaved their populations, threatened the naval power of Rhodes, and seized control of the Black Sea trade lanes, which were of vital importance to the grain trade of both Rhodes and Athens. Rhodes declared war and persuaded Attalus I of Pergamum, an old friend of Rome, to do likewise. After a number of naval engagements Attalus and the Rhodians concluded that they were unable to defeat Philip without outside help. In 201 B.C. they appealed to Rome and sent embassies to wait upon the senate. The senate was in a more receptive mood than it had been the year before, when it had rudely rebuffed an Aetolian embassy bringing complaints against Philip.

The ambassadors charged Philip with aggression against Pergamum, and took advantage of the hysterical atmosphere caused by the Hannibalic War and the bitter resentment engendered by Philip's opportunistic alliance with Hannibal after Cannae. They accused Philip of having made a secret pact with Antiochus III to carve up the foreign possessions of Egypt and insinuated that the pact was ultimately aimed at Rome. Though this "pact" may have been a propagandistic lie to scare the Romans, it fell on willing ears. In the elections for 200 B.C., P. Sulpicius Galba, whose profitable enslavement of captured towns during the First Macedonian War had become notorious, was elected consul for the second time, with Macedon as his provincial command.

The Second Macedonian War, 200 to 196 B.C.

After Galba took office in 200 B.C., he laid before the Centurate Assembly a proposed declaration of war against Macedonia, which was overwhelmingly turned down. Many Romans did not want another war. They were exhausted after the long war with Carthage. Their minds had not yet been fully contaminated by propaganda when the war bill was first presented. It would take time to make them fall in line. Meanwhile, the matter would be taken out of their hands and they could do nothing about it.

Even after the assembly had rejected the first request for war, a commission of three senators went ostensibly to investigate the situation in the East, but really to provoke Philip, who was now attacking Athens, into war by presenting him with demands unauthorized by the Roman people. The commission demanded that he should not attack any Greek city and ordered him to pay reparations to Attalus I as if he had attacked Attalus first. Since Philip could not honorably accept these outrageous demands, he continued his military operations. Actually, war between Rome and Philip was a foregone conclusion before the Centuriate Assembly met for the second time to vote on a formal declaration, which was more acceptable to the voters after Scipio's

tired veterans were exempted from further service. Thus, aristocratic Roman leaders determined on war had involved two nations in a war which neither wanted and for which there was little cause.

Roman Motives The reasons why many Roman senators and eventually the *comitia centuriata* wanted to wage an unprovoked and aggressive war against Philip aptly illustrate the general motives for Roman imperialism after the Second Punic War. Previously popular explanations for the Second Macedonian War, such as a need for more territory or a sentimental desire to preserve the Greek way of life against Macedonian conquest, can be ruled out. The Romans already had more land than they could use in Spain and even northern Italy, and they did not keep an inch of Greek territory after the war was ended. Similarly, except for a few, such as Scipio Africanus, Titus Flamininus, Aemilius Paullus, and some others, most of the Roman senators did not particularly admire the Greeks—not the Claudii, not the Fabii, not Cato the Elder, and those allied with them who dominated the senate when it provoked war against Philip.

Apologists for Rome have stressed the defensive nature of Roman motives. It is easy to dismiss that explanation as self-serving or naive, but one must try to see the situation through Roman eyes. The two wars with Carthage, especially the second, had reinforced traditional Roman fear of strong neighbors. Philip certainly had aroused this fear against himself by allying with Hannibal after Cannae. Objectively valid or not, the fear that Philip, like Pyrrhus and other ambitious Hellenistic monarchs before him, had Alexandrian visions of conquering Italy was a real concern to many. It was a theme stressed by both the Pergamene and Rhodian ambassadors and by the leaders who asked the Centuriate Assembly to declare war.

Along with that fear also went a desire for revenge against Philip, especially since he had escaped any serious loss in the First Macedonian War. The aristocratic values of the Romans instilled a deep sense of collective pride and dignity that was jealously guarded. Any slight—great or small, real or imagined—had to be avenged to protect Roman honor.

Although the Romans were not so greatly influenced by concern for markets and raw materials as modern imperial powers have been, economic motives existed. As the *lex Claudia* of 218 indicates, a significant number of Romans and their allies in Italy had grown wealthy, or at least prosperous, as a result of overseas trade and territorial expansion during the First and Second Punic Wars. Such individuals would not have been reluctant to speak and vote in favor of a war that could expand their economic opportunities or reduce competition in the eastern Mediterranean. In addition, the Greek East was the source of the most skilled and intelligent slaves. Galba had already profited handsomely from capturing slaves during the First Macedonian War, and the Roman market for such slaves was growing rapidly. Another war with Macedon would also be the source of other valuable booty, which always attracted many Romans, noble and common. In addition, as the experience with Carthage had shown, rich states could be made to pay lucrative indemnities when defeated in war.

Overseas wars had also whetted aristocratic ambitions at Rome. The great military glory won by Scipio against Hannibal had given him preeminent *dignitas* and *auctoritas*. Publius Sulpicius Galba and those who would be eligible for consulships after him could hope to equal Scipio's exploits in another great overseas war. Finally, the huge armies involved in such wars also increased the numbers of ex-soldiers who could become useful clients in the political struggles of the Forum, while the acquisition of rich and powerful friends abroad would increase the resources and prestige necessary for success in competition with other aristocrats. Those who advocated another war with Philip probably were not unmindful of those facts.

The First Two Years, 200 to 198 B.C.
The Romans landed in Illyria in the fall of 200

B.C. but did little fighting until the next year, and even then fought no important battles. Their only success was in persuading the Aetolians, inveterate enemies of Philip, to enter the war. During the first two years the other Greeks remained neutral except the Athenians, whom Philip had earlier attacked. Philip was highly respected as a general. If his Greek neighbors had joined the Romans and lost, Philip's vengeance would have been devastating. Many Greeks, therefore, waited to see which horse they should back in an uncertain race.

Titus Quinctius Flamininus   In 198 B.C., when the new consul, Titus Quinctius Flamininus, arrived to take command, the war took a major new turn. He spoke Greek with a faultless accent and could write it well too. He had fought under Marcellus, one of the best Roman generals, against Hannibal. At the age of 23 he had been placed in command of the Roman garrison at Tarentum with the rank of propraetor. His magnetic personality, his enthusiasm, and natural wit befitted the true diplomat. His somewhat careless and unkempt appearance served to bring out the charm of his personality. He was above all a master of the propaganda slogan. No sooner had he arrived than he electrified the Greek world with the slogan of "Freedom and self-determination of all Greeks." This was indeed a most unusual Roman!

Flamininus maneuvered Philip out of nearly all Greece except the key fortresses of Demetrias in Thessaly, Chalcis in Euboea, and Corinth in the Peloponnesus. Philip, now confined to Thessaly, sought a peace conference with Flamininus. Although the two men understood and admired each other, the conference itself achieved nothing and broke up over Philip's refusal to surrender the three fortresses, which he had inherited from his ancestors. Flamininus, however, was rewarded for his military success by being made a proconsul to continue the war.

The Battle of Cynoscephalae, 197 B.C.
The war was decided the next year at Cyno-

scephalae (Dog's Heads), a ridge of hills in Thessaly. The two armies were about equally matched. The right wing of the Macedonian army made a brilliant breakthrough on the Roman left, but the Roman right routed the Macedonian left before it had been able to close ranks. The Romans gained the victory, however, when a quick-thinking tribune detached some maniples from the rear of the successful Roman right and attacked the ponderous phalanx of the Macedonian right wing from behind. Accordingly, the greater tactical flexibility of the Roman legion's manipular organization proved decisive.

Peace Terms   Philip lost the battle of Cynoscephalae and the war. He had no other army, Macedon was exposed to invasion, and peace had to be obtained at any price. The terms were better than expected, for Flamininus and the majority of Roman senators did not want to destroy the Macedonian state (as the Aetolians demanded) now that Philip had been humbled. Macedon served as a buffer against the restless Balkan tribes to the north. Also, Philip might be a useful ally to Rome some day, perhaps more useful than the Aetolians.

Late in 197 B.C. Philip was compelled to recognize the freedom and independence of the Greeks, to withdraw all his garrisons from Greece, the Aegean, and Illyria, to surrender his fleet, to reduce his army to five thousand men, and to pay an indemnity of one thousand talents, half to be paid at once and the rest in ten annual installments. The infuriated Aetolians demanded the whole of Thessaly as their share of victory, but Flamininus would concede them only Phocis and the western part of Thessaly and, even worse, allowed Philip to make jokes at their expense during the peace negotiations.

The Proclamation of Flamininus   In July of 196 B.C. Flamininus made a grand appearance at the Isthmian Games at Corinth and, as proconsul, proclaimed in the name of the Roman senate the promised freedom and independence of the Greek states. They were to be sub-

ject to their own laws, without garrisons and without tribute. A pandemonium of joy and thanksgiving broke loose, unparalleled since the day Alexander proclaimed the right of all Greeks to return to their homes. Gold coins, imitating the famous staters of Alexander, were struck bearing the portrait of Titus Flamininus. In some cities he was even worshipped as a god—the first Roman ever to receive divine honors—a point not lost on other ambitious Roman aristocrats.

For a while some of the Greeks, especially the pro-Roman aristocrats, enjoyed their newly proclaimed freedom enormously. As a Roman aristocrat, Flamininus understood and admired the aristocrats of Greece and desired to perpetuate their domination of the masses. He knew little about the poor and cared less. He regarded their struggle for the cancellation of debts, the redistribution of land, and other social and economic reforms as subversive activity.

Flamininus was even prevailed upon by his aristocratic Greek friends to declare war on Sparta. Nabis, the king of Sparta, whose character biased sources have sought to blacken, was an able and energetic man, who in 206 B.C. had resumed the reform program begun by Cleomenes III twenty years before. His object was to increase the number of landholding citizens who could serve in an enlarged Spartan army and restore ancient Spartan glory. He abolished the malignant plague of debt, broke up the large estates, distributed the land fairly, enfranchised the helots (Spartan serfs), and proclaimed liberty to captives and slaves. His kingdom had become a refuge to homeless exiles. Though Sparta had in a short time become a fairly strong power, she was unable to resist the might of Rome. Flamininus reaped even greater glory, Roman soldiers carried off much plunder, and the Roman treasury received a hefty indemnity of five hundred talents.

Flamininus and the Romans had no romantic notions about Greek freedom. Their concern was to keep Greece, with its strategic location and valuable manpower, politically fragmented and out of the hands of any strong power without the trouble and expense of annexing it themselves. Indeed, they expected that as grateful clients the various Greek states would follow Roman policy and preserve the status quo. Unfortunately, there was always someone trying to upset it within Greece and take advantage of the situation from without.

The War with Antiochus the Great, 192 to 189 B.C.

No sooner had Flamininus pulled his legions out of Greece and celebrated a glorious triumph in Rome than the senate became alarmed at the activities of Antiochus III. While Philip had been occupied with fighting Rome, Antiochus had dangerously upset the Hellenistic balance of power. He attacked and defeated the Egyptians at Panium in northern Palestine in 200 B.C. Seven years later he concluded a marriage alliance between his daughter, Cleopatra I, and the young Egyptian king, Ptolemy V. After he had confirmed his peace with Egypt by this marriage, Antiochus began to annex the few still free coastal cities of Asia Minor. He occupied Ephesus, though it had been held by Egypt for more than a century. In 196 B.C. he crossed the Dardanelles and occupied several towns in Thrace. Since all these cities had once belonged to the empire of Seleucus I, Antiochus believed that he had a perfect right to reoccupy them.

The attempt of Antiochus to recover the empire of Seleucus I alarmed Pergamum, which had also once formed part of the old Seleucid domains. The new king, Eumenes II, decided to follow his father's example of appealing to Rome, and it was not until near the end of his reign in 167 B.C. that he realized that Rome, once she vanquished all her enemies, would then deprive Pergamum and all the other small states of their freedom and independence.

In response to the appeals of Eumenes and of some Greek cities in Asia Minor, the senate authorized Flamininus to negotiate with Antiochus in 196 B.C. Flamininus warned the king to keep his hands off the independent Greek cities in Asia Minor, not to cross the Dardanelles, and to evacuate all towns recently taken from Egypt. The king replied correctly that Flamininus had no right to speak on behalf of the Greek cities in Asia Minor, and that if the Romans would leave him alone, he would gladly leave them alone. The Romans were not yet ready to go to war, but influential men were laying the basis of future action, which was eagerly anticipated and promoted by Scipio Africanus and his supporters.

About this time (196 B.C.) Hannibal, forced into exile from Carthage (p. 110), arrived at Ephesus. In response to a question from Antiochus, Hannibal replied that the only chance for victory against Rome lay in the creation of a united front of all her enemies. Antiochus would have to come to terms with Philip V, with Egypt, with Pergamum —perhaps even make concessions. Antiochus thanked Hannibal for his sage advice and ignored it. He decided to ally himself instead with the little powers of Greece, a decision that was to prove extremely unwise.

Antiochus III Invades Greece, 192 B.C. In Greece the disgruntled Aetolians had become violently anti-Roman, particularly because the peace settlement restricted their favorite occupation—plundering their neighbors. They tried to enlist Philip's help in throwing off the hated Roman yoke, but remembering how they had urged Flamininus to dismantle his kingdom, he rejected their overtures. Antiochus was so ill-advised as to accept their invitation; he landed in Greece in 192 B.C. with a puny force of ten thousand men and was promptly elected Aetolian commander-in-chief.

By his actions Antiochus had triggered the responses that characterized Roman imperialism—fear, vengefulness, greed, and desire for glory. The Romans immediately made common cause with Philip against Antiochus by offering to cancel the unpaid balance of his war indemnity and promising him any Thessalian cities that he might capture from the Aetolians. Thus they employed one of the maxims that they had learned in their long history of warfare, *divide et impera* (divide and rule), advice no doubt seconded by Cato, who was serving as an advisor to the Roman commander, Manius Acilius Glabrio, when he landed in Greece in 191.

Allied with Philip, Pergamum, Rhodes, the Achaean League, Numidia, and even Carthage, the Romans had little trouble in defeating Antiochus, whose last stand was at Thermopylae, a position historically impossible to hold. After his defeat at Thermopylae, Antiochus made his escape to Chalcis and set sail for Ephesus.

The Results of the War   The failure of Antiochus had two important results: the invasion of Asia Minor by the Romans, and the immediate resurgence of the Scipionic group in Roman factional politics. The spectacular successes of Flamininus naturally gave the Fabian faction (to which he probably belonged) immense prestige, although Scipio Africanus was most critical of the peace settlement. Later events seemed to justify Scipio, and in the years 191 and 190 B.C. only pro-Scipionic consuls were elected.

In view of the probable magnitude of the coming struggle with Antiochus, it would have been advantageous to elect Scipio Africanus, the greatest living Roman general, to the consulship. Since Africanus had been consul in 194 and was not eligible for reelection until ten years later, the people elected instead his younger brother, Lucius Cornelius Scipio, in the expectation that the latter would appoint him as legate and permit him to assume actual command. Lucius did just that.

Early in 190 B.C. the Scipios sailed from Brundisium with a small army, took command of the larger army already in Greece, and began their march through Macedonia to the Dardanelles. Under the usual Roman policy of *divide et impera,* the Scipios secured Philip's active assistance. Philip allowed the Romans to pass through his country and helped them by supplying provisions, building bridges, and repairing roads.

The conquest of the East would have been impossible for the Romans without command of the sea, which they secured partly through the tactical skill of their admiral, Gaius Livius, and the effective assistance of the Rhodian and Pergamene navies, and also partly through the stupidity of Antiochus himself.

The first decisive naval battle was fought off Cissus between Ephesus and Chios, the next off Dide, Pamphylia. Antiochus committed the inexplicable blunder of placing Hannibal, one of the greatest land generals, in command of the fleet. He was defeated by the smaller but more efficient Rhodian fleet. A few weeks later Antiochus' main fleet was destroyed off Myonnesus, between Teos and Samos, and Scipio's army crossed the Dardanelles without naval opposition.

Antiochus Offers Peace Terms   Antiochus offered to abandon Thrace, break off relations with the Aetolian Greeks, and recognize the independence of the Greek cities in Asia Minor, as Flamininus had demanded seven years before. In addition, he agreed to pay half the costs of the war. There was a time when the Romans would have made peace with him, had he merely agreed not to cross the Dardanelles and refrain from attacking the cities of Thrace. Now his far more sweeping offers came too late. Nothing would satisfy the ambitious Scipios short of the surrender of all Asia Minor north and west of the Taurus Mountains and payment of the entire costs of the war, which terms Antiochus rejected.

The Battle of Magnesia   The battle for Asia took place near Magnesia on the Sipylus in 190 B.C. It was easily won by the Romans, despite the absence of the Scipios because of illness. Antiochus was hampered by poor generalship, poor equipment, and lack of coordination among the various units of his huge but ill-assorted army. At Magnesia Antiochus lost the war and the Seleucid empire lost its power.

The Peace Treaty of Apamea, 188 B.C.   A peace treaty was finally worked out at Apamea in 188 B.C. The king was obliged to give up all his possessions in Asia Minor north of the

Taurus Mountains and west of the Halys River, to surrender his navy, and to pay fifteen thousand talents, one of the largest indemnities exacted in ancient times. Some of the vast territory surrendered in Asia Minor by Antiochus to the Romans, who were not yet prepared to administer so large an area, went to the Greek cities and the Republic of Rhodes in return for their help; but the lion's share went to Pergamum, whose original size was increased tenfold to an area almost equal to Great Britain's. The new kingdom of Pergamum, writes Polybius, was now inferior to none.

The Aftermath   Antiochus the Great was assassinated after robbing a temple at Susa in 187 B.C. After Magnesia, Hannibal escaped first to Crete and then to Bithynia, which was at war with Pergamum. He won a naval battle for his friend, Prusias I of Bithynia, but Flamininus finally hunted him down and compelled Prusias to promise his surrender. Hannibal frustrated the plan by taking poison in 183 B.C. and dying as proudly as he had lived.

Earlier in the same year his greatest opponent, Scipio Africanus, also died under unhappy circumstances. Cato, jealous of Scipio's military achievements, had never agreed with Scipio's aggressive overseas policy and unorthodox political career. He kept up relentless political and judicial attacks on Scipio, his family, and his friends. In 183 B.C., Africanus finally retired to his country estate and died a short time later.

Philip V had done comparatively well since his defeat at Cynoscephalae, although he did not reap many permanent advantages from his disgraceful alliance with Rome against Antiochus. He received only a few paltry talents and the promise of a few towns in Thessaly—a promise that the Romans ultimately failed to keep. He did try, when it was almost too late, to cultivate good relations with the other Hellenistic states—Egypt, Syria, and even Pergamum. He even changed the Macedonian constitution to permit the towns under his rule the right of local self-government so

that he might pose as the champion of the oppressed masses in Greece.

Philip also set about building up the economic life of Macedon. He encouraged agriculture, sank new mines, reopened old ones, and encouraged the people to raise larger families. To increase the population still more, he brought in Thracian settlers from the Balkan regions that he had recently annexed. These measures were intended to increase the military power of his kingdom.

Philip's last days were far from happy. He had put his own son Demetrius to death on charges of treason that were later found false. After learning the horrid truth, Philip, tortured with remorse, could no longer sleep and fell an easy to victim to illness. He died in 179 B.C. and his eldest son, Perseus, succeeded to the throne.

The Third Macedonian War, 171 to 167 B.C.   The Third Macedonian War was caused partly by the reawakening power of Macedonia, partly by the intrigues of Eumenes, and partly by the chaotic conditions in Greece after the dismal defeat of Antiochus and the Aetolians, all of which gave convenient pretexts for war to the ambitious aristocrats in the senate, who saw Macedon as their next opportune target after intervening wars in Spain and northern Italy had come to a close. The Greeks, moreover, had perverted the freedom proclaimed at the Isthmian Games of 196 into chaos and anarchy, a danger to themselves and a constant source of worry and annoyance to the senate.

Greece was torn apart by the class struggle between the haves and the have-nots. The petty and venal aristocracy, whom Flamininus had hoped would guide the Greek cities onto the path of freedom and self-government, were as much responsible for the anarchy as the demagogues, who kept fanning the smoldering embers of popular discontent. In vain Eumenes tried to persuade the Greeks to preserve law and order by pretty phrases and prettier gifts of gold.

The first three years of this war provided

a pitiable exhibition of incompetence on both sides. The Roman commanders marched to and fro to no purpose and made mistakes that a more resolute and daring enemy than Perseus could have turned into defeats as disastrous as those of the Caudine Forks, Trasimene, or Cannae.

Perseus was a good soldier but no general. In time of peace he might have been a good king, though he lacked the energy and decisiveness of his father. His forty-three thousand men were twice the number that Hannibal had when he rocked Rome to its foundations. Moreover, Perseus had in his treasury the equivalent of almost ten thousand talents. (After his defeat he still had about fifty-eight hundred left, which fell into the hands of the Romans.) He could have hired twenty or thirty thousand Celts, had he been willing to spend money. He might even have bought the support of Eumenes II, not to mention that of the Greeks. His excessive caution and misguided hope that he might avoid a serious confrontation with those Romans who were intent on war prevented him from taking these opportunities.

Lucius Aemilius Paullus and the Battle of Pydna, 168 B.C. Lucius Aemilius Paullus was allied with the Scipios and had a sincere appreciation of Greek art and culture. He had been consul in 182 B.C. and accepted the second consulship in 168 only on condition that his conduct of the war not be hampered by unsolicited and unwanted advice. He brought Perseus to a decisive battle at Pydna.

The battle of Pydna was a repetition of Cynoscephalae. The solid mass of the Macedonian phalanx charged the Roman legions on level ground and pushed them up the hilly terrain behind. Nevertheless, the force of its own momentum broke the phalanx apart on the higher and rougher ground. The Roman maniples, still intact, penetrated the resulting gaps, circled the enemy's flanks, and cut the disordered Macedonians down. This battle demonstrated once more, as did those at the Allia, at the Caudine Forks, at Heraclea, at Cynoscephalae, and at Magnesia, that the

phalanx, supreme in the days of Epaminondas and Philip II, was now a thoroughly obsolete battle formation.

Perseus, a most pathetic figure, was brought to Rome as a prisoner and was forced to walk, clad in black, in the triumphal victory parade of Aemilius Paullus. He was subsequently interned for life and died around 165 B.C. Rome, however, profited so greatly from the confiscation of Perseus' treasury and the yearly tribute imposed on the Macedonians that all Roman citizens ceased to be subject to direct taxes.

Macedon after Pydna In Macedon the Romans decided to try an experiment apparently modeled after the Greek leagues. They abolished the monarchy and replaced it by four independent republics—separate, partially disarmed, and deprived of the rights of alliance, intermarriage, or trade with each other. The Romans also made the royal mines and domains the property of the Roman state, closed the royal gold and silver mines for ten years, forbade the export of timber, and exacted an annual tribute of one hundred talents, which was half the amount of the land tax formerly paid to the kings.

The Macedonians were far less concerned about having their form of government changed than about the unity of their country. They had never regarded their monarchy as an oppressive evil but as the symbol of their national unity. The Kingdom of Macedon had more nearly resembled a nation than any other state in the ancient world. It was not a land of city-states like Greece or Italy; it was not a loose confederation of cities like the Achaean League; nor was it a universal state held together solely by the monarchy like the empire of the Seleucids. It was one people in ethnic background, language, religion, customs, and government. The Roman experiment violated the very nature and traditions of the Macedonian state.

The Fourth Macedonian War, 149 to 148 B.C. It is little wonder, then, that within two decades the Roman experiment failed. Andriscus, an upstart pretender, probably the son of a clothmaker, was able to convince the people that he was the son of Perseus, and they rallied around him. He restored the monarchy in 149 B.C., reunited the kingdom, and even overcame a small Roman army sent against him. After defeating him with a larger army, the Romans converted Macedon into the province of Macedonia in 148 B.C. and thereby ended the political existence of Macedon for all time.

Greece after Pydna, 168 B.C.

The Roman treatment of Macedon was mild compared with the punishment inflicted upon Greece. In Aetolia the Romans lent troops to their contemptible henchmen to carry out a purge of Macedonian sympathizers, probably the most intelligent and democratic elements of the population. In Achaea they deported to Italy one thousand of the leading citizens, including the historian Polybius, whose names they found among the papers that Perseus had neglected to destroy. For sixteen years the Achaean hostages were kept interned without a trial or hearing and were not released until after seven hundred of them had died. In 167 B.C. the most horrible and revolting brutality was inflicted upon Epirus, against which Rome had no legitimate complaint, where seventy towns were destroyed and one hundred and fifty thousand people were dragged off to the slave market, to the profit of Aemilius Paullus and his soldiers.

The worst was yet to come. In 146 B.C. Lucius Mummius arrived in Corinth. To punish this city and the Achaean League for rebellion against Rome, he turned his troops loose upon it, sacked it, and razed it to the ground. He massacred many of its inhabitants, sold many more as slaves, and shipped its priceless art treasures to Rome.

After the destruction of Corinth, the Romans in 146 B.C. dissolved the Achaean and most of the other Greek leagues to break the last desperate but hopeless attempts of the Greek people to win back their independence.

They destroyed the militant democracies and set up petty tyrants or aristocratic oligarchies in their place. Each city-state now had separate relations with Rome, but the governor of Macedonia was empowered to intervene, to settle disputes, and to preserve public order. A century later, Augustus made Greece a separate province.

Rhodes and Pergamum

After Pydna (168 B.C.) the hand of Rome also fell heavily upon Rhodes, the proud and wealthy republic that for a century had kept the eastern seas free of pirates. Rhodes had appealed to Rome for help against Philip V and had later given Rome valuable naval assistance in the war against Antiochus III. This faithful friend at last made one mistake. Just before Pydna she tried to mediate between Rome and Perseus, not so much out of sympathy toward Perseus as out of fear that Rome might become the unbalanced power in the eastern Mediterranean. Rome took offense at this attempted mediation. A praetor even proposed a declaration of war, and it might even have been passed had not old Cato stood up and made a strong plea in defense of the Rhodians.

Although Rhodes humbly repented of her mistakes, dragged the pro-Macedonian leaders to the scaffold, sent Rome a massive golden wreath in thanksgiving for deliverance from war, and begged for an alliance, she did not escape Roman vengeance. She was stripped of the territories in Asia Minor given her after Magnesia (an annual loss of one hundred and ten talents) and prohibited from importing shipbuilding timber from Macedonia. Delos was given to Athens in 167/6 B.C. and made a customs-free port. The resulting competition from Delos reduced the income of Rhodes as a banking, shipping, and commercial center from 166 to about twenty-five talents annually. The loss of revenue from her Asiatic possessions and from harbor dues and banking so crippled the finances of Rhodes that she was compelled to reduce her navy and was no longer able to keep piracy in check in the eastern seas.

Eumenes II, king of Pergamum, who had done so much to betray the Hellenistic world into the ruthless hand of the Romans, incurred the senate's displeasure because of suspected collusion with Perseus. He was punished by confiscation of territory and hounded by hostile Roman commissions sent to Asia Minor to gather evidence against him. Thus did Rome reward her most devoted and servile ally in the Near East.

When Eumenes died in 159 B.C. he was succeeded by his brother, Attalus II, who followed Eumenes' policy of friendship and subservience to Rome and of philanthropy toward the Greek city-states. He continued also to promote Pergamum as a cultural and intellectual capital and maintained a Greek cultural offensive against the resurgence of native Near-Eastern cultures. He was followed in 138 B.C. by Attalus III, whose parentage is uncertain. Like Louis XVI of France, he preferred his studies and hobbies to being a king. He did serious research on botany, zoology, medicine, scientific agriculture, and gardening. Having no direct heirs, he bequeathed his kingdom to the Roman people and thereby closed, with his early death in 133 B.C., the history of Pergamum as a separate state.

The Seleucid Monarchy   After Magnesia in 190 B.C., the defeated empire of the Seleucids had rapidly disintegrated. Everywhere the native peoples were on the march —the Arabs, the Jews, the Iranians, the Parthians, and the Hindus. Even the Greek colonies of the East were becoming increasingly Eastern in spirit, religion, and government. The blow that Rome struck at Magnesia against the stability of the Seleucid Empire served to accelerate the inevitable process by which the culture of the Greek ruling minority was absorbed into that of the native majority. This blow was all the more damaging to Hellenism because of the very nature and character of the Seleucid monarchy itself.

The Seleucid Empire was not a national state like Macedon, nor a city-state like Athens or Rome. It was rather a universal state consisting of many ethnic groups, languages, and even forms of government. All were more or less loosely held together by the military prestige, personality, royalty, and divinity of the Seleucids, the heirs of Alexander the Great and of the Persian kings. The power of the king and his claim to royalty and even to divinity rested ultimately upon military victory—a sign both of royal virtue and divine favor. Defeat in war signified the loss of these vital prerequisites and tended to destroy the claim of the Seleucid monarchy to the loyalty and allegiance of the various regional rulers, provincial governors, satraps, and native kings. Therefore, the defeat of Antiochus III at Magnesia dealt a shattering blow to the unity and stability of the Seleucid Empire.

Most of Asia Minor had gone to Pergamum and Rhodes. Armenia broke away. The Parthians seized large areas of Iran. Further to the east, the huge kingdom of Bactria, having snatched the eastern portions of Iran, broke away. New Arab kingdoms arose in southern Palestine, Transjordan, and southern Syria. Two decades or so later a new Jewish state sprang up in Judea.

The Jewish Revolt of the Maccabees   Antiochus IV (175 to 164 B.C.), a younger son of Antiochus III, had tried to turn Judea into a strongly Hellenized city-state as a buffer between Egypt and Syria. This program aroused some discontent among the Jews, but no open revolt occurred until Antiochus decided to devote the temple of Jahweh to the worship of Baal Shamin ("Lord of the Heavens"), a universal deity whom the Greeks identified with Olympian Zeus and the Hellenized Jews with Jahweh. Simultaneously, he revoked the decree of his father, Antiochus III, which had permitted the Jews to live and worship according to the law of Moses.

A priestly landowner named Judas Maccabaeus and his brothers, Jonathan and Simon, aroused non-Hellenized Jews to rebellion, gathered together an army, and inflicted a series of defeats upon the king's troops. Aided by the death of Antiochus IV in Armenia late in 164 B.C. and by the subsequent disruption of the Seleucid empire, the Maccabees rooted out every last vestige of Hellenism in Jerusalem and restored the ancient temple state. In 161 B.C. the Romans saw a chance to erect a barrier to further Seleucid ambitions in Palestine and Egypt by recognizing the Jewish temple state as an ally.

A Review of Roman Imperialism in the East, 200 to 133 B.C.

After the Second Punic War, Rome's attention was drawn permanently to the East out of the desire of many Romans for revenge against Philip V of Macedon for supporting Hannibal and out of fear that one of the Hellenistic successors of Alexander the Great might become so powerful that he would seek to expand in the West. Other Romans, who may or may not have shared these motives, favored Roman intervention in Eastern affairs in the hope of securing personal glory, political advantage, financial gain, or a combination thereof.

The Romans were not imperialistic in the sense that they wanted to seize the territories of Greece and the Hellenistic monarchies. They did everything that they could think of to avoid a direct takeover. Certainly, however, they were imperialistic in wanting to subordinate the Hellenistic East to their own interests by the use of proxies like Aetolia, Rhodes, and Pergamum, or by the force of their own armies when other tactics failed. On the other hand, the attempts of smaller Hellenistic states to use Rome as much as she used them and the expansionistic moves of the kings of Macedon and Seleucid Syria excited Roman suspicions and invited Roman military intervention.

The Romans were always successful in their Eastern wars because the individual Greek states and kingdoms were never able to set aside their own ambitions and petty jealousies to present a united front against Rome. Many Roman leaders in their ambition to win military glory and other benefits of victory became arrogant in the exercise of power and took every advantage of Greek weakness to divide and rule. Moreover, the Greeks, smug in the confidence of their superiority over the "Western barbarians," failed to adopt Roman military improvements and thereby reduced their individual chances of success in battle against Rome's legions.

In the process Rome destroyed the Hellenistic states politically by policies designed to weaken them. She also ruined them economically by wholesale plundering and the imposition of profitable indemnities. Therefore, the vitality of Hellenistic culture was steadily sapped, and the Greek East went into a long period of decline.

XI

Roman Imperialism in the West, 200 to 133 B.C.

While the Romans pursued an imperialistic policy that sought to avoid territorial takeovers in the East, they were actively engaged in territorial imperialism in northern Italy and Spain. Although the same motives applied to the Western wars as to the Eastern, the Romans also consciously sought territorial acquisition in northern Italy and Spain because they had no other possible means to exercise control over areas that experience had shown were vital to Roman security and had to be kept out of potentially hostile hands. In both northern Italy and Spain, people were still loosely organized in agrarian tribes. There were no large city-states or territorial monarchies that the Romans could manipulate to maintain control indirectly. There was no sophisticated political elite whom they could coopt and no shared body of concepts or values that could provide a basis for peaceful coexistence. Therefore, outright conquest was the only possible solution from the Roman point of view right from the start.

Northern Italy The Gallic tribes of northern Italy had periodically attacked Roman territory or sided with Rome's enemies ever since 390 B.C. Under the leadership of

Gaius Flaminius just before the Second Punic War, the Romans had begun to satisfy the need for both land and security by systematically subduing the Cisalpine tribes and colonizing the area that they called the near side of the Po, *Cispadana* (as opposed to the *Transpadana*). This effort had been interrupted and undone by the war with Hannibal, whom the Gauls supported. As soon as the Romans were free of the Second Macedonian War, therefore, they began to settle the score with the Gauls of northern Italy and founded colonies on both sides of the Po between 197 and 175 B.C. For example, they occupied and colonized Mediolanum (Milan) in 196 B.C., and in 190 reinforced the two early colonies of Placentia (Piacenza) and Cremona, both vital strongholds during the Second Punic War, with a total of six thousand Roman and Latin settlers. The following year saw a Latin colony of three thousand settlers established at Bononia (Bologna), and in 183 B.C. Parma and Mutina (Modena) each received two thousand Roman colonists. Small market towns and administrative centers rapidly sprang up as the country became settled by the many individual farmers who were encouraged to move north and take up land.

After the conquest and settlement of the

central region of northern Italy, the Romans turned to the coastal areas. In 181 B.C. they founded a Latin colony at Aquileia, at the head of the Adriatic, which served as a springboard for the later conquest of Istria and the Dalmatian coast. During the late Republic and early Empire, Aquileia was one of the busiest shipping and commercial harbors of Italy (see map on p. 71).

On the west coast, or the Italian Riviera, the conquest of the hardy but culturally backward Ligurian tribes was a long and difficult operation attended by several Roman defeats, some victories, and some notorious atrocities. Throughout the early part of the second century B.C., the Ligurian country had been a happy hunting ground for Roman generals looking for triumphs, some of which they obtained by making war upon friendly and inoffensive tribes. The two notorious slave catchers Marcus Popilius Laenas and his brother Gaius (p. 142) had a peculiar weakness for such wars.

By 172, after a series of campaigns, the Romans had brought both the Italian and the French Riviera under their control as far as the borders of Massilia. They had founded colonies at Pisa in 181, perhaps at Luca in 178, and at Luna (now the Italian naval base of La Spezia) in 177 B.C. While these Roman and Latin colonies were being planted along the Ligurian coast in the north, forty thousand Ligurians were moved south and settled on vacant public land near Beneventum in central Samnium (see map, p. 71).

The building of roads was equally important for the occupation and settlement of the north. A very active road builder as well as colonizer was Gaius Flaminius, the consul of 187 B.C. Following in the footsteps of his famous father, who was killed at Trasimene, he built the New Flaminian Way from Arretium (Arezzo) to Bononia. Not to be outdone, his consular colleague, Aemilius Lepidus, built the famous Aemilian Way, which ran from Ariminum (Rimini), the terminus of the Old Flaminian Way, through Bononia as far as Placentia.

Several years later (171 B.C.) the Cassian

Way was built from Rome to Arretium, where it joined the New Flaminian Way, to provide a strategic thoroughfare to northern Italy as far as Aquileia. About two decades later, another important road, the Postumian Way, was constructed across northern Italy to connect the cities of Genua (Genoa), Placentia, Cremona, and Verona. Many secondary roads were built, and in a short time northern Italy had become an integral part of peninsular Italy. The wars ceased, and the use of the Latin language spread. Rome was rapidly becoming the capital of a united Italy.

The Subjugation of Spain   When the Romans had driven the Carthaginians from Spain in the Second Punic War, they decided to hold on to that country in order to prevent any other state from using it as a base for another attack on Italy. They were also influenced by tales of its fabulous mineral wealth and the remarkable fertility of its soil. They hoped to extract enough wealth from Spain to pay for the costs of its occupation and recoup the staggering losses suffered from the Second Punic War and, perhaps, to finance future wars as well.

The Romans encountered unexpected difficulties. Not only were there in Spain no large self-governing states or kingdoms that could be held responsible for the collection of tribute or the maintenance of law and order, large areas that the Carthaginians had claimed in the interior and in the western part of the peninsula had never been subdued or even explored by them. The tribes living in these backward areas had long been in the habit of raiding the richer and more civilized parts of Spain formerly controlled by the Carthaginians and now by the Romans. To protect their recent gains, the Romans were obliged to make further conquests.

But Spain was cut up by its mountains into thousands of small communities and as many separate clans. Communications among them were difficult, and access to them was practically impossible. The Romans could not conquer them in a few pitched battles, as they had conquered Macedon or Asia Minor, because the Spaniards formed small armed bands skilled in making sudden raids and vanishing as rapidly as they came. The Romans were completely baffled by this guerrilla warfare, which the Spaniards loved to wage. War raged almost continuously until 133 B.C., and even then Spain was not fully subdued until the time of Augustus.

Nearer and Farther Spain   For purposes of administration and defense, the senate decided in 197 B.C. to divide Roman Spain into two separate provinces known as Nearer (Hither) and Farther Spain, each to be governed normally by a praetor but, in time of war and crisis, by a magistrate of consular power. The Mediterranean seaboard from the Pyrenees to a point slightly south of New Carthage (Cartagena) comprised Hither Spain, rich in silver mines but agriculturally somewhat poor. Farther Spain, roughly coextensive with Andalusia, embraced the fertile Guadalquivir valley as far north as the silver mining region of the Sierra Morena range. Neither province extended very far into the interior, and both were quite well known, having been visited from the Late Bronze Age onward by Phoenician, Greek, and Etruscan traders and sailors.

The costs of provincial administration and defense were defrayed by revenue derived from tribute and regular taxes. The tribute *(stipendium)* was imposed on all tribes, semiurban communities, and a few municipalities such as Malaca (Malaga) and Gades (Cadiz). It was not collected by tax farmers, as in other provinces, but by government agents (prefects). It consisted sometimes of farm products, such as wheat or barley, but more often of payments in silver or gold, partly in bullion and partly in coined money. Up to 195 B.C. the amount of the tribute varied from year to year according to the needs of the provincial government and the rapacity of the governor. As a rule, it was too high for primitive rural communities and often provoked unrest and rebellion. The regular tax, on the other hand, was fairly low, being only a twentieth of farm crops and payable in kind. In addition to tribute and

taxes, all communities were required to furnish troops to the Roman army.

In the year in which the two provinces were created, war broke out in both because of the extortions and tyrannies of the Roman praetors. The Romans, who had been welcomed as deliverers under Scipio, proved less tolerable than the Carthaginians had been. Even Gades and Malaca, finding themselves denied the promised status of allies, supported the inland tribes in the fight for independence.

Cato the Elder's Governorship of Nearer Spain   In 195 B.C., Cato, now consul, arrived in northeastern Spain with an army of fifty thousand men. Though he was successful in stamping out the rebellion in his own province and even subdued the region as far west as the headwaters of the Tagus, his military achievements were not as outstanding or as permanent as his economic and administrative reforms (which applied to both provinces since he was the senior magistrate).

He did not reduce the tribute but fixed it once and for all for each administrative district, so that the people would know long in advance what they would have to pay. More important, he reopened the mines, which had been shut since the Carthaginian defeat, and placed most of them under public ownership, operation, and control to provide new income for the provincial administrations and employment for the poorer people living in New Carthage and other mining districts.

Tiberius Sempronius Gracchus, 180 to 178 B.C. Tiberius Gracchus, son-in-law of Scipio Africanus and father of the famous reforming tribunes Tiberius and Gaius Gracchus (see pp. 155–166) was another governor whose fame rests not on military achievements but on his reforms, fairness, and sympathy. To remove the causes of unrest, he founded many new towns and villages and gave the peasants and workers in Hither Spain good land for settlement. The faith and confidence that he inspired among the people kept them contented and peaceful for twenty-five years.

The peace and order that Tiberius Gracchus had established in Spain were destroyed by the brutalities of the later governors. The senate refused to punish their crimes, in spite of bitter denunciations by Cato and the repeated appeals of the Spanish people, whose resentment festered until the end of the first century B.C.

The Third Punic War, 149 to 146 B.C.

While the Romans were trying to crush the native peoples' understandably bitter resistance to their rule in the Iberian peninsula, events in North Africa were leading to the final and sorriest chapter in the history of Rome's conflict with Carthage. Even after Zama, Carthage had continued to prosper despite her loss of military and political power. She was still a busy shipping and industrial center and controlled all the trade between Africa and the Hellenistic world. Now that peace and order prevailed in North Africa, she enjoyed a better market for her industrial products than ever before. The crops grown on her farms and plantations were the envy of the world. Her commercial and diplomatic relations with Rome had steadily improved. In an effort to please and cooperate with the Romans, the Carthaginians had scrupulously observed all their treaty obligations. They had disavowed Hannibal and had supplied grain for the Roman armies on numerous occasions. They had helped Rome wage war against Philip V, Antiochus III, and Perseus by furnishing both military and naval assistance. Perhaps they would have remained on good terms had it not been for the ambitions and aggression of Massinissa, who unscrupulously expanded his kingdom of Numidia at the expense of the Carthaginians, whose hands were tied by Rome.

Massinissa The Romans had used the smaller power Massinissa as a check on Carthage in the same way that they had used the smaller Hellenistic states to exercise indirect control over Macedon and the Seleucid Empire. The end result was also the same. The smaller power tried to manipulate Rome and helped to precipitate a major war.

The treaty between Rome and Carthage after Zama left Carthage in possession of many ports and trading posts along the African coast but confined her to the northern half of Tunisia within frontiers known as the Phoenician Bounds, which enclosed an area of about thirty thousand square miles. Massinissa, on the other hand, was permitted to occupy any land that either he or his ancestors had previously held. Another clause forbade Carthage to wage even defensive war without the consent of Rome. Massinissa, with Roman connivance, took full advantage of both clauses of the treaty.

One by one, Massinissa had seized most of the Carthaginian coastal colonies from Morocco to the western frontiers of Cyrenaica. Not permitted to resist these aggressions by armed force, Carthage appealed to Rome, who sent commissions to arbitrate. These commissions sometimes decided in favor of Massinissa and sometimes left the dispute unsettled. By 154 B.C., Massinissa had whittled Carthage down to about five thousand square miles, or one-sixth of her former area. In answer to an urgent Carthaginian appeal, the Romans sent a boundary commission supposedly headed by Cato. The commission left the matter undecided but, before returning to Rome, made an inspection tour in and around Carthage.

The proud city—overflowing with wealth and luxury, teeming with fighting men, filled with arms and military supplies, and humming with busy shipyards—is said to have stirred in Cato an unreasonable hatred. He demanded an immediate declaration of war, and thereafter ended all his speeches, regardless of the subject, with the hysterical refrain: *censeo Carthaginem esse delendam* ("In my opinion Carthage must be destroyed!").

Motives for War   For some Romans, like Cato the Elder, an irrational fear and hatred may well have prompted support for a declaration of war against Carthage, their great enemy in two previous wars. Cato at least had often opposed unjustified imperialistic adventures in the East. Again, however, economic considerations, though often denied, and the traditional aristocratic desire for glorious triumphs must not be underestimated among the motives of the senatorial majority that ignored the pleas of P. Cornelius Scipio Nasica Corculum to spare Carthage. Cato, for example, had lucrative investments in shipping firms and companies engaged in foreign trade. (He used a dummy to get around the *lex Claudia* of 218 B.C., which forbade senators from engaging in foreign trade.) Carthaginians were the Romans' major foreign competitors in the West. Carthage was also a major exporter of agricultural products, which, since Carthage was only three days' sail from Rome, could compete successfully in the Roman market with produce from the large rural estates of Roman senators. Perhaps most significant of all, however, in 152 Carthage had finished paying the huge indemnity imposed after the Second Punic War. If the rich, fat goose was no longer going to lay golden eggs, many Romans might have found it attractive to carve up the goose itself. Certainly the general victorious in a war with Carthage would celebrate a magnificent triumph and contribute a vast hoard of plunder to the commonwealth.

There is no reason to doubt Polybius' statement that a majority in the Roman senate had been bent on war well before the event. All that was lacking was a pretext that could decorously mark naked aggression. Such a pretext was conveniently provided as a result of Rome's tacit encouragement of Massin-

issa's unscrupulous seizures of Carthaginian territory. In Carthage, popular, anti-Roman leaders, exasperated by the aggressions of Massinissa and the indifference of Rome, had seized power from pro-Roman oligarchs in 151 B.C. They exiled the adherents of Massinissa and attacked his sons, who had been sent to demand the restoration of the exiles. In 150 B.C. war broke out between Carthage and Massinissa with disastrous results for the poorly trained and badly led Carthaginian army. Worse still, in waging war against Massinissa, the Carthaginians had violated the treaty of Zama and gave Rome a convenient excuse for war.

Hearing that the Romans were preparing to send an army to Africa, the Carthaginians made haste to undo the mischief that they had done. They returned their pro-Roman oligarchs to power, and executed the popular leaders. Envoys from Rome arrived to investigate the situation and obscured Roman intentions by vague replies when the Carthaginians asked how they could make amends. Meanwhile, the Roman senate, goaded by Cato, prepared for war, which the *comitia centuriata* finally declared in 149. The Carthaginians sent ambassadors to Rome to request peace terms. The ambassadors were told that Carthage would be permitted to retain her territory and independence, provided that she surrendered three hundred noble hostages and carried out all future orders of the consuls. The consuls demanded the surrender of all arms and weapons. After receiving the surrender of the war engines and military equipment, the consuls grimly announced the senate's secret final terms: the Carthaginians must abandon and destroy their city and rebuild at least ten miles from the sea—a death sentence for people who made their living by commerce. The Romans calculated that such an outrageous demand would produce the desired war.

The Siege of Carthage and Rise of the Younger Scipio Africanus   Beside themselves with fear and rage, the Carthaginians prepared to defend their beloved city. Supplies of food were hurriedly gathered from the surrounding countryside and brought into the city, where the people were toiling day and night to make new weapons. Prisons were opened, slaves freed, and even the temples were turned into factories as the Carthaginians frantically prepared for siege.

The siege lasted three years. Carthage was situated in an excellent defensive location, and its walls were enormously thick and strong. The Romans received no help from old Massinissa, hostile at this usurpation of the fruits of a lifetime of ambition and intrigue. The badly disciplined Roman armies were led by incompetent commanders. One young lieutenant, however, distinguished himself. He was Publius Cornelius Scipio Aemilianus, the son of Aemilius Paullus and the adopted grandson of Scipio Africanus.* So impressive were his exploits that when he returned to Rome in 147 B.C. to stand for election as curule aedile—he was only about thirty and ineligible for any higher office—a special law was passed clearing the way to his election as consul and placing him in command of the besieging army.

The young consul finally took Carthage by storm in the spring of 146 B.C. For six days and nights the struggle raged inside the city from street to street, from house to house, until the beautiful old city was a sea of flames. The last to fall was the citadel, from which emerged fifty thousand people. All were sold as slaves, and Carthage became the province of Africa Proconsularis.†

---

* He had also served Rome well when he was asked in 148 B.C. by the dying Massinissa to arrange the future of Numidia. Scipio divided Numidia among the old king's three sons and thereby averted the menace of a strong, united kingdom to the future security of Rome.

† The common belief that the city was leveled to the ground and a plow run over it is based on the exaggerated account of Orosius (fifth century A.D.). Actually, the ruins remained for centuries afterward. In fact, Plutarch tells us that Marius once sat among them. They remained on such an immense scale that for centuries the old walls, temples, and other buildings were a quarry of ready dressed stone. Far more thorough agents of demolition than Scipio's soldiers were the builders of Roman Carthage, which was founded on the Punic site in 28 B.C., and the insatiable stone hunters of later centuries.

Surveying the final destruction of the once magnificent city, Scipio, according to the historian Polybius, who was there, wept, not for the suffering of the Carthaginians, which he was only too happy to inflict, but at the thought that Rome might someday suffer a similar fate. At that time, however, Rome was invincible, and Scipio could stanch his tears with pleasant thoughts of returning home in glory as Rome's most admired citizen.

The Viriathic and Numantine Wars in Spain, 151 to 133 B.C.

At the same time that Scipio was destroying Carthage, wars of resistance in the Spanish provinces were raging again. This time the Lusitanians, native inhabitants of Farther Spain, had found a skillful and inspiring leader by the name of Viriathus, who was able to frustrate the Romans for a decade. His name, even after two thousand years, remains synonymous with freedom among the people of Portugal (ancient Lusitania). Viriathus was a shepherd and a hunter who knew the mountains, glens, and winding paths through which he led ten thousand guerrilla soldiers. For eight years he and his followers held the Romans at bay and cut down one army after another. Again and again he would attack and then fade away into the darkness by paths that the Romans could never follow.

In 141 B.C. Viriathus had entrapped a Roman army of fifty thousand men, whom he spared in return for a treaty respecting the freedom and independence of his people. He could not know to what depths of infamy the majority of senators had sunk; the treaty was ratified and, the next year, broken. The Romans bribed two traitors to slit the throat of the sleeping Viriathus, and the Lusitanians, left without a leader, submitted to the iron yoke of Rome. Some of the captives were transported to found a Latin colony along with Roman veterans at Valentia (Valencia), where they could not easily resist Roman authority again.

In 137 B.C. the new governor of Farther Spain, Decimus Junius Brutus, brought an army and a fleet against the Callaici in north-western Spain (Galicia) but did not permanently occupy the area. Instead, he left the Tagus River as the boundary of Farther Spain and merely fortified the town of Olisipo (Lisbon) at its mouth.

The Siege of Numantia The war in Nearer Spain raged around the Celtiberian fortress town of Numantia. Even for its small garrison of about four thousand men, Numantia was easy to defend because of its location on a hill at the junction of two rivers that flowed between deeply cut banks through thickly wooded valleys. While besieging Numantia in 137 B.C., the Roman commander Mancinus saw his army of twenty thousand caught in an ambush by four thousand Celtiberians and was forced to sign a treaty, which the youthful Tiberius Gracchus, son of the former governor with the same name, had persuaded the Numantines to accept. This treaty of 137 B.C., which saved a large Roman army from utter destruction, was later shamelessly broken.

After several such defeats, the Romans in 134 B.C. sent to Spain the best general of his time, Scipio Aemilianus, the destroyer of Carthage, who was looking for another opportunity to earn military glory and prestige among his fellow citizens. He reformed and retrained the demoralized Roman army, drove away the plunder buyers, bootleggers, and prostitutes, and surrounded Numantia with a double-ring wall five miles long, set with towers, and guarded by seven camps. He then proceeded to starve Numantia into unconditional surrender and set the town on fire.

The destruction of Numantia in Spain and the inheritance of Attalus' kingdom of Pergamum in Asia Minor in 133 B.C. terminated the remarkable period of a little less than seventy years during which Rome had acquired imperial control over much of the Mediterranean world. It was often a brutal process, but it would be naive to think that the Romans had never been brutal before. Subjugating others, particularly those of different cultural backgrounds, often produces brutality, and brutality in subjugating others certainly was not unprecedented in Roman history. The destructions of Alba Longa and Veii, for example, were prominently featured in patriotic historical tradition. Nevertheless, even with allowance for personal bias or rhetorical exaggeration in the sources, the level of brutality that Roman commanders used against both highly civilized and less civilized peoples does seem to have increased as Rome expanded abroad. Frustration that people of different cultural backgrounds like the Greeks, Carthaginians, and Spanish tribes would not conform to Roman preconceptions of peace and order, ambition to outdo others in military honor, greed, and the need to keep abreast of political rivals in wealth all combined to increase the Romans' use of mass enslavements, wholesale massacres, and total destruction to subdue their adversaries.

An increase in brutality against non-Romans, however, was not the only change produced by Rome's imperial expansion. The changes produced in Rome's internal life were even greater and often equally lamentable, as the following chapters will make clear.

XII

The Internal Effects
of War and Imperialism

By war and conquest Rome had established her dominion over the Mediterranean world and thus completed the political and economic unification begun by Alexander the Great and continued by the Hellenistic monarchies. In less than a century and a half since the outbreak of the First Punic War, she had passed from city-state to empire. Zama, Cynoscephalae, Magnesia, and Pydna mark the triumph of Rome's armies on three continents. She had reduced the most powerful kingdoms to vassalage and subservience. Vast streams of gold, silver, slaves, and other tribute flowed into her hands. Before her, nations trembled. While Roman cultural life became much more varied and sophisticated in the process, this phenomenon of world conquest and expansion had begun to work revolutionary effects upon the economic, social, political, and ethical life of the Roman people, which set the stage for the destruction of the Republic itself.

Agriculture One of the most spectacular transformations occurred in agriculture. In the early centuries of the Republic, agriculture was not only the principal occupation of the Roman people; it was also a way of life. To its influence Cato the Elder attributed all the moral virtues of the early Romans. The early consuls and dictators, Cincinnatus and Manius Curius, whose example Cato loved to imitate, worked with their hands, as did the other farmers of their time.

With the help of his sons and perhaps a slave or two, the farmer was able to produce all the food that his family required, as well as most of their clothing, shoes, and other necessities. The occasional sale of a few bushels of grain or a couple of pigs would enable him to buy what he could not produce on the farm.

By the middle of the second century B.C. farm life in Italy had undergone a radical change. This change had been hastened by Hannibal's invasion. For fourteen years Punic and Roman armies marching up and down the peninsula lived off the land, seized or destroyed crops, killed livestock, and burned down thousands of homes and farm buildings. Military activity and war-enforced neglect also destroyed vital drainage systems that had been built by the patient labor of generations. As a result, low-lying areas returned to swamp and marsh, perfect breeding grounds for malarial mosquitoes. Malaria became endemic in these areas and further reduced a rural population already decimated by warfare.

The human losses were terrific. The approximately 285,000 Roman citizens listed before the First Punic War had declined to 214,000 by the year 203 B.C. and to 144,000 in 193. This decline reflected not only battle losses but the large number of men serving in the armies abroad, the majority of whom had come from the farms. Many of the farmer-soldiers would never return. The security of army life and the sight of strange and exciting places were more pleasant for some than the dull farm routine. Others returned to find homes ruined and fields overrun with briars and weeds. Not a few farms had been seized for debt or by some greedy neighbor. Returned soldiers lucky enough to find houses and fields intact could not raise money to buy the necessary oxen, tools, and seed. Many were discouraged and drifted into Rome to find employment. Others went back into the army or returned to the provinces where looting and trading paid better than farming. Although the number of citizens did increase after the Second Punic War, the downward pressure on the number of small farmers remained severe.

Despite the enormous property and manpower losses, the number of family-sized farms in ancient Italy could have been restored within a few decades, had not the Roman conquest of the Mediterranean basin generated new economic forces that made the old style of agriculture untenable in several sections of Italy. Typically, Italian agriculture had been dominated by the small peasant proprietor whose principal crop had been grain. Although the impact on Roman farmers of grain that could be more cheaply imported by sea from provinces like Sardinia, Sicily, and, after 146 B.C., Africa has been overexaggerated, the economic impact of expansion did work against the small cultivators in many cases.

Rome's overseas expansion had placed the Roman and local Italian aristocrats in a very advantageous position to expand their estates into large-scale, capital-intensive operations often called *latifundia* (sing. *latifundium*), although the term is not found in Roman writers before the first century A.D.

Large operations specializing in the raising of such animals as cattle, sheep, and pigs spread rapidly in southern Italy, Etruria, and in some parts of Latium. In other parts of Latium and particularly in Campania, large estates specializing in the production of olives or wine grapes became very common. Both cases represented a type of large agricultural enterprise in which great amounts of money were invested in labor, equipment, and land for the purpose of achieving, under unified management and control, the specialized production of certain livestock or cash crops for sale in local or foreign markets.

Wherever large-scale commercial agriculture developed, it depended on five main elements: abundant capital and land, cheap labor, special equipment, efficient organization and management, and expanding markets. All of them were available to the Roman and local Italian aristocrats as a result of Rome's overseas expansion.

Capital and Land   The plunder and tribute from overseas conquests, subsequent commercial expansion, the official exploitation of provincial resources, and the exactions of corrupt provincial officials produced an enormous influx of investment capital at Rome. Some of the acquired capital was invested in shipping, commerce, and industry, but most was invested in real estate (especially farm land) since it was for senators the only kind of investment permitted by the Claudian Law of 218 B.C., and for members of the equestrian class, the *equites,* the main road to political advancement and social recognition.

The so-called Licinio-Sextian legislation of 367 B.C., which restricted the growth of the large estate, had never been strictly enforced and was almost completely ignored after the Second Punic War. The state encouraged such investment, for it had some fourteen million acres of land (most of it confiscated after the war), at least nine million acres of which were good farming land. Since the state found it easier to deal with large investors, it leased most of the public land for long terms at small stipulated rents to rich and powerful landowners, who after a few generations came to regard the leased lands as private property and even ceased paying rent to the state.

The growth of *latifundia* in Campania, southern Latium, and parts of Etruria was favored by two separate government policies: the importation of wheat from Sicily and Sardinia and the colonization of the north for purposes of defense. Wheat imported by sea from the provinces as tribute (Rome exacted from Sicily an annual tribute of a million bushels before the Second Punic War), as rent collected from tenants on arable land confiscated by the Roman state, or as the result of outright grain confiscations by powerful Roman officials could be sold in Rome at prices with which the small and medium size grain growers of Campania and Latium could not compete. Lacking the capital to engage in the more profitable forms of agriculture, many sold or abandoned their farms and took advantage of the government's colonizing program in the north and northwest. These abandoned farms were bought up at extremely low prices by rich investors, who consolidated them into *latifundia* ranging at first from sixty to two hundred acres, and later to as many as five hundred acres. The risk of crop failure, crop surplus, or insufficient labor at harvest time encouraged owners to acquire several *latifundia* located in different regions, rather than to operate an extremely large one.

It is erroneous, however, to imagine that the independent peasant proprietors disappeared everywhere in Italy. As indicated, they were extensively displaced in the South, Campania, Etruria, and parts of Latium. Nevertheless, in the area of Latium around Rome itself many were able to make the inexpensive transition from growing grain to producing garden crops for the expanding Roman market, and the same must have held true around other sizeable cities. In the rich Po valley to the north, the small peasant farm whose principal crop was grain remained the norm. Nevertheless, the number of people adversely affected by the spread of *latifundia* in many places was large, and the problem was compounded by the increase of slavery occa-sioned by the wars of the third and second centuries B.C.

Slave Labor   The wars of conquest solved the labor problem that they created by substituting for the depleted free manpower the hundreds of thousands of war prisoners. In times of peace a lack of war prisoners was made up for by the victims of pirates and professional kidnappers, whose tasks were made easier by the connivance of Roman officials and the destruction of Rhodian naval power, which had formerly kept them in check.

Use of slave labor encouraged the production of such crops as required attention all year round, yet which involved the simplest processes of cultivation so that even the dullest hands could learn by routine, and such crops as permitted maximum concentration of labor in the smallest possible area in order to reduce the high cost of supervision. Olive trees and grape vines were ideal crops under these circumstances. Wheat and barley were not suitable because they have a relatively short growing season, require a great deal of labor at planting and harvest time, and do not permit use of the gang system, whereby a single supervisor can direct the work of the greatest number of slaves in the smallest possible area. (Some wheat was grown because the *latifundium* aimed to achieve the ideal of self-sufficiency, but it was rarely produced as a staple.)

The competitive advantages of systematic slave labor were many. It was a stable supply of manpower, always available when and where needed, and easily replaced. Slaves, unlike tenants, could not be drafted for military service. Still more important, they could be organized, concentrated, and combined in any way the owner saw fit. Because the owner could appropriate any physical or value surplus earned by slaves, he was able to produce at prices only slightly above the cost of maintaining them.

The Marketing of Farm Products
Rome's conquests and her political unification

of the Mediterranean world contributed as much to the development and expansion of markets as to the mobilization of capital and labor. As early as 167 B.C. and as late as the time of Sulla (87 to 80 B.C.), Italian wine and oil were exported to Delos and to other islands as well as cities in the eastern trading area. Though the volume of these exports was at first probably small, they do show that by the middle of the second century B.C. Roman farm products had begun to compete in markets hitherto the exclusive monopoly of the Greeks.

The chief market for Italian farm products was western and northern Europe. Wine exporting to France, where a six-gallon jug cost as much as a slave, must have been a very lucrative business, and began surprisingly early. The remains of a Greek ship, which probably foundered around 230 B.C., have been discovered among a group of islands south of Marseilles. It was laden with Campanian tableware and about ten thousand large jars of wine, some of Greek vintage but most of it red Latian produced on the Sabine hills.

Far larger than the export trade, of course, was the local consumption of wine, oil, and other farm products. The demand in Rome and other cities must have grown apace with the influx of wealth and population. The Campanian cities were becoming industrial centers. The port of Puteoli was beginning its spectacular growth as an industrial center and a gateway of world trade. The large number of wineshops and bars in the small (twenty-five thousand people) city of Pompeii just before its destruction in 79 A.D. gives some idea of the quantities of wine and other farm products which must have been consumed in the larger cities of Capua, Puteoli, Naples, and, of course, Rome.

Urban Growth and the Plight of the Poor   This growth of urban economic activity attracted to Rome and the other cities of Italy many of those people from the countryside who were being displaced by economic pressures. While large holders often put unfair pressure on smaller neighbors to obtain their land, the attraction of employment in a city or the chance of starting a small business like a wine shop, food shop, fulling and dying shop, bakery, pottery, foundry, or other craft shop often encouraged the small landowners to sell out voluntarily to escape the harsh economics of small farming.

Naturally, the rapid influx of people to the cities created serious problems. Despite the growth of the urban economy, there were not always enough jobs for the newcomers, especially the unskilled. Unemployment and underemployment caused hardship for many. Housing was in high demand and short supply so that rents were steep for even the worst accommodations in hastily constructed apartment blocks called *insulae*. This situation encouraged overcrowding, which in turn produced serious problems in health, sanitation, and safety. Not only did the flimsy buildings often collapse, but many were also firetraps that burned in large numbers without adequate fire protection. Similarly, the lack of any organized police force encouraged the growth of crime, which the hardship of life fostered. As a result of these conditions, the urban poor of Italy understandably became increasingly discontent and a threat to public order and political stability.

The situation became especially acute at Rome itself in the latter part of the second century B.C. The economy of Rome did not rest on any productive base. Its great growth during the first sixty years of the century had depended upon the profits of overseas expansion, which had fueled a great construction boom in the city. Successful generals often immortalized their deeds by using part of their booty to build votive temples to the gods whose aid they had sought, basilicas for public use, roads, and aqueducts. The senate also appropriated large amounts of the revenue from the sale of booty, war indemnities, tribute, and state-owned mines to beautify the city and construct useful public works. Therefore, there was a significant demand for labor to attract people from the country to the city.

After the destruction of Carthage and Corinth in 146 B.C., however, there were no more profitable wars for some time. As they dragged on, the wars against relatively poor Spanish tribes, for example, probably did not even recover their own expenses, while they disrupted the regular tribute. In 135 B.C. a slave rebellion in Sicily also required an expensive military effort. Accordingly, there was a drastic decline in both private benefaction and public expenditure in the 130s and a serious depression of the city's economy, which greatly aggravated the plight of the urban poor.

Decline of Military Strength As small landowners left the country for the city, fewer men were left who met the property qualification for service in the Roman army. The resulting military weakness became apparent by the mid-second century B.C. Roman consuls found it increasingly difficult to recruit soldiers, especially for unpopular and dangerous wars in Spain from 154 to 133. In response to popular pressure, tribunes obstructed military recruiting and harassed returning generals with prosecutions and charges of incompetence, fraud, and even treason. After antirecruitment riots in 144, one tribune even tried to prevent a consul from departing for Spain, and in 138 tribunes actually imprisoned the two consuls to prevent them from drafting more troops. Clearly, Rome's ability to field armies was being reduced.

Widespread Discontent and Slave Revolts While the results of Rome's successful wars of conquest ironically were making Rome militarily weaker, they were also helping to increase the number of those desperate enough to challenge Roman authority in armed revolt. The people of the Hellenistic East were in particularly difficult circumstances as a result of Roman wars and conquests. Between 201 and 136 B.C., Greece, Egypt, Syria, and other parts of the Near East may have lost as much as twenty to twenty-five percent of their population. Houses fell into decay, large tracts of land lay fallow or were turned into pasture for want

of labor. From 210 to 160 B.C., while wages remained low, the prices of food, rent, and other necessities rose and in times of crop failure, even skyrocketed. Prices finally went down again because of the lack of buying power but not before the people had undergone intense suffering.

Slave Revolts One of the most discontented and potentially dangerous groups was made up of the huge number of slaves that then existed. Bondsmen and slaves had been part of Roman society since its early days, but their numbers had been small and their treatment usually mild because they lived with and worked along side their masters at home and in the fields. They had been part of the family in every sense. Unfortunately, the great influx of slaves and wealth and the consequent growth of large, market-oriented, slave-worked estates as a result of Rome's overseas expansion vastly altered the conditions of slavery during the second century B.C.

Skilled and educated household and urban slaves were still well treated, but the large numbers of anonymous slaves who worked in the fields, forests, and mines of great landlords and commercial operators were treated like animals. Food and clothing were of the poorest quality, and family life was denied them. When concentrated in groups, they were often chained up in underground prisons at night. Beatings were common. Moreover, because their only value was as the cheapest labor possible, they did not even have the hope of being allowed to acquire any money from the fruits of their labor to purchase eventual freedom. Under these conditions, therefore, it is not surprising that many slaves escaped to become robbers and brigands and even raised serious revolts. Indeed, their ability to do so was considerable because the supervision of rural slaves was often poor and many of them were former soldiers captured in war.

Slave revolts began breaking out all over the Roman world after 138 B.C. In Italy a revolt was suppressed after the crucifixion of 450 slaves at Minturnae, 150 at Rome, and 4000 at Sinuessa. An uprising at the great slave market of Delos was put down by force of arms, another at the silver mines of Laurium near Athens, where for some months the rebellious slaves had set up an independent state and even issued their own coinage. In Pergamum, the war (132 to 129 B.C.) of Aristonicus, the bastard son of Eumenes II, and his Stoic "Sunstate" against Rome was simply a major revolt of slaves, proletarians, and soldiers. Worst of all was the slave revolt in Sicily, where normal slave thuggery and mugging had swelled into full scale war near 136 B.C. under the leadership of a Syrian slave named Eunus, who by vomiting fire and uttering oracles was able to persuade his 70,000 (some say 250,000) followers that he was Antiochus, the king of the Syrians. Only after several years of hard fighting, the murder of many landlords, and much damage to property were the Romans able to crush this revolt and extinguish its last sparks in 131 B.C.

The Equites   While not desperate enough for armed rebellion, other groups were unhappy with their situations by the last third of the second century B.C. One of these groups was the *equites,* the "knights," who are often called the equestrian class, *ordo equester.* By the third century, the term *eques,* "knight," had been extended to any citizen of full birth whose property was equal in value to that of those who were enrolled in the equestrian centuries of the *comitia centuriata.* These men included wealthy nonsenatorial landowners, such as members of the local Italian aristocracy whose families had obtained Roman citizenship, and those people who had prospered with the times. Some invested in contracts to build roads, bridges, temples, and other public works, to supply the legions with food and equipment, or to exploit the resources or collect the taxes of Italy and the provinces. Others participated in banking, shipping, and large-scale commercial enterprises, such as the export of wine, the manufacture of fine pottery, and the production of bricks.

In practice, of course, no rigid distinction can be made between well-to-do landowners and people engaged in business pursuits. Landowners invested some of their surplus income in business, and people who made money in business usually sought financial security and social status by investing a large share of their profits in land. One reason why the techniques of Roman business and manufacturing never advanced further than they did is that the goal of many businessmen was not to reinvest their profits in ways to improve their productivity, but in estates and villas so that they could live the lives of gentlemen on their rents and agricultural income and even aspire to senatorial office for themselves or their sons.

The most highly developed areas of Roman business were the financial operations. The huge influx of wealth turned Rome into the banking and money-lending center of the Mediterranean. Well-organized partnerships of investors often made loans to shipowners to finance their cargoes. More frequent and more profitable were loans to provincial taxpayers and whole cities that were hard pressed to pay their taxes or tribute. While the official rate on such loans was usually limited to twelve percent, the actual rate could reach twenty-four or even forty-eight percent. Indeed, whole kingdoms sometimes became indebted to Roman moneylenders at these rates as client kings endeavored to pay for the support that secured their thrones.

Roman bankers became very sophisticated. Individuals could keep open accounts with bankers and use bankers' orders or letters of credit instead of cash. In that way payments could easily be made by bookkeeping entries instead of with cash, which in large amounts would have been a cumbersome and dangerous impediment to large transactions.

The most highly organized of all were the companies of *publicani,* publicans, who contracted with the state to construct public works, operate state-owned mines or forests, and collect taxes. These companies were granted the special privilege of legal incorporation so that their existence was continuous regardless of who the investors were. In order to raise working capital, the principal partners, *socii,* offered shares, *partes,* to the public. The company would then submit a bid to the censors for the right to collect a particular tax or to obtain some public contract. In the case of taxes, the highest bidder won, and the investors' profit would be the difference between what they paid and the actual yield of the taxes collected. In the case of other contracts, the profit would be the difference between what the state paid the company and what it actually cost to do the work. Naturally, there was a temptation for the *publicani* to squeeze the taxpayers as much as they could and to cut corners on public works in order to increase profits. Such work itself was, of course, beneath the dignity of the investors themselves and was left to slaves, freedmen, and laborers supervised by a hired manager, *magister.*

One source of discontent among the *equites* was that, for those who wanted to, it was very difficult to move upward into the senatorial aristocracy and almost impossible to break into the ranks of the consular nobility. The senators and especially the nobles jealously guarded their exclusivity. While members of the great noble families might support an equestrian for one of the lower offices of the *cursus honorum,* they expected such a man to remain a grateful and subservient client who would help them in their rivalries with fellow nobles. They reserved the supreme honor of the consulship for themselves and greatly resented a *novus homo,* new man, who managed to be the first of his family to reach the consulship. While most equestrians probably were content with their status, many must have resented the slight to their class in general implied in the nobility's attitude toward those of their number who wanted to achieve high honors at Rome.

In particular among the *equites,* the *publicani* resented any check that members of the senate might impose on attempts to maximize the amount of taxes collected or of profit made on state contracts. Moreover, the *publicani* were vulnerable to extortion at the hands of magistrates and provincial governors, who could threaten to interfere with their activities unless they handed over a share of their profits. *Publicani* subjected to such treatment often found the legal system unresponsive to complaints because the juries who heard them were staffed exclusively by the senatorial class, to which magistrates and provincial governors belonged.

Accordingly, as the equestrian order grew with the prosperity generated by Roman expansion, its members developed interests that sometimes led to dissatisfaction with the senatorial leaders.

Freedmen   Another group that came to resent the senatorial leaders by the end of the second century B.C. was the growing number of freedmen that resulted from the great increase in slavery. Not all slaves were forced to work under harsh conditions on *latifundia,* or in mines, quarries, and other places requiring exhausting physical labor. Large numbers of trained, educated people captured from the lands of the eastern Mediterranean were used in domestic service as bookkeepers, secretaries, doctors, tutors, cooks, butlers, waiters, maids, hairdressers, and footmen, or as skilled craftsmen like potters, carpenters, masons, decorators, tailors, and jewellers. A vast retinue of such slaves was a mark of status, and the wealthy often competed to impress their peers with the numbers that they owned.

More than any other ancient people, the Romans were also willing to free slaves, particularly in the case of skilled household slaves, with whom masters lived on intimate terms and who could become productive citizens upon gaining freedom. Many masters hired out skilled slaves and allowed them to keep part of their earnings as their *peculium.* When a slave had accumulated a large enough *peculium,* he or she could often purchase freedom. A female slave might be granted freedom after producing a certain number of children. Often a slave was manumitted, given freedom, after a number of years of faithful service, and large numbers were manumitted in the wills of deceased owners. In fact, manumission was so common, that the state collected a handsome revenue from a five-percent tax on the value of manumitted slaves.

The masters who freed their slaves also had something to gain from their generosity. The prospect of freedom in return for faithful service encouraged slaves to be docile and work hard. Many wealthy Romans helped their exslaves set up their own businesses in return for a share of the profits. At the very least, the nature of Roman society being what it was, any exslave was expected to be a loyal client to his former master. For the dead slave-owner, that meant that his tomb would be well cared for by those whom he had freed, that his memory would be kept green, and that his shade would receive the proper ritual offerings. For the living, the increase of clients through manumission had important political implications, for freedmen were automatically granted citizenship. Although freedmen (but not their sons) were barred from public office, as voters and political agents freedmen clients could be very helpful to an office seeker. Therefore, politically ambitious owners had a real incentive to manumit slaves.

It was this political impact of freedmen that caused them problems, however. Lower-class, free-born citizens would naturally resent the dilution of their voting power by the influx of freedmen into the tribes of voters, and many senators feared that their rivals might gain an advantage from having a large number of freedmen clients in the Tribal Assembly. (Freedmen in the *comitia centuriata* were less of a worry because exslaves would not usually be wealthy enough to qualify for the highest centuries, which had the most power in voting.) Therefore, the issue of tribal enrollment for freedmen became a source of political controversy.

Customarily, freedmen were enrolled in only the four urban tribes, where their impact would be outweighed by the less populous but more numerous rural tribes dominated by landowners. In 312 B.C., however, the famous censor Appius Claudius Caecus (the Blind) sought to strengthen his *clientela* by enrolling freedmen in all of the tribes. Many senators denounced this action, and the censors of 304 removed the freedmen from the rural tribes and confined them to the urban ones again. Naturally, the freedmen resented such a move. Some subsequent censors sided with them, but no permanent change was achieved.

The Italian Allies The Italian allies were also a group embroiled in political controversy and conflict as a result of Rome's imperial expansion. Initially, the alliances with varying degrees of privileges and duties that the Romans had granted the conquered peoples of Italy worked to the general satisfaction of both sides. During the second century B.C., however, the allies found their status more and more burdensome as Rome expanded overseas. They too had suffered enormous losses of manpower during the Second Punic War, and now the Romans were calling upon them to spend long years in wars overseas. Moreover, since the indemnities and tribute imposed upon the conquered went to Rome, the allies were receiving only a minor share of the profits of those wars while Rome was getting rich. In 177 B.C. the allies' share was even reduced when the Romans began to reward individual allied soldiers with only one-half as much captured booty as Roman citizens received. After 173, allied settlers in new Roman colonies were also given smaller lots of land than Roman citizens.

Roman leaders became more high-handed in their treatment of the Italian allies as Rome became more and more secure in Italy itself and Romans grew accustomed to dominance abroad. Allied soldiers were more subject to harsh and arbitrary discipline at the hands of Roman commanders. Roman magistrates began to demand free accommodations and entertainment when they travelled through allied territory. In 186 B.C. the Roman senate set a dangerous precedent for unilateral interference in the allies' domestic affairs through a decree that suppressed throughout Italy secret Bacchic cults, whose popularity among slaves and the poor caused the Romans to consider them subversive. In short, the Romans more and more began to treat their allies in Italy as subjects. That eventually led to allied demands for citizenship and ultimately to violent rebellion when the Romans obstinently refused to grant this just demand.

Advancement of Women   One group whose position did improve in the third and second centuries B.C. was upper-class women. One of the reasons for this improvement was the greatly increased wealth of the aristocracy as Rome acquired and exploited a vast empire. Husbands gained status by their wives' ostentatious displays of wealth. The wife of the elder Scipio Africanus was notorious for such display, and she died richer than her own brother. In 215, during the Second Punic War, the *lex Oppia* limited how much expensive clothing and ornamentation a woman could wear in public. In 195, however, women made mass protests, and the law was repealed, supposedly despite old Cato's vehement objection. As a result of wartime casualties, many women came to possess vast wealth as widows, and in 169 a law was passed to limit female inheritances, but its impact seems to have been limited.

As families became richer and daughters' doweries and inheritances greater, aristocratic families did not want to lose control of such wealth. Therefore, the old-fashioned marriage with *manus,* which transferred a wife to the complete control of her husband, became increasingly rare, and marriage contracts usually contained the stipulation that the dowry be returned to the wife's family if she predeceased her husband. In this way, a woman now lived with a man who did not have legal supervision over her, while those who did, her male blood relatives or legal guardian, were physically separated from her. Such a situation allowed shrewd and capable women a

great amount of room to maneuver. Many of them, surrounded by loyal and able personal slaves, took full advantage of this situation.

The increased level of education among upper-class women also contributed to their independence and influence. The growing wealth and sophistication of aristocratic families prompted them to acquire the most highly trained tutors for their children. The large staffs of domestic slaves meant that girls were not needed for household chores, and were, therefore, allowed to attend the lessons that might have been denied them in earlier times. Also, Roman aristocrats were now being exposed to the Hellenistic Greek model of the educated woman. Soon, a number of educated women were patronizing literary circles and running salons, as did aristocratic women of France in the eighteenth century.

Women's independence also increased because their close male relatives and husbands were often far away in the army or on official business for long periods. Many men were killed or died overseas. Distantly related or nonrelated male guardians often did not have enough personal interest to exercise close supervision over the complex affairs of the women left behind, so that for all practical purposes a wealthy, well-educated aristocratic woman could live as she wished.

One of the most famous Roman women of the late second century B.C. combines many of the characteristics and accomplishments of such women. She was Cornelia, daughter of the elder Scipio Africanus and mother of the Gracchi (see pp. 159–160). Her husband, Tiberius Sempronius Gracchus, had a highly distinguished public career. Cornelia was rich in her own right, but when Tiberius died her wealth increased. Well educated under the influence of her philhellene father, she provided the best education possible for the three of her twelve children who survived to maturity, and was well known as a patronness of writers and philosophers. Her own cultured letters were read for generations after her death. Her wealth, family name, and personal accomplishments even brought her an offer of marriage from Ptolemy VII (Physcon) of Egypt, but she preferred her independence as a Roman widow and turned him down.

Political Developments

The Senate   The general political effect of Rome's wars and expansion from 264 to 133 B.C. was to increase and entrench the power of the senatorial aristocracy despite some superficial attempts at reform. Shortly after the end of the First Punic War certain reforms were made in the organization of the *comitia centuriata* that probably were intended to give greater voice to those enrolled in the second highest census class. Men of this class had contributed greatly to the financial support of the costly struggle with Carthage and no doubt were able to extract some political gain as a result (see p. 97).

Since the difference in wealth between the first two census classes was not extreme, this reform represented only a minor step in the liberalization of the Roman constitution. The trend for the next century, moreover, was one of increased domination of the Republic by the wealthy senatorial landowners. They shared the same economic interests, and their great wealth assured them of loyal clients who would do their bidding in the assemblies.

Initially, most people had been satisfied with the senatorial aristocrats' control of Rome. The men of the senate had gained enormous prestige for their leadership during the dangers of the first two Punic wars and their successful prosecution of profitable overseas expansion. Ironically, however, just as the Romans needed creative leadership to help solve the problems fostered by war and expansion, the consular nobility that dominated the senate had become almost a closed caste often more concerned with preserving their own power and prestige and pursuing their own narrow rivalries than with promoting the welfare of Rome as a whole.

In the century before the First Punic War, the regular election of plebeians to the consulship had brought a number of new families into prominence within the senatorial

leadership. By 264 B.C., however, these newcomers had begun to coalesce with the old patrician families to prevent further additions to their ranks, and the consular nobility became an exclusive oligarchy dominated by a handful of powerful noble families. For example, in the one hundred years from 232 to 133 B.C., there were two hundred and eleven consuls, including suffect consuls elected to replace those who had died in office. All came from only fifty-three *gentes*, and one hundred and forty-five came from only twenty-seven, while ninety-one came from a mere eleven. It is even more significant, however, that, based on the male line of descent, a maximum of fifty-one individual families and separate groups of closely related families represented the twenty-seven *gentes* that account for one hundred and forty-five consuls, and a maximum of twenty-five individual families and separate groups of closely related families represented the eleven *gentes* that account for ninety-one consuls. If ties of marriage, adoption, and descent in the female line were also considered, the exclusivity of these families would appear even more striking. Finally, of the nineteen *gentes* represented by only one consul from 232 to 133, seventeen were plebeian. Of those seventeen, fourteen had had no previous consuls, two had had only one, one had had only two, and eleven produced no more consuls in the remaining two centuries of the Republic. Of the six who did have successors, only one had a significant number with five, while three had only one, one had two, and one had three. Clearly, therefore, it was not only difficult for families from nonconsular plebeian *gentes* to reach the consulship, but it was also difficult for them to maintain their consular dignity in competition with their more entrenched rivals from older consular patrician and plebeian families.

A few powerful families were able to monopolize the office of consul because the number of consuls was not increased, despite the greatly increased need for high executives as a result of overseas expansion. Instead, the senate greatly increased the practice of proroguing (prolonging) a consul's or a praetor's military command or provincial governorship after his normal year of office. Magistrates whose terms of service were prorogued became promagistrates. Such men were able to use their extended terms to capitalize on the opportunities that their positions gave them to acquire clients and financial resources to further their domination of high offices.

The result was a very unhealthy political situation for Rome. Unchecked by any challenges from without, the nobility competed with increasing intensity among themselves for dominance within the senate and for the corresponding prizes of *gloria* (glory), *dignitas* (esteem), and *auctoritas* (prestige) that came with high office and military triumph. Simultaneously, the holding of high office helped a man to amass the resources of money and patronage needed to maintain or increase his family's advantage in competition with other nobles.

Political Groupings Political struggles within the nobility were not organized on the basis of political parties with formal organizations and programs. While rivals might well have different ideas concerning domestic issues or foreign affairs, their supporters were organized on a highly personal basis of family connections, personal friendship, mutually advantageous coalitions, and patronage. Some individuals and families might build up a relatively stable faction of personal supporters that would last for some time. Others might last only for one electoral campaign. Patterns of cooperation or rivalry between certain individuals, families, or groups of families can sometimes be traced, but usually the detailed data necessary for drawing firm conclusions about the factional alliances involved in any particular political event do not exist.

Changing Political Behavior As the social and financial rewards of political power increased with the power and wealth of Rome, the temptations increased to violate the customary rules governing political behavior in order to secure competitive advantage. Values and behavior necessary to preserve a republi-

can form of government gradually began to disintegrate under the pressure. The way was imperceptibly opened for one man to overcome his competitors and dominate all in the manner of Hellenistic monarchs, whom Roman nobles had replaced as the masters of the Mediterranean world.

A good example of the process can be seen in the career of the elder Scipio Africanus during the Second Punic War. After Scipio's father and uncle had been killed in Spain, the senate gave the young Scipio a proconsular command to continue the war there, even though he was only twenty-five and had held no office beyond the aedileship. His successful prosecution of the war in Spain emboldened him to return to Rome and run for the consulship in 206 B.C., although he was far younger than normal and had never held the praetorship, as was normal for a consular candidate. His popularity as a military hero and his promise to invade Africa if elected guaranteed his victory, despite the opposition of rival families and conservative-minded senators who objected to his unorthodox career.

Scipio's opponents sought to block him by placing him in charge of the disgraced survivors of Cannae and denying him public funds for any invasion. He used his popularity to raise enough funds and volunteers to man, equip, and train a first-rate army to invade North Africa in 204 B.C. Such power and independence in one man did not bode well for the Republic, which depended upon the willingness of political rivals to work within the established political ground rules.

Other ambitious individuals were quick to follow the path taken by Scipio as they sought to equal or surpass his achievement. For example, T. Quinctius Flamininus had never been elected to any office beyond the junior one of military tribune, but he was made a propraetor in charge of Tarentum in 205 B.C. and while not yet thirty was elected consul for 198 B.C. to prosecute the Second Macedonian War.

The extraordinarily rapid rise of such young men as Scipio and Flamininus prompted their rivals and many other senators, who saw in their careers a danger to the Republican system, to procure laws to enforce what custom and tradition could no longer safeguard. Shortly after Flamininus was elected consul, the praetorship was made a prerequisite before holding the consulship (ca. 197 B.C.). In 180 the curule magistracies were systematically regulated by the *lex Villia Annalis:* minimum ages were set for holding the curule aedileship, the praetorship, and the consulship—probably thirty-six, thirty-nine, and forty-two, respectively—and a minimum interval of two years between the end of one office and the holding of another was required. The status of the quaestorship at this time is not clear, but a minimum age of twenty-five may have been fixed for it, and it became the normal, if not mandatory, first office of the senatorial *cursus honorum.* Finally, in 151 B.C. a law was passed to forbid reelection to the consulship.

Still, the temptation to violate traditional political norms intensified with political competition. The increasing use of questionable campaign practices is reflected in the *lex Baebia* of 181, which attempted to regulate them. Efforts by wealthy nobles to extend their private *clientelae* and impress the people through their wealth evidently necessitated the *lex Orchia,* also in 181, which restricted the number of guests that one could invite to dinner. The ineffectiveness of such laws, however, is revealed by the passage of even more stringent regulations on entertainments in 161 and the imposition of the death penalty for bribery in 159 B.C.

When the prizes are large and the temptations correspondingly great, mere laws are not enough to restrain undesirable behavior. At Rome, the legal restraints on political behavior were especially weak in any case. The political system at Rome was not based on a written constitution that could be altered only after a lengthy process allowing due consideration and requiring the overwhelming approval of those responsible for making any changes. "Constitutional" matters were either merely customary or regulated by normal, *ad hoc* legislative acts like the *lex Villia Annalis.* All that an ambitious and popular leader had to do to circumvent such restraints was to procure a new law in his favor. For example, in 148 B.C. Scipio Aemilianus, the younger Africanus, was granted a special enactment to run for the consulship although he met none of the conditions set by the *lex Villia Annalis.* Another special law also gave him the command against Carthage, an action that breached the customary right of the senate to assign consuls to military commands. Finally, in 135 B.C. he was granted an exemption from the law that forbade repetition of the consulship so that he could take charge of the war against Numantia.

Other ambitious men dispensed with legality altogether. In 189 B.C., for instance, the consul Gnaeus Manlius Vulso exceeded his authority in attacking the Galatians. In 173, M. Popillius disobeyed express senatorial orders and attacked the Ligurians in order to obtain military laurels. He then used his political connections to escape punishment for his misdeeds.

One of the great problems with Republican provincial administration was how to control the actions of governors who abused their authority for political purposes. Individual governors were practically laws unto themselves in their provinces. They were far from the watchful eyes of their senatorial colleagues, and since they enjoyed supreme judicial and military power in their provinces, the provincials were at their mercy. Since they usually were to govern a particular province for only a year or two, they often had no interest in securing the long-term welfare of their charges; too often they were interested in using their power to extort as much money as they could from hapless provincials so that they would have the resources to advance their careers, pay off their debts, and maintain their status among competing peers back home. That is not to say that there were not many responsible and fair Roman governors who refused to put selfish interest above duty, but the bad ones were numerous enough to cause discontent in the provinces and concern in the senate.

The problem had become acute enough

by 149 to inspire the tribune L. Calpunius Piso to establish Rome's first permanent jury court, the *quaestio perpetua de rebus repetundis,* a tribunal in which provincials could bring charges of extortion against a former governor before a jury of senators and sue for the restitution of their losses. Unfortunately, this court often inspired greater rapacity on the part of ambitious governors, who wanted to make sure that they had money to bribe the jurors in the event of prosecution and still have enough left for other purposes. Also, the court became a weapon in the factional competition within the nobility as men tried to destroy their rivals by supporting their prosecution for extortion, the penalty for which was loss of citizenship and exile.

The entire Republican administrative system tended to intensify political competition at the expense of the kinds of sound, long-range policies needed to cope with the great and rapid changes produced by Rome's expansion. With the exception of the eighteen-month censorship, all of the higher magistracies were held for only one year. No one held office long enough to be able to put into effect consistent, long-range policies, and there was great pressure to think only in terms of what was expedient for gaining election to the next office.

This problem might not have been so serious if the senate had been a united body providing well-planned and uniform guidance, but it was not. It was often rent by factionalism and personal rivalries that were manipulated in the struggle for high office, which endowed the successful candidates with the prestige necessary for playing a leading role within the senate. Therefore, present politics rather than the future welfare of the Republic often dominated senators' actions. In simpler times, with less complex and fewer problems to face, this situation was not dangerous. But, when Rome had to cope with rapid socio-economic changes and the government of a far-flung empire, it became a fatal weakness and contributed to the worsening of the crises that these changes had helped to produce. Between 133 and 27 B.C. political in-fighting among the nobility often prevented solutions to the problems of discontented groups, and discontent increased so that political stability was undermined still further.

XIII

Roman Culture, 300 to 100 B.C.

Rome and Roman culture underwent a remarkable period of growth in the third and second centuries B.C. The influx of wealth as Rome assumed control of Italy and then an overseas empire stimulated the physical expansion of the city and the development of its architecture. Increased contact with the sophisticated Greeks of southern Italy, Sicily, and the Hellenistic East also helped to raise cultural life in general way beyond that of early Rome and began the process of creating a Mediterranean-wide Greco-Roman culture.

Development of Coinage Both the growth of the Roman economy and the influence of the Greeks can be seen in the development of Roman coinage. After the expulsion of the last Etruscan king (ca. 500 B.C.), the Romans had reverted to a basically subsistent agrarian economy that did not produce enough surplus wealth to support a high level of public works and cultural activity. Except for independent craftsmen, small shopkeepers, and a few traders, the majority of Romans, even aristocrats, had lived on and farmed their own soil outside the city. The low level of this agrarian economy before 300 B.C. is illustrated by the fact that the Roman word for money,

pecunia, is derived from the word *pecus,* cattle or sheep, which provided the standards of value in a pastoral, agrarian economy. In the fifth and fourth centuries B.C., irregular lumps of bronze, *aes rude,* which had to be weighed at each transaction, often took the place of actual cattle or sheep as a medium of exchange. Later, rectangular pieces of cast bronze replaced the irregular lumps, and the state guaranteed the purity of the bronze by a distinctive sign stamped into the metal. The stamped bronze was called *aes signatum.*

By 289 B.C. the economic needs of Rome had increased to the point where the Romans created a board of three moneyers, *triumviri monetales,* to supervise an official mint located in the temple of *Juno Moneta* on the Capitoline Hill and from whose name the words *mint* and *money* are ultimately derived. While it produced *aes signatum,* which was not true coinage because only its purity, not weight or value, was indicated by the stamp, this mint also introduced Rome's first real coins, called *asses* (sing. *as*) or *aes grave* ("heavy bronze"). These coins were circular in shape and were issued in units of one Roman pound, *libra* (ca. 11 oz.) or fractions thereof, as indicated by a standard mark.

Gradually reduced in size, the bronze *as*

(Top) The quadrigatus, a silver didrachma of the third century B.C., with the head of Janus on one side, (left) and on the reverse side Jupiter (holding a thunderbolt) and Victory in a quadriga (four-horse chariot) with ROMA inscribed below. (Bottom) A type of denarius introduced in 217 or 215 B.C. showing the head of the war goddess Bellona, and on the reverse side Castor and Pollux on horseback with ROMA inscribed below. (Courtesy The American Numismatic Society, New York).

remained the common coin used throughout the Republican period. Nevertheless, as the Romans became more deeply involved with the Greeks of southern Italy, especially during the war with Pyrrhus, they found it necessary to mint silver coins comparable to the silver coins commonly used by the Greeks. Whatever the precise date for the first issuance of such coins, the need for them would have become particularly great to finance the war against Pyrrhus, which took place in the territory of the southern Italian Greek city-states, where silver, as opposed to the bronze money of central Italy, was the primary medium of exchange.

The earliest Roman silver coins were two-drachma pieces, didrachms, and were clearly modelled on the silver coinage of Campania. During the Second Punic War, as the Roman economy became integrated with that of the entire Mediterranean world, the Romans introduced a lighter silver coin called the *denarius* (pl. *denarii*). With a small reduction in weight a few years later, the *denarius* was equal

to the Athenian drachma, which had been the most widely circulated coin in the Mediterranean up to that time. From about 170 B.C. the *denarius,* with its fractions the *quinarius* (one-half) and the *sestertius* (one-quarter), became the standard silver coinage of the Roman Republic. Six thousand *denarii* equalled a talent. Some idea of what these monetary units were worth in economic terms can be gained from the fact that a denarius was about the average daily pay of a hired laborer.

Architecture and Art   Prior to the Punic Wars and Roman expansion into the Greek East, the city of Rome was little more than a provincial farming town and regional market. Except for its defensive walls, which had been constructed probably with the help of Greek craftsmen after the Gallic sack around 390, and a few major temples, which had been built under the influence of Etruscan designs, there was little in the way of serious architecture at Rome. After the Gallic sack, Rome had been rebuilt as haphazardly as it had grown up before. The majority of residents had continued to live in flimsy, flammable wattle-and-daub cottages, although the wealthy enjoyed more substantial houses with a central *atrium* open to the sky to provide light and fresh air. The larger homes, however, still did not have the gardens and colonnades that became the hallmarks of wealthier homes later. It was only in 338 B.C. that balconies were added to the upper floors of the shops, *tabernae,* around the Forum. Shortly thereafter, the ramming beaks, *rostra,* of ships captured at Antium (340 B.C.) were attached to the speakers' platform in the Forum. Both of these improvements gave the Roman civic and commercial center a more impressive appearance, but Rome still looked nothing like the major Greek cities of southern Italy.

By 300 B.C., however, the Romans had begun to undertake the kinds of great building projects for which they are famous. In 312, under the censor Appius Claudius Caecus, the Romans started the famous paved road that bears his name, the *Via Appia*. It was a military

The temple of Fortuna Virilis (214 B.C.) in the Forum Boarium at Rome. Its Ionic columns and the lines of its roof reveal the influence of Greek temple architecture. (Courtesy Fratelli Alinari, Florence)

road to link Rome with Capua and was the model for the great system of Roman roads that eventually extended all around the Mediterranean world. In the same year Appius Claudius started work on the first of Rome's aqueducts, the *Aqua Appia,* which was about a mile in length. In 272 B.C. it was dwarfed by the *Anio Vetus,* which carried fresh water for over fifty miles from the Sabine Hills.

During the third and especially the first half of the second century B.C., the rapid expansion of Rome stimulated building by both public officials and private benefactors. Victorious generals used large amounts of their booty to construct numerous roads, aqueducts, temples, public buildings, triumphal arches, and town houses that turned Rome into a major metropolis in the Hellenistic manner. The Greek influence can be seen in the adoption of Greek-style temple facades, the increased use of marble and other stone, and the use of the basilica design for public and commercial buildings.

Captured Greek statues adorned buildings both public and private, and when the demand outstripped the supply of Greek originals, Greek craftsmen were hired to make copies of Greek works or produce statues of Roman gods and heroes in the Hellenistic style. In the second century B.C., the late Hellenistic interest in portraying real people and the Romano-Etruscan practice of preserving the likenesses of ancestors in wax masks (*imagines*) and funerary portraits combined to produce a distinctly Roman style of realistic portrait sculpture in stone and bronze. Many fine examples of these portrait busts have survived, so that the features of many leading figures of the late Republic are familiar.

Greek fresco painting also had a major impact on Roman art. The Etruscans had already introduced the Romans to this type of wall decoration, but in the third and second centuries B.C. Greek artists were the most accomplished in this medium of painting. They were hired to depict in public buildings great events in Roman history, like the victories in the wars with Pyrrhus and Carthage. In the homes of the rich, fresco paintings and murals reproduced from Greek works illustrated scenes from Greek literature and provided beautiful still lifes, landscapes, and decorative designs just as fine prints and wallpaper are used in modern homes.

Literature In early Rome, literature in any significant sense of the word did not exist. Writing, like most everything else, was primarily for practical, mundane purposes such as keeping financial accounts, recording laws, noting important yearly secular and religious events, and preserving oracles and religious rituals. Beginning in the third century B.C., however, the Romans were increasingly influenced by the advanced literary culture of the Greeks. While many Romans like Cato the Elder affected to scorn the "weak Greeklings" whom they had conquered, they learned Greek in increasing numbers, as did even Cato himself, for several reasons.

First of all, Greek was the international language of the wider world of which Rome had become an important part after the conquest of Italy and Carthage. In order to deal with the leaders of Greece and the Hellenistic kingdoms as equals, it was necessary for Roman senators to understand and speak Greek. Second, there was a certain curiosity and a practical need on the part of the Romans to find out more about the Greeks, whom they increasingly conquered and had to control. Third, despite their feelings of moral and military superiority, many Romans must have felt a certain amount of awe and admiration before the accomplishments of an older, more refined culture and wished to imitate it. Finally, Greek literature had a certain practical and social value for the Roman upper classes. Greek allowed for the formulation and expression of far more complex concepts and ideas than early Latin and could provide a model for expanding the expressiveness of Latin itself in an increasingly complex world. Greek orators had perfected the principles of persuasive rhetoric, which were very useful to Roman aristocrats in senatorial debates, speeches at trials, and addresses to Roman voters in the Forum. Furthermore, a knowledge of Greek and appreciation of Greek literature was a mark of social distinction, which helped the upper classes set themselves apart from the lower and gave them the sense of their own superiority that all elites crave. These factors created a demand for teachers of Greek, who were supplied in the form of educated Greek captives serving as tutors in the homes of their wealthy captors. Those who were later freed often set up grammar schools, where they dispensed their wisdom to the sons of aspiring nonaristocrats for a fee.

Livius Andronicus (ca. 284–ca. 204 B.C.) One of these teachers was Lucius Livius Andronicus, who had been born in Tarentum about 284 B.C. and had been brought to Rome in 272 as a slave in the house of a Roman senator named Lucius Livius (Salinator?). Upon being freed he had added his patron's name to his own, as was the custom, and became Lucius Livius Andronicus. Andronicus became not only a teacher of Greek and Latin, but a translator and adaptor of Greek literature for Roman audiences. One of his earliest works was an adaptation of Homer's *Odyssey* into Latin Saturnian meter. Saturnian meter was native to Latin poetry and was an accentual meter based on the stress placed on syllables within a word, not a quantitative meter like that of Greek poetry, which is concerned with the kind of vowel, whether open or closed, in a syllable and how long the syllable is held in speech.

The *Odyssey* was a very good choice to adapt for Roman readers. Its description of travel in exotic lands appealed to Romans, whose horizons were just then extending beyond the narrow confines of Italy. Also, unlike the *Iliad,* it did not dwell on the Greek defeat of the Trojans, whom the Romans by now were claiming as their ancestors. Odysseus' wanderings and hardships even provided the models for those of Aeneas, who supposedly had led the Trojan refugees to Italy. Therefore, if not the first piece of Greek literature adapted to Latin, Andronicus' *Odyssey* was the first to attain wide popularity at Rome. It continued to be used as a textbook by schoolmasters for centuries. In the late first century B.C., the poet Horace once recalled having to memorize passages from it when he was a boy.

In 240 B.C. the aediles, who were planning the annual festival of the Roman Games, *Ludi Romani,* wanted something special with which to celebrate the recent end of the First Punic War. They asked Livius Andronicus to adapt a Greek tragedy and a Greek comedy for the Roman stage. He not only wrote the texts but performed as the chief actor. His efforts aroused great enthusiasm and set the trend for Roman drama ever after.

The Creativity of Roman Literature The fact that all subsequent Roman authors freely borrowed from the Greeks has often led people to charge that Roman literature is wholly derivative and not worthy of respect. That is not a legitimate view. The ancient Greek and Roman concept of creativity is different from the modern. For an ancient artist the supreme challenge was to work within a given tradition in order to refine it and improve it, not to create something startlingly new. What the best Roman authors did was to adapt Greek literary forms to the expression of distinctively Roman themes and ideas. Roman literature was intensely patriotic, even nationalistic, portraying the glories of Roman history and the values that distinguished Romans from other people.

Naevius (ca. 270–199 B.C.) The first native Roman to achieve success as an author was Livius Andronicus' slightly younger contemporary Gnaeus Naevius. He was proficient in tragedy, comedy, epic, and satire. He continued to use the native Saturnian meter and was Rome's first nationalistic poet. He wrote the first important plays that dealt with events of Roman history, *fabulae praetextae,* rather than Greek mythology. He also wrote the first patriotic Roman epic. Appropriately enough, Naevius' subject was the First Punic War, in which he had served. He wove in legends which told of Rome's founding by descendants of Aeneas and thus provided Vergil (70–19 B.C.) with useful material for the *Aeneid.* In his plays Naevius often made critical comments about contemporary political figures. Among those offended was the powerful family of the Caecilii Metelli. In 206 B.C., Quintus Metellus

retaliated by having him imprisoned. He was freed only after writing two apologetic plays. He then lived as an exile at Utica in North Africa, where he died. His fate set greater limits to the use of personal invective on the Roman stage in contrast with the license of Greek Old Comedy.

Ennius (239–169 B.C.) The heir of Naevius as a master of tragic, comic, and epic poetry was Quintus Ennius. He was a native Italian born at Rudiae in southern Italy. The fortuitous circumstance of being a native Italian living near the Greek cities of southern Italy and under Roman domination made him trilingual, knowing Oscan, Greek, and Latin. His talent was equally diverse. He had a thorough understanding of Greek thought, a real ear and feeling for language, and a genuine admiration for Rome. His love of Rome overcame the anti-Hellenism of Cato the Elder, who brought him to Rome in 204 B.C., after they had served together in the Roman army on Sardinia. At Rome Ennius quickly became acquainted with other leading Romans, such as the elder Scipio Africanus, who acted as his patrons.

Ennius' tragedies were more admired than his comedies. They reveal the influence of Euripides in their subjects, rationalism, and critical liberalism. He also wrote some philosophical books and some shorter poems of a satirical nature. His greatest achievement, however, was his patriotic epic poem entitled the *Annales.* In eighteen books, the *Annales* dealt with the tales of Rome's past and the history of the Second Punic War. Thus, Ennius carried on the process of integrating the legends of Rome's founding with real history. The poem's major innovation was the use of quantitative meter on the Greek model instead of the native Saturnian meter. In both respects, therefore, Ennius served as another of Vergil's major models.

Specialization after Ennius
Pacuvius (ca. 220–130 B.C.) and Accius (170–ca. 85 B.C.) Marcus Pacuvius and Lu-

cius Accius tried to carry on the Naevian and Ennian tradition of mastering all major poetic genres, but they concentrated their greatest efforts on tragedy. Pacuvius was Ennius' nephew. Extensive fragments of his plays survive and reveal that they had good intellectual content, impressive characterization, and powerful language. Accius seems to have shared these characteristics, so that later Horace and Quintilian counted him among Rome's greatest writers.

Lucilius (ca. 180–103 B.C.) In contrast to Pacuvius and Accius, Gaius Lucilius concentrated his attention on satire, which is Rome's most important contribution to the genres of Western literature. It grew out of a strong native tradition whereby famous people had hoped to avoid excessive pride and the jealousy of the gods by having their faults as well as their virtues pointed out in a jesting manner during such events as triumphal celebrations and funeral processions. Lucilius really made the genre of satire in its modern sense: sharp, biting, witty commentary on the social and political life of various people and the times in general. As a close friend of the younger Scipio Africanus, Lucilius had access to many of the important men who looked to Scipio for leadership. He was particularly critical of Scipio's opponents, as one might expect. While his Latin was not elegant, Lucilius had a natural, vigorous sense of humor that was highly appreciated by the later satirists Horace and Martial and the critic Quintilian.

Plautus (ca. 254–184 B.C.) and Terence (ca. 195–159 B.C.) Tragedy and comedy were the first literary genres to reach their highest stage of development at Rome. In contrast to early tragedy, however, which is known only through fragmentary quotations and comments in later works, Roman comedy is represented by a body of twenty-seven complete plays, twenty-one assigned to Titus Maccius Plautus and six belonging to Publius Terentius Afer. Few facts are known about the life of Plautus. Even his real name was unknown until 1815, when the oldest manuscript of his plays was discovered. He was not a native-born Roman but an Umbrian from the Italian town of Sarsina, a fact that shows how Roman culture, as in the case of Livius Andronicus and Ennius, was enriched by the incorporation of conquered and allied peoples into the Roman state. Just as with modern New York, London, or Paris, few of the great literary figures associated with ancient Rome were natives of the city itself.

A little more is known about Plautus' younger contemporary Terence. According to the early second-century A.D. biographer Suetonius, Terence was an African who had been born at Carthage and brought to Rome as the young slave of a senator named Terentius Lucanus. It is possible, therefore, that Terence is the Western world's first Black author. Terentius is said to have recognized the young man's intellectual gifts and set him free after giving him a good education. Terence's talents brought him to the attention of Scipio Aemilianus, the younger Africanus, who helped him to launch his career. Unfortunately, his talent was soon extinguished when he died during a trip to Greece in 159 B.C.

The comedies of Plautus and Terence, and of others whose works are preserved only in fragments, underline the growing impact of Greek culture on the Romans in the late third and throughout the second century B.C. Both authors freely borrowed their plots, situations, and characters from the Greek New Comedy of the Hellenistic era, especially as represented by Menander, Diphilus, and Philemon, but Plautus infused his plays more with the native comic traditions of Italy, which Roman intellectuals had not yet learned to despise, as they did when the influence of older Greek culture became even stronger in the latter two-thirds of the second century B.C. Despite the external trappings of urbane Greek New Comedy, Plautine comedy is basically farce inspired by the native Italian Atellan farces and the ribald humor of the Etruscan Fescennine verses. It is rich in slapstick, fast-paced wordplay, and satirical comment on matters of public concern, elements which are lacking in the surviving examples of New Comedy. The latter was much more genteel and philosophical in nature.

Terence, the younger author, reveals the greater impact of Hellenism on the younger generation of Romans in the second century B.C. He was patronized by aristocrats like Scipio Aemilianus, who had received a more thoroughly Greek education than their predecessors and had begun to look down on their native culture before it had a chance to reach a greater level of sophistication built on its own foundations. Terence's plays are much more intellectual and less farcical than the plays of Plautus. Terence's Latin reflects the speech of the educated upper class rather than the less polished, more racy talk of the man in the street. His plays try to teach the psychological lessons of New Comedy. They make good literature but not such entertaining stage productions as those of Plautus. That is why Terence sometimes had trouble holding the attention of his audiences, as he complained in the introductions to his *Phormio* and to his *Mother-in-Law*. Moreover, it is significant that after Terence there are no more important writers of Roman comedy. The growing Hellenism of the educated elite prejudiced them against writing in a manner that would appeal to a mass audience. They turned to other forms of writing, while the average Roman enjoyed revivals of Plautus' and occasionally Terence's old plays, which have continued to inspire comic playwrights down to the present.

The plays of Plautus and Terence are not only important as major contributions to Western comic drama but are also historical reflections of the great cultural, social, and economic changes that affected Rome with the aquisition of an empire. Obviously, the influence of Greek New Comedy on Roman authors mirrors the impact of Greek culture in general. Moreover, New Comedy appealed to the Romans precisely because of the parallels that they saw with their own times. The prominence of slave characters corresponds to the tremendous increase of slavery in Roman society. The conflicts between fathers and sons or husbands and wives that often provide the plots are similar to the conflict between the more cosmopolitan younger generation of Romans like Scipio Aemilianus and Romans of the old school like Cato the Elder and emphasize the growing independence of upperclass women. The prominence of merchants, high-living young men, and gold-digging mistresses mirror the great influx of wealth that Rome was experiencing. The plays may have been set in Greece, but the topics were as much Roman as Greek.

Prose Literature   It took much longer for Roman prose to reach its highest development than it did comedy. In fact, the first significant Roman prose authors were historians who wrote in Greek after the Second Punic War. Many of the early Roman historians are called annalists because they organized their works on the year-by-year official records kept by the College of Pontiffs. The two earliest known historians, Quintus Fabius Pictor and Lucius Cincius Alimentus, were both Roman senators who had served in the Second Punic War; Alimentus had even been captured by Hannibal. They both wrote histories from the founding of Rome down to their own times. They were particularly interested in the Punic Wars and sought to portray the policies and actions of Rome's leaders in the best possible light.

Greek was the logical choice of language for them for several reasons. First, the only models for writing prose history were Greek, and it would have been easier to use existing Greek vocabulary and concepts than to create new ones in Latin. Second, the use of Greek made their works available to both Rome's educated elite and the Greeks, who were becoming more interested in Rome as Roman power grew but seldom bothered to learn Latin, which they considered too crude and beneath their dignity. Third, Roman writers wanted to counteract the favorable view of Carthage that Greek historians presented in their accounts of the Punic Wars.

Cato the Elder (234–149 B.C)   The first Roman to compose an important history in

Latin was Cato the Elder. It was entitled *Origines, The Origins,* and covered the early history of Italy and the founding of Rome as well as the recent past. For the recent period, by leaving out the names of others and including parts of his own speeches, Cato deflated other prominent men and glorified himself. In one famous episode Cato underscored the omission of famous names by giving only the name of Surus, one of Hannibal's elephants. Besides his history of Rome, Cato made many other important contributions to Latin prose. He wrote major works on law, medicine, and agriculture, the last of which, the *De Agricultura,* survives as the earliest extant work of Latin prose and a valuable source of information on Roman life and economic history in the second century B.C. Cato also published a book on rhetoric and was the first Roman to publish his own speeches.

Rhetoric The publication of Cato's speeches and his work on rhetoric emphasize the growing importance of the art of rhetoric and rhetorical training. With the growth of Rome as a world power, the state needed officials and leaders capable of clearly expounding problems and policies to the voters, in senatorial debates, and in dealing with foreign governments. The increased complexity of Roman life also meant more lawsuits and, therefore, a need for more trained advocates to plead them. Naturally, great Greek masters of oratory and rhetoric like Demosthenes, Isocrates, and Thucydides served as models of the formal practice of these arts at Rome.

Philosophy Hand in hand with rhetoric and oratory at Rome, an interest grew in philosophy, which meant Greek philosophy, of course. Philosophical systems were useful to the practical-minded Romans because they could provide the conceptual and logical structures for developing ideas in a speech, sharpen skill in debate, or clothe personal or partisan purposes with high-sounding phrases. The formal study of philosophy at Rome also received a big boost in 155 B.C. when the Athenians sent an embassy made up of the heads of three major philosophical schools: Critolaus the Peripatetic, Diogenes the Stoic, and Carneades the Academic sceptic. While waiting for an opportunity to address the senate they gave a series of public lectures that aroused much interest.

Carneades the Academic made the greatest impression. As a sceptic he had no absolute dogmas or guides on ethical and intellectual questions. He substituted a system of probabilty, and in an eclectic spirit set out to combine the best aspects of all philosophical schools in order to improve the human condition. To show the weakness of absolute dogmas, he argued one side of a question one day and convinced the audience that he was right and then, just as convincingly, argued the other side on the following day. Cato the Elder was scandalized and expressed fear that this sceptical approach would undermine traditional Roman morals.

More compatible with traditional Roman values was the philosophy of Stoicism. The Stoic doctrines of a divinely created world brotherhood and order and its stress upon duty, the upholding of established authority, and the natural rule of the wise were tailor-made for Romans seeking to justify their growing empire to themselves and others. These ideas had been popularized by Panaetius of Rhodes, who lived for some time as a guest of Scipio Aemilianus and his famous friend Gaius Laelius, who was often called *Sapiens,* "The Wise ," because of his Stoic learning. Another Stoic, Blossius of Cumae, was the tutor of the tribunes Tiberius and Gaius Gracchus and may have had some influence on their reforms to aid the poor in 133 and 123 B.C. (see pp. 156–160).

The fourth major school of Hellenistic Greek philosophy, Epicureanism, did not find many important adherents at Rome until after 100 B.C. The tendency to go to extremes in adopting Epicurus' doctrines about the lack of divine punishments and the primacy of pleasure as life's goal horrified traditional-minded, conservative Roman aristocrats. Therefore, as early as 173 B.C. the senate banished Epicureans from Rome.

The Romans themselves made no notable original contributions to philosophy. They had little patience with the intricacies and hair-splittings of philosophical controversies. They mostly received the established systems of the Greek schools, chose what suited their purposes, and applied it to their lives. For example, those who were concerned with law adopted the rigorous dialectic of the Stoics in order to give structure and order to Roman law.

Law   By 200 B.C. skill in Roman law required more than simple knowledge of the Twelve Tables. About that time Sextus Aelius Paetus published a systematic legal work in three parts: the text of the Twelve Tables; various interpretations that had clarified and expanded the application of those laws over the years; and detailed presentation of the various forms of lawsuits and their appropriate *formulae*. In the last part of the second and early first century B.C. various members of the family of the Mucii Scaevolae rose to prominence as *jurisconsulti*, interpreters of the law, who trained students in law and gave advice to those seeking clarification of legal points. The greatest of these men was Quintus Mucius Scaevola the Pontiff, a teacher of Cicero, who systematized such matters as wills, damages, contracts, and legal procedures. His methods and systems provided the basis for all further such legal work.

Religion   While law was becoming more structured and logical under the influence of Greek philosophy, Roman religion was becoming more emotional and uninhibited under the influence of ecstatic mystery cults from the Greek East. The worship of the Greek god Dionysus, or Bacchus as the Romans called him, had become very popular among the Greeks of southern Italy by the third century B.C. The drunken, orgiastic revels of this cult provided a welcome emotional release from the harsh, unremitting routine of daily life faced by the poorer classes,

especially the women. Many conservative Romans were not only shocked by the uninhibited behavior of Dionysiac worshipers, but as the cult spread they feared that its secret, orgiastic meetings masked a conspiracy against Roman rule in Italy. In 186 B.C. the senate passed a decree (still extant) against the Bacchants and forbade, under penalty of death, more than five people to meet together for private worship in Rome or Italy without permission from the praetor.

The senators also sought to restrain the overwrought emotionalism of the worship of Cybele, the Great Mother, that had been imported to Rome in 205 B.C. during the dark days of the Second Punic War after consultation of the Sibylline Books. The cult of the Great Mother centered around the death and resurrection of the god Attis, who was both her son and husband. The rites symbolized the annual death and rebirth of vegetation. The actual cult object was a black stone brought from Pessinus in Asia Minor and housed in a temple on the Palatine. Wild celebrations associated with it were performed by gorgeously clad eunuch priests and included riotous outdoor parades, ecstatic dances to the beat of drums and cymbals, and castrations and self-mutilations performed at the climax of religious fervor. Roman leaders were properly horrified and, despite the state's official sponsorship of the cult, denied Roman citizens the right to participate.

Similar attempts, often futile, were made to restrain other eastern cults, such as that of the Egyptian Isis, but still they kept coming. Their arrival often coincided with periods of great social and economic stress and upheavals accompanying Roman expansion, in face of which the sober religion of Rome's simpler past was unable to meet the psychological needs of the average person. Therefore, partly in response to the needs of the people as well as a result of increased wealth, the state greatly expanded the size and scope of religious festivals, *ludi*, at Rome. They included circus races, perhaps at one point a magical attempt to influence the cycle of the seasons and the rotations of the heavenly bodies associated with them, gladiatorial combats (introduced in 264 B.C. from Etruria, where they were part of funeral rites for departed spirits to supply them with blood and vitality), and dramatic performances, the first of which were held at the *Ludi Romani,* September games in honor of Jupiter, in 240 B.C. Other major festivals were the *Ludi Plebeii,* Plebeian Games, in November and also for Jupiter; the *Ludi Apollinares* for Apollo in July; and the *Ludi Megalenses* in honor of the Great Mother, the *Ludi Cereales* for Ceres, and the *Ludi Florales* for Flora, the goddess of plants, all in April. Except for the *Ludi Apollinares,* these festivals were put on by the aediles and brought them so much public recognition and popularity that they had an interest in expanding the number of days and events involved, often at their own expense, as time went on.

The educated Roman elite lost faith in the old Roman gods and mythologies. They often cynically exploited the priesthoods and official religion for political purposes. For them, Greek rationalism replaced the old faith. Many adopted the ideas of the Hellenistic thinker Euhemerus. He argued that the gods were simply human beings who, like Hercules, had by their superhuman deeds become saviors of the world. His work on the origin of the gods was so popular that Ennius translated it into Latin. It had a significant impact on the Roman aristocracy's ambition for fame and glory and is the underlying assumption behind the deification of Roman emperors later on.

Education Expanded cultural and intellectual life created a need for more formal education at Rome. In the early days, when Roman life was primarily rural for aristocrat and peasant alike, education such as it was had centered around home and family. Slaves were not used as tutors. The mother and other female relatives trained the children until at least the age of seven. After that, girls remained under their mothers' tutelage to learn about household managment, while boys accompanied their fathers into the fields and Forum to learn how to make a living and be good citizens. Fathers considered it one of their gravest duties to furnish precepts and examples from which their sons could learn their roles as citizens. Plutarch, in his biography of Cato the Elder, gives a splendid picture of how meticulously a traditional Roman reared his son.

At fifteen, a young male became a man and put on the *toga virilis,* toga of manhood. Soon the young man left his father's personal care. A young aristocrat was often placed by his father in the hands of an old and distinguished friend to further his training for public life. Then, after a year or two, at about seventeen, the young aristocrat entered military service. First, as a soldier in the ranks, he learned how to fight and obey orders. Then, he joined a general's staff to learn the techniques of command. After that, the young man apprenticed himself to another older man at Rome to complete his training in political life.

The purpose of this system was not only to provide a basic education in practical matters, but also to inculcate the rigid system of Roman moral values and service to the state as passed on in the ancestral customs, *mos maiorum.* This ideal is seen for example in the Roman attitude toward athletic training. Greeks fostered athletics for health, beauty, and personal satisfaction in excelling through competition as much as for military training. Roman physical education centered primarily on training for war, and conservative Romans were shocked at the nudity and self-indulgence associated with Greek athletics.

In the third and second centuries, however, with the increasing interest in Greek culture, Romans began to adopt features of Greek education. Wealthy Romans began to use learned Greek slaves to instruct the young in Greek language and literature. Greek freedmen set up grammar schools to teach the children of those who could not afford slave tutors. At first only Greek was taught, but as Latin literature became established Latin grammar schools appeared too. In the second century professional Greek philosophers were even coming to Rome to offer instruction at a higher level. By the end of the second century aristocratic Romans were no longer satisfied with the instruction available at Rome and were beginning to finish their formal education by studying with one of the famous masters of philosophy or rhetoric in Greek cultural centers like Athens or Rhodes.

That is not to say that the old mode of education disappeared. Rather, as the early years of Cicero show in the first century B.C., the two existed side by side. The old system still sought to instill Roman youths with the old traditions and values, while training in Greek studies gave them useful intellectual tools and cultured grace. In this way, the Romans created the Greco-Roman cultural blend that has left a lasting impression on Western language, literature, art, and thought.

XIV

The Gracchi and the Struggle over Land Reform, 133 to 121 B.C.

By 133 B.C., the socio-economic changes resulting from the Punic Wars and Rome's rapid expansion overseas were producing serious problems and discontent among a number of groups. The attempts of Tiberius Sempronius Gracchus and his brother Gaius to deal with some of these problems and satisfy the interests of disaffected elements ushered in a century of increasingly violent political upheavals that helped eventually to destroy the Roman Republic. Therefore, the careers of these two men and the circumstances surrounding them constitute one of the most intensively studied subjects in Roman history.

Sources for the Period of the Gracchi, 133–121 B.C. Unfortunately, the sources for this crucial period are not nearly so extensive or reliable as for the preceding one. There is no extant contemporary source. Although he lived through the Gracchan crisis and it colored the later stages of his writing, Polybius ended his history with the year 145/44 B.C. The continuation of Polybius down to about 78 B.C. by Posidonius (see p. 258) is lost. Even the most extensive secondhand account, Books 58 to 61 of Livy, which would have preserved much valuable detail from contemporary or

nearly contemporary sources, is also lost except for the brief summaries of the *Periochae* and the sparse outlines derived from him in the late Empire (see p. 515). The few relevant fragments from Books 34 and 35 of Diodorus Siculus and from Books 24 and 25 of Cassius Dio have little value. The same is true for Book 2 (sections 2–7) of Velleius Paterculus. The only extensive accounts are Plutarch's biographies of Tiberius and Gaius, which are naturally limited in scope, and sections nine to twenty-six in Book 1 of Appian's *Civil Wars* (Books 13 to 17 of his history as a whole).

The Lack of Military Recruits Traditionally, the Roman legions were recruited from landowning citizens (*assidui*) whose property, usually small family farms, was equal to a certain minimum value. This requirement was supposed to ensure that they could provide the weapons and equipment necessary for legionary warfare.* Despite successive lowering of the minimum qualification, by 133 B.C. the casualties from a century of almost constant

---

* Men without the requisite wealth were used as rowers in Roman fleets or as craftsmen and other service personnel necessary in large armies.

warfare and the decline of small farmers as a result of accompanying economic changes had combined to reduce dangerously the number of recruits available for legionary service.

In 145 or 140 B.C., Gaius Laelius, a close friend of Scipio Aemilianus, had tried to relieve the problem by proposing a law to reinforce the Licinio-Sextian laws of 367, which supposedly limited to 500 iugera (about 320 acres) the amount of public land that an individual could hold, and to resettle on surplus land people who had lost their farms. When he met with vehement opposition from many fellow senators, he decided to withdraw his proposal and avoid an obviously sensitive issue. In 133, however, Tiberius Sempronius Gracchus refused to avoid a confrontation under similar circumstances.

The Tribuneship of Tiberius Gracchus, 133 B.C.

When the 30-year-old Tiberius Gracchus took office as tribune of the people in 133 B.C., he bemoaned the impoverishment of Roman citizens and worried about the loss of recruits for Roman legions. Without consulting the senate, he immediately introduced before the *concilium plebis* his famous agrarian bill designed to break up the large estates created out of public land and to divide them among landless Roman citizens. It had been drafted not by Tiberius, the mere spokesman, but by Appius Claudius Pulcher, the "first man" (*princeps*) of the senate, and by two learned jurists, P. Licinius Crassus and P. Mucius Scaevola, the consul of 133 B.C. It ordered the state to repossess all public land in excess of 320 acres plus an allowance of 160 acres for each of two sons. The holders of estates between 320 and 640 acres were guaranteed clear title, unencumbered by taxes or rent, and reimbursement for any improvements, such as buildings or plantings, on the land to be repossessed. The repossessed land was to be assigned to landless citizens in lots varying in size probably from nine up to eighteen acres and was to be subject to a nominal rent payable to the state. The allotments were inalienable and entailed against sale or transfer.

Although it was unusual and was bound to inflame opinion against Tiberius in the senate, his failure to consult that body was neither unconstitutional nor unprecedented. In 232 B.C., Gaius Flaminius had obtained enactment of his agrarian law without consulting the senate (see p. 96). Therefore, since a majority of the senators were probably opposed to any such law, it must have seemed pointless to bring it up there at all. Far more rash and revolutionary was Tiberius' later refusal to abide by the veto of a fellow tribune.

The Land Bill Vetoed   On the day of the vote, the farmers flocked in from the country in unprecedented numbers. After a moving speech, Tiberius ordered the clerk to read the bill to the people. Suddenly Octavius, a fellow tribune, interposed his veto on behalf of the bill's opponents. Tiberius adjourned the assembly in the hope that Octavius would change his mind before the next meeting. The following day Octavius again vetoed the bill. Because the assembly was on the verge of a riot, friends persuaded Tiberius to submit the bill to the senate. When it met with predictably overwhelming and bitter opposition, Tiberius came away more determined than ever to win his cause and took a series of ever more radical steps to parry the traditional constitutional weapons used by his opponents.

The Deposition of Octavius   To gain passage of his reform, Tiberius had to overcome Octavius' veto. To ensure enough popular support (and perhaps also to get back at his opponents in the senate, who, whatever their motives for opposing him, were also wealthy landholders), Tiberius altered his original proposal to make more land and money available for land distribution. The exact changes are unclear, but perhaps they included reduction or elimination of compensation for the confiscation of improved land and of the amount of land that could be retained for children. If this action did not induce his opponents to persuade Octavius to remove his veto against the original proposal, Tiberius could count on the bill being so attractive to voters in the *concilium plebis* that they would support a daring move to depose Octavius and so nullify his veto.

Octavius persisted in his veto. Tiberius argued that he was working against the interests of the plebs instead of for them as a tribune should and took the fateful step of calling for a vote of removal. The favorable votes of eighteen of the thirty-five tribes would decide. Even at the last minute Tiberius gave Octavius a chance to relent. When the first seventeen tribes had voted against Octavius, Tiberius held up the voting for a moment to appeal to his colleague to change his mind. The latter remained obdurate. The voting resumed, and Octavius was divested of his tribunate and forcibly removed from the tribune's bench.

The Agrarian Commission   To carry out the provisions of the land act, Tiberius asked the people to appoint a commission of three members consisting of himself, his younger brother, Gaius, and his father-in-law, Appius Claudius. The commission was later granted full judicial powers with *imperium* to determine what lands were public and what private, to repossess all public land not exempt by the law, and to distribute it to new settlers. Ample funds were required to pay the salaries of surveyors and other officials as well as to help the new settlers make a start by providing them with housing, tools, work animals, seed, and even subsistence till the crops were harvested. Now Tiberius' opponents in the senate, which traditionally controlled appropriations, had a chance to stop him. They appropriated operating expenses of only a denarius and a half a day. Tiberius took another radical step to thwart them.

The Pergamene Treasure   Attalus III of Pergamum had upon his death willed his personal fortune and kingdom to the Roman people (see p. 122). This matter usually would have been handled in the senate, but Tiberius,

casting about for new sources of money, at once requested the people to make these funds available for the use of the commission.* Thus thwarted, his opponents began to threaten his life. To prepare the ground for violence, they circulated the rumor that he was planning to declare himself king and had retained for that purpose the diadem, scepter, and royal vestments of the Pergamene kings.

Tiberius Campaigns for a Second Term   To protect his legislation from annulment and to save himself from certain prosecution and probable death, Tiberius offered to run for a second term, a step contrary to recent custom but not unconstitutional since the sovereign people could reelect him in spite of law or custom just as they had, in violation of custom, elected his grandfather, Scipio Africanus, to supreme command during the Second Punic War.

Frustrated and embittered by Tiberius' refusal to abide by traditional political rules, his enemies were bent on his defeat and destruction. Tiberius was vulnerable because he had not won the support of the wealthy equestrian class or the city voters. The country voters who supported him might be too busy with their crops to turn up on election day. In his campaign speeches he hastily endeavored to win the majority that he needed by promising, it is said, to shorten the term of military service, to extend the right of appeal from the courts to the people, to admit jurors of equestrian rank to the court established by the Calpurnian Law in 149 B.C., to try governors for extortion in the provinces,† and to compensate the Italian allies for losses suffered through the land reform law. Although these

---

* It is not completely certain whether such a bill was ever passed or whether the mere threat to deprive the senate of control over provincial revenues caused that body to open up the state treasury for the use of the commission.

†The *lex Calpurnia* of 149 B.C. instituted a standing court composed of fifty jurors drawn entirely from the senate and presided over by a praetor to try cases for the recovery of damages from governors and other officials accused of extortion in the provinces *(quaestio de rebus repetundis)*.

promises have often been considered pure demagoguery, they held out the hope of reforms that were badly needed.* Apparently, they were not radical enough to win the overwhelming support of the city voters. They were too few and too late.

Even so, the early voting ran so strongly in his favor that opposing partisans interrupted the voting by vetoes and bogus religious "omens." Just when the assembly seemed about to break out in open riot, Fulvius Flaccus pushed his way through the milling throng to inform Tiberius that the senate was holding an emergency session in the Temple of Faith. Opponents, he said, had accused Tiberius of wanting to be king and invoked an ancient law under which Tiberius was to be killed as a tyrant!

Scaevola, the consul, had refused in horror to take part in the murder, but Scipio Nasica Serapio and some other senators rounded up a mob of sympathizers and slaves and hurried to the Forum. The tribunes of the people, who might have interposed their sacred persons between Tiberius and the mob, scurried out of the way. Picking up legs of broken chairs and benches, Scipio Nasica and his men rushed toward Tiberius and clubbed him and three hundred of his followers to death. They threw the bodies into the Tiber.

While the bodies of the slain were floating down the Tiber, Popillius Laenas, the consul of 132 B.C., set up a special court to try the Gracchan partisans. The more outspoken ones were executed. To forestall popular retribution, Scipio Nasica was whisked out of danger and sent on a diplomatic mission to Pergamum, where, as Head Pontiff, he safely performed his pontifical duties in absentia. There, in 132 B.C., he died—too soon to see the train of political violence and civil war that he had helped to set in motion.

*Some scholars believe that these proposals have been anachronistically attributed to Tiberius in light of his brother's proposals ten years later. Yet, given Tiberius' political needs at this time, they are perfectly reasonable moves for him to make.

Tiberius' Motives   The struggle over Tiberius Gracchus' land reform bill has often been simplistically portrayed as a struggle between Tiberius on the one hand and the Roman senate on the other: Tiberius appears as some kind of ideologically motivated democratic liberal or radical reformer in the modern mold; the senate merely represents the corporate interest of a wealthy landed oligarchy seeking to protect its financial interests without any regard for the social and economic problems of Rome. Such a view is untenable. Tiberius did not start out with some scheme of radical reform in mind. His reform was essentially a conservative one, designed to restore Roman military manpower, which had always depended on the free class of landowning peasants, and to halt the spread of estates run by slaves, whose increasing numbers posed a serious threat to internal peace and security, as witnessed by the slave revolt in Sicily from 136 to 131 and a brief uprising of slaves in Campania.

Insofar as his law would stem the migration of dispossessed rural citizens into the city and even attract back to the countryside some of those who had already come to the city, Tiberius may also have hoped to alleviate some of the unemployment and attendant sociopolitical stress existing in Rome itself. The flow of booty that had sustained economic growth at Rome had ceased with the sacks of Carthage and Corinth in 146. Since then, Rome's wars, mainly against poor tribesmen and slaves, had become an economic burden. The urban economy, always heavily dependent upon expenditures for publicly and privately funded construction projects, had become seriously depressed.

Tiberius' reforms, therefore, were not based on consideration of some abstract radical ideology, although it is quite possible that his education at the hands of Greek and Stoic teachers like Diophanes of Mytilene and Blossius of Cumae provided him with arguments to support the rightness and justice of his cause. Nor was Tiberius fighting the senate as an institution or seeking to destroy the primary role of the senatorial aristocracy in governmental affairs. Tiberius himself was a member of the consular families that dominated the senate. The senate was not a monolithic bloc opposed to Tiberius and serving only the interest of the wealthy senatorial landowners. It is often overlooked that powerful members of the senate drafted his initial reform bill. No doubt many of those senators who opposed Tiberius did so to protect their own extensive land holdings. Others, however, saw his actions as threats to the "constitution" in which they genuinely believed. Still others opposed him on the basis of personal and factional politics.

The "institutional fallacy" in historical analysis must be avoided. No institution, class, or state does anything. The Senate of the United States, for example, does not ever do anything. A majority, sometimes all, of those senators who vote on a given issue decide if an action is to be taken or not, and each senator has a unique combination of motives for voting the way he or she does, although each may share many of the same motives with others to one degree or another. Tiberius Gracchus' determination to pursue agrarian reform in the face of bitter opposition from many of his fellow nobles cannot be understood without reference to the personalities and careers of individual senatorial aristocrats.

As expected of members of his class, Tiberius Gracchus was a politically ambitious young noble. A number of factors made him particularly so. His father, now dead, had reached the pinnacle of public success. He had been consul twice, celebrated two military triumphs, earned much good will as a governor in Spain, reached the coveted censorship, and been a member of the prestigious priestly board of augurs. It was the duty of Tiberius, the oldest surviving son, to equal or surpass the achievements of his father and preserve the *dignitas* of the family. Moreover, the Sempronii Gracchi had been closely associated in politics with the Cornelii Scipiones since the time of the Hannibalic War. Tiberius' mother, Cornelia, was the daughter of the elder Scipio

Africanus, victor over Hannibal. Well educated and talented herself, she had had the distinction in widowhood of turning down an offer of marriage from the King of Egypt. Ambitious for her sons, she obtained the rhetorician Diophanes of Mytilene and Blossius of Cumae, a Stoic philosopher, as their tutors. She is said to have urged her sons to live up to the glory of both sides of the family and make her known not only as the daughter of Africanus, but mother of the Gracchi! Finally, Scipio Aemilianus, the younger Africanus and famous destroyer of Carthage, was not only Tiberius' first cousin by adoption but also was married to Tiberius' sister Sempronia. (Because Cornelia was also the daughter of the sister of Scipio's natural father, she and Scipio were first cousins, and he was a first cousin once removed of Tiberius and Sempronia.)

At first, the connection with Scipio Aemilianus served Tiberius well. As a youth he had accompanied Scipio to Carthage and won his praise for valor, which would have impressed the voters when he ran for the quaestorship in 138. Nevertheless, there was ill will between Tiberius' immediate family and Scipio over an issue of inheritance produced by their complex relationships. Also, the marriage to Sempronia, which probably had been designed to restore friendly relations, had turned out unhappy and merely made matters worse. As so often happened in the Roman aristocracy, complex interrelationships that had arisen from close political cooperation between families in earlier generations led to personal animosities that embittered political differences and rivalries in later generations.

Probably two or three years after he returned from Carthage, Tiberius became betrothed to the daughter of Scipio's chief rival for preeminence within the nobility, Appius Claudius Pulcher. In 137, Tiberius served as quaestor in Spain under C. Hostilius Mancinus, whose close relative, L. Hostilius Mancinus, was an enemy of Scipio. Mancinus and his whole army were disgracefully captured by the Numantines. Because of his father's reputation, Tiberius was the only one with whom the Numantines would negotiate a treaty. He obtained the release of the whole Roman army and saved much precious manpower for Rome. It looked as if Tiberius would gain the kind of fame and honor that would advance his career.

Tiberius was bitterly disappointed. When he brought the treaty to the senate for ratification, Scipio Aemilianus strenuously opposed it and helped persuade a majority of senators to reject it. Furthermore, Mancinus, Tiberius, and the other officers were prosecuted for cowardice. Tiberius and the others secured acquittal, but Mancinus was ordered stripped, bound in chains, and handed over to the Numantines. (The Numantines showed their contempt of Rome by sending him back.) While hostility to the Hostilii Mancini may well have been a factor in Scipio's actions, even more important was his desire to keep the war going so that he could obtain command of it and gain the glory of avenging Rome's disgrace with another great victory, which he did in 134 and 133 after obtaining exemption from the law forbidding second consulships.

In his ambition, Scipio had been quite willing to sacrifice the career not only of Mancinus but also of Tiberius Gracchus. In fairness to Scipio, he did help Tiberius escape Mancinus' fate, but the whole episode had dealt a tremendous blow to Tiberius' prestige, and he can hardly have appreciated Scipio's poor attempt to show some shred of familial piety. Now he was desperate to find a means of saving his political career and, no doubt, obtain some revenge on Scipio. Land reform was the perfect vehicle. As already seen, it was urgently needed to help solve some of Rome's pressing socio-economic and military problems. In his campaign for the office of tribune, it would be a very popular issue with a large bloc of voters. Once he was elected and succeeded in obtaining a law for redistribution of land, those who received land could become a valuable source of loyal clients who would help him in future elections. Finally, the proposed agrarian commission would give Tiberius and his backers, like Appius Claudius Pulcher,

control over the very land that Scipio would need to reward his veterans once he returned from Spain. Instead of being beholden to Scipio for obtaining grants of land, the veterans would be expressing their gratitude toward Tiberius and his fellow land commissioners.

Personal animosities and political maneuvering within the senatorial aristocracy, therefore, go a long way to explain the actions of Tiberius Gracchus and some of the leading opponents of his reform. Tiberius was certainly sincere in his desire to alleviate some of Rome's pressing problems through land reform. But for any politician the most attractive reform is one that is not only just but also politically beneficial to the politician himself. Tiberius was an ambitious son of a great noble father and mother and needed to gain popularity and build a loyal following of clients in order to save his career from the disgrace of having his treaty with the Numantines rejected in the senate. Once set on the path of reform, he could not give up in the face of powerful opponents. To have suffered a second political defeat would have meant the end of his career within the senatorial elite. That is why, every time his opponents tried to use traditional constitutional means to stop him, Tiberius resorted to more and more untraditional practices to thwart them.

His refusal to quit was made more adamant by the desire to use land reform as a weapon against Scipio Aemilianus (the younger Africanus) since there had long been bad blood between them and since Scipio for his own selfish means had led the move to reject Tiberius' treaty with Numantia. Conversely, Scipio's allies sought to protect Scipio's interests from Tiberius, who was being backed by one of Scipio's chief rivals in the senate, Appius Claudius Pulcher. Naturally, Scipio's allies would have found ready cooperation from those senators who were more concerned with their own economic or political self-interest, the constitutional implications of Tiberius' actions, or the principle of land redistribution in general.

The Land Commission and its Impact

That the land commission set up to administer the Sempronian land law was allowed to function even after its creator was slain is another indication that much of the opposition to Tiberius in the senate was not based on ideological opposition to reform or narrow economic self-interest but on personal and factional politics. Since the man who would have reaped the most political benefits from the reform was now dead, it was no longer a threat to his rivals. Indeed, they now tried to reap for themselves the benefits of *gratia* and increased clientage among those who received allotments. The consul Popillius Laenas even boasted of what he had done to carry out the law. On a milestone in Lucania he caused the statement to be inscribed that he was ''the first to compel the shepherds to make way for the plowmen.''

The commissioners appointed after the death of Tiberius were two active supporters of Tiberius, M. Fulvius Flaccus and C. Papirius Carbo. They worked with zeal and energy, and within six years the commission may have settled over seventy-five thousand men, which would have been an increase of twenty percent in the manpower available for military service. The Gracchan land law seems temporarily to have achieved the objective of strengthening the military power of Rome.

The work of the commission was hard and probably involved some injustice, for after the passage of time and with the poor methods of keeping records in ancient times it was seldom easy to determine what land was public. However conscientiously the commissioners consulted the old land registers and summoned neighbors to testify, probably in some cases they seized private property and in other cases confiscated the only good land that the owners possessed. The complaints must have been numerous and bitter.

Rome's Allies and the Death of Scipio

The grievances of Roman citizens probably were not given a sympathetic hearing, but those of the Latin and Italian allies,

however, could not have been brushed aside so easily. To have ignored the complaints of the allied states might have constituted a violation of their treaty rights with Rome, disturbed peaceful relations, and perhaps even invited revolt. To the allies, in some cases, whether as individuals or as communities, Rome had assigned public lands by lease or by outright grant. In other cases, wealthy allied landowners simply had encroached on otherwise unoccupied Roman public land, as had wealthy Romans. In either case, when the allies looked for a patron to champion their interests, they found one in Scipio Aemilianus, the destroyer of Carthage and Numantia. Realizing the value of their military help and anxious to extend his network of clients, he gladly consented to press their claims before the senate and succeeded in having the judicial powers of the commissioners transferred to the consuls, at least as far as the Latin and Italian allies were concerned. If the consuls preferred to go off on long campaigns to avoid involvement in irksome land disputes, the work of the commission would be brought to a standstill.

Scipio's meddling with the land problem in 129 B.C. did not help his popularity. In fact his popularity had waned since he had spoken before an assembly against Carbo's bill to legalize reelection to the tribuneship.* In the course of the debate, Carbo asked him what he though of the murder of Tiberius Gracchus. Scipio replied, ''If Gracchus intended to seize the government, he has been justly slain.'' When the crowd greeted this remark with jeers and catcalls, Scipio roared, ''I have never been scared by the shouts of the enemy in arms. Shall I be frightened by your outcries, you stepsons of Italy?''

In May 129 B.C., Scipio announced that he was going to make a speech about the Latin and Italian allies. It is not known whether he

---

* Though Carbo failed to get this bill passed, he had succeeded two years earlier in passing the secret ballot law (131 B.C.). No bill was more potent in weakening the hold of politically entrenched nobles, because now they could not easily hold those whom they benefitted to account at voting time.

intended to talk about the land law or about the granting of Roman citizenship. He went home early to work on his speech. The next morning he was found dead in bed. Whether he died from natural causes or was, as rumored, the victim of foul play by one of the Gracchans, perhaps aided, by Sempronia, Scipio's wife and sister of Tiberius Gracchus, was never known.

While previously the Romans had been fairly generous in granting citizenship to upper-class individuals in the Latin and Italian towns, there had never been any widespread desire for Roman citizenship among the allied communities. The increasingly inequitable relationship between Roman citizens and the allies (see pp. 138–139), however, seems to have been brought into sharper focus by the activities of the Gracchan land commission. A number of Latins and Italians began to press more actively for citizenship. Their overt agitation in Rome made them quite unpopular, and in 126, with senatorial approval, a tribune pushed a bill through the assembly to legalize their expulsion.

Fulvius Flaccus took up the cause of citizenship for the Italian allies. As consul (125 B.C.), he proposed the grant of citizenship to any of the allies that wanted it. When all classes opposed his idea—especially the common people, who did not want to share their privileges with the Italians—Fulvius dropped his bill and went off on a campaign in southern France to conquer new lands for farm settlement, a scheme dear to the hearts of those who sought popularity among the voters since the days of Gaius Flaminius.

In the same year, the allied town of Fregellae rose up in rebellion. What, if any, connection this event had with the question of Roman citizenship for the Italians is unclear. The events in Rome may simply have aggravated a particular local conflict among the Fregellans. At any rate, the revolt was crushed with the help of Fregellan "loyalists," who were rewarded, while the rest were stripped of their property and the town destroyed.

Although no other town revolted, the events at Fregellae may have heightened interest in the question of citizenship among other Italians. At Rome, feelings were intensified. Attempts were made to punish those who were suspected of having inspired and encouraged the revolt. Even Gaius Gracchus, who had just returned from Sardinia, was accused, but was able to prove his innocence.

Gaius Gracchus, Tribune of the Plebs, 123 to 122 B.C.   The powers and capabilities of Gaius Gracchus were known and feared years before he became tribune. Those who had opposed Tiberius considered him a menace because of his influence over crowds and his membership in the land commission set up by his brother. His enemies were naturally relieved when it fell to his lot in 126 B.C. to go as quaestor to Sardinia, whose pestilential climate, it was hoped, might do him no good, but he returned to Rome in 124 B.C. In spite of hostility from powerful fellow nobles, he campaigned for the tribuneship and was elected. Once more the country voters poured into the city, as they had done ten years before to support his brother. They voted him into power again in 122 B.C., although he was not an official candidate at that time.

The motives of Gaius Gracchus in promoting reform were essentially those of his brother Tiberius, with two major additions. First, there was the desire to avenge the murder of his brother and repair the damage to his family's honor. Second, he wanted to build a far more broad and complex coalition of socio-economic groups not normally part of the political process in order to gain the breadth of political support whose lack had proved fatal to Tiberius. That would help him to win the offices necessary to repair his family's tattered *dignitas*.

The two years of the tribuneships of Gaius Gracchus were politically the most memorable of the Roman Republic and perhaps the most crucial in the history of the Roman people. He converted the tribuneship, hitherto dominated by the same small number of noble families that also dominated the senate, into an instrument of almost absolute power, whereby an ambitious rival, usually from some other noble family, could effectively circumvent their control. A century later (23 B.C.), the Emperor Augustus strengthened his position against opposition from the old republican nobility by invoking not the powers of a consul but the power of a plebeian tribune (*tribunicia potestas*).

The Reforms of Gaius Gracchus

Upon taking office, Gaius Gracchus proceeded to stir the fury of the people against his brother's murderers, who had violated the sacrosanctity of a tribune, and against the procedure by which Popillius Laenas had condemned his brother's followers to death without appeal to the people. The *concilium plebis* responded by passing a bill that prohibited the senate from creating extraordinary tribunals to condemn political offenders without appeal to the people. Under a retroactive provision of this law, Popillius Laenas was condemned and exiled.

Revenged, Gaius Gracchus proceeded to carry out his more constructive program of reform, which was designed to build a solid coalition of political supporters to advance his own career in competition with fellow nobles while dealing intelligently and realistically with the social and economic problems generated by the Roman conquests. The most pressing problems concerned the spreading unemployment and slums, the periodic fluctuations in food prices, the decline of military strength and efficiency, the frequent slave revolts, the continuing problem of provincial administration, and the dissatisfied allies. Therefore, he attempted to organize a coalition of the middle class, the proletarian city voters, and the farmers.

The Farm Vote To win the farm vote, Gaius revived and amplified his brother's legislation. He restored to the land commission the judicial powers which Scipio Aemilianus had perhaps justly persuaded the senate to remove. Most of the public land had by now been assigned, but he was able to benefit the farmers by an extensive road-building program, under which a network of secondary roads was created linking farms with markets, villages with towns, and towns with Rome. These roads not only enabled farmers to obtain employment but also permitted them to move their crops more easily and cheaply to markets and thus improved trade. Also, by facilitating travel to Rome and, therefore, attendance at assembly meetings, they promoted a fuller participation in affairs of government. The extraordinary speed with which this project was completed under Gaius' personal direction further increased the fears of the senate.

The City Vote To gain the political support of the city masses, Gaius persuaded the assembly to pass the famous *lex Frumentaria* or Grain law, which provided that the state should buy and import grain from overseas for sale on demand in fixed monthly amounts to citizens residing in Rome at six and one-half *asses* per *modius* (a price which was roughly equivalent to one-half of an unskilled worker's daily wage for about one-quarter of a bushel), a price not far below the average market price in Rome and often much higher and never below the regular producer prices in such surplus areas as Egypt, Sicily, northern Italy, and Spain. This law, the most severely critized of all the Gracchan reforms, did not constitute a dole; it was passed solely to promote price stabilization for the benefit of the consumer (not, as now, for the producer). A considerable amount of the wheat consumed in Rome came in as tribute and cost the state only the expenses of transport, naval convoy, and storage. The Grain law also provided for the construction of warehouses and wharves in Rome, a measure designed to relieve unemployment along with implementing the subsidy for grain.

The Grain law also had a more subtle purpose. It was designed to weaken the clientage of entrenched fellow nobles and increase that of Gaius by using public money. In periods of high food prices, candidates for high office had regularly bought votes by the provision or promise of cheap grain. The Grain law helped to restore the independence of Roman citizens and rendered more effective the secret ballot law of 131 B.C. And, it also earned *gratia* for Gaius among the voters resident in Rome.

Some other important laws were passed which also brought needed relief to poorer citizens and politically valuable gratitude to Gaius. The Military law *(lex Militaris)* required the government to clothe and equip Roman soldiers without deductions from their pay, shortened the term of military service, and forbade the draft of boys under seventeen years old. This law was intended to improve army morale, always a concern of the Gracchi, and to win the political support of soldiers, allies, and voters with small incomes. Furthermore, in 122 B.C. the weight of the denarius was reduced. This measure not only meant that in real terms Roman citizens had to pay less in fixed rents and taxes, but also significantly reduced the tribute of the Roman allies without special legislation.

Gaius Gracchus' laws authorizing commercial and agricultural colonies in Italy and across the sea were intended to relieve the overpopulation in Rome and provide economic opportunities for farmers, traders, craftsmen, and small businessmen unable to make a living. The sites selected were Capua, Tarentum, and Carthage. The most ambitious of these projects, as authorized by the Rubrian law, was the founding of Junonia near the cursed site of Carthage, where six thousand colonists drawn from Rome and the rest of Italy were to be settled on farms of 125 acres. Gaius went to Africa to supervise in person the initial stages of the settlement, which first established officially the principle of emigration.*

---

* Gaius' opponents were strongly opposed to Junonia and, by the use of propaganda and the appeal to superstitious fears of the curse of 146, managed to persuade the people after Gracchus' death to repeal the Rubrian Law authorizing the scheme. Had it been completed, he would have created a loyal colony of overseas clients in the vital grain-growing area of North Africa. Thus, he had anticipated by almost a century the policy of Augustus and the later emperors.

Equestrian Interest: Provincial Taxes and Jury Service   In an effort to drive a wedge between wealthy equestrians and his rivals, who dominated the senate, Gaius appealed to the economic interests of key members of that class by two important laws.

Those *equites* who had significant interests in business and particularly in tax farming (contracting to collect taxes for the state in return for a share of the proceeds) were already irked by the senatorial aristocracy's control over finance, provincial administration, and especially over the rich revenues of the new province of Asia. After Attalus III had willed his kingdom of Pergamum to Rome in 133 B.C., the senate decided to collect direct taxes of fixed sums payable by the communities to the governor and by him, in turn, to the Roman treasury. Gaius had a law passed overturning this arrangement and directing instead that the taxes of Asia take the form of a tithe as in Sicily (see p. 94). Unlike the system employed in Sicily, where the tithe was collected locally, the Gracchan law stipulated that the censors should auction the lucrative contracts for the tithes of Asia to tax-collecting companies in Rome for five-year terms.

The new system of taxation provided the Roman treasury with immediate funds and, theoretically at least, was less burdensome to the provincial taxpayers than fixed taxes since payments in kind would fluctuate with good or poor crops. It was also beneficial to the Roman tax collectors since clauses were added protecting them against losses due to war and other calamities. It naturally benefited the richest men of the equestrian class, for the right to bid was open only to those owning property worth in excess of 400,000 sesterces (roughly equal to the daily wages of 100,000 unskilled workers). This Gracchan law increased the economic power of the wealthiest equestrians, who were expected in turn to use some of their wealth to advance their benefactor's political career, while at the same time it weakened the power of rivals within his own class.

Another move which tended to divide the equestrians from Gaius' rivals within the nobility was the Acilian Law, sponsored by one of Gaius' supporters, which excluded senators, the relatives of senators, and all curule magistrates from the juries of the standing courts established under the Calpurnian Law of 149 B.C. to try provincial governors for extortion.* This law, therefore, transferred jury service from the senatorial class to the equestrian class. It achieved its intended purpose of widening the breach between the latter and Gaius' rivals, but it made it easy for equestrian business interests to punish good governors for preventing the wholesale exploitation and plundering of the provinces by businessmen.

The Italian Question   In his second term as tribune, Gaius Gracchus introduced a bill which further shows Gaius' attempts to appeal for support from major groups by remedying pressing social and economic problems. If he had succeeded he would have created a vast army of voter-clients throughout Italy. The bill, which proposed to extend Roman citizenship to the Latins and Latin rights to the rest of the Italians, was scuttled by the selfish ignorance of the Roman populace and the malice of Gaius' enemies within the senate.

Livius Drusus   During the seventy days that Gaius was in Africa to lay the groundwork for the colony of Junonia, his enemies within the nobility had been planning the destruction of both the Italian citizenship bill and its author. They found in the tribune M. Livius Drusus, member of a prominent noble family, a brilliant agent of their scheme. An eloquent speaker, Livius Drusus pandered to the selfish interests of the Roman populace by pointing out that the benefits of citizenship would be diluted by extending them to greater numbers, and he threatened to veto the Gracchan bill extending citizenship to the Italians.

---

* The justification for the Acilian Law was the charge that the senatorial juries acquitted governors commonly believed guilty.

That threat prevented it from being brought to a vote because Gaius knew that it was unpopular and would not pass. Livius then presented a bill to protect Italian soldiers from mistreatment by Roman army officers, which was an important advance, but a shabby substitute for the citizenship bill.

He subsequently introduced a bill which promised to found twelve colonies in Italy, each to consist of three thousand colonists selected from the poorest class. The land was to be rent free. He also proposed to release from payment of rent the settlers who had been allotted land under the law of Tiberius Gracchus. The proposal to found twelve colonies in Italy was never intended to be carried out since there was not enough public land left in Italy to permit so ambitious a scheme. After it had achieved its purpose of destroying Gaius Gracchus, it was speedily dropped.

The Fall and Death of Gaius Gracchus
When Gaius returned from Africa, he discovered that Livius had succeeded in splitting the once solid ranks of the city electorate, who had supported him. Too long had Gaius stayed in Africa; too late did he realize the extent of the conspiracy against him. His immense popularity had made him overconfident and forced his rivals into close cooperation against him. Also, Fulvius Flaccus, whom he had left in Rome to look after his interests, was a violent and tactless man who had done a great deal of damage to Gaius' cause by his reckless and turbulent acts. Gaius was defeated in his attempt to run for a third term. Only his membership in the African commission (granted *imperium* by the Rubrian Law) stood in the way of political enemies now resolved to take his life.

To remove the protecting power of the *imperium,* they hastened to bring about the annulment of the Rubrian Law authorizing the founding of Junonia. Though still holding an official position as commissioner, Gaius lacked the authority to summon the people or the power to resist the threatened repeal. He wished to avoid acts of violence, which might give his enemies the excuse for authorizing extreme measures against him. Nevertheless, the newly elected consul, Lucius Opimius, the destroyer of Fregellae and a vehement opponent of Gaius, deliberately provoked an incident. As Opimius was preparing to offer a sacrifice in the porch of the Capitoline temple, one of his attendants, who carried the utensils required for sacrifice, stood opposite Gaius and cried out the traditional formula ordering all "bad citizens" to leave the porch. A Gracchan follower thereupon cut the man down with his sword and thus gave Opimius the pretext that he had been seeking.

Armed with a final decree of the senate (*Senatus Consultum Ultimum*), virtually declaring a state of martial law (see p. 168), Opimius organized a posse of senators and their slaves and, assisted by a force of Cretan archers, attacked the Gracchan followers, who had taken refuge on the Aventine. Here the Gracchans were routed and 250 of them killed. Fulvius Flaccus was killed as he attempted to escape. Gaius also attempted to escape but, seeing the hopelessness of his position, ordered his slave to kill him. Supposedly, his severed head was filled with melted lead and brought to Opimius, who paid its weight in gold. Afterward, pseudolegal trials resulted in the execution of three thousand Gracchan followers.

Thus died Gaius Gracchus, who, in his two years of office as tribune of the people, had temporarily broken the monopoly of power enjoyed by a small number of nobles who had dominated the senate and the popular assemblies. He had concentrated in his hands many executive powers and functions. He had supervised the distribution of grain to the populace, selected the juries of the courts, awarded contracts for and superintended the construction of highways, presided over meetings of the senate, supported and campaigned for candidates to the consulship, and converted the tribuneship into an office more powerful than the consulship itself. Some of his reforms were truly measures of enlightened statesmanship. Others were dictated by political calculation and must be described as frankly opportunistic. Most were combinations of both.

In death, the Gracchi were mightier than in life. By killing them, their enemies had unwittingly exalted the two tribunes into figures of heroic proportions. Allowed to live they might have been the sooner forgotten. Instead, statues were erected to them in public places, and the spots where they had fallen became hallowed ground. Prayers and sacrifices were offered to them as to gods. Even the proudest noble, regardless of his private opinions, dared not speak of them in public except in respect and veneration. The common people revered them for having brought hope into a world of misery and exploitation. Ambitious fellow aristocrats, seeking advantage against rivals, followed their political strategy.

XV

The Breakdown of the System, 121 to 88 B.C.

The careers of the Gracchi reveal a major reason why the reforms necessary for preserving the stability of the Roman Republic were extremely difficult to make. Reform, however altruistic or patriotically motivated, could not be separated from the highly personalized, factional competition within the Roman aristocracy. Laws always bore the name of the man who proposed them. Therefore, any law that brought about significant reform benefitting a large number of discontented people would bring the man who proposed it a large increase in supporters among the voters. Envy, jealousy, and political self-interest would cause many current or potential rivals for public office and esteem to resist the attempted reform with every weapon at their disposal—even including violence and, as the competition intensified, eventually civil war. The Republican system began to lurch from crisis to crisis without hope of a solution to its problems.

Sources for the Period from 121 to 88 B.C. As for the Gracchi, the literary sources for this period are also in disarray. The brief summaries of Livy Books 62 to 76 in the *Peri-*

ochae and the epitomes largely derived from him in the late Empire provide only a bare outline, as does Velleius Paterculus (Book 2.8–17). The fragments of Books 34 and 35 of Diodorus Siculus have some information on events from 111 to 104 B.C. and large fragments from Books 36 and 37 are valuable for the years from 104 to 88. The fragments of Books 26 to 29 in Cassius Dio are useful for events from 114 to 88, and there are some fragments on the Jugurthine War (111–104 B.C.) in Book 8 of Appian. The only lengthy extant sources are *The Jugurthine War* of the mid-first century B.C. historian Sallust (see pp. 267–268), sections 27 to 54 of the first book from the part of Appian's history known as the *Civil Wars,* and Plutarch's lives of Marius and Sulla, part of which are based on Sulla's *Memoirs.* Some inscribed boundary stones, road markers, fragmentary inscriptions of laws, and excavations of colonial settlements help us to understand the process of land distribution after Gaius Gracchus, and Cicero's speech *Pro Rabirio Perduellionis* discusses the civil strife of 101 and 100 B.C. Cicero knew many of the major figures during this period and made numerous references to them in his works, especially his philosophical dialogues and rhetorical treatises (see pp. 264–267).

Optimates and Populares   In analyzing the political struggles that marked the century of Roman history after the Gracchi, two labels are often applied to the protagonists. Those ambitious individuals who followed the Gracchi's example of building public support by promoting reforms and policies that benefited significant discontented groups of voters or potential voters are often referred to as *populares* (sing. *popularis*). In Roman political rhetoric this label was applied to such people by more traditionally minded aristocrats or those whose current domination in the senate was guaranteed by the status quo. They did not approve of seeking popularity among large groups of voters on public issues. Instead, they preferred to rely on the traditional political tools of family reputation, personal alliances with other aristocrats, and the marshalling of clients whose loyalty had been won by individual services. They called themselves *optimates,* the best people, in contrast with the *populares,* whom they accused of using dangerously demagogic tactics. The *optimates* naturally disliked anyone who sought a base of power that they did not control, and many may honestly have feared that *popularis* actions would eventually lead to the creation of a popularly supported tyrant and destroy the Republic.

In no way should the terms *populares* and *optimates* be taken as representing anything like modern political parties with their formal institutional structures and acting within some explicit philosophical framework or theory of government. They do not even signify cohesive factions. The terms mainly indicate in a broad way the two different types of political tactics employed by individual political figures at any given moment in the history of the late Republic.

Insofar as the labels *optimates* and *populares* mean anything, they can be applied only in the context of particular political conflicts between individuals or personal factions. The social origins and the goals of the people so labelled were mostly the same. They almost always came from the senatorial aristocracy and sometimes from ambitious equestrian families allied with a powerful noble. Their goals were to retain or increase power and prestige in competition with their peers. Individual *optimates* were often just as much rivals with each other as they were with individual *populares,* and vice versa. For example, individual *optimates* might temporarily ally themselves and their factional supporters against a *popularis* who threatened to outstrip them all, but as soon as he was eliminated they would usually resume intense competition among themselves. Nor were *populares* opposed to the dominant role of the senate in the Roman government. They themselves usually were members of the senate. They were looking for ways to establish their own dominance in the senate by utilizing the office of tribune of the plebs and appeals to the mass of voters outside the senate. Many may also have been convinced of the rightness or justice of their positions, but in no way were they seeking to overthrow the power of the class to which they mostly belonged.

Therefore, the political conflicts of the late Roman Republic cannot be viewed as struggles between the senate as a monolithic institution and outside democratic leaders or reform groups. The question was what individual or group of factional allies would control the senate, which controlled Rome. Not even Julius Caesar, for example, ever sought to abolish the senate. In the civil war that Caesar precipitated at the end of the Republic many senators supported him. He fought against those fellow senators who opposed him in the competition for glory and prestige, *dignitas.* Having beaten them, he merely packed the senate with his loyal supporters to ensure his personal domination.

After the death of Gaius Gracchus, his opponents, who can be broadly classed as *optimates,* were willing to let his legislation operate once he could not benefit from it at their expense. They did not repeal the Grain Law, and they changed neither the selection of jurors for the extortion courts nor the administration of provincial taxes. Even the land laws, including those pertaining to the founding of colonies, though modified, were not overthrown.

The Senatus Consultum Ultimum

The reign of terror that had followed the slaying of Gaius Gracchus seems temporarily to have silenced anyone who might have challenged his optimate opponents. When Opimius was prosecuted for murder before the people, he was acquitted, and this acquittal seemed to confirm the legality of the Ultimate Decree of the Senate, *Senatus Consultum Ultimum (S. C. U.)*. This decree advised the consuls to take whatever steps they deemed necessary to preserve the safety of the state, and could be construed as a decree of martial law suspending normal constitutional procedures. The senate's right to issue such a decree, however, was not based on any legal statute or ancient customary practice.

Therefore, the question of its validity remained open and subject to the political passions of the moment. *Popularis* politicians shunned it because of its origin as a weapon against the Gracchi and its lack of legal sanction by a popular assembly, but the *optimates* always considered it a perfectly constitutional weapon against *popularis* rivals during the late Republic. Since they were dominant at this point, their view temporarily prevailed and even Popillius Laenas, who had been exiled by the people for killing the followers of Tiberius Gracchus, was now allowed to return to Rome.

Post-Gracchan Land Legislation

Three successive laws gradually modified the Gracchan land legislation in the interest of all groups affected. The first, probably in 121 B.C., permitted the settlers to sell the farms allotted to them. Although this law tended to nullify the purpose of guaranteeing that there would be enough men to meet the property requirements for military service and permitted the rich proprietor to buy or force the sale of small neighboring properties, it was not necessarily unpopular. Trying to earn a living on a small holding was not easy. It would be even more difficult if it were divided among heirs into smaller holdings. Many settlers probably would have been pleased to sell for ready cash.

The second law (perhaps in 118 B.C.) abolished the land commission (whose work probably was already done), halted further division of public land in Italy, and guaranteed legal possession of lands already distributed on payment of a small rent to the state. That would have pleased both large and small proprietors and would have been especially welcome to the Italian allies, at whose expense any further distribution of *ager publicus* in Italy probably would have come. Finally, in 111 B.C. a third law, probably the *lex Thoria,* partially preserved in an inscription, abolished all rentals ordered by the law of 118 B.C., declared as private property all public lands assigned by the Gracchan commission up to 320 acres, and guaranteed to colonies and municipalities secure tenure of lands already granted. It also forbade further encroachment on public pastures and strictly regulated the number of animals grazed on those lands. Relief from rents benefited both large and small proprietors, and allies in the municipal towns appreciated the secure tenure of lands granted to them. Small farmers would have welcomed the attempt to keep large neighbors from encroaching illegally on additional public land, and both large and small operators would have benefited from the regulation against destructive overgrazing.

Colonization

The Gracchan program of land settlement in Italy was strongly reinforced both before and after the tribunate of Gaius by the conquest, colonization, and settlement of lands beyond the borders of Italy. Thousands of Roman colonists still remained around Carthage even after the abrogation of the Rubrian law. In 123 B.C. the Spanish conquests had been tightened up with the capture of the Balearic Isles, which had become a haven for pirates. They were attached administratively to Nearer Spain through a prefect, and two settlements—not colonies but probably containing some veterans—were made at Palma and Pollentia on Majorca.

The greatest activity was in southern Gaul. The Romans first intervened there in 125 B.C. during the consulship of M. Fulvius Flaccus in answer to repeated complaints from Massilia about the Ligurians and the Saluvii. Their subjugation gave the Romans control of a road leading from Italy to the Rhone valley, which they dominated from a strongly fortified base established in 122 at Aquae Sextiae (Aix) by the settlement of Roman veterans.

The pacification of southern Gaul was largely the work of Gnaeus Domitius Ahenobarbus. Domitius occupied all southern Gaul, exclusive of the small territory of Massilia, from the Alps to the Pyrenees and in 120 B.C. organized it into the Roman province of Transalpine Gaul, later called Narbonese Gaul *(Gallia Narbonensis)* or simply the Province (hence modern Provence). He also constructed a permanent military highway, the *Via Domitia,* from the Rhône to the Spanish Pyrenees. On this route a Roman citizen colony of discharged veterans was established in 118 B.C. at Narbo, the first Roman colony, apart perhaps from Junonia at Carthage, to be founded outside the Italian peninsula. The founding of Narbo not only provided the commercial operators a trading center in southern Gaul, but also provided new lands for settlement by the small farmers of central Italy. In this way, the number of properly qualified military recruits might be maintained, and those who sold their Gracchan allotments in Italy might use the proceeds to capitalize a fresh start in the rich province of Gaul.

For some time, therefore, there was no public issue that aroused enough discontent for anyone to exploit in the *popularis* manner of the Gracchi. In 114 B.C., however, the death of a Vestal Virgin struck by lightning aroused popular religious superstitions. A tribune named Sextus Peducaeus took advantage of the situation by introducing a law to take jurisdiction in the investigation of the matter away

from the college of pontiffs and establish a special court of inquiry presided over by a former censor. Three Virgins were found guilty of violating their vows of chastity and condemned to be buried alive. Nevertheless, popular passions were not satisfied until the Sibylline Books were consulted in the senate and both a Greek and a Gallic man and woman were sacrificed to the gods.

The Jugurthine War, 111 to 104 B.C.

It was, however, the outbreak of an unpopular and difficult war that provided the first major opportunity for *popularis* exploitation. This war, known as the Jugurthine War after Rome's adversary Jugurtha, occurred in the North African kingdom of Numidia between the years 111 and 104 B.C. and was marked initially by corruption, poor diplomacy, and inept generalship against a wily and audacious foe. Like his grandfather, Massinissa, Jugurtha was a lion of the desert, a good athlete, a skilled rider and hunter, and a born soldier. He had fought under Scipio Aemilianus at the siege of Numantia and had become acquainted with many young Roman officers, from whom he learned all he needed to know about the state of Roman society.

The problem began when King Micipsa died in 118. He left Numidia jointly to Jugurtha and two other sons, Adherbal and Hiempsal. After a brief attempt at joint rule, the three princes agreed to split the kingdom, but secretly Jugurtha plotted to take the whole of it for himself. He had Hiempsal murdered and made war on Adherbal, whom he defeated and drove out of Numidia. Adherbal fled to Rome and appealed to the senate. Though many of the senators listened to his words with politeness and sympathy, they were reluctant to interfere. Others were strongly in favor of Jugurtha, especially after they had been contacted by his agents, who came plentifully supplied with gold. After some debate the senate decided to partition Numidia and in 116 B.C. appointed a commission to go to Africa to arrange the details. The commission awarded the richer, eastern half to Adherbal. This part contained the capital, Cirta (modern Constantine, Algeria), an important center of the grain trade with Rome and home of many Italian and Roman merchants of equestrian status.

Three years later, when Jugurtha invaded the eastern territory and besieged Cirta, Adherbal again appealed to Rome but without success. Cirta fell, Adherbal was tortured to death, and the foreign merchants were massacred. This massacre incensed both the common people of Rome and the *equites*. Therefore, it became a politically exploitable issue. Finally, in 111 B.C., the tribune Gaius Memmius openly accused some senators of receiving bribes from Jugurtha and attacked the senate so vigorously that the majority of senators instructed the consuls to ask the *comitia centuriata* for a declaration of war against Jugurtha.

The consul L. Calpurnius Bestia raised an army and invaded Numidia in mid-111 B.C. He put up a good show initially but quickly worked out a peace settlement very favorable to Jugurtha. Bestia's peace reeked of bribery and corruption. The tribune Memmius demanded an investigation and obtained a law to bring Jugurtha to Rome under safe conduct to testify. Jugurtha came, but another tribune conveniently forbade him to speak when Memmius asked him to reveal whom he had bribed. Jugurtha overplayed his hand, however, by procuring the murder of his cousin Massiva, who was living in Rome and urging the senate to recognize him as king of Numidia. A majority of senators felt compelled to repudiate Bestia's peace and renew the war.

In 110 B.C., the consul Spurius Postumius Albinus and his brother Aulus set out for Africa with a large undisciplined and poorly trained army. Predictably they were able to accomplish nothing. Then, when Spurius returned to Rome to conduct the elections for 109, Jugurtha lured Aulus and the army into a trap and forced them to surrender. He demanded that Rome evacuate Numidia within ten days and acknowledge him as an ally.

The news of this disaster further enraged the people. The humiliating peace terms were at once rejected. A tribune named Gaius Mamilius Limetanus put through a bill setting up a special court composed of jurors selected from the equestrian class, but presided over by the distinguished noble M. Aemilius Scaurus, to investigate those accused of corruption or collusion with Jugurtha. The court condemned Bestia, Spurius Postumius Albinus, and Lucius Opimius and sent them into exile.

Quintus Caecilius Metellus, 109 to 108 B.C. The African command was at last assigned to a competent general: Metellus, one of the consuls of 109 and a member of the most powerful noble family in Rome at the time, was incorruptible and an excellent disciplinarian. His first duty was to whip a thoroughly demoralized and undisciplined army into an efficient fighting machine. Only then, making forced marches under the burning desert sun, did he invade Numidia.

Hoping to lure Metellus into ambush, Jugurtha retreated. Finally, Jugurtha launched his surprise attack, which was beaten off with heavy losses. In Rome the failure of Metellus to capture Jugurtha was misunderstood. The business interests hoped for a speedy termination of the African war, but they did not understand the difficulties of desert warfare. Neither, of course, did the people. They were inclined to accuse Metellus of prolonging the African war for his own glorification.

This unjust accusation was not only entertained in Rome but was carefully encouraged by the activities of Gaius Marius, one of Metellus' senior officers. He urged the merchants of North Africa to write letters to their friends and agents at Rome in protest of Metellus' conduct of the war.

Gaius Marius (157–86 B.C.) If the Roman people did not understand the difficulties of North African warfare, Gaius Marius did and was calculating and unscrupulous enough to exploit them in a *popularis* manner. Born outside of Arpinum, a little town south of Rome, Marius was the son of a wealthy equestrian landowner. His ambition was to reach the consulship at Rome and ennoble his family. He was an excellent soldier and knew how to win popularity among the common recruits, who would remember him at election time. Even after he had become their commander, he slept on the same hard ground as the troops. His rough and ready appearance and his use of common idiom also endeared him to the average man.

He had been with Scipio Aemilianus at the siege of Numantia. His courage, his physical endurance, the care that he took of his horse and equipment, and the attention that he gave to details about the camp earned Scipio's respect. Later he became a client of the powerful Metelli family, who helped him to become a tribune for 119 B.C. At that point, however, he deserted his patrons.

He won the admiration of the common people by his defiance of the aristocracy and his threat to arrest the consuls, one of whom was a Metellus, for opposing his bill to make it more difficult for patrons to influence the ballots of their clients. His noble patrons were outraged and helped to ensure his defeat in his campaign for the aedileship. He managed with some difficulty and much bribery, however, to get elected to a praetorship in 115 B.C., after which he was sent as a propraetor to Farther Spain, his first military command.

Marius' praetorship entitled him to admission into the upper ranks of the senate. His money and success earned him a useful marriage into the ancient patrician family of the Julii Caesares. His wife was the aunt of the future Julius Caesar. He also was able to mend fences with his offended former patrons, and Metellus appointed him as a staff officer in the war against Jugurtha. Even so, without any noble ancestors of his own, Marius would have found the consulship beyond his reach, except perhaps under most unusual circumstances —circumstances he set about creating.

Marius Campaigns for the Consulship
Whatever gratitude Marius may have felt

toward Metellus for appointing him chief of staff and any admiration the two men may have had for each other as soldiers rapidly disappeared when Metellus scornfully refused to grant Marius leave to go to Rome to campaign for the consulship. Supposedly Marius had been encouraged to seek the consulship by the words of a priest at Utica, "Ask and ye shall receive, seek and ye shall find." Concrete help came from the equestrian merchants in North Africa. Their letters to friends and agents in Rome complained about the slow progress of the war and urged the election of Marius to the consulship and appointment to the Numidian command. Finally, to get rid of a disgruntled officer, Metellus granted Marius leave to go to Rome, where he was elected consul for 107 B.C. Marius, the first of his family to reach the consulship, was a *novus homo,* new man, resented deeply by the old nobility. To add insult to their injury, he also was given the North African command by a plebiscite against the will of Metellus' supporters in the senate.

In recruiting troops for service in North Africa, Marius tried to solve the problem of military manpower by accepting as volunteers all who were physically fit regardless of property qualifications. This move was the logical outcome of a long process of lowering the property qualification for service in order to keep up the supply of recruits. It had occasionally been resorted to in past emergencies. After Marius it became a regular practice.

Inadvertently, however, this change had serious political consequences. Roman legions became manned more and more by propertyless volunteers personally loyal to their commanders, upon whom they depended for their welfare and whose clients they had become. Successful generals could now more easily compete with their political rivals by mustering the votes of loyal veterans or using them to intimidate their opponents. The value of military commands was thereby raised and the temptation to provoke some foreign military crisis to obtain one became even greater. More ominously, a successful military commander backed by an experienced and personally loyal army was in a greater position to resort to civil war against his political rivals if the usual constitutional means failed.

Marius in Africa　Marius made no move until he had trained his raw recruits. The training completed, he made long and fatiguing marches through the hot waterless wastes. He captured many towns and fortresses until he had reached the extreme western borders of Numidia, fully six hundred miles from his original base. There he seized Jugurtha's war treasure stashed away on the lofty summit of an almost unassailable rock, and compelled Jugurtha and his ally and father-in-law Bocchus, the king of Mauretania, to fight pitched battles with the Romans. In two bloody battles Marius broke the military power of Numidia and Mauretania and turned king Bocchus to thoughts of peace and friendship with Rome. Still the war could not be considered won until he had captured Jugurtha himself. He entrusted this highly dangerous task to his quaestor, the capable noble Lucius Cornelius Sulla, who persuaded Bocchus to lure Jugurtha into an ambush. Marius brought the captured Jugurtha to Rome to walk in royal robes and in chains before his triumphal chariot and had him killed a few days later in the horrible dungeon of the Tullianum. As a reward for his treachery, Bocchus received the western and drier part of Jugurtha's kingdom, the eastern part going to Gauda, the half-witted brother of Jugurtha. The business interests of Marius' equestrian friends and relatives were satisfied at last. Numidia was safe for Roman investment and exploitation.

The War with the Cimbri and the Teutons, 105 to 101 B.C.　Marius was now the most popular military hero. After the Jugurthine War, he was immediately given a command to repel the far more serious threat of war in the North. He was elected consul for the year 104 B.C. and for the next four years thereafter, sometimes in his absence from Rome and always in violation of the law requiring a ten-year interval between consulships.

What drove the people to violate both law and precedent in the election of Marius?—the threat of an invasion by the Germanic tribes of the Cimbri, the Teutons, and the Ambrones, who had by their mass migrations convulsed central and western Europe for more than a decade. Driven from their homelands of Jutland and Schleswig by overpopulation and tidal inundations, the three Germanic tribes loaded their families into leather-covered wagons and migrated southward. Equipped with copper helmets, tall, narrow shields, and long iron swords, they were accustomed to rush into battle in serried ranks linked to one another with chains. They struck terror into the heart of the average Roman.

These homeless hordes marched in search of land or plunder. From eastern France the Cimbri, the Teutons, and their allies approached the Roman province of Transalpine Gaul, where they attacked and broke the army of consul M. Junius Silanus in 109 B.C. Before the battle they had requested the senate to grant them land for settlement and offered to serve in the Roman armies as mercenaries. These reasonable requests, which the Roman emperors of a later time would gladly have granted, the senate rejected.

Two years later, another tribe, the Tigurini, crossed the Rhône and moved into southwestern France, where they met, defeated, and killed the consul L. Cassius Longinus and sent his army under the yoke. After the Tigurini had evacuated southwestern France, the people of Tolosa (Toulouse) rebelled and placed the Roman garrison in irons. In 106 B.C. the proud aristocratic consul, Quintus Servilius Caepio, recaptured the city by treachery and looted the temple of 100,000 pounds of gold and 110,000 pounds of silver. This treasure was later lost, either hijacked on the road to Massilia or embezzled, as he was accused, by Caepio himself.

The Battle of Arausio, 105 B.C.　The Germans again begged land for settlement and permission to enroll in the Roman army. Again the request was coldly rejected. Alarmed by the German invasion of Transalpine Gaul and the threat of an invasion of Italy, the senate ordered the consul Mallius Maximus, a *novus homo* like Marius, to join forces with Caepio. Caepio refused to cooperate with or take orders from Mallius. This refusal was a huge factor in the subsequent defeat of the Roman army with losses estimated at some eighty thousand men. The disaster revived memories of the Allia and the Sack of Rome. The "Cimbric terror" of 105 B.C. swept Marius into power and kept him there for five years, in violation of all constitutional precedent.

Marius Reorganizes the Legion   In terms of warfare, Marius' most important military reform was the reorganization of the Roman legion to meet the tactical problems presented by the Germanic tribes. Before his time the legion normally consisted of three thousand regular infantrymen and twelve hundred lightly armed skirmishers. He abolished the skirmishers and increased the legion to between five and six thousand men, all heavily armed. The old division into three distinct lines of *hastati, principes,* and *triarii* had practically lost its meaning, and Marius, if he retained them at all, probably amalgamated them in the *cohort,* a new tactical unit of from five to six hundred men or one-tenth of a legion. He also abolished the old maniple of 120 men or of two centuries of 60 men each as a separate legionary unit. Three maniples of 200 men—each maniple corresponding to one of the three old battle lines—now united to form the new cohort. The cohorts of Marius may be called supermaniples strong enough to fight separately but numerous enough to be deployed in various tactical combinations. Thus, without losing its flexibility, the legion acquired a compactness and cohesion symbolized by the new standard that Marius introduced, the famous silver eagle.

The soldiers were trained to fight as duelists in the cut-and-thrust technique used by gladiators. They were toughened up by long marches and by a great deal of fatigue duty, such as ditch digging. Thus, by a mixture of hard training and a rough and ready camaraderie, Marius created a formidable military machine which could also become an effective political weapon.

Roman Victories   The Germans planned to attack Italy on three widely separated fronts: the Teutons and Ambrones by way of southern France, the Cimbri, after circling around the northern slopes of the Alps, by way of the Brenner Pass and the valley of the Adige, and the Tigurini by way of the Julian Alps and Venetia. Dividing their forces in this way proved fatal. First, Marius defeated the Ambrones and Teutons in 102 B.C. Then, he crossed the Alps in 101 B.C. to reinforce Quintus Lutatius Catulus, who had retreated south of the Po in the face of the Cimbri. Together they annihilated the Cimbri at Vercellae (probably near Turin). The Tigurini wisely retreated home without a fight. Marius now appeared truly heroic.

The Slave Revolt in Sicily, 104 to 99 B.C.

Had the Germans invaded Italy and set at liberty a million slaves or more, the consequences might have been similar to the revolt of the slaves in Sicily which took five years to suppress. In 104 B.C. Marius asked the Roman client-kings of Asia Minor to send troops to assist in the defense of Italy against the Germanic invaders. When the kings sent back word that most of their subjects had been kidnapped and sold as slaves by the pirates and that many of them were in Sicily, Marius and the senate ordered the governor of Sicily to release the slaves held illegally. After the release of several hundred persons, the governor allowed himself to be browbeaten by the landowners and harshly ordered the rest of the slaves applying for freedom to go back to their masters. They did not go back; instead they took to the hills and prepared to resist. Under the leadership of Tryphon and Athenion, the slave revolt swelled into full scale war and for four years (104 to 101 B.C.) the slaves had control of the country. Before the end of the Cimbrian war released enough troops to put down the rebellion, 100,000 lives had already been lost.

Piracy in the Eastern Mediterranean
Even before the suppression of the Sicilian slaves, the Romans had to deal with piracy in the eastern Mediterranean. Ever since the destruction of Rhodes as a naval power, the pirates and slave traders of Cilicia and Crete enjoyed unrestricted freedom of the seas and conducted kidnapping raids upon the coastal regions of Syria and Asia Minor to supply the great slave market of Delos (where ten thousand slaves are said to have been sold every day) and Roman purchasers. Finally in 102 B.C., two years after King Nicomedes III of Bithynia had complained to Rome about the abduction of one-half of his able-bodied subjects, the praetor Marcus Antonius (grandfather of the famous Mark Antony) was commissioned to attack and destroy the chief bases and strongholds of the eastern Mediterranean pirates. After destroying the pirate strongholds, he annexed the coastal part of Cilicia as a Roman province and base of future operations against the pirates. These measures may have checked but did not destroy the evil of piracy, for in 100 or 99 B.C. the Romans had to close to pirate ships all ports and harbors under their control.

The Political Fall of Marius Just returned from glorious victories, Marius was the object of adulation and even worship: he was seen as "another Camillus" and the savior of Rome. He enjoyed the unfailing support of a devoted army and found before him a populace that cried out for leadership. He had held five consulships; he wanted his sixth and seventh.

Marius entered his sixth consulship in 100 B.C. Unfortunately for him, however, Rome was at peace. All of his jealous enemies in the senate now felt free to work against him. To overcome their opposition to legislation benefiting his veterans, equestrian supporters, and Italian clients, Marius had to rely on two opportunistic *populares,* Gaius Servilius Glaucia and Lucius Appuleius Saturninus, who were prepared to go to greater political extremes than Marius would have liked.

Lucius Appuleius Saturninus, 103 to 100 B.C. Saturninus was an eloquent speaker, an able man, and an ambitious noble whose career had suffered a serious setback. As a quaestor in 104 B.C., he had had charge of the grain administration at Ostia. When, through no fault of his own, grain prices rose and a famine was imminent because of the Sicilian slave revolts, rivals in the senate removed him from his post and replaced him with one of their own factional allies. Saturninus, therefore, became an active supporter of Marius in a attempt to gain popularity and a position of strength against his rivals.*

When Saturninus entered upon his first tribuneship in 103, he sponsored a law assigning 66 acres of land in Africa to each of Marius' African veterans. A colleague of his, acting in concert with his opponents, attempted to veto the bill, but after a shower of stones promptly withdrew his veto. Saturninus had no patience with obstructive tactics or legal technicalities. Fists and stones were more effective than vetoes or religious "omens."

During his first tribuneship, Saturninus introduced a law that made it a criminal offense to compromise, injure, or diminish the honor or dignity *(maiestas)* of the Roman people. This was very dangerous legislation. Under it Saturninus brought action against Caepio and Mallius for losing the battle of Arausio in 105 B.C. In the case of Caepio the law was needed since the old law against treason *(perduellio)* did not cover insubordination to legally constituted authority, which jeopardized the safety of the army and the very existence of the state. Caepio was an extremely unpopular person for other reasons. During his consulship in 106 B.C., he secured the

---

* Another politician injured in the same factional conflicts within the senate was Cn. Domitius Ahenobarbus, a tribune of 104 B.C. Angry because he was not co-opted into the college of pontiffs to succeed his father, he brought Aemilius Scaurus to trial for the improper performance of sacred rites. When he failed to convict him, he secured the passage of a law (the *lex Domitia*) which made all the priestly offices elective by seventeen tribes, chosen by lot, instead of by priestly nomination. In this way, Domitius outmaneuvered his rivals and was the first Pontifex Maximus to be elected by the people.

passage of a law (later repealed in the tribuneship of Glaucia in 104) restoring senators to the juries of the extortion courts. He was also held responsible for the mysterious disappearance of the sacred treasures seized at Toulouse. When Caepio was tried before the people for these crimes and misdemeanors, two tribunes, who attempted to veto the proceedings, were driven off by violence, and Aemilius Scaurus, a prominent optimate and *princeps senatus,* was hit on the head with a stone.

In 100 B.C., the year of his second tribunate, Saturninus embarked upon a full program of social legislation. This program included a grain law (possibly dating back to his first tribunate of 103), which restored the regular monthly grain distributions suspended after the death of Gaius Gracchus at a selling price below the market rate. The bill seems to have been carried over the vetoes of his fellow tribunes and the violent opposition of the quaestor in charge of the treasury. His second bill provided for the founding of veteran colonies in Sicily, Greece, Macedonia, and possibly Africa. A third law assigned land once occupied by the Cimbri and Teutons in Gaul (possibly Transalpine Gaul) to veterans who had fought under Marius.

Lastly, Saturninus proposed a general mobilization of Roman forces against the Cilician pirates and against Mithridates VI of Pontus, a command that was intended for Marius. To this batch of laws, Saturninus appended a clause requiring all senators to take oath within five days to obey these laws—on pain of loss of their seats, exile, and a fine of twenty talents. In spite of vetoes, "omens," and violence, the laws were passed.

To most of these laws Marius' and Saturninus' enemies in the senate offered strenuous and determined opposition. They suborned tribunes to interpose vetoes, which Saturninus brushed aside with, "Let the voting proceed." Then by courier the opposing senators informed the presiding magistrate that they heard thunder in the distance, a religious "omen" long employed to block necessary legislation. Saturninus asked the courier to advise the hostile senators to keep quiet lest the thunder turn into hail.

The Fall of Saturninus and Marius   All eyes were fixed on Marius to see if he would take the oath of obedience appended to the bill assigning land in Gaul to his veterans. At the last minute he did take the oath to observe the law "as far as it was legal." This express reservation turned the law into a farce. All the senators who took the oath would be able to make the same reservation. Marius' blunder lay in his indecision. He wanted to cooperate with the popular leaders, but at the same time he did not like to offend the powerful senators who opposed Saturninus. Marius thus reveals what was typical of most *populares.* He was quite willing to seek popularity by opportunistic means in order to gain high office and status, but he shared the same basic aristocratic outlook as his foes. Having achieved equality with his former noble opponents and rivals, he instinctively cooperated with them in preserving the political status quo.

Before the end of his second tribuneship, Saturninus had lost the support of both the equestrian class and the city masses. The *equites* disliked his radical and revolutionary methods and feared that he might next attack the sanctity of private property. The city voters turned against him because his agrarian law of 100 B.C. had granted too many benefits to the veterans, many of whom were Italians. Hostile senators were not slow to take advantage of the mistakes, vacillations, and petty hatreds of Marius, Saturninus, the *equites,* and the city voters and to involve them all in a common ruin. The popular leaders, particularly Saturninus and Glaucia, had naively supposed that they could with impunity employ violence and assassination.

Knowing now that their lives were worth nothing the moment they stepped down from office, Saturninus and Glaucia campaigned successfully for the tribuneship and consulship, respectively, in defiance of the Villian law requiring a two-year interval between the offices of praetor and consul (see p. 142). In order to rid himself of a possibly successful opponent, Glaucia hired gangsters to kill the former tribune Gaius Memmius. The senate declared a state of emergency and ordered Marius to take action under the *S. C. U.*

Marius did not want to injure or destroy Saturninus, Glaucia, and the other popular politicians to whom he and his veterans owed so many benefits. To save their lives and follow the senate's orders at the same time, he locked them up in the senate building. An angry mob of nobles and *equites* climbed up to the roof, ripped off tiles, and pelted his prisoners to death. Marius was ruined. Distrusted and disliked by his old enemies among the nobles and despised for his weakness by his former friends, he was obliged to look on helplessly as the senate declared the laws of Saturninus null and void. This action apparently ruined Marius' career and gave second thoughts to those who would seek political advantage through *popularis* tactics. It is not surprising that he suddenly "remembered" that he had to go to the East to fulfill a vow.

The Decade of Reaction The stormy opening of the last century of the Republic soon died down. It was followed by a decade of inaction and stagnation. The slave revolt in Sicily that began in 104 B.C. was triumphantly suppressed in 99 B.C. A Spanish uprising of 97 to 93 B.C. was also brilliantly handled. The veterans of Marius were still unsatisfied and the demand of the Italians for citizenship was answered by their expulsion from the city in 95 B.C. In the interest of making it more difficult for *populares* to utilize tribunician legislation, a law was passed in 98 B.C. to require an interval of seventeen days between the promulgation of a piece of legislation and its enactment by the *concilium plebis*. This provision would allow those whose political power was guaranteed by the status quo to marshall enough opposition to defeat a law that they did not like. The new law also forbade the enactment of an omnibus bill *(lex Satura)* that included more than one subject in its provisions, such as Saturninus may have tried to pass. Finally in 92 B.C., P. Rutilius Rufus, who assisted Mucius Scaevola

as deputy governor of Asia, was tried and convicted for extortion. His "offense" in the eyes of the equestrian jurors was that he had assisted the stern and righteous governor in drawing up a model edict and in preventing the tax-farming companies from plundering the people of the province. The conviction of this upright man seems to have proved that it was dangerous for a provincial governor to be other than an opportunist. Such were the main events of this passive and melancholy decade prior to the rise of the Younger Livius Drusus.

The Attempted Reforms of Livius Drusus, 91 B.C. The monotony was broken in 91 B.C. by the tribune Livius Drusus the Younger. He was more brilliant and, perhaps, idealistic than his father, who in 122 B.C. had helped to bring about the downfall of Gaius Gracchus. Livius Drusus' reforms had two major components: (1) an increase in the size of the senate by recruiting new members from the equestrian class; and (2) the extension of Roman citizenship to the Italian allies. He proposed to double the senate's membership by the admission of 300 of the richest and most prominent men of the equestrian order. This reform had as its aim the fusion of the two highest classes representing nobility and wealth. To remove the chief source of friction between these two classes, he proposed that jurors for the extortion court be chosen partly from the enlarged membership of the senate and partly no doubt from the *equites* enrolled in the first eighteen centuries of the Centuriate Assembly. To his proposed reform of the courts he added a special clause making corruption or the acceptance of bribes a criminal offense.

These proposals naturally met with a chilly reception from some of the powerful vested interests in the senate and the united opposition of the equestrian class, and could not possibly be carried through the assembly unless Drusus succeeded in winning the support of the masses. To gain this support he proposed the public distribution of grain at low prices, the founding of colonies in Italy and Sicily (as his father had once proposed), and the renewed distribution of public land to individual colonists. To defray the expenses of his grain law he proposed to debase the silver coinage with an eighth part of copper. All these laws seem to have been passed but whether separately or in an omnibus bill is uncertain.

Nor is it certain how, if, and when he introduced the bill to extend Roman citizenship to the Latin and Italian allies. As a separate law, it stood no better chance of passage than it had in the time of Fulvius Flaccus or of Gaius Gracchus. The urban voters were just as strongly opposed to it as ever; the *equites* did not want to share their control of the courts or tax-gathering privileges in the provinces with the Italian upper class; nor some of the short-sighted senators their office-holding rights with the aristocracy of the local Italian towns. It is more likely that Drusus hoped to be able to tie it in with other more popular proposals. Of the need, wisdom, and justice of the law there can be little question. The Italian allies had supplied more than half the soldiers who had fought Rome's battles but had no share in the Roman higher offices, no say in determining Roman policies, had received no benefits that Roman citizens enjoyed in the distributions of public lands, no protection against the abuse and tyranny of Roman generals and officers, and no right of appeal in cases tried by Roman judges.

In the end, the rest of the legislative proposals of Livius Drusus fared no better than the abortive proposal for Italian citizenship. The judicial law was enacted and seemed at first to meet general approval in the senate, though the die-hard traditionalists, who bitterly opposed the admission of the wealthy nonaristocrats to their exclusive body, had wanted nothing less than a repeal of the Gracchan law and full restoration of jury service to the senate. Some of those who currently dominated the senate also did not want the addition of a large number of new senators, whose loyalty they could not control. Other members, who had been able to profit from the financial speculations of the *equites,* did not want the Gracchan law disturbed. At last, the opposition, led by the consul L. Marcius Philippus, grew strong enough to declare the laws of Livius Drusus null and void on the ground that they had been passed through violence and unconstitutional methods.

Even after the nullification of his reforms, Drusus seems to have been determined to propose a special law granting citizenship to the Italian allies. But, before he was able to bring the bill to a vote, he was stabbed to death near the entrance of his house by an unknown assassin. Thus died Livius Drusus the Younger, a tragic example of how explosive a mixture politics and reform were in the late Roman Republic.

The Italian or Social War, 90 to 88 B.C. The justice that Livius Drusus the Younger had failed to procure for the Italian allies by legal means was achieved in a war that could easily have been avoided if the Roman aristocracy had been able to put aside their own rivalries and selfishness. Never since the Samnite and Pyrrhic Wars, not even in the blackest days after Cannae, had Roman supremacy in Italy been more violently shaken than in the months that followed the stabbing of Livius Drusus. With his death vanished the last hope of the Italian allies of securing the rights and freedoms of citizenship by peaceful means. The praetor Gaius Servilius Caepio went to the Abruzzi and addressed the people of Asculum (Ascoli) in a violent harangue against their agitation for citizenship and their revolutionary societies. The Asculans, enraged by the insolence of his threats, tore apart Caepio and his lictors, and massacred all the Romans who lived in the town. The war which Livius Drusus had tried to prevent had begun.

The revolt spread like wildfire through the Abruzzi down into the southern Apennines. First the Marsi rose to arms, then their neighbors, the Paeligni, Marrucini, and Frentani; in the North, the unenfranchised Picenes and Vestini; in the South, the Samnites, the Lucanians, and Apulians. From the Po to the straits of Messana the Italian people rose up in arms. Only the landlord-ridden sections of Umbria and Etruria remained at peace, as did the more Romanized Latins and Campanians, and the Greek coastal cities from Naples to Tarentum.

Preparation for War   Among the insurgents the Marsi and the Samnites were the fiercest. Together with their allies they declared their independence and set up a confederacy called Italia, whose capital was at Corfinium in the Abruzzi about 75 miles due east of Rome. Their government, modeled on that of Rome, consisted of a senate of 500 members representing the various tribes and towns and of two consuls and twelve praetors elected annually by their senate. The new state issued its own coinage showing usually on one side either Bacchus or a female head representing Italia and on the other a swearing in of troops or the Italian bull goring the Roman she-wolf.

The Italian confederacy raised an army of 100,000 men, many of them hardened soldiers trained in the tactics and discipline of the Roman army. They had as their commanders two excellent generals, the Marsian Q. Pompaedius Silo, and the Samnite C. Papius Mutilus. In the spring of 90 B.C., the Italian armies advanced westward, the Samnites against Campania and the Marsians against Latium, in order to cut Rome off from the south.

In waging war against the Italians, the Romans had several important advantages. Their control over the ports and harbors of Italy as well as their command of the sea gave them access to the manpower and resources of the provinces and enabled them to recruit Gauls, Spaniards, and Numidians. In a short time they were able to raise and equip about 150,000 men. Another advantage was their ability to operate within interior lines of communication, and their control of the road system enabled them to shift troops from one point to another more quickly than the insurgents. Within insurgent territory the Romans held strong enclaves of resistance in colonies of Roman citizens and towns that had already been granted citizenship over the years, which could threaten or impede the Italian war effort.

Military Operations   Even with these advantages, the Romans fared badly in the first year of the war. Some of their defeats arose from many senators' hostility and spite toward Marius, their most capable military leader. He was recalled from his self-imposed exile in Asia, but instead of being placed in command of the army sent eastward against the Marsi, he was made only a *legatus,* deputy commander, under the consul P. Rutilius Lupus, who had little military skill or experience. The consul, rejecting Marius' advice to take time to train his troops, attacked immediately, and was defeated and killed. Only the military genius of Marius saved the main Roman army from complete disaster. Even then he was obliged to share the supreme command with Q. Servilius Caepio, who was later lured into an ambush and killed.

The Roman Grant of Citizenship to the Italians   The war continued to go badly for the Romans until later in 90 B.C. when one of the consuls, Lucius Julius Caesar (cousin of the more famous Gaius Julius Caesar) did what should have been done in the first place. He returned to Rome and carried a bill called the *lex Julia* to confer citizenship on all Latins and Italians still loyal to Rome and to those who would at once lay down their arms. In 89 B.C. the tribunes, M. Plautius Silvanus and C. Papirius Carbo, put through a more comprehensive bill, the *lex Plautia-Papiria,* granting citizenship to all free persons resident in any allied community who would register before a Roman praetor within sixty days. A third law, the *lex Pompeia,* proposed by Gnaeus Pompeius Strabo (a consul of the same year and father of Pompey the Great), extended citizenship to all free persons residing in Cisalpine Gaul south of the Po and Latin rights to those living north of the river. The revolts began to collapse.

Strabo was a very good general and an

opportunistic politician who backed whatever side in Roman politics seemed most personally advantageous at the moment. Militarily and politically his son, who along with later famous figures like Cicero and Catiline served on Strabo's staff, was much like him but more personally charming. At one point it was only the young Pompey's pleas that saved his father from death at the hands of mutinous soldiers. Strabo ended the war in the North by capturing Asculum and, it was charged, misappropriated the booty. In 88 B.C., Strabo was guilty of complicity in the murder of his cousin, the consul Q. Pompeius Rufus, who was supposed to take over Strabo's command. Thereupon, Strabo continued to fight until the Marsi and their allies were defeated in central Italy.

On the southern front, Sulla, as the other consul of 88, took over the command from Lucius Julius Caesar and decisively defeated the Samnites under Papius Mutilus in southern Campania. After sweeping all the Samnite forces out of Campania, he carried the war into Samnium. His victorious march was checked finally by a reverse at the hands of the famous Marsian general, Pompaedius Silo, who later was killed in a battle with Q. Metellus Pius. The death of the great Marsian marked the end of the war except for sporadic local resistance. The longest to hold out was Nola in Campania, which lay besieged for many years.

The Aftermath of the Social War
The war had exacted a heavy price for the shortsightedness and petty politicing that had blocked Livius Drusus' proposal to grant citizenship to Rome's Italian allies. The human and property losses must have been almost as great as those inflicted by Hannibal. The economic hardships were extremely severe.

Food was scarce and prices high; rich and poor were oppressed by debts that they had no means of paying; and the city was crowded with Italian refugees. The city praetor of 89 B.C., A. Sempronius Asellio, attempted to give the debtors some relief by issuing an edict which revived the fourth century B.C. law prohibiting interest. He was killed by a mob of angry creditors.

The war had actually been a civil war and had pitted against each other communities that in some cases had been fighting side by side for 200 years. It set a dangerous precedent for civil warfare in Italy and trained a generation of leaders who were willing to resort to it in pursuit of personal political goals.

As for the problems that produced war, the majority of senators seemed to have learned little from the experience. With the war almost over, it was politics as usual. There was a move to limit the voting power of the new citizens by enrolling them in only eight or ten of the thirty-five tribes of citizens. This shortsighted action merely fueled more divisive struggles that rent the Republic in the following years.

Nevertheless, the war produced some good results. It added almost 500,000 new citizens to the rolls. From the Po river to the straits of Messana all free men were now Romans, and all the many different ethnic elements would in time be fused into a single nation. Local self-government was still continued and all communities and municipalities enjoyed the right to elect their own boards of four magistrates *(Quattuorviri)*. Gradually they would adopt Roman private and public law as well as a common Latin language. The grant of universal Roman citizenship was a giant stride toward national unification and the development of a common Latin culture that characterized Italy in later centuries.

XVI

Marius and Sulla: Civil War and Reaction, 88 to 78 B.C.

The foreign and domestic crises since the time of the Gracchi reveal some of the basic problems with the Roman Republic. It was ruled by an aristocratic class of large landowners whose main activities were the accumulation of wealth and prestige through the winning of high office and military leadership in competition with each other. The acquisition of a great overseas empire had intensified the competition by increasing the value of the prizes for which the aristocrats competed. It also produced a number of major social, economic, and administrative problems with which neither they nor the institutions of the Republic could cope.

Because the higher offices, including the chief executive and military office of consul, were only held for one year, each year was an election year. It was very difficult to develop any consistent policies or programs, and almost every act would be judged in the context of personal rivalries and short-term electoral politics. Therefore, useful and necessary reforms were extremely difficult to effect. Military operations were often bungled because a man was too anxious to gain a victory during the limited time available or a competent man was replaced before he could accomplish his

goals. (This problem was tacitly realized when Marius was elected to five successive consulships during the invasions of the Cimbri and Teutones.) Often the provinces were unscrupulously exploited by governors who had their eyes on amassing money for the next election or paying off the debts incurred in the last one, so that provincial unrest was aggravated.

Since the senate was the arena in which members of the aristocracy competed, it was not easy for objective or rational solutions to problems to be generated there. Nor were the popular assemblies any more capable. They met infrequently, only at the summons of a magistrate, attendance was difficult and sporadic for citizens who lived any significant distance from Rome, and they could easily be packed or manipulated according to the rivalries and passions of the moment.

As a result of all these factors, increasing problems produced increasing instability, which merely increased the problems and led to further instability. A good example of this syndrome can be found in the First Mithridatic War. It broke out near the end of the Social War, in part because Rome now looked weak, and it touched off such a bitter rivalry between

Marius and Sulla for command that it precipitated an increasingly brutal series of civil wars.

Sources for the Years 88 to 78 B.C.

As for the previous period, the only two major sources are Appian and Plutarch. Appian covers the First Mithridatic War (88 to 85 B.C.) in Book 12 (*Mithridatic Wars,* sections 1–63) and the turmoil at Rome from 88 to 78 in Book 13 (*Civil Wars,* Book 1, sections 55–107). Plutarch's lives of Marius and Sulla are particularly important, and pertinent information is also found in the early portions of his biographies of Sertorius, Lucullus, Pompey, Crassus, Caesar, and Cicero. Velleius Paterculus presents a summary in Book 2 (18–29) of his *Histories,* and Books 77 to 90 of Livy are summarized in the *Periochae* and later epitomators. There are a few fragments from Books 30 to 35 of Cassius Dio and sizable fragments from Books 37 to 39 of Diodorus Siculus. There also survive some interesting fragments on the First Mithridatic War from the first-century A.D. Greek historian Memnon of Heraclea in Pontus. For the Mithridatic War some official documents of both Sulla and Mithridates have been preserved on inscriptions. For internal affairs, numerous references scattered throughout the works of Cicero make him a valuable contemporary witness.

Mithridates VI Eupator (134–63 B.C.)

In granting citizenship to the Italians to end the Social War, the senatorial leadership had been prompted not only by the adverse military situation in Italy, but also by the aggressive actions of Mithridates VI, King of Pontus. He had taken advantage of the resentment that often-corrupt Roman rule in the eastern provinces had aroused and of Rome's involvement first with Germanic invaders and then in the desperate Social War. His goal was to overthrow Roman rule in the eastern Mediterranean and create an empire of his own on the model of Alexander the Great's. By 90 B.C. he had gained control of all but the western coast of the Black Sea and most of the interior of Asia Minor. At that time, however, the Romans were thoroughly aroused by his simultaneous seizures of Bithynia and Cappadocia. Therefore, the senate sent a special envoy, Manius Aquilius, to compel Mithridates to withdraw from both kingdoms and recognize Ariobarzanes as the lawful king of Cappadocia and Nicomedes III, son of Nicomedes II, as king of Bithynia. That done, Aquilius did a very foolish thing. He incited Nicomedes to raid Pontus in order to seize enough loot to reward the Romans for their intervention in Bithynia.

Mithridates Makes War on Rome   When Aquilius persuaded Nicomedes to invade Pontus (88 B.C.), Mithridates, after several unheeded protests, decided to strike. Quickly defeating Nicomedes, he swept the weak Roman forces aside and invaded Pergamum. He captured Aquilius and paid him the money that he had demanded by pouring molten gold down his throat. Many in Asia Minor welcomed Mithridates as a deliverer and a savior and seized the chance of making the Romans pay dearly for their forty years of oppression. By prearrangement they slaughtered many Italians, mostly tax agents, money lenders, and merchants, although the figure of eighty thousand given in the sources is probably highly exaggerated.

The conquest of Asia Minor was not enough. Mithridates would not feel secure unless he added Greece to his dominions. He knew that the Romans were hated in Greece almost as much as in Asia and had sent his agents to Athens and other cities to make propaganda for his cause. Meanwhile, his powerful navy had broken out into the Aegean and made a descent on Delos, where he ordered the massacre of twenty thousand Italian merchants and slave dealers. That massacre and the seizure of property permanently destroyed the prosperity of the island. Athens, too, was ready for revolt and, under the leadership of the philosophers Athenion and Aristion, overthrew its pro-Roman oligarchic government and made common cause with Mithridates, whose general, Archelaus, occupied the Piraeus (port of Athens) and from that base conquered most of southern Greece. Another Pontic army was entering Greece from the North. Such was the dangerous situation in the East as Rome slowly rose from the ruins of the Social War.

The Rise of Sulla (138–78 B.C.) Two well-known and experienced Roman generals, Marius and Sulla, were most eager for the command in the war against Mithridates. Marius wanted to recover the popularity that he had enjoyed after the Jugurthine and Cimbrian Wars but had later lost. Sulla, from an old patrician family that had not been prominent within the consular nobility for some time, wanted the command because he believed that the war would be easily won and a source of power, fame, and also fortune. His rivalry with Marius went back at least as far as his capture of Jugurtha, on account of which he tried to claim at Marius' expense much of the credit for ending the Jugurthine War. He was closely allied with Marius' optimate enemies in the senate, and they had assured his election to the consulship of 88 B.C. and an important command in the Social War, while Marius had to settle for a legateship. Now Sulla's powerful friends procured him the coveted command against Mithridates.

The Tribuneship of P. Sulpicius Rufus, 88 B.C. The question of the Mithridatic command might well have been settled if it had not been for the political aims of the tribune P. Sulpicius Rufus, a close friend and admirer of Livius Drusus the Younger. Sulpicius had strongly opposed the restriction of the newly enfranchised Italians to eight of the thirty-five tribes. Though a member of one of the most ancient and illustrious patrician families and an heir to immense wealth, Sulpicius had given up his patrician status (89 B.C.) in order to qualify for election as tribune. Like Gaius Gracchus, he was an orator of remarkable power, a little inclined to be showy perhaps but, Cicero declared, by far the best he had ever heard.

As tribune of the people, Sulpicius Rufus made four proposals which seem to have been presented in one omnibus bill: (1) to enroll the new Italian citizens as well as the freedmen in all the thirty-five tribes; (2) to recall all exiles; (3) to exclude from the senate all members owing bills in excess of two thousand denarii in order to prevent bribery and corruption; and (4) to replace Sulla with Marius in the command against Mithridates. The first law was the least acceptable. He was able to muster the support of twelve tribes (he needed eighteen): the four urban ones, to which Aemilius Scaurus had, in 115 B.C., assigned the freedmen, and the eight in which the Italians already had votes. To gain the support of the six other required tribes, he had to make a deal with Marius, who might, in exchange for the command against Mithridates, be able through the votes of his veterans to swing the six needed tribes required for a majority. The bill became law, though not without considerable opposition and violence.

Sulla's March on Rome At first Sulla tried to prevent the passage of these laws by declaring religious holidays in order to suspend all meetings of the assembly. Exasperated by the repeated use of that religious weapon, Sulpicius and his armed followers rioted. Ironically, Sulla escaped by taking refuge in the house of Marius. After Sulla had publicly revoked the religious holidays, Marius, like an old soldier doing a good turn for another, allowed him to escape from his house with the expectation that he would go into exile. Instead, Sulla hastened to his army, which was then besieging Nola, and persuaded it to march on Rome. The increasingly bitter factional struggles among ambitious politicians had led to outright civil war for the first time in the annals of the Roman Republic. It is a great irony that this act was made possible in part by the military reforms of Marius, which had increased the personal dependence of the soldiers upon their commanders and weakened their loyalty to the state.

During the ensuing reign of terror, Sulla set fire to all the sections of the city that offered resistance and put to death many innocent people. Sulpicius attempted to escape but was betrayed. He was murdered and his head stuck up on the rostra in the Forum. Marius also fled and reached the coast of North Africa after some narrow escapes.

The victorious Sulla rescinded the laws of Sulpicius Rufus. Although he introduced a law for the relief of debtors by reducing the maximum rate of interest to ten percent, he then made a number of reactionary changes designed to make it impossible for anyone outside his group of optimate friends to challenge their dominant position within the senatorial aristocracy. He made the Centuriate Assembly the primary legislative assembly by revoking the right of tribunes to introduce legislation in the *concilium plebis*. The Centuriate Assembly was also reorganized so that the centuries of the senatorial and upper middle class and those of the first assessment class had a clear majority. Another reactionary step was the requirement that magistrates consult the senate before introducing new legislation.

Sulla's attempt to interfere with the consular elections failed, though he did manage to extract a promise from one of the newly elected consuls, Lucius Cornelius Cinna, not to tamper with any of Sulla's constitutional changes already made. After Sulla had carried out these changes, he departed for the East to make war against Mithridates.

Cinna's Consulship, 87 B.C.

Hardly was Sulla gone from Italy's shores than Cinna annulled the laws of Sulla and reenacted those of Sulpicius. He enrolled the Italians in all thirty-five tribes against the opposition of the *optimates,* including his colleague, Gnaeus Octavius. After some rioting, Octavius drove Cinna from the city and had him declared a public enemy by a vote of the senate. In so doing his enemies committed a very serious blunder for they gave him the opportunity of appealing to the Italian voters and winning the support of the army still besieging the Campanian town of Nola. He recalled Marius from Africa and, imitating Sulla's deadly example, marched on Rome.

Marius and his Reign of Terror

Recalled from Africa, the elderly Marius, now well over seventy, stormed Ostia, the seaport of Rome, cut off the food supplies of Rome, and starved her into surrender. Marius, brutalized by years of war and slaughter, embittered by ingratitude and neglect, and maddened by his recent experiences in Italy and Africa as a hunted outlaw, gave full vent to his rage and lust for blood. For days he ranged the city like a raving lunatic. His followers struck down all the nobles and senators whom he hated. Their mutilated corpses littered the streets and their heads, dripping blood, decorated the rostra. Their houses and property were confiscated and auctioned. His outrages made even Cinna quail and finally stop them. In 86 B.C., Marius at last achieved his long-cherished ambition of a seventh consulship, but he did not long enjoy his victory. He fell ill and died a few days after taking office.

The Significance of Marius

For a *novus homo,* Marius had had an unusually great impact on Roman history. His military service in making the Roman army more tactically effective, in defeating Jugurtha, and in annihilating the threat of Germanic invasion made him an authentic hero. Politically, however, he was more of a villain. The problem was not with his opening military recruitment to the propertyless and its negative political consequences. That would have happened anyway. Rather, the problem was that his only goal was to achieve and continue to hold the consulship. He had no real program to deal with Rome's pressing problems. Therefore, he only made them worse and undermined faith in the political system. Although he was not the first to resort to outright civil war, his willingness to follow Sulla's example in that case helped to set precedents for violence that greatly aided in the destruction of the Republic. Moreover, his reputation as a military hero and the popular policies of Saturninus, Sulpicius, and Cinna, who had become associated with him, created among his veterans, the urban masses, and new Italian citizens a large body of people who could be manipulated by appeals to his name in the increasingly bitter factional struggles of the late Republic.

Cinna's Time (Cinnanum Tempus)

After Marius' sudden death in 86, Cinna was in effect left as a dictator. Foregoing elections, he appointed Lucius Valerius Flaccus as consul to replace Marius, and for 85 and 84 he simply appointed himself and Gnaeus Papirius Carbo to the consulship. Cinna attempted, however, to use his power much more responsibly than Marius ever had in order to secure his position. He overturned Sulla's reactionary laws and tried to satisfy the legitimate grievances of those who supported him. He obtained the election of censors who registered the new Italian citizens equitably in all thirty-five tribes. Flaccus introduced a law that forgave three-quarters of all debts, while financial stability was protected by restoring the value of the coinage, which had been thrown into disarray during the recent upheavals and debased by corrupt moneyers.

Under Cinna the senate and courts continued to function, and many nobles supported him. Those who did not support him prudently kept a low profile and waited to see what would happen with Sulla, who, despite being stripped of his command against Mithridates, ignored Cinna's government and continued to press the war. Cinna attempted to come to an amicable agreement, but Sulla would have none of it. As Sulla went from victory to victory and assumed control of the East with all of its resources, support began to shift toward him at Rome, and Cinna was forced to take a harder stand and prepare for another disruptive civil war before dying suddenly in 84 B.C.

Sulla's Operations against Mithridates

Having landed thirty thousand men in Greece in 87 B.C., Sulla had captured and looted Athens in 86 after a winter of siege. Then, using superior Roman tactics, he had defeated the Hellenistic phalanxes of Mithridates in central Greece at Chaeronea and Orchomenus during the summer. After Chaeronea, the consul Flaccus, whom Cinna had sent to take over command from Sulla, arrived in Greece with another army, but he accomplished nothing. He lost some of his men at sea in encounters with the fleet of Mithridates. He lost still others by defection to Sulla, who refused to obey legitimate orders to surrender his command. Flaccus, after an oral agreement, promptly set out for Asia by way of Macedonia and Thrace. No sooner had Flaccus crossed the Hellespont and arrived in Bithynia than his soldiers mutinied at the instigation of Flaccus' own legate, C. Flavius Fimbria, and murdered him. Elected by the soldiers' council to take over the command, Fimbria exhibited surprising energy and talent. In a night attack he defeated the army of Mithridates' son and marched against Pergamum. Mithridates, realizing that he had already lost the war not only because of the defeats of his armies but because of the revolts stirred up in Asia Minor by his despotism and tyranny, sued for peace.

Sulla wanted peace so as to be free to get back to Italy and take revenge on the followers of Marius and Cinna. The peace that he made in 85 B.C. at Dardanus in the Troad was the softest that a Roman was ever known to make, especially with an enemy like Mithridates, who had robbed and murdered innumerable Roman and Italian citizens. All that Mithridates was required to do was abandon his conquests in Asia Minor, surrender eighty of his warships, and pay the comparatively trifling indemnity of two thousand talents. Far harsher terms were imposed on the province of Asia, from which was exacted an indemnity of twenty thousand talents and five years' back taxes. Sulla billeted his army on the towns during the winter of 85 to 84 B.C. and required them to pay each soldier sixteen drachmae a day, which apart from the food and clothing also required of them must have amounted to at least another twenty thousand talents. To raise these vast sums the province had to turn to the Roman money lenders and fell victim to a crushing burden of debt.

Sulla's Return to Italy, 83 B.C.   After making peace with Mithridates, Sulla took over the army of Fimbria, who later committed suicide. Placing that army under the command of Lucius Licinius Murena to serve as a permanent garrison in the province of Asia, Sulla set sail for Italy. Accompanied by his army of from thirty to forty thousand men, more loyal to him than to their country, he stepped ashore at Brundisium in the spring of 83 B.C. To oppose Sulla, the ex-consul Carbo had raised two armies of fifty thousand men, mostly raw recruits, undisciplined, and not very loyal or reliable. They were also poorly led, for the two consuls in command, L. Cornelius Scipio and C. Norbanus, knew little about war. Sulla defeated the army of Norbanus with little trouble; Scipio's deserted to him. The only anti-Sullan who might have defeated him was Quintus Sertorius, but the other opponents of Sulla had found him too disturbing a critic and at the earliest opportunity had shipped him off to Spain instead.

The leaders who joined Sulla after he left Asia Minor were much superior to their opponents in military capacity and experience. The first was his brother-in-law, Quintus Caecilius Metellus Pius, who brought with him a number of recruits from his hiding place in North Africa. Next came the young Marcus Licinius Crassus at the head of a small army returning from Spain. Gnaeus Pompeius (Pompey), the young son of Pompeius Strabo, was an even more valuable addition both in the number of troops that he brought and in military skill. On his own initiative he had raised three legions in Picenum and on reaching Sulla was hailed, young as he was, with the flattering title of *Imperator*. After Pompey had won several victories, Sulla somewhat facetiously called him *Magnus*, "the Great," and the title stuck.

To bolster their tottering regime, the anti-Sullans elected as consuls for 82 B.C. Cn. Papirius Carbo and Gaius Marius, the adopted son of the dead Marius. Neither one was a first class general though both were fairly successful in gathering recruits, especially in Etruria and Samnium, where the elder Marius had enjoyed great support. Carbo went south and rallied thousands of Samnites to his cause, while Marius attracted many veterans by the magic of his father's name. Choosing separate combat areas, Carbo directed operations in the north, Marius outside Rome. In his efforts to block Sulla's advance up the Appian Way, Marius fought a hard but losing battle and was forced to take refuge in Praeneste. Sulla immediately dashed north and met Carbo at Clusium (Chiusi) in Etruria. Although he did not win a decisive victory, he succeeded in breaking the morale of Carbo's army, already somewhat undermined by the successes of Metellus in northern Italy and of Pompey and Crassus in Umbria. Carbo, seeing the futility of further struggle, escaped to North Africa.

Carbo may have given up too quickly. The war was far from being over and even victory might still have been won. Had Carbo had the military sense of a Marius, he might have, even with his battered army, followed Sulla as he hastened south to meet a huge Samnite army outside of Rome. At the battle of the Colline Gate, the Samnites, fighting with insane fury far into the night, crumpled the left wing, which was under Sulla's personal command, and had Crassus, in command of the right wing, not been victorious, Sulla might never have become dictator of Rome. Carbo's arrival at that crucial moment might have spared Rome the horrors of a Sullan triumph.

Sulla's Reign of Terror, 82 B.C.   The bloody battle at the Colline Gate ended all effective resistance in Italy. Then a reign of terror began, during which thousands of persons suffered death often accompanied by torture. Next door to the temple of Bellona, where Sulla was addressing a meeting of the senate, six thousand Samnite prisoners, whose only crime was that they lost a battle for what they believed was freedom and justice, were tortured to death. As the screams of the dying broke into his speech and distressed some of the senators to the point of fainting, Sulla grimly explained that only some criminals were punished at his orders.

The Proscriptions   To ruthlessness he added method. He posted lists of his intended victims, some carefully selected by himself, other suggested by his henchmen; some were listed for political reasons, others to avenge private injuries and others for no other reason than that the proscribed owned large and valuable properties. The proscribed were to be hunted down as outlaws, murdered, and a price set on their heads. Sulla confiscated their property and revoked the citizenship of their children. Among the thousands he doomed to die were ninety senators, fifteen men of consular rank, and twenty-six hundred *equites,* whose property was distributed among Sulla's supporters and veterans. As beneficiaries of his murders they would, when required, rally around him or loyally support the oligarchy, whose power he proposed to restore. He secured additional supporters by freeing ten thousand slaves who had belonged to his victims. He generously rewarded some freedmen. One, for example, was allowed to buy an estate worth about 1.5 million denarii for about twenty-five hundred.

Unfortunately, the murder and spoliation of rich individuals failed to provide enough money or land to enable Sulla to redeem his promises of pay, pensions, and farms to his discharged veterans. He compelled cities, towns, and other communities to contribute their share to the cause, especially those suspected of having resisted his seizure of power or of having supported his enemies. Their punishment was in proportion to the duration and strength of their resistance and opposition. The cities that offered only mild opposition were required to pay fines, have their walls torn down, and surrender most, if not all, of their territory. Others, such as Praeneste in Latium or Florentia (Florence) in Etruria, which resisted him long and stubbornly, were destroyed and their inhabitants sold into slavery. He also turned the richest and most thickly populated districts of Sam-

nium into a desert. Although the confiscations and enslavements were heaviest in Etruria and a few other parts of central and northern Italy, Samnium remained for long a desolate waste. Such were the atrocities that resulted from the increasingly bitter rivalries within the Roman ruling elite. The Roman Republic had come to a sorry state of affairs.

Sulla's Changes of the Constitution
In 82 B.C., a few days before his arrival in Rome, Sulla had demanded and secured the formal passage by the Centuriate Assembly of a law known as the *lex Valeria* to appoint him dictator for an undefined period for the purpose of drafting laws and "reconstituting" the state. The assembly, confirming that which had already been established by military force, revived an office held only once since the middle of the third century (by Fabius Maximus Cunctator in 217 B.C.), and legalized his murders, confiscations, and other atrocities. Unrestrained by law or custom, by the right of appeal, or by tribunician veto, Sulla's dictatorship could be terminated only by his death or resignation. He had the power of life and death, and his *imperium* was absolute.

In 81 B.C., Sulla increased the membership of the senate, which had been somewhat reduced by the civil war and the series of assassinations conducted by Marius, and by Sulla himself. The 300 new members came from the first eighteen centuries of the Centuriate Assembly and from the rich, landowning *equites* of the Italian municipalities. To maintain the senate's membership at a level of 500 or more, he increased from twelve to twenty the quaestors, who were eligible for seats in the senate after their term of office. The main object of expanding the senate's membership was to make a larger number of persons available for jury service, which he transferred from the *equites* to the senate. In expanding the membership of the senate and in making senators alone eligible as jurors, Sulla was actually carrying out a proposal of Livius Drusus the Younger. Moreover, this move not only opened up the senate to equestrians from the local Italian aristocracy, but it packed the senate with grateful clients loyal to Sulla and those who had supported him in the civil war.

Reform of the Courts   In his reform of the courts, Sulla went much further than Livius Drusus. He abolished trials before the popular assemblies and assigned all trials to a system of standing courts, whose juries were manned by senators. He raised the number of special jury courts for the trials of major crimes to seven (namely, the *quaestio de repetundis* dealing with extortion; *de maiestate,* with treason; *de ambitu,* with bribery in elections; *de falsis,* with forgery; *de peculatu,* with embezzlement of public property; *de sicariis et veneficis,* with murder; and *de vi publica,* with assault and battery). To provide enough judges to preside over these standing courts he increased the number of praetors from six to eight. The reform of the courts was the greatest and the most permanent of Sulla's reforms. It clarified and recast the law dealing with serious crimes and laid the foundation of Roman criminal law.

Changes in the Magistracies   To regulate the system of office holding and prevent the unorthodox careers that had increased political competition to destructive levels, Sulla reenacted, in a considerably modified form, the *lex Villia Annalis* of 180 B.C., which prescribed a regular order of holding office *(cursus honorum)*—first the quaestorship, then the praetorship, and finally the consulship. He reaffirmed the rule prescribing an interval of ten years between successive consulships. His revised law advanced the minimum age for the quaestorship to 30, for praetorship to 40, and for consulship to 43. During their year of office the eight praetors and two consuls were to remain in Italy and were prohibited from raising armies. In the following year the senate would assign them provinces to govern as proconsuls and propraetors.

Changes were made in the tribuneship which destroyed the effectiveness of that office and the temptation to use it in a *popularis* manner. Sulla crippled it most by disqualifying a tribune from holding any higher office, in order to make it unattractive to able and ambitious men. He limited the veto power of a tribune to the protection of personal rights and restricted or abolished his right to propose laws or prosecute cases before the Tribal Assembly.

The Reorganization of the Provinces   Before the time of Sulla there were nine provinces, six in the West (Sicily, Sardinia-and-Corsica, Nearer Spain, Farther Spain, Africa Proconsularis, and Gallia Transalpina) and three in the East (Macedonia, Asia, and Cilicia). Cyrenaica, though accepted in 96 B.C. as a legacy from its king, Ptolemy Apion, was not formally organized as a province until 74 B.C. A tenth province was created by Sulla, who detached Cisalpine Gaul from the rest of Italy and sent a governor and a garrison to guard it against the raiders who periodically descended from the Alps.

It was also to provide enough governors for the ten provinces that Sulla had increased the number of praetors from six to eight. They, like the two consuls, would automatically become provincial governors after their year of office in Rome. To fortify the power of the senate even more and prevent ambitious governors from creating personal armies strong enough to seize control of the state, Sulla limited the term of governor to one year and prohibited him from making war beyond the frontiers of his province without express authorization from the senate. He hoped thus to give the senate full control over the armed forces and limit the war-making potentiality of consuls and praetors in both Italy and the provinces. In the case of a major conflict the senate would raise the armies, choose the general, and grant him "extraordinary command." What Sulla did not foresee was that the real danger to the future of senatorial control would arise not from the provincial governors but from generals given the "extraordinary commands."

Sulla's Consulship, Abdication, and Death   After Sulla had fully reorganized the government to his own satisfaction and had created a system designed to maintain the dominance that he and his partisans had achieved, he stood for election as consul for 80 B.C. and headed the government both as consul and dictator. The following year he resigned his dictatorship and retired to his country estate near Puteoli (Pozzuoli) in Campania, where he hoped to pass the rest of his life in ease, luxury, and pleasure. He did not enjoy himself long. In 78 B.C. the sixty-year-old Sulla died of a stroke and was cremated in Rome after a most magnificent funeral. Before his death, he had dictated the epitaph to be inscribed upon his tomb, "I have always rewarded my friends with good, my enemies with evil."

The Failure of Sulla   Sulla had named himself Felix, which means "Lucky." He was even more fortunate in death for he never saw the utter futility of the major part of his work. He died in the happy belief that he had created a system that would produce a stable government for Rome under the control of the friends whom he had rewarded. They were to dominate the senate, and the constitutional avenues that previously had allowed other ambitious members of the senatorial class to challenge the dominant leaders were to remain blocked. The constitution that he tried to make permanent had some admirable features, such as the reform of the courts, the admission of new senators from the equestrian class, and the rational ordering of the magistracies and provincial government, but it was doomed to failure. It did nothing to solve the basic social, economic, and imperial problems that politicians who did not want to play the political game by his rules could exploit in building bases of power to challenge those whom he had left in control. No sooner had the ashes of his funeral pyre cooled than the whole carefully designed superstructure of his constitution began to collapse upon the sand beneath it.

Throughout the 70s and 60s B.C., a series of domestic and foreign crises gave ambitious individuals opportunities to gain so much popularity, clientage, and military power that those who controlled the senate became powerless to restrain them. The constitutional safeguards that Sulla had created to check the destructive competition for personal preeminence that had led to civil war in the 80s were inadequate. In fact, they were part of the problem because they also restricted the rights and privileges of the *equites* and the common people, and ambitious politicians could gain popularity by supporting repeal of the safeguards that were supposed to keep them in check.

Furthermore, Sulla had left a legacy of bitterness and hate that created many enemies for the oligarchs who succeeded him. The most bitter enemies of these oligarchs were the sons, relations, and friends of the senators and wealthy *equites* who had suffered proscription, exile, or confiscation of their property. Their main motivations were a desire for revenge and the hope of gaining power for themselves. In the forests of Etruria roamed bands of once-peaceful and well-to-do farmers whose lands had been confiscated by Sulla for distribution among his veterans. In the city of Rome, the poor had been deprived of their subsidized grain. Many *equites* had suffered financial ruin and had been deprived of jury service in the extortion court.

As the years passed, no group was more frustrated and rebellious than Sulla's own veterans who had been given confiscated land but had no knowledge of farming or desire for the monotony of rural life. They were soon enmeshed in debt and became one of the most discontented and potentially dangerous elements in Roman society. They were only too happy to support anyone who promised them personal gain without regard to constitutional proprieties. It is not surprising, therefore, that crises soon confronted the Republic.

XVII

Personal Ambitions and Public Crises, 78 to 60 B.C.

In creating a constitution designed to secure the oligarchic domination of a select group of nobles within the Roman senate, Sulla had alienated, frustrated, and embittered numerous groups within Roman society. Their hatred, frustration, and desire for revenge, however, could not have found expression without leaders, and in the generation after Sulla, given the political opportunities presented, leaders came. These leaders opened up another round of upheavals and civil wars that led to the destruction of the Republic by 30 B.C.

Sources for Roman History from 78 to 30 B.C. The years from 78 to 30 B.C., which will be covered in this and the following three chapters, are the best documented in Roman history. Until his death in 43, Cicero's numerous speeches, essays, and letters provide volumes of invaluable information by a keen observer and participant in events (see pp. 198–199). Cicero's letters also include letters to him from other important participants or observers. Caesar's commentaries—the *Gallic War* (first seven books) and the *Civil War*—and others by some of his officers—Book 8 of the *Gallic War,* the *African War,* the *Alexandrian*

War, and the *Spanish War*—are the second largest group of contemporary works and cover the conquest of Gaul and the civil war from 58 to 46 B.C. Another valuable contemporary witness is Sallust, whose *Histories* covering the years from 78 to 67 is preserved only in fragments, but whose account of Catiline's conspiracy (63 B.C.) is extant. Cornelius Nepos was another contemporary historian. Unfortunately, his biography of Cicero is lost, but his life of Cicero's devoted friend Atticus is extant.

The poems of Catullus (see pp. 262–263) and the didactic epic *De Rerum Natura* (*On the Nature of Things*) by Lucretius (see pp. 263–264) help to reveal the atmosphere at the time of Caesar's rise, and the *Eclogues* and *Georgics* of Vergil (see pp. 306–307) do the same for the time of Caesar's heir, Octavian, the future Emperor Augustus. Fragments of a biography of Augustus' early life by the late-first-century B.C. writer Nicolaus of Damascus also survive. Most of Augustus' own official summary of his career, *Res Gestae Divi Augusti,* had been preserved because it was set up on stone inscriptions in various cities. The most complete version is the *Monumentum Ancyranum* from Ankara in modern Turkey.

Later writers also supply abundant material. The mid-first-century A.D. commentary by Asconius on some of Cicero's speeches, particularly some lost ones, is extremely valuable. The biographies of Caesar and Augustus by the early-second-century A.D. author Suetonius, who often quotes from contemporary writers and documents, are veritable gold mines. So too are Plutarch's biographies of Sertorius, Lucullus, Pompey, Crassus, Cicero, Caesar, Cato the Younger, Brutus, and Antony, which are often based on contemporary sources like Asinius Pollio (see p. 310). Although Livy Books 91 to 133 survive only in the summaries of the *Periochae* and in the brief late Imperial histories and Diodorus Siculus is lost except for some fragments of Book 40 (71 to 63 B.C.), there are extensive narrative sources. In the five books of the *Civil Wars* (Books 13 to 17 of his history), Appian narrates the years 78 to 35 from section 107 of the first book to the end of the work. Beginning with events of 69 B.C., Cassius Dio is complete for the remaining years (Books 36 to 50). Also, Velleius Paterculus' narrative, though still brief, is much fuller for this period than before (Book 2.30–85).

The Rebellion of Lepidus, 78 B.C.

The first attacker of the Sullan oligarchy was Marcus Aemilius Lepidus, consul in 78 B.C. and a member of a most ancient noble family. Initially he had belonged to Sulla's inner circle. He had increased his wealth by buying at cut rates the property of those proscribed by Sulla. Afterward, as governor of Sicily, he so shamelessly plundered that province that he narrowly escaped impeachment, the threat of which thrust him into the leadership of the rebel opposition.

Hardly had the torch kindled Sulla's funeral pyre than Lepidus proposed the recall of all exiles, the resumption of cheap grain distributions to the poor, the return of all confiscated properties to the former owners, and the restoration of the powers of the tribunes. The first two proposals Sulla's heirs in the senate somewhat unwillingly accepted; the last two they vigorously and successfully opposed.

Soon the exiles began to return; first came Marcus Perperna, then the young Lucius Cinna, and a young man named Gaius Julius Caesar. Political clubs sprang up, and the barrooms and whorehouses of the city hummed with political plots and conspiracies.

Those who controlled the senate were in a difficult position. To eliminate Lepidus, they sent him to northern Etruria to suppress an armed rebellion near Florence, where the evicted farmers had emerged from hiding and had driven the Sullan veterans off their lands. To carry out his assignment, Lepidus went to Cisalpine Gaul and raised an army. Leaving his legate, M. Junius Brutus, in charge of northern Italy, he marched to Etruria where, instead of suppressing the rebels, he invited them to join his army and marched on Rome. To the senatorial order that he disband his army he replied with the demand of a second consulship and the restoration of the tribunes' powers.

In 77 B.C., his opponents responded by sending their loyal consul Catulus to oppose Lepidus, and Pompey the Great fought Junius Brutus. Catulus, with the aid of Sulla's veterans, drove Lepidus away from Rome back to Etruria, while Pompey defeated Brutus and put him to death. Pompey then moved down into Etruria and defeated Lepidus at Cosa. His cause lost, Lepidus escaped with the remnants of his army to Sardinia, where he soon afterward died. His legate, Marcus Perperna, took the army to Spain and joined Sertorius, who had been waging full-scale war against the Roman government since 80 B.C.

The War against Sertorius (ca. 122 to 73 B.C.)

Quintus Sertorius is clearly one of the most interesting military commanders in the history of Rome. Under Marius he had fought in the Cimbrian and Social Wars and had learned how to train and discipline troops. For eight years, with units made up of a few Roman officers and some native Spanish troops, he had repeatedly frustrated the armies of provincial governors sent out against him in Spain.

Had the Marian leaders, who had mismanaged the war against Sulla in 83 B.C., only utilized the military and political talents of Sertorius instead of shipping him off to Spain, they might have changed the history of the Republic. Had Sertorius been in command of those brave Samnite fighters at the Colline Gate, Sulla might have been denied his grim victory.

Sertorius in Spain, 82 to 73 B.C.   In order to challenge those who controlled the senate at Rome, Sertorius attempted to Romanize the native nobility and earn the provincial's loyalty. He accepted many Spaniards and Lusitanians as Roman citizens, admitted some of their leaders into his opposition senate, and established a school for the education of the upper class youth.

By war, diplomacy, and sheer force of personality, he had acquired an authority over the Spanish people such as no native chieftain (not even Viriathus) had ever wielded. He taught the thousands who flocked to his standards to fight as Roman soldiers without destroying their aptitude for guerrilla warfare. He appealed to their superstitions by pretending that he received all his secret information from a white fawn, a gift of Diana, which followed him everywhere. By tact, justice, and moderation, he won the devotion of the Spanish people, controlled the major part of the country, and outwitted Sulla's generals, even the great Metellus Pius, time after time.

Despite his battles against Roman armies, Sertorius never felt that he was really at war with Rome or the Romans but only with Sulla's government. After Sulla's death he was eager for reconciliation, but Sulla's political heirs were determined to continue the war, which had been under the command of Sulla's old ally Quintus Caecilius Metellus Pius since 79 B.C.

The Rise of Pompey the Great (106–48 B.C.)   Metellus had not been able to make much progress against Sertorius by 77, when Pompey the Great returned to Rome after de-

feating Lepidus. Pompey refused a senatorial order to disband his army and practically demanded to be sent to Spain to join Metellus against Sertorius. A majority in the senate agreed, although many senators were reluctant because they were friends of Metellus or feared to entrust so dangerous a weapon as a major provincial command to a young man not old enough to hold even the lowest office of the *cursus honorum*. Pompey received consular *imperium* and the chief command in Nearer Spain.

As the heir of Gnaeus Pompeius Strabo, Pompey was the largest landowner in the district of Picenum. Therefore he had a large number of clients and vast personal resources. Although he was personally charming and seems to have inspired great loyalty and love in his children and most of his several wives, he was also extremely ambitious and missed no opportunity to use his resources to advance his personal career. Typically, at the age of twenty-three, after Cinna had refused to grant him the recognition that he wanted, he had raised a large private army and joined Sulla. Later, he willingly divorced his first wife when Sulla wanted him to marry a more politically acceptable partner. Nor did he speak up for former friends who had helped him in trouble when Sulla struck them down before his very eyes. His zealous hunting of Sulla's enemies even earned him the nickname *adulescentulus carnifex,* young butcher. Then, when Sulla asked him to disband his army after killing Carbo and his followers in Sicily and North Africa, he refused and successfully demanded that Sulla grant him a triumph, for which he was ineligible under Sulla's own laws. It was then that Sulla gave him the facetious title *Magnus,* which Pompey opportunistically turned to his own advantage.

As a general, Pompey was not brilliant, and his detractors said with some justice that his victories were prepared by others who had fought before him. Still, Pompey often succeeded where others had not because he planned methodically and seldom attacked unless he had secured an overwhelming numerical superiority. As a statesman, Pompey was somewhat inept and shortsighted. He spoke poorly and awkwardly at times and often fell back on silence because he could think of nothing to say. He had no ideology or political program. His main ambition was simply to be admired as the Republic's greatest hero and enjoy the political prestige that such heroes naturally acquired. He certainly did not want to destroy the Republic that produced him, and he would have been appalled if he had realized that he was helping to do so.

Pompey in Spain, 76 to 71 B.C.   When Pompey arrived in Spain in 76 B.C., he found the military situation more formidable than he had expected. Sertorius, a superior tactician and field general, succeeded in defeating him twice, even with fewer men. On one occasion, only the timely arrival of old Metellus saved Pompey's army from annihilation. Pompey sent off a bitter letter to the Roman senate to demand strong reinforcements, which finally arrived. With their help and after the treacherous assassination of Sertorius by Perperna in 74 or 73 B.C., Pompey at last wound up the Spanish campaign.

Though a less skillful tactician than Metellus, Pompey seems to have been a better advertiser, for when the war was over public opinion gave Pompey the victory. The triumphant Pompey promptly executed Perperna for the murder of Sertorius. Yet he wisely followed the example of Sertorius and dealt with the Spanish people with great justice. His honorable peace terms restored prosperity to Spain and were long and gratefully remembered by the Spanish people.

The Great (Third) Mithridatic War, 74 to 63 B.C.   While Metellus and Pompey were fighting Sertorius in Spain, the eastern end of the Mediterranean was also ablaze with war. In late 75 or early 74 B.C., the childless king of Bithynia, Nicomedes IV, bequeathed his kingdom to the Roman people. The senate accordingly declared Bithynia a Roman province. This action provoked Mithridates VI of Pontus, who feared that Roman control of

Bithynia would block his access to the Aegean Sea. Mithridates moved swiftly and occupied Bithynia before the Roman armies arrived.

War had long been expected by both sides. The Roman senate had only reluctantly ratified Sulla's easy peace terms after the first war, and Murena, Sulla's legate in Asia, had touched off the brief Second Mithridatic War in 83 and 82 by an unauthorized attack until Sulla had recalled him. Subsequently, Mithridates had engaged exiled Roman officers, who had been supporters of Marius, to modernize his army and made alliances with his son-in-law, Tigranes II of Armenia, with the pirates of Crete and Cilicia, and with Sertorius in Spain.

When war broke out with Rome in 74 B.C., the pirates flocked to Pontus and helped Mithridates build up a formidable navy. Sertorius had sent some of the former Roman officers to train the Pontic army to fight with Roman tactics. Tigranes did nothing—at least not yet.

Lucullus in Command, 74 to 66 B.C.   Lucullus, consul of 74 B.C., was of a very old aristocratic family that had fallen into relative obscurity before Sulla. He loyally served Sulla in civil wars, however, and had been well rewarded. He was now closely linked with the innermost circle of *optimates* who controlled the senate. After his consulship, he was slated to be governor of Cisalpine Gaul but contrived to have himself transferred to the provinces of Cilicia and Asia and the command of the Roman army in the war against Mithridates. His consular colleague, M. Aurelius Cotta, received Bithynia as his province and command of the fleet.

At the same time Marcus Antonius (father of Mark Antony), was given an extraordinary command to suppress the pirates of Crete and Cilicia, the naval allies of Mithridates. He failed most miserably. The pirates of Crete compelled him to sign a disreputable treaty, which was repudiated in the senate. He later died in Crete.

Cotta, in his first year, also got involved in difficulties. Hoping to carry off a big victory

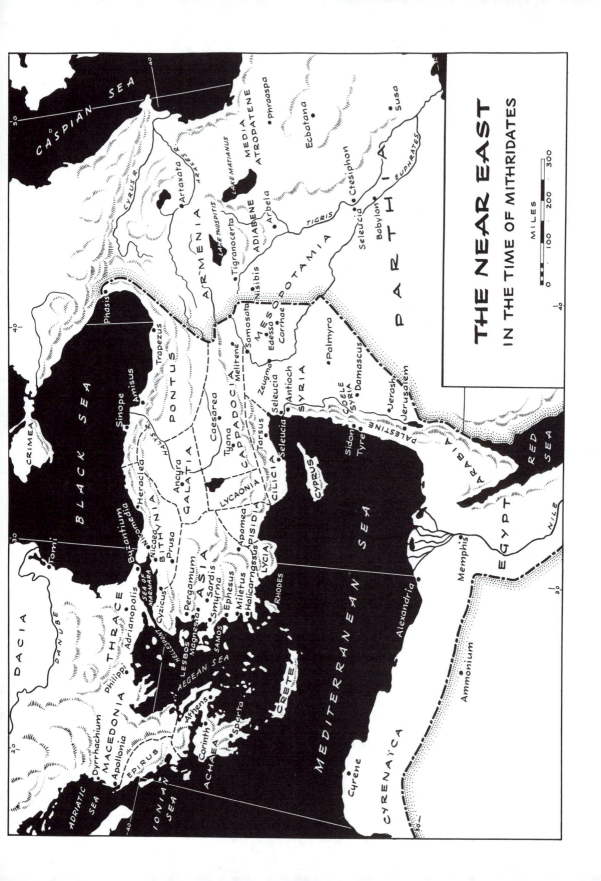

THE NEAR EAST
IN THE TIME OF MITHRIDATES

MILES

0   100   200   300

before Lucullus should reach the battle area, he impatiently began military operations against Mithridates, who attacked by land and sea, killed three thousand of Cotta's men, burnt or captured nearly seventy of his ships, and shut him up in Chalcedon, a city on the Bosporus opposite Byzantium, now Istanbul.

Lucullus arrived and, with fewer than thirty thousand infantrymen and sixteen hundred cavalry, he forced Mithridates to raise the siege of Chalcedon and won a magnificent series of victories against tremendous numerical odds. Had Mithridates at once retreated to the familiar mountain terrain of Pontus, he might have lured the Romans into ambush. Instead he suddenly bolted westward and laid siege to the big city of Cyzicus, where he was himself trapped and where he lost most of his enormous army. After chasing Mithridates out of Bithynia, Lucullus invaded Pontus in the fall of 73 B.C. In 72, at Cabira, he inflicted a disastrous defeat upon Mithridates, who fled in exile to the court of his son-in-law, Tigranes, king of Armenia.

While lieutenants completed the reduction of Pontus, Lucullus returned to the Roman province of Asia to relieve its cities of the crushing indemnity levied by Sulla and the extortionate loans that they had been forced to contract with Roman moneylenders to pay it. He assisted the city treasuries by imposing a tax of 25 percent on crops and special taxes on houses and slaves. He fixed the maximum interest rate on loans at 12 percent, disallowed two-thirds of the debts, gave four years to pay them without interest, and issued a ruling that no debtor had to pay more than one-quarter of his income. These regulations rapidly restored the economic health of the province but infuriated the financiers at Rome, who worked for his downfall.

The Downfall of Lucullus Permanent peace was impossible without the capture of Mithridates. When Tigranes refused demands to surrender Mithridates, Lucullus invaded Armenia in 69 B.C. without authorization from the senate. He scored a brilliant victory over the much larger forces of Tigranes at his capital of Tigranocerta and set out on a long, painful march against Artaxata, the second capital. He never got there. An iron disciplinarian, Lucullus had not endeared himself to his troops. He had driven them hard and had forbidden them to loot captured cities. Marching through the mountains of Armenia in the snows of an early winter heightened their discontent. Agents of financial interests hurt by Lucullus' policies and Publius Clodius, an opportunistic brother-in-law and member of his staff, provoked a mutiny. Lucullus was forced to retreat for the winter to Mesopotamia, where he won his last victory in the brilliant siege and capture of Nisibis and all the rich booty it contained.

Even while Lucullus was falling back from Artaxata, the ever-resourceful and indomitable Mithridates was gathering a force of eight thousand men. He advanced into Pontus as liberator and avenger and easily destroyed the small Roman garrisons stationed there. The weak and feeble Tigranes, after reoccupying Armenia, again invaded Cappadocia. Lucullus could do nothing. His men refused to fight. He appealed to Rome for more men but got none. He appealed to the new governors of Cilicia and Asia, who also refused. The disastrous effects of the mutiny nullified eight glorious years of victory. Finally, after much political intrigue and maneuvering, Lucullus was relieved of his command first by Acilius Glabrio and then a year later by Pompey. Lucullus, though cheated of the final victory, did eventually obtain the triumph that he deserved and found consolation in his wine cellar, his fish ponds, and his cherry trees,* while he seized every opportunity to oppose Pompey, who had capitalized on his difficulties to gain charge of the war.

Spartacus and the Slave War in Italy, 73 to 71 B.C.   While wars were raging at both ends of the Mediterranean, a dangerous slave revolt broke within Italy itself. In 73 B.C.

---

*Lucullus brought back the cultivated cherry from the East to Italy. That is why the botanical name of the tree is *lucullus*.

Spartacus, a Thracian slave possibly of royal descent, led a band of gladiators out of the barracks of a training school at Capua. They fortified themselves in the crater of Vesuvius and called upon all farm slaves to join them in a fight for freedom. Many thousands did, especially the Gauls and Germans whom Marius had captured in the Cimbrian war. No strangers to arms and warfare, they were a dangerous and desperate lot, big brawny rascals brutalized by hard labor and harsh treatment on the large estates. The cowhands and shepherds, who came to Spartacus from the big estates in the South, were well armed. The others soon obtained arms by buying them from the pirates and unscrupulous traders or capturing them from the Roman armies sent to subdue them. Their force grew to seventy thousand, as they ranged over the country, broke open the slave prisons, and armed the slaves.

The slaves' rebellion was able to gain momentum because Rome's best soldiers were pinned down in Spain and Asia Minor. The Romans were now locked in a desperate struggle to maintain their power against a loosely coordinated uprising that spanned the whole Mediterranean. Sertorius, Mithridates, and the Mediterranean pirates had already taken some cooperative steps. Now the pirates were supplying arms and material to the rebellious slaves in Italy. If Sertorius had been willing to support Mithridates' claim to Roman territory in the East, and if the pirates had had time to do more for the slaves in Italy before Spain was pacified, the Roman domination of the Mediterranean world might have been broken before it had been completely consolidated.

The government, which had thought the slave revolt would be easily quelled, soon learned that Spartacus commanded a large army and was a master strategist as well. Defeat followed defeat. After Spartacus had vanquished the armies of four praetors and two consuls, the senate in desperation appointed Marcus Licinius Crassus to take command and assigned him six new legions in addition to remnants of the four consular legions that Spartacus had shattered.

Marcus Crassus (ca. 115–53 B.C.)

Like Pompey and Lucullus, Crassus had been a Sullan partisan. He had even played the decisive role in Sulla's crucial victory at the Colline Gate. Accused of manipulating the proscriptions for himself, however, Crassus had lost favor with Sulla and Sulla's most important allies. Now, Crassus was in a very difficult position. For three generations his family had enjoyed great prominence among the nobility. His father and brother had died while opposing Marius, and he was the only one left to carry on the family honor. He would have to do it on his own. Therefore, he had set about to acquire the financial resources essential for success in the intense competition of aristocratic politics.

Crassus' financial operations earned him an unfair reputation for greed in ancient times because it was not considered proper for a Roman aristocrat to be so directly concerned with making money. Crassus had to make money, however, if he wanted to compete for high office. Pompey, and eventually Caesar, became much richer through the profits of war, an employment considered very honorable. Crassus, on the other hand, invested in profitable agricultural land, mines, and business loans. He maintained a large staff of highly trained slaves, who could be rented out to those who needed temporary help. He also used them to repair and rebuild property that he bought at bargain prices as a result of the many fires in overcrowded and flimsily built Rome.

Many believe that Crassus maintained a private fire brigade (there was no public fire protection) that would not put out a fire until the unfortunate owner agreed to sell his property to Crassus at a reduced rate. There is no ancient evidence for this story. It was not, however, unusual for wealthy men to maintain private fire brigades in their role as patrons of the less fortunate. Crassus may have done so too, but it would not have been worth the ill will created to refuse to put out a fire before the owner sold.

Crassus was very skilled at earning good will. He was famous for his willingness to defend anyone in court, even though advocates could receive no fees. He often loaned money to people without interest and in that way earned the loyalty of many lesser-known members of the senate. As a result, Crassus had patiently advanced his career and had reached the praetorship in 73 B.C., a few years after he was first eligible. In 72 the command against Spartacus gave him the chance to earn the kind of fame that would advance him further. He even used his own money to recruit more soldiers.

After he had trained his men, Crassus pursued Spartacus to the southern part of Bruttium. Eventually he tried to fence him off by a walled entrenchment across a small neck of land on which Spartacus had encamped. One dark winter night Spartacus broke out and marched into Lucania. Crassus was discouraged, and the Romans, more frightened than ever, had already recalled Pompey from Spain. Crassus was determined to do something before Pompey arrived and stole all the glory. Spartacus' army proceeded in two separate detachments—one consisting of Germans and Celts, the other of Thracians and Near Easterners. First, Crassus defeated the Celts and Germans in two separate engagements. Then, he caught up with Spartacus and forced a pitched battle. Spartacus, who had defeated nine different Roman armies in two years, was finally beaten. He died in battle, and his body could not be identified, so great was the slaughter.

Pompey, on his way back from Spain, encountered a detachment of five thousand slaves who had escaped to Etruria, and destroyed them. This minor feat of arms enabled Pompey to claim credit for ending yet another war, much to Crassus' chagrin.

The Consulship of Pompey and Crassus, 70 B.C.

Pompey and Crassus, both victors, marched to Rome and encamped their armies outside the gates. Each expected military honors; both wanted the consulship. Crassus, praetor in 73 B.C., was eligible for the office. Pompey was six years too young to be a consul

and had not yet held any of the lower offices that the law required for a consular candidate. The senators could grant Pompey's demands only by violating the Sullan constitution, on which their power was based. Yet they could not reject the demands without the risk of having legions enter Rome. The hope of playing Crassus off against Pompey was equally vain. Although the two were political rivals, they realized that their hopes for consulships could be fulfilled only by cooperation at this point. To increase their popularity and put further pressure on their opponents in the senate, they supported popular demands for the restoration of full powers to the tribunes of the plebs and the placing of non-senators on juries. Pompey received a dispensation from the legal requirements, and both he and Crassus were elected consuls for 70 B.C.

The consulship of Pompey and Crassus completed the ruin of the Sullan constitution, which had been under attack for several years. The optimate leaders of the senate had made some concessions to popular pressure in the hope of defusing discontent. In 75 the consul Gaius Aurelius Cotta had carried a law permitting the tribunes to hold higher offices. The consuls of 73 B.C., a year of scarcity and high prices, sponsored a bill to distribute five pecks of grain a month to forty-five thousand citizens at the price set by Gaius Gracchus. Pompey and Crassus now proposed and carried a law to restore to the tribunes all the powers taken away by Sulla. (Pompey hoped that the tribunes would later help him to secure desirable commands. They did not disappoint him.) The tribunes then proposed a law to restore citizenship to all who had fought under Lepidus and Sertorius. The consuls revived the censorship, dormant since Sulla's time, and the newly appointed censors promptly ejected from the senate sixty-four of Sulla's partisans.

Near the end of this historic consulship, the praetor L. Aurelius Cotta, an optimate who sought to save something from the wreck, drafted and carried a law to break the senatorial monopoly of jury service and to draw jurors in equal numbers from the senate, the *equites,* and the *tribuni aerarii* ("tribunes of the treasury''). About the *tribuni aerarii* almost nothing is known. They were probably inferior to the *equites* in rank, but like the *equites,* belonged to the upper non-senatorial classes, which henceforth supplied two-thirds of the jurors.

The Trial of Gaius Verres, 70 B.C.

The issue of who should sit on juries was underlined by the famous trial of Gaius Verres in 70 B.C. An old supporter of Sulla, he had become a praetor for 74 B.C. and had received the governorship of Sicily for the following three years. As governor he had cheated, blackmailed, plundered, and even murdered people, some of whom were clients of Pompey. When injured Sicilians charged him with extortion in 70, he assumed that Sulla's old supporters in the senate would procure his acquittal. So did many others, who saw this trial as a test of the integrity of senatorial jurors.

Powerful friends rallied to Verres' support. They persuaded Quintus Hortensius Hortalus, the most famous orator of the day, to defend him. They used the most ingenious tricks and dodges in a vain attempt to quash the indictment or postpone the trial until one of them could preside. They even tried to obtain a friendly prosecutor. They, however, were met at every turn by an eager young orator, Marcus Tullius Cicero, who saw a chance to do Pompey a favor by protecting his Sicilian friends, bolster his own clientele among the Sicilians, and gain fame as an orator by beating Hortensius through successfully prosecuting Verres.

Marcus Tullius Cicero (106–43 B.C.)

Cicero, the son of a prominent *eques,* was born in 106 B.C. at Arpinum. He had received a fine education, had traveled extensively, had studied philosophy and rhetoric in Athens, Asia, and Rhodes, and had trained himself for the Roman bar. He became one of the world's most renowned orators and greatest literary figures. His writings consist of many legal and political speeches, of which his *In Catilinam* and

Philippics are the most famous, essays such as *On Old Age* (*De Senectute*) and *On Friendship* (*De Amicitia*), many philosophical and political treatises, of which the best known are the *De Legibus* (*On the Laws*), *De Re Publica* (*On the State*), and *On Duties* (*De Officiis*), and works on oratory such as the *De Oratore* (*On the Orator*) and the *Brutus.*

More important from the historical standpoint are his *Letters.* They describe the events of this period not only from year to year but often even from day to day. It is doubtful whether any period of history has been so carefully recorded until the advent of the modern daily newspaper. Cicero's letters are more than historical documents: they reveal the soul of a man as well, his deepest feelings, his weaknesses, and his strength of character. And strength of character he had. But on the basis of these *Letters* he sometimes has been unfairly judged by modern historians, yet not many men have had the courage, the basic assurance, and the honesty to reveal themselves, unless it be St. Augustine in his *Confessions.*

Throughout his lifetime Cicero continued to unveil the offenses and scandals of the optimate oligarchs, although he never wholly deserted them or ceased to look up to them. His ideal was to join them and convince them to be true, impartial servants of the common good. Nor was he a political coward. In 80 B.C. he defended a young man who was threatened by one of Sulla's henchmen. He had a genuine sympathy for the oppressed people of the provinces. For that reason, as well as to advance his career through a spectacular trial, he undertook the case against Verres in 70 B.C. and marshalled such a mass of damning evidence against him that the great Hortensius gave up the defense. Verres fled into exile to Massilia, where the mullets were delicious and the climate delightful. Not a really harsh punishment for a man who had robbed the Sicilian people of millions and had even crucified a Roman citizen.

Cicero's second Verrine oration, never delivered but published as a pamphlet, describes how Verres was able to amass a fortune by plundering his province. He made false accusations against well-to-do persons and intimidated the judges to hand down verdicts of confiscation against the property of the accused, which he then seized for himself. He sold justice as well as priesthoods and municipal offices to the highest bidder. He made partnerships with the tax collectors to extort without redress as much money as the traffic would bear. He lent public money at scandalous rates of interest and paid little or nothing for the wheat he bought from the Sicilians for resale to the Roman government at regular market prices. His extortions extended to works of art, which he collected from individuals, cities, and even from temples. All who resisted or opposed his thefts and extortions he imprisoned, or crucified.

The disclosure of the iniquities of Verres supplied opponents of the Sullan oligarchs and the system that they controlled with all the ammunition needed. That Verres was not acquitted, however, may have helped to make Cotta's compromise of sharing the seats on juries among the senators, *equites,* and *tribuni aerarii* acceptable to the voters. After this reform and the restoration of full tribunician powers, the constitution had for the most part been restored to its pre-Sullan state.

After their historic consulship of 70 B.C., both Pompey and Crassus looked for further ways to enhance their fame and prestige when the next public crisis should arise. Pompey never attended meetings of the senate, where he was most unwelcome, but he was always accompanied on his rare appearances in the Forum by a mass of clients and retainers, to the mingled awe and pride of the populace. He was their idol and mighty protector of their rights. Crassus worked diligently behind the scenes to increase his wealth and network of grateful friends on whom he could depend when the need arose. Eventually, one of those friends was an abitious young man by the name of Gaius Julius Caesar.

Caesar (100–44 B.C.)   Caesar was born on July 13, 100 B.C. into a family that was very ancient, very patrician, but which for centuries had been politically obscure.* He had strong *popularis* antecedents. His aunt Julia had been the wife of Marius; an earlier Julia had been wife of Fulvius Flaccus, a Gracchan land commissioner. His own wife was Cornelia, Cinna's daughter, whom he had once refused to divorce in the face of Sulla's command.

Caesar's later fame has led many historians to exaggerate the importance of his early career. His exploits and narrow escapes probably have been romanticized. He may have spoken in favor of restoring the tribunician powers in 70 B.C., but he had little to do with the overthrow of the Sullan constitution. Nevertheless, he certainly took advantage of its unpopularity and the common people's high regard of the dead Marius. For example, as a quaestor in 69, Caesar dared to display the images of Marius, which Sulla had banned, and even dared to extol the deeds of Marius and Cinna at the funerals of his aunt Julia, Marius' widow, and of his own wife Cornelia, Cinna's daughter. Later in the same year, he went to serve in Spain, where he set about to make a name for himself and build up a useful group of Spanish clients. Still, Caesar could not hope to make a mark at Rome without the help of men more powerful than he. For Caesar, whose background made him suspect among many of Sulla's heirs, it would be useful to attract favorable attention from men like Pompey and Crassus.

Opportunistic Tribunes   Other young men were seeking to make their marks too. Several took advantage of the opportunities offered by the office of tribune, whose powers Pompey and Crassus had restored. In 67 B.C., the tribunes Gaius Cornelius and Aulus Gabinius were particularly active. The first law of the tribune Cornelius obliged praetors to administer justice according to the principles

* According to Suetonius, *The Divine Julius* (6.1), Caesar boasted of his descent from the immortal gods and from King Ancus Marcius (*ab Anco Marcio*). Although some scholars have argued for 102 or 101 as the date of his birth, the traditional date of 100 B.C. is now commonly accepted.

that they had laid down in their edicts on taking office—an enactment of supreme importance and the foundation of uniform law and equity throughout the provinces. His second law imposed a fine and future exclusion from office for persons guilty of bribing the electorate. His third, as finally passed, made it illegal for the senate to exempt individuals from the laws unless a quorum of two hundred members was present. Of his other proposals, later carried by his colleague Gabinius, the first forbade the lending of money to foreign and provincial envoys to enable them to secure audience in the senate by bribery, and the second compelled the senate to give priority to the reception of embassies during its February meetings to protect the Roman allies against dilatory political tactics. These excellent and salutary laws, enacted in spite of the violent opposition of many leading senators, who stood to lose significant financial and political advantages, seemed to justify the freeing of the tribunes from the restrictions imposed by Sulla.

Still, men like Cornelius and Gabinius were not simply public-spirited reformers. They were doing just what Sulla had feared. As competitors in senatorial politics, they were using the restored powers of the tribunate to get around the dominant senatorial leaders, just as the Gracchi and others had done earlier. Part of their strategy was to attract the favor of other powerful senators, like Pompey and Crassus, who also stood outside the group of Sulla's optimate political heirs, who dominated the senate.

Pompey's Commissions against the Pirates and Mithridates, 67 and 66 B.C. The fame of Gabinius rests largely upon the passage of a law in 67 B.C. to deal with the scourge of piracy in the Mediterranean. Previous attempts to suppress it had proved ineffective (see p. 193) and the menace had recently reached dangerous proportions. Pirates had attacked large coastal cities in Italy itself; had destroyed a large Roman fleet near Ostia; and so infested the waters around Sicily

that grain ships supplying the city of Rome no longer ventured to sail. Food prices had risen and the people, threatened with famine, resolved to clear the seas.

The bill that Gabinius laid before the assembly provided for the appointment of a supreme commander of consular rank to take command with extraordinary powers for three years over the waters and coasts of the Mediterranean basin and gave him an authority, superior to that of the provincial governors, over all coast lands extending fifty miles from the sea. As finally enacted, the law authorized him to draw from the public treasury six thousand talents, raise a fleet up to five hundred ships, if necessary, recruit an army of 120,000 infantry and 5000 cavalry, and appoint a staff of 24 subcommanders (*legati*) of praetorian rank and two quaestors.

The consul C. Calpurnius Piso and other senators strenuously opposed this bill because of the enormous powers that it gave to one man, but the populace mobbed the consul. One of the tribunes vetoed the bill but withdrew his veto when threatened with the treatment that Tiberius Gracchus once dealt out to Octavius. The bill passed. After it became law the majority of senators appointed Pompey to take the command. They had little choice for there was no one else of equal competence, and, although not expressly named in the law, he was the person whom Gabinius and the voters had in mind.* Gabinius in turn was amply rewarded for his efforts on Pompey's behalf. Pompey chose him as a legate in 66 and ensured that he would reach the consulship in 58.

Pompey threw himself into the campaign against the pirates with tremendous energy. He divided the Mediterranean and Black Seas into thirteen naval districts, each under one of his subcommanders, so that any pirates able to slip out of one net might get caught in another. His excellent organization and the vast concentration of ships, men, and supplies enabled him to sweep the western Mediterranean clean

---

* So great was the confidence in his leadership that grain prices fell the very day he received the command.

in forty days. Sailing into eastern waters, he forced the pirates to fight a naval battle off the shores of Cilicia and there completely destroyed them. Before three months had passed, he had not only swept them off the seas but had destroyed all their bases, strongholds, and installations on land.

Pompey owed his swift victory over the pirates not only to the overwhelming superiority of his armaments but also to his treatment of captives. Instead of following the usual Roman practice of crucifying or selling them into slavery, he adopted the more humane methods that he had used successfully in Spain: he settled all those who surrendered on farms or in villages in Asia Minor. Many of the basic social and economic causes of piracy were thus eliminated, and the resettled pirates later became some of Rome's most loyal and useful subjects. Some were among the first in the East to receive Roman citizenship. They also became loyal clients of Pompey, who later, in his civil war with Caesar, based his strategy on the tremendous support that he enjoyed in the East.

For some time the war against Mithridates had not been going well. Lucullus, despite his brilliance as a field commander, had been unable, because of his mutinous troops, to prevent the Pontic king from reoccupying his kingdom. The newly appointed governors of Cilicia and Bithynia were so incompetent that Lucullus retained the command. Pompey, who was already in the East with a large army and fleet, was the logical successor.

While Pompey's friends and enemies in the senate were arguing about giving him the appointment, the tribune Gaius Manilius made a bid for popularity and Pompey's powerful favor by proposing his famous law, the *lex Manilia,* conferring upon Pompey the supreme command of all Roman forces in Asia Minor. Other ambitious young men sought to cash in on the situation too. Caesar was in favor of the law, and Cicero delivered the *Pro Lege Manilia* on its behalf, a famous oration that he later published. The Council of the Plebs adopted the resolution amid wild enthusiasm, for Pompey was now the idol of the populace as well as of the equestrian class. Though many in the senate, especially the leading *optimates,* opposed the sweeping provisions of the law, no one dared to speak in public against the appointment of this very popular general.

Pompey's Conquest of the East, 66 to 62 B.C.

Like a buzzard come to enjoy another's kill, Pompey arrived to take over the command of Lucullus, who had already shattered the armies and destroyed the prestige of Mithridates and Tigranes. With an army of fifty thousand men, about twice as many as Lucullus ever had, and a navy cruising about in the Black Sea, Pompey overtook and destroyed the inferior forces of Mithridates, who fled first to Armenia and, when refused haven by Tigranes, to the distant Caucasus. Pompey did not attempt immediate pursuit.

Pompey next invaded Armenia and advanced upon Artaxata, where he accepted the abject surrender of Tigranes and acknowledged him as an ally and friend of the Roman people. In the spring of 65 B.C. he attempted the pursuit of Mithridates, whom he failed to overtake. He advanced as far as the Caucasus and conquered the Albanians and Iberians, who dwelt between the Black and Caspian Seas. Abandoning his attempted march to the Caspian, he returned to Pontus, which he divided into two parts. He joined the western part as far as the river Halys to the province of Bithynia and assigned the eastern part to an allied prince.

Meanwhile, Mithridates had made his way through the Caucasus to the Crimea. Here that persistent and daring king attempted to raise a huge army for the invasion of Italy by way of the Balkans and the eastern Alps, a grandiose idea carried out five centuries later by Attila the Hun. By the inhuman cruelty of his conscriptions Mithridates provoked his subjects to rebel. Shut up in his palace, with all hope of escape or mercy gone, he murdered his wives and daughters and then took his own life. His son, Pharnaces II, turned the body over to Pompey, who buried it in the tombs of the Pontic kings and thereby enhanced his growing new reputation as a just and humane conqueror.

Pompey in Syria, 64/3 B.C.   News of the death of Mithridates reached Pompey in Syria, where he was fighting to stamp out the anarchy which had reigned there since Lucullus had driven out Tigranes II and restored Antiochus XIII to the decrepit throne of the Seleucids, whose eastern territories had been taken over by the resurgent Iranian peoples under the aggressive leadership of the Arsacid kings, founders of the Parthian Empire, which became Rome's chief rival in the East. Tyrants had seized control of the cities; robbers and pirates harassed the people. Pompey disposed of these nuisances and annexed Syria and Phoenicia as a Roman province.

Turning south into Palestine, Pompey found two brothers, Hyrcanus and Aristobulus, fighting over the Judean throne of the Maccabees. Both rivals gave him presents and sought his favor. In Rome's interest he took the side of the rather feeble Hyrcanus, who was supported by the Pharisees, against his more able pro-Parthian brother, the leader of the Sadducees. In making this choice, Pompey, who knew nothing about Jewish theology, unwittingly contributed to the ultimate triumph of the Pharisees over the Sadducees.

The Sadducees, composed mainly of the rich landed aristocracy and of the priestly caste, were conservative fundamentalists who accepted literally the text of the Written Law contained in the Torah or first five books of the Bible. The Pharisees accepted the Written Law too, but included a mass of interpretations and oral traditions handed down by the Scribes. The Pharisaic Rabbis or Teachers later produced the great commentaries of the Law known as the Mishna and the Talmud. In deciding in favor of Hyrcanus on purely political grounds, Pompey may have set the future course of Judaism.

Pompey's Achievements in the Near East
Pompey's work in the Near East was done—

a work which long endured. Because the existing records are poor and barren, little is known of his military strategy and tactics, and only the main outlines of his achievements are even dimly visible. Rapidly, smoothly, but with overwhelming force, he completed the task begun by his more brilliant but less flexible predecessor. Pompey did not attempt the impossible, as Lucullus had done. Parthia's hostility did not provoke him, nor did Egypt's weakness invite him. Few generals with the forces at Pompey's disposal ever acted with more self-restraint.

Yet his command in the Near East was historic and his achievements solid and enduring. He extended Rome's empire from the Mediterranean to the Euphrates. He poured into the Roman treasury more revenue from a foreign war than any of his predecessors. In return for the taxes and indemnities he imposed upon the people of the East, he gave such peace and security as they had never enjoyed since Alexander. He cleared the seas of pirates and made them safe for commerce, delivered Syria from anarchy, and all Asia Minor from the scourge and fear of war. More important still, he encouraged city life by granting privileges to numerous existing cities and restoring or founding scores of others.

During Pompey's absence, Lucullus and his other optimate opponents in the senate were bitter and resentful toward him. They prosecuted the former tribunes Cornelius and Manilius, who had favored him. On the other hand, they had little power to inflict real harm, and many feared that with his overwhelming military power Pompey would return like another Sulla and crush his enemies.

The Maneuverings of Crassus and Caesar

Crassus did everything that he could to build up a position of countervailing political and military power. One of his schemes was to increase his own influence in Spain and undercut Pompey's by persuading the senate to send his agent Gnaeus Calpurnius Piso to replace the suddenly deceased governor of Nearer Spain in 65 B.C. The tactless Piso was soon murdered, however, and Crassus made no further moves on that front.

Crassus was more successful in electoral politics. He himself obtained the office of censor for 65 B.C., and he supported other friendly candidates for high office. Among them was Caesar, who won an aedileship. Crassus may also have contributed to the support of P. Cornelius Sulla, a nephew of the dead dictator, and P. Autronius Paetus, who had been elected consuls. A crisis was precipitated when these two consuls-elect were convicted of bribery under the so-called Calpunian law of 67 B.C. Their election was invalidated and they were barred from office. According to Cicero, they then conspired with L. Sergius Catalina (Catiline) to murder their replacements on New Year's Day, 65 B.C. This supposed plot, known as the First Catilinarian Conspiracy, never existed. Cicero was merely twisting certain facts in a later piece of campaign rhetoric designed to blacken his electoral rival Catiline, as well as Caesar and Crassus, who were supporting Catiline.

Meanwhile, Caesar was winning popularity and entertaining the multitude with money supplied by Crassus. For their delectation he had the Forum decorated, exhibited 320 pairs of gladiators, and armed the criminals condemned to fight the lions in the arena with silver-decorated weapons. Early one morning, people entering the Forum saw gleaming gold statues of Marius and his trophies set up everywhere. The old veterans gathered around, tears of pride streaming down their cheeks. Caesar's efforts had begun to bear fruit.

Crassus' ultimate purpose in building a base of popular support was to create an army that would give him the same kind of political strength that Pompey enjoyed. One of the best Roman recruiting grounds was northern Italy. Using the power of censor, he proposed to enroll as full citizens, in all the voting tribes, the people of Cisalpine Gaul north of the Po, a move already advocated by Caesar in 68. Crassus was vetoed by his fellow censor, Quintus Lutatius Catulus, a staunch optimate who trusted neither Pompey nor Crassus and his

friends. The impasse was so unbreakable that both Crassus and Catulus resigned. Even so, the proposal won for Caesar and Crassus the continued gratitude of the people north of the Po and future armies were easily recruited there.

Another of Crassus' schemes earlier in 65 concerned Egypt, which was said to have been bequeathed by will to the Roman people in 80 B.C. He drafted a bill declaring Egypt a province, which cleverly appealed to several groups. It would have given Crassus or his agent Caesar the right to raise an army, the Roman populace a rich source of grain, and equestrian financial interests a store of untapped wealth. Nevertheless, it was foiled through the efforts of Catulus and Cicero, who was then one of Pompey's staunchest supporters and did not trust the aims of men like Caesar and Crassus.

The Elections of 64 B.C.   Foiled, frustrated, and out of office in 64, Crassus and Caesar sought to gain control over the executive machinery of the Republic by backing Catiline and one C. Antonius Hybrida, who were now running against Cicero for the consulship of 63 B.C.

Catiline was already a man of some fame, or rather, notoriety. Although descended from an ancient and illustrious lineage, Lucius Sergius Catiline was (if Cicero's and Sallust's accounts are to be believed) a scoundrel, a murderer, and a master of every known vice. He had supported Sulla and had played a notorious role in Sulla's bloody proscriptions. After serving as propraetor in the province of Africa in 67 B.C., Catiline was accused of extortion and brought to trial in 65.[*] Bribery secured him an acquittal, and he went on to stand for the consulship in the elections of 64. But at the last minute Catiline alarmed the electorate by his violent behavior and his radical talk about the cancelling of debts, and

[*] The prosecutor at the trial was Publius Clodius Pulcher, who had helped to undermine Lucullus in Asia Minor. Cicero, though convinced of Catiline's guilt, had at first thought of defending him and even worked out a deal with Clodius but then dropped the idea.

Cicero, who had widespread equestrian support, won the election by a large majority. Antonius was a successful but poor second, Catiline a close third. Although the success of one of his candidates (Antonius) made the election seem at first to be a partial triumph for Crassus, it had actually been a total defeat: Cicero soon won the allegiance of Antonius by assigning him to Macedonia, a far richer consular province than that which Antonius had originally drawn.

The Rullan Land Bill, 63 B.C.   The defeated but irrepressible Crassus and Caesar conceived another scheme, a land law tremendous in scope and extremely radical, whose proposal they entrusted to an obscure tribune, P. Servilius Rullus. Among its many vague and complicated clauses the bill provided that seventeen tribes chosen by lot out of the total thirty-five appoint ten commissioners of praetorian rank. They were to be vested for five years with final legal authority to terminate leases on the rich revenue-producing public lands of Campania for distribution to the poor and to purchase other lands for the same purpose from state funds accruing from the sale of public properties acquired in Italy and the provinces since the year 88 B.C. and from the seizure of recent war booty, including that from Pompey's prospective conquests in the East. The law also empowered the commissioners to adjudicate titles to land and compensation thereof, to found colonies, to enroll and equip troops, and to occupy Egypt by military force. Its real purpose was to corner the land that Pompey would need to reward his loyal veterans and to provide Crassus and Caesar with an immense amount of patronage and the power to raise armies in order to rival Pompey's power.

On the first day of his consulship, Cicero attacked Rullus' bill with arguments both sound and specious by employing devastating ridicule, misrepresentation, and alarmist propaganda. Using all the tricks of a demagogue, he even persuaded the people in whose interests the bill was supposedly framed that it

was too dangerous to vote for. The bill was voted down.

At this point, Caesar cooperated with Titus Labienus, a tribune of 63 B.C., who carried a bill to bring suit against Rabirius for treason (*perduellio*), in fact for the murder of the tribune Saturninus in obedience to the final decree of the senate (*Senatus Consultum Ultimum*) 37 years earlier. Caesar had nothing against Rabirius, who was an old obscure senator. His object was to attack the validity of the final decree, under which the consuls had put to death declared enemies of the state without an appeal to the people. Convicted in a special court permitting appeal to the people, Rabirius was tried before the Centuriate Assembly. Cicero made an eloquent plea on his behalf (*Pro Rabirio Perduellionis*). Just before the voting was to begin, a praetor lowered the red flag over the Janiculum and thereby dissolved the assembly. The old man was allowed to go home in peace, but Caesar had focused hostile popular attention on a weapon that those in control of the senate relied upon as their ultimate defense against *popularis* rivals like himself. Labienus carried a law to restore the election of priests to the special Tribal Assembly of seventeen tribes, as under the *lex Domitia* of 104 B.C. (see p. 175) which Sulla had revoked. Caesar supported the bill and the popularity he thereby gained helped him in his election as Pontifex Maximus. That was a triumph for so young a man, especially since one of his opponents was Catulus, Crassus' former colleague in the censorship and one of the most respected optimate members of the senate. Yet another reverse followed the triumph: Caesar's proposal to recall and reinstate the Sullan exiles was blocked by Cicero.

The Catilinarian Conspiracy, 63 B.C.

Catiline again ran for the consulship, in the elections for 62 B.C. Initially, he probably still had the backing of Crassus and Caesar, although his rhetoric was more radical and alarming than what they were prepared to support in actual practice. While his demands for a general scaling down of debts repelled creditors and investors, they had a strong attraction for debtors, ruined aristocrats, Sulla's veterans, and the sons of the persons whom Sulla had proscribed. The more support Catiline received from idlers, hoodlums, criminals, and exiles, the more he caused the well-to-do and respectable citizens to fear him as a public nuisance, if not a dangerous enemy. Cicero did his best to whip up the fear that Catiline, if elected, would resort to violence and revolution.

Upon losing the election, Catiline, frustrated and desperate, formed a conspiracy to overthrow the government, rumors of which reached Cicero. More definite information arrived through the mistress of one of Catiline's accomplices. Also, Crassus secretly visited Cicero and entrusted to him a number of compromising letters that he had received from the conspirators.

Still, Cicero's first denunciation of Catiline before the senate was based largely on surmises. Even when he reported that Catiline's lieutenant, Manlius, was busily recruiting an army of malcontents in Etruria to seize control of the government, his evidence was dismissed as incomplete by the senate, which refused to issue a *Senatus Consultum Ultimum* until the news arrived in Rome the next day that Manlius had indeed recruited a substantial army in Etruria. Cicero had not lied.

Cicero refrained from using the emergency decree and waited instead for Catilines's next move. Catiline called a secret meeting of his fellow-conspirators to make the final arrangements. He assigned some to start fires within the city, others to foment uprisings through Italy, and he named the day on which Manlius was to march. Two *equites* volunteered to carry out the assassination of Cicero and other important political leaders.

But the mistress of the false accomplice reported the plans to Cicero. When the would-be assassins arrived at his house, he was ready for them. That same day he called an emergency session of the senate and delivered his *First Catilinarian Oration* in the presence of Catiline himself. The following night Catiline left Rome to join Manlius in Etruria. The great majority of senators thereupon declared him a public enemy.

Catiline was gone, but dangerous men still remained in the city. They could have been even more dangerous had they had the energy and daring of Catiline. Cicero knew their identity, but lacked the evidence to place them under arrest until they made their supreme blunder. They made overtures to envoys from a tribe of Allobroges from Gallia Transalpina in the hope of enlisting cavalry support for Catiline. The envoys betrayed the conspirators by securing signed agreements from them, which they promptly turned over to Cicero. Acting with great speed, Cicero ordered the conspirators arrested and brought before the senate, where he made them acknowledge their signatures and secured their confessions.

The news of the arrest and confession of the five conspirators spread through the city. Every time Cicero appeared in public he got a thunderous ovation. Next morning throngs waited outside the senate house to hear the prisoners' fate. Those suspected of being in league with Catiline—even Caesar—were in danger.

The Debate in the Senate   Even the senate was in turmoil. Silanus, the consul elect, moved that the prisoners be put to death, and at first the majority were in favor of the motion. Then Caesar rose. He acknowledged the guilt of the prisoners but, in keeping with his opposition to the *Senatus Consultum Ultimum,* wondered if execution might not be both illegal and politically dangerous. He moved that they be imprisoned for life in some Italian municipality instead and their property confiscated. His eloquence persuaded a majority of the senators to change their opinions. Even Cicero seemed on the point of voting for Caesar's motion. Then Cato the Younger (Uticensis), great-grandson of Cato the Elder, took the floor and attacked the weakness and irresolution of his colleagues. So stinging were his words that a majority of the senators finally voted for the death penalty. That same day the conspirators paid for their crimes in the gloomy torchlit prison of the Tullianum.

The Death of Catiline, 62 B.C. The executions brought the conspiracy to an end. Two-thirds of Catiline's army melted away. The three thousand who were left fought and died on the plains of Pistoia (northwest of Florence) around their proud standards, the eagles of Marius. Catiline was among the slain.

Cicero's Hopes for the Future   Cicero of Arpinum had attained sudden glory. For delivering Rome from danger he was voted a thanksgiving festival and given the title *Pater Patriae,* Father of His Country. Without the support of a proud family name, great wealth, military talents, or strong political following, he had entered the senate, reached the consulship, and ennobled his family—a proud achievement, in proclaiming which he sometimes became tiresome even to his friends. The experience must have had its uncomfortable moments: he was admitted, but not accepted; admired for his eloquence, but ridiculed for his self-adulation. The first *novus homo* since Marius, Cicero cannot but have been hurt by the aloofness of his colleagues, by their tacit assumption of superiority, and by their frequent rudeness.

Difficult as it must have been for so proud a man to accept such treatment, Cicero was nevertheless convinced that the preservation of republican government depended on maintaining the supremacy of the senate. The ancient nobility was to give it prestige and continuity with the past, and new men—like Cicero himself—were to bring to it energy, intelligence, and an awareness of present problems. Peace, stability, and freedom depended on the continued harmony *(concordia ordinum)* between the senatorial aristocracy and the wealthy equestrian class of both businessmen and local Italian landed aristocracy. In a slightly expanded form, the concord of the orders was an alliance of all good law-abiding citizens against revolutionary attacks upon property and the status quo. He also insisted upon the *consensus Italiae,* by which he meant that Rome should conduct her affairs in conformity with the interests and sentiments of Italy as a whole—that is, of the class of local Italian notables, from which Cicero himself had come.

Of the ideals underlying all Roman political life Cicero was the most eloquent spokesman and supplied the vocabulary. The greatest of these was *libertas,* the spirit and practice of constitutional government, under which a man belonging to the governing elite could pursue a career to which birth entitled him as a right, maintain his *dignitas* (rank, prestige, and honor), practice freedom of speech, and display the virtues of honesty, independence of spirit, and generosity to friends and clients *(magnitudo animi)*. In short, *libertas* was almost a form of government, which respected law and constitutional forms and perpetuated the special privileges of the governing class. When *libertas* obtained, then there would also be *otium cum dignitate*—peace, tranquillity, and security for all classes and for each its own dignity and influence.

Cicero's concept of the ideal state was one governed according to law. To the magistrates was to be allotted executive power; to the senate, authority; to the people, liberty. It was to be a state in which the people might live and work in peace and security, and the governing class find fulfillment worthy of rank and dignity. All classes were to flourish, undisturbed by social strife or civil war. Such a state, Cicero believed, could be neither a monarchy nor a participatory democracy on the Athenian model, but only a free aristocratic republic.

The Crises of the Republic   Toward the end of 62 B.C. Pompeius Magnus, the conqueror of the East, landed at Brundisium. He at once disbanded his powerful army, with which he might have seized dictatorial power, as Sulla had done. His action belies the monarchic ambition sometimes attributed to him.

This fiction is based on the literal and serious acceptance of *rex* and *regnum,* two terms of political invective freely and loosely hurled. They were used to arouse hatred against such popular leaders as the Gracchi, Saturninus, and Cinna. They were hurled at Sulla, though he restored the supremacy of the senate and, at the end of two years, more or less voluntarily relinquished his dictatorship; at Crassus, who sought only to protect himself against Pompey; and even at Cicero, who because he was a *novus homo* from Arpinum, was maliciously called "the first foreign king at Rome since the Tarquins."

Against no one has the charge of monarchic ambition been more frequently hurled than against Julius Caesar, who has been described as having perversely dedicated his whole life to the goal of kingly power. He probably never had such a long-range program but had more immediate goals: the acquisition of money to pay his debts (he owed 25 million denarii before he went to Spain) and as a source of patronage; the maintenance of his *dignitas;* and the winning of *gloria* in politics and war. When a Roman achieved those goals, he did not need or want the useless and invidious *ornamenta* of a king. To Caesar, to Pompey, and to every other Roman *nobilis* the very name of king was still anathema.

The opening days of the year 61 B.C. looked bright for the future of the Republic. The senate had shown unexpected strength and resolution in dealing with the Catilinarian conspiracy. The equestrian class had, in Cicero, a brave and eloquent spokesman, whose *concordia ordinum* seemed an answer to social and civil strife, although not a substitute for needed reforms. A most hopeful sign was Pompey's dismissal of his army and his refusal to seize dictatorial power. Cicero might yet have saved the Republic, could Pompey but have been induced to support the policy of *concordia.*

But these were empty hopes: the jealousy of Crassus, the hostility of the optimate leaders of the senate toward Pompey, Pompey's own ineptness, and Cicero's unconquerable vanity all contributed to the breakdown of the tenuous harmony. Upon his return to Rome, Pompey attended a meeting of the senate with the expectation of being hailed as another Alexander. Crassus solemnly rose and, pointedly ignoring Pompey, dramatically declared Cicero the savior of Rome. Cicero, his vanity flattered, promptly forgot all about Pompey and went on to speak at great length of his own illustrious deeds instead. Cicero had already alienated Pompey by earlier boasts and thereby denied himself crucial support for his *concordia ordinum.* Thus, he had unwittingly shattered his own hopes of reconstructing the Republic.

Pompey's modest demands, when finally presented to the senate, met bitter opposition. He understandably wanted land for his veterans and ratification of his *acta* or arrangements made in the East. The consul Metellus Celer, whose half-sister Pompey had just divorced, opposed him and so did the exconsul of 69 B.C., Metellus Creticus, who held a grudge because Pompey had interfered with his command in Crete during the pirate war in 67. Lucullus, emerging from his princely gardens, vindictive and rancorous, insisted on debating Pompey's proposals in detail, not *en bloc* as Pompey requested. He had the support of Crassus, who was a jealous rival, and Cato the Younger, who saw Pompey's power as a threat to the Republic.

Cato the Younger (95–46 B.C.) Not one of the optimate leaders of the senate opposed Pompey's requests with more rancor than Cato the Younger. Narrow-minded and pedantic, yet honest and fearless, he was one of the few Stoics who lived by the philosophy they professed. In the vice-ridden capital, he reflected almost to the point of parody the harsh virtues of his ancestor, Cato the Elder (Censorius). Although he was still only one of the lowliest senators—a group which Cicero scornfully called *pedarii* ("footmen")—Cato's moral courage soon gained him recognition as the spokesman of the optimate heirs of Sulla, and his forceful character won him a power greater than that of any other member of the senate. Because of Cato's obstructive tactics, ratification of Pompey's *acta* was delayed.

After destroying the possibility of good will between Pompey and the optimate leaders of the senate, Cato proceeded to alienate Crassus and the equestrian financial interests by blocking passage of a bill for the relief of tax-collecting companies which had optimistically bid too high for the taxes in Asia and were now requesting a reduction of their contract payments to the treasury. Cicero, though he privately considered the petition outrageous and impudent, had nevertheless supported the bill for the sake of his policy of *concordia ordinum*.

Cato further antagonized the *equites* by forcing passage of a bill which declared as criminal offense the acceptance of bribes by *equites* serving on juries (it had long been so for senators). Again Cicero, as politicians so often must, betrayed one principle for the sake of another: although he thought the bill a fair measure, he opposed it as being detrimental to harmony.

Cato's next object of attack was Julius Caesar. Caesar, on his return from Spain, had requested the right to declare his candidacy for the consulship *in absentia,* in addition to receiving the triumph already voted for his military successes. It was legally impossible for him to have both in the time available: a recent law compelled potential candidates to declare their intentions in person before the magistrate in charge of the election, but to cross the city limits would have meant forfeiture of his triumph.

When Caesar learned that Cato opposed the petition, he decided to forego the triumph and stand for the consulship instead. Fearing that Caesar might win the election and thereby be eligible for a province and control of a provincial army, Cato persuaded the senate to assign the mountain roads and forests of Italy as the provinces of the consuls of 59 B.C. If Cato had deliberately set out to destroy the Republic, he could not have been more successful.

Cato and his allies ultimately drove Pompey, Crassus, and Caesar into a coalition that made each of them more powerful than he otherwise could have become. Then, with each aiming for supreme honors, the natural rivalries that were bound to reemerge resulted in the dictatorship of Julius Caesar, who paved the way for the principate of Augustus, which ended the Republic forever. The natural ambitions and rivalries of Roman nobles had reduced Republican politics to a vast game of musical chairs in which only one man would ultimately be left to dominate the rest.

XVIII

The Rise of Caesar,
60 to 52 B.C.

Having surprised Cato and his other optimate enemies by foregoing a triumph to run for the consulship in 60 B.C., Caesar marshalled all of his charm, skill, and resources to guarantee victory. His earlier cultivation of Marius' old followers now bore fruit. After his governorship of Spain, he also seems to have had fairly abundant funds of his own for bribery, in addition to those provided by another candidate, Lucceius, Pompey's friend. Caesar's optimate enemies, determined to defeat him, decided to raise their own bribery fund (to which even the incorruptible Cato contributed) to ensure the election of Bibulus, a stubborn and somewhat dull-witted man but son-in-law of Cato. Countering them, Caesar also secured the aid of Crassus and Pompey (probably independently of each other at first). Both of them had, like himself, been thwarted and injured by their optimate enemies in the senate, and they were happy to support a candidate who promised to act favorably toward them as consul. Thus supported, Caesar had little trouble winning election. Lucceius, however, lost to Bibulus, and that posed problems.

The So-called First Triumvirate The election of Bibulus revealed the strength of Caesar's opponents. It was probably only after

the election that Caesar, to strengthen his position as much as possible, persuaded Pompey and Crassus to cooperate together in the coalition that modern writers often call the First Triumvirate. Actually, it is inaccurate to refer to their coalition as a triumvirate, which in Roman terms denoted a legally constituted board of three men with some clearly defined authority. The later triumvirate of Octavian, Antony, and Lepidus, which is often called the Second Triumvirate, was such a board (see pp. 336–337). The informal coalition of Pompey, Crassus, and Caesar, the proper Roman term for which would be *coitio* or *factio,* was not. The whole difficulty with the word triumvirate might have been avoided if Caesar had succeeded in his attempt to add Cicero as a fourth member of the coalition, but Cicero, rightly seeing it as an attempt by three individuals to thwart established constitutional mechanisms, honorably refused.

The three others privately swore that each would seek only those ends not objectionable to the other two. The personal aims of the three were fairly clear: Pompey wanted land for his veterans and ratification of his *acta* in the East; Crassus desired a reduction of the tax contracts of his equestrian friends; Caesar sought command of a province and an army.

At the start, Caesar was clearly less powerful than either Pompey or Crassus. He had a certain long-term advantage, however, because Pompey and Crassus could never completely forget their rivalry and Caesar could maneuver between them. He soon strengthened his position by marrying his daughter, Julia, to Pompey and taking to wife Calpurnia, the daughter of Lucius Calpurnius Piso Caesoninus, who became a consul in 58 B.C. In that and following years, with the help of Pompey and Crassus and others, Caesar obtained passage of legislation favorable to himself that enabled him eventually to amass enough political, military, and financial power to surpass the other two partners in the coalition.

Caesar's Legislation   In 59, however, Caesar's first task was to make good on his promise to obtain the legislation that would fill the needs of Pompey and Crassus. At the start of his term, Caesar sensibly tried to obtain his goals without any unnecessary offense to his opponents and began by being studiously polite to both the optimate-controlled senate and to his optimate colleague, Bibulus. He consulted them on all matters, accepted their suggestions and amendments, and proposed only moderate bills. His friendly behavior may have been interpreted as weakness, or Caesar himself may have tired of the cautious approach, for he soon resorted to more direct methods. When even his moderate bills were endlessly debated and obstructed in the senate, Caesar had Cato, the leader of the opposition, arrested. Upon reflection, however, he apparently decided not to turn the righteous Cato into a martyr, and had him set free.

As a last resort, Caesar presented his land bill for the settlement of Pompey's veterans to the assembly. Bibulus promptly vetoed it. Using the consular right of fixing the days of movable holidays, Bibulus declared all remaining days on which the assemblies could meet during the year to be feast days, and the last constitutional path for the three dynasts had thereby been cut off.

Disregarding this legal obstacle, Caesar presented his land bill to the assembly a second time. The Forum was filled with eager spectators, most of them Pompey's veterans. The law was proposed; three tribunes interposed vetoes. The crowd's murmur rose to an angry roar. Dramatically, Caesar halted the voting and asked Pompey what other action he was prepared to take. Pompey placed his hand on his hip and declared that he would not hesitate to draw his sword. Bibulus, who had pushed his way into the Forum, jumped to his feet. But before he could say a word, the angry mob had broken his fasces and someone dumped a basket of filth over his head. The assembly passed the bill, and Caesar declared it carried.*

The humiliated Bibulus retired from public life and spent the rest of his term shut up in his home. Some wag acutely observed that from then on the names of the two consuls were no longer Bibulus and Caesar, but Julius and Caesar.

Now unopposed, Caesar carried out the rest of his legislative program with speed and efficiency. A law was passed which provided for the distribution of Campanian public lands among twenty thousand needy citizens—the only requirement being that each have at least three children. A bill was passed to ratify *en bloc* all Pompey's settlements in the East; another bill remitted one-third of the contract payments that the tax collectors of Asia, Crassus' friends, had to submit to the treasury.

Caesar also obtained passage of legislation favorable to himself. One of his partisans, the tribune Publius Vatinius, secured passage of a bill that granted Caesar immediate proconsular power for five years over the provinces of Cisalpine Gaul and Illyricum and an army of three legions. Caesar began at once to recruit his army and held it in readiness near Rome. His opponents within the senate were powerless: they could have declared the law null and void if a meeting of the senate had been summoned by a magistrate, but no one summoned it. Nor could it pass a *Senatus Con-*

---

* The authors of the bill had foresightedly included a clause, similar to that inserted into the land bill of 100 B.C. of Saturinus, which required all senators to swear obedience to the law. They all did, including Cato.

sultum Ultimum, which would have been useless anyway, for there was no one to enforce it except Bibulus, who had no troops. After that, no senator dared oppose any of Caesar's measures for fear of incurring his wrath. Those who still attended meetings summoned by Caesar were considerate and polite: when the governor of Transalpine Gaul suddenly died, they voluntarily assigned that province to Caesar.

One of the most enlightened of Caesar's early laws ordered the publication of the *Acta Diurna,* a daily bulletin which contained the texts of all currently enacted laws as well as condensations of the debates and proceedings of the senate and popular assemblies (*Acta Senatus et Populi Romani*). Sold in the streets, posted in the Forum, and sent to all the towns of Italy and to provinces, this publication kept the people informed about foreign and domestic problems. Caesar's purpose in ordering publication of the *Acta Diurna* was also personal, however. Now the actions of his enemies in the senate would be made visible to the average citizens, among whom he was very popular. Therefore, his enemies would think twice before taking what might prove to be very unpopular actions against him.

The most statesmanly law of Caesar in 59 B.C. was the *lex Julia de Repetundis,* which regulated the administration of the provinces, drastically controlled extortion, and forbade governors, under pain of heavy penalty, to accept presents, sell or withhold justice, transgress the limits of their provinces without authorization, or fail to deposit their official edicts: two copies in the provinces and one at Rome. This excellent law served to protect the people of the provinces from oppression and promote their well-being and prosperity. Still, it too had a partisan purpose, for it would make it more difficult for his enemies to abuse the provinces in an attempt to obtain power and resources against him and would make the danger of prosecution greater if they did.

The Banishment of Cicero, 58 B.C.

Before leaving for Gaul, Caesar wanted to make sure that his opponents in the senate would not venture to annul the Julian laws of 59 B.C. With his compelling oratory, Cicero was a man who might successfully lead such an attack. In an effort to prevent Cicero from freely speaking his mind, Caesar offered him a remunerative position in the Land Commission. That offer rejected, Caesar then invited Cicero to accompany him to Gaul as his legate. When Cicero turned down this and other offers, Caesar finally decided to leave Cicero to the devices of the tribune Publius Clodius. He was the same man who had helped to undermine Lucullus' command against Mithradates in 67. Loose and dissolute, clever and audacious, he was one of the most potent rabble-rousers in Roman history. His armed gangs ruled the streets of Rome. He was a patrician Claudius by birth but used the plebeian spelling Clodius to gain popularity. Also, early in 59 B.C. Caesar, as Pontifex Maximus, and Pompey, as an augur, presided over his adoption by a plebeian family so that he could become a tribune and frighten Cicero into silence when the latter refused to cooperate with them.

The Bona Dea Affair   Clodius had a very special reason for hating both Cicero and Cato. Late in the year 62 B.C. Roman women were celebrating at the house of Julius Caesar, the Pontifex Maximus, the annual festival of the Bona Dea, from whose rites men were rigorously excluded. Clodius, alleged to have been the lover of Caesar's second wife, Pompeia, at the time, managed to enter the house disguised as a woman. His presence was detected, and a scandal ensued. As a result, Caesar declared that "Caesar's wife must be above suspicion," and divorced Pompeia. Instead of treating the escapade as a joke (Cicero privately regarded it as such), Cato brought Clodius to trial on a charge of sacrilege. When called as a witness, Caesar, not wishing to make an enemy of a popular and powerful political figure, refused to testify, but Cicero, testifying at the trial, ruined Clodius' attempt to establish an alibi. Conviction seemed certain, but Crassus bribed the jurors to vote for acquittal. Clodius never forgave Cato for bringing him to trial, or Cicero for testifying against him.

Clodius' Attack   One of the first bills that Clodius carried abolished the use of "omens" for the obstruction of legislation. Another of his laws provided for the distribution of free grain to the needy. But Clodius is remembered for the notorious law which was part of his revenge against Cicero: it forbade the use of fire and water to all persons who had put Roman citizens to death without trial or appeal to the people. The law attacked not only Cicero, who had ordered the execution of the Catilinarian conspirators, but also the *Senatus Consultum Ultimum,* the senatorial decree whose legality had been debated since the time of the Gracchi. Cicero, who had believed himself immune from attack, was stunned: he and his friends vainly pleaded with the consuls, Piso (Caesar's father-in-law) and Gabinius (Pompey's client), to intercede. He appealed to Pompey, who had once promised him protection, but Pompey, according to Plutarch, slipped out of his house upon Cicero's approach. His pleas denied, Cicero had no choice but to leave Italy.

Clodius next disposed of Cato by a law assigning him to govern the distant island of Cyprus. Clodius dryly observed that Cato was the only man in Rome honest enough to administer the royal treasures of that new province. Cato, who could not justify breaking a duly constituted law, stoically complied.

The removal of his two ablest opponents ensured for Caesar the perpetuation of the recently enacted Julian Laws of 59 B.C., and he finally set forth for his proconsular provinces.

Caesar in Gaul   Caesar, waiting outside Rome for Cicero to be exiled, now hurried north and took command of the legion stationed in Transalpine Gaul, often called the Province or Narbonese Gaul, the eastern part of which is now Provence in southeastern France. Caesar hoped to use his governorship of Transalpine Gaul to pursue great wars and

conquests that would earn him undying glory, a large following of loyal veterans, and huge financial resources from booty, all of which were extremely useful in the even more important political battles of the Forum, as the careers of Marius, Sulla, and Pompey had amply demonstrated. At this time, Transalpine Gaul was ideally located for fulfilling these hopes. It bordered the rich and populous lands of the free Gallic tribes, and the political situation both within and without their territory was in an unsettled state that could give ample pretexts for the neighboring Roman commander to intervene "to protect the vital interests of Rome."

Geography   Transalpine Gaul, shaped somewhat like an inverted "L," followed the Mediterranean shoreline from the Alps to the Pyrenes, whence its northern boundary swung around in an arc to Geneva about two hundred miles north of the sea. North of the Province lay free or "long-haired" Gaul (*Gallia Comata*). It embraced what is now all central and northern France, Belgium, and most of Holland and the German Rhineland. According to Caesar, this territory was divided into three parts: the first was Aquitania, which lay in the southwest between the Garonne and the Pyrenees. Its people were related to the inhabitants of the Iberian peninsula (probably the modern Basques) with a considerable Celtic admixture.

The second part embraced all central and northern France and the neighboring German regions as far east as the Rhine, not including the northeastern area. The people were almost purely Celtic, who had been coming over the Rhine from southern Germany, Austria, and Bohemia, probably from the seventh century B.C. onward, and had either driven out or absorbed the original inhabitants. The third was the northeastern region extending from the Seine and the Marne to the estuary of the Scheldt and the Lower Rhine. There lived the warlike Belgians, a mixed group of Celts and some Germans, most of whom had crossed the Rhine late in the second century B.C. The three Gallic nations differed from one another in ethnic origin, language, customs, and institutions.

Social and Political Organization　As a primarily agricultural people, the vast majority of Gauls lived in villages and small towns. There were some larger manufacturing or mining communities, but most of the few larger towns were trading posts, which had sprung up at the mouths and bends of major rivers and junctions of trade routes. In the interior, some towns like Bibracte, Gergovia, and Alesia, were on steep-sided hilltops, easily defended refuges in time of prolonged danger but often abandoned after the period of crisis had passed. Probably few of the Gallic towns ever became real cities until Gaul had been Romanized.

The Gauls, as a whole, were politically weak and unstable. Their largest political unit was the tribal state (*civitas*), a loose confederation of more or less independent clans. There were nearly one hundred such states, and they often fought with each other. Also, they were unstable internally. Most had abolished monarchic rule about fifty years earlier and were rent by feuding noble factions. The resulting confusion and disorder made the Gallic tribes vulnerable to conquest by either aggressive German tribes from across the Rhine or imperialistic Romans.

Defeat of the Helvetians, 58 B.C.　Such were the economic, social, and political conditions in Gaul when Caesar arrived in the Province. At that moment, the Helvetians (Helvetii) of western Switzerland were ready to set out on a long-projected trek across Gaul to the West, to a land richer and more spacious than their own and far away from the aggressions of Ariovistus and the Germanic tribes in southwestern Germany. They had burnt their homes and villages behind them and, in the spring of 58 B.C., stood poised on the banks of the Rhône.

Here was an opportunity for Caesar to display his military talents. Claiming that the migration of the Helvetians would threaten the security of the Province by creating turmoil in free Gaul and would leave their old territory open as an avenue for German tribes to invade Italy, Caesar refused to let them cross. There is a pass that winds around the Jura mountains along the right bank of the Rhône, a route narrow and difficult, where ox-pulled wagons may pass only in single file. After being repulsed on the Rhône, the Helvetians, intending to follow the Saône before crossing and swinging west, took that road. Caesar reacted with the speed and determination that became his hallmarks as a general and the key to his rise as the dominant power at Rome. After a series of minor skirmishes, the two armies clashed in a decisive battle during which the Romans all but destroyed the Helvetian army. Caesar compelled the survivors to return to their native homeland, except for the Boii, whom he allowed to settle in Aeduan territory, at the request of the Aeduan leaders.

Ariovistus　There began almost immediately a procession of envoys from many states of central Gaul to Caesar, some to offer congratulations for his recent victory, others to implore his aid against Ariovistus, a powerful German king who had already reduced two states to vassalage and whose aggressions were daily growing more menacing. Caesar at once began negotiations with the king, in whose rudeness and arrogance he found a plausible pretext for war. Bold, swift marches, a few skillful maneuvers, and a single battle ended in the utter rout and destruction of the Germans. Thus, in one brief summer, Caesar had destroyed two major enemies and had made Rome the arbiter of *Gallia Comata*. After quartering his legions at Besançon for the winter, he hastened to Cisalpine Gaul to hold the November sessions of his gubernatorial court and recruit two more legions for another campaign.

The Belgic War, 57 B.C.　Caesar's selection of eastern Gaul for winter quarters had aroused the fears and hostilities of the Belgians. A letter from his most trusted legate,

Titus Labienus, about their warlike preparations sent the proconsul hurrying back over the Alps with two more legions. Again, speed and resolute action were decisive. The Belgian force proved too unwieldy for unified command and soon ran short of supplies. Torn by mutual jealousies and dissension, the Belgians broke up and dispersed after only one minor skirmish. Caesar could now subdue the Belgian states one by one.

Meanwhile, young Publius Crassus, Crassus' eldest son, whom the proconsul had sent with one legion to western Gaul, had compelled all the tribes along the English Channel and the Atlantic seaboard to submit to Rome. Gaul was prostrate at the feet of the conqueror. Even the Germans beyond the Rhine sent hostages and promised to obey his orders. On receiving report of these triumphs, the senate decreed a public thanksgiving of an unprecedented fifteen days.

The Political Situation in Rome, 58 to 56 B.C.

While Caesar was winning battles, Rome itself was the scene of disorder and violence. Constitutional government had broken down. The senate was too weak to govern, Pompey the Great too inept. Clodius had by his free grain law made himself the idol of the slums and his armed gangs ruled the streets. They besieged and burnt down houses, hissed at or spat upon political opponents, pelted them with stones or stomped them to death.

No sooner had Caesar left for Gaul than Pompey and Crassus began to quarrel. The former, in order to restore his ebbing popularity and win the support of the nobility, began to agitate for the recall of Cicero from exile. Clodius, aroused to fury, incited a series of riots, and the ensuing jeers, insults, and threats drove the general from public life temporarily and confined him to his house. Crassus, who had no liking for Cicero and helped to keep Clodius supplied with funds, although he by no means controlled him, chuckled over his rival's discomfiture with malicious glee.

Cicero's Recall, 57 B.C.   Clodius, as tribune, could veto every proposal for the return of Cicero and continued to incite his followers to riot whenever such a bill came up before the assembly.

Pompey returned to the political arena during the summer of the Belgic War: he entered into correspondence with Caesar and began to attend assembly meetings in the Forum once more. Usually he was escorted by a large group of followers (many of them veterans of his Eastern wars), headed by the tribune T. Annius Milo. Pompey called upon Cicero's brother, Quintus Cicero, to guarantee that the orator, if permitted to return, would do nothing to upset either the rule of the so-called triumvirs or the Julian laws. Pompey's efforts bore fruit, and that same autumn a bill for Cicero's return passed the *comitia centuriata* with uproarious acclaim. The success of the bill had depended somewhat on the victory of Milo and his followers during a bloody scuffle with the followers of Clodius.

Cicero's return was met with thunderous applause from the watching throngs who scattered flowers in his path. The senate undertook to rebuild (at public expense) his house, which had been destroyed by the followers of Clodius. Unfortunately the same hoodlums drove away the workmen, demolished the reconstructions, and set fire to his brother's house, next door.

After Cicero's return, a sudden and dangerous shortage of grain frightened the optimate leaders of the senate, and they agreed to place Pompey in charge of the food supply. He was given command of a fleet to transport grain and was offered an army, but he solemnly demurred in order not to appear too eager for what he really did want. The *optimates* simply took him at his word. His friends, though exasperated by his lack of frankness, saw a good opportunity for him to acquire an army when Ptolemy the Fluteplayer, king of Egypt, driven from his throne by the citizens of Alexandria, formally requested Roman aid. Unfortunately for Pompey's ambitions, someone took the trouble to consult the books of the Sibyl and found it there forbidden to use an army to restore a king of Egypt. Much relieved, the majority of senators let the matter drop.

The Conference of Luca, 56 B.C. Caesar was undoubtedly kept informed of the political situation in Rome through correspondence with Pompey, Crassus, and others. He knew that Cicero and Clodius (the latter with the connivance of Crassus) were both attacking the Julian laws of 59 B.C., though for different reasons. He knew from a visit of Crassus to his winter quarters at Ravenna in early April of 56 that Pompey, with Cicero's encouragement, was veering over to the *optimates*. With the coalition of Pompey, Crassus, and Caesar threatened, the time had come for Caesar himself to act. He met with Pompey and probably also Crassus at Luca in mid-April of 56.

It was agreed that Pompey and Crassus should stand for the consulship of 55 B.C., probably that Pompey should afterward be governor of the two Spains for five years while Crassus for an equal period should be governor of Syria with the right to wage war against the Parthians, and that Caesar's proconsulship be renewed for another five years. They also agreed that Cicero's acid speechmaking be curbed and the mobs of Clodius and Milo restrained. The conference over, Caesar swept off for Transalpine Gaul.

The Gallic Wars Continued, 56 to 55 B.C. Caesar found the Veneti of Brittany in full revolt. A shipbuilding and seagoing people who lived by trading with Britain, they presented a formidable naval threat. The Romans, however, soon discovered that long poles with hooks on the end could render the enemy's ships helpless by pulling down their rigging as Roman ships maneuvered alongside. The seapower of the Veneti broken and the conquest on land rapidly completed, the proconsul turned east to meet a new menace emerging from the wilds of Germany.

In the late fall of 56 B.C., two German tribes pushed savagely westward by the advance of the Suebi, crossed the Rhine. Their numbers have been exaggeratedly reported as 400,000. Probably there were no more than 100,000, 25,000 adult fighting men and the rest women and children. The Romans entered into negotiations with the leaders of the tribes, but a treacherous attack by the German cavalry provoked Caesar to arrest the still-negotiating German chiefs and lead an overwhelming Roman attack which resulted in the ruthless slaughter of the leaderless tribes.

A series of swift maneuvers, beginning with the rapid building of a large wooden bridge across the Rhine, sufficed to overawe the remaining Germans. Then, in late summer of 55 B.C., Caesar invaded Britain, an event more memorable in British history than in Roman. He may have had several motives: curiosity, a desire to punish the Britons for helping the Gauls, or to impress Roman society by conquering, like Alexander the Great, a land of mystery at the edge of the world, and perhaps a desire to pacify the conquered Gallic leaders by making them partners in the invasion of Britain. Though his expedition was of little military value and meant no expansion of Roman power, it so flattered Roman pride that the senate decreed another public thanksgiving, this time lasting twenty days.

The next year Caesar again invaded Britain. With a new fleet of specially constructed ships, he landed five legions and two thousand cavalry on the shores of Kent. He pushed inland swiftly. But disaster struck: word arrived that wild storm winds and high tides had pounded his anchored fleet upon the beach. Encouraged by the news, the Britons rallied for a counterattack under the leadership of their famous war-king, Cassivellaunus, skilled in ambush and guerrilla tactics. Caesar repulsed the British attacks and again driving inland, crossed the Thames and stormed and captured the king's main stronghold. The Britons sued for peace. Hostages and a formal promise of tribute were the terms, but it would be almost another hundred years before Britain became a Roman province. Caesar then returned to Gaul to deal with the new and dangerous unrest brewing among the Gallic chiefs.

Final Conquest, 54 to 52 B.C.   In the fall of 54 B.C., Caesar called a meeting of the Gallic leaders at Samarobriva (Amiens). There he learned that their chief complaint against Roman authority was that it cramped their age-old right of warring upon and plundering their neighbors. Proud of their glorious past, they were angered by Roman subjugation. Moreover, Caesar's perpetual demands for grain in a year of poor crops were driving them to desperation.

Sensing their dangerous mood, Caesar dispersed his legions in a wide arc among the Belgians. The dispersion of the legions strongly tempted the tribes to revolt, and in the late fall of the same year, the Nervii, Treveri, and Eburones attacked the legions encamped in their lands. Caesar's savage reprisals against the Belgians, his execution of certain Gallic leaders, the oppressive severity of his rule, and the encouraging reports of turmoil in Rome, aroused the tribes of central Gaul.

The Revolt of Vercingetorix   In 52 B.C., under the leadership of Vercingetorix, the son of a former Arvernian king, the Gauls began their war for independence. The revolt began with a frightful massacre of Italian merchants at Orléans and spread rapidly over all Gaul. It aroused the Aedui, Rome's oldest and strongest friends. It also threatened the Province. Returning in haste from the Cisalpina, Caesar found himself cut off from his legions stationed for the winter in the North. After arranging for the defense of the Province, he made a fast but painful march through deep mountain snows into *Gallia Comata* and the home state of Vercingetorix, a strategy which diverted the latter from his original plans and indirectly enabled Caesar to recover the initiative and join his legions in the North.

Realizing that his armies were hopelessly inferior to Caesar's veteran legions, Vercingetorix devised and at first carried out guerrilla and scorched-earth strategy—the burning of towns and villages, the disruption of communications, the capture of convoys, the destruction of foraging parties, and hit-and-run attacks on the Roman army.

Had the Gallic leaders permitted Vercingetorix to pursue his strategy consistently, he might have paralyzed Caesar's army and perhaps even driven him out of Gaul altogether. They could not bear to see their beautiful town of Bourges either fired or captured; when Caesar besieged it with gigantic siegeworks and circumvallations, he took it by storm and destroyed a large Gallic army. Then Caesar again invaded the home territory of Vercingetorix and besieged the hill fortress of Gergovia, where the Romans suffered their first defeat of the war.

Undaunted, Caesar met the crisis with courage and intelligence. He coolly exploited his opponent's every mistake. Emboldened by his victory at Gergovia, and partly to placate his jealous and recalcitrant Aeduan allies, Vercingetorix abandoned his own guerrilla tactics and unsuccessfully adopted those of open warfare. Defeated, Vercingetorix next led his army to the hill fortress of Alesia, which Caesar promptly besieged by setting his men to work with pick and shovel to dig entrenchments nine miles long and studded with twenty-three redoubts.

The Siege of Alesia, 52 B.C.   Failing to hamper Caesar's siege works, Vercingetorix ordered his cavalry, with muffled hooves, to steal away one night, each to his own part of the country and there recruit a relief army in the cause of national independence. Informed by spies, Caesar had an elaborate second line of circumvallation constructed to keep the relieving army out—wide and deep river-inundated trenches interspersed with bastions and towers; beyond and further out, innumerable turf-concealed pits and booby traps, the most ingenious system of defense works ever constructed until the wars of the twentieth century.

The Gauls answered the call for help. From almost everywhere men kept streaming toward the appointed marshaling center. A vast assembled host marched to Alesia. Day after day raged the battle of Alesia, the battle of Gaul to decide the future of Europe. Cavalry engagements, sorties by the besieged army inside of Alesia, assaults upon the outer defense works by the relieving army occurred simultaneously or in rapid succession. The Romans, hard pressed at times everywhere, were in one particular sector almost overwhelmed. A hard-riding messenger breathlessly told Caesar of the breakthrough; the defenders weary, exhausted; the defense works collapsing under the weight of the mass attack. Into that salient Caesar threw six cohorts, then seven more, and hurried himself to the spot with more reinforcements. The cavalry was ordered to follow; additional cavalry units were ordered to hit the enemy rear. Labienus threw in every available man. The legionaries, exhausted and on the point of surrender, caught sight of Caesar's scarlet battle cape fluttering in the wind, took

heart, and pressed home a furious attack. The enemy broke and ran, vanishing into the night. Except for some minor (though at times rather difficult) mopping-up operations, the battle of Gaul was over.

The battle for supremacy at Rome, however, was now beginning in earnest. In Gaul, Caesar had established the military and financial basis for realizing his ambition of being the most powerful and respected man in Rome. In so doing, he had increased the fear and jealousy of his erstwhile partners, Pompey and Crassus, and the optimate leaders of the senate. All of them began to look for ways to counter Caesar. Eventually, these maneuverings convinced him to stake everything on civil war, for which he was now even better prepared than his enemies realized.

XIX

Caesar Wins and Is Lost, Mid-50s to 44 B.C.

While Caesar was overawing the Germans across the Rhine, invading Britain, punishing the Belgian tribes, and putting down Vercingetorix, major political developments important for Caesar's future were taking place at Rome. From the Conference of Luca in 56 B.C., Crassus and Pompey had gained renewed strength that promised to keep them on a par with Caesar. Both would again stand for the consulship and would again command armies and provinces. Their enemies were stunned: Cicero, bound to preserve the peace, turned quickly from invective to softer words of praise and thanksgiving. With Caesar himself Cicero kept up a frequent correspondence; borrowed money from him; and sent him his latest works, the *De Oratore* perhaps, which he could admire, as well as some poems, which he could not.

The Struggle for Preeminence In the last years of the Republic, four things clearly mattered—the consulate, the armies, the tribunate, and the role of the preeminent statesmen, which many aspired to play—above all Cicero, Cato, Pompey, Crassus, and Caesar. All strove for prestige and power; none desired to precipitate violence or revolution.

In 55 B.C., with Pompey and Crassus as consuls, the tribune C. Trebonius carried a law (the *lex Trebonia*) assigning the consuls their provinces for five years as apparently agreed upon at the Luca conference. Pompey received the two Spains but decided, perhaps on Caesar's advice, to remain in the vicinity of Rome to watch the course of events. At last he could recruit legions. Some he would send under his legates to Spain, others retain in Italy. Never again would he make the mistake of disbanding them too soon, as he had in 61 B.C. after his return from the East. Crassus, Pompey's rival and colleague, received the province of Syria with the right to make war as he saw fit. Parthia was not mentioned in the law, but it was an open secret that he was preparing a war against that rival power on Rome's eastern border.

The Downfall of Crassus Crassus lost no time in setting out for his province. Even before the end of his consulate he left Rome for Syria and, early in the spring of 54 B.C., invaded Mesopotamia with an army of thirty-five thousand men. He crossed the Euphrates, captured and garrisoned a few border towns, and returned to winter quarters in Syria, where he could train his troops. They were still raw recruits, who would have to face the full force of the Parthians now that they would no longer enjoy the advantage of surprise attack. He also took advantage of the pause in military operations to replenish his war chest by looting the Temple of Jerusalem and other rich shrines in his province.

In the spring of 53 B.C., Crassus again crossed the Euphrates. His objective was a full-scale invasion of Parthia and the capture of Seleuceia. Crassus rejected the idea of attacking Parthia through Armenia and, contrary to what is usually thought, followed a well-known and strategically sound route, along which he had placed garrisons the year before. Crassus' army was already approaching the garrison at Carrhae on the Belikh River when the Parthians finally attacked. If Publius Crassus had not led the vital cavalry too far from the main army, the Romans might well have withstood the assault. With Publius and the cavalry lost, however, Crassus was forced to retreat. He reached Carrhae with the bulk of his army, but the town was not strong enough to withstand a major siege, and he ordered a further retreat north to hilly terrain more favorable to Roman infantry.

On this retreat his inexperienced troops were slowed by a fatal loss of discipline. Crassus was captured and killed only two miles from the safe walls of Sinnaca, and his grisly, bleeding head was displayed at the Parthian court during the performance of the *Bacchae* of Euripides. Seven legions met destruction, their proud eagles set up in Parthian temples. Of an army of almost forty thousand men only ten thousand made good their escape into Syria through the skill of Gaius Cassius Longinus, one of Caesar's future assassins.

The Dissolution of the Coalition   The death of Crassus completely upset the delicate political equilibrium that had existed after Luca. Henceforth, Pompey and Caesar would drift steadily apart. The personal bond which had been sealed by Pompey's marriage to Julia, Caesar's only daughter, was broken in 54 B.C. by the untimely death of that charming and tactful lady.

Caesar's meteoric rise threatened Pompey's prestige and dominance. To maintain his position, Pompey needed the support of the senatorial leaders. Their hope of wedging the two strong men apart seemed about to be realized. To close the ever widening breach, Caesar asked for the hand of Pompey's only daughter, and was coldly rebuffed. Pompey himself married Cornelia, the young widow of Publius Crassus and daughter of Metellus Scipio, a man from the inner circle of the optimate leadership of the senate.

Meanwhile disorder prevailed in Rome, corruption and electoral bribery without restraint. The year 53 B.C. began without consuls, 52 likewise. Violence and rioting made the streets unsafe. Milo was running for the consulship, Clodius, with Pompey's support, for the praetorship. The bribes were lavish. Blood flowed. The year expired. No elections and no magistrates. Authority had broken down. Rome was in anarchy.

The Death of Clodius, 52 B.C.   The murder of Clodius during a brawl between his retinue and Milo's caused further riots. Egged on by Clodius' widow, Fulvia, a mob in the Forum seized his body, carried it to the senate house, and used the building for his funeral pyre. Pompey exploited the widespread fear and outrage that was aroused. Most people agreed that only Pompey was capable of restoring order and should be given emergency powers. His friends proposed a dictatorship, but that was too much for the *optimates* to accept. Cato and Bibulus came up with a compromise that saw Pompey elected sole consul for 52 B.C. In this way he had great latitude for action but was still subject to tribunician veto and would be held legally accountable for his acts.

Pompey Sole Consul, 52 B.C.   Pompey quickly obtained passage of several laws designed both to restore order and to weaken his rivals. The first was aimed at punishing the perpetrators of the recent violence, even his former ally Milo, who was expendable now that Clodius was dead and who was a rival of electoral candidates whom Pompey preferred to him. The second attacked bribery and was retroactive to 70 B.C., an aspect that troubled Caesar's friends. Both laws included harsher penalties and swifter procedures than previous ones.

Cicero was only too happy to defend Milo when he was charged under the new law against violence, *de Vi,* for the actions leading to Clodius' death. To make certain that no one disrupted the trial to help Milo, Pompey surrounded the court with armed troops. Cicero was so flustered at their sight that he forgot what he wanted to say, and Milo, convicted, went into exile to Massilia. Cicero, who was sometimes amazingly insensitive, sent him a polished version of the speech that he had hoped to give!

Pompey also obtained passage of a law that required a five-year interval between a magistracy and the governorship of a province. While this law was sincerely designed to reduce bribery at Rome and protect the provincials from extortion by forcing a man to wait too long between expenditure of bribes and a chance to recoup his money, it also worked to Pompey's personal advantage. Under normal circumstances Caesar could not have been superseded in his Gallic command without it being designated as consular prior to the election as consul of the man who would succeed him. That would give him as much as eighteen months to choose his options. Under Pompey's law Caesar's command could be reassigned immediately, and Caesar would have to depend upon Pompey's influence to see that it did not happen. In the meantime, Pompey had strengthened himself by having his command of the Spains extended for five more years. Also, to cover the five-year interval before the current magistrates could hold governorships, Pompey required all exconsuls and expraetors of more than five-years' standing who had never held governorships to do so. That enabled him to send influential men like Cicero and Bibulus to overseas governorships and make the *optimates* look to him even more for guidance at Rome.

Pompey's basic strategy from 52 B.C. onward was to demonstrate his strength to both Caesar and the *optimates* and to force each to cooperate with him for protection against the other. In this way Pompey would guarantee his own preeminence. For example, Caesar, in order to avoid prosecution for any of his previous acts by retaining his *imperium* as proconsul until he could return to Rome as consul again, had persuaded the ten tribunes of 52 to obtain a law allowing him to declare *in absentia* his candidacy for a second consulship, for which he would be eligible in 49 B.C. Pompey, however, subsequently strengthened the law requiring all candidates for high office to declare themselves personally in Rome to the magistrate in charge of the election. Caesar's friends protested and pointed out that the new provisions of the law would have precedence over the previous law favoring Caesar. Pompey then replied that Caesar was excepted from the new law and probably illegally had a codicil so stating engraved on the official public copy. This act publically demonstrated that Caesar was dependent on Pompey's good will, and it cautioned the *optimates* not to take for granted a man who could alter a law at will.

Prelude to Civil War   A series of complicated maneuvers followed in 51 B.C. as some of the *optimates* tried to remove Caesar from his command immediately. Pompey persuaded the senators not to raise the issue until March 1, 50 B.C. In this way Pompey could claim not to have violated his own law of 55 that extended Caesar's command for another five years, yet his stance was a threat to Caesar's hope of retaining his provinces and army while keeping his *imperium* and running *in absentia* for the consulship.

Caesar was not so easily kept subordinate, however. In 50 B.C., the consul Aemilius Paullus and the ten tribunes seemed to favor Caesar. The most brilliant of the tribunes was C. Scribonius Curio, an eloquent speaker and a master of intrigue who had married Fulvia, the fiery widow of Clodius. He was recklessly extravagant and some sources allege that Caesar won his support by paying his huge debts. Bribed or not, Curio was Caesar's subtlest weapon and could, under pretense of neutrality, block all action unfavorable to Caesar.

Three other clever and ambitious young men, Caelius Rufus, Dolabella, and Marcus Antonius (Mark Antony), supported the proconsul. Like Curio, Caelius was a fine speaker, worldly and sophisticated. He had been both Cicero's friend and a lover of Clodius' notoriously dissolute sister Clodia. Dolabella, debauched and sinister, was Cicero's son-in-law. Marcus Antonius, though pleasure-loving and licentious, was a brilliant soldier and strategist and was well liked by Caesar, whom he had followed over the mountains and through the plains and forests of *Gallia Comata.*

The major attempt to cripple Caesar, in March of 50 B.C., failed. The consul Paullus, in collusion with Curio, faked a noisy and angry debate over the provinces and thereby forestalled the discussion of all other matters. The "nonpartisan" Curio astutely demanded that both Caesar and Pompey relinquish their commands and surrender their armies for the security of the Republic. He became a popular hero overnight.

Although irked by Curio's tactics and frustrated by his vetoes, Pompey refused to admit defeat. He persuaded the optimate leaders of the senate that troops were needed in the East to fight the Parthians, and that body accordingly decreed that he and Caesar should each supply a legion. Although ostensibly fair, the decree actually profited Pompey, for he had to give up nothing while Caesar was forced to relinquish two legions (one of his own and one lent him two years earlier by Pompey for service in Gaul). When the troops arrived in Italy, Pompey decided that they were no longer needed in the East and stationed them (under his command) at nearby Capua instead.

On December 1, the consul Gaius Mar-cellus appeared before the senate and moved that Caesar be stripped of his command. Curio did not interpose the expected veto. The motion carried. With mounting confidence, Marcellus then proposed that Pompey be permitted to retain his command. Again Curio remained silent; again the motion passed. Then Curio rose. He too had a proposal. Condemning all military dictatorships, he pointed out the injustice of penalizing only Caesar, and proposed that both Caesar and Pompey be made to step down. His motion carried by an overwhelming 370 to 22. Enraged, Marcellus cried, "Have it your way, since you want Caesar for your master!" and he stormed out of the senate. Curio then went to the Forum to address the assembled populace. His eloquence served him well: he was wildly applauded and pelted with flowers by his enthusiastic audience.

Next day Marcellus summoned a special meeting of the senate. He spoke of rumors of Caesar's arrival in Cisalpine Gaul and of a possible march on Rome. The senate must act at once, he urged, to proclaim a state of emergency and declare Caesar a public enemy. The two legions stationed at Capua must march to defend the capital. Curio, insisting the rumors were false, vetoed the motion. Marcellus in turn moved a vote of censure against Curio as a subversive and an obstructionist. When the motion failed to pass, the consul took it upon himself to go to Pompey. He handed him a sword and commissioned him to lead the two legions against Caesar. Pompey accepted the commission, but with a singular lack of enthusiasm.

One crisis followed another: debates in the senate, public mediation, private negotiations. Caesar offered to resign his command provided Pompey would resign his. But the *optimates* ignored the proposal, engineered his declaration as a public enemy, and obtained passage of the *Senatus Consutum Ultimum.* The new tribunes, Marcus Antonius (Mark Antony) and Quintus Cassius, their veto censured and their very lives in danger, fled the city with Curio and Caelius and went to join Caesar.

Caesar Crosses the Rubicon Meanwhile, Caesar had arrived in Cisalpine Gaul with one Roman legion and some detachments of German and Gallic cavalry. He set up his headquarters at Ravenna and awaited the arrival of the two legions that he had summoned from Further Gaul. Once more, swift and decisive action tipped the balance in Caesar's favor as it had against the Gauls. When Caesar heard of the senate's action, he decided to act without further delay. He had camped on the bank of a small stream, the Rubicon, which separated the Cisalpina from Italy. As he stood with his assembled troops on the northern bank, the significance of what he was about to do became clear to him. Once across the river there would be no turning back: the invasion of Italy would have begun. Resolutely he declared, "The die is cast," and led his men across the Rubicon.

While Caesar claimed to be acting in defense of the lawful rights of the tribunes, a more powerful appeal to his loyal veterans was the request that they help him to avenge his enemies' affronts to his own *dignitas*. Constitutional matters were not unimportant, but the struggle for personal preeminence at Rome was paramount. The same was true for Pompey.

Caesar's decision to invade Italy with only one legion and in the dead of winter was a calculated risk: the mobilization of Italy had just begun. The hastily recruited troops that were being sent against him would be untrained and perhaps unwilling to fight. He also knew that Pompey had only two trained legions and they were the ones that had served under Caesar in Gaul: they might be counted on to desert.

Caesar swept down the eastern coast. Large districts surrendered to him, even Picenum, Pompey's own barony. As he advanced, Pompey's own recruits surrendered and joined Caesar. At Corfinium Domitius Ahenobarbus, defying Pompey's orders, pigheadedly attempted a stand. The siege of Corfinium was brief. The garrison of fifteen thousand men mutinied and Domitius himself surrendered. Caesar let the man go.

Caesar's swift advance and his easy capture of Corfinium (considered a strong base) created a panic among the followers of Pompey. They had abandoned Rome weeks before and, speeding to the coast, neglected to take the state treasure. Pompey hastened to Brundisium with all the troops that he could muster and embarked for Greece.

Caesar arrived too late: the army had already escaped to fight again on other fronts. Caesar left Brundisium and started for Rome.

Caesar's swift conquest of Italy had been made possible by his absolute and uncontested command of his forces, the loyalty of his retired veterans, and his generous treatment of both civilians and captured soldiers. Still, the tasks ahead were stupendous, for Pompey, with undisputed command of the sea, could cut Rome off from the grain supplies of Sicily and North Africa and starve her into submission. Pompey had many battle-hardened legions in Spain and could also draw upon the vast resources and manpower of the East, where he had made and unmade kings. With these forces he could launch a two-pronged attack on Italy. And what if Gaul, recently conquered and weakly held, should raise up another Vercingetorix? Such were the problems confronting Caesar as he hurried to Rome.

Before reaching Rome, Caesar stopped off to call on Cicero to persuade him to come back to Rome and support the new regime by lending it both dignity and prestige. Not quite sure yet which side would win and not able to reconcile his principles with Caesar and Caesar's supporters, Cicero refused. Much disappointed, Caesar went on his way.

Caesar Reorganizes the Government Caesar entered Rome for the first time in nine years and at once set about reorganizing the government. Summoning all senators still in Rome, he invited their cooperation to avoid bloodshed. Some responded willingly, others less so. They did accept the law granting citizenship to the people living north of the Po, to whom Caesar owed much.

Caesar speedily arranged for the temporary administration of Rome and Italy. He appointed the praetor M. Aemilius Lepidus, son of the rebel leader whom Pompey had defeated in 77 B.C., to take charge of affairs in the city. He made Marcus Antonius governor of Italy and commander-in-chief of all the armed forces. He sent Curio to secure the grain supplies of Sicily and North Africa and Dolabella and Gaius Antonius, younger brother of Marcus, to Illyria to block a possible attempt by Pompey to invade Italy from the northeast. Caesar ordered the doors of the state treasury opened and unceremoniously removed the tribune who attempted to intervene. So much for the rights of tribunes! The administration of Rome and the soundness of his finances thus assured, Caesar set out for Spain, which was controlled by forces loyal to Pompey.

Caesar in Spain, 49 B.C.

Caesar had first to break the opposition of Massilia, which not only endangered the line of communication between Spain and Italy but which also might encourage the resurgence of rebellion in Gaul. Leaving part of his army to reduce the city by siege, he hurried on to Spain. Despite some initial difficulty there, the Gallic and Germanic cavalry, whose loyal service proved the value of his years in Gaul, assured victory. Within forty days he had subdued the Pompeian forces in Spain. On the way back, he accepted the surrender of Massilia, which became virtually an imperial possession of Rome.

News of Caesar's victory in Spain aroused wild enthusiasm at Rome and greatly increased his political power. A special law, proposed by Lepidus, had invested him with a temporary dictatorship. The populace rejoiced; his followers triumphed. If Curio had not been killed in an attempt to seize Africa from Pompey's loyal ally Juba, King of Numidia, Caesar's joy would have been unbounded.

Caesar's Second Consulship, 48 B.C.

Two important matters engaged Caesar's attention in Rome—the consular elections and social reforms. Dictator for eleven days in December, he secured his own election as consul for 48 B.C. with P. Servilius Isauricus, a partisan of neither camp, as his colleague.

Caesar's most pressing problem was the relief of debtors and the revival of credit and business undermined by the civil war. For many, the grain dole was the sole salvation. He enacted a law to the effect that creditors be obliged to accept real estate at prewar valuations, that all paid interest be deducted from the principal (a loss to creditors of roughly twenty-five percent), and that all interest payments be suspended for one year. In order to make money circulate more freely and encourage lending at twelve percent interest as decreed by the senate in 50 B.C., he reenacted an old law forbidding the hoarding of more than fifteen thousand *denarii*.

The most humane and enlightened of Caesar's acts was the recall of persons exiled by Pompey and the restoration of civil rights to victims of Sulla's cruel proscriptions. Proposed by praetors or tribunes, the laws rectifying long-standing injustice were duly passed by the Tribal Assembly. The procedure was regular, correct, quite constitutional in fact. Those who benefitted became his friends; those who objected could not accuse him of unconstitutional acts.

Pompey Prepares for War, 49 B.C.

While Caesar was winning control of Rome and the West, Pompey had built up a large force in Greece and Epirus. By the end of 49 he had nine legions under training and two others on the way from Syria. Pompey's commands against the pirates and Mithridates were now proving their long-term worth. From the provinces and dependent peoples of the East, Pompey, "the king of kings," had impressed an additional force of three thousand archers, twelve hundred slingers, and seven thousand cavalry, a fleet of five hundred warships, numerous transports, and a huge magazine of grain and war materials. With this enormous army and vast armada Pompey stood poised for the invasion of Italy when Caesar suddenly struck across the Adriatic and landed in southern Epirus.

Caesar's Invasion of Greece, 48 B.C.

On January 4, 48 B.C., in a season when few ventured on the sea even in daytime, Caesar sailed from Brundisium with seven legions. He slipped past Pompey's patrols at night and landed safely south of the port of Dyrrhachium (Durazzo) the next day. His speed and daring, Caesar's trademarks, surprised the methodical and slow-moving Pompey, who was on his way to occupy Dyrrhachium as a springboard for his invasion of Italy. Both generals raced to that strategic port. Pompey won.

Even worse for Caesar, Pompey's admiral, Calpurnius Bibulus, the consul of 59 B.C. and old enemy of Caesar, had waylaid, captured, or burnt many of his transports, crews and all, on their way back to Brundisium to bring over Antonius' legions. Caesar's half-starved army, cut off from seaborne supplies, had to march and fight on empty bellies. Plague and malaria threatened. Clearly everything favored Pompey—command of the sea, a larger army, superior cavalry, and accessible supplies.

Caesar resorted to negotiations and proposed that they both disarm and let the senate and people work out the details of peace. In this way, neither would be surrendering to the other. Pompey could never accept, as Caesar probably realized. Pompey's *dignitas* had already suffered from what many saw as an ignominious retreat from Italy. He had to prove that he was not a coward, as he would have been branded if he had accepted an offer of peace from an opponent in Caesar's precarious military position.

The Battle of Dyrrhachium   Forced to fight at Dyrrhachium, Caesar overextended his siege line and had to retreat in face of Pompey's superior numbers. By long, fast marches, Caesar moved into central Thessaly to deprive Pompey of his naval support and encamped at Pharsalus. Instead of seizing the opportunity to invade undefended Italy and

deprive Caesar of his political and military base, Pompey chose to follow. Pompey was confident of victory: Caesar had only twenty-two thousand men; Pompey had forty-seven thousand and a cavalry seven times the size of his opponent's. Caesar was equally confident: his army, though smaller, was well trained, experienced, and fiercely loyal.

The Battle of Pharsalus, 48 B.C.   The two armies met on a sultry summer morning. Caesar attacked quickly, blocked Pompey's anticipated flank attack, and turned Pompey's flank instead. Then, Caesar flung into action his strategic reserve. The enemy line buckled and finally broke. In scattered confusion Pompey's men ran to their camp. Pompey himself was already there and soon fled. Caesar set out after him. He never found Pompey alive.

The Death of Pompey, 48 B.C.

Pompey sailed from Lesbos, where he had met his wife, Cornelia, and his younger son, Sextus, and headed for Egypt. There some of his old soldiers still lived; there he might find money, help, and new opportunity to recover his lost power.

He arrived in Egypt at a most unfortunate time: the country was convulsed by civil war. Two young rulers, Ptolemy XIII*, a boy of thirteen, and his coregent, elder sister, and nominal wife, Cleopatra VII, were fighting over a throne left them by their father, Ptolemy the Flute Player. The harmony of the early years of their dual reign had been shattered by the efforts of the eunuch, Pothinus, young Ptolemy's vizier, who had prevailed upon the boy king to drive Cleopatra off her throne and banish her from Alexandria. She fled to Syria, where she raised an army, and had returned to fight for her inheritance. The two armies were about to engage when Pompey cast anchor at the mouth of the Nile and requested the king's permission to land.

_____
* Sometimes called Ptolemy XII.

The king's advisers invited him to land. As he was stepping ashore a renegade Roman stabbed him in the back. The advisers cut off his head and pickled it in brine as a gift to Caesar and left the body to rot on the shore. Three days later Caesar arrived.

Caesar in Egypt, 48 to 47 B.C.   When Caesar came ashore, he appeared with the dread *fasces* of a consul to show that Egypt was now subject to the authority of the Roman people. Presented with Pompey's head he turned away in disgust. He wept, ordered the head reverently buried and the perpetrators of the murder executed for daring to do violence to a leader of the Roman people. Caesar had never hated Pompey. They were both men of great charm, and their purely personal relations had often been warm. Ultimately, however, it had simply been impossible for both of them to occupy the same political position at Rome that each craved.

Caesar's high-handed actions at Alexandria aroused the populace against him and made life uncomfortable for Roman soldiers. After Caesar, captivated by the brilliant and charming Cleopatra, had peremptorily restored her to her throne and had demanded from the Egyptians payment of a debt owed by her late father, Pothinus and other advisers of Ptolemy XIII ordered out the royal army and kept Caesar under siege for several months. Unable, with his one small legion, to cope with an army of twenty thousand men as well as with the mobs of Alexandria, Caesar was in dire peril until the arrival of the two legions that he had earlier summoned. The last one to arrive was a mixed force of Jews, Syrians, Arabs, and Cilicians hastily collected by Mithridates of Pergamum, reportedly one of the many bastard sons of old Mithridates VI of Pontus.

When Mithridates, advancing from Syria, had reached the Nile, Caesar took over command and crushed the Egyptian army. Ptolemy fled and was drowned in the Nile. The Alexandrians submitted. The crown passed to Cleopatra and another brother, Ptolemy XIV, who became her dynastic husband. In the spring of 47 B.C. Caesar left Egypt.

From Egypt Caesar passed through Syria, Cilicia, and Cappadocia on his way to Pontus, where he planned to settle accounts with Pharnaces, disloyal son of Mithridates VI (p. 201). Taking advantage of the civil war, that despot had emerged from southern Russia, had overrun Pontus, Lesser Armenia, and Cappadocia, and had committed mayhem and other outrages upon Roman citizens. He had recently defeated Cn. Domitius Calvinus, the governor of Asia. In a five-day campaign Caesar tracked him down and annihilated his army at Zela. In a letter written to his friend Matius in Rome, Caesar proclaimed this swift and decisive victory with the laconic *"Veni, Vidi, Vici"* ("I came, I saw, I conquered"). After rewarding Mithridates of Pergamum for his services in Egypt, Southern Russia, and Asia Minor at the expense of Pharnaces, and settling other affairs in Asia Minor, the conqueror hastened back to Italy.

Caesar in Italy, 47 B.C.   Many tasks awaited Caesar's hand on his arrival in Italy in the summer of 47 B.C. after an absence of eighteen months. He had to restore order, solve several social and economic problems, find ways and means of raising money, restore discipline among his own legions, who were tired of fighting, and finally take an army over to Africa to subdue the large Pompeian forces assembled for an eventual invasion of Italy.

At Rome, Mark Antony had been unable to handle the dangerous problem of debt. Caelius Rufus had raised the standard of revolt when his proposals for relief failed, and he was killed. The next to take up the debtors' cause was Dolabella, Cicero's now-divorced son-in-law. Elected tribune for 47 B.C., he proposed the repudiation of all debts and the abolition of rents. Riots and murders followed. Acting on complaints of the creditors and a decree of the senate, Antonius' troops quelled Dolabella's followers and left eight hundred dead in the Forum. Even these drastic measures did not stop Dolabella. Meanwhile, mutinous soldiers had already begun to march on Rome when Caesar arrived.

On the arrival of the dictator a sudden stillness seemed to descend upon the city. The mobs disappeared from the streets at once. Peace and order reigned within the city, but outside the mutinous legions were camped on Mars Field. To their surprise, Caesar suddenly appeared and addressed them. Crowding around the speaker's platform, they saluted. He asked them what they wanted. To be discharged, they replied. This demand he immediately granted, then went on to say he would fulfill his promises and more on the day of his triumph. After pointedly addressing them as ''Fellow citizens'' instead of as ''Fellow soldiers,'' he turned on his heel to go. Stung by the rebuke, they stood mute, repentant, ashamed; then began to beg and implore him to take them back as his soldiers. He willingly relented and gave them their orders to march.

Turning next to social and economic problems, the cause of the recent disorders, the dictator neither disapproved of Dolabella's attempt to solve them nor strongly condemned Antonius' drastic action against the attempt, though he quietly chose Lepidus as his next master of the cavalry, an older and more level-headed politician. His program of debt relief was a moderate adaptation of Dolabella's. He remitted for one year all house rents up to 500 *denarii* in Rome and 125 in Italy and deferred for a year all interest in arrears since 49 B.C.

The African Campaign, 46 B.C.

After Pharsalus Cato had regrouped Pompey's shattered forces and taken them to Africa. Forced by a storm to land in the Cyrenaica, he led his army for hundreds of miles through the desert from Benghazi to Tripoli and thence to Tunisia, where he joined Varus and Juba. After this astonishing military feat, Cato misguidedly resigned the command in favor of Metellus Scipio, Pompey's father-in-law, a higher-ranking officer but one of demonstrated incapacity. Scipio, joined by Caesar's old legate Labienus with eighteen thousand

cavalry, stood together with Juba's forces to contest Caesar's mastery of the world.

In the fall of 47 B.C. Caesar sailed from Sicily to Africa with five legions and two thousand cavalry. Although this force was greatly reduced by a storm, Caesar successfully established a beachhead. Then, having collected more troops, though still outnumbered, he lured the inept Scipio onto unfavorable ground near Thapsus and annihilated his army.

The Death of Cato, 46 B.C.

When Cato received news of Thapsus, he saw the approaching end of the free state.

Although he might have obtained Caesar's calculated pardon, he could not bring himself to ask, and preferred to take his own life instead. His suicide was a cruel blow to Caesar and took some of the glory from his triumph.

''O Cato,'' he exclaimed, ''I envy you your death; You denied me the chance to spare your life.'' Cato became a legend, his martyrdom a cult; even the despots of the later Empire were wont to array themselves in the robes of that self-slaughtered saint.

Caesar's Homecoming and Triumph, 46 B.C.

The news of Thapsus had preceded Caesar's return to Rome. His followers were in ecstasies. The Forum rang with jubilation. Caesar had reached the pinnacle of preeminence for which he had been aiming: the senators decreed a thanksgiving of forty days and voted seventy-two lictors to attend him at his triumph—three times the usual number; they renewed his dictatorship for ten years and appointed him Prefect of Morals for three years with powers of a censor; he received the right to express his opinion in the senate first, so that every timid and self-seeking politician could take his cue; and his statue, cast in bronze, was to stand on the Capitol opposite to that of Jupiter himself. He rejected most of the other religious and monarchical honors allegedly showered upon him. Some of them are of late report and fictitious, undoubtedly suggested by the history of later Caesarism.

Soon after his arrival at Rome in 46, Caesar celebrated his long-awaited triumphs. There were four, each celebrated on a different day, over the Gauls, Egyptians, Pharnaces, and Juba, but none over Pompey or Scipio. Caesar had no wish to call attention to the defeat of fellow Romans in the civil war that he had started. Gigantic parades, the distribution of millions of *denarii* among soldiers and civilians, twenty-three thousand tables loaded with food and wine for the plebs, elaborate shows, games, and gladiatorial combats, a naval battle in an artificial lake, and a mock battle between two armies on Mars Field were among the highlights of the grandest display ever seen in Rome. Caesar was undisputedly greatest. Almost.

The Spanish Campaign, 45 B.C. One more campaign had to be fought. Late in 46 B.C., Caesar embarked for Spain with eight legions. Taking advantage of uprisings against Caesar's governor, Q. Cassius Longinus, Pompey's two sons, Gnaeus and Sextus, and Labienus, who had escaped from Africa, had raised a major revolt.

Failing to draw the Pompeians into a battle by attacking their fortified towns, Caesar finally caught up with them at Munda (between Seville and Malaga), where his men had to deliver their attack uphill. The battle was one of ferocious savagery as fear and hate on both sides supplied energy to their desperate valor. Superior discipline and generalship at last gave Caesar the decision. Labienus died in battle and Gnaeus Pompey was caught three weeks later.* This was Caesar's hardest battle, his last. He was now the undisputed military champion of the world.

Caesar's Work of Reconstruction   If by war Caesar had saved his life, honor, and dignity, he would now have to save the Roman state from chaos and ruin, heal its wounds, and give to it such peace, justice, and stability as it

*Sextus lived to fight years later against Caesar's successors.

had not known for almost a century. Otherwise, the very source of his fame and glory would have been destroyed.

Armed with the powers of the ancient Roman dictator and with those of a tribune of the people, which Gaius Gracchus had shown so well how to use, he undertook the task of transforming the Roman Republic and its empire into a centralized world state. Unlike Sulla, he did not attempt to resurrect the pre-Gracchan constitution, which events of the past 100 years had shown to be impossible to maintain under circumstances quite different from those that had given it birth. What Caesar, with his customary daring and decisiveness, did not realize, however, was that many Romans did not yet recognize that fact or wish to be functionaries in a state controlled by him.

Some of Caesar's reforms were administrative or governmental, some social and economic; others belonged to neither category. Some affected Rome alone, some Rome and Italy, others the empire as a whole. The overall effect of his reforms was to reduce the absolute dominance of the city of Rome and to integrate Rome with Italy and Italy with the rest of the empire while they reinforced his own supremacy over all.

Before he even began his work of reform, Caesar had removed one fatal weakness of the late Republic: separate control of the civilian government and provincial armies. Caesar was both chief executive of the state and commander-in-chief of the army. After his rise to supreme power, no governor of a province could act the tyrant, no victorious general would dare to use his army as a personal or private instrument for the overthrow of the constituted civil authority of the state. In his own person as chief executive, Caesar had at once united the civil and military authority of the state. He sought to prevent anyone from doing what he himself had done with the command of Gaul.

Administrative Reforms   The most important of Caesar's administrative reforms had to do with the senate. Traditionally and constitutionally the senate had been a purely advisory council serving first the kings, later the early consuls. During and after the Punic Wars it had necessarily assumed greater control of Rome's increasingly more complex affairs, which increased the competition for leadership among the senators as a whole and thus contributed to the last century of turmoil. To eliminate the senate, however, would have been beyond even Caesar's daring, and it would have destroyed the very body whose expertise and cooperation were needed to run Rome's vast empire. Instead, Caesar raised its membership from six hundred to nine hundred and filled the extra seats with old friends, wealthy equestrians, and even Romanized provincials. In admitting the newcomers into the senate, Caesar had broken down the barriers between Rome and Italy. Rome and Italy for the first time became one, the dominant partners within Rome's empire, and even provincials could aspire to ultimate membership in the senate. Moreover, all of the newcomers were bound to have felt gratitude and loyalty toward Caesar, and they were expected to look out for his interests.

Caesar took a giant stride toward the unification of Rome and Italy when he drafted the Julian Municipal Law *(lex Julia Municipalis)*, which was divided into three parts and first enforced after his death. Two of its sections refer to Rome, the first dealing with the reduction of free grain recipients from 320,000 to 150,000, the second with the upkeep and repair of streets and roads in Rome and suburbs. The third relates to the Italian towns, specifically to the age and other qualifications of municipal councilors or senators and to the taking of the local census. The law provided for local self-government and relieved the Roman city praetors of the burden of law enforcement throughout Italy. It laid the basis for the later extension of the municipal system of government to the provinces.

Caesar also increased the number of quaestors from twenty to forty and of praetors from eight to sixteen. This change was useful for keeping up membership in the enlarged senate, providing more provincial administrators, and allowing more of his friends to reach high office quickly.

Social and Economic Reforms The immediate purpose of many of Caesar's social and economic reforms was to provide useful employment for those whom he had cut off from the grain dole and to relieve the congestion of population in Rome (then approaching 700,000). He also had to provide for his war veterans. In a society whose industrial capacity was low, Caesar had only two alternatives—public works and colonization.

The object of Caesar's building program in Rome was not only to provide unemployment relief but to make Rome the beautiful and magnificent capital of a great empire. The chief architectural achievements of the period were the Basilica Julia, a covered hall to house the law courts, and the Forum Julium with galleries all around it and a temple of Venus Genetrix in the center. He had plans drafted for a new senate house, a large meeting place for the popular assemblies, a fine public library, a splendid theater, and an enormous temple of Mars.

Even more gigantic were the projects planned for Italy: an artificial harbor at Ostia for seagoing ships (a project later undertaken by Claudius), a road across the Apennines to the head of the Adriatic, and the draining of the Fucine Lake and the Pontine Marshes (a feat often attempted later but never accomplished until modern times).

To promote further the economic recovery of Italy, he compelled by law all wealthy citizens to invest half their capital in land and also enacted that at least a third of the cowhands and shepherds employed on cattle and sheep farms be men of free birth.

Colonization and Romanization To relieve unemployment, remove excess population from Rome, and find homes for a large number of war veterans, he resumed, on a much larger scale, the colonizing work of Gaius Gracchus outside Italy. In all he founded no less than twenty colonies and provided homes in the provinces for at least 100,000 Roman citizens. In Spain the chief colonies were Hispalis (Seville) and Tarraco (Tarragone); in France, Arelate (Arles), Nemausus (Nîmes), Arausio (Orange); and Lugdunum (Lyons); in Africa, Cirta and Carthage; in Greece, Corinth; in Switzerland, Geneva. To promote the commercial importance of the new Corinth, he planned to have a canal cut across the isthmus. Further east, he founded colonies at Sinope and Heraclea on the Black Sea.

Following the example of Marius, he granted citizenship to the soldiers whom he had recruited in southern Gaul. He enfranchised doctors, teachers, librarians, and scholars who came to Rome from the provinces, and granted Roman or Latin status to many provincial towns—full Roman citizenship to Gades (Cadiz) and Olisipo (Lisbon), Latin rights to thirty other Spanish towns, to Tolosa (Toulouse), Vienna (Vienne), and Avenio (Avignon) in Gaul, and to all the towns of Sicily. He also founded schools and public libraries in many towns of the western provinces, whence came a century or so later some of Rome's greatest writers.

Even these works do not encompass all that Caesar did for the provinces. In the East he reduced the burden of taxation and transferred, as far as possible, the right of collection from the harsh and corrupt Roman tax-farmers, hitherto the curse of provincial administration, to the municipal governments. In Asia and Sicily he replaced the traditional tithe by a land tax of fixed amounts. To stimulate the growth of a true money economy in the provinces, he supplemented the silver denarius with a new gold coin worth 25 denarii called the *aureus,* which was destined to play an important economic role in the empire of the future. All of the colonies and actions favorable to the provinces not only were fair solutions to long-standing problems, but also increased the reservoir of clients and good will available to support his rule throughout the empire.

Reform of the Calendar The most lasting of all Caesar's reforms was a new calendar based, not as formerly on the phases of the moon with a year of 355 days beginning on March 1st, but on the Egyptian solar calendar, with a year of 365¼ days beginning on January 1st. The new calendar, worked out by the Greek astronomer Sosigenes of Alexandria, is still in use with a few minor corrections added in 1582 by Pope Gregory XIII. In honor of Julius Caesar the senate decreed that the month of his birth formerly called Quintilis (the "Fifth") be named July. Later Sextilis (the "Sixth") became August in honor of Augustus, Caesar's heir and successor. Even this reform directly benefitted Caesar, however. The vagaries of the old calendar had given priests and magistrats many opportunities to delay and obstruct the actions of political rivals. The regularization of the calendar made it impossible for anyone to use such tactics against Caesar.

By February of 44 B.C., Caesar had obtained unprecedented power. By a decree of the subservient senate, he assumed the title *Dictator Perpetuus,* Dictator for Life. This "reform" was totally incompatible with the old Republic and alarmed many who still valued the old traditions.

The Assassination of Julius Caesar, March 15, 44 B.C.

Caesar hoped that with stability and security assured by his sweeping reforms he would be free to pursue a scheme of conquest that would make him even greater than Alexander the Great. The last act of his military career was to be a campaign against the Dacians, who lived north of the lower reaches of the Danube, and against the Parthians in the East, who had defeated and destroyed the army of Crassus at Carrhae in 53 B.C.

His very success, however, had driven many senators to desperation, lest he eclipse

Denarius of Brutus. (Left, obverse) Head of Brutus, with the words **BRUT. IMP** *and the mint master's name. (Right, reverse) Two daggers and pileus (cap worn by liberated slaves), and the words* **EID. MAR** *(Ides of March). (Courtesy The American Numismatic Society, New York)*

Denarius of Julius Caesar. (Left, obverse) Head of Caesar wearing the veil of a pontiff. (Right, reverse) Venus, with the mint master's name. Struck in 44 B.C. *(Courtesy The American Numismatic Society, New York)*

them forever. Some had probably voted him excessive honors in the hope of arousing a violent reaction against him. If so, they succeeded. Over sixty senators, led by Gaius Cassius Longinus and Marcus Junius Brutus, incensed at his growing power and unfailing popularity with the people, plotted to kill him at a meeting of the senate on the Ides (15th) of March, 44 B.C., three days before his scheduled departure for the East. Some of the conspirators were pardoned Pompeians like Brutus and Cassius, but the majority were Caesar's old friends and officers. It is said that a soothsayer stopped him on the way to the site of the meeting, ironically a hall in the portico attached to Pompey's theater, and warned, "Caesar, beware the Ides of March!" Undaunted, Caesar continued on his way.

When Caesar took his seat, a number of the conspirators crowded around him as if to make petitions. When the first blow struck, he rose from his chair in surprise and anger, but his cries were of no avail. Bleeding from countless wounds, Caesar died at the foot of Pompey's statue. He had beaten Pompey in the competition for preeminent *dignitas* at Rome, but his undisguised attempt to make his preeminence permanent had unleashed the forces of his own destruction.

The Question of Monarchy

There is abundant evidence that during the last two years of his life Caesar was planning to establish some kind of monarchy. He took or

allowed to be taken a number of steps to exalt him above ordinary mortals. With his reform of the calendar in 46, the month of his birth was renamed July. Numerous statues of himself were set up. One showed him standing on a globe, symbol of the world, and another was placed in the temple of Rome's first king, the Deified Romulus (Quirinus). In 45 and 44 he issued coins showing a royal diadem and other symbols of kingship. Other coins in 44 bore his portrait, an unusual, if not unheard of, practice at Rome, but a common practice of Hellenistic kings.

Caesar's assumption of a previously unprecedented lifetime dictatorship on February 14, 44 made him a king in all but name only. Along with this dictatorship he received such royal honors as the right to wear a triumphal robe (which was derived from the robes of Etruscan kings) and a laurel crown on public occasions and to use a gilded chair instead of the ordinary magistrate's curule chair. Finally, Caesar was voted his own special priest

Denarius of Julius Caesar. (Left, obverse) Head of Caesar with a laurel crown and the words **CAESAR, DICT. PERPETVO.** *(Right, reverse) Venus, with the mint master's name. (Courtesy The American Numismatic Society, New York)*

(*flamen*), and Marcus Antonius was appointed to the position.

It may well be that some of these measures were prompted by his enemies in order to provoke a reaction against him. Nevertheless, he could have refused them if he had wanted to. It would seem, therefore, that he was only trying to disguise the obvious and deny the hated title of king, *rex,* while assuming the position when he rebuked a crowd for hailing him as *rex* earlier in 44 and, ostentatiously refusing a royal diadem offered him by Antonius at the Lupercalia festival on February 15, ordered it publicly recorded that he had refused royalty.

One cannot say, however, that Caesar had been planning from an early point in his career to overthrow the Republic and establish a monarchy. There is not any hint of such a plan in his own latest writing, the *De Bello Civile* (*On the Civil War*), which probably was written in 48 or 47 B.C. Before the civil war, Caesar was merely acting like any other Roman noble in his quest for preeminence *within* the Republic. It was only after the civil war that Caesar found himself faced with the problem of protecting the position that he had achieved while creating a stable government for Rome and the vast polyglot empire that she had become. Previously, Sulla's reforms had failed. Some form of monarchy was the logical alternative, and Caesar's quick mind always cut to the heart of the matter when confronted with a problem.

The Significance of Caesar Despite his quick mind, however, too much should not be made of Caesar as an individual. He was not a unique phenomenon, only the culmination of a long series of ambitious nobles who had striven for supreme *dignitas* and *auctoritas* at Rome. For a long time the military opportunities presented by Roman imperialism had been placing power in the hands of a narrowing circle of rival dynasts backed by large armies of loyal veterans. Caesar had narrowed the competition further during fourteen years of almost continuous warfare by creating the largest and most cohesive body of veterans that Rome had yet seen. Whoever could command their loyalty after him would then be in a position to command Rome.

XX

The Last Days of the Republic, 44 to 30 B.C.

The assassination of Caesar had solved nothing. It merely set the stage for another destructive civil war to determine who would be the most important man in Rome. At Brutus' insistence, the conspirators had planned nothing other than to murder the "tyrant," Caesar. They naively thought that the old Republic would return miraculously to life. The senators adjourned in distracted alarm and stole away to their homes. The two arch-conspirators, Brutus and Cassius, still exulting, arrived to address the populace and found the Forum almost deserted. The few who lingered there were sullen, hostile, and apathetic, and listened to their words in a dazed and stony silence. The uneasy conspirators retired to the Capitol and there barricaded themselves in to plan their future moves.

The Rise of Mark Antony (ca. 82–30 B.C.) Sensing a chance to act, Marcus Antonius (Mark Antony), Caesar's colleague in the consulship of 44, improvised a bodyguard, came out of hiding that night, and persuaded Caesar's widow, Calpurnia, to hand over all of his papers to him. Antonius has often been portrayed as a boozing, boorish, bully of the worst kind. As did many young men of his class, he had led a self-indulgent youth that did nothing to enhance his reputation. It must be remembered, however, that his faults, weaknesses, and early follies have been exaggerated by the propaganda of his enemies, especially Cicero and Augustus, which shaped the "official" version of events reflected in the majority of surviving sources. Antonius had many good qualities as a soldier, general, and politician. His shrewdness and diplomacy helped to avoid serious trouble in the next few days.

While Antonius was securing Caesar's papers, M. Aemilius Lepidus, governor-designate of Nearer Spain and Narbonese Gaul, who had been outside the gates of Rome with a newly recruited legion, was preparing to besiege the conspirators on the Capitol. The next morning Antonius sensibly persuaded Lepidus to refrain and took charge of his troops. They then conferred with others of Caesar's old officers and friends and established contact with the conspirators. Both factions also kept in communication with Cicero, the elder statesman, who had declared for Caesar's murderers immediately after the killing.

The outcome of the various conferences was a meeting of the senate on March 17th, over which Antonius presided. He remained cool and shrewd, reasonable, objective, and conciliatory. Many of the senators wanted Caesar condemned as a tyrant, his assassination approved as necessary and just, his body flung into the Tiber, and all his acts declared null and void. Briefly replying, Antonius urged them to reject such measures as extreme, unwise, and impracticable; proved to them that they owed to Caesar offices, provinces, and political futures; hinted at the danger of uprisings in Rome, Italy, and the provinces; and appealed to them to open their ears and listen to the people outdoors howling for vengeance and the blood of the conspirators. The appeal to fear and self-interest prevailed. Even the adherents of Brutus and Cassius in the senate voted to give all Caesar's acts the force of law, to proclaim an amnesty for the conspirators, and to grant Caesar the honor of a public funeral. After the meeting, Antonius invited the conspirators to a banquet. The toasts that they drank seemed to proclaim more loudly than senatorial resolutions that at last an era of peace, concord, and good feeling had dawned.

March 20th was the day of Caesar's funeral. Marcus Antonius delivered the traditional oration. His speech was brief, factual, and undramatic.* A reader recounted Caesar's mighty deeds, and his will was made public. His benefactions to the Roman people included gardens across the Tiber bequeathed as a public park and three hundred sesterces in cash to each Roman citizen. The chief beneficiary of Caesar's recorded will was not Antonius but Gaius Octavius Thurinus, Caesar's grandnephew, who became his son by testamentary adoption. He was the grandson of a rich banker from the small Latin town of Velitrae, whom Caesar's sister, Julia, had married. Decimus Brutus, one of the assassins, was mentioned jointly with Antonius as a minor heir.

With consummate showmanship, Antonius displayed Caesar's bloodied toga and a wax image of the corpse with its oozing wounds. The angry crowd went completely berserk and surged forth into the streets to find the conspirators. (By mistake, they tore apart one innocent bystander.) Returning to the Forum, the mob burned Caesar's corpse and the senate house too, and far into the night they kept vigil over the ashes of their hero and benefactor.

Such being the mood of the populace, the Forum was not a safe place for the conspirators. Nor was Rome. Still playing a cool and cagey game, Antonius allowed them to proceed to the provinces that Caesar had allotted them: Decimus Brutus to the Cisalpina, Trebonius to Asia. Cassius and Marcus Brutus had not yet gone to their provinces, but lingered forlornly among the towns of Latium in a vain effort to recruit support for their cause.

At this time it seemed that Antonius would succeed Caesar. Though disappointed that Caesar had not made him his principal heir, he profited much from his possession of the dictator's private funds, papers, and rough drafts; much more still from his own skillful diplomacy and conciliatory spirit. He procured for Lepidus the high pontificate. He was not violent toward the conspirators. He had some liking for Marcus Brutus, accepted Dolabella, with whom he had violently quarrelled over the question of relief for debtors, as his consular colleague, and reluctantly permitted Dolabella to demolish an altar and pillar set up in the Forum for Caesar's worship. He had the office of dictator forever abolished and assigned to Dolabella, in accordance with Caesar's wish, the province of Syria. With the senate concurring, he took the province of Macedonia and all the legions that Caesar had mobilized for his intended invasion of the Balkans and of Parthia. Antonius' tact and reasonableness certainly had helped save Rome from chaos after Caesar's death, and for that all could be thankful.

Still, Antonius was an ambitious man. He could not resist using his position as consul and executor of Caesar's estate to show special favor to his friends and spend money for his

---

* Quite unlike that popularized by Appian, Plutarch, and later by Shakespeare.

own benefit. These actions caused men like Cicero, who wanted to guide the ship of state himself, to doubt his motives and work against him.

The Opposition of Octavian (63 B.C.- A.D 14)

Even more, it was the unexpected challenge of Caesar's heir that prevented Antonius from smoothly consolidating a position of supremacy. Caesar had sent Octavius to Apollonia in Epirus for military training in preparation for the projected Parthian war. Only eighteen and of a rather delicate constitution, he boldly determined to return to Italy and take advantage of any opportunity that the sudden turn of events might offer. When he learned that he had been made Caesar's principal heir and adopted as his son, he gladly followed the usual Roman practice and took the name Gaius Julius Caesar Octavianus. To capitalize on the magic of the name, he always called himself Caesar, as do most of the sources. (Modern writers call him Octavian when writing of the period after 44 and before he received the title Augustus in 27 B.C.) Octavian immediately demanded his inheritance, much of which Antonius had already spent. Seriously underestimating the unimpressive looking young man, Antonius contemptuously rebuffed him. More determined then ever, Octavian undermined loyalty to Antonius among Caesar's veterans by playing upon the magic of his new name and by exploiting their resentment of Antonius' leniency with Caesar's assassins.

To strengthen his position, Antonius obtained passage of a law giving him command of Cisalpine and Transalpine Gaul for five years and transferring Caesar's legions there from Macedonia, his original assignment. Obviously, Antony was hoping to dominate Italy and Rome from this advantageous position, as Caesar had done before him. Pressure from many of Caesar's old officers and soldiers, who did not want to fight each other or lose the political advantages of a united front, kept Antonius and Octavian from intensifying their feud.

Still, Antonius' troubles increased. His new provincial command aroused the fear and jealousy of Marcus Brutus and Gaius Cassius. In July, they demanded more significant provinces than Crete and Cyrene. His patience worn thin, Antonius refused their demands and issued such strong threats that they abandoned Italy in order to recruit armies among Pompey's old centers of support in the East. Moreover, Pompey's son Sextus, who had escaped the Pompeian disasters in Africa and Spain, was now seizing control of western waters and raising a revolt in Spain once more. Antonius was becoming worried, and he began to resent Cicero's absence from the senate, which many would interpret as that influential orator's criticism of Antonius' actions. Indeed, Cicero did feel that the Republic was being subverted, a feeling sharpened by his own lack of power.

Cicero's Defense of the Republic

On September 1, 44 B.C., Antonius publicly criticized Cicero's neglect to attend meetings of the senate. In reply, Cicero delivered a mildly critical speech but irritating enough to provoke the increasingly sensitive Antonius to an angry attack upon Cicero's past career. Cicero in turn wrote and published an undelivered second speech, in which he branded Antonius as a tyrant, ruffian, drunkard, and coward, a man who flouted morality by kissing his wife in public. Likening his speeches to Demosthenes' famous orations against Philip of Macedon in fourth-century Athens, Cicero dubbed them *Philippics*. Twelve other *Philippics* followed, an eternal monument to Cicero's eloquence but filled with misinformation and misrepresentation. Antonius did not hear them at all. He had other things to do.

Rome had become unbearable for Antonius. Down to Brundisium he went to meet the four legions that he had summoned from Macedonia. He intended to send them north to drive Decimus Brutus out of Cisalpine Gaul, which the latter refused to hand over to Antonius despite the recent law. Antonius' consular year (44 B.C.) was near its end.

Should he delay, he might be left without a province or legions to command. Brutus and Cassius had proceeded to the East to take over rich provinces and the large armies stationed there. Cassius had defeated Dolabella and had driven him to suicide. Lepidus, in Nearer Spain, was a shifty and precarious ally; Lucius Munatius Plancus in *Gallia Comata* and Gaius Asinius Pollio in Farther Spain were even less dependable. To make matters worse, Octavian had marched on Rome, and two of Antonius' Macedonian legions, seduced by bribes and promises, had declared for the young rebel, whom Cicero eagerly embraced as a means, later to be discarded, of destroying Antonius.

The Siege of Mutina, 44 to 43 B.C. Antonius hastened north and entrapped the recalcitrant and unyielding Decimus Brutus in Mutina (Modena), to whose relief the senate finally sent in January the two new consuls, Aulus Hirtius and Gaius Vibius Pansa, former comrades of Antonius under Caesar. At Cicero's clamorous demand, the senate also sent the young Octavian armed with propraetorian power and granted senatorial rank. He was promised rich rewards: money and land for his legitimized troops and for himself the right to stand for the consulship ten years before the legal age.

The three armies finally forced Antonius to abandon the siege of Mutina but were unable to prevent his retreat across the Alps into southern Gaul, where he hoped to gain the dubious support of Lepidus and Plancus. Both consuls lost their lives at Mutina, Hirtius killed in battle, Pansa later dying of his wounds. Their deaths left Octavian master of the field.

Mutina was a day of glory for the Republic. Triumph, exultation, delirium! The enemy was on the run. The armies of the Republic would shortly track him down. Dolabella dead, the entire East fell into the hands of Brutus and Cassius. Decimus still held the Cisalpina, and Sextus Pompey was supreme at sea. Soon the Republicans would close the ring and dispose of Octavian too. Then would come

the day for the glorious restoration of the Republic and of constitutional government —so Cicero believed, but he was cruelly deceived.

After Mutina, the senate declared Antonius a public enemy. For the soldiers, the living and the dead, who had fought for Decimus Brutus and the Republic, the senate decreed a thanksgiving of fifty days, never until then decreed in a war of Roman against Roman. Upon Brutus and Cassius it conferred superior command (*imperium maius*) over all Roman magistrates in the East. To Decimus Brutus the senators voted a triumph and supreme command over all the armies in Italy. Even to Sextus Pompey, though really nothing but a successful pirate, they extended a vote of thanks and an extraordinary command over the Roman navy; but for Octavian, who had rescued Decimus Brutus from siege and defeat, they proposed only a minor triumph or *ovatio* and an inferior command. Even this they finally voted down, refused to reward his troops, and repudiated the promised consulship. Through their own folly they drove Octavian back into the arms of the other Caesarians.

Octavian punished the slights and studied disdain of the senate by imperiously demanding a triumph, the consulship promised to him, and rewards for his troops. The senate refused. Octavian marched on Rome. He had eight legions and when the two legions brought over from Africa to defend the senate declared for him, all resistance collapsed. Octavian entered Rome and had himself elected consul with Quintus Pedius, an obscure relative, as his colleague to fill out the deceased consuls' terms.* Octavian was not yet twenty.

The first act of the new consuls was to rifle the treasury to pay each soldier twenty-five hundred denarii; the next was the passage of a law instituting a special court to try Caesar's murderers as well as Sextus Pompey. At the same time, Octavian, who needed allies, had the senate's decree against Antonius

---

* Consuls elected to fill out others' terms were called suffect consuls.

revoked. That done, he hastened north to meet Antonius.

Meanwhile, Antonius himself had been neither idle nor unsuccessful. The debacle at Mutina had brought out the leadership, courage, endurance, and self-discipline that had earned Caesar's respect and the loyalty of his troops. After a hard and painful march into southern Gaul, he confronted the far larger army of the aging Lepidus, the governor of Nearer Spain and of Narbonese Gaul, who maintained control over his men solely because of his professed loyalty to Julius Caesar. The two armies lay encamped on either side of a small river.

Antonius cleverly played upon the sympathies of Lepidus' men, many of whom had served with him under Caesar in Gaul. Begrimed, haggard, and thickly bearded, he stole into the camp of Lepidus and addressed the men. Thereafter, the two armies began gradually to fraternize and soon Antonius was in real command. He used the same tactics in approaching the army of Plancus, the governor of *Gallia Comata,* and returned to Italy with twenty-two legions. He occupied Cisalpine Gaul without opposition, for the defending army of Decimus Brutus deserted. Brutus himself attempted to escape to Macedonia, but he was trapped and slain by a Gallic chief.

When Antonius and Lepidus returned to Cisalpine Gaul, they found Octavian already there with eleven legions. They greatly outnumbered the young pretender, but they did not even try to fight them. Their men might refuse to fight against one who bore Caesar's magic name. Lepidus arranged a conference instead.

The Triumvirate of Octavian, Antony, and Lepidus   After some preliminary negotiations, the three leaders met on a small island in a river near Bologna and agreed upon a joint policy. Carefully avoiding the emotionally charged name of dictatorship, they decided to form themselves into an executive committee with absolute powers for five years for the reconstruction of the Roman state

(*tresviri rei publicae constituendae*). The *lex Titia* to that effect was carried by a friendly tribune on November 27, 43 B.C. The consulship survived in name with traditional prestige, title, and conferment of nobility but with greatly reduced powers. Octavian and Pedius agreed to resign the office, and two nonentities took their place. To strengthen the alliance, Octavian also married Clodia, the daughter of Antonius' wife Fulvia, widow of Publius Clodius

Octavian was not the dominant member in the triumvirate, as the division of provinces reveal. Antonius secured Cisalpine Gaul and *Gallia Comata,* Lepidus *Gallia Norbonensis* and the two Spains. Octavian received a more modest and doubtful portion: North Africa and the islands of Sicily, Sardinia, and Corsica, all disputed and some already seized by the outlawed adventurer Sextus Pompey.

The Proscriptions, 43 B.C.   A few days later the triumvirs sent a chill of horror through Roman society by a proscription as coldblooded and loathsome as that of Sulla and with little better excuse. Among their victims were 130 senators and perhaps 2000 *equites.* The excuse alleged was the avenging of Caesar's murder, but the real reason was the confiscation of wealth and property in order to raise money for their forty-three legions and for the inevitable campaign against Marcus Brutus and Gaius Cassius. When the triumvirs found that the wealth of their victims was insufficient for their needs, they imposed a capital levy upon rich women, laid crushing taxes upon the propertied classes in Italy, and set aside the territories of eighteen of the richest cities in Italy for veteran settlements.

In addition to the triumvirs' greed and rapacity was a desire to wipe out political enemies. Their most distinguished victim, at Antonius' virulent insistence, was Cicero. Unlike some of the proscribed, he lingered until too late. Abandoning his final flight, Cicero calmly awaited his pursuers along a deserted road and was murdered on the seventh of December, 43 B.C., a martyr to the cause of the dying Republic. His tongue and right hand, the orator's most potent instruments, were nailed to the rostra in the Forum, a brutal reminder of the price that one could expect to pay for opposing the triumvirs.

Cicero may have been vain and short-sighted in his attack on Antonius, but he was one the few men in the late Republic who had a vision of politics beyond the narrow aristocratic struggle for personal honor and prestige. His ideal of a republic governed by an enlightened elite drawn from meritorious aristocrats and equestrians throughout Italy seems hopelessly naive and paternalistic today. Still, it was an ideal, a consciously constructed vision of a better world based on concerns beyond his own narrow self-interest. That could be said of few, if any, of his fellow senators, even the posturing Stoics Cato and Brutus.

To buttress their regime of terror and violence, of confiscation and proscription, the triumvirs packed the senate with men whose nonsenatorial origin would make them loyal clients of themselves. They made the consulship the reward of graft or crime and nominated within a single year several pairs of consuls. To the praetorships, which Caesar had increased to sixteen, they added fifty more.

Formally taking office on the first of January, 42 B.C., the triumvirs compelled the senate and the magistrates to swear an oath to observe Caesar's acts, dedicated a temple to him in the Forum, and by a special law elevated him among the gods of the Roman state under the name of the Divine Julius. Octavian could now call himself *Divi Filius* ("Son of a God").

Philippi, 42 B.C. After crushing all resistance in Italy, the triumvirs determined to make war on Brutus and Cassius, who by a systematic and ruthless looting of the eastern provinces had accumulated a huge war chest. With nineteen legions, some of them Caesarian veterans, and with numerous mercenaries, the conspirators had taken up at Philippi on the Macedonian coast, a strong position flanked on the north by mountains, on the south by a marsh. Their navy dominated the seas.

Eluding the Republican naval patrols, Antonius and Octavian landed in Greece with twenty-eight legions and advanced to Philippi, where in the fall of 42 B.C. two battles took place. In the first, Brutus defeated Octavian, but Antonius defeatd Cassius. Thinking all was lost, Cassius fell on his sword. The loss of Cassius, by far the abler general, was ruinous to Brutus. Instead of letting winter and famine destroy the enemy, he yielded to the impetuous clamor of his officers and offered battle three weeks later. It was a fatal mistake. After a hard and bloody battle, the triumvirs emerged victorious. Brutus took his own life. Antonius, when he came upon the corpse, pulled off his purple cape and reverently laid it over his fallen enemy but former friend.

Philippi was the decisive victory. It laid the Roman world at the victors' feet. To Antonius, the real victor, went the glory and the major share of the spoils. Lepidus, on the other hand, who was reported to have been secretly negotiating with Sextus Pompey, now began his sudden slide to impotence and obscurity. Accusing him of disloyal intrigues with Sextus Pompey, Antonius robbed him of *Gallia Narbonensis,* while Octavian took the two Spains. Antonius and Octavian agreed to shunt him off to Africa, provided he could prove his loyalty and conquer the province. Antonius thus had control over the entire East and all the Gallic provinces, though he later surrendered Cisalpine Gaul, which now became fully part of Italy. Octavian had still to reconquer his original provinces of Sicily and Sardinia, which Sextus Pompey had seized.

After the reassignment of provinces came the more unpleasant tasks, the hardest and most unpopular of which fell to the lot of Octavian. He had to return to Italy to disband the troops and by confiscation find land for the resettlement of over 100,000 veterans. Antonius elected to go to the East to regulate its affairs and raise the money promised to the legions. The more calculating and farsighted Octavian had clearly perceived, no doubt, that

Italy was still the key to empire and to ultimate supremacy.

Antonius and Cleopatra

Antonius had an assignment more pleasant than he had anticipated. After his arrival in the East, he had extracted considerable money from the rich cities of Asia by arranging for nine-years' tribute to be paid in two, and had set up or deposed kings as seemed advantageous to himself and Rome. Finally, he came to Tarsus in Cilcia, where Cleopatra, whom he had earlier summoned to explain why she had aided and financed the conspirators, was soon to arrive. She arrived in a splendid barge with silvery oars and purple sails, herself decked out in gorgeous clothes and redolent with exquisite perfumes. It is easy to follow propaganda and legend and see Antonius hopelessly seduced and subservient to a sensuous foreign queen. Passion not withstanding, however, both pursued rational political interests. Each had something to gain by cooperating with the other—Cleopatra the support of Roman arms against her rivals, Antonius Egyptian wealth to defray the costs of a projected war against Parthia and rivalry with Octavian.

The Siege of Perusia (The Perusine War), 40 B.C.

Unlike Antonius, Octavian was beset with difficulties in Italy. He arrived weak, ill, despondent. The eighteen cities previously earmarked for soldiers' settlement proved insufficient to satisfy the veterans, and the evicted owners angrily protested. Expanded confiscations further increased the groundswell of discontent. The populace of Rome was also in a disturbed and angry mood. Sextus Pompey, who still controlled the seas, had begun to shut off grain supplies. Discontent, confusion, insecurity, and want threatened the stability of the state. Soldiers and civilians were at each other's throats. Octavian himself once almost fell into the clutches of a battling mob.

Intrigue aggravated the difficulties, unpopularity, and danger of Octavian. The firebrand Fulvia (ex-wife of Clodius and Curio and now the wife of Marcus Antonius) and Antonius' brother Lucius, a consul of 42, attempted to whip up against Octavian the suspicion and hatred of both veterans and landowners. In so doing, Fulvia and Lucius hoped to destroy Octavian and catapult the absent and unsuspecting Antonius to supreme power. They well knew that Antonius would disavow their acts and would refuse to repudiate his agreements with Octavian, but they hoped to force his hand.

Fulvia and Lucius eventually went too far and drove Octavian to make war on them. His loyal generals Quintus Salvidienus and Marcus Vipsanius Agrippa, who soon became his right-hand man, maneuvered them into the Etruscan hill town of Perusia (Perugia) and put them under siege. Antonius, ignorant of their aims and doings, made no move. Two of his legates marched from Gaul but gave them no concerted or effective help, and starvation quickly forced them to surrender. Although Octavian ruthlessly executed all but one member of Perusia's town council, he spared the lives of Lucius and Fulvia. He sent Lucius as governor to Spain, where he soon died. He allowed Fulvia to visit her husband in Greece. There she, too, soon died.

Since Antonius' remaining legate in the two transalpine Gallic provinces had now died, Octavian sent some of his victorious forces to seize them.[*] The dead legate's son surrendered without a fight, and Agrippa was placed in charge. Now, militarily, Octavian was virtually in charge of all of western Europe.

Still, it was not the end of troubles for Octavian. Pillage, fire, mass executions, and military control of provinces had not solved his problems nor made him safe from danger. His atrocities served only to increase the hatred and discontent in a land still seething with revolt and held in the grip of famine, turmoil, and despair. The hostile fleets of Sextus Pompey menaced Italy's coasts, assailed the provinces, and interrupted grain shipments. Oc-

---

[*] The larger province, which Caesar conquered, is now commonly called Transalpine Gaul, and the older transalpine province is usually referred to as Narbonese Gaul, from Narbo, its chief city.

tavian seemed doomed, caught up in the web of his own duplicity, trapped, and destroyed at last.

In his extremity Octavian sought accommodation with Sextus Pompey, master of the seas. Apparently he was unaware that Antonius, taking Fulvia's advice, was also making overtures to Sextus. To make his negotiations appear more sincere, Octavian put aside Clodia, Fulvia's daughter, whom he had earlier married, and took instead Scribonia, many years his senior but an aunt of Sextus Pompey's wife.

The Pact of Brundisium, 40 B.C.

Antonius had been in Egypt while Octavian was fighting his brother and Fulvia. News had also reached him that the Parthians, led by Quintus Labienus, son of Titus, Caesar's famous lieutenant in Gaul and later enemy, had overrun Syria, Palestine, and parts of Asia Minor. Not yet prepared to fight the Parthians, Antonius sailed for Greece to confer with Fulvia after she left Italy. Fulvia persuaded him to receive envoys from Sextus Pompey and accept the proffered alliance. Only than did Antonius proceed to Italy to recruit legions for war against the Parthians.

By previous agreement Antonius and Octavian were to use Italy as a common recruiting ground. How worthless that agreement was Antonius discovered when he found Brundisium closed against him by Octavian's troops. Frustrated and angry he landed troops and besieged that port. Simultaneously, his Republican ally, Sextus Pompey, struck against southern Italy. When Octavian appeared at Brundisium to oppose his colleague, Caesar's old legions refused to fight and fraternized instead. There followed negotiations, conferences, and finally a new agreement known as the Pact of Brundisium, which renewed the triumvirate. A redistribution of provinces left Octavian in control of Illyricum as well as of all the western provinces, Antonius of the East, and Lepidus of Africa. Italy was to remain, theoretically at least, a common recruiting ground for all triumvirs.

To seal the pact, Antonius married Octavia, the fair and virtuous sister of Octavian. The covenant between the two powerful rivals filled Italy with joy and thanksgiving. All Rome rejoiced. A golden age of peace and concord seemed near—so men hoped.

The rejoicings were premature. Sextus Pompey, who felt that Antonius had played him false, was threatening Rome with famine. Taxes, high prices, and food shortages provoked riots. The people clamored for bread and peace. When Antonius and Octavian prepared to attack Sextus, popular reaction was such that they were forced to negotiate with him.

The Treaty of Misenum, 39 B.C. At Misenum (near Naples) in the autumn of 39 B.C. the triumvirs met with Pompey, argued, bargained, and banqueted. They agreed to let him retain Sicily and Sardinia, which he had already seized, and gave him Corsica and the Peloponnesus as well. They also allowed him compensation for his father's confiscated lands and promised him a future augurship and consulate. In return, he agreed to end his blockade of Italy, supply Rome with grain, and halt piracy on the high seas.

The Predominance of Antonius, 39 to 37 B.C.

The power and popularity of Antonius was now at its height. His influence was especially strong among the senatorial and equestrian orders, old-line Republicans, and most men of property throughout Italy, while that of Octavian was stronger with the Roman populace and the veterans. Moreover, time was on the side of Octavian. Years of Antonius' absence in the East would cause his influence to wane in the West.

For the present however, the West looked bright to Antonius. Pompey would surely counterbalance the growing power of Octavian—so thought Antonius as he set out for Athens in company with Octavia, his young and loving bride. There he spent two winters enjoying to the full domestic happiness and the culture of that old university town.

From there he directed the reorganization of the East. To the Balkans he sent Asinius Pollio to subdue the Parthini, to the East Ventidius Bassus and Herod (the latter king of Judea since 40 B.C.) to drive out the Parthian invaders of Syria, Palestine, and Asia Minor. Moving with the speed of Caesar, Ventidius shattered the Parthians in three great battles and rolled them back to the Euphrates. There Ventidius stopped.

Having restored Roman prestige in the East, Antonius moved to subjugate the Parthians and avenge Carrhae. In 37 B.C. he sent Canidius, another of his great marshals, to pacify Armenia. Canidius even carried Roman arms beyond Armenia to the Caucasus. Returning to Armenia, he awaited the arrival of Antonius. He waited long, for new troubles in the West compelled Antonius to postpone his invasion of Parthia. Octavian was the cause.

Octavian Consolidates His Power

To Italy the Treaty of Misenum had brought peace and a brief respite from piracy, shore raids, and famine, but to Octavian it meant even greater benefits. Exiled Republicans returned home, aristocrats of ancient lineage, allies worth his while to court and win. The peace was of short duration, however. Octavian did not want peace. Sextus Pompey was an enemy to be destroyed. Octavian's first act of war was to accept the province of Sardinia from a traitor whom Pompey had failed to liquidate; his second was to divorce Scribonia.

Livia For love and politics Octavian promptly married Livia Drusilla, young, beautiful, rich, politically astute, and anxious to secure the future prominence of her family and her children. Livia is another of the numerous strong-willed and influential aristocratic women, such as Clodia (sister of P. Clodius and wife of Metellus Celer), Servilia (stepsister of Cato, mother of M. Brutus, and reputed mistress of Caesar), and Fulvia (wife first of Clodius, then of Curio, and last of Antonius), who had a major impact on late Re-publican politics. Her father was Livius Drusus Claudianus, who linked the great Claudian *gens* with the family of the Livii Drusi through adoption into the latter. Livia herself had married Tiberius Claudius Nero, from another branch of the Claudii, who had fought against Octavian in the Perusine War. Now, both she and her husband decided to pin their families' futures on Octavian. Livia had already borne her husband one son, Tiberius Claudius Nero, the future emporer Tiberius, and she was pregnant with his second son, Nero Claudius Drusus, when by mutual consent he divorced her and betrothed her to Octavian. Octavian was so anxious to consummate this advantageous union with Livia that he divorced Scribonia on the very day that she bore him his only child, Julia, whom he would later use in numerous dynastic marriages. Livia became one of Octavian's most trusted advisors, whom he consulted at every major turn for the rest of his life.

The Breadth of Octavian's Support Octavian's marriage to Livia and the noble connections that she secured helped him to broaden his support among the senatorial elite and undermine that of Antonius, whose own family was far better connected with the aristocracy than Octavian's had been. On the other hand, Octavian's origin from an equestrian family of Italian background had been a great asset to him. It gained him friends among the equestrian class, who had long resented the exclusivity of the old Republican nobility. From this class came two of his most loyal and important supporters, the wealthy patron of the arts who helped to mold public opinion in his favor, Gaius Cilnius Maecenas, and the architect of many of his military victories, Marcus Vipsanius Agrippa. Moreover, he received great sympathy in the countryside of Italy, from which Roman armies were recruited.

The Treaty of Tarentum, 37 B.C. Octavian was unable to finish alone the war that he had started against Sextus Pompey. His attempted invasion of Sicily in 38 B.C. was a fiasco, and Pompey destroyed two of his fleets.

These reverses compelled him to recall the indispensable Agrippa from Gaul and to invoke the aid of Antonius. Though angry at Octavian for his unprovoked aggressions and for delaying his own campaign against the Parthians, Antonius loyally left Athens with a large fleet and came to his aid. The two triumvirs, both resentful and suspicious of each other, met at Tarentum. Through the patient diplomacy of Maecenas and the alleged good offices of Octavia, they concluded an agreement and renewed their triumvirate, which had lapsed on December 31, 38 B.C., for another five years. In exchange for the 120 ships that Antonius contributed for the war against Pompey, Octavian promised twenty thousand Roman soldiers for service in the East. Antonius never got them.

The Defeat of Sextus Pompey, 36 B.C. The ships lent by Antonius and added to those constructed and equipped by Agrippa enabled Octavian to mount a three-pronged amphibious attack upon Sicily: Octavian and Agrippa sailed from Puteoli, Statillius Taurus from Tarentum, and Lepidus from Africa. The operation proceeded according to plan except for a crippling defeat suffered by Octavian at sea. Agrippa and Lepidus both landed and quickly overran the island, while Agrippa forced Pompey to fight a sea battle at Naulochus near the Straits. His fleet destroyed, Sextus escaped to Asia Minor.

Octavian had already overcome one rival, and soon he would another. Lepidus, with twenty-two legions under his command and hungry for glory, insisted on accepting the surrender of Sicily in person. When Octavian objected, he ordered him off the island. Bearing the magic name of Caesar, Octavian boldly entered the camp of Lepidus and persuaded his legions to desert. Then he stripped Lepidus of any real power, and committed him to honorary confinement at Circeii. There Lepidus died twenty-four years later.

The Triumphant Return of Octavian A sincere and joyous welcome at Rome awaited the homecoming of the victorious Octavian, who had ended wars in the West, restored the freedom of the seas, and liberated Rome from the danger of famine. Though he had crushed the liberty of the old nobility, he brought the blessing of strong and ordered government to a populace exhausted by their civil wars.

A grateful and idolizing people heaped honors upon Octavian, even epithets and adorations of divinity: his statues were placed in Italian temples, a golden one in the Roman Forum, and he received the sacrosanctity of a plebeian tribune in addition to the military title of "Imperator Caesar," which he had already usurped.

Octavian had already attained a success beyond reasonable expectation. Frail in health and utterly lacking in military skill, he had triumphed over seemingly insuperable odds. He owed his success to his own coolness, tenacity, good looks and distinguished bearing, his knowledge of men, an ability to take advantage of his opponents' mistakes, an unusual skill as a propagandist, and monumental deceitfulness. He had exploited Caesar's name, Cicero's eloquence, and the prestige of the Republican senate. He had also used and often deceitfully abused Lepidus, Marcus Antonius, Sextus Pompey, the Roman populace, Caesar's veterans, such loyal friends as Agrippa and Maecenas, and even his own wives.

Antonius in the East

Marriage to Cleopatra, 37 B.C. Having been tricked into spending the better part of two years helping Octavian win mastery of the West while he gained nothing, Antonius returned to the East, to which he henceforth committed himself fully in order to secure his independent power. This commitment was strikingly symbolized by his marriage to Cleopatra at Antioch in 37 B.C. He did not, however, divorce Octavia. He did not want to end his valuable relationship with her, and from the Roman point of view, he did not need to. Roman law did not recognize as valid marriages between Roman citizens and complete foreigners. Therefore, in Roman eyes, Octavia remained his legal wife and Cleopatra only his mistress. Although Octavian condemned Antonius for this action in his later propaganda, he took no public notice of it at the time, and Octavia remained loyal to her husband until civil war between him and Octavian became unavoidable.

Antonius, of course, was using the marriage with Cleopatra to bolster Roman and, therefore, his own power in the Greek East against Parthia. By becoming coruler of the only remaining independent successor state of Alexander the Great's empire, he was able to lay legitimate claim to that empire, much of which the Parthians controlled. This marriage also allowed Antonius to manipulate popular religious ideas to his advantage. He had already sought favor with the Greeks by proclaiming himself to be Dionysus, the divine conqueror of Asia in Greek mythology. Now, for the Greeks, he and Cleopatra became the divine pair Dionysus and Aphrodite. To the native Egyptians they appeared as Osiris and Isis.

The religio-political significance of the marriage is also revealed by Antonius' acknowledgement and renaming of the twins whom Cleopatra had previously borne to him. They became Alexander Helios (Sun) and Cleopatra Selene (Moon). The choice of Alexander as part of the boy's name clearly shows the attempt to lay legitimate claim to Alexander the Great's old empire, while the names Helios and Selene had powerful religious implications for his and Cleopatra's political positions. According to Greek belief, the Age of Gold was connected with the sun deity. In Egyptian mythology, Isis (the role claimed by Cleopatra) was mother of the sun. Finally, the Parthian king bore the title "Brother of the Sun and Moon," who were powerful deities in the native religion. Accordingly, Antonius was probably identifying these potent Parthian symbols with himself in order to strengthen his anticipated position as king of conquered Parthia.

Reorganization of Eastern Territories Antonius also strengthened his hand in 37 B.C. by

reorganizing the eastern half of Rome's empire. In the past the dependent kingdoms of the East had owed allegiance not to Rome but to their patron, Pompey the Great. The Parthian invasion had clearly revealed the weakness of that relationship and the disloyalty of the native kings and dynasts to Rome. Antonius did not disturb the provinces of Asia, Bithynia, and Roman Syria, but he assigned the rest of the eastern territories to four client kings, dependent on Rome but strong enough by means of their heavily armed and mail-clad cavalry to guard their frontiers against invasion.

To Cleopatra he gave Coele-Syria, Cyprus, and part of Cilicia, territories not more extensive than those given to others but immensely rich. Yet, even they did not satisfy the ambitious queen, who wanted in addition the kingdom of Herod I, who ruled Judea. Antonius firmly rejected this demand, although he did give her Herod's valuable balsam gardens at Jericho. Cleopatra had now regained control over much of what Ptolemaic Egypt had ruled at its height under Ptolemy II Philadelphus. She emphasized this point by naming the son whom she bore to Antonius in 36 B.C. Ptolemy Philadelphus.

The Parthian Campaign, 36 B.C. Antonius' marriage to Cleopatra in 37 had greatly strengthened his position in the reorganized East in preparation for his great invasion of Parthia. He was, however, neither subservient to her nor dependent upon the financial resources of Egypt at that point. He prepared his expedition with the resources of the Roman East and embarked upon it against the advice of Cleopatra in 36. His plan was not to cross the flat plain of Mesopotamia, as Crassus had done, but to invade by way of Armenia, where the hilly terrain would put the Roman legions at an advantage over the deadly Parthian cavalry and where Canidius was awaiting his arrival with sixteen seasoned legions. The loyalty of Artavasdes, the Armenian king, however, was essential to the success of the enterprise.

Loyalty was too much to expect from Artavasdes. When Antonius had begun his march of five hundred miles to Phraaspa, the capital city of the Medes (about one hundred miles south of present-day Tabriz in the Ajerbaizan), the treacherous king withdrew his cavalry and allowed the Parthians to attack and destroy two Roman legions left behind the main army to bring up the baggage and the siege train. The lack of siege equipment made the capture of Phraaspa impossible. Food running low and winter near, Antonius retreated to Armenia and was harassed all the way by Parthian sneak attacks. He finally straggled back to Syria with a loss of more than twenty thousand men and would have lost even more but for his superb generalship and the discipline of the legions.

The loss of trained troops prevented Antonius from resuming operations until 34 B.C., and even then he was able only to overrun Armenia, whose treacherous king he vengefully seized and deposed. He made Armenia a Roman province and formed an alliance with the Medes, who had revolted against their Parthian overlords. The Parthians remained unsubdued and Carrhae unavenged. Alarming reports of trouble in the West compelled Antonius to abandon his Parthian enterprise, never to attempt it again.

Despite his failure against the Parthians, Antonius was still strong in the East and the dominant partner in a divided empire. He also had considerable popular support remaining in Italy and an impressive following of Roman senators, Caesarians, Pompeians, and such staunch republicans as Cn. Domitius Ahenobarbus, L. Calpurnius Bibulus, and several kinsmen of Cato and Brutus. Nevertheless, the defeat in Parthia made Antonius dependent on Cleopatra and Egypt to repair his losses. That situation gave Octavian a chance to undermine his support gradually by propaganda and to weaken him further.

The Approach of Civil War   It is fair to say that between the masters of the East and the West a clash was inevitable. Both protagonists, just like Pompey and Caesar, were too proud to tolerate the appearance of backing down before each other. Beyond that, however, the truth of the situation lies buried beneath a thick, hard crust of defamation, lies, and political mythology. Had Antonius instead of Octavian won the eventual civil war, the official characterizations of the protagonists would have been equally fraudulent but utterly different. Antonius would have been depicted as a sober statesman and a loving husband and father, not a sex-crazed slave of Cleopatra, and as the savior of the Republic from ruin and destruction, not a tyrant striving to subject the liberties of the Roman people to Near Eastern despotism.

Octavian tightened the noose around Antonius. He refused to send the four legions that he had promised in the Treaty of Brundisium (see p. 239) and returned only the seventy ships that survived of the one hundred and twenty that Antonius had lent him against Sextus Pompey. Even Sextus Pompey tried to take advantage of Antonius' Parthian defeat by attacking Asia, where he was finally captured and killed in 35.

The Divorce of Octavia   Octavia, however, remained intensely loyal and set out with a large store of supplies and two thousand fresh troops to aid her husband in the spring of 35. At Athens a message from Antonius ordered her to return to Rome while sending on the troops and supplies. It was a bitter blow. Still, she dutifully obeyed and continued to look after his interests. It is not that Antonius did not care for her. He was not inhuman, but he was even more concerned with challenging her brother for supremacy in the Roman world, and Cleopatra had more to offer in achieving that goal than Octavia could. It was not, however, until late in 32 B.C., when Cleopatra's influence was at its height, just before the climactic battle against Octavian, that Antonius finally divorced her, a move that lost him much of the support that he still had in Italy.

Preparations for War   After punishing the treacherous Artavasdes by conquering Armenia in 34, Antonius celebrated an extraordinary triumph at Alexandria. In a ceremony known as the Donations of Alexandria, he confirmed Cleopatra and her children in their possession of the territories that he had given them and recognized Cleopatra as supreme overlord of all. He and Cleopatra then spent the winter of 33 and 32 B.C. at Ephesus in preparation for the great battle with Octavian. It was not, however, easy for even so crafty a politician as Octavian to go to war against Antonius, who had both consuls of 32 and half the senate on his side and was elected consul for 31 B.C. To prove Antonius a menace to Rome was still difficult. Cleopatra was more vulnerable. She was portrayed as a detestable foreign queen plotting to make herself empress of the world and was reported to have said that she would some day hand down justice from the Capitol. In all her alleged machinations Antonius was made to seem only her doting dupe!

The breach between the two triumvirs constantly widened. In a bitter exchange of letters each hurled recriminations against the other, charges of broken promises, family scandal, and private vices. Poets, orators, lampoonists, and pamphleteers entered the fray at the expense of truth and justice.

The two consuls of 32 B.C., Sosius and Domitius Ahenobarbus, both friends and partisans of Antonius, had earlier received from him dispatches requesting the senate's confirmation of all his acts in the East and his donations to Cleopatra and her children. Antonius also promised, for propaganda purposes, to resign from the triumvirate and restore the Republic. Fearing its political repercussions, the consuls withheld the contents of the dispatch, though Sosius, in a bitter speech before the senate, roundly condemned Octavian and moved a vote of censure against him. A tribune promptly interposed his veto.

A few days later Octavian appeared before the senate in person with an armed bodyguard. He denounced Antonius and his agents, the consuls. Then he dismissed the senate with the promise to present incriminating evidence against Antonius at the next meeting. The consuls and more than three hundred senators at once fled from Rome to Antonius. Octavian suffered them to depart.

The Will of Antonius   Meanwhile Plancus, hitherto a strong adherent of Antonius, had with several others deserted Antonius and fled to Rome. The defection of Plancus, who had never yet proved wrong in his choice of a probable winner, was ominous, sensational, and to Antonius most disconcerting. To Octavian he brought a precious gift, none more urgently needed, namely the knowledge that Antonius had deposited with the Vestal Virgins his last will and testament. Octavian promptly and illegally extorted that will from the Vestal Virgins and read it at the next meeting of the senate. The will allegedly confirmed the legacies to the children of Cleopatra, declared that her son Caesarion was a true son and successor of Julius Caesar, and directed that Antonius after death be buried beside Cleopatra in the Ptolemaic mausoleum in Alexandria.*

Genuine or forged, the will gave to Octavian his greatest propaganda victory. It confirmed the most vicious rumors against Antonius, befuddled his friends, and filled the patriotic citizenry with loathing and horror.

Octavian Declares War, 32 B.C.   Capitalizing on the popular revulsion against Antonius, Octavian now resolved to mobilize the power of the West against the East. By various means—local agitations, propaganda, patriotic appeals, and some intimidation, perhaps—he contrived to secure from the municipalities first of Italy and later of the Western provinces an oath of personal allegiance. Fortified by this somewhat spurious popular mandate, he declared Antonius stripped of his *imperium* and of his consulate of 31 B.C. Late in the fall of 32 B.C., in order to avoid the appearance of initiating another civil war of Roman against Roman, Octavian declared

---

* Though regarded as genuine by some classical scholars, more than one historian has judged the will of Antonius to be an obvious forgery.

war on Cleopatra and spent the rest of the winter in preparation.

Antonius himself had meanwhile not been idle. He had assembled at Ephesus a vast apparatus for war—thirty legions mostly of Italian origin, twelve thousand cavalry, five hundred ships, and large stores of grain and supplies. Toward the end of 32 B.C., he and Cleopatra sailed for Greece and took up battle stations at Actium, at the entrance of the Ambracian Gulf, in which lay the main part of his fleet.

On paper, Antonius should have won the battle of Actium. He was an excellent general and commanded an army numerically equal in both infantry and cavalry to that of Octavian. He also had one of the biggest and strongest fleets the ancient world had yet seen.

His weakness overbalanced his strength. His ships were too heavy and slow, their crews untrained and inexperienced in recent naval warfare. Not one of his admirals was the equal, in skill and daring, of Agrippa, one of the greatest naval strategists in Roman history.

More serious still would be the lack of morale among Antonius' troops, if confronted with the patriotic fervor that Octavian seemed able to inspire in the West. While most legionaries admired Antonius as a man and soldier, they hated war against fellow citizens. His officers detested Cleopatra and in private cursed Antonius for not being man enough to send her back to Egypt. They did not know how much he depended upon her for money, grain, and supplies. She in turn feared to let him out of her sight lest he abandon her and go back to Octavia. Antonius was doomed.

The Battle of Actium, 31 B.C.

The details of the battle of Actium, one of the most famous and decisive of world history, are not known. Its phases, duration, and character are obscure or controversial. Despite the efforts of ancient writers to embellish or dramatize it, it was evidently a miserable affair, scarcely worthy of the name of battle. It took place at sea and involved a pitifully small number of ships.

The land armies never fought at all. Actium was famous and decisive only because it marked the end of the Republic and the beginning of the Empire.

Agrippa set up a blockade that caused a severe famine and an outbreak of plague in Antonius' camp; his commanders were divided and quarreling among themselves; his troops were paralyzed by treason and desertions. Antonius himself had become distracted by his cares, and he continued to place undue importance on his ponderous ships instead of reviving his famed leadership on land. At the height of the already hopeless battle, Antonius caught sight of Cleopatra's ship heading out to sea.* The distraught Antonius instantly followed the queen. His men, left leaderless, soon succumbed to bewilderment and surrendered some days later to the victorius Octavian.

The victory of Octavian was so complete that he felt no immediate need to pursue the fugitives to Egypt. He turned his attention to mutinous legions in Italy instead and crossed the sea to appease their demands for land and money.

The Deaths of Antonius and Cleopatra

It was not until the summer of 30 B.C. that Octavian, desperate for money, went to Egypt. The legions of Antonius put up only a brief resistance. Alexandria surrendered. While Octavian was celebrating his recent victory, news arrived that Antonius had committed suicide. A few days later Cleopatra followed suit. Thus passed the last of the Ptolemies, a dynasty that had ruled Egypt for almost three hundred years. Egypt became part of the Roman Empire, and its rich treasures fell into the hands of Octavian, who had defeated some of the greatest militarists of the age and was now undisputed master of the

---

* The reason for Cleopatra's precipitate departure is not known. Some attribute it to despair at having received word that Antonius was killed. Others, less romantic, maintain that the battle had clearly taken a turn for the worse and Cleopatra was fleeing to escape capture.

world. After a century of civil war, peace had come at last.

The End of the Republic

In form, the Roman Republic, with its diffusion of powers among the citizen assemblies, collegiate magistracies, and senate of aristocratic equals, still remained. In reality, power had become concentrated in the hands of one man, the total antithesis of republicanism. Many reasons have been offered to explain why the Republic collapsed. Ancient authors like Sallust, Cicero, and Plutarch offered moral explanations that often have been favored in modern times: having conquered most of the Mediterranean world, the Romans no longer had the fear of external enemies to restrain them, and they lost their old virtues and self-discipline through the corrupting influences of the alien cultures to which they had become exposed and the great wealth and power that they had attained. Many modern historians have seen the Republic's fall primarily as the work of Julius Caesar in single-mindedly pursuing some long-planned monarchic design or mystical sense of destiny.

Still others have seen the problem primarily in institutional terms: the institutions of a small agrarian-based city-state were inadequate for coping with the great social, economic, administrative, and military problems that came with vast overseas expansion. Some, however, would argue that there can be no general explanation of the Republic's fall because it was essentially an accident: the Republic had weathered the upheavals from the Gracchi to Sulla, made the necessary adjustments to changed conditions while maintaining its basic character, was functioning quite normally, and would have continued to do so if two egotistical, stubborn, and miscalculating men had not chanced to precipitate the civil war that destroyed it.

None of these explanations is adequate. To a certain extent, all history is accident, but that does not mean that general causes cannot be found or are not important. Accidents occur and have an impact within a general context that make them possible. For example, in one sense the oil crisis that afflicted many nations in the 1970s was an accidental result of politics and warfare in the Middle East, but there would not have been any oil crisis without a whole host of general technological, economic, social, and cultural developments that had taken place in those nations during the previous century to make oil such an important commodity. Similarly, one must look at the outbreak of the particular civil war that destroyed the Republic in the context of general, long-term social, economic, political, and cultural developments.

Those who emphasize the inadequacy of old Republican institutions for coping with the new problems of a vast empire have an important point. Institutions that arise from or are designed for a particular set of circumstances will eventually cease to function satisfactorily under radically altered circumstances. For example, the old eighteenth-century New England town-meeting form of government is totally impractical in twentieth-century Boston. Old institutions may be modified and adapted up to a point and remain basically what they were, but that process can be carried only so far before they are transformed into something quite different. After four hundred years of change, the British monarchy of Queen Elizabeth II is not the same as that of Elizabeth I.

Similarly, after two hundred years the old Republican system had ceased to work and minor modifications had not helped to preserve it. Annual magistrates limited by collegiate veto and guided by a senate of narrow outlook and experience were not capable of waging long-term overseas wars and governing distant provinces in alien lands. The use of practically independent pro-magistrates and extraordinary commanders, often with extended terms of duty, to deal with these problems placed in the hands of individuals unprecedented amounts of economic, political, and military power. They could then be used to overcome normal constitutional checks and destroy the equilibrium within the ruling elite that had kept the old system in balance. The tremendous social and economic changes that had accompanied two hundred years of imperialism had also greatly altered the composition of the popular assemblies and made them more susceptible to ambitious manipulators in search of personal advantage over their peers. Sulla's attempt to restore the old system in the face of changed conditions merely doomed it to failure.

Institutional inadequacies alone, however, do not explain the fall of the Roman Republic. Institutions do not exist or function apart from the people who control them. The character, abilities, and behavior patterns of the people who control vital institutions do have a bearing on how well those institutions function under given circumstances. For example, during the Great Depression, the American Presidency was not an effective instrument of popular leadership under Herbert Hoover, but it was under Franklin Roosevelt, however one judges the ultimate worth of his policies. Therefore, individual leaders like Julius Caesar are important. Although he was not pursuing any mystical sense of destiny or long-meditated monarchic ambitions, he did have particular personality traits, such as self-assurance, decisiveness, and speed, that made him particularly successful in the political and military competition that was destroying the Republic.

Nevertheless, individual differences should not be overemphasized. Caesar was operating within a general cultural context that shaped his thoughts and actions in ways that were typical of fellow nobles like Pompey, Crassus, Catiline, Clodius, Cato, Curio, Antonius, and Brutus. They were all deeply concerned with the personal *gloria, dignitas,* and *auctoritas* that were the most highly valued prizes of the nobility.

Therefore, although mere moralizing is too simplistic, moral considerations, in terms of how the values of a culture affect human behavior, are important in explaining the fall of the Republic. The dominant values of a culture shape the general ways in which individuals who share that culture perceive the world around them and act in it. Such values

often arise in response to a particular set of historical circumstances during a formative period and then are perpetuated, reinforced, and amplified in the customs, religion, folklore, art, literature, and institutions that develop along with them. As conditions change over a long period of time, values that produced what may be viewed as positive behavior in earlier times often produce what may be viewed as negative behavior (even as defined by other values in the culture) under new conditions and lead to a period of crisis and change.

For example, during the Dark and Archaic Ages of Greece (ca. 1000 to ca. 500 B.C.), the emerging Greek city-states developed the deeply held values of independence, self-sufficiency, and military success that ensured their survival and promoted their growth, which reinforced their values. Their very success, however, brought them into increasing conflict with each other in the Classical Age (ca. 500 to ca. 300 B.C.) because they could not remain self-sufficient under the changed economic conditions that their growth had generated and could no longer expand except at each other's expense. The only way to achieve the peace that each would have agreed to be desirable would have been to surrender their highly valued independence and give up the ideal of military success as the proof of their independence and self-sufficiency. Such values were too deeply ingrained in their culture, however, and they continued their self-destructive warfare, which allowed Philip of Macedon to destroy the independence that each vigorously fought to preserve.

In the early Roman Republic, the great emphasis on and competition for *gloria, dignitas,* and *auctoritas* produced generations of leaders who eagerly defended the state against hostile neighbors, expanded Roman territory to satisfy a land-hungry population, and ably served the state as priests, magistrates, and senators. So long as Rome expanded within the relatively narrow and homogeneous confines of Italy, there was little opportunity for aristocratic competition at Rome to get out of hand, and the values that fueled it were reinforced while the highly desired stability of the state was maintained. These same values then contributed to overseas expansion along with accompanying disruptive socio-economic changes at home, both of which made it possible for individual aristocrats to acquire dispro-portionate resources for competing with their peers. In eagerly seeking these resources in accordance with long-held values, Republican aristocrats raised their competition to levels destructive to the very state that they cherished.

XXI

Life and Culture in the Late Roman Republic, ca. 100 to ca. 30 B.C.

The political turmoil of the first century B.C. was matched by social, economic, and cultural ferment. In the countryside of Italy, the problems that had contributed to the Gracchan crisis of the previous century were often made worse by the series of domestic wars inaugurated by the Social War in 90 B.C. The provinces suffered from the ravages of war, both civil and foreign, and from frequently inept or corrupt administration. In Rome and Italy, people's values and behavior changed as the old social fabric frayed. The *mos maiorum* lost its old strength, and the state's cults lost their power. Nowhere, however, was change more evident than in art and literature. Creative, thoughtful individuals responded to the social, economic, and political turmoil with new attitudes, forms, and concepts that mark the late Republic as a period of great creativity as well as crisis.

Land and Veterans Whatever success Gracchan land-redistribution legislation may have had in the late second century B.C., the problems that it sought to alleviate were just as bad throughout much of the first. The economic and military pressures that had impoverished many small farmers earlier still ex-

isted, and facts do not support the thesis that beginning with Marius powerful generals largely solved the problem by enrolling landless men in their armies and providing them with land upon discharge. Those who did receive allotments usually lost them again from a combination of economic pressures, confiscation in civil war, and military conscription. Large-scale, long-term settlements had to wait until after 31 B.C., when the civil wars of the Republic finally ceased.

Until then, instead of receiving their own land to farm, a number of landless or indebted peasants became free tenants, *coloni,* on great estates. This trend is evident primarily in central and southern Italy, where the great estates were concentrated and where the danger of rebellion among large concentrations of slaves had been emphasized by the revolt of Spartacus. Some owners, therefore, found it safer and more productive to settle *coloni* as cultivators on part of their land in return for a yearly rent.

Agriculture In the rural districts of Italy, the small farmers concentrated primarily on the cultivation of grain, whose surplus production could be sold in nearby towns, and the raising of a few vegetables, some poultry, and an occasional pig for domestic consumption. Near large towns and cities, a peasant could engage in market gardening or the specialized production of poultry, honey, and flowers. The great estates concentrated on raising sheep, cattle, and pigs to supply wool, hides, and meat for urban markets and Roman armies, or on the growing of grapes for wine and olives for oil. Vintage wines from Campania were equal to the best from Greece, and the less prized wines of northern Italy found a ready market in lands across the Alps.

Wealthy landowners also began to experiment with more exotic crops either for profit or ostentatious display on their own tables. Lucullus deserves to be remembered for transplanting the sweet cherry and the apricot from Asia Minor to Italy, orchards of which expanded rapidly along with those of other fruit-bearing trees. Many large estates were turned into hunting preserves to supply their owners with choice wild game, and seaside properties became famous for their ponds of eels, mullet, and other marine delicacies.

In the Western provinces, immigrants from Italy had a great impact on agriculture. In Sicily and North Africa, Roman landowners intensified the production of grain for export to the insatiable Roman market. Settlers in Spain and Gaul were establishing olive groves, vineyards, and orchards that would eventually capture the provincial markets of the exporters in Italy. The provinces of the East, however, were severely depressed as a result of the devastation, confiscations, and indemnities resulting from the Mithridatic wars and the civil wars of the 40s and 30s.

Industry and Commerce Manufacturing and trade in the East had also been severely disrupted by the wars of the late Republic. Many Italian merchants and moneylenders in Asia Minor lost their wealth and their lives in the uprising spurred by Mithridates in 88 B.C. Delos, which the Romans had made a free port to undercut Rhodes in 168, never recovered from being sacked in 88 and 69. When commerce did revive between the Levant and Italy, it was carried largely by Syrian and Alexandrian traders, who maintained sizable establishments at Puteoli to service Rome and Italy.

Italians, however, dominated the Western trade. The export of grain from Africa and Sicily was in the hands of numerous Italian merchants. Italian traders dominated Utica at the time of its capture by Caesar's forces in 46, and 300 Italian businessmen were resident in Thapsus. Itinerant Italians also carried Italian wine, pottery, and metalwork across the Alps in return for silver and slaves.

Industry remained basically an affair of handcrafts practiced by individual artisans working with a few slaves and apprentices in small shops. Technological development was almost nonexistent. Two of Italy's most important industries, the production of bronze goods and ceramic tableware, were concentrated respectively at Capua in Campania and Arretium in Etruria. Capua produced fine bronze cooking utensils, jugs, lamps, candelabra, and implements for the markets of Italy and northern Europe. Using molds, the Arretine potters specialized in the mass manufacture of red, highly glazed, embossed plates and bowls known as Samian ware. It enjoyed great popularity all over the Western provinces, which eventually set up rival manufacturing centers of their own.

The copper mines of Etruria were becoming exhausted in terms of the prevailing techniques of exploitation, but the slack was more than taken up by production in Spain, where private contractors operated the mines on lease from the state. Tin, which was alloyed with copper to form bronze, was imported from Cornwall in the British Isles along a trade route that had been opened up by the father of Marcus Crassus during his governorship of Spain in 96 B.C.

In Rome and Italy, the building trades profited enormously from the conquests of Sulla, Pompey, and Caesar and the ensuing profits that accrued to other nobles. The wealth that Sulla brought back from the East or confiscated from his Marian enemies at home financed many public works in Rome, such as the rebuilding of the senate house, new paving in the Forum, reconstruction of the temple of Jupiter on the Capitoline, and the construction of the Tabularium, a public record office. Sulla also endowed his numerous veteran colonies, such as Pompeii, with suitable public buildings, while his great Sanctuary of Fotuna at Praeneste is one of the outstanding achievements of Roman architecture (see pp. 260–261). Pompey constructed Rome's first stone theater and the adjoining portico, where Caesar was killed. Caesar himself initiated another reconstruction of the senate house, which had been burned at Clodius' funeral in 52. He also planned the Saepta Julia, an enclosed hall for voting purposes, the Basilica Julia in the old Forum, and a completely new forum, the Forum Julium.

Wealthy nobles covered the Palatine with sumptuous townhouses. Elsewhere in the city, speculators put up huge blocks of flimsy, multistoried apartment buildings, *insulae,* to house the rapidly expanding population, which now neared a million. Land at Rome became so valuable that Crassus made a fortune from buying burned-out or fire-damaged properties at low prices and then repairing them with his own construction crews for resale at a profit.

The business that produced the biggest profits other than war was finance, both public and private. The numerous annexations in Asia Minor greatly expanded the business of tax-farming, which was carried on by companies of *publicani* (see pp. 136–137). Wealthy *equites* were heavily involved as partners in these companies, and sometimes senators, though officially forbidden, were involved as silent partners or through intermediaries. Moneylending, often to provincial cities who needed money to pay the *publicani,* or to client kings, who needed to borrow to stay solvent after paying huge sums in buying Roman support for their thrones, was a huge source of profits to wealthy financiers. With rates as high as twenty-four or forty-eight percent, even the greatest nobles were tempted to exploit this source of revenue. Pompey loaned

some of the huge fortune that he had acquired in the East to Ariobarzanes, whom he had confirmed as king of Cappadocia. In 52 B.C. Cicero was shocked to learn that Marcus Brutus was the Roman who indirectly pressured him to use his power as governor of Cilicia to force the Cypriot city of Salamis to make payment on an illegal loan at forty-eight percent interest.

On the other hand, there were many lenders, mostly well-to-do *equites,* who engaged in the more normal business of advancing money to merchants and shipowners to finance trade or to Roman aristocrats to finance their careers. One of these men was Cicero's confidant, publisher, and banker, T. Pomponius Atticus. While they were businessmen, they shared the basic outlook of the aristocracy and used much of their profits to invest in land and live like gentlemen. Atticus, for example, acquired vast estates in Epirus, which allowed him to spend the turbulent years from 88 to 65 at Athens (hence his cognomen, Atticus), where he was safe from the political storms of Rome. When he returned to Rome, he patronized the arts and literature from his house on the Quirinal and made so many important contacts that he was protected on all sides during the subsequent civil wars.

The Concentration of Wealth Atticus, with his great wealth, illustrates one of the striking features of the late Republic, the concentration of wealth in a few upper-class hands and the ever-widening gap between rich and poor. This trend had already been evident since at least the time of the Punic Wars, but it was greatly accelerated by Marius' and Sulla's introduction of proscription. In times of civil war, those on the winning side, or at least not on the losing side, could acquire the property of proscribed individuals at a mere fraction of their normal value either through favoritism or because the sudden increase in property for sale temporarily depressed prices. When property values rose with the return of normalcy, their net worth increased enormously. For example, Marcus Crassus had inherited a relatively modest fortune of three hundred talents upon the deaths of his father and remaining brother in the civil war of 87. After siding with Sulla in 83, however, he took advantage of Sulla's proscriptions in order to acquire valuable properties. Then, through shrewd management, he increased his wealth still further, so that his vast real estate holdings alone were worth more than seven thousand talents in 55 B.C.

The profits of war and imperial administration that accrued to the nobility were even greater. Despite his failure to defeat Mithridates totally, Lucullus had amassed enough wealth from Asia Minor to live like a king in numerous villas after his recall to Italy. He became so famous for his conspicuous consumption that the term "Lucullan" has come to characterize rich living. The wealth acquired by Pompey and Caesar during their respective conquests in the East and Gaul made them far wealthier than even Crassus, whose only hope of staying even was to conquer the wealthy empire of Parthia.

Provincial governors often abused their power to amass personal fortunes in order to compete with their aristocratic rivals for high office and social status. Verres, the notorious governor of Sicily from 73 to 71, was reported to have said that the illegal gains of his first year were to pay off the debts that he had incurred in running for his praetorship of 74, those of the second year were to bribe the jury to acquit him of his crimes, and those of the third were for himself. Significantly, the art works that he had plundered from Sicily were said to have earned him a place on Antonius' proscription list in 43. Even an honest governor, such as Cicero had been in Cilicia in 52, was able to profit handsomely from office. In addition, though a man of relatively modest means among the Roman nobility, Cicero acquired enough through inheritances, gifts, and favorable loans from other nobles whom he defended in court to buy a townhouse on the Palatine for 3.5 million sesterces and at least eight well-appointed country villas. He, too, of course, lost them along with his life in the proscriptions of 43.

To finance their political careers and maintain the style of life expected by their peers, many nobles borrowed heavily against their properties and future prospects. At one point, before he became immensely wealthy in Gaul, Caesar was almost seventy-five million denarii in debt and his opponent Curio about fifty million. Catiline was so hopelessly in debt after buying acquittal on charges of extortion as a provincial governor and two unsuccessful campaigns for the consulship that revolution was his only hope of avoiding financial ruin. Many of his fellow conspirators were in similar straits.

Life for the Rural and Urban Poor
While wealthy *equites* and senatorial aristocrats enjoyed sumptuous townhouses and country villas, the assiduous attention of innumerable domestic slaves, private baths, personal libraries, vintage wines, and exotic delicacies, the rural and urban poor led a hand-to-mouth existence. When not harassed by rapacious neighbors, bad weather, conscription, or dispossession in civil war, the free peasant or tenant farmer could get by. Sometimes he could even earn a little extra by working for hire on the estate of a wealthy neighbor at harvest. His wife worked as hard as he did as she helped at peak seasons in the field, tended the kitchen garden, ran the house, and bore children. Even if she survived the dangers of childbirth under unsanitary conditions, she grew old before her time.

The urban masses were often worse off. Increasingly they were crowded into ill-lit, poorly ventilated, unsanitary tenements prone to fire and collapse. In Rome there was also the danger of flood, since the Tiber often overflowed its banks. While there were a number of middle-class shopkeepers, such as bakers, fullers, metal smiths, potters, shoemakers, and wine and food vendors, there were more unskilled or semiskilled people who seldom found steady work. Occasional employment could be found on construction projects, on the docks, and doing odd jobs for the more fortunate. The low level of ancient technology in the production and transportation of goods and the concentration of wealth in a few hands, however, prevented the development of large-scale industries and mass markets to provide high levels of employment.

As clients of the rich, many of the poor were helped by gifts of food (*sportulae*) and occasional distributions of money (*congiaria*). At election time, one could look forward to selling one's vote as the use of the secret ballot and intense electoral competition increased the use of bribery. Public festivals and triumphs could also produce helpful bonuses. Crassus, for example, feasted the whole city of Rome to celebrate his victory over Spartacus and gave each Roman citizen a three-months' supply of grain. The public distribution of free grain to several hundred thousand Roman citizens also helped to prevent starvation, but since it was limited to adult men, it was not enough to sustain their families. Hunger must have been a constant condition faced by many, and abortion and infanticide, especially of girls, were frequent to limit the number of mouths to feed.

Fire and Violence   Life in the cities was precarious in other ways too. There was no public fire department to control the numerous fires that swept through crowded slums. Nor was there a police force to prevent the growing crime and violence that poverty and crowded conditions bred. Private associations might try to provide local protection, and some wealthy individuals earned popularity by maintaining private fire brigades, as Crassus is believed to have done and as did a certain Egnatius Rufus later. The rich surrounded themselves with private bodyguards when they traversed the city, especially at night. The poor had to rely mainly on their own efforts or those of family and friends to protect themselves or secure justice from those who committed crimes against them. The principle of self-help was still widely applied. There was no public prosecutor, and the courts, with their cumbersome procedures, were mainly for the rich.

Politically inspired violence also increased greatly in late Republican Rome. The most notable examples, of course, are the civil wars and proscriptions, during which many thousands were killed. Increasingly, however, important trials, political meetings (*contiones*), elections, and legislative meetings of the assemblies were marred by violence. Rival politicians hired gangs to intimidate and harass each other. In 66, for example, thugs so intimidated the prosecutors of the extribune Cornelius that they dropped the case. In 65 Catiline took part in an armed attempt to save the extribune Manilius from prosecution. Caesar rammed through his legislation in 59 with much violence aimed against opponents like Cato and Bibulus. P. Clodius perfected the art of political violence in 58 B.C. by organizing poor citizens into clubs (*collegia*), modelled on legitimate private associations and used them to harass his enemies like Pompey, whom they beseiged in his own house, and Cicero, whose house they tried to keep from being rebuilt after his return from exile in 57.

Public entertainment also reflected the increase of violence. Sulla and Caesar both added festivals to the Roman calendar, part of whose games were chariot races, which excited spectators with high-speed wrecks and the frequent deaths of charioteers. Gladiatorial combats sponsored by candidates for office had become such a common feature of life that special schools for training and supplying gladiators became big business. Blood-thirsty crowds also delighted in staged beast hunts (*venationes*), animals for which were imported from all over the empire. As dictator, Caesar invented a new source of violent entertainment, *naumachia,* staged naval battles on man-made lakes created for the occasion.

Slaves and Freedmen   Slavery in Rome and Italy continued to grow in the first century B.C. The kidnapping activities of pirates before 67, Pompey's conquests in the East, and Caesar's conquests in Gaul had produced a flood of slaves, who were in constant demand for various rural and urban, business and domestic occupations (see pp. 133, 137). The Romans finally learned their lesson after the dreadful uprisings of mistreated rural slaves in Sicily (104 to 99 B.C.) and under Spartacus in Italy (73 to 71 B.C.) and improved the treatment of such slaves to prevent future outbreaks. Household slaves and those with skilled trades or professions continued to enjoy many advantages. Those in the service of wealthy and powerful masters fared better than the majority of free citizens. They ran their owners' estates, acted as their business and political agents, and were well rewarded for their loyalty. Many of them acquired considerable personal wealth and even owned slaves of their own.

Roman masters continued to be generous in freeing slaves, especially personal and domestic slaves, whom they came to know and love as members of their own families, personal friends, and bedmates. A good example was Cicero's personal secretary Tiro, whom he treated as a son and eventually freed. Tiro served Cicero faithfully as a freedman, invented a system of shorthand (still extant) to cope with his copious dictation, wrote a biography of him after his death, and helped to collect his correspondence for publication. Because freedmen became the loyal clients of their former masters, however, efforts to give them membership in all the voting tribes were bitterly resisted and always failed. The tribune Sulpicius failed in such an attempt in 88, and Manilius aroused such resentment in a similar attempt as a tribune of 66 that he tried to blame it on others.

Italians   and   Provincials   Unlike freedmen, the Italians, who had won the franchise as a result of the Social War, were able to obtain equitable enrollment in the voting tribes. Cinna performed that service between 86 and 84, and Sulla wisely did not anger the Italians by trying to undo the justice that had finally been done. Still, for the average Italian, being allowed to vote on a par with other Roman citizens was a right of little use. The difficulty of going to Rome to exercise the franchise regularly was too great. For the local Italian landed aristocracy, who now became

Roman *equites,* it was another matter, however. They joined the older *equites* in demanding a greater voice in public affairs. Sulla's addition of 300 *equites* to the senate did not appreciably alter the status of the rest, who continued to feel that the noble-dominated senate was not doing enough to protect their legal and financial interests. With Pompey's support, their agitation won them a third of the seats on juries in 70, and under Caesar in 59 they received a reduction of the overbid contracts for Asian taxes, which were threatening to bankrupt a company of *publicani* whose stock was held by many *equites* and whose collapse might have started a financial panic. Men like Cicero (who came from the equestrian class), Pompey, Crassus, and Caesar eagerly sought *clientelae* among the wealthy equestrian landowners of Italy. Their money, votes, and influence could be highly useful in the struggles of the Forum.

Similarly, powerful Roman aristocrats courted wealthy provincials, provincial cities, and even entire provinces as clients. Tiberius Gracchus had been able to extricate Hostilius Mancinus' army from Numantia because the elder Tiberius Gracchus had won the loyalty of many Spaniards during his term as governor. Similarly, Crassus' father had obtained so many clients in Spain during his governorship that Crassus was able to find a safe refuge in Spain from Cinna. Both Pompey and Metellus Pius secured Spanish clients by granting citizenship to numerous Spaniards during the war against Sertorius. Moreover, Pompey's actions during the pirate and Mithridatic wars won him so many clients in the eastern provinces that he calculated upon their support to enable him to defeat Caesar in 49 and 48.

Education   By the first century B.C. Rome had developed a fairly extensive system of education, although its availability was limited by the ability to pay since the state contributed no support. Primary schools (*ludi literarii*), were open to both boys and girls. There they learned the fundamentals of reading, writing, and arithmetic, often painfully, since corporal punishment was frequently applied. Between the ages of twelve and fifteen, girls and boys took different paths. A girl would often be married to an older man at about fourteen, and unless she were of the wealthy elite, formal education stopped. Roman boys moved on to the secondary level under the tutelage of a *grammaticus,* who taught them Greek and Latin language and literature. No Roman of the first century B.C. could be considered truly educated if he did not speak and write Greek as fluently as Latin and did not know the classical Greek authors by heart.

Since the Romans had come to dominate Italy and the western Mediterranean by the first century B.C., it was essential for people to know Latin. Therefore, schools of Latin and even Greek, for those who had real ambitions, were becoming common everywhere. They spread the Latin language and Greco-Roman culture widely and produced a remarkably uniform culture among the upper classes of Italy and the western provinces. As earlier, the masters of the primary and secondary schools were frequently freed Greek slaves who had been tutors in the houses of the wealthy. Their pupils were often offspring of middle- and upper-middle-class fathers like those of Cicero, Virgil, and Horace, who had ambitions for their sons to enter Roman politics and rise in social standing.

The prevalence of private tutors among the aristocracy meant that aristocratic girls often received instruction at the secondary level along with their brothers. Sometimes they were even able to participate in the higher training of rhetoric and philosophy, if, as with Sempronia, sister of the Gracchi, their families brought men accomplished in these fields into their homes and supported them in return for instructing their children. Many aristocratic sons as well as those of nonaristocrats were sent to professional rhetoricians for instruction at the highest level.

For a long time Greek rhetoric dominated the higher curriculum. Right at the beginning of the first century there was a movement to create a parallel course of professional instruction in Latin rhetoric. In 92, however,

the censors banned teachers of Latin rhetoric, perhaps out of fear that rhetorical skills, the foundation of political success, might be made too accessible to the lower orders. Julius Caesar finally lifted the ban when he became dictator.

Frequently an upper-class young man capped his formal education with a tour to the great centers of Greek rhetoric and philosophy at Athens and Rhodes. Both Cicero and Caesar studied under the Greek rhetorician Apollonius Molo at Rhodes. Cicero developed a love of philosophy at Athens, which in later years he tried to communicate in Latin through his philosophical treatises. He sent his son, Marcus, to Athens also, but it is clear from Cicero's letters that young Marcus soon found other pleasures more appealing than the study of philosophy. Still, Marcus must have picked up enough education to hold his own in aristocratic society, for he reached the consulship as a colleague of Augustus in 30 B.C.

Women in Late Republican Society

As already seen, upper-class women benefited intellectually from the schooling and tutors supplied their brothers. While fathers did not send their daughters for the final stage of education to places like Athens or Rhodes, some accomplished and loving fathers, like Hortensius, Cicero, and the younger Cato, took great personal interest in providing their daughters with higher training. Cicero was inconsolable over the death of his beloved Tullia. For a while he even contemplated building a shrine for her worship. Cato's daughter, Porcia, was like her father in outspoken Republicanism. She supported her first husband, M. Calpurnius Bibulus, in his opposition to Caesar. She insisted that she participate with her second husband, Brutus, in the planning of Caesar's assassination, and after her death Cicero delivered a powerful eulogy for her. Hortensia, the daughter of Cicero's oratorical rival Hortensius, broke all precedent in 42 when she personally appeared in the Forum to argue against the imposition of a special tax on wealthy women to pay for the war against

Woman with a stylus and wax writing tablet; wall painting from Pompeii, A.D. *40–50. (Courtesy Archaeological Museum, Naples)*

Brutus and Cassius. She gained public support and won her point. Pompey's last and most beloved wife, Cornelia, daughter of Metellus Scipio, earned praise because she was well read, could play the lyre, and, most significantly, was adept at geometry and philosophy.

Just as dynastic marriages gave shrewd and ambitious royal women more power and status in the Hellenistic Greek world, so the need for powerful marriage alliances in the growing competition for power among the aristocracy of the rapidly expanding Roman Republic gave upper-class Roman women opportunities for power and prestige. Cornelia, Pompeia, and Calpurnia, Caesar's wives; Fulvia, wife of Clodius, Curio, and Marcus Antonius; Octavia, sister of Octavian; and Livia, Octavian's last wife are prime examples.

One of the most visible signs of the increased power and independence of upper-

class women in the late Republic is their sexual liberation. Earlier, a woman like Cornelia, mother of the Gracchi, though quite independent, had held to the ideal of a virtuous Roman matron and widow. During the first century B.C., as traditional values began to break down rapidly under intense political and economic competition, many women became infamous for their uninhibited sexual behavior. Pompey divorced his third wife, Mucia, because she had been notoriously unfaithful while he was fighting Mithridates. Caesar's second wife, Pompeia, was caught in the famous affair with P. Clodius. One of Clodius' sisters, Clodia, the wife of Metellus Celer, was notoriously promiscuous. Among her many lovers were the poet Catullus and Cicero's young friend Caelius Rufus. On his deathbed her husband claimed that she had poisoned him, and on another occasion Lucullus produced testimony that she and her sister, Lucullus' wife, had incestuous relations with their brother. Sallust claims that a number of talented and dissolute women even became involved in Catiline's conspiracy, and he describes one, a certain Sempronia, in titillating detail. These independent, strong-willed, and unconventional women of the late Republic have their counterparts in many of the empresses of the imperial era.

Lower-Class Women There were three major categories of lower-class Roman women: slaves, freedwomen, and poorer freeborn women. Female slaves were usually used as household servants, such as nurses, weavers, hairdressers, handmaidens, cooks, and housekeepers. Usually they were available to masters for sexual purposes, to which neither they nor their wives necessarily objected. In such an arrangement wives had less fear of pregnancy and, often, freedom from husbands who had been forced upon them and whom they did not love; also, a responsive female slave might expect eventual freedom from a grateful master. Women slaves could own property, even other slaves. Marriages to other slaves were not legally recognized but were often very stable, even when a couple had been separated by sale. A woman slave who saved enough money to buy her freedom or had freedom granted would often then purchase her separated husband and free him.

The most unfortunate group of female slaves was that of the prostitutes. Prostitution was extensive, and prostitutes were often the unwanted female children of slaves and poor free citizens who were sold by masters and parents to procurers who raised them for that purpose alone. In general, they had little to look forward to. Even if they obtained their freedom they were not trained to do anything else and might be worse off without an owner who had an interest in providing a minimum level of shelter, food, and physical security.

Large numbers of female slaves were eventually freed because they were usually household slaves, to whom masters were traditionally more generous. Some stayed on as free retainers with their former owners, others practiced the trades that they had learned as slaves, and some rose to a comfortable status by good marriages, generous patrons, or hard work. Often a master would free a slave woman in order to marry her. Marriage to freedwomen carried no stigma in all but the highest classes, and was not unheard of even there. Cato the Elder's second wife was a freed slave.

Ironically, the slaves and freedwomen of the aristocracy often had far greater opportunities in life than freeborn women of the poorer citizen classes. Women of the working poor often had to be content with the lowliest jobs. Laundry work, spinning and weaving, turning grindstones at flour mills, working as butchers, and selling fish are frequently recorded. Inscriptions from Pompeii list some other occupations, such as dealer in beans, seller of nails, brickmaker, and even stonecutter. Many women worked as waitresses in taverns or servers at food counters, where they may also have engaged in prostitution on the side. The names of waitresses and prostitutes are found scribbled on numerous tavern walls with references to their various virtues or vices, attractions or detractions as the case may be. For many unskilled poor women, prostitution was the only source of livelihood, and, unlike slave prostitutes, who had at least the protection of a brothel, they had to practice their trade unprotected out of doors in the public archways, *fornices,* whence comes the word *fornicate.*

Especially among the poor, daughters were often considered a useless burden and exposed at birth or sold into slavery. Even when such extreme steps were not taken, girls received less attention. That combined with the high incidence of death in childbirth as a result of adolescent marriage, poor health care, and unsanitary living conditions made life for a poor woman very precarious indeed.

Law As the Republic had expanded and life became more complex, it had become too cumbersome to have all important cases tried in the popular assemblies. It had become desirable to establish standing jury courts, *quaestiones perpetuae,* each presided over by a praetor or *iudex quaestionis* to try various crimes. Significantly, the first was the extortion court, *quaestio de rebus repetundis,* in 149 B.C. Two to four more were created before the time of Sulla, who raised the total to seven (p. 188). Many of the crimes involved were related to political life, and prosecutions in these courts often had political motives, as the speeches of Cicero and what is known of other orators' works clearly show. That is why control of the seats on juries became such a divisive issue in the late Republic.

The law itself became more fair and equitable in the late Republic, although access to it was generally limited to people of means. The rather narrow Civil Law, *ius civile,* of the Twelve Tables and subsequent legislation did not always apply in cases where non-Romans were involved, as was increasingly the case with the expansion of Roman power. Roman praetors, therefore, incorporated into their edicts, which set the precedent for future cases, elements taken from the laws of other people, *ius gentium,* and their own concepts of equity. The formulas of procedure that praetors developed in such cases were so superior to the rigidly prescribed actions of the Civil Law that the formulary procedure had been introduced to the Civil Law as early as 150 B.C. Improved rules of evidence were also devised for the jury courts, and the Stoic doctrine of Natural Law, *ius naturale,* influenced the formation of law more and more in the direction of fairness and universality.

Religion and Philosophy   In the late Republic the personal cults of family and field still inspired meaningful religious feeling, especially among the average citizenry. The official cults and practices of the state were no longer a living religious force for either the lower or upper classes. It was already apparent in the second century that the aristocracy cynically manipulated the religious calendar, augury, divination, the taking of auspices, and the interpretation of the Sibylline oracles in order to perpetuate its dominance. In the first century cynical practices became even more blatant as political rivals within the aristocracy used the state religion to further their own personal or factional interests.

Hostility to Foreign Cults   Nor was the aristocracy willing to renew the official religion by sanctioning popular foreign cults and mystery religions. They might not be so easy to control as the traditional cults. A senatorial decree banned proselytizing Jewish immigrants in 139 B.C. and did not tolerate synagogues until the influx of Pompey's Jewish captives in 61. The prohibition of the Egyptian worship of Isis and Serapis was vigorously enforced in 58 by the destruction of unauthorized altars to Isis on the Capitoline. The first new god to be recognized at Rome since Cybele, the Great Mother (*Magna Mater*), in 104 B.C. was the assassinated Julius Caesar in 42 B.C. for obvious political motives.

The increasing exposure of Roman aristocrats to the rationalism of Hellenistic Greek philosophy probably contributed to their cynical attitude toward the old state religion. On the other hand, their declining faith probably caused them to become more interested in exploring philosophical alternatives. Stoic philosophy, especially as modified in the late second and early first centuries B.C. by the philo-Roman Panaetius of Rhodes and his pupil Posidonius of Apamea, appealed to Romans like Cato the Younger and Brutus, who saw support for traditional Roman morality in Stoic ethics. Panaetius emphasized the virtues characteristicly ascribed to a Roman noble: magnanimity, benevolence, generosity, and public service. In 87 B.C., as a Rhodian ambassador to Rome, Posidonius had developed a dislike of Marius. Therefore, in his historical writings he favored Marius' optimate enemies and their outlook, which further endeared his Stoic teachings to men like the younger Cato. Cicero and Pompey had both sat at his feet in Rhodes, and Posidonius was so impressed with

Pompey that he appended a favorable account of Pompey's wars to the fifty-two books of his continuation of Polybius.

Posidonius saw Rome's empire as the earthly reflection of the divine commonwealth of the supreme deity. Its mission was to bring civilization to less advanced people. Statesmen who served this earthly commonwealth well would join philosophers in the heavenly commonwealth after death, an idea that Cicero adopted in his *Republic* to inspire Roman nobles to lives of unselfish political service. Posidonius also believed that the human soul was of the same substance as the heavenly bodies, to which it returned after death. His scientific demonstration of the effect of the moon on earthly tides reinforced this idea and gave great impetus to astrology at Rome. The growing popularity of these ideas, therefore, made it less difficult to accept the notion that the comet seen soon after Caesar's death was his soul ascending to heaven.

Epicureanism   Ironically, Caesar himself and a number of other Romans at this time had adopted the skeptical, materialistic, and very un-Roman philosophy of Epicurus, who had argued that such gods as there were lived beyond this world and took no part in it. He believed that the soul is made up solely of atoms that disperse among the other atoms of the universe upon death. Therefore, he stressed that death is not to be feared and that men should shun the cares of marriage, parenthood, and politics to live quietly in enjoyment of life's true pleasures. Among the Romans, Epicureanism was popularized by Philodemus of Gadara, who came to Italy after the First Mithridatic War and settled on the Bay of Naples at Herculaneum in association with his patron L. Calpurnius Piso Caesoninus, Caesar's father-in-law. Charred papyrus rolls containing some of Philodemus' writings have been found in the remains of Piso's villa, which was destroyed 150 years later by the famous eruption of Vesuvius.

Roman Epicureans were less restrained in taking their pleasures than Epicurus himself

would have approved, yet the Epicurean ideal of a life of pleasant retirement in one's garden may help to explain why Sulla at the height of his power retired and why Lucullus, Caesar, and Sallust lavished so much attention on their pleasure gardens. Perhaps Caesar's Epicureanism also explains his lack of concern when he was warned of plots and bad omens shortly before his assassination.

Peripatetic and Academic Schools   The Peripatetic and skeptical Academic schools of Aristotle and Plato were much less popular at Rome than others. Crassus, however, maintained the Peripatetic Alexander in his household, and Cicero was greatly drawn to the Academic school with its emphasis on the testing of ideas through rational inquiry and debate. Still, in general Cicero was eclectic. He greatly favored Stoic ethics and attitudes, and Peripatetic influences, especially in political thought, can be found too (p. 264). Cicero and other Roman philosophical writers were not trying to advance original ideas; they were mainly interested in making available to fellow Romans the ideas that they admired and found useful in the works of Greek thinkers.

Art and Architecture   As with philosophy, the Romans of the late Republic often imitated the art of the Greek masters. Roman governors and generals ransacked the cities of the Greek East for the paintings and sculptures of famous Greek artists. When originals were not available, well-to-do Romans commissioned copies. Italian stonecutters became adept at the standardized reproduction of famous statues. Artists recreated famous paintings in frescoes, with which the affluent increasingly decorated the walls of their homes, as can be seen from the ruins at Pompeii. Still, native Roman and Italian traditions in realistic portraiture and landscape scenes flourished and became more sophisticated in technique.

Of the visual arts, it was architecture in which the Romans were most creative in the

View of the Roman Forum with the remaining columns of the Temple of Saturn in the right foreground, the Senate House in the center, and the Arch of Septimus Severus to the left of both. (Courtesy of the Italian Travel Office)

first century B.C. They combined native Italian and Etruscan elements with Hellenistic Greek principles to create a distinctive form of architecture. Hellenistic architects stressed the articulated combination of different architectural units into a symmetrical whole along a central axis. The best Greek examples are the acropolis of Pergamum and the Temple of Zeus at Priene.

The buildings of Sulla show the first evidence of this influence. The Tabularium, Record Office, commissioned by Sulla and finished by Catulus in 78, was carefully sited on the brow of the Capitoline just behind the Forum. It not only gave a central backdrop to the Forum, but its colonnaded upper story provided a clear architectural link between the buildings of the Forum and the others on the Capitoline to create an articulated whole. Sulla's most splendid building project, however, was the highly articulated and symmetrical complex known as the Sanctuary of Fortuna Primigenia at Praeneste. Much of it came to view when Allied bombs in World War II destroyed later buildings on the site. The whole sanctuary rose up the side of a hill in terraces. Each terrace was architecturally defined in its own symmetrical style on either side of a central axis. The fourth terrace was

approached from either side by a pair of unique curved ramps leading to a central staircase on the axis. The whole culminated in a little round shrine centered at the top, behind a semicircular set of steps and a curved colonnade.

When Pompey built Rome's first stone theater in 55, this design and his own travels in the East may have inspired him or his architect to design the theater along similar lines. The theater itself, unlike Greek theaters, which were built into solid hillsides, was a freestanding semicircle with the stage and backdrop on the chord and the seats rising in tiers on the arc. To overcome opposition to permanent theaters, Pompey apparently included on the center of the topmost tier a shrine to Venus Victrix. Articulated with this theater was a portico that attached to the back wall of the stage. Two parallel colonnades provided shelter for audiences in case of unexpected rain or places where meetings could be held. The senate was meeting there when Caesar was assassinated before the statue of its builder.

Caesar himself had planned the Basilica Julia to the east of Sulla's Tabularium and across from the rebuilt Basilica Aemilia and approximately parallel to it. In accordance with the new fashion, these roughly parallel

Model of Sulla's Temple of Fortuna Primigenia at Praeneste, which shows the careful symmetrical arrange-
ment of different shapes and architectural elements along a central axis extending from the "notch" at the
center of the covered inclined ramps up the central staircases to the semicircular colonnade at the top. (Courtesy
Fototeca Unione, Rome)

buildings introduced greater axial symmetry to the Forum. Caesar also built an entirely new and symmetrical forum known as the Forum Julium in 46 B.C. It was a rectangle completely surrounded by a colonnade with a peristyle temple of Venus Genetrix set toward the back along the longitudinal axis. Centered in front of the temple on the same axis were an equestrian statue of Caesar and a fountain with statues of nymphs grouped about it. This symmetrical forum set the pattern for all fora subsequently built by the Roman emperors.

The combination of both the Roman arch and vault with the Greek column in the structure of Sulla's Tabularium and Sanctuary of Fortuna Primigenia also set a trend for later Roman architecture. The walls of Pompey's

theater rose up on three tiers of arches, each framed in half-columns: the first with Doric, the second with Ionic, and the third with Corinthian capitals. The facade of the Colosseum received the same treatment over 100 years later. Also, just as in Pompey's theater, the tiers of seats in the Colosseum are supported on vaults.

The Romans achieved greater flexibility of design and larger size in their buildings than the Greeks because they used brick and concrete, which are particularly suitable for constructing the arches and vaults that permit more massive structures. The Romans even built columns out of brick and then faced them with stucco or sheathed them with stone. Concrete allowed decorators to achieve numerous textures on exposed surfaces by inserting shaped or colored stones in various patterns. On the most important buildings, however, at Rome and elsewhere in Italy, architects began to use a greater variety of handsome stone too. Cream-colored travertine limestone from Tibur and the brilliant white marble of Luna (Carrara) came from Italy. Other white and colored marbles of all hues were imported from Greece, the Aegean islands, Asia Minor, and Africa. Rome and Italy in the late Republic had begun to appear like the imperial centers that they had become.

Late Republican Literature　By the first century B.C. writers of Latin comedy, tragedy, and historical epics like Plautus, Terence, Naevius, Accius, Ennius, and Pacuvius had already reached ''classical'' status. Creative younger writers were turning to other genres. Indeed, the Roman populace, swollen by uneducated rural poor and exslaves or immigrants of diverse cultural heritage could no longer appreciate sophisticated comedy or the deep questions posed by tragedy. Dramatic entertainments at Roman festivals lapsed back to simple farce, slapstick, and mime that could be appreciated on the most basic level.

Traditional Roman epic had lost its audience too. Many among the upper classes had become more individualistic in outlook, grown self-indulgent on the spoils of empire, or disillusioned by the civil strife around them. They now had little taste for patriotic epics that celebrated old-fashioned virtues and Roman strength.

The *Novi Poetae* and Catullus　Many young aristocrats, thoroughly educated in all Greek literature, caught up in the fast pace and unconventional mores of cosmopolitan life, and conscious of the difference between themselves and older, more staid generations, became interested in other, more appealing types of literature. Among such youths in the first half of the first century B.C. were a number of poets who have come to be known

as the *Novi Poetae* (''New Poets'') or Neoteric Poets from some references in Cicero, a traditionalist who disapproved of them. It is not known if they referred to themselves as the New Poets or felt any special identity as a group, but it is likely that they did. Many of them were pupils of Valerius Cato, a *grammaticus* and also a poet. They often mentioned each other in their poems and even commented on each other's work.

The *Novi Poetae* modelled their works on the personal and emotional writings of the Alexandrian lyric and elegiac poets. They also delighted in the learned, obscure, and exotic allusions to mythology, literature, and geography that characterized the Alexandrians. They did not write for a large public but for themselves. That is why the works of all but one of them (including the epigrams of Cornificia, the only woman associated with them) have perished except for a choice line or two quoted by some grammarian or commentator on another work.

Catullus (ca. 85–ca. 54 B.C.)　The one New Poet whose work has survived, albeit in a single manuscript from his home town, is Gaius Valerius Catullus of Verona. Little is known of his life. He was born about 85 and died around 54 B.C. His participation in public life was limited to a year of service on the staff of Gaius Memmius, governor of Bithynia in 57, and to some scurrilous poems about Caesar, with whom he was reconciled shortly before he died. Nevertheless, these two people and others addressed in his poems show that he moved in the highest circles of the aristocracy.

It was in such circles that Catullus met a woman with whom he had a torrid love affair. He called her Lesbia, but she was really Clodia, sister of the notorious P. Clodius and wife of Metellus Celer. Apparently Clodia's beauty and charm were equalled only by her promiscuity, as Catullus discovered to his bitter sorrow.

The passionate love and hate, joy and sorrow produced by this relationship inspired many of Catullus' most famous poems. Their emotional intensity still burns with a gemlike flame across the ages to kindle a response that reaches a universal human level. Many are written in elegaic couplets. The most famous is number 85:

I hate and I love. You ask, perhaps, why.
I know not, but feel it happen and am crucified.

This poem and others like it were probably the main inspiration for Cornelius Gallus, who perfected the use of elegy for love poetry, subjective erotic elegy, in the Augustan Age (p. 308).

Catullus' poetry encompasses many other themes as well. Number 101 is a touching lament for his dead brother, whose grave he visited in Asia Minor. In poem 96 he consoles a friend whose wife has just died, and he can move from a lighthearted drinking song in 27 to a celebration of the beauties of his home at Sirmio, to which he has just returned, in number 31. He could even write a reverential hymn to Diana (34) and a long poem charged with ecstatic frenzy on the god Attis (63). Number 64, on the mythical marriage of Peleus and Thetis, is a masterful little epic, *epyllion,* in the Alexandrian manner. Moreover, in all of his poems Catullus shows himself to be a serious craftsman by being the first to adapt many Greek lyric meters to Latin poetry.

Lucretius (ca. 94–ca. 55 B.C.)

One of the contemporary poets who did not share the interests of Catullus and other *Novi Poetae,* although he may have known them, was the Epicurean Titus Lucretius Carus. Even less is known about Lucretius than about Catullus. He was born about 94 and died probably in 55 B.C. His patron was Gaius Memmius, the same man whom Catullus served in Bithynia. A house excavated at Pompeii indicates that Lucretius' family may have lived in the area around the Bay of Naples, where Philodemus and other Epicurean philosophers were concentrated. In a letter, Cicero mentions Lucretius' poetry favorably, but not his subject. Romantic legend has it that Cicero published Lucretius' work after the latter had died. Equally unfounded is the story popularized by Tennyson that Lucretius had been driven mad by a love potion and composed his work in lucid intervals before committing suicide.

Lucretius not only was a dedicated Epicurean but was also a deeply patriotic Roman. He had little in common with passionate young sophisticates like the *Novi Poetae* and their essentially private literary world. Instead, Lucretius tried to renew the genre of patriotic epic. Yet his epic was not a traditional Roman historical epic, like those of Ennius and Naevius, but a didactic epic like the poems of Hesiod and such early Greek philosophers as Parmenides and Empedocles. In fact, the latter's poem *On Nature* may have been the direct inspiration for Lucretius' work, the *De Rerum Natura (On the Nature of Things)* in six books of dactylic hexameter verse. Lucretius' purpose was uniquely Roman, however. He was appalled at the destructive power politics that were leading to violence, instability, and even civil war at Rome. By teaching his fellow Romans the quietistic philosophy of Epicurus, Lucretius hoped to save them from destroying themselves.

Accordingly, Lucretius used the traditional divine invocation required by epic convention at the beginning of his work to express the desire for peace. He asked Venus, symbol of the creative power of nature, to seduce Mars, the personification of destructive war, and beg that he grant peace to Rome. In the rest of the poem, however, the gods do not play any role. With a missionary zeal rare in either Greece or Rome, Lucretius used Epicurus' rationalistic atomic theory to destroy the irrational fears and superstitions that led people to violence and crime. By imparting knowledge of the true nature of reality, Lucretius hoped to convince people that the competition for wealth, fame, and power in order to achieve immortality, or the frenetic search for pleasure to blot out the fear of death are completely vain. Therefore, he argued, people should lead quiet lives, avoid all excess, and preserve the philosophic calm that alone guarantees true happiness free from either pain or anxiety.

As an atomist, Lucretius held that the universe is made up of empty space and atoms —solid yet invisible particles, infinite in number and differing only in size and shape —which swerve and collide as they fall through space, and cluster together to form all animate and inanimate things: the earth, the stars, plants, animals, the bodies and even the souls of men. All things, even the human soul, must come from something or become something else, for, as the individual object dies or disintegrates, its constituent atoms—themselves eternal and indestructible—separate and drift away into space once more. Death, even that of the soul, being nothing but atomic separation, is a process of nature—inevitable, but not to be feared. All sensation and consciousness simply cease.

Nor, maintained Lucretius, are the gods to be feared, who, though they do exist, dwell apart in celestial space and do not concern themselves with human affairs. The only thing to be feared is passionate emotion, which clouds the reason and leads to extremes of behavior, the inevitable result of which is pain. Passion and pain both disrupt reason, but reason secures the understanding of Epicurus' philosophy, which is the only source of real, lasting happiness in life.

Lucretius' philosophical message is completely derived from Epicurus. His originality lay in adapting his message to a Roman context, expressing it in poetic language of great power and beauty, and raising the Latin dactylic hexameter verse to a new level of smoothness and flexibility. In the next generation, Vergil, Rome's greatest epic poet, who studied Epicureanism extensively as a young man, owed a great debt to Lucretius. Not only does Vergil's published hexameter verse show clear parallels with that of Lucretius, but the theme of the destructiveness of passion and the powerful scenes that reveal its force in the *Aeneid* vividly recall Lucretius' *De Rerum Natura*.

Cicero (106–43 B.C.) Even Cicero, who viewed Epicureanism as a threat to all the values that had made Rome strong, recog-

nized the talent in Lucretius' verse. Philosophically, however, Cicero's taste ran to the Stoic and Academic schools. One of Cicero's great contributions to Western literature and thought is his philosophical works. In them he made the Latin language a vehicle for popularizing Greek philosophy among the literate people of his day. Cicero does not deny that his philosophical essays were, for the most part, copies or adaptations of Greek works (as Cicero himself frankly admits in a letter to Atticus). But they were enlivened by anecdote and written in a supple and polished style which has caused them to be read and reread over the centuries.

Among them are *On the Definitions of Good and Evil,* in which he discussed Epicurean, Stoic, and Platonic philosophy; the *Tusculan Disputations,* a discourse on the essentials of human happiness; *De Natura Deorum (On the Nature of the Gods),* which deals with Stoic physics. The best known of his treatises are the two short dialogues, *De Amicitia (On Friendship),* and *De Senectute (On Old Age).*

Cicero's enlightened philosophy, worthy of the name *humanism,* deals with human beings, their essential nature, the validity of their perceptions and their place in the universe. From Cicero's Stoic insistence on proper regard for all people stems the modern idea that all are created equal.

Cicero wrote two treatises on political science, the more important of which, *De Re Publica (On the State),* is an imaginary dialogue between Scipio Aemilianus and his friends. Its unfinished sequel, *De Legibus (On the Laws),* was a discussion by Cicero, Atticus, and Quintus Cicero. Both treatises set forth political theories based partly on Stoic teachings, partly on the scepticism of the New Academy as outlined in the *De Officiis* and other philosophical works, and to a large degree on Cicero's own idealized concept of the Roman Republican constitution.

The New Academy upheld the doctrine of its founder, Carneades (ca. 214–129 B.C.), that some ideas are more probable than others. Although Cicero was an avowed adherent of the New Academy, he was strongly attracted to Stoicism because he saw in it a close affinity to the Roman moral code. He admired the Stoic doctrine of duties and its sublime belief in fortitude. Cicero unreservedly accepted Reason as the governing principle of the universe and the foundation of natural law. True law, or reason in harmony with nature, is superior to civil or international law. It is the basis of human brotherhood and it is based, in turn, on the natural concept of universal justice implanted in the hearts of men. Cicero's concept of the ideal Republic was consistent with his philosophical ideas. He held that a state guided by an enlightened leader of outstanding prestige, a *princeps civitatis,* with a senate and citizenry observing their separate functions would guarantee a form of government not only stable but capable of reconciling individual freedom with social responsibility. Such a state would combine the best features of monarchy, aristocracy, and democracy and in it all social classes would work together for the common good.

Like Lucretius, Cicero was trying to prevent the Roman aristocrats from ruining the Republic with their destructive rivalries for power and *dignitas.* The *princeps,* through the moral authority of his prestige, would be able to stand above and control the factional rivalries of other ambitious aristocrats. Unlike Lucretius, however, Cicero argued in the *De Re Publica (On the State)* that virtuous behavior on behalf of the state would be rewarded with a blessed afterlife among the gods.

Cicero himself was a *novus homo* recently risen from the local Italian aristocracy, which made up the bulk of the Roman equestrian class. Therefore, he also viewed Roman politics with sympathy for their needs and desires. The grievances of this large and influential class were often exploited in the rivalries of the Forum, as seen in the careers of Gaius Gracchus, Livius Drusus the Younger, Sulpicius Rufus, Marius, Pompey, Crassus, and Caesar. Cicero advocated harmonious relations between the senatorial aristocracy and the equestrian class, a *concordia ordinum,* so that *equites* of talent and political ambition would not be kept from successful careers at Rome

and the senate would look out for equestrian business and financial interests. In this way the *equites* would have every reason to support the political *status quo,* which Cicero thought would guarantee the stability of the Republic.

Cicero's Oratory   It was Cicero's talent as an orator that helped him to break into the exclusive circle of the consular nobility at Rome. For him, moreover, oratory, as the statesman's practical tool for persuading his fellow citizens, was even more important than philosophy. He raised the art of oratory to its highest level as an active force in Roman public life.

Cicero combined substance and style. After delivering a speech, he would polish and refine it for publication by professional copyists, who supplied an even wider audience. Often, note-takers using shorthand would copy a speech as he delivered it in order to supply those who could not wait for the official version. Cicero's sonorous, rolling, rhythmic periods, his pungent and even scurrilous wit, and his marvelous figures of speech constantly delighted a population steeped in an oral culture in which books were rare and mass mechanical or electronic media nonexistent. The art of public speaking, therefore, was a treasured heritage built up by generations of skilled orators. Cicero himself, however, so surpassed his predecessors and contemporaries that only scattered fragments quoted from their speeches by later writers survive.

As in other forms of art, the Romans based their formal oratory on Greek models. In Cicero's day adherents of two rival Greek oratorical styles, the Attic and the Asiatic, vied for popularity. The Asiatic style tended to be florid, grandiloquent, and overwrought, the Attic more simple and restrained. The speeches of Cicero's older contemporary Hortensius, whom he replaced as Rome's leading orator, exemplified the former style; the spare prose of Caesar's *Gallic War* exemplified the latter.

Probably no orator always used the same unvarying style, least of all Cicero. He could be crisp and pointed, grand and verbose, or anywhere in between. Cicero's greatest skill as an orator was in fitting his style to his subject and knowing just what was required for maximum effect as the occasion demanded. For example, in his defense of Sextus Roscius of Ameria, *Pro Roscio Amerino* (80 B.C.), he made a strong case against one of Sulla's henchmen, who had framed Roscius for murder in order to get his property. Sometimes he used a highly colored and contrived style to play upon the jurors' emotions, but in his summation he made a simple, direct, and clear indictment of Sulla's man that was politically difficult and all the more effective for being sincere. In the first of his speeches against C. Verres, the rapacious exgovernor of Sicily, Cicero wasted no time on artificial grandiloquence but let the damaging facts speak for themselves in forceful language that sent Verres scurrying into exile before certain condemnation.

The five speeches of the second *actio* of the *Verrine Orations* were, therefore, never delivered. When Cicero reworked the notes on these speeches for publication he embellished them with all the stylistic virtuosity at his command: sometimes he employed a simple expository style to present the facts, sometimes he took a middle course calculated to charm as much as to instruct, and at other times he pulled out all of the rhetorical stops to sweep everyone away on a hot tide of indignation over Verres' crimes.

Indeed, Cicero was a master of his audience's emotions, and he often used this skill to obfuscate and mislead when his case was weak or his purpose polemical, as, for political reasons, they often were. For example, the first of Cicero's four speeches against Catiline (63 B.C.) is a masterpiece of biting invective based on much suspicion about Catiline but too little evidence to warrant strong action. Cicero's political purpose was to stir hostility among Catiline's fellow senators and panic him into showing his hand. By emotional appeals to patriotism, fearful images of murder and conflagration, devastatingly malicious inuendo, and pure bravado Cicero succeeded.

Such was the power of Cicero to overpower the emotions of an audience with sheer rhetoric that the usually self-controlled Caesar was totally nonplused as he listened to Cicero's defense of Ligarius, *Pro Ligario* (46 B.C.), and dropped the papers in his hands. The fourteen *Philippics* aroused in their object, Mark Antony, such undying hatred that no one could induce him to spare Cicero during the proscriptions of 43. Yet, even Antony probably felt the emotional pull of Cicero's patriotic appeal at the end of the *Second Philippic*, although he would have realized that it was designed to manipulate him.

Works on Oratory　In the period between the Conference of Luca (April, 56 B.C.) and the feverish outburst of the *Philippics* (44 to 43 B.C.), Cicero's opportunities to exercise his oratorical talents were severely limited. He turned them to writing about his craft in a series of instructive works on the theory and practice of oratory: *De Orator* (*On the Orator*, 55 B.C.), *De Optimo Genere Oratorum* (*On the Best Type of Orators*, 52 B.C.), *De Claris Oratoribus* (*Brutus* or *On Famous Orators*, 46 B.C.), *Orator* (*The Orator*, 46 B.C.), and *Topica* (*Topics*, 44 B.C.). When added to his early work *De Inventione* (*On Invention*, 84 B.C.), they form an invaluable record of oratory in the late Roman Republic and the principles followed by its greatest practitioner.

Letters　Cicero was also a prolific letter writer. He was a keen observer of the political scene as well as one of its participants. Comments to others in his letters provide an invaluable firsthand source for the crucial last years of the Republic from 68 to 44 B.C. The private thoughts of a great man do not always live up to his public image, and Cicero provides no exception to the rule. His excessive vanity, his lack of judgment at critical moments, and his willingness to sacrifice truth to political expediency are there for all to see in sixteen books of letters *Ad Atticum* (*To Atticus*), sixteen books *Ad Familiares* (*To His Friends*), three *Ad Quintum Fratrem* (*To His Brother Quintus*), and two *Ad Brutum* (*To Brutus*). Nevertheless, these letters are also full of wit, charm, learning, and grace that have made them a model of epistolary style over the centuries for those who write letters with an eye to posterity.

Poetry Few people remember that Cicero was also a poet. As a young man he seems to have experimented with a number of different meters and genres in the Alexandrian manner, much like the later *Novi Poetae*. All of these works are lost, but most of an early didactic hexameter poem, the *Aratea,* survives. It is a free translation of the *Phaenomena,* a verse rendition of astronomical lore by the Hellenistic Greek poet Aratus. Cicero also wrote an epic poem on the life of Marius and two on events of his own life: the *De Consulatu Suo* on his consulship, and *De Temporibus Suis* on his exile and restoration. The last two found little favor, probably more for their vanity than for any weakness as poetry. In the *Aratea,* however, Cicero was the first writer since Ennius to make a serious attempt at epic verse. His hexameters are more graceful than Ennius' stilted lines, and Cicero's influence, among others, can be seen in the hexameters of Vergil.

Sallust (86–ca. 34 B.C.) Cicero was an *eques* who had broken into the nobility and believed in its basic worth even while he criticized its selfishness and exclusivity. The historian C. Sallustius Crispus, Sallust, was an *eques* who failed to reach the dignity of the consulship and was far less charitable. He, too, had come from a small Italian town, Amiternum in central Italy, and had started on a senatorial career through the *cursus honorum*. He probably was a quaestor in 55, and then in 52 he hoped to advance his career by earning popularity as a tribune. He associated himself with Publius Clodius, the unscrupulous *popularis* politician and personal enemy of Cicero. When Clodius was murdered in 52, Sallust played a leading role in burning down the senate house at his funeral and opposing Cicero, who defended Milo, Clodius' murderer, in court.

Needless to say, there was little love lost between Sallust and Cicero or Clodius' op-timate enemies. The optimate censor of 50 B.C., Appius Claudius Pulcher, ironically Clodius' brother, expelled Sallust from the senate. Sallust sought to restore his position by serving Julius Caesar in the civil war against Pompey and Caesar's optimate enemies. His reward was election to the praetorship in 46 and governorship of the revamped province of Africa. He enriched himself scandalously at the provincials' expense and was tried for extortion. Caesar's influence seems to have saved him, but his political career came to an end. Even Caesar apparently did not think of favoring him for the consulship, and his career was certainly lost with the assassination of Caesar a few months later.

Instead, Sallust retired to luxurious gardens and villas financed by his ill-gotten gains and spent the rest of his life in writing moralistic historical monographs condemning the Roman nobility's ambition, corruption, and greed. Hypocrisy? Perhaps. But the disappointing end to Sallust's own ambitions seems to have driven him to reflect on the conditions that had produced the political turmoil in which it had occurred and to present the lessons that he drew to his countrymen, as Thucydides had once done for the Athenians. The glory that he failed to achieve in politics Sallust hoped to replace with the glory of writing profound works of history that would make his countrymen see the errors of their ways and would also put Roman historiography stylistically on a level equal to that of the best Greek historian, Thucydides. To do that in an age without formal academic institutions, research fellowships, or royalty contracts required the wealth of a leisured aristocrat.

Sallust wrote three historical works: first the *Bellum Catilinae* (*The War of Catiline*), second the *Bellum Jugurthinum* (*The Jugurthine War*), and finally the *Historiae* (*Histories*), whose five books covered events from 78 to 67 B.C. and may have been unfinished at his death. The first two works are extant, while only fragments of the *Histories* remain. Two letters addressed to Caesar are also attributed to Sallust, but their authenticity is often doubted for numerous reasons. They may well be later compositions produced in imitation of Sallust under the influence of the rhetorical training that dominated Roman education in the Imperial Age, as is the spurious *Invective Against Sallust* attributed to Cicero.

The War of Catiline gave Sallust an opportunity to present in a single character all the failings of the old nobility, whose corrupt, selfish, and partisan leadership was destroying the state. In the character of Catiline all of the old Roman virtues are presented as corrupted into their opposites: he was willing to provoke civil war with his considerable talents in order to satisfy his own greed and ambition. In *The Jugurthine War* Sallust castigates the venality and incompetence of noble leaders who place partisan political advantage above the interests of the state.

The same themes were carried on in the *Histories,* which dealt with the growth of destructive violence and civil strife in the struggles of greedy and ambitious nobles after the death of Sulla. Sallust attributes the origin of these problems to opportunities for great wealth, power, and glory that came with the acquisition of a great empire and after the destruction of Carthage removed any strong foreign enemy whose threat would require internal unity at Rome to oppose it. While Sallust may be criticized for not seeing the origin of the Republic's problems far earlier than the destruction of Carthage and for overemphasizing the aristocracy's failure to maintain idealized Roman standards in the face of temptation, he shows some awareness that the increasingly desperate social and economic conditions of the lower classes were also a serious factor in the growing instability of the Republican system. That is more than can be said of many of his contemporaries.

Sallust was not the first Roman to write a historical monograph, but he did succeed in setting the stylistic standard for which he strove. He consciously revived the archaic language of Cato the Elder with its concrete, pungent vocabulary. In sentence structure he imitated the concise, abrupt style of Thucydides. He favored sharp verbal contrasts and striking antitheses to create memorable, epigrammatic phrases and quotable *sententiae.*

Also in the manner of Thucydides, Sallust expressed many of his views through speeches attributed to the people who took part in the events that he described. This rhetorical approach to history stamped the style of major Roman historians thereafter, as seen in the works of Livy, Tacitus, and Ammianus Marcellinus. In an age where oratory was the main medium of communication, this characteristic would not seem so artificial as it does now. As connoisseurs of rhetoric, Sallust's audience also would have enjoyed these rhetorical interludes in the narrative of events.

Caesar (100–44 B.C.)   Julius Caesar is usually remembered as a glorious conqueror and an assassinated ruler, but he was also an accomplished orator and consummate literary stylist. His success as a general and politician were based in no small part on both. They enabled him to win the loyalty and devotion of his troops, acquire votes, and overcome the arguments of his political foes. Caesar favored the straightforward, lightly adorned Attic style. He used neither the abrupt, sententious style of Sallust nor the highly colored, ornate writing that Cicero thought appropriate for history. Neither did Caesar concentrate on the personalities and moral characters of those who participated in events. He believed that chance was as big a factor in events as the characters of the participants, and he let actions speak for themselves without overt moralizing on his part.

By 50 B.C., Caesar had published the first seven books of *De Bello Gallico (On the Gallic War).* The eighth book was later written by his loyal legate Aulus Hirtius. *De Bello Civili (On the Civil War),* in three books, was probably written in late 48 or early 47 B.C., but was not published until after Caesar's death.

Caesar's description of these wars was a unique combination of history and commentary. Unlike the dry, factual military reports which had prevailed since the time of Alexander the Great, Caesar's commentaries were elegant, rhetorical, and vigorous. No historian has been able to rework them without sacrificing their author's personality and genius. The purpose of *De Bello Gallico* has never been clear. It was once held that it was the military report of the democratic general to the people who had given him his command. Most scholars no longer share this opinion; they hold that Caesar was more likely seeking to impress members of his own class. The common modern view—that Caesar wrote to justify his war in Gaul as a defensive measure—seems hardly correct. For the Romans, no justification or apology was required for a war against barbarians. In waging it the proconsul fulfilled his major duty: the maintenance and extension of the power and dignity of the Roman people. If the commentaries have a motive other than military, it is not apology but more likely self-glorification.

The Civil War was different in both tone and purpose. The consciousness of war guilt is evident, for civil war was the worst of crimes in Roman society, and it was necessary to show that it had been waged only under extreme provocation. According to Caesar's account, a small group of ultrareactionaries had perversely driven him to defend his honor and dignity and the good name and best interests of the Roman people. The men are shown as cruel and vain, cowardly in battle and ignominious in defeat. They begged for mercy; he spared their lives. There are no outrageously false statements in the account, but the truth may be said to have been tested for elasticity.

Literature, from 40 to 31 B.C. During the period of military despotism after Caesar, oratory, being neither useful nor esteemed, languished and declined. Cicero, Caesar, Calvus, and Hortensius all were dead and in the new age had no peers. Gaius Asinius Pollio and Marcus Valerius Messala Corvinus, the best orators of their day, were very good but not great (see pp. 309–310).

Of the prose writers the most notable was Sallust. Of lesser stature were M. Terentius Varro, T. Pomponius Atticus, and Cornelius Nepos.

Varro (116–27 B.C.) The most learned and versatile of all ancient writers was Varro. He wrote with indefatigable industry on a great variety of subjects—history, law, religion, philosophy, education, linguistics, biography, literary criticism, and agriculture. His greatest work was probably the *Antiquities Human and Divine,* which contained a vast array of knowledge as well as many errors. It was in this work that Varro fixed the canonical date for the founding of Rome by Romulus as April 21, 753 B.C. Of his numerous works the only ones to survive are his three valuable books on agriculture, six of his twenty-five books on the Latin language, and many fragments of his *Menippean Satires,* a medley of prose and verse on almost every subject under the sun. In 36 B.C., at the age of eighty, he brought out his monumental work on the theory and practice of farming, a treatise of inestimable value for an understanding of Roman social and economic history.

Atticus (109–32 B.C) and Nepos (ca. 99–ca. 24 B.C.) Varro based part of his research into early Roman history on a chronology of Rome produced by Cicero's old friend T. Pomponius Atticus. This interest in history had prompted Cicero to request that Atticus write a history of his consulship and the suppression of Catiline, but Atticus politely declined. Cornelius Nepos, born about 99 B.C., was a friend of both Cicero and Atticus. He too wrote a Roman chronology, but his main contribution was the popularization of the Greek genre of biography at Rome. He had come to Rome from Cisalpine Gaul early in his life but never became involved in politics, so that he survived unmolested until his death around 24 B.C. In 34 B.C. he published the first edition of his sixteen-volume *De Viris Illustribus (On Illustrious Men),* which contained short biographies of generals, statesmen, writers, and scholars both Roman and non-Roman. He published a revised version after the death of Atticus and added a tribute to his dead friend in the form of an appreciative biography. Only twenty-five of the biographies have survived; the best is that of Atticus. Also of great interest is a biography of Rome's old foe Hannibal, which tells how the jealousy of powerful Carthaginians and the suspicions of many Romans finally drove Hannibal into exile and suicide.

Nepos' style is very easy to read. That he wrote about many Romans and non-Romans and even non-Greeks shows a breadth of outlook that is not common among Roman authors. Unfortunately, like most ancient biographers, he is interested more in drawing moral lessons rather than historical accuracy. Therefore, he often omits valuable historical details and uncritically reproduced errors in his sources.

Politically, the last generation of the Roman Republic had been a disaster. They had failed to meet the challenges produced by the acquisition of a vast empire and the great social and economic changes that it had stimulated. Culturally, however, they must be credited with great creative success. In art, architecture, rhetoric, literature, and scholarship they were worthy successors to the Greeks of earlier generations. They had advanced the distinctive blending of Greek and native Italian traditions that was the hallmark of Roman culture to the point where the next generation could produce a new Golden Age, which rivaled that of classical Greece and became the dominant cultural force in western Europe for centuries.

XXII

The Principate of Augustus, 29 B.C. to A.D. 14

Octavian's acquisition of undisputed mastery of the Roman world by 29 B.C. is a convenient point for beginning a new period in Roman history. The system of government characteristic of the Republic, traditionally founded in 509 B.C., had now given way in reality to the rule of one man, who came to be known as *Imperator* (''emperor''). Therefore, although the Republic had long ago acquired a vast empire, the establishment of a system of government controlled by an emperor marks the beginning of the Roman Empire.

The first 300 years of the Empire are usually dealt with under the subheading Principate, from the word *princeps,* one of the emperors' chief titles up to A.D. 282. The implication of this title was that the emperor, though the acknowledged head of state, was only *primus inter pares,* first among equals within the Roman nobility, and that he governed in cooperation with them. The period after 282, however, is often called the Dominate, because the emperors were undisguisedly autocratic, the title *princeps* was completely abandoned, and the title *dominus,* lord and master, prevailed.

Sources for the Augustan Principate   Most of the information for the political history of Augustus' rule comes from Suetonius' biography of Augustus, Books 52 to 56 of Dio's history, Book 2.86–123 of Velleius Paterculus' brief compendium, and Augustus' own *Res Gestae.* Unfortunately, Livy's eyewitness account down to A.D. 9, Books 134 to 142 of his history, receive the briefest summaries of all in the *Periochae,* and, therefore, their loss is even more acutely felt.

The literary works of the great authors of the Augustan Age (see pp. 305–312) are rich sources for the social, economic, cultural, and intellectual life of the period, as are abundant archaeological remains and the numerous Latin and Greek inscriptions, documents on Egyptian papyri, and coins that have survived. Of great importance for provincial matters is a long Greek inscription from Cyrene, which contains four edicts of Augustus and a senatorial decree and is known as the *Edicts of Cyrene.*

The Triumphal Return to Rome, 29 B.C.   In the late summer of 29 B.C., Octavian returned to Rome in triumph. The senate ratified all his acts, proclaimed his birthday a future holiday, and decreed the erection of triumphal arches at Brundisium and at Rome. The poets hailed the mighty conqueror. On three successive days he held triumphs for Dalmatia, for Actium, and for Egypt, all surpassing in pomp and splendor the triumphs of Julius Caesar. For the first time since the end of the First Punic War in 241 B.C., the doors of the temple of Janus stood closed as the mute but visible sign of peace on land and sea. After a century of civil war and violence, men could at last breathe freely, work, and enjoy peace and prosperity without fear of confiscation, proscription, or violent death.

Problems to Be Faced   Although peace reigned within the empire, the imperial frontiers had yet to be protected lest the barbarians massed beyond the Rhine and the Danube swarm into the rich and peaceful provinces of the Empire. Imperial defense called for a firm policy of aggressive war.

The Roman armies themselves were an even greater potential menace to internal peace and stability than the barbarians. Under the command of ambitious and ruthless generals, they could again turn and rend the state, as they had in the recent past. After Actium, Octavian found himself the master of seventy legions, of which less than thirty would suffice for Imperial defense without bankrupting the weakened treasury. Over these he needed to retain supreme and undivided command and disband the rest. He then had to deal with the problem of finding land on which to settle the veterans of more than forty legions without confiscation of private property or higher taxes, as well as with the heavier and more manifold problem of reconstruction: the creation of a strong central government; the revival of the prestige and authority of the senate, whose power Caesar had weakened; the maintenance of control over the army by the chief of state; the creation of an Imperial administrative service; the regulation of public finance and the administration of the provinces and control over foreign affairs; the problem of finding and securing a suitable successor to himself; the revival of the ancient moral code and the regeneration of the state religion. To carry out all these tasks might well have taxed the strength of a human dynamo.

The sickly Octavian compensated for his poor health by the willpower, determination, political astuteness, and ruthlessness that he had demonstrated from the beginning of his slow and arduous climb to power.

He had returned from the East a popular idol, with a prestige and power such as even Caesar had never possessed. East and West were bound to him by oaths of allegiance, and he had supreme command of the biggest and best army in Roman history, as well as access to the revenues and resources of a rich and mighty empire. The confiscated treasures of the Ptolemies might alone have sufficed to provide land and bonuses for his veterans, feed and amuse for a time the populace of Rome, and even revive the economic prosperity of Italy by permitting the removal of taxes and the initiation of a vast program of public works.

In addition to his financial resources, Octavian had an *auctoritas*, a prestige and a dignity unique in Roman history. At first the "soul" of Julius Caesar, "cleansed" of earthly sin and "translated" into a comet, had been called upon to aid Octavian in his struggle for power. Such "divine" aid was now no longer needed, for Octavian, a war hero and popular idol, was also the unchallenged leader of a powerful political faction and the acknowledged source of all patronage and power.

Even before he had returned from Egypt and the East, the senate and people had been outdoing themselves in voting Octavian special honors, privileges, and titles. He received, along with triumphal arches, games, supplications, and statues, the tribunician right to aid citizens, apparently not only within the first milestone of the city but also throughout the whole Empire; the right to hear judicial appeals; the power to grant pardons in criminal cases tried in popular courts; and the right to raise men to patrician status.

Special Titles   First among the imposing string of titles that Octavian possessed was *Caesar*, his adopted name. The coinage clearly proves that he retained the name even after Actium. Though then no longer needed, indeed temporarily abjured by him and almost blotted from the record, it had yet a great future, illustrious, imperial, even absolutist, later becoming a title worn by all succeeding emperors and, in more recent centuries, by the Kaiser of Germany and the Czar of Russia.

The title *Imperator*, also part of his nomenclature, was a proud and ancient title. A commander-in-chief of a victorious army had always been hailed as *Imperator* and retained the title until after his triumph. Marius, Sulla, Pompey, and Caesar had frequently held it, and Octavian received it twenty-seven times before his death for victories won either by himself or by his legates. Unlike Caesar, Pompey, and all the other generals of the Republic who had this title bestowed upon them, Octavian adopted it as a *praenomen* and permanently retained it as part of his official nomenclature in order to emphasize his military past. Though repudiated by his immediate successors, Tiberius, Caligula, and Claudius, with and after Vespasian, *Imperator* became the standard title of all Roman rulers and survives as the English word "emperor."

Although it never became part of his official nomenclature, outstanding among the titles of Ocatvian was *princeps civitatis* ("first man of the state"), a term usually shortened to *princeps*, from which are derived the words "principate" and "prince." Though it later came to signify something like "monarch" or "emperor," it was neither unique nor new; there had been other *principes*. During the Republic the term *princeps* had meant an ex-consul who had been recognized as a leading senator and a person of great prestige and venerability, *auctoritas*.

The Evolution of the Principate In 29 B.C., Octavian was in a very difficult political and constitutional position. He had allowed the legally constituted triumvirate to lapse on December 31, 33 B.C. in order to deny its powers to Antonius. During the next year Octavian's position was purely personal. He justified his public acts by the oath of personal loyalty sworn by most of the inhabitants of Italy and many in the municipalities throughout the West. Such a purely personal position was

dangerously unorthodox, however, and he sought a more legitimate stance by obtaining election to one of the consulships for 31. He continued to be reelected consul each year thereafter. Still, as consul he claimed precedence over his colleagues on the basis of the earlier personal oath and was accompanied by all twenty-four lictors, as dictators had been before the abolition of that office by Antonius.

To counteract criticism Octavian had promised to give up his extraordinary position and restore the normal operation of the Republican constitution when the war was over. In 29 it was time for Octavian to start making good on that promise, or at least appear to be doing so. If he did not, he could expect the same fate as Julius Caesar or at least some dangerous and difficult opposition. On the other hand, Octavian personally wished to retain the dominant position that he had just won and patriotically realized that if he did not, further destructive power struggles would probably result. Octavian's task, then, was to restore the old Republican constitution enough to satisfy many, high and low, who earnestly desired it, without surrendering so much power that he would undermine his own hard-won supremacy and risk the return of the instability that had characterized the previous century of Republican government.

It was a difficult and delicate balancing act that he had to perform on a very thin rope and without a safety net. He had good examples of what not to do: Sulla had been too reactionary and anachronistic in designing his constitution; Caesar had pursued one-man rule too obviously; Pompey and Antonius had never gained adequate trust from the nobility. Still, Octavian had no model of what to do. His cautiousness, patience, determination, and shrewdness would be taxed to their fullest as he tried to work out an acceptable form of government over the next ten years.

Initial Reforms Octavian took the first visible step on the road to political reconstruction when he and Agrippa took office as consuls on January 1, 28 B.C. He surrendered twelve of his extraordinary twenty-four lictors and handed them over to Agrippa to indicate that equality had been restored to his consular colleague in accordance with normal Republican practice. The next step was to acquire a grant of censorial power for himself and Agrippa in order to register citizens and revise the roll of the senate. Revision of the senate was imperative if his claim to restoring constitutional normalcy was to have any credibility. The senate had been the centerpiece of the old constitution and the pride of the old nobility, whose good will and cooperation Octavian urgently needed. The senate had recently lost much prestige, however, because Caesar and the triumvirs had greatly increased its size with the addition of many obscure and unworthy individuals in return for political services. Those were now the kind of men that Octavian wanted to eliminate. He did not purge anyone on the basis of Republicanism or lack of support in the civil war. That would merely have raised hostility among those who wished to restore the independence of the senate and whom he wished to please. Octavian and Agrippa succeeded in reducing the size of the senate from about one thousand to about eight hundred this time. With further purges in 18 and 13 B.C., Octavian ultimately lowered it to six hundred, the figure established by Sulla.

By reducing the number of quaestors in 28 B.C. from forty back to the twenty set by Sulla, Octavian ensured in any case that membership in the senate could not have been maintained at one thousand by the practice of admitting exquaestors. He also tried to ensure the worthiness of future new members by restricting the quaestorship to men at least twenty-five years old, of senatorial family and good moral character, who had had military training and possessed property worth at least 800,000 sesterces (later 1 million). Men of equestrian rank could also hold the quaestorship if they had held one or more of certain inferior magistracies. Octavian pleased traditionalists by cutting back the number of praetors from sixteen to the Sullan eight. Finally, he lowered the minimum ages for the praetorship and consulship to thirty-two and thirty-five respectively.

Octavian made admission into the equestrian order dependent, as before, upon a minimum property valuation of 400,000 sesterces. To invigorate both the equestrian and senatorial orders with new blood, Octavian adopted Caesar's policy of admitting a few rich and aristocratic residents of the Italian *municipia* and even of the Roman colonies of Gaul and Spain. Future emperors would continue that policy on a much more extensive scale.

The Settlement of 27 B.C. On the thirteenth of January, 27 B.C., Octavian dramatically appeared before the purged and rejuvenated senate and offered to surrender all his powers to the senate and the Roman people. That solemn and dramatic act, seemingly portending the full restoration of the Republic, aroused, as he probably expected, more trepidation than joy. Overwhelmed by the noble gesture, the majority of the senators, probably inspired by his close friends, prevailed upon him to accept proconsular power for ten years over the large and geographically separated single province of Spain, Gaul, Syria and Egypt, where most of the legions were stationed. As with Pompey during the pirate war, Augustus had the right to appoint legates of consular and praetorian rank and to make war and peace as he saw fit.

In the new division of power, the senate resumed control over Rome and Italy and over the provinces of Sicily, Sardinia and Corsica, Illyricum, Macedonia, Greece, Asia, Bithynia, Crete-Cyrene, and Africa. Octavian was to govern the "imperial" provinces through his own legates or deputies, while the senate controlled the "senatorial" provinces through proconsuls recruited from the ranks of exconsuls and expraetors.* The *princeps,* who continued to be elected consul each year, probably

---

* The so-called senatorial provinces were, according to Dio (53.12.2 and 53.13.1), generally peaceful and, unlike the "imperial" provinces, did not require a garrison of legionary troops. This distinction did not always hold, for the proconsuls of the senatorial provinces of Africa, Illyricum, and Macedonia had legionary troops under their command at various times during the early Principate.

maintained effective control over the governors of the "senatorial" provinces either through his *auctoritas* or the weight of his *imperium* as both consul and proconsul. He thus retained as much real power after his so-called restoration of the Republic as he had had before.

Three days after Octavian's "surrender" of power, the senate met to honor the restorer of the Republic. A laurel wreath was to be placed above the door posts of his house and a golden shield inscribed with his virtues of valor, clemency, justice, and piety was to be hung up in the senate. An even greater honor was the conferral upon him of the name *Augustus* ("Revered"), of exalted connotation and religious association.

Further Reforms The new Augustus, in turn, exalted the senate and augmented its powers. He restored its control over public finance and even the right, for a time at least, of coining money in gold and silver. Some time after 23 B.C. the senate became a supreme court to judge cases of extortion in the senatorial provinces and to hear appeals from Italy and the provinces. Though Augustus continued to recognize the popular assemblies as law-making bodies, he permitted the senate to issue decrees having the force of law without ratification by the people. Officially, the senate became a full partner in the government. Theoretically, it was even more: the ultimate source of power of the *princeps*. What it had granted it could also take away.

Unanticipated Problems Hoping that he had effectively solved the constitutional problems that he confronted, Augustus left Rome in late 27 to take control of urgent military operations in his provinces of Gaul and Spain. He was not to return for almost three years. During that time, however, it became increasingly clear that his constitutional sleight of hand had not been so effective as he had hoped. Many of the old nobles were not happy with it. In 26, for example, while he conducted wars in Spain, he had tried to retain control of events in Rome by reviving the ancient office

of Prefect of the City. His appointee was Marcus Valerius Messala Corvinus, a former partisan of Brutus and Cassius before he had switched to Antonius and finally Augustus. The office had its roots in the pre-Republican monarchy, however, and had fallen into disuse with the growth of the praetorship after 367 B.C. Messala held the office for only six days before he resigned it as unconstitutional. (Eventually Augustus did succeed in reviving the office, but he abandoned it for now.) Obviously the old Republicans were beginning to grumble.

The lavish honors that Augustus' friends continued to propose in the senate further aroused resentment among the old nobility. After Augustus returned from Spain because of poor health in late 24, they were even more offended when in early 23 he interfered in the treason trial of a senatorial governor and obtained his condemnation. Shortly thereafter an assassination plot hatched by disgruntled nobles was discovered. It was quietly suppressed, but before Augustus could do anything to remedy the source of discontent he fell gravely ill.

The Settlement of 23 B.C. Upon his recovery, Augustus made further constitutional adjustments in order to preserve both himself and political stability. The major irritant to the old nobles was Augustus' continued tenure of the consulship. That was too reminiscent of Marius and Caesar, whose careers were not pleasing to traditionalist Republicans. Moreover, the consulship was the goal of every ambitious senator. By holding one of the consulships himself year after year, Augustus was reducing by half the consulships available to others. After consulting with members of the senate, Augustus resigned his consulship on July 1, 23 B.C. In return he received (or possibly reemphasized) the full tribunician power, *tribunicia potestas*. He had enjoyed tribunician sacrosanctity since 36 and the right of aiding citizens, *auxilium,* since 30. In 30 he had been voted full tribunician power but either refused it or did not make use of it. Now, he made it the official legal foundation of his position, and from this date he numbered the years of his principate by the number of years that he had held the *tribunicia potestas* (abbreviated "T.P." on his coins).

The power of a tribune gave Augustus many important rights and privileges: he could convene meetings of the senate; present legislation for approval by the *concilium plebis*; and submit motions in writing to the senate, which took precedence over all other business. Nevertheless, he needed more powers to make up for the loss of the consulship. Though no longer consul, Augustus was allowed to retain the consular right to nominate candidates for office. In addition, of course, he had the same prerogative as any high-ranking individual to endorse candidates once their candidacies had been accepted. Once elected, however, all incoming magistrates were required to swear that they would uphold all past and future public acts of Augustus. Also, he was granted the right to nominate jurors to the various standing courts, which gave him additional control over the administration of justice. Finally, to make up for his loss of the consulship, his proconsular *imperium* was strengthened. Augustus was allowed to retain it in the city, and it was made *maius* ("greater") so that he could still override other provincial governors and exercise command over all legions if need be. This *imperium* was renewed at intervals of five or ten years in 18, 13, and 8 B.C. and A.D. 3 and 13.

Other adjustments were also made in 23 B.C. Augustus increased the number of praetors from eight to ten, the two new ones being placed in charge of the city's treasury. To provide two additional governorships for the increased number of expraetors that would result, he transferred to the senate control of *Gallia Narbonensis* (Provence) and Cyprus. (Provinces annexed after 23 needed garrisons and were kept by him.) If not in 23, then some time later, the senate acquired the right to try fellow senators accused of political or criminal offenses. Suits brought against senatorial governors by provincials simply for the restitution of allegedly misappropriated property were allowed to be tried by a small *ad hoc* committee of fellow senators. The ghost of Sulla would

have been pleased!

Acquisition of Further Powers   While traditionalist nobles might have approved of the changes made in 23, the populace of Rome did not. In 22 a combination of flood and famine made life very difficult for the ordinary citizens. They were not impressed by how the senate handled matters and riotously demanded that Augustus be given a perpetual consulship or dictatorship and that he take up the censorship and curatorship of the grain supply, *cura annonae,* himself. He refused the consulship, dictatorship, and censorship, but with his vast resources, he was able to alleviate the grain shortage within a few days. Also in 22, because it was less dignified for the senate to be summoned by a person with only tribunician power, Augustus accepted the consular right to summon the senate.

In the spring of 22, Augustus departed to take care of affairs in the provinces, and the senate was left to handle affairs without him. Later that year, the people refused to elect more than one consul, and he had to intervene. He refused to accept the other consulship but persuaded the people to accept his own personal nominee, a noble with good Republican credentials. Much the same also happened in 21, 20, and 19. Also in 19, candidates whom Augustus rejected for the quaestorship refused to withdraw. Worse still, Egnatius Rufus, who had become very popular by organizing a fire department for Rome at his own expense and sponsoring splendid games as aedile, illegally ran for the consulship right after his praetorship. A majority of senators passed the *Senatus Consultum Ultimum* and begged Augustus to return and restore order.

The Settlement of 19 B.C.   Augustus' return on October 12, 19 B.C. was declared a national holiday. He was voted further consular powers: perhaps the right to appoint a prefect of the city in his absence; the use of twelve fasces; and the right to sit on a curule chair between the two annual consuls. It must have become clear to Augustus and many traditionalist nobles as well that he had given up too much in 23. Now he had regained anything of importance that he had lost in giving up the consulship. Although he still did not have the title of consul, he was in effect a third consul. The nobles could now happily vie for the two annual consulships, and the common people could be reassured that their hero was in control when they saw him acting with the powers of a consul and being treated like one.

Minor Alterations after 19 B.C.   The settlement of 19 B.C. was the last major series of constitutional adjustments and changes in Augustus' power. Occasional alterations were made over the years, however. In 18, Augustus revised the rolls of the senate once more and reduced it to six hundred members, and he had the right of judicial appeal transferred from the people to himself. In 15 B.C., he acquired the sole right to coin gold and silver. In 12 B.C., when his old triumviral partner Lepidus died, Augustus was elected *Pontifex Maximus* in his place. That office gave him great prestige as head of the state religion, and it was kept by all subsequent Roman emperors, even Christian ones, until Gratian (ca.A.D.375). Further prestige accrued to Augustus in 2 B.C., when the senate voted him the title *Pater Patriae,* "Father of his Country," an honor formerly voted Cicero after the suppression of the Catilinarian conspiracy.

After 18 B.C., therefore, the form of the Augustan principate was fairly well fixed and the stability of the state seemed secure. Augustus himself was confident enough to celebrate the beginning of a new era with the holding of the Secular Games of 17 B.C. Like many ancient peoples, the Romans believed that the history of the world moved in a cycle of epochs (*saecla*: hence the word "secular"). Each *saeclum* was often calculated at 100 or 110 years, and the tenth of the cycle was thought to inaugurate a new Golden Age. With a little prompting from Augustus, who was a member, the board of priests who were in charge of the Sibylline Books indicated that the tenth era of the current cycle was about to begin in 17 B.C. The celebration of magnificent festival

games in honor of the event would give Augustus the perfect opportunity to advertise the end of the evil period of political chaos and civil war and the dawn of an era of peace and prosperity under his newly "restored" Republic. The message was clear. The wounds of civil war had now been healed, and health had returned to the body politic. No more fitting symbol of that idea can be found than the fact that the most important religious element of the whole celebration, a joyous hymn to Apollo, was composed by Horace, a man who had once fought against Augustus at Philippi.

The Nature of the Principate   Augustus had succeeded in creating with his principate a stable form of government that enabled the Roman Empire to enjoy a remarkable degree of peace and prosperity for two centuries. A question that has exercised generations of historians, therefore, is what kind of a government it was. Augustus himself tried to convince people that the old system of the Republic had been restored. Superficially it had. The senate, the magistrates, and the Roman people continued to perform many of their old functions in the familiar way. Augustus' many offices and powers almost invariably had precedents in the Republic. Nevertheless, it was the simultaneous and continuous possession of them that gave him more power than anyone in the Republic (except perhaps dictators) had ever held.

Given Augustus' great personal and constitutional power, the respect that he always showed the senate as an institution, and his eager solicitation of its cooperation in running the Empire, many have characterized Augustus' constitutional settlement as a dyarchy, an equal rule between *princeps* and senate. That, too, is wide of the mark. No matter how much Augustus tried to disguise it or others were willing to overlook it, Augustus was the dominant force at Rome. Cassius Dio, a Greek from the Eastern provinces who wrote a comprehensive history of Rome from the beginning to his own time under Septimus Severus and who was much less squeamish about monarchy than a native Roman, said simply that the Augustan principate was a monarchy.

That judgement is closer to the truth but not wholly satisfactory. It needs refinement and qualification. Augustus' position certainly was monarchic, but it was not like that of the Persian, Hellenistic, or Parthian kings, who provided the standard models of monarchy in both Augustus' and Dio's day. Augustus and his successors did not hold their positions by right of dynastic succession, although in practice dynastic considerations were important, and their powers were not based on any absolute sovereignty of the ruler. Their powers were based on laws and decrees passed by the traditional sources of legitimate authority at Rome—the senate and the people. Gradually, as the traditions of the Republic faded further and further into the past, the force of these restraints weakened in the face of the emperor's overwhelming constitutional powers, financial resources, and raw military force, and the later emperors became absolute monarchs in every way. The principate of Augustus and his successors in the first two centuries A.D., however, was more like an elective, constitutional monarchy. Their powers were bestowed and limited by laws not of their own making. The choice of a successor to the previous emperor had to be ratified by the senate, and his powers were voted anew. The senators could be compelled to give their votes by the threat of military force, but that shows that their votes still meant something. Moreover, if an emperor acted like an arbitrary despot, the traditions of the Republic were still strong enough to foster dangerous conspiracies against him and might even result in his condemnation as a public enemy by a vote of the senate, as happened in the case of Nero. Sovereignty still lay in the hands of another constitutional body.

In the last analysis, of course, the constitutional settlement created by Augustus was uniquely itself. The man who had clawed his way to the top as a ruthless opportunist in civil war had created an enduring monument of statesmanship. He had performed a delicate constitutional balancing act with consummate patience and skill as he bent and shifted to counteract the conflicting forces that would have toppled others from the tightrope of power. He created a veiled monarchy that was strong enough to ensure his own power and the stability of the state, while it preserved enough characteristics of the free Republic to satisfy many Romans' deep respect for the traditional constitutional forms and institutions that had been the focal point of their public lives for centuries. If politics is the art of the possible, then Augustus became one of its greatest masters.

The Problem of Succession   There was one problem that gave Augustus more difficulty than all the rest. The political crisis of 23 B.C. and his almost fatal illness drove Augustus to concentrate attention upon the urgent problem of the succession. Legally and constitutionally, the choice of a successor was not his right, but that of the senate and the Roman people, to whom he owed his power. Nevertheless, he feared that his failure to deal with the problem might, after his death, bring about a civil war between rival candidates for the throne. Also, he naturally hoped to find a successor in his own family and of his own blood. Unfortunately, he had no sons and only one daughter, Julia, who had been married in 25 B.C. to his eighteen-year-old nephew M. Claudius Marcellus, Octavia's son, by her first husband. Augustus assiduously promoted the political advancement of his son-in-law so that he would have accumulated the experience and prestige that would make him the natural one to replace Augustus upon his death. At nineteen, Marcellus was already a member of the senate. In 23 B.C. he was elected curule aedile and served also as a pontiff, and then was scheduled for election to the consulship, although he was ten years younger than the legal age.

The election of Marcellus to the consulate was a virtual certainty. He not only enjoyed the backing of Augustus, but had made himself immensely popular during his aedileship by the magnificence of his games and shows. When Augustus fell gravely ill in 23, however, Marcellus was still too young to succeed. The *princeps,* therefore, handed his signet ring to Agrippa to indicate that he should carry on in his place. Under the circumstances, that was the only prudent thing to do. As Augustus' loyal aide and most successful general, Agrippa would have had the military backing necessary to prevent a destructive power struggle in the vacuum that otherwise would have been created if Augustus had died at this point.

When Augustus recovered, he procured for Agrippa *imperium* over all the Imperial provinces and sent him to the East to superintend the affairs of Syria and strengthen the defenses against the Parthians. Not long after Agrippa had departed for the East, Marcellus died (23 B.C.).

The suddenness of Marcellus' death at this point has prompted speculation (ancient and modern) that Agrippa and/or Augustus' wife, Livia, had a hand in it. Such speculation seems more to reflect malicious gossip aimed at discrediting later emperors descended from them than anything else. Agrippa's loyalty to Augustus had always been unswerving, and he had been rewarded far beyond what a man of his equestrian origin could normally have expected. To risk what he had achieved by plotting against the heir apparent seems both out of character and far too risky. Nor does it make sense to see Livia involved in any such plot either. To be sure, her son Tiberius was only two years younger than Marcellus, so that he might have appeared at least as reasonable a choice for Augustus' successor as Marcellus. Still, it is doubtful that Augustus had chosen Marcellus without Livia's approval, upon which he always depended heavily in major decisions. As later actions show, both he and Livia saw flaws in Tiberius that made him only the second choice for succession when other reasonable candidates were available.

After the death of Marcellus, Augustus took steps to see that others, preferably of his own family, were available. In 21 B.C. he sent for Agrippa and prevailed upon him to divorce

his wife and marry Julia. In 18 B.C. he had obtained the extension of Agrippa's *imperium* over the senatorial provinces as well and even had the tribunician power conferred upon him for five years. Agrippa, always the faithful deputy, was now son-in-law, coregent, and heir presumptive to the Augustan throne. Nor was that all. In 17 B.C. the *princeps* adopted, under the names of Gaius and Lucius Caesar, the two young sons of Julia and Agrippa to settle the problem of succession not just for one but for two generations to come.

In 12 B.C., however, Agrippa's heart failed, and he died. Agrippa's two sons, Lucius and Gaius, whom the *princeps* had adopted as his own, were still too young to take part in affairs of state. The farsighted plans of the *princeps* to choose a successor seemed to have gone awry.

Tiberius would have to be given a more prominent role, if only as a stopgap. Tiberius himself had served Augustus well on numerous military assignments and had held the consulship in 13 B.C. He seems to have been comfortable as a loyal subordinate. He might have happily accepted a secondary role as regent for Augustus' young adopted sons if Augustus had not made him divorce his beloved Vipsania, Agrippa's daughter by his first wife, and marry Julia, the young widow of Marcellus and Agrippa. Tiberius did not like her gay and frivolous ways, nor did she like her new husband—grim, austere, and reserved. Julia, pushed about as a political pawn from one husband to another, soon turned for comfort to more experienced lovers.

Tiberius was enraged by her conduct and the resulting insults to his dignity. Still, Augustus came to rely on him more and more. Tiberius' popular and talented younger brother, Drusus, was killed by a fall from his horse after a successful invasion of Germany in 9 B.C. In 8, when Augustus' *imperium* over his provinces was renewed for ten years, Tiberius seems to have been given a share, which would have given him command of the bulk of the Empire's legions in an emergency. In 6 B.C., Tiberius even obtained the tribunician power for five years. Clearly, Tiberius would be in a position to take Augustus' place in the event of a crisis.

The five-year grant of tribunician power neither appeased Tiberius nor averted the impending personal crisis over Julia. Rather than being upset over Augustus' steps to advance the careers of his young adopted sons, Tiberius may have felt that it was not necessary for him to put up with his unhappy personal situation any longer. Bitter and morose, Tiberius retired to Rhodes to sulk for almost a decade. That Tiberius seems to have broken under the strains placed upon him may confirm Augustus' judgement that he was not really the best man to bear the great burdens of the principate. Finally, however, Augustus, himself grown disturbed by Julia's flagrant adulteries, had her exiled to a desert island in 2 B.C. He executed some of her paramours (who were more guilty of conspiracy against the regime than of vice) and banished others. Even Tiberius interceded on Julia's behalf, but unsuccessfully. The *princeps* would not relent.

Again fate intervened in favor of Tiberius and shattered Augustus' hope of a successor of his own blood. In A.D. 2, the year of Tiberius' return from Rhodes, Lucius Caesar died on the way to Spain. Two years later Gaius, after a treacherous attack in Armenia, died of his wounds. The *princeps* had no choice but to turn to Tiberius. In grief and frustration he adopted Tiberius as his son in A.D. 4 and obtained a ten-year grant of the tribunician power for him as well as a grant of *imperium* in the provinces.

Over the years, Tiberius clearly acquired the position of a coregent as Augustus became older and more frail. In A.D. 13, when Tiberius' tribunician power was renewed along with another grant of *imperium* for both him and Augustus, there was no question that he was Augustus' equal partner. When Augustus died a year later, Tiberius was already in place and the smooth succession for which Augustus had carefully planned automatically took place.

Unfortunately, in his attempt to secure the eventual succession of a member of his own family, Augustus complicated things for the future. At the same time that he adopted Tiberius, he adopted Agrippa's surviving son, Agrippa Postumus, who was also the son of his daughter Julia. He also required Tiberius to adopt Germanicus, the son of his dead brother, Drusus. Germanicus' mother had the blood of Augustus' family because she was a daughter of Augustus' sister, Octavia, by Marcus Antonius. The tie was also strengthened by having Germanicus marry Agrippina, a daughter of Julia and Agrippa. Tiberius' own son, also named Drusus, who was not a blood relative to Augustus, was relegated to an inferior position because he was only a Claudian. Augustus' attempts to manipulate the succession in favor of his own Julian side of the imperial family created unfortunate tensions and rivalries in later generations.

XXIII

Systematic Reform under Augustus

Aside from the difficult task of creating an acceptable constitutional solution to Rome's political crisis and providing a successor to himself, Augustus also had to work out an effective and efficient system of administration for the city of Rome and its vast empire, whose population has been estimated at between seventy and one hundred million. Under the Republic, both the city and the provinces had been administered rather haphazardly by the yearly magistrates and provincial promagistrates on short-term assignments. Theoretically, the whole senate, with its collective wisdom, was supposed to offer sound guidance and provide coherence. In practice, that was not always the case. With the growing complexity of affairs, the senators did not have the time to give adequate attention to many problems. Other senators often had not gained any more direct familiarity with problems during their short tenure of various offices and posts than those whom they were supposed to advise. Finally, communications to the provinces were slow, so that governors were often left to face crises on their own. In the past, this situation had helped to create emergencies that ambitious men could exploit for their own aggrandizement. Also, the Republican practice of not paying high officials any salary greatly increased the temptation to engage in graft and corruption, which contributed to provincial unrest. Therefore, Augustus was anxious to institute administrative reforms.

Evolution of an Administrative System Between 27 and 18 B.C. Augustus had secured the appointment of a senatorial committee to assist him in preparing the agenda for meetings of the senate. This committee, often called the *concilium principis* (Council of the Princeps), consisting of the consuls, one representative from each of the other magistracies, and fifteen senators selected by lot, was to change every six months. As reorganized in A.D. 13 and reinforced by members of the imperial family and from the equestrian order, the committee began to assume functions formerly belonging to the senate. Even as reorganized, it was not a true cabinet or privy council. Meeting more or less publicly, it was an administrative, not a policy-making, body.

The real predecessor of the later imperial privy council, however, was not this clumsy, rotating committee of the senate, which was abandoned by Augustus' successor, but small coteries of top-flight administrators, close friends of Augustus, high-ranking senators, legal experts, and other specialists, who met informally and behind closed doors. They decided the policy of the government, the legislation to be presented before meetings of the senate and the popular assemblies, the candidates whom it might please Augustus to recommend at the coming elections, the next governor of such and such a province, and all matters pertaining to public finance, foreign affairs, law, religion, and the administration of the empire.

The Beginning of an Imperial Bureaucracy

One of the outstanding achievements of Augustus was the creation of a permanent administrative staff for the Empire, a task begun early in his reign but still uncompleted at the time of his death. The trained and salaried staff that he slowly built up was the predecessor of the imperial bureaucracy, which enabled the later emperors to maintain executive control over the Roman world state.

The idea of trained administrators was not entirely new. Since the Second Punic War provincial governors, administrators, and even the proprietors of large and scattered estates had employed their freedmen and personal slaves as secretaries, accountants, and business managers. Pompey had engaged such assistance in his administration of the grain supply and in the government of his provinces. Augustus had inherited from Caesar a large corps of trained slaves and personal agents, the nucleus of the complex bureaucratic organization that he was later to extend over all the empire.

Never until the principate of Augustus had the need for trained administrators been more urgent—in Rome, for the administration of such vital services as the grain supply (*cura annonae*), the grain dole (*frumentatio*), the water supply (*cura aquae*), police and fire protection, the prevention of floods, the construction and maintenance of streets and marketplaces, and the erection and repair of temples and public buildings; in Italy, for the preservation of law and order and for the construction and maintenance of such public works as roads and bridges; in the provinces, for the management of the emperor's private estates, the collection of taxes, the supplying of the armies with provisions and equipment, public works, and the imperial postal system (*cursus publicus*).

Senators in Imperial Administration

In his administrative organization, Augustus employed people of every social class—senators, equestrians, freedmen, and even slaves. The Police Commissioner (*praefectus urbi*), who had under his command a police force, the first in Rome's history, of three cohorts of one thousand men each, was at first always a senator of consular rank; so was the Water Commissioner, whom Augustus appointed in 12 B.C. to supervise, with the assistance of two other senators, the 240 slaves whom Agrippa had trained to service the aqueducts and water mains of the city. Another board of five senators dealt with the flood problem along the Tiber. Two senators of consular rank presided until A.D. 6 over the vitally important grain commission, which had branch offices at the port of Puteoli near Naples as well as in the grain-producing provinces.

Equestrians in Imperial Administration

Although Augustus, especially in the early years of his principate, conferred upon senators positions of dignity and prominence, he drew many of his top-ranking administrators from the equestrian class. The *equites* had acquired valuable experience, especially in the fields of finance, taxation, and commerce, of which senators had little knowledge. For more than a century the *equites* had been exploiting the natural resources of the Empire (mines, forests, and fisheries), had set up large banking, shipping, industrial, and commercial monopolies, and through their tax-farming companies had unmercifully wrung taxes from the provinces.

Now somewhat restricted as tax gatherers by the reforms of Caesar and Augustus, they were glad of the opportunity of rendering a more useful and honorable service. Augustus, in turn, welcomed their services because he regarded them as more reliable and less politically dangerous than senators, and more dependent upon him for patronage and future advancement. Eventually, faithful service could advance an *eques* to membership in the senate where, as a *novus homo* obligated to Augustus, he helped keep that vital body loyal to him.

The careers open to equestrians were military, judicial, financial, and administrative. A young *eques* usually began his career as a prefect of an auxiliary cavalry squadron, advanced to tribune of a cohort or legion, then to prefect of a cohort. A prefect of the engineers (*praefectus fabrum*) could also look forward to a future of some importance.

Military service often varied in length. *Equites,* such as the historian Velleius Paterculus, usually served eight years. Others served longer. Some even chose the military life as a career: *equites* frequently commanded legions on garrison duty, particularly in Egypt, a land forbidden to senators. After a year or two in the regular army, some *equites* served as attorneys in the civil administration; others as officers with the Praetorian Guard (the Imperial guard—preserver of law and order in Rome and Italy), *cohortes urbanae* (the urban police), or the *vigiles* (fire department), which Augustus organized after Egnatius Rufus had become dangerously popular by providing such a service himself; or, more frequently still, as procurators, or imperial agents in the provinces.

In the Imperial provinces a procurator was the emperor's financial agent, his tax collector and paymaster; in the senatorial provinces, his financial agent, manager of his private estates, and collector of the revenues therefrom. He also served as a special observer. A corrupt and rapacious governor had to be exceedingly wary, lest he be liable to stern retribution at termination of office. The procurator was often more powerful even than a governor of consular senatorial rank.

As prefects, *equites* might also govern provinces, especially the more backward and turbulent ones, such as Rhaetia and Noricum north and east of the Alps, not to speak of Egypt, the richest and most important of all, the eminence and power of whose prefect even the very proudest senatorial governor might envy.

Second in power to the prefect of Egypt were the two prefects (also of equestrian rank) whom Augustus had in 2 B.C. placed in joint command over the nine cohorts of the Praetorian Guard. Under Tiberius the joint Praetorian prefecture was eliminated in favor of a single Praetorian prefect. Under later emperors, the Praetorian prefect became chief of staff of all armies, head of the bureaucracy, the highest judge of appeals in the Empire, eventually the maker and unmaker of emperors, and on occasion ascended the throne himself.

Two other prefectures, created around A.D. 6, were less important, but often served as stepping stones to higher office. One belonged to the commissioner of the grain administration, the other to the prefect of the *Vigiles,* a corps of seven cohorts, each consisting of one thousand former slaves, who patrolled the streets at night and guarded the city against riot or fire.

Freedmen in Imperial Administration   The rise of the *equites* in Imperial administration was neither as rapid nor as spectacular as that of the freedmen, some of whom ultimately attained positions more powerful than those held by equestrians, senators, consuls, or provincial governors.

At first the freedmen performed the more menial tasks. Their willingness to take orders, their subservience and loyalty proved in the end their greatest asset. By dint of hard work, thrift, loyalty, and intelligence the freedmen gradually began to forge ahead and occupy positions of opulence and power under later emperors.

The bureaucratic tasks of imperial correspondence became their monopoly. As a result of the growing needs and complexity of a great empire, the services rendered by freedmen finally proved more essential to imperial administration than military commands or governorships. The routine work of the various bureaus created by Augustus required large numbers of accountants, auditors, secretaries, and clerks. In this vast organization freedmen held the higher and better paid jobs, slaves the more menial and obscure. The secretarial bureaus, as important to the Roman Empire as the departments of state, treasury, war, and commerce to a modern state, remained the monopoly of the freedmen class and a source of immense power.

Many of them were shrewd and skillful managers, who soon came to determine how much the state should spend on armaments, on aqueducts, temples, palaces, games, and spectacles; how much on roads, bridges, harbors; the weight and fineness of gold or silver coin; the taxes or tribute provinces must pay; even the salaries governors, prefects, procurators, and other civil servants should receive.

Finally, certain freedmen in high positions began to receive petitions and requests from every part of the Empire—complaints of extortion from provincial councils, applications for offices or priesthoods, prayers for manumission, petitions for imperial decorations. The option of ignoring or bringing such petitions to the emperor's notice gave these freedmen officers positions of real patronage and power.

Manipulation of the Popular Assemblies In directing the administration of Rome and the Empire, it was important for Augustus to influence the popular assemblies in their electoral and legislative functions. As did any prominent man, he had the right to canvass voters on behalf of candidates whom he favored. Through his consular *imperium* he shared with the consuls the right to accept or reject men who wished to be candidates. These two rights, *commendatio* and *nominatio,* in combination with his great personal popularity and *auctoritas* gave a major advantage to people whom he preferred.

Still, Augustus did not always get his way by these means, and he was reluctant to interfere too much in consular elections lest he offend the nobles, who continued to dominate the consulship for a number of years and often employed bribery and violence to do so. In

A.D. 5, therefore, he induced the consuls to propose the *lex Valeria Cornelia,* which altered the procedure for voting in the Centuriate Assembly. It established in honor of the dead Gaius and Lucius Caesar ten centuries comprised of the six hundred senators and the three thousand *equites* enrolled as jurors. They were to vote first and indicate their preference for two consular candidates and twelve praetorian. The remaining centuries would then usually follow their lead in the rest of the voting. From that time on, the majority of *equites* in these ten tribes usually secured the election of "new men," who were much to Augustus' liking.

The common people were pleased with Augustus' attempts to influence the outcome of elections. They wanted him to have loyal magistrates and demanded to know whom he preferred. In A.D. 8, when he was no longer strong enough to canvass for candidates in person, he began to post lists of those candidates whom he commended to the voters.

Augustus' power to influence legislation was also great. By virtue of his *tribunicia potestas* or consular *imperium,* he could submit bills directly. Usually, however, he preferred to have friendly magistrates submit desired bills, as in the case of the *lex Valeria Cornelia* above.

Military Reforms The armed forces presented Augustus with an even more serious problem than administrative reform. In the late Republic, client armies loyal to their personal commanders had been a major factor in the ability of ambitious commanders to wage civil war. Augustus himself was simply the end of a long line going back through Caesar and Pompey to Marius and Sulla. To have allowed this situation to continue would have undermined Augustus' own power and the peace that he earnestly wished to give Rome. In 27 B.C. he greatly reduced the chances of being faced with a challenge from some ambitious noble commander by having assigned to himself the provinces that contained the most legions, which he placed under the immediate command of his own loyal equestrian legates.

Moreover, all soldiers were required to take an oath of personal allegiance to Augustus.

Reduced Size of Army Augustus' first step in dealing with military problems, however, had been to reduce the sheer number of men under arms and provide them with their expected grants of land. Both of these steps were necessary to reduce the risk of civil disorder from unoccupied and disgruntled soldiers and to reduce the crushing economic burden that the huge armies of the civil war placed upon the exhausted treasury. After Actium, Augustus had demobilized about 300,000 men and cut the number of legions from over sixty to perhaps twenty-eight (about 160,000 men).

He avoided the harsh confiscations that had accompanied his settlement of discharged veterans in 41 B.C. and established new colonies in Italy and throughout the Empire to provide land for his veterans, who also helped to increase the security and Romanization of the surrounding areas. The vast wealth of Egypt gave Augustus the funds necessary to carry out this colonization scheme without increasing taxes or denying compensation to those whose land was used for colonial settlements.

A Retirement System Eventually, however, it became impractical to give all veterans land upon discharge. First, to have continued that practice on a regular basis would have required an expensive system of administration to acquire and distribute the land. Second, since the population of the Empire was probably between seventy and one hundred million and the provinces were no longer being depopulated by warfare, the supply of land suitable for distribution was becoming limited and, consequently, increasingly expensive to obtain. Confiscating good land without adequate compensation to previous owners would have set the stage for more unrest, as in the past; yet, to have settled veterans on cheap waste or marginal land would have been equally bad. Many would have failed or given up and, understandably bitter, would have become a threat to internal peace and tranquillity.

Therefore, beginning in A.D. 13, Augustus began to reward many veterans with a system of monetary payments to provide them with financial security upon discharge. Praetorian guardsmen received grants of 5000 denarii and ordinary soldiers 3000, the equivalent of almost fourteen years' pay. That is far more money than the average person could have saved in a lifetime. Moreover, soldiers were encouraged and later required to save some of their pay in a fund kept at legionary headquarters. If spent wisely, their savings and discharge bonuses alone, on the average, would have supplied the daily needs of veterans for as long as they might expect to live after retiring at thirty-five or forty years of age. On the other hand, a retired veteran could invest his money in a small farm or open up a small shop to support himself in retirement. A higher-paid centurion might even have enough from his bonus and savings to acquire equestrian status and pursue a career in higher offices after retirement. The auxiliary troops, however, did not fare as well. Since their bonus, if any was small, their greatest reward was the diploma of citizenship.

During the years from 7 to 2 B.C., Augustus paid discharged veterans no less than 400 million sesterces from his own funds. Even his resources could not stand that kind of expense forever. Therefore, in A.D. 6 he shifted the burden to the state by setting up a special fund *(aerarium militare),* to which he contributed 170 million sesterces of his own money for a start and funded it for the future with the revenues of a five percent sales tax, as well as the gifts and legacies received from his subjects and clients. This move not only relieved the personal finances of the *princeps* but also strengthened the soldiers' loyalty to the state, to which they now looked for their rewards. The value of this system became clear when, as happened under Nero, attempts that were made to substitute poor land for cash in order to save money resulted in unrest among veterans.

Professionalization The armies of the Republic had always been temporary units recruited for particular emergencies and commanded by yearly magistrates or temporary promagistrates. This system had become both inefficient for defending Rome's far-flung territories and dangerous to the state because of the power that it put in the hands of men whose interests were mainly in advancing their own political careers. Augustus created a permanent professional army commanded by men loyal to him and Rome. Terms of service and rates of pay were regulated. Regular soldiers received 225 denarii a year and, at first, were required to serve sixteen years. To relieve the strain on manpower and reduce the drain on retirement funds, however, the term was raised to twenty years, though, in practice, men might have to wait even longer before receiving their discharge.

The backbone of the army was the corps of professional officers comprised of the centurions. They were the lowest commissioned officers and commanded the individual cohorts of the legions. They were often promoted from the ranks of the noncommissioned officers and received triple pay and bonuses. The ranks from military tribune on up, however, were held by equestrians and younger members of the senatorial class in preparation for higher civilian careers. The highest officers were usually members of Augustus' family or nobles of proven loyalty.

The individual legions were made permanent bodies with special numbers and titles. Through the use of identifying symbols for each legion, soldiers were encouraged to develop strong loyalties to their units and strive to enhance their reputations. Each legion tended to be permanently stationed on some sector of the frontier, and around their camps many of the important cities of later Europe grew up.

Legionary soldiers were recruited primarily from Roman citizens in Italy and heavily Romanized areas such as Spain and southern Gaul, although freshly enfranchised natives were also used in the East. Each Roman legion was accompanied by an equal number of auxiliary forces, particularly cavalry, from warlike peoples in the less-developed parts of the Empire and from allied peoples, who often supplied whole units with native officers. Regular pay for auxiliaries was only seventy-five denarii a year, and their term of service was twenty-five years.

The combined total of legionary and auxiliary forces under Augustus was between 250,000 and 300,000 men, not too large an army for defending a frontier at least four thousand miles long. Of the twenty-eight legions, at least eight guarded the Rhineland and seven the Danubian region. Three legions were in Spain, four in Syria, two in Egypt, one in Macedonia, and one in Africa. The equivalent of two others were scattered in cohorts in Asia Minor, Judea, and Gaul.

The Praetorian Guard   In Italy itself, however, Augustus stationed the nine cohorts of the Praetorian Guard. They were specially recruited Roman citizens and were called the Praetorian Guard after the bodyguard of Republican generals. Each cohort probably contained five hundred (later one thousand) men. Three were stationed near Rome and six others in outlying Italian towns. As privileged troops, the praetorians served for only sixteen years and received three-hundred and seventy-five denarii a year, with five thousand upon discharge. Many praetorians were promoted to legionary centurions.

Vigiles and Cohortes Urbanae   The *vigiles* and *cohortes urbanae,* whose duties were to fight fires and maintain public order in Rome, were organized along military lines but were not considered as part of the military. The *vigiles* consisted of seven cohorts of one thousand men apiece, and each was in charge of two of the fourteen regions into which Augustus divided Rome. There were three urban cohorts of one thousand to fifteen hundred men each. The *vigiles* were recruited from freedmen and were commanded by an equestrian Prefect of the Watch (*praefectus vigilum*). The *cohortes urbanae* were freeborn citizens and were commanded by the City Prefect (*praefectus urbi*), a senator of consular rank.

The Imperial Roman Navy The war with Sextus Pompey and the battle of Actium clearly demonstrated the need for a permanent Roman navy. To suppress piracy, defend the shores of Italy, and escort grain transports and trading ships, Augustus created two main fleets, one based at Misenum on the bay of Naples, the other at Ravenna on the Adriatic. He had other bases also, especially at Alexandria, and for a time one at Forum Julii (now Fréjus) in southern Gaul. The fleets, manned by a few slaves or freedmen, but largely by Dalmatians, were under the command of prefects who were sometimes equestrians but more often freedmen. Auxiliary river flotillas patrolled the Rhine, the Danube, the French rivers, and the Nile.

Financial Reconstruction Before the principate of Augustus, the civil wars of the late Republic had depleted the funds of the old senate-controlled state treasury, the *aerarium Saturni,* and exhausted its revenues. The old system of tax collection, corrupt and inefficient at best, had completely broken down, and the absence of any formal budget, regular estimate of tax receipts and expenditures, or census of taxable property only made an already bad situation worse.

Upon that depleted and exhausted treasury fell burdens both numerous and heavy under Augustus: funds for the grain administration that furnished free grain to 200,000 proletarian families in Rome; money for public games and religious festivals; funds for the construction and repair of roads and streets; for maintenance of the water supply and sewers, and the police and fire departments of the capital. Maintenance of these services required enormous sums of money. In addition, the ever mounting costs of imperial defense, administration, and the provision of pensions for war veterans rendered a reform of the financial system absolutely imperative.

Despite the urgent need for action, Augustus at first moved most slowly and circumspectly, wishing to avoid in every way the suspicion of ruthlessly trampling upon the an-

cient prerogatives of the senate. In 28 B.C. he requested a transfer of control over the state treasury from inexperienced quaestors to ex-praetors selected at first by the senate but to two additional annual praetors after 23 B.C. Because his greater income enabled him to subsidize the state treasury he soon acquired virtual control over all the finances of the state.

Not content with that, Augustus, after 27 B.C., set up for each imperial province a separate account or chest called a *fiscus* (literally "fig basket"), into which he deposited the tax receipts and revenues of the province for payment to the legions. The *fisci* not only helped him, as sole paymaster, to assume complete mastery of the armies, but enabled him to take control over the financial administration of the Empire. Years later Claudius united the several *fisci* into a single and central *fiscus,* which then became in fact and in law the main treasury of the Roman Empire.

In A.D. 6 Augustus established a third treasury, the *aerarium militare,* to provide pensions for discharged war veterans (see p. 285).

Augustus had still a fourth fund, the *patrimonium Caesaris,* of fabulous size, though not strictly a treasury. It consisted of Caesar's private fortune, the confiscated properties of Antonius, the vast treasures of Cleopatra, the revenues from Augustus' private domains in the provinces, and the numerous legacies left him by wealthy Romans. (The legacies alone amounted to the enormous sum of 1.4 billion sesterces.) These funds gave him control over the entire financial administration of the Empire.

Social Reforms Although his constitutional, administrative, military, and financial reforms were a great success, Augustus' social and religious reforms were conspicuously lacking in either success or permanence. Most were futile, some reactionary. Their purpose was to halt the growing self-indulgence and lack of public spirit in high society and promote the moral regeneration of the Roman people—laudable objectives but not to be attained by legislative action or imperial decree.

Most praiseworthy was his attempt to improve the treatment of slaves. According to a story of Cassius Dio, Augustus was dining one day at the home of Vedius Pollio, a rich freedman who had acquired the habit of feeding the lampreys in his fish pond with erring slaves. As Vedius and Augustus were eating, a waiter accidentally broke a precious crystal goblet. Enraged, Vedius ordered that the slave be thrown into the fish pond. The trembling slave knelt before Augustus and begged for his intercession. Augustus, moved, asked Vedius to have fetched all the crystal goblets in the house. When they had been placed before him in glistening array, he sent them all smashing to the floor. Vedius flushed, but said not a word. The point was clear.

In contrast to his attempts to ease the lot of slaves, Augustus assaulted human freedom and dignity by his revival of the law of treason *(maiestas),* vague, flexible, and sweeping, comprehending all offenses from conspiracy against the state to insult or even disrespect to the emperor in speech, writing, or deed. Informers, *delatores,* received one-fourth of their victims' property. In light of Caesar's assassination, conspiracies, such as that uncovered in 23 B.C., and the numerous civil wars of the previous century, Augustus was understandably anxious about plots against himself and the state. He was sensible and restrained in applying the law of *maiestas,* but in the hands of less secure, intelligent, and mentally stable emperors, the law was to become an instrument of tyranny and repression.

Less noxious but less effective were the attempts to control promiscuity and regulate marriage and family life. The two Julian laws of 18 B.C. and the *lex Papia Poppaea* of A.D. 9* were specifically designed to curb immorality, speed up the birth rate, and revive ancient Roman virtue.

The new laws prohibited long engagements and divorce; required all bachelors and spinsters to marry as soon as possible, all

widows below fifty and all widowers below sixty to marry within three years. Failure to comply carried many penalties and disabilities: partial or complete ineligibility to receive legacies or hold public office and exclusion from public games and spectacles. Married persons who were childless, impotent, or sterile incurred similar disabilities, while those with three or more children could advance rapidly in their public careers and social life. For example, women who had borne three or more children were freed from guardianship.

The total effectiveness of the law, however, was somewhat diminished by the conferral of the special and fictitious "right of three children" (*ius trium liberorum*). Persons of influence might claim this right. Thus, the unmarried poets Vergil and Horace, Augustus himself with only one child, the Empress Livia with two, the married but childless Maecenas, and even the two bachelor consuls who lent their names to the *lex Papia Poppaea,* did not have to comply with the provisions of the law.

The new laws made adultery a criminal as well as a private offense. A *pater familias* might kill adulterous females under his power along with their paramours, a husband could kill his wife's lover. A man who refused to divorce a wife caught in adultery or who knowingly married an adulteress was equally guilty before the law. Flagrant adulterers suffered penalties varying from fine and loss of property to banishment and even death.

Although Augustus himself finally admitted that his marriage laws neither curbed immorality nor raised the birth rate, his legislation was not wholly without result: it enriched the treasury and favored the rise of a class of informers, who were to remain the bane of social life in future years.

In the field of social legislation three other laws deserve mention—the *lex Fufia Caninia* of 2 B.C., the *lex Aelia Sentia* of A.D. 4, and the *lex Junia Norbana* probably of 17 B.C. The first two prohibited the mass emancipation of alien slaves, who might swell and swamp the ranks of Roman citizens and, as it said, through intermarriage "defile" and "pollute" the "purity" of the Italian stock.

---

* This last was a complete and systematic codification of all previous laws and edicts pertaining to marriage and adultery.

This unattractive ethnocentrism of Augustus was probably part of his character as a person whose origins were in rural Italy, but it also served the political purpose of preserving the privileges of the Italians, who had loyally supported him in the civil war. The Junian law relegated slaves freed without proper formalities to the status of second-class citizens, the so-called Junian Latins. They could attain the privileges of full citizenship only by fulfillment of marriage vows and procreation of children.

Benefits for the Poor The great mass of poor citizens that had built up at Rome since the second century B.C. had been a significant factor in the instability of the late Republic. Augustus had blunted their direct political power by effectively gaining control of the popular assemblies himself. On the other hand, he still had to cope with the potential that they represented for violence and disorder. To limit their numbers, he had contemplated eliminating the distribution of free grain, which attracted the poor from the countryside, but he decided against such a potentially provocative move. Instead, he merely reduced the number eligible for free grain to 200,000 and set up a more efficient system of procuring and distributing the grain needed to keep the recipients happy and the price reasonable for the rest. At his own expense, he also expanded the number of games and public entertainments, such as the increasingly popular gladiatorial contests. In this way, Augustus set the Imperial policy of "bread and circuses" (*panem et circenses*) that kept the poor citizens of the city of Rome loyal clients of the emperors and a valuable reservoir of support against the old nobility.

Religious Reforms In his reformation of the ancient state religion, Augustus resurrected long-neglected ceremonies and priesthoods. It was a difficult undertaking. The primitive Roman animism, the worship of the spirits of stream, field, house, grove, and crossroad, which had gradually merged with Greek anthropomorphism, was past resuscitation. Its revival could only be artificial, unreal, impermanent. The masses of the common people, except perhaps in the most out-of-the-way Italian communities, had long ago turned to the more exotic and exhilarating religions of Egypt and the Near East. The cultured and sophisticated upper classes had turned to Philosophy—Stoic or Epicurean, Sceptic or Cynic.

In 28 B.C., Augustus undertook the repair of all temples in Rome (eighty-two, according to his own statement). The previous year had witnessed the dedication of the new temples of the Divine Julius (in the old Forum)

Sculptured relief from the Ara Pacis, *with fruitful Earth and babes flanked by the East and West Winds and surrounded by symbols of peace and prosperity.* (*Courtesy Museo delle Terme, Rome*)

and of Apollo (on the Palatine), a fitting tribute since both gods were protectors of the Julian dynasty, givers of victory, and saviors of the state from civil war. In 2 B.C. Augustus had erected a new temple of Mars the Avenger in the newly built Forum of Augustus.

The repair of crumbling temples was a prelude to the revival of many half-forgotten religious rites of Old Rome. In 27 B.C. Augustus reconstituted the college of the Arval (Plowing) Brethren, who once led the people each year at the end of May in the *Ambarvalia,* a solemn yet joyous procession around fields to implore divine blessing on growing crops, and who also conducted the celebration of the festival of a primitive field goddess known as the Dea Dia. Augustus also revived the priesthood of the Flamen Dialis with all its old taboos (see p. 40).

The revival of archaic rites may have helped revive the spirit of piety and valor, but could not immediately evoke loyalty or devotion to the new government or create propaganda for monarchic Augustan rule. Accordingly, in 13 B.C. the senate voted to erect an altar of Augustan Peace *(Ara Pacis Augustae).* One of the sculptured panels of this superb monument shows Augustus proceeding in solemn pomp to offer sacrifice; another panel shows Mother Earth seated on a rock and holding on her lap two children and the fruits of the earth. The altar seems to suggest peace with the gods and on earth peace and plenty, blessings which flowed from the martial valor of Augustus and his dauntless devotion to duty.

Augustus was able to push the new religious program with more zeal and vigor after 12 B.C., when he succeeded Lepidus as Pontifex Maximus. By 7 B.C. he had the city divided into fourteen regions and the regions into wards or precincts *(vici).* The *vicomagistri* or ward masters, usually of freedmen status, not only assisted the aediles in fighting fires but officiated at the shrines dedicated to the worship of the *Lares Compitales,* now called the *Lares Augusti,* guardian spirits of the crossroads and household. At each shrine the *vicomagistri* also offered sacrifices to the Genius of Augustus, his guiding spirit, just as the *genius* of the *pater-*

familias was traditionally honored in the household worship of the *lares* and *penates.* These religious demonstrations were spontaneous enough but subtly helped organize public opinion behind the government.

Some Italian cities, especially in the Greek South, did erect temples to Augustus, but he did not encourage such overt expressions of divinity in Italy. He preferred to promote the cult of his *genius* and encourage its maintenance by colleges of six minor magistrates called *Seviri Augustales.* These magistrates were usually local freedmen, who were expected to contribute to the cult and festivals associated with it in their towns. This honor helped to compensate for Augustus' strict enforcement of the traditional ban on their holding of regular magistracies, and they willingly undertook its expense in return for the increased social prestige that it offered.

During a reign of forty years, therefore, Augustus instituted reforms that touched every part of Roman life. Trying not to attempt too much too soon, but proceeding by gradual steps and building on precedents, Augustus succeeded in a radical reformation of Rome. He created a complex administrative system that reserved many positions of highest status to satisfy the old nobility but brought the equestrians of Italy into real positions of power and made them a loyal part of the system, with chances of obtaining senatorial status as *novi homines.* In some ways, slaves and freedmen were more restricted, but they too had important roles to play in an increasingly professional administrative system and could hope for enhanced status for themselves or their children through loyal service. The urban poor played a much more limited role in urban life, but they were kept content with generous benefits. The army became a permanent professional force, and the finances of the state were made more rational and secure. Attempts at reforming the personal morality of individuals did not enjoy great success, but Augustus gave renewed influence to the state religion and promoted the cult of his *genius* as a way of fostering widespread loyalty to his regime.

XXIV

Imperial Stabilization
under Augustus

While Augustus had been working out his unique constitutional settlement and making extensive internal administrative, military, financial, and social reforms at Rome, he also had been forced to pay extensive attention to the pacification of certain provinces and the establishment of defensible boundaries for the Empire as a whole. Under him the basic boundaries of the Empire were fixed, and policies to Romanize the provinces were consistently pursued. Augustus gave great impetus to the consolidation of the Mediterranean world into a unified state and single cultural unit, whose impact on the history of Europe and the Middle East is still felt.

Improved Provincial Administration
One of the sources of instability in the late Republic had been an unprofessional system of provincial administration that produced a rapid turnover of personnel who, at best, could not spend enough time to do their jobs well and, at worst, milked the provincials as much as they could in the short time available. Such a system bred disloyalty and distrust, which made it easier for Rome's enemies to stir up revolts. The loyalty of the provinces required stable, efficient, and honest administration

with due regard for the provincials themselves. To ensure such administration Augustus kept firm control over the governors, imperial as well as senatorial, strengthened the laws against extortion, and reformed the system of taxation by instituting a census of property at regular intervals. By breaking up the large provinces of Transalpine Gaul, Spain, and Macedonia, he achieved greater administrative efficiency and control. He curbed the power of the tax-farming companies and gradually transferred the collection of direct taxes to procurators assisted by local tax officials. These reforms made possible particularly in the East a rapid economic recovery and commercial expansion and helped Augustus win the loyalty of the provincial peoples.

The *princeps* respected local customs, and gave the provinces considerable rights of self-government, which encouraged the growth of urban communities out of villages, hamlets, and temple lands. More important still, he allowed the town councils and the councils of the provincial cities and tribes (*concilia* or *koina*) freedom of assembly and the right to express gratitude or homage and bring their grievances to the attention of emperor or senate.

Egypt was a special case. For millennia it had been the personal estate of its kings. To

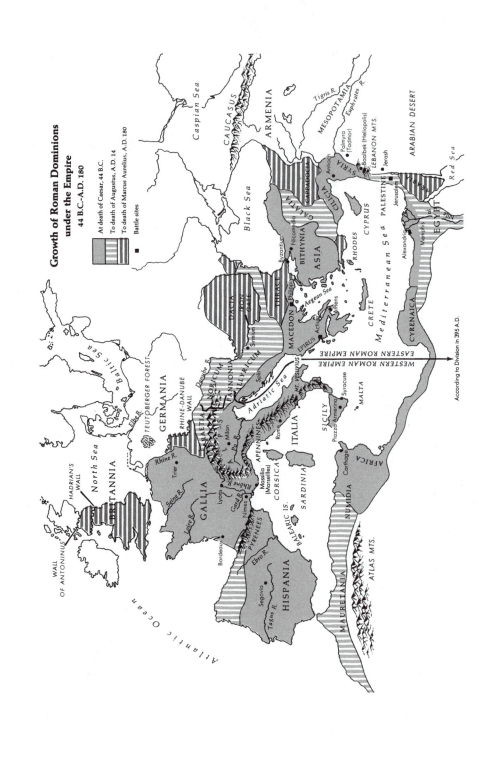

**Growth of Roman Dominions
under the Empire**
44 B.C.–A.D. 180

At death of Caesar, 44 B.C.

To death of Augustus, A.D. 14

To death of Marcus Aurelius, A.D. 180

■ Battle sites

have imposed a new system might have been disruptive, and it was to Augustus' advantage simply to take the place of the ancient pharaohs and Hellenistic Ptolemies in order to keep Egypt's vast wealth and vital grain out of the hands of potential challengers. Therefore, he treated it as part of his personal domain and declared it off limits to Roman senators without special permission. He and his successors administered it through special prefects of equestrian rank.

New Territories and Provinces   Another aspect of Augustus' policy of providing peace and stability for the Empire was to round out the conquest of the Mediterranean basin and extend Imperial borders to the most defensible geographic frontiers. By the time he finished, there were twenty-eight provinces, ten of which were senatorial and eighteen Imperial. From the Roman point of view, his policy was a great success and earned him much prestige in a society that valued military prowess highly. It was not, however, always a pretty story in human terms. A century later, the historian Tacitus grasped the reality faced by the native peoples whose independence and homelands were destroyed in the process of creating the Roman Peace (*Pax Romana*) when he said of the Romans, "They created a desert and called it peace."

The West   It was in the West that Augustus applied the policy of conquest most consistently. The West was the less-civilized part of the Empire, and, therefore, means of control other than brute force were often lacking. There were still large areas near Italy that the Romans had not yet attempted to take over. In order to protect Italy, the heart of the Empire, and secure efficient communications with the rest of the Empire within naturally defensible boundaries, Augustus set out methodically to conquer them.

Spain   In 27 B.C., Augustus personally set out to subdue the Cantabrians and Astur-

ians of northwestern Spain, who had been raiding the settled populations to the east and south for years despite Roman efforts to stop them. In 26 he mounted a massive three-pronged attack that resulted in much hard fighting and overstrained his always delicate health. His lieutenants met with little success until Agrippa took charge and finally suppressed the recalcitrant tribespeople through massacre and enslavement.

Gaul   In Gaul, Caesar's thorough conquest left Augustus nothing more than minor campaigns in Aquitania and administrative reorganization. In 22 B.C. he transferred the Province, Gallia Narbonensis, to the senate. He divided old Gallia Comata into three administrative parts: Aquitania, Lugdunensis, and Belgica, each under a separate legate subject to the governor, who had his headquarters in Lugdunum (Lyons).

The Alpine Districts   Though the Roman Empire now extended from Gibraltar to the Euphrates, the Alpine region had remained unsubdued and menaced Italy. Wild and warlike tribes continued to raid their peaceful neighbors to the south and held passes essential to direct communication between Italy and Gaul. In the year 25 B.C., the *princeps* sent Terentius Varro Murena against the Salassi, the most dangerous of all Alpine tribesmen. A decisive victory and ruthless enslavement removed the menace. Thereafter, a colony of veterans at Aosta guarded the Great and Little St. Bernard Passes and made possible the construction of a road through the Little St. Bernard from Italy to Lugdunum.

Next came the turn of the northern and eastern Alps. In 17 and 16 B.C., P. Silius Nerva, able governor of Illyricum, began the conquest of Noricum (modern Tyrol, Styria, and Salzburg). The task was completed from 16 to 14 B.C. by the Emperor's two stepsons, Tiberius Claudius Nero and Nero Claudius Drusus, who, in a brilliant and converging campaign, consummated the conquest of both Noricum and Rhaetia (eastern Switzerland and western Tyrol) and all the tribes living near the headwaters of the Rhine and Danube. Noricum and Rhaetia became Imperial provinces, at first governed by prefects, after 8 B.C. by procurators. The upper Danube became the northern boundary of the Roman Empire.

The Danubian Lands   Long overdue was the conquest of the Balkans. The two provinces of Illyricum (modern Albania and parts of Yugoslavia) and Macedonia had often been invaded by the Pannonians, who dwelt in what is now Hungary, northern Yugoslavia, and eastern Austria, or by the Dacians and Bastarnae of Rumania and northern Hungary. In addition, the Dalmatians of Illyricum, never completely pacified, were usually in full revolt against Roman authority.

The suppression of the rebellious Dalmatians and the subjugation of the Pannonians first fell to M. Vinicius, the capable proconsul of Illyricum in 14/13 B.C. He was replaced in the winter of 13/12 B.C. by Agrippa. Agrippa, his health shattered by the rigorous winter campaign, died, leaving his mission unfinished. The conquest was finally completed by Tiberius after four hard years of fighting from 12 to 9 B.C. He had carried the Roman standards to the southern bank of the middle Danube and incorporated Pannonia with Illyricum.

The eastern Balkans had also long been a troubled area. In 30 and 29 B.C. M. Licinius Crassus, grandson of the victim of the debacle at Carrhae in 53 B.C., had, as governor of Macedonia, subdued Thrace (now Bulgaria) and had driven the land-hungry Bastarnians back over the Danube, for which a jealous Augustus granted him a long-delayed and paltry triumph. The peace did not last long, for in 13 B.C. Thracian uprisings, an invasion of Macedonia, and massive raids by the Dacians over the Danube compelled Augustus to summon an army from Galatia. Its commander, the able but hard-drinking L. Calpurnius Piso, restored order in the area after three years of fighting (13 to 11 or 12 to 10 B.C.). Later, sometime between 9 B.C. and A.D. 6 Cn. Cornelius Lentulus and Sextus Aelius Catus made raids north across the Danube and trans-

planted fifty thousand Dacians to Moesia, which extended along the south bank of the Danube from Illyricum to the Black Sea. In A.D. 6, Moesia became a separate province governed by legates of Augustus.

By these conquests Augustus moved the border of the Empire away from northeastern Italy and greatly shortened communications between the vital Rhineland and the East. Moreover, although less economically valuable than many provinces, the Danubian lands soon proved to be the best recruiting grounds in the Empire. In later centuries many of the emperors who heroically fought to preserve the Empire from barbarian attacks came from this region.

Failure on the German Frontier   Augustus' only failure on the frontiers was in Germany. The restlessness of German tribes persuaded Augustus to cross the Rhine and push the frontier to the Elbe, and later, if possible, to the Vistula, so as to shorten the line of defense to the Danube by three hundred miles or more. The operations of his stepson Drusus from 12 to 9 B.C. spectacularly accomplished the initial goal. Unfortunately, Drusus broke his leg in 9 B.C. after falling from a horse and died of complications. Tiberius then handled matters effectively in Germany until he was called away to suppress a serious rebellion in Pannonia and Illyricum from A.D. 6 to 9. In 9, however, the harsh policies of Tiberius' successor in Germany, Quinctilius Varus, stirred up a revolt there. The German leader Arminius ambushed three legions in the Teutoburg Forest. Few escaped, and Varus committed suicide.

News of the Teutoburg disaster reached Rome. The *princeps,* dazed, sorrowing, broken, old, kept moaning to himself, "Quinctilius Varus, give me back my legions." The Teutoburg debacle and the lack of manpower and money to replace the three lost legions persuaded the *princeps* to abandon hope of conquest in Germany and, despite all later successes of Tiberius and Germanicus, to relinquish the ambition of making the Elbe a frontier of the Empire in Europe. That decision, final, momentous, and irrevocable, was financially and administratively, though probably not strategically, sound. The longer border and the nearness to Italy of the triangular territory between the headwaters of the Rhine and the Danube made that frontier more difficult to defend from barbarian attacks and made breakthroughs more dangerous threats to Italy and the Western provinces.

North Africa   Caesar had enlarged the old province of *Africa Proconsularis* by the annexation of Numidia. Augustus, however, convinced that the enlarged province was too difficult to defend, consigned the western part of it to the kingdom of Mauretania (modern Algeria and Morocco) and placed upon the vacant throne of Mauretania Juba II of Numidia, who had married Cleopatra Selene (Moon), daughter of Antonius and Cleopatra. Juba, a Latin author in his own right and a connoisseur of art, proved an enlightened and cultivated ruler. He raised the cultural level of his own country and West Africa, defended his realm against the wild tribes of the desert, and assisted Augustus in the work of founding twelve Roman colonies, of which Tingi (Tangier) was the most notable, along the Moroccan coast.

The East   The problems of the Near East differed widely from those of the West. The East, heir to a very old and advanced civilization, was proud of its traditions and was still a powerful creative force. The Parthian Empire was a territorially vast, polyglot state embracing an area of 1.2 million square miles from the Euphrates to Lake Aral and beyond the Indus. Within recent memory Parthia had inflicted three stinging defeats upon the Romans, and was still considered a potential menace. As an organized state, however, it was capable of being dealt with through sophisticated diplomacy as well as force.

After Actium, an insistent clamor arose for a war of revenge against Parthia. Without openly defying the demands of public opinion and the patriotic sentiments of authors like Vergil and Horace, Augustus accepted the

logistical impossibility of waging war in Spain, Germany, and along the Danube and of conducting at the same time a major campaign against Parthia. The Empire lacked the manpower, resources, and communications for such an undertaking. Augustus would try other methods first.

Client Kingdoms   To strengthen Roman power and neutralize Parthia, Augustus continued the policy of Antonius, which maintained client kingdoms as buffer states between Parthia and the Roman provinces. After Actium, Augustus had consigned large territories to Amyntas the Galatian (Galatia, Pisidia, Lycaonia, and most of Cilicia). He had also confirmed possession of eastern Pontus and Lesser Armenia to the enlightened Polemo and had awarded to the despicable Archelaus the huge realm of Cappadocia. He enlarged Judea, the kingdom of Herod I, the so-called Great (37–4 B.C.), a wily and efficient ruler who built a splendid temple at Jerusalem but was also an accomplished murderer of wives and sons.

Eventually all the client kingdoms became provinces. When Amyntas was killed in 25 B.C. while rounding up some savage tribes in the Taurus Mountains, Rome acquired the vast province of Galatia and Pamphylia. A decade after Herod's death, Augustus made Judea and Samaria an imperial province or rather a Syrian subprovince, governed by prefects, the most famous of whom was Pontius Pilate, who held office A.D. 26 to 36 at the time of the crucifixion of Christ.

Armenia and Parthia   Only in one kingdom, Armenia, had Roman influence deteriorated after the death of Antonius. Subdued and annexed as a province in 34 B.C., Armenia had slipped away from Roman control just before Actium and had come under the brutal rule of Artaxias, who forthwith slew all Roman residents in Armenia. Augustus did not avenge their deaths and, for over a decade, made no effort to recover the region, though it provided the best land routes leading from Parthia to Asia Minor and Syria. He watched and waited.

In 20 B.C., Artaxias was killed. Augustus immediately sent Tiberius into Armenia with an army. He placed Tigranes III, a pro-Roman brother of the late king, on the throne. At the same time, he frightened the Parthian king into surrendering the battle standards and all surviving Roman soldiers captured at Carrhae or after. A rattle of the saber temporarily restored Roman prestige in the East and wiped away the stain upon Roman honor. Augustus, therefore, shrewdly declared a great victory and silenced further demands for war by advertising his feat on coins with such slogans as *signis receptis* (the standards regained), *civibus et signis militaribus a Parthis recuperatis* (citizens and military standards recovered from the Parthians), and *Armenia recepta* (Armenia recaptured).

All was quiet in the East until the death of Tigranes in 1 B.C. The Armenian nationalists, aided and abetted by the Parthians, enthroned a king of their own choice without even consulting Augustus. He at once sent Gaius Caesar, armed with full proconsular power over the entire East, into Armenia at the head of a powerful army. Gaius subdued the Armenians and compelled the Parthians, by show of force and by diplomacy, to recognize Rome's preponderant interests in Armenia. After that magnificent feat, Gaius Caesar died (A.D. 4) of wounds that would not heal.

Parthia, as well as Augustus, had reasons for avoiding war. Torn by the dissensions of rival claimants to the throne and continually menaced by Asian migrations, Parthia was in no position to attack and willingly endured diplomatic defeat rather than risk actual conflict. Diplomacy and intrigue, it was thought, might succeed; overt aggression might fail and would surely be costly.

Parthia and Rome also had common economic interests that would have been ruined by war. Both were interested in opening the Euphrates valley as a caravan route for trade with India, central Asia, and China. Under joint Parthian and Roman protection, Palmyra was rapidly becoming a large and prosperous caravan city with fine streets, parks, and public buildings. Other cities— Petra, Jerash, Philadelphia, and Damascus— were beginning to enjoy the rich benefits of caravan trade.

Africa and the Red Sea Zone Egypt, richest of all Augustan annexations and producer of one-third of the Roman annual grain supply (five million bushels), remained relatively quiet except for some skirmishes on the Ethiopian border. C. Cornelius Gallus, Egypt's first prefect, a distinguished general, elegiac poet, friend of Augustus, of Pollio, and of Vergil, led an expedition against the Ethiopians in 29 B.C.* A later prefect, C. Petronius, repulsed counterattacking invaders from Ethiopia and in two campaigns (27 and 22 B.C.) drove them back into the Sudan and destroyed their holy city of Napata. In agreement with Candace, their queen, the *princeps* finally fixed the southern boundary of Egypt near the First Cataract, where it remained for the next three hundred years.

About this time (25 to 24 B.C.), the *princeps* sent Aelius Gallus, probably prefect of Egypt, on an expedition down the Red Sea against the Sabaeans, who dwelt near Aden and in Saudi Arabia. The purpose of this expedition was to gain naval control of the Straits of Bab-el-Mandeb in order that Alexandrian merchants might break the Sabaean monopoly of trade with India in precious stones, spices, cosmetics, and other commodities. That expedition, though badly handled by Gallus, paved the way for more successful ones later. Strabo the Geographer tells us that from Myos Hormos, a port on the Red Sea, there annually sailed 125 ships, some to Zanzibar and East Africa, many to western India, others to Ceylon, and some as far east as the shores of the Bay of Bengal and possibly Indochina. Excavations conducted at Pondicherry and Arikamedu in eastern India have revealed the amazing scope of this Roman commerce (see p. 395).

---

* Statues of Gallus and boastful proclamations of his exploits incised on pyramids incurred the wrath of Augustus and condemnation for treason by the senate. He took his life in 27 B.C.

Road Building Road building went hand in hand with conquest, imperial defense, and provincial communication. Though road building for military purposes did not originate with Augustus, he devoted much attention to it and was the first to extend the network from Italy to the provinces. By 27 B.C. he had completed the repair and reconstruction of the Italian roads (much neglected since the time of Gaius Gracchus), especially the Flaminian Way—main thoroughfare between Rome and the North and a vital artery of the Empire. After the conquest of the Alpine and Danubian regions, he began the construction of a road north from Tridentum (Trent) on the Adige in the Venetian Alps to Augusta Vindecilorum (Augsburg) on the Lech in Rhaetia (Bavaria). Other roads ran through the Alps between Italy and Gaul. The completion of this program brought Switzerland, the Tyrol, Austria, Bavaria, and Gaul into close and rapid communication with Italy.

The Imperial Post (*Cursus Publicus*) Road building made possible another Augustan achievement—the imperial postal service (*cursus publicus*), much like that of ancient Persia, for transfer of official letters and dispatches and the carrying of officials, senators, and other privileged persons. The expense of this service—relays of horses and carriages and the provision of hotel service for official guests—fell upon the towns located along the great highways, a grievous burden upon many towns but most conducive to Imperial communication and centralization of administration.

Colonization Another valuable instrument in the work of conquest and empire was the colony. Throughout his political career from 43 B.C. to A.D. 14, Augustus had founded twenty-eight colonies in Italy and perhaps eighty in the provinces. The Italian colonies, composed mainly of war veterans, were centers of tremendous loyalty to the new regime. Augustus seems to have abandoned Caesar's policy of commercial colonies and founded few, if any, civilian or commercial colonies outside of Italy. Most of his colonies were for settlement of veterans or to serve as fortresses or military outposts at strategic points to hold down and secure conquered territory. In the Alps, Gaul, and Spain especially, they served as garrisons in wild, uncivilized regions, though they later helped to spread the use of the Latin language and of Roman law among the conquered peoples and thus became important agents of Romanization. Around some sprang up large and prosperous communities, the original foundations of well-known modern cities: Barcelona, Zaragoza, and Merida in Spain; Vienne, Nîmes, and Lyons in France; and Tangier in Africa.

Urbanization of the Provinces The most striking feature of Augustus' provincial policy was the urbanization of the West. In the East he simply followed the policy initiated by Alexander the Great and continued by the Hellenistic kings, Pompey, Caesar, and Antonius. That policy Augustus extended to Gaul and Spain and revived in Africa. In Gaul, hilltop towns, fortified refuges, and market places were dying out, giving place to towns built on the flatlands, at river bends and fords, and at road junctions.

Augustus had social and political motives for promoting town and city life in the provinces, for the towns served as centers for diffusion of Roman culture. Furthermore, like modern county seats, they often controlled territories within a radius of fifty miles or more and so served the central government as convenient administrative units for the collection of taxes and other useful functions. No doubt, too, Augustus realized that since the towns owed their privileged position to the central government, they would in turn support the new Imperial regime with vigor and enthusiasm.

Growth of the Imperial Cult The growth of emperor worship throughout the Empire was also useful in strengthening ties of loyalty to both Rome and Emperor. The people of the Eastern provinces had long been used to worshipping their rulers as gods. After the Hellenistic empires and native kingdoms had been taken over by the Republic, the Eastern peoples had honored provincial governors with divine honors. When Augustus became ruler of the Roman world, many Easterners began to establish cults for his worship.

Augustus, however, was reluctant to have himself worshipped too directly. It may have been distasteful to him as a religiously conservative Roman, and it certainly would have entailed the political risk of alienating jealous or conservative nobles. He insisted therefore that official provincial cults for his worship be linked with the goddess Roma. By 29 B.C. temples of such cults already existed in the East at Nicaea, Ephesus, Pergamum, and Nicomedia, along with quinquennial festivals known as *Romoia Sebasta.* Later, with his encouragement, such cults also existed in the Western provinces too, notably at Cologne in Germany, Lyons in *Gallia Comata,* and Tarraco in Spain.

Maintenance of these cults was the responsibility of provincial assemblies, which met once a year at the shrine of Rome and Augustus for a festival. The festival was managed by a high priest elected from among the leading aristocrats of the province. In this way, the provincial elite became identified with and loyal to both Rome and the Emperor.

By the end of his life, therefore, Augustus had brought about the pacification of the Roman provinces internally and organized their efficient administration. He had fixed the boundaries of the Empire, with a few notable exceptions, for the future and organized a system of defense that kept them secure for almost 200 years. By cautiously promoting the growth of emperor worship, he had also found a means of building a basis for imperial unity that bridged the different local and ethnic traditions of a huge polyglot empire.

The Death of Augustus   At last after a political career of almost sixty years, on August 19 of A.D. 14 in the little Campanian town of Nola, Augustus died. And death overtook him not unprepared. He was ready, serene, cheerful; not plagued by doubt, guilt, or remorse. Dying, he jokingly quoted to his friends words from a Greek drama: "Have I played my part well? Then clap your hands and take me off the stage." Played his part well? Indeed he had, and the grateful Roman senators willingly conferred upon him the divinity that he had tactfully refused to claim overtly while he was alive.

XXV

Life and Culture under Augustus

The Augustan Age witnessed a general quickening of economic life throughout the Mediterranean. The ending of the civil wars, the suppression of piracy at sea and of banditry and lawlessness in Italy, and the Augustan program of road building in Italy and the provinces brought about a remarkable expansion of agriculture, industry, and commerce. Italy was for a time the chief beneficiary of the new expansion, for the East had not yet recovered from the effects of past wars and exploitation, and the Western provinces were still too young to take full advantage of the new order. Italy therefore continued to dominate the Mediterranean world both economically and politically.

Agriculture In Italy the main impact of Augustus' rule was peace and the prosperity that came with it, but the basic characteristics of agriculture earlier in the first century B.C. remained the same (see p. 219). After Actium, Augustus avoided the disruptive confiscations that had marked his attempts to settle veterans after Philippi. New colonies in the provinces provided land for many veterans, and the ranks of the small farmer stabilized throughout Italy. Large estates, however, continued to

flourish, as is evident from the *De Re Rustica* published in 36 B.C. by Marcus Terentius Varro, and their patterns of distribution, products, and labor continued as before.

Industry Knowledge of craftsmanship in the Augustan age is still defective and spotty. The excavations of Pompeii and Ostia have yielded some information about the industrial life of small cities and one port, but little or nothing is known about that of the larger cities and other harbors—Rome, Brundisium, Naples, Puteoli, Capua, Tarentum, and Aquileia—in which excavation is either impossible or has scarcely begun.

The excavation of the so-called Street of Abundance in Pompeii has clearly shown the quickening effect of Augustan peace and prosperity upon industry in Italy. Before the Principate that street had been entirely residential; by A.D. 79 (the year of the eruption), the ground floors of most of the houses had been converted into small factories or shops, many of them engaged in the clothing business—fulling, cleaning, and dyeing. The powerful fullers' guild had its display and sales rooms in a large exchange building nearby.

The most interesting of the shops ex-

Pompeii, the Street of Abundance, with workshops and stores. (*Courtesy New York Public Library Picture Collection*)

cavated in Pompeii were the bakeries because therein is preserved the equipment used in every step of the ancient bread-making process—grinding, kneading, and baking. The shops are distributed quite evenly throughout the city, one in almost every block, some of them fairly large with four or five mills, a kneading machine, and oven. One shop had a capacity of apparently two thousand loaves per day. With a few slight repairs the mills can still grind wheat into flour. One of the ovens contained, when excavated, the very loaves, now somewhat charred and carbonized, that were baking at the moment of the eruption.

Not even the largest of the Pompeian milling and baking shops (of which there were almost forty) would compare in size with the enormous bread-making establishment of M. Vergilius Eurysaces at Rome. As contractor (*redemptor*) for the state, he employed scores of workmen, both slave and free. His tall and unique monument, still to be seen near the Porta Maggiore, has bas-reliefs representing all the various operations of the bread-making process. Thus, Pompeii with its small shops and guilds had a typical small-town economy (not unlike that of a late medieval town), and the fullest description of its crafts producing for local trade would fail to convey an adequate idea of some of the larger industries of Roman Italy that almost reached the stage of mass production and shipped their products to distant markets from Jutland to the Caucasus, from Britain to India.

The Glass Industry   The thriving glass industry had been revolutionized around 40 B.C. by the Syrian (or Egyptian) invention of the blow pipe which made possible the production not only of beautiful goblets and bowls but even window panes, useful in northern climes at once for admittance of daylight and exclusion of winter's cold. From the glass factories of Campania or of the Adriatic seaport of Aquileia came wares that found their way from Trondheim fiord in Norway to the southernmost borders of the Soviet Union. Augustan Italy enjoyed temporarily an exclusive monopoly of Western glass exports. A half century later Gaul began to compete and the factories first of Lyons and finally of Cologne on the Rhine exported small bowls with cut geometrical designs not only to Denmark but to the lands near Danzig (Gdansk) and the tributaries of the Danube and the Theiss.

Arretine Pottery   Italian pottery repeats the history of glass. The factories engaged, at Arretium in Etruria and later at Puteoli, in the manufacture of a tableware known as *terra sigillata,* a red-glazed pottery of beautiful ornamentation, had in the time of Augustus and Tiberius achieved mass production and enjoyed an export monopoly from the British Midlands to Arikamedu in southeastern India. One Arretine factory had a mixing vat with a capacity of ten thousand gallons and might well have employed as many as forty expert designers and a much larger number of mixers, potters, and furnacemen. Even then branch factories were being established in southern and eastern Gaul, in Spain, Britain, and on the Danube, which eventually broke the proud monopoly in western and northern Europe and even in Italy itself.

The Metal Industries   Augustan Italy led the world in the manufacture of metalware. The chief centers of the iron industry were the two great seaports of Puteoli and Aquileia. The iron foundries of Puteoli smelted ores seaborne from the island of Elba and by repeated forging manufactured arms, farm implements, and carpenters' tools which were as hard as steel. Easy access to the rich iron mines of recently annexed Noricum (Austria) stimulated at Aquileia the· manufacture of equally excellent farm implements for sale throughout the fertile Cisalpina and for export

to Dalmatia, the Danubian region, and even Germany.

For the manufacture of silverware (plates, trays, bowls, cups, and candelabra), the two leading centers were Capua and Tarentum; for bronze wares (statues, busts, lamp stands, tables, tripods, buckets, and kitchen pots and pans), Capua, where operators employing perhaps thousands of workmen had evolved a specialization and division of labor usually associated with modern industry. The immense export trade of Capua to Britain, Germany, Scandinavia, and south Russia continued unabated until Gaul had established workshops first at Lyons, and around A.D. 80, further north in the Belgica and the Rhineland.

Building Supplies and Trades   The extensive building program of Augustus and the large sums spent on beautifying the world's capital stimulated the manufacture or extraction of building and plumbing materials—lead and terra-cotta pipes, bricks, roof tiles, cement, marble, and the so-called travertine, a cream-colored limestone quarried near Tibur. Some of these crafts seem never to have developed large, systematized methods of production. The makers of lead pipes, for instance, were small shop owners who, with the help of a few slaves, filled orders as they came in, buying the lead and making the pipes, and also laying and connecting them.

On the other hand, the making of bricks and tiles had reached the highly specialized stage, especially on senatorial and imperial estates, which competed with private enterprise in the production of materials for public works. Almost nothing is known about the organization of the enterprises which made cement, a mixture of volcanic ash and lime and a cheap and flexible building material in great demand.

The queen of building materials was marble. Not only did the Romans import the famous marble of the Greek Aegean, the fine white, purple-veined varieties of Asia Minor, the serpentines and dark red porphyries of Egypt, and the beautiful, gold-colored marble of Simitthus in Numidia, but they also began at this time to quarry marble in Italy: the famous white marble of Carrara in Etruria and all those remarkable varieties found in the Piedmont, in Liguria, and near Verona, noted for their colors—brilliant greens and yellows, or mixed reds, browns, and whites.

The Roman Imperial Coinage

The Augustan age not only marked the political and economic unification of the Mediterranean region and a tremendous expansion of industry and world commerce but also witnessed new developments in the creation of a stable and abundant coinage to serve ever-expanding economic needs both within the Empire and far beyond its frontiers.

Before Actium the coinage had been in a somewhat confused state. During the mid-80s B.C., the mint in Rome had suspended all issues in bronze (an alloy of copper, tin, and lead) because of the scarcity of tin, and in the early 30s had suspended all issues in gold and silver (*aurei et denarii*). Various mints in Italy and the provinces sporadically and inadequately coined money for business and the payment of armies.

In the decade after Actium, Augustus struck coins of various denominations, styles, and types in gold, silver, and bronze: first in the East at Ephesus, Pergamum, Apamea, Antioch in Syria, and elsewhere; later in the West at Emerita (Mérida) in Spain and at Nemausus (Nîmes) in Gaul.

Sometime after 23 (probably in 19) B.C., Augustus began to lay the foundations of a genuine imperial coinage, one of the most notable achievements of his principate. He reopened the mint at Rome and instituted a college of three mint officials (*tresviri monetales*), who struck (at the joint direction of the *princeps* and the senate) coins in gold and silver as well as in brass or orichalcum (an alloy of copper and zinc) and in pure copper. The brass and copper coinage (perhaps token money without relation to actual metal value) helped satisfy the Empire's long-standing need for small change. In addition to the mintages at Rome,

Augustus issued, during his stay in Gaul in 16 to 13 B.C., a huge bronze coinage at Nîmes. A major emission, issued contemporaneously at Antioch in Syria, bore in reverse the legends S C (*senatus consulto*) and C A (*Caesaris auctoritate*), showing that the "clear-cut" distinction between Imperial and senatorial provinces is a modern myth. In the coinages at Rome, *princeps* and senate likewise worked together. One Imperial gold *aureus* had the value of 25 silver *denarii*, a *denarius* had the value of four bronze *sestertii* or 12 *asses* during and after the principate of Augustus. Local issues by provincial governors, allied kings, and autonomous cities and tribes in gold (Bosporan kingdom of southern Russia) and especially in silver and bronze supplemented the Imperial coinage, though with a variously reduced valuation.

The Augustan coinage had an important propaganda or publicity value in addition to its purely economic function, for it provided the newborn regime a flexible yet easily controlled, a subtle yet compelling method of influencing public opinion. Its kaleidoscopic variety of types kept the public informed of the ideals and ever-changing policies and objectives of the government. People all over the Empire would use and inevitably look at the coins, which could vaguely yet effectively suggest what the government from time to time wanted to be felt and believed. New coin types appearing as frequently as modern stamps kept before the public eye the exalted figure of Augustus sometimes as an associate of Roma (ROM. ET. AUG), as the victor at Actium (IMP. X. ACT), as the preserver of citizens' lives (CAESAR. COS. VII. CIVIBUS. SERVATEIS), as the defender of the *libertas* of the Roman People (LIBERTATIS. P. R. VINDEX), or as the recoverer of the standards lost to the Parthians in 53 B.C. (SIGNIS RECEPTIS).

As media of publicity and mass propaganda, which must have shifted with each changing nuance of imperial policy and achievement, the coinages were more effective and malleable than the arts, for even the most wonderful works of architecture and sculpture were too stiff and static to serve as propaganda devices. Moreover, comparatively few of the

Empire's seventy to one hundred million inhabitants ever saw them, whereas people everywhere daily used and handled the coins.

The coinages were also more tractable and amenable to rapidly changing purposes, policies, and resolves of the government than literature, for writers, especially poets, have an unfettered, independent spirit, seldom captive to a ruler's shifting moods or yoked in service to the state.

Architecture and Art As master of Italy and the West, Octavianus continued Julius Caesar's work of beautifying Rome. To this period belong the first public library, a temple to Apollo on the Palatine, a new theater, the rebuilding of the Regia, the completion of the Basilica Aemilia, and the repair of the temple of Hercules. Agrippa, an engineer as well as soldier and admiral, began the repair of the aqueduct *Aqua Marcia* and, as aedile in 33 B.C., the construction of the aqueduct *Aqua Julia* and other public works.

In the Augustan principate Roman art, a blend of Italic, Etruscan, and Hellenistic elements, acquired its distinctive Roman and Imperial character. The conditions which favored this development were the peace and economic prosperity of the period, the publication of Vitruvius Pollio's classic *De Architectura* (ca. 27 B.C.), which has exerted a profound influence on the architecture of Europe until modern times, and the great building activity of Augustus himself. In his *Res Gestae* he briefly refers to the temples that he had constructed and the 82 he had repaired. Before his death he remarked that he "had found Rome a city of brick and left it one of marble," a claim undoubtedly accurate with respect to temples and public buildings but not to the huge blocks of flimsy tenements constructed of small timber and sun-dried brick.

The most important structures erected during the Augustan principate were the Temple of Divus Julius at the eastern edge of the old Roman Forum; the Temple of Mars the Avenger in the newly constructed Forum of Augustus, the first of the four great Imperial

forums; the magnificent Temple of Apollo on the Palatine, the first great building in Rome to be constructed entirely of the gleaming white Carrara marble. Completed in 28 B.C., it contained two libraries, one for Greek books, the other for Latin. Also imposing are the Theater of Marcellus, with its three rows of arcades supported by Corinthian columns and with a seating capacity of twenty thousand; the Baths of Agrippa, the first of a long series culminating in the enormous Baths of Caracalla and Diocletian (all adorned with mosaics, paintings, and statues, and equipped with hot and cold baths, steam rooms, swimming pools, gymnasiums, libraries, and recreation rooms); and the huge Mausoleum of Augustus shaped like a mounded Etruscan tomb (*tumulus*). Erected beside the Tiber in 28 B.C., it served as the Imperial family tomb from the death of Marcellus in 23 B.C. to that of Nerva in A.D. 98. The Pantheon ("Shrine of all the Gods") was erected by Agrippa in 27 B.C. and, though reconstructed by Hadrian in the second century A.D. (see p. 384), still bears on its facade the famous inscription: M . AGRIPPA . L . F . COS TERTIUM FECIT (Marcus Agrippa, son of Lucius, built [this] in his third consulship). Erected after 13 B.C., the Altar of Augustan Peace (*Ara Pacis Augustae*), whose marble panels contain perhaps the finest sculptured reliefs in the history of art, portrayed the themes of restored peace and prosperity and had a unique sculptured relief of the Imperial family and officials depicted as taking part in the dedication ceremonies of the altar itself.

As portrayers of the leading ideas and achievements of the government (peace, prosperity, victory, religion) as well as masterpieces of art, the panels of the Altar of Peace are equalled only by the celebrated portrait statue of the Augustus from Prima Porta. He is wearing a decorated breastplate that portrays the Parthian surrender of the captured standards to Tiberius, the final conquest of Spain and Gaul, the fecundity of the earth (*Terra Mater*), and Jupiter's protecting mantle over all. Similar, if not identical, ideas are conveyed by marble altar from Roman Carthage with Roma seated on a heap of arms and contem-

Statue of Augustus Imperator with sculptured breastplate (ca. 20 B.C.), from the Villa of Livia at Prima Porta. (Courtesy The Photographical Archives of the Vatican Museums and Galleries, Rome)

plating an altar with a horn of plenty (*cornucopiae*), staff of peace (*caduceus*), and globe (*orbis terrarum*) resting upon it; by the exquisite Vienna cameo (*Gemma Augustea*) and the Grand Camée de France showing respectively a triumph of Tiberius and the ascension of Augustus into Heaven; by two silver cups from Boscoreale showing the submission of the Germanic Sugambri to Augustus and Tiberius; and by a silver dish of Aquileia, which shows the Emperor surrounded by the four seasons and by all the symbols of the fertility, plenty, and prosperity of the Golden Age.

The building activity of the Augustan period was not confined to Rome. A study of the ruins of the cities of northern and central Italy reveals that the Augustan age was a period of economic prosperity and of great building activity by the local aristocracy. The Western provinces, especially Gaul, copied or borrowed from the newly erected monuments of Rome. To the time of Augustus belong the famous Etruscan-like temple at Nîmes, (Nemausus) the so-called Maison Carrée, notable for its harmony, symmetry, and delicate finish; possibly also the lofty Pont du Gard, which rises on three tiers of arches 160 feet above the deep gorge of the river Gard and carries on its top an aqueduct that brought fresh water to Nîmes; an unfortified city gate (Porte de Mars) at Reims (Durocortorum); and at Orange (Arausio) an arch of triumph and an immense theater, whose colonnade and central niche housed a colossal statue of Augustus.

La Maison Carrée at Nîmes.
(Courtesy French Government Tour-
ist Office)

Literature The Augustan Age was one of the great periods of world literature and comparable to that of Pericles in Athens, of Elizabeth I in England, and of Louis XIV in France. It has therefore been usually called the Golden Age because during the Augustan principate Roman literature acquired its highest perfection in form and expression. Although this period did not produce any literary figures (apart, perhaps, from Vergil) of the stature of Homer, Aeschylus, Plato, Thucydides, or even Lucretius, the term "Augustan Age," as applied to English literature of the early eighteenth century, has come to connote the "correct" and "classical" expression of the gracious elegance and polished *urbanitas* of everyday human life in an aristocratic society. It therefore denotes a period in which literature was in perfect harmony with the aims and ideals of the governing class. As

Pont du Gard, Nîmes. (Courtesy French Government Tourist Office)

in the past, therefore, Roman literature of the Augustan Age often reflects a patriotic concern with Rome's history and contemporary subjects of political importance.

Augustan Rome provided conditions highly favorable to literature. After a century of chaos and civil bloodshed, an era of general peace and ordered government evoked the gratitude, pride, and enthusiasm of the Roman people. It offered themes for literary glorification: a heroic past and a great and glorious present. Already the political capital of the world, it was rapidly becoming the cultural center, attracting students, scholars, and writers from abroad.

Unlike the age of Caesar, in which prose writers predominated (Cicero, Caesar, Sallust, Nepos, and Varro), the Augustan Age was notable for its poets (Vergil, Horace, Tibullus, Propertius, and Ovid). It was essentially an age of poetry. Even Livy's great history of Rome, *Ab Urbe Condita,* was no exception, for it was regarded by some critics as an epic in prose form. The *Ab Urbe Condita* began where the *Aeneid* of Vergil left off.

Vergil (70–19 B.C.) Publius Vergilius Maro was the son of a northern Italian farmer near Mantua. He was originally trained for a career in the courts, which he gave up to study philosophy with Siro the Epicurean at Naples. After Siro's death, however, he turned to poetry.

In 38 or 37 B.C., Vergil published his *Eclogues* (*Bucolics*), ten short pastorals in the style of the Hellenistic Greek poet Theocritus, poems idealizing country life and the loves and sorrows of shepherds. They were more than pretty pastorals, however. For example, the first and the ninth refer to the dispossession of small farmers to settle Octavian's veterans after Philippi. The fifth and the ninth also refer to the deification of Julius Caesar, while the fourth predicts the return of the Golden Age with the birth of a child. The sixth is reminiscent of Lucretius with its exposition of Epicurean philosophy, and the tenth is a tribute to fellow poet Cornelius Gallus (see p. 308).

The *Eclogues* had brought Vergil to the attention of Gaius Cilnius Maecenas, a wealthy equestrian of Etruscan descent, patron of literature, and close friend of Augustus. With Maecenas' support, Vergil began, and by 29 B.C. had completed, his *Georgics,* a didactic poem in four books, like Hesiod's *Works and Days.* Not intended as a technical handbook, like Varro's, the *Georgics* nevertheless describe with realism and firsthand experience the various activities of the farmer—the plowing, the harvest, the care of vines and orchards, the breeding of cattle, and the keeping of bees. The poem was a hymn of praise to Italy's soil and sturdy farmers and to Augustus for restoring the peace so essential for prosperous agriculture and human happiness.

After completing the *Georgics,* Vergil spent the next decade in the composition of his greatest work, the *Aeneid,* a national epic in twelve books, the first six of which correspond to Homer's *Odyssey,* the last six to the *Iliad.* Written in the smoothest and most beautiful narrative and in stately hexameter verse, the *Aeneid* unfolds the destiny of Rome from the burning of Troy and the landing of the hero Aeneas in Latium to its rise as a great world empire, of which the Augustan Age was the culmination. It glorifies as the fulfillment of decrees of fate the achievements of the Roman people from Aeneas to Augustus. Though Aeneas, the legendary ancestor of the Julian family, is nominally the hero, the real theme is Rome: her mission is to rule the world, to teach the nations the way of peace, to spare the vanquished, and to subdue the proud. The fulfillment of this mission requires of all its heroes the virtues that made Rome great: courage, piety, devotion to duty, constancy, and faith. Vergil's emphasis upon these virtues was in line with the Augustan reformation of morals and the revival of ancient faith (*prisca fides*).

In contrast, Vergil, like Lucretius before him, condemns the lust (*cupido*) and blind emotion (*furor*) that he saw as the causes of prior civil strife. It is these destructive forces that hinder Aeneas and the Trojans from fulfilling the glorious destiny that Jupiter has decreed for Rome and that the virtuous hero Aeneas must overcome. Unfortunately, Vergil usually portrays these evil forces in feminine terms that help perpetuate the negative stereotype of women in Western literature.

It is the furious anger of Juno at the Trojans because long ago Paris had not chosen her as the most beautiful goddess in the famous contest with Minerva (Athena) and Venus (Aphrodite) that causes constant disasters for Aeneas and his fellow Trojans. At Carthage, on whose shores Juno's storm has wrecked Aeneas' fleet, it is Dido's Juno-inspired passion for Aeneas that threatens to divert him from his manly task until Jupiter reminds him that he has more important things to do than dally in the seductive embraces of a foreign queen. When Aeneas dutifully abandons Dido, her passionate love turns to furious, self-destructive hatred, and her dying curse makes Carthage Rome's implacable enemy forever.

At one point, even the Trojan women, tired of the rigors imposed by Aeneas's heroic mission, weakly succumb to Juno's temptations and the prospect of settling on the hospitable shores of Sicily and try to burn the Trojan fleet. When they finally do get to Italy, the Trojans become embroiled in a desperate war with the native peoples because the Rutilian king Turnus, jealous over Aeneas' betrothal to Lavinia, daughter of King Latinus, is enflamed with lust for war and revenge at Juno's bidding by the Fury Allecto, one of the most powerfully portrayed female demons in literature.

On his deathbed Vergil requested the burning of the *Aeneid,* for he considered it not yet perfected, but Augustus countermanded that request and ordered it published.

Horace (65–8 B.C.) Another great poet of the age was Quintus Horatius Flaccus, son of a fairly well-to-do freedman of Venusia in Apulia. A sincere believer in a good education, his father sent him to school in Rome and later to higher studies at Athens. There he met the noble Brutus and, like many young idealistic Romans studying abroad, he fought for the Republic at Philippi. Afterward he returned to Rome penniless and got a job in a quaestor's office which, though boring, gave him the time and means to write poetry.

By 35 B.C. he had composed some of his *Epodes,* bitter, pessimistic little poems in iambic meter (in imitation of the Greek poet Archilochus), and the first book of his *Satires* (which he called *Sermones,* informal "conversations" in colloquial style and in hexameter verse), in which he pokes fun at the vices and follies of the capital. His earliest poems, though caustic, sometimes vulgar, and even obscene, were written in such a clear and incisive style and with such wit and cleverness as to win the admiration of Vergil, who in 38 B.C. introduced him to Maecenas.

At first Maecenas provided Horace an income sufficient to enable him to give up his job and spend his time writing poetry, roaming the streets, and observing life in the metropolis. He later (33 B.C.) presented the poet a house of twenty-four rooms and an extensive estate worked by eight slaves and five tenant families in the Sabine country near Tivoli. There Horace could loaf, drink wine, enjoy the solitude of the country, and write poetry.

In 30 B.C., Horace published his second book of *Satires,* in which he is more mellow and less caustic than in the first. Meanwhile, he had begun and for seven years thereafter continued to work on his *Odes.* The first three books, which appeared in 23 B.C., comprised eighty-eight poems of varying lengths and in a score of meters, most of which he derived from Greek poets like Sappho, Alcaeus, Archilochus, and Anacreon and adapted to Roman lyric form.

The *Odes* (*Carmina*), a monument "more durable than brass and loftier than the pyramids of Egyptian kings" (*Odes* 3.30.1–2), on which the fame of Horace chiefly rests, touch lightly on many subjects, their variety adding yet another charm to artistry, compactness, pure diction, fastidious taste, and lightness. Some are so-called "wisdom poems" containing moral exhortations which he himself took seriously: since Youth and Beauty touch us and soon are gone, let us enjoy them now;

since envious time keeps running out, seize the occasion (*carpe diem,* "snatch the day," *Odes* 1.11.8). Others discourse on friendship, the brevity of life, religion and philosophy, drinking wine, and making love, which for Horace was a pastime lightly comic, not an all-consuming passion as for Catullus.

Horace was not a descriptive nature poet or a landscape word painter like Vergil in the *Eclogues* and *Georgics,* though now and then, in the manner of Gerard Manley Hopkins, he flashes pictures that sparkle and soon are gone: a snowy mountain glistening in the distance, a vine-clustered elm, a herd of long-horned, black-muzzled cattle grazing peacefully under Campagna's cloudless skies.

Among his *Odes* are the long, solemn, so-called Roman poems, Pindaric in their splendor, wherein he praises the old virtues resurrected by Augustus: moderation and frugality, valor and patriotism, justice, piety, and faith. In proclaiming these virtues as the sole hope of Rome's salvation, Horace anticipated the implementation of the Augustan policy of social regeneration by at least five years.

In his later years, Horace wrote two books of *Epistles,* which were sermons on morals, religion, and philosophy rather than real letters, such as those written by Cicero. Though some of these so-called letters are charming and even entertaining, others seem stodgy, uninspiring, even repellent, but they commended themselves to critics of the English "Augustan Age" because of their wit, geniality, *urbanitas,* pretty phrasings, and paradoxes. The longest and most famous of these letters, the so-called *Art of Poetry* (*Ars Poetica*), sets forth the principles for writing poetry, especially tragedy. From this Alexander Pope in the eighteenth century drew many of the principles he versified in his *Essay on Criticism.*

The Latin Elegy The elegiac couplet consisting of a hexameter alternating with a pentameter had served in Greek and Latin literature a variety of purposes—for drinking songs, patriotic and political poems, dirges, laments, epitaphs, votive dedications, epi-

grams, and love poetry. Following the innovations of Catullus (see pp. 262–263), the first Roman to use the elegy extensively for love poetry was probably Gaius Cornelius Gallus (ca. 69–26 B.C.). His four books of *Amores* firmly established the subjective erotic elegy. Until 1978, none of Gallus' poems were known to exist. That year, in Egypt, a piece of papyrus was discovered that contained one complete four-line poem and most of a second. While not major poems, they do help to see Gallus more clearly in the literary context of the age and his influence on others.

After Gallus came Albius Tibullus (54?–19 B.C.), Sulpicia (50? B.C.), Sextus Propertius (50?–ca. 15 B.C.); and Ovid, Publius Ovidius Naso, (43 B.C.–A.D. 17/8). For smoothness and elegance Quintilian (ca. A.D. 35?–97?) the Roman professor of rhetoric, liked Tibullus best. Some modern critics would agree.

Of Tibullus there is known only the little he tells about himself in his two books of sixteen elegies addressed to Delia and to Nemesis—two slum-bred tramps who alternately made him swoon with ecstasy or drove him to madness by their vile temper and infidelities. Tibullus did not belong to the circle of Maecenas but to the smaller circle of the illustrious noble Marcus Valerius Messalla Corvinus (see p. 310). He seems to have been handsome, elegant and rich, but rather neurotic and sometimes even morbid. His two passions in life were girls and the peace and beauty of the country. The attraction of the first was often stronger than that of the second. In spite of his problems he was a remarkable poet, clear, brilliant, never trite. His verse was smooth, elegant, musical, and he was a master of the elegy of love and of lament.

Some would prefer the Umbrian-born Propertius. His love was Cynthia, wellborn, beautiful, gifted. To her he addressed four books of elegies, the chief burden of which was how she had bewitched him and how she was sole cause of his joy and pain. In spite of her charm, her suspicions, rages, and infidelities drove him away to some other girl.

Superior in some ways to Tibullus as a stylist, Propertius is a peculiar poet, bewildering and hard to understand. Frequently he abruptly veers off into some obscure Greek myth, which dulls the most passionate climacteric. Boldest and most original of poets, he yet manages somehow by his recondite allusions to destroy the fine effects achieved by the hard brilliance and sparkle of his verse.

The only poetess to survive from the Augustan Age is Sulpicia, the ward and probably niece of Messalla. Her date of birth can only be approximated to that of her contemporaries, and it is not known how long she lived. Six exquisite short elegies bearing her name are preserved in the manuscripts of Tibullus. They are addressed to Cerinthus, the otherwise unknown object of her unpretentious affections. Notable for their directness and candor, they distill more true feeling than the longer poems of her more celebrated contemporaries.

The most sensual and sophisticated of the elegists was Ovid, who came to Rome from the little town of Sulmo in the remote mountain region of the Abruzzi. His family were well-to-do equestrians, and for a while he pursued the career in the courts for which he had been trained. He eventually devoted himself to poetry, however. His style was very light, and he became the most prolific of the Augustan poets. He had no particular patron, was friends with both Tibullus and Propertius, and became part of a rather high living set with low morals.

The two most informative and important of Ovid's works were the *Metamorphoses* (*Transformations*) and the *Fasti,* the first written in hexameters, the second in elegiacs. The *Metamorphoses,* a collection of 250 stories in fifteen books, is a storehouse of information about Greek mythology and the source of inspiration to poets and painters ever since. More than that, however, the *Metamorphoses* was Ovid's answer to Vergil's *Aeneid,* an epic history of the world that culminated patriotically in the change of Julius Caesar from a man to a god. The *Fasti* or *Calendar* described and explained the astronomical, historical, and religious events associated with each month of the year, one book per month. It nicely complemented

Augustus' attempt to revive the many priesthoods and religious observances that had fallen into disuse. Unfortunately, the work is unfinished and covers only the first six months.

Among his earliest works were the *Amores* or *Love Elegies,* written in the style of Tibullus, with less sincerity but with more polish and virtuosity and greater mastery of erotic verse. One of his most original undertakings was the *Heroides* a group of fictitious poetic letters from famous legendary women to absent husbands or lovers and presenting the womens' view of things. Then came his masterpiece, the *Art of Love,* a salacious handbook, perversely didactic, which explains all the arts of seduction and surveys all the known aspects of heterosexual experience from rape to incest. This thorough piece of research, which the two Julias (daughter and granddaughter of Augustus) both appreciated, gave offense to the *princeps* as an insult to the laws dealing with moral reform and the sanctity of marriage. The *princeps* remembered. Later, in A.D. 8, when Ovid became implicated in a scandal involving the younger Julia, Augustus ordered them banished: Julia to some rocky island in the Adriatic, the poet to the cold and barbarous town of Tomi (now Constantza) on the Black Sea (his works removed from the public libraries and consigned to the flames). From Tomi, Ovid wrote with unusual depth of feeling two books of poems in graceful and melodious verse: the *Tristia* ("Sorrows") and the *Ex Ponto* ("Epistles from Pontus") in which he complains bitterly of the ice and snow on that dismal, treeless rock and the barbarity of the knife-wearing *Getae.* At Tomi after many years of useless and pathetic begging for permission to return from exile, Ovid finally died (A.D. 17/18).

Latin Prose Writers   The most notable prose writers of the Augustan age were the soldier and statesman Gaius Asinius Pollio (76 B.C.–A.D. 5), the literary patron Marcus Valerius Messalla Corvinus (64 B.C.–A.D. 8), the Emperor Augustus himself (63 B.C.–A.D. 14), and the patriotic historian Titus Livy (59 B.C.–

A.D. 17). Although not so great an orator as Cicero, Pollio had enjoyed an important military and political career as a partisan of Caesar and then of Mark Antony before siding with Octavian. He retired from public life after the treaty of Brundisium (40 B.C.) proved ineffective and founded Rome's first public library in a hall adjacent to the temple of Liberty. He was a minor poet as well as an orator, but his importance is as a historian. He had firsthand knowledge of many important events and access to many valuable sources. Therefore, he wrote a critical and authoritative history of the civil wars from 60 B.C. to the battle of Philippi. He was scrupulously honest and wrote in an admirably plain style alleviated with rhythmic phrases and unexpected abruptness and ellipses. While most of this valuable work is lost, it directly or indirectly is a major source for Plutarch's biographies of Caesar and Antony and Appian's *Civil Wars*.

Messalla, a respectable orator in his day and devotee of poetry, had served under Cassius at Philippi and then sided with Octavian, for whom he wrote attacks (now lost) on Antony. He wrote an independently minded firsthand account of the civil war following Caesar's assassination that would be very valuable to have. Unfortunately, it too is lost, and few traces of its influence can be found.

Augustus was an excellent prose stylist. In his *Res Gestae* the *princeps* wrote with clarity, brevity, and precision without shrinking from a slang or colloquial phrase that might express his meaning more accurately and vividly. This precious document officially records the achievements and honors of Augustus and formulates the constitutional position of the *princeps* in the reorganized state as he wished it to be viewed.

The supreme prose writer of the Augustan Age was the historian Livy. He came from Patavium (Padua) in the Cisalpine region of Italy. He eventually became part of the Imperial literary circle and tutor to the future Emperor Claudius. Of his 142 books on the history of Rome from its founding to the death of Drusus in 9 B.C., there are extant Books 1–10 (from the landing of Aeneas in Latium to

293 B.C.) and 21–45 (218 to 167 B.C.). Short summaries or epitomes (written probably in the fourth century A.D.) indicate the contents of all the books except 136 and 137. In a swiftly flowing Ciceronian style blended with Sallustian and poetical phraseology and with great dramatic power, Livy records the mighty deeds of the Roman people and Rome's divinely ordered march to world conquest. Beginning with a stern preface in which he denounced the luxury and vices of his own age, he proposed to show that Rome's success and greatness resulted from patriotism and virtue: pious devotion to the gods, valor in war, self-control, constancy, *gravitas,* and the sanctity of family life. (His work was in full accord with the social reforms of Augustus.) In spite of numerous defects as a historian—uncritical use of sources, failure to consult documents and other primary sources, ignorance of economics and military tactics, and failure to interpret primitive institutions in their proper social setting—Livy succeeded in giving the world a valuable picture of Roman history and character as many Romans wanted to see it, a fact that is itself of great significance for the modern historian of Rome.

The Impact of Augustus on Latin Literature   In a society where writers depend on wealthy or powerful personal patrons, those patrons have a great impact on literary production. Directly, or indirectly through Maecenas, the impact of Augustus was great indeed. That is not to say that he dictated what people wrote. Livy, for example, was no hack writing official history for Augustus. He wrote with a genuine patriotism that happened to coincide with Augustus' own needs and policies. The same can be said for Vergil, Horace, and Propertius, but that is what helped to attract the interest and patronage of Maecenas and Augustus, which in turn enabled them to pursue their writing and ensured a public audience for and the survival of their works. Indeed, Augustus personally intervened to secure the publication of the *Aeneid* against Vergil's own wishes. This situation was not necessarily harmful, but it raises the question of how many other writers, either through lack of connections or because of incompatible views, were lost because they could not find a powerful patron.

Augustus, of course, tolerated disagreement and was too intelligent to exercise any real censorship. Propertius, for example, often resisted Maecenas's requests that he write on something favorable to Augustus. Augustus himself even joked with Livy about the latter being a Pompeian in his political sympathies, but Augustus was safely dead before Livy wrote about the sensitive events after Actium. It may not be coincidental that under Augustus' successors the summaries of the relevant books (134–142) in the *Periochae* give them the shortest shrift of all. More directly, however, the career of Cornelius Gallus was cut short because he committed suicide after Augustus expressed official displeasure over the way in which he tactlessly publicized his military accomplishments as the first prefect of Egypt. Gallus' disgrace, therefore, may help to account for the disappearance of his work until the recent discovery of a few lines on an Egyptian papyrus (which may be contemporary with his own life). Although official disgrace had no such effect on Ovid's work, it did prevent him from finishing the *Fasti* and may well have denied the world better works than the pathetic *Tristia* bemoaning his exile and begging for release.

Greek Writers Educated men from the Greek-speaking parts of the Empire continued to produce much literature for Greek audiences. Of special note are two who worked in Rome under Augustus. The first is Diodorus Siculus (the Sicilian). He wrote a history of the world in forty books from the earliest days to Caesar's conquest of Gaul. It is not a particularly distinguished work of history as such, but it is important because in addition to covering Greece and Rome, it also treats Egypt, Mesopotamia, India, Scythia, Arabia, and North Africa, about which most ancient authors say little. Moreover, because Dio-

dorus compiled his work from important earlier historians whose works are lost, his history gives an indication of what they wrote.

More important for the history of Rome and Italy is Dionysius of Halicarnassus, who taught Greek rhetoric at Rome from 30 to 8 B.C. and established an influential literary circle. His most famous work is the *Roman Antiquities*. It covered the history of Rome from its founding to the *First Punic War* in twenty books. While the work suffers from rhetorical exaggeration, it preserves valuable material from lost Roman annalists on that period of Roman history, which is most poorly documented.

Dionysius is even more valuable as a literary critic who influenced the tastes of the day. His essay *On the Arrangement of Words* discusses the artistic ordering of words, and his *On Imitation,* which is only preserved in fragments, sets forth the principles to be followed when imitating earlier authors, a practice considered essential for developing a good style. In an essay on the style of Thucydides, he also reveals the impact that Thucydides had on writers of the late first century B.C., while a letter to C. Pompeius, in which he criticizes the style of Plato, reveals some of the stylistic controversies of the period. Especially valuable is his partially preserved *On The Ancient Orators,* which presents biographical and stylistic information about the classical Attic orators.

Also important was a Greek from Pontus named Strabo (64/63 B.C.–ca. A.D. 25). His forty-seven books of history, exclusive of that covered by Polybius, are unfortunately lost, but his *Geography* in seventeen books survives. It covers the known world of the time. While it is not always based on the best available mathematical, astronomical, and geographic research of the day, it presents in readable form much interesting geographical and historical information that would otherwise be lost.

Technical Writings Handbooks and technical manuals of all types became increasingly popular from Augustus' time onward.

The *De Architectura* of M. Vitruvius became the standard handbook for Roman architects and exercised great influence on the neoclassical architecture of the Renaissance and later classical revivals. Verrius Flaccus, the tutor of Gaius and Lucius Caesar, compiled the earliest Latin dictionary, *De Verborum Significatu,* and Marcus Agrippa set up a large map of the Roman Empire in the Forum, for which he wrote a detailed explanation in his *Commentaries* that summarized the results of Greek geographic research and Roman surveying. A few years later, under Tiberius, Aulus Cornelius Celsus compiled an important encyclopedia, whose section on medicine still survives as a valuable summary of ancient Greek medical knowledge.

Jurisprudence   The Augustan Age marks the end of the so-called Hellenistic period of Roman legal science or jurisprudence and the beginning of a new period known as the Classical, which lasted until the reign of Diocletian.

The Hellenistic Period   In the Hellenistic period of Roman law, which began around 200 B.C. and ended with Augustus, Roman legal science had come under the powerful stimulus of Greek jurisprudence, philosophy, and rhetoric, which, acting as a catalyst, released the natural and national energy of Roman jurisprudence. This period saw the rise of nonpriestly jurisprudence and the gradual replacement of state priests and pontiffs by laymen as professional jurists, consultants, and interpreters of the law. One of the earliest secular jurists was Sextus Aelius Paetus Catus, who published the *Tripertita,* containing the text of the Twelve Tables with commentary (see p. 152).

The greatest of all legal works published during the Republic was the *Civil Law* (*Ius Civile*) of Q. Mucius Scaevola the pontiff, who was consul in 95 B.C. The *Civil Law* in eighteen books was the first systematic exposition of private law and down into the second century A.D. served as a model for legal commentators.

It thereby laid the basis not merely of Roman law but of future European jurisprudence.

The Classical Period   The Classical period, beginning under Augustus, lasted about 250 years. It saw the creative ideas of the Republic elaborated in great detail. Genius was now slowly giving way to professionalism. As the old Roman families of high pedigree and proud public achievement gradually became extinct, new jurists and legal experts from Italian and even provincial towns came to the fore. Though some jurists held high office in the early Principate, after Vespasian's time (A.D. 69–79) another type more commonly appeared—the salaried officials of the Imperial bureaucracy. Many of the jurists were practising consultants, writers, and professors of law.

Responsa   Augustus did not abolish the custom established by the early pontiffs and later jurisconsults of giving expert opinions or rulings (*responsa*) on legal questions. Wishing to preserve that custom, he gave a few select jurists the right to give responses reinforced by his own personal authority (*ius respondendi ex auctoritate principis*). Most praetors and judges respected and accepted these responses, but were under no legal obligation to do so. Unauthorized jurists were still free to give responses and magistrates and judges to accept them. Like so many other innovations of Augustus, official authorization of jurisconsults did not endure beyond the reign of Trajan (A.D. 98–117).

Law Schools   As Roman society became more complex and jurists more active in civil and criminal cases than during the Republic, the demand for legal education increased correspondingly. In the first century A.D. two law schools sprang into being. One said to have been founded by Capito (*consul suffectus* of A.D. 5) was actually a foundation of C. Cassius Longinus, who died shortly after A.D. 69, but the school is often called Sabinian after Masurius Sabinus, a famous teacher of Cassius. The other school was probably a foundation of M. Antistius Labeo in the time of Augustus even though it later received the name of Proculian from a certain Proculus, who allegedly taught law during Nero's reign.

The Augustan Achievement Law flourishes only in times of peace. Although Augustus had started his career as another factional leader in civil war, he made up for the destructiveness of his early years by earnestly trying to construct for Rome a better future. The restoration of peace and orderly government after Actium and the economic upsurge that followed laid the groundwork for a brilliant efflorescence of art and literature, which Augustus himself did much to inspire and encourage. Augustan art not only achieved complete Romanization, but acquired an empire-wide character, as shown by the sculptures on the Altar of Carthage and numerous monuments in *Gallia Narbonensis*. In Vergil, Horace, Propertius, and Ovid the Latin language was perfected as a poetic medium, and Latin literature became one of the great literatures of the world.

XXVI

The First Two Julio-Claudian Emperors: Tiberius and Gaius (Caligula), A.D. 14–41

The Julio-Claudian Dynasty Augustus established the longest and most complex dynasty of Roman emperors until the dynasty of Constantine and that of Valentinian and Theodosius 300 years later. Augustus' dynastic successors are called the Julio-Claudians because of their connections with the Claudian family of Augustus' wife Livia and his own Julian family. Of the four Julio-Claudian emperors, Augustus' immediate successor, Tiberius, son of Livia by her first husband, was the only one without Julian ancestry. The other three, Gaius (popularly known as Caligula), Claudius, and Nero were members of both families. The four reigns fall conveniently into two pairs each of twenty-six and one-half years: Tiberius and Gaius (A.D. 14–41) and Claudius and Nero (A.D. 41–68).

In order to understand fully the characters of these important Emperors and the intrigues and complexities of their reigns, it is necessary to keep in mind the intricate relationships of the Julio-Claudian family as seen in the accompanying genealogical chart. In his tenacious attempt to provide a successor closely related to himself by manipulating the marriages of his daughter Julia, his sister Octavia's children, and Livia's children, Augustus created not only a confusing web of relationships but also jealousies, rivalries, and intrigues that bedeviled and even warped those who managed to attain the office of *princeps* that he created. Had he been able to foresee Caligula or Nero, he might have modified his dynastic ambitions.

Sources for the Julio-Claudians There are only two surviving ancient writers who give significant continuous accounts of the whole Julio-Claudian period. The first wrote in Latin, the second in Greek. They are Suetonius in his *Lives of the Twelve Caesars* and Cassius Dio in Books 57 to 63 of his *Roman History*. Both authors lived after the events that they describe. Suetonius was born about A.D. 69, right around the end of Nero's reign, and died around 140. He practiced law for a time and was the Emperor Hadrian's Secretary in Charge of Correspondence from ca. A.D. 119 to ca. 122. He was dismissed by Hadrian as a result of some scandal and spent the rest of his life writing in retirement. Cassius Dio, a member of the Greek aristocracy of Nicaea in Bithynia, was born about A.D. 150 and died around 235 after a distinguished senatorial career including two consulships and two provincial governorships.

THE JULIO-CLAUDIAN DYNASTY (Emperors are shown boldface)

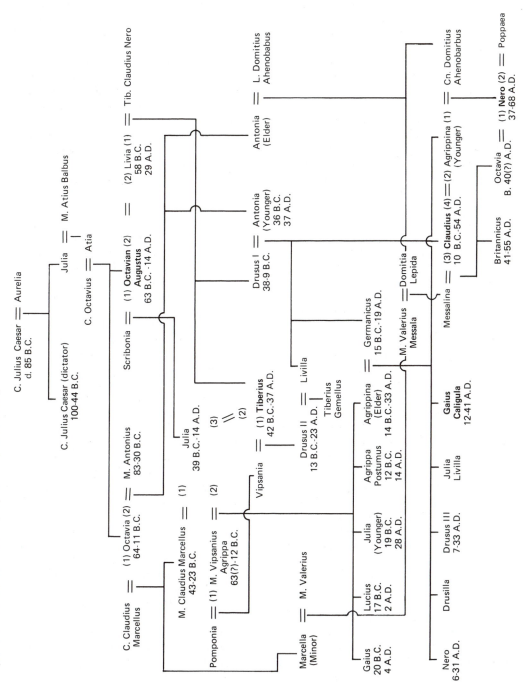

As a child, Suetonius would have heard some firsthand information about the Julio-Claudians from his elders, and while serving Hadrian he had access to archival documents, which he often quotes, and so provides some very valuable information. As a high-ranking senator, Dio also had access to much official information, but he seems not to have made much use of it. Both he and Suetonius were primarily dependent upon the narratives written by earlier authors. Since the earlier writers were mainly from the senatorial aristocracy, who often resented their loss of real power and privileges under the Principate, the words of Suetonius and Dio often reflect a negative bias toward the Julio-Claudians. Moreover, both Suetonius and Dio had an unfailing attraction to the sensational and scandalous. Therefore, in their works, the plain unvarnished truth often takes a back seat to the baseless rumors, damaging innuendoes, and malicious fabrications that they often found in other writers.

Other important literary sources exist for individual Julio-Claudian emperors. Velleius Paterculus, who was a loyal cavalry officer under Tiberius, presents a very favorable account of Tiberius' reign in the last part of the second book of his *History of Rome.* For Caligula, the Jewish historian Flavius Josephus in his *Jewish Antiquities,* Books 18 and 19, and the Jewish scholar Philo of Alexandria in his *Against Flaccus* and *Embassy to Gaius* present good contemporary accounts of certain events. Book 19 of Josephus' *Jewish Antiquities* and Books 2 to 7 of his *History of the Jewish War* also cover events under Claudius and the Jewish revolt under Nero. The philosopher Seneca the Younger, who had been exiled under Claudius, is believed to have written a scathing satire of that Emperor, the *Apocolocyntosis (Pumpkinification),* while the various philosophical and literary works of Seneca and the numerous nonhistorical writings of other authors reveal much about the social, economic, cultural, and even political history of the period (see pp. 373–375).

A far more detailed and greater literary source than any of these others is the *Annals* of Tacitus in its surviving books. Originally covering events from A.D. 14 to 69, only Books 1 to 6 (with most of Book 5 missing), covering the reign of Tiberius, and Books 12 to 16 covering the reign of Nero to 66, survive. Just as Edward Gibbon, who greatly admired Tacitus, has exercised a profound influence on modern historians of the Roman Empire because of a superb literary style combined with an intense personal viewpoint, so has Tacitus. The dark, negative images that he presents have left an indelible print on the minds of succeeding generations.

A conscientious historian cannot accept Tacitus' views of people and events uncritically. Many factors caused him to portray Tiberius and Nero in the worst possible light. Tacitus reached maturity under the reign of Domitian (A.D. 81–96), whose last years were oppressive and tyrannical and who was particularly hostile to that group of senators who wished to preserve the independence and dignity of the senate. Tacitus himself was a part of this group and wrote for them and their heirs. He absorbed and perpetuated the hostility that many old senatorial families harbored toward the Principate. This hostility was strengthened by his own experiences under Domitian, and he tended to interpret the actions of previous emperors in terms of the despotism that he had experienced. In fact, he became rather cynical and disillusioned about life in general, as can be seen from his remark that "the gods care little for our well-being, but much for our punishment." Expecting the worst, Tacitus easily saw it when the opposite could not be clearly proven.

In fact, having been trained in oratory and law and been a successful advocate in the courts, Tacitus approached history as a prosecuting attorney who was determined to seek justice for the wronged and punishment for the wicked. He claimed that the historian had the moral duty to "Preserve the record of virtuous men and to make evil men and evil deeds fear judgment at the bar of posterity." Therefore, he used all the tricks of his trade to present the most convincing case against those whom he suspected of being wicked. It is often necessary, therefore, for the modern reader of

Tacitus to act the roles of both the defense and the jury—the one to highlight the favorable evidence that Tacitus is usually willing to admit as he builds a stronger case against it, the other to arrive at a balanced evaluation of both sides of the case.

The modern historian is also aided in this task by the abundant archaeological research that has brought to light numerous coins, artifacts, monuments, inscriptions, and the remains of whole cities and towns from this period. This physical evidence illustrates the social, economic, and administrative developments that the ancient literary sources slight in favor of investigating the emperors' personalities, high politics, court intrigue, and wars. From the nonliterary evidence it is possible to estimate what was happening to the more ordinary inhabitants of the Empire under their rulers, whose primary duty was to protect them and promote their welfare.

Tiberius (A.D. 14–37)   The full name of Tiberius was Tiberius Claudius Nero. He was fifty-five years old when he succeeded Augustus in A.D. 14 and already past the prime of life for those times. On the one hand, he had the invaluable experience of many years as a successful general on the frontiers and as Augustus' virtual coemperor during the past ten years. On the other, bitterness and disillusionment combined with a character that made him both proud and content with being second in command left him ill-suited for the difficult job that he had to undertake at this late point in his life. As a proud descendent of the mighty Claudii, he was ready to do his duty to Rome and the honor of his family, but his pride made him stiff and reserved, while the fear of sole responsibility made him insecure and joyless.

Joy was something of which Tiberius had known little, and what little he had experienced had never lasted long. Born in 42 B.C. during civil war, he spent the first two years of his life with his parents in exile. In 38, his mother, Livia, persuaded his father to divorce her so that she could marry Octavian, who seems to have disliked the shy lad with the slow, halting speech and to have preferred his younger brother, Drusus, who had a more jovial and appealing personality. These early experiences made Tiberius a gloomy man, cynical and resentful.

Nor did manhood bring him respite from trouble. Hard work and successful generalship won him neither recognition nor reward. He found himself repeatedly passed over in favor of younger men. After a happy marriage with Vipsania, Agrippa's daughter, he yielded to Augustus' insistence that he divorce the woman whom he loved to marry Julia, who despised him. To escape from that marriage more, perhaps, than from the favoritism that Augustus had begun to show toward Julia's sons by Agrippa, Lucius and Gaius Caesar, Tiberius went into self-imposed exile at Rhodes, where he remained for nine years. His adoption by Augustus after the deaths of the young Caesars and his later assumption of tribunician power and the proconsular *imperium* could not efface all the slights, snubs, and indignities he had suffered in the past. At his accession he was still a soured and disillusioned man. It is no wonder that many of the nobles in the senate with which he was supposed to work neither liked nor trusted him and were always willing to place his actions in the worst light for the historical record.

Many, for example, believed that he was simply being a hypocrite when he declared that he was reluctant to become the new *princeps*. Perhaps he was merely imitating what Augustus had done in 27 B.C. to make it look as if the senate really was in control, but he may well have been deeply ambivalent about taking on the burdensome role. He must have realized that he did not have Augustus' tact and probably feared the inevitable situations in which he would have no precedent to guide him through the political and constitutional ambiguities that Augustus' new form of government necessarily entailed. He eventually accepted with the proviso that he had the right to step down when a suitable successor could be found. Unfortunately for him and Rome, the suitable ones all died before they were ready to relieve him of his heavy burden.

The principate of Tiberius began ominously with the execution of Agrippa Postumus, the grandson of Augustus but a brutal and intractable person, whom Augustus had exiled to a barren island in A.D. 7. Unarmed but with the strength of an ox, Postumus savagely resisted the centurion dispatched to the island to put him to death. It is not known who decided or ordered the killing—Augustus, perhaps Livia, or Tiberius. Suspicion fell upon Tiberius. So Tacitus reports in his *Annals* and calls the execution the "first crime of the new principate" (*primum facinus novi principatus*).

Already Tacitus has subtly cast Tiberius as a murderous tyrant by stating the suspicion against Tiberius in this case as strongly as possible. But it is quite likely that Augustus had advised that Postumus be executed, and there was good reason to do so. He would have made a very bad emperor, and if he were to remain alive after Augustus, there were those who, for their own ambitions or dislike of Tiberius, would have promoted his claim. Such a situation would have created dangerous political instability for Rome.

The Mutiny of the Legions   Shortly after the accession of Tiberius, the legions stationed in Pannonia (Hungary) and those in the Lower Rhineland mutinied in protest against the long terms of service, wretched pay, and discipline enforced by beatings and brutalities. Tiberius sent his son Drusus (II) to Pannonia to quell the mutiny there, and Germanicus, his nephew, adopted son, and heir, to the Rhineland. Drusus, acting with dignity and courage, successfully restored discipline, but Germanicus resorted to weak emotional displays and theatrical threats of suicide, which inspired little respect.

Germanicus   To restore the morale of the troops, to emulate the deeds of his father, Tiberius' brother, Drusus, and to avenge the defeat of Varus in the Teutoburg Forest (see p. 294), Germanicus was determined to renew the attempt to conquer Germany. Although he conducted three successful campaigns from A.D. 14 to 16 and defeated Varus' old foe, Ar-

minius, he was unable to occupy German territory permanently. Tiberius realized that the military ventures of Germanicus were a drain upon the Empire's manpower and resources. His personal knowledge of Germany convinced him of the wisdom of the Augustan policy of making the Rhine a permanent frontier. He therefore called Germanicus back to Rome and renounced the conquest of Germany. He preferred to rely instead on the diplomatic talents of his son Drusus (II). This reversal of policy soon bore fruit. Arminius and Maroboduus, the powerful king of Bohemia, began to quarrel and then to fight. Maroboduus lost his kingdom and fled to Italy as a refugee. Arminius fell victim to an assassin's dagger. Bohemia became virtually a client kingdom of Rome.

After receiving Germanicus at Rome with highest honors (including a splendid triumph), Tiberius sent him to the Near East with powers transcending those of all governors and legates in that area. The purpose of the mission was to negotiate with Artabanus III, the ambitious and aggressive king of Parthia, to place upon the now-vacant throne of Armenia a king friendly to Rome, and to superintend the annexation of the kingdoms of Cappadocia, Cilicia, and Commagene as Imperial provinces. Germanicus carried out these difficult tasks with consummate efficiency and success.

All might have ended well had not Tiberius feared that Germanicus might impulsively embroil the Empire in an all-out war with Parthia. To act as a brake upon the warmaking proclivities of that brilliant but impulsive youth, he sent Cn. Calpurnius Piso to the East as governor of Syria. The choice was most unfortunate, for Piso hated Germanicus and refused to acknowledge him as a superior officer or obey his orders.

Germanicus was guilty of mistakes too. Without authorization from Tiberius he went to Egypt, where he accepted divine honors and opened reserve granaries for the relief of starvation in Alexandria. Although that generous act did not endanger the food supply of Rome, his journey to Egypt seemed contrary to the policy of Augustus and naturally irritated the suspicious and legalistic mind of Tiberius, who complained bitterly before the senate.

On his return to Syria, Germanicus found that Piso had contemptuously disobeyed all his orders, and he had no alternative but to order him out of the province. Shortly after Piso's expulsion, Germanicus took sick at Antioch. In his illness and delirium, he accused Piso of attempting to destroy him by sorcery and poison and, calling upon his wife and children to avenge his murder, died.

The body of Germanicus was hastily cremated, and Agrippina the Elder, his wife, set out for Rome with the ashes. Piso seized the opportunity to make a bold stroke for the province of Syria, but he was defeated and brought to Rome. There he was brought to trial before the senate on three charges: the murder of Germanicus, insubordination in disobeying a superior officer, and his attempt to recover a province from which he had been ordered to depart. Although acquitted of the charge of murder, he was convicted and condemned on the others. Upon hearing of the senate's judgment, Piso committed suicide.

Agrippina suspected Tiberius of complicity in Germanicus' death on the grounds that he was jealous of Germanicus' popularity and wanted to clear the way for his own son Drusus (II) to succeed. These suspicions were furthered by Tiberius' (and Livia's) unwillingness to participate in the extensive public mourning for Germanicus. (Tiberius would have found it difficult to eulogize an impetuous man who had acted unwisely on significant occasions; he might have felt that his own austere personality would suffer in the eyes of the public by comparison with the affable, outgoing man being mourned; and he and Livia may genuinely have wished to remain in the background so as not to appear to be competing with Agrippina, her children, and her dead husband for public attention.) Furthermore, Piso's suicide convinced others that he really was guilty of poisoning Germanicus (Piso probably was only trying to avoid execution so that his property would go to his heirs instead of being forfeited to the state), and it made his

friends in the senate suspect that he had been made a scapegoat for Tiberius. For the rest of his reign, therefore, Tiberius had to contend with the slanders of Agrippina, who, along with her children, was a figure around whom those senators who disliked Tiberius could rally.

Sejanus   A man who took advantage of the situation for his own self-aggrandizement and made it even worse for Tiberius was Lucius Aelius Sejanus. Sejanus is one of the most infamous and sinister personalities in Roman history, but he is also a prime example of how the Principate opened up the high levels of government to the equestrian class, whom the restrictive Republican nobility had generally excluded. Sejanus' father had risen to be a prefect of the Praetorian Guard before him, and Sejanus eventually became his colleague. The Guard soon became for Sejanus an instrument of great power and terror, especially after he had persuaded the *princeps* to make him its sole prefect after his father's death and to concentrate all of its nine cohorts, hitherto scattered throughout Italy, in new barracks on the eastern outskirts of Rome. Growing ever more presumptuous, he aspired to marriage within the Imperial family and eventual succession to the throne. His first step was the seduction of Livilla, the wife of Drusus (II). In 23, Drusus died suddenly. Apparently it was a natural death, but the coincidence led to the accusation of foul play in the light of Sejanus' later machinations.

To clear the way to the throne and remove all potential rivals, Sejanus next plotted the ruin and death of Agrippina and her three sons, Nero (not the future emperor), Drusus (III), and Gaius (Caligula). Deviously and with devilish cunning, he aroused the Emperor's suspicions of that violent and vindictive woman, whose hatred for Tiberius was public knowledge. The intrigues of Sejanus against Agrippina became increasingly bold in 26, when Tiberius, at Sejanus' urging, decided to leave the hectic capital and ensconce himself on the lovely and inaccessible island of

Capreae (Capri) in the bay of Naples. Sejanus opened his offensive against Agrippina by attacking her friends, charging them with treason, and driving them into exile or death by suicide or execution. After the death of the old Empress Livia in 29 (at the age of eighty-six), he apparently convinced Tiberius of Agrippina's involvement in a plot against the throne. Thereupon, the senate (after two letters from Tiberius) exiled Agrippina to the island of Pandateria and her eldest son, Nero, to Pontia, where he killed himself soon after. Her second son, Drusus (III), committed to a prison in Rome in 30, starved himself to death three years later. The only consolation that Agrippina and Drusus might have enjoyed was that they lived long enough to learn of the downfall and death of the agent of their ruin.

Sejanus' attempt to glide gently into power had been a notable success until he overreached himself. In 31 he was consular colleague of Tiberius and received from the senate the proconsular *imperium,* through which he was able to extend his patronage by the disposal of honors and provinces. He now formed a double matrimonial connection with the Imperial family: he won Tiberius' consent to wed either Livilla or her daughter by Drusus (II), the princess Julia, and betrothed his own daughter to the son of Claudius (the future Emperor). In Rome the statues of Sejanus and Tiberius stood side by side, and altars to clemency and friendship conjointly commemorated their virtues. Only one obstacle now blocked the way to the throne: Agrippina's third son Gaius (Caligula), whom Tiberius had recommended in a letter to the senate as heir to the throne. Sejanus sought to remove that obstacle by a plot against the life of Gaius. Then suddenly something went wrong.

Antonia, the younger daughter of the triumvir Marcus Antonius and grandmother of the young prince Gaius, secretly sent her freedman Pallas to Tiberius, who promptly summoned Gaius to the safety of Capri. Then he sent Naevius Sutorius Macro, prefect of the *vigiles,* to Rome to take over command of the Praetorian Guard and convey to the senate a long and wordy letter. The letter, read out by the consul, began with mild praise of Sejanus. Praise became criticism, criticism reproof, and the reproof ended in sharp denunciation and a peremptory order for arrest. The senate at once voted condemnation and death. The populace hailed the fall of Sejanus with frenzied joy, pulled down his statues, dragged his body through the streets, and flung it into the Tiber. Many of his friends and supporters fell victim to the infuriated mob.

The treason of a long-trusted minister was a cruel blow to Tiberius. Others were soon forthcoming: Apicata, the divorced wife of Sejanus, maddened by the Praetorian Guards' execution of her eleven-year-old son and their raping and strangling of her little daughter, committed suicide. Before doing so she wrote Tiberius a letter with the tale that Sejanus and Livilla had murdered Drusus (II), the heir to the throne. The former slave attendants of Drusus, when put to torture, understandably confirmed the charge, and Tiberius believed that he had become the unwitting accomplice in a conspiracy against the state with unknown ramifications. He resolved to eradicate and destroy it.

The Law of Treason (*Maiestas*)   A mighty weapon lay at Tiberius' hand—the law of treason (*maiestas*), not of his own making but the product of a long process of evolution from the early Republic to the principate of Augustus. *Maiestas* originally covered all offenses against the safety of the state, such as betrayal to an enemy or physical assault upon a magistrate. By the time of Julius Caesar, the law came to include all offenses against the dignity of the state. In the Principate, it covered not only high treason (*perduellio*) but a variety of rather ill-defined charges, which ranged from arrogance, sacrilege, and slander to extortion, adultery, incest, rape, and murder.

Under a law of such flexibility it is not surprising that 106 persons should have been brought to trial during the long reign of Tiberius. Tiberius often favored acquittal or disallowed convictions already handed down by the lower courts or by the senate, and only thirty-five of those charged were actually convicted. It is a gross exaggeration, therefore, to say that Tiberius' principate was a tyranny or reign of terror. Nevertheless, he did set a precedent for future abuses by others.

The Informers (Delatores) The worst aspect of the treason trials during the principate of Tiberius was the practice of permitting private citizens to initiate prosecutions for financial rewards (usually one-fourth of the convicted defendant's property). The use of *delatores* (informers) was a miserable system of law enforcement because it encouraged unscrupulous persons to trump up charges against the rich, but it was a necessary evil since there was no public prosecutor or state police. Tiberius himself once remarked that the abolition of rewards to professional accusers would wreck the entire system of existing law enforcement.

Yet it would be erroneous to suppose that many *delatores* rose from poverty to riches. Of fourteen recorded prosecutors, who later appeared as defendants on charges other than that of calumny, only one had ever informed against more than one person. The informer's profession was apparently neither busy nor lucrative—nor safe. It was invariably one of considerable risk. Tacitus himself reports how lucky some informers were to suffer merely the loss of an expected reward. On several occasions, Tiberius had false accusers and calumniators punished, sometimes exiled. They brought ruin upon others and in the end upon themselves.

Tiberius and the Senate: The Increasing Power of the *Princeps* The increase of *delatores* and treason trials in Tiberius' reign, especially after the disillusioning revelations that accompanied his self-imposed exile on the Isle of Capri and the fall of Sejanus, embittered Tiberius' already precarious relations with many senators. Throughout his reign, Tiberius' relations with the senate were full of irony. They reveal a serious paradox in the nature of the Augustan principate that could

not be resolved except in the direction of increased power for the *princeps*.

Conscientiously following Augustus' model, as he always tried to do, Tiberius earnestly attempted to make the senate a meaningful partner in the government of the Empire. He styled himself as an equal citizen with the senators and refused such honors as the *praenomen Imperator* and the title *Pater Patriae*. If a worthy senator fell into such financial difficulties that his status as a senator was threatened, Tiberius generously provided the money to remedy the problem. Before abandoning Rome for Capri, Tiberius had tried to attend all meetings of the senate. He encouraged freedom of speech and debate. At least once, he ended as a minority of one when a vote was taken.

Tiberius also increased the powers and responsibilities of the senate. For example, he transferred to it the age-old prerogative of the Centuriate Assembly: the function of electing the consuls and praetors, the most prestigeous magistrates. He made the senate a supreme court of justice, especially for the trial of influential persons accused of treason and of both Imperial and senatorial provincial governors accused of extortion and corruption. Though some treason trials even as late as A.D. 20 took place in the regular praetors' courts, Tiberius preferred to have such cases tried in the senate because it was less vulnerable to bribery and intimidation by powerful defendants.

He also made it a practice to consult the senate on all affairs of state—finances, public works, the raising and disposition of armies, the appointment of generals and governors, and the conduct of foreign affairs. Yet all of these attempts to make the senators responsible partners in government did not really work. Despite Tiberius' attempt to be an equal citizen with them, they knew that in the last analysis his powers as *princeps* were far greater than theirs, and his very attempts to encourage senators to speak their minds freely only added to the suspicion that he was trying to set traps for those who did not like him. A remark addressed to Tiberius by Gnaeus Piso aptly illustrates the problem: "I would ask you sire: when are you going to vote? If first, you set me an example to follow; if last, I am afraid that I may unintentionally disagree with you." No matter how much Tiberius might try to disguise the fact, the senators knew that they were the clients of the powerful *princeps*, and it was impossible for them to forget it. Their distress was highlighted after Tiberius retired to Capri and they had to wait for his letters to find out what he wanted them to do.

An Insolvable Problem   While it is easy, therefore, to accuse many senators of servility, as even Tiberius did when, in a moment of frustration at their refusal of responsibility, he called them "men ready to be slaves," there was no real incentive to counteract the pressures in that direction. While at the same time a well-intentioned emperor like Tiberius tried to uphold the prestige of the senate or encourage the senators to take responsibility and act independently, he could not give them the real power and rewards that were the true basis of prestige and incentives for assuming responsibility. The office of *princeps* depended upon a monopoly of the highest powers, greatest military forces, and most strategic provinces. Those, however, were the very things which brought prestige and for which senators freely strove under the free Republic. If an emperor were to share them with other senators now, however, he would inevitably create rivals to himself. That was something a conscientious emperor could not risk and a despotic one would not tolerate. As a result, even under an emperor who respected the senate, the tendency was for senators to abdicate the responsibilities that he was willing for them to have. Therefore, even a well-meaning emperor had to assume more direct responsibility himself. In this way, the senate was weakened even further, so that it was even less able to resist the usurpations of a despotic *princeps*. Eventually, the power to flatter an emperor was all that the senate had left.

Stoic Opponents   There were, of course, a significant number of senators who resented this situation bitterly. They were descendants of the old Republican nobility or members of newer senatorial families from the conservative districts of northern Italy, who, like their famous compatriot, the historian Livy, idealized the virtues of the Republic in its heyday. Their heroes were Cato the Younger and Caesar's assassins Cassius and Brutus. Like their heroes, they often professed the philosophy of Stoicism, which became associated at Rome with Republican opposition to the Principate. When persecuted for their opposition they frequently sought a martyr's death in suicide, which became the ultimate, though futile, act of protest.

The historian Cremutius Cordus was such an individual under Tiberius. He wrote a history of Rome in which he praised Brutus and called Cassius "the last of the Romans." As a result, in 25 he was prosecuted for *maiestas*. Tiberius attended the trial in the senate, and his grim face showed that he disapproved of Cremutius' defense. Cremutius, therefore, gave up and starved himself to death. A majority of senators then sought favor with the Emperor by ordering the aediles to confiscate all copies of his history and burn them. Secretly, however, some saved copies that were published after Tiberius' death and helped to inspire more martyrs under later emperors.

Tiberius the Administrator   The fame of Tiberius rests chiefly on his knowledge of and skill in Imperial administration. He followed the foreign policy of Augustus by relying wherever possible on diplomatic rather than military tactics, as when he compelled Germanicus to abandon the conquest of Germany and restrained him from involving Rome in a war with Parthia. The Augustan conquests in central Europe and the East required a pause for consolidation. By strengthening the defenses along the Rhine and other frontiers and by suppressing revolts in Gaul, in Thrace, and in North Africa, he kept the Empire at peace and at an unprecedented peak of prosperity.

To promote the material welfare of the provinces, he kept tribute and taxes at a minimum, and, by strict financial economy (the curtailment of expensive spectacles and ambitious building projects), he was able to reduce taxes and yet build up a large surplus in the treasury. Unfortunately, his reduced spending on games, spectacles, and grandiose building projects made him unpopular among the common people of Rome. In an effort to procure a more honest and efficient collection of provincial taxes, he restricted the tax-farming companies to the collection of customs dues and severely punished all provincial governors guilty of extortion, floggings, and confiscation of private property, or of corrupt administration. Some of the governors found guilty of such injustices committed suicide rather than face the wrath of the Emperor.

Tiberius appointed able and conscientious men to govern the Imperial provinces. As an incentive to honest administration, he increased governors' salaries and lengthened their terms of office so that they would get increasingly familiar with their duties and with local conditions. Many of the governors held office from five to ten years, some even longer. C. Poppaeus Sabinus was in charge of the newly united Imperial province of Macedonia, Achaea, and Moesia for twenty years, and C. Calvisius Sabinus was legate of Pannonia for almost twenty-four. As a result of this policy, cases of extortion and corruption arose less frequently in the Imperial provinces than in the senatorial, where governors normally held office for only one year.

Tiberius encouraged the provincial assemblies (*concilia*) to send delegates to Rome to lodge complaints before the Emperor and the senate about the conduct of governors, legates, and procurators in both the Imperial and senatorial provinces.

Tiberius prohibited the Gallic cities from issuing silver coins in order that a uniform Imperial coinage might be established to facilitate trade and the exchange of goods over wider areas. To expedite frontier defense and encourage travel, communication, and commerce, he embarked upon an extensive road-and bridge-building program in Gaul, Pannonia (Hungary), Moesia (Bulgaria), North Africa, Egypt, and particularly in Spain, where flourishing cities sprang up at road junctions and terminals.

The new economic prosperity of the provinces, the efficient collection of taxes, and careful financial administration increased revenues and created a large surplus in the treasury which enabled the Emperor to give prompt and liberal relief to disaster-stricken areas in both Italy and the provinces. Even after making these and other large grants from the treasury, Tiberius was able to reduce an unpopular sales tax from one to one-half percent and to leave behind in the treasury the sum of 2.7 billion sesterces (3.3 billion according to some authorities).

Last Years and Succession   Tiberius spent the last ten years of his reign in almost continuous seclusion on the Isle of Capri. Three times he journeyed to the outskirts of Rome, but he could never bring himself actually to enter it again. His preference for Capri led to malicious rumors that he spent his time in every vice and debauchery that a perverted mind could invent. Suetonius delighted in publicizing them, but they are baseless. Tiberius actually spent his time working for the Empire or enjoying more cultured pursuits. For example, he surrounded himself with scholars and artists, such as the famous Alexandrian scholar Thrasyllus, who tutored the Emperor in astrological lore.

One of the most serious questions of state with which Tiberius had to wrestle in his last years was that of a successor. The death of Germanicus and the deadly plottings of Sejanus against Drusus (II) and the family of Germanicus had left as possible choices only Germanicus' son Gaius Caligula and Tiberius' own grandson, Tiberius Gemellus, son of Drusus (II). In A.D. 35, at age 75, Tiberius tried to resolve the problem. Although he had saved Caligula by taking him to Capri, Tiberius may not have thought that his character was suitable for that of a *princeps*. Moreover, his refusal, for whatever reason, to give Caligula any official duties, through which he could have gained experience, made him even less suitable, and growing up with a reclusive emperor governing by letters to the senate certainly would have given Gaius a strange model to follow. Tiberius probably would have preferred Gemellus as his ultimate successor, but in 35 he was only sixteen. Caligula was not only older but also could trace his ancestry back to the family of Augustus and Caesar through both of his parents, whereas Gemellus could do so only through his mother. Finally, Caligula was the son of the popular Germanicus, so that he enjoyed great support from the common people and the soldiers. It would have been too dangerous to pass over Caligula completely. Therefore, Tiberius made Gemellus and Caligula his joint heirs.

In 37, when Tiberius felt that he was nearing the end, he attempted to return to Rome. He reached only Misenum across the bay from Capri. There he fell into a coma and died. Unsubstantiated rumors reported that when Tiberius momentarily revived, the Praetorian Prefect Q. Naevius Sutorius Macro had him smothered in his bedclothes. The story was probably fabricated after Caligula had turned out to be a murderous tyrant, but it received circumstantial support from the fact that Macro had been the one who nominated Caligula as the new *princeps* at a meeting of the senate right after Tiberius' death.

Caligula* (A.D. 37–41) The senators accepted Caligula's nomination without objection, and they showed their disapproval of Tiberius by refusing to proclaim him a god as they had done in the cases of Augustus and Caesar. Caligula, whose official name was Gaius Julius Caesar Augustus Germanicus, certainly had much to recommend him. Not only did he en-

joy popularity as Germanicus' only surviving son, but one of his grandfathers was Agrippa, Augustus' great general. (Caligula himself, however, was reportedly ashamed of Agrippa's equestrian origin.) Also, one of his great grandfathers was Marcus Antonius, whose reputation had improved as the civil wars faded into the past. Another great grandfather was Augustus himself.

His lineage, therefore, probably overshadowed his recent past, which may have given a thoughtful observer pause, or if it did, such observers thought it best to keep quiet. In his later teens he had lived with his grandmother, Antonia, who threw him into constant companionship with three young Thracian princes, with the young Herod Agrippa I of Judea, and with Ptolemy of Mauretania, a grandson of Antonius and Cleopatra. From them he may have acquired his Eastern conception of absolute monarchy. During his stay at his uncle's court at Capri he practiced the arts of dissimulation and obsequiousness, which probably had been necessary for him to survive during Sejanus' reign of terror.

Popular Start   After the long, stern, and puritanical reign of Tiberius, however, the people welcomed their new ruler with gladness and thanksgiving. He, in turn, delighted the populace by distributing the legacies of Livia and Tiberius, by abolishing the unpopular sales taxes (already slightly reduced by Tiberius), and by his splendid spectacles, games, chariot races, and wild beast hunts. He even restored to the popular assemblies their ancient right of electing magistrates. He pleased the senate by his deference and courtesy and by his conciliatory attitude toward the nobility. He abolished all impending trials for treason, curbed the infamous activities of the *delatores,* recalled the exiles of Tiberius, and piously had the bones and ashes of his mother Agrippina and his brother Nero brought back from the islands for interment in the mausoleum of Augustus. He adopted his cousin and cobeneficiary, Tiberius Gemellus, as his son and heir, shared the consulship with his uncle Claudius, and had his three sisters honored throughout

---

* Literally, "Little Boot," a name bestowed on him as a child in the Rhineland by his father's soldiers because his mother, Agrippina, liked to dress him in the uniform of a legionary soldier, complete with little military boots. (*Caligulae,* the diminutive of *caligae,* means "heavy top boots.")

the Empire. To cap it all, he stirred the patriotic fervor of all classes by announcing preparations for the conquest of Britain and Germany. A serious illness, however, forced him to postpone this enterprise and shattered men's hopes for a glorious reign of concord and felicity.

Increasing Despotism Ancient sources (especially Suetonius) imply that after his recovery Caligula became mentally deranged and succumbed completely to the temptations of supreme power. His close brush with death certainly could have triggered his subsequent vehement insistence that he was a god incarnate. While he may have acted like a madman, however, there was method to his madness. His acts were those of a man who wanted to show that he was more powerful than a mere mortal. Also, Tiberius' failure to receive deification may have been a lesson to Caligula to make certain that such an important matter not be left to chance.

He began to play the role of an unrestrained despot and indulged in acts of cruelty, megalomania, and caprice. He insulted and humiliated the senate, stripped it of military control over *Africa Proconsularis,* and deprived it of its exclusive right of coinage in Italy by removing the Imperial mint from Rome to Lyons. He forced individual senators to swear that they would lay down their lives for him and his sisters, to wait upon his table dressed as slaves, trot beside his chariot in their togas, and even kiss his feet in homage. Like the Pharaohs of ancient Egypt (whom he greatly admired and imitated), he asserted the right of eminent domain over the property of his subjects (he introduced taxes in the Egyptian manner on shopkeepers and craftsmen), reportedly lived in habitual incest with his sisters (a report that is not farfetched if he was modelling himself after Egyptian Pharoahs, who often married their sisters, and after Zeus of Greek mythology, who was both the husband and brother of Hera), and longed to be worshipped as a god on earth, the New Sun, *Neos Helios* (Egyptian coins represent him as a sun god).

He loved to sit in the Temple of Castor and Pollux and receive divine worship or converse with Jupiter and the other gods. Eventually, he had a temple erected to himself out of public funds, and not only appointed his favorite horse, Incitatus (which he believed to be a reincarnation of Alexander the Great's Bucephalus), as high priest of his cult, but even had him made a member of the senate. In 39 he had a bridge of ships built across the Bay of Baiae and celebrated its completion by riding over it and wearing the breastplate of Alexander, whose vast military enterprises he wished to imitate. At the height of the celebration, a great many people became drunk and, as boats overturned, some drowned.

Financially, Caligula was equally unrestrained. He squandered money on perfume baths, banquets, and fabulous drinks, and on horse races, shows, and gifts to the populace. His pleasure barges on Lake Nemi contained baths, gardens, gem-studded sterns, and the costliest of furnishings. These and many other extravagances soon exhausted the huge surplus that Tiberius had accumulated in the treasury. To obtain new funds he resorted to extraordinary taxes (on foodstuffs, law suits, and the earnings of porters, panders, and prostitutes), forced legacies, and confiscations. He accordingly revived the treason laws as a means of confiscating money and property.

Among his victims were his father-in-law Junius Silanus, Tiberius Gemellus, his adopted son and heir, Naevius Sutorius Macro, the prefect of the Praetorian Guard who had helped him to the throne, and several members and partisans of the Claudian family. His uncle Claudius escaped only because he seemed to be a harmless dolt.

Caligula's megalomaniacal behavior inspired plots against him. In 39, for example, one of his army commanders in the Rhineland, Cn. Cornelius Lentulus Gaetulicus, conspired to place upon the throne M. Aemilius Lepidus, the widower of Caligula's own dearly beloved sister Drusilla. Caligula had both men executed and exiled his other two sisters, the Younger Agrippina and Julia Livilla, both of whom were involved in the plot. He also brought Calvisius Sabinus, the governor of Pannonia, to trial for tampering with the loyalty of the army under his command.

After suppressing the conspiracy in the Rhineland, Caligula crossed the Rhine in late 39 to discourage future German border raids, but in 40 his long-planned invasion of Britain came to nothing more than a march to the Strait of Dover and the erection of a lighthouse (two hundred feet high) at Boulogne, which remained standing until 1544.

Caligula's Foreign and Provincial Policies

Though Caligula was autocratic and capricious in foreign and provincial affairs, he generally favored the policies of Pompey and Marcus Antonius rather than that of Augustus and Tiberius. In the East, for example, he preferred client kings to provincial governors, who might enter into conspiracies and create armies for rebellion against the throne. He abandoned Greater Armenia as a Roman sphere of influence and allowed Parthia to control it in exchange for Parthian recognition of Rome's interests in the East. He restored Commagene, which Tiberius had annexed as a province, to Antiochus; he made his three young Thracian friends client rulers respectively of Thrace, Pontus and the Bosporus, and Lesser Armenia; and placed Herod Agrippa (I) over the whole of the kingdom formerly ruled by his grandfather Herod the Great. In Africa, on the other hand, Caligula foolishly deposed and executed Ptolemy, the client king of Mauretania (western Algeria and Morocco), and made his kingdom a Roman province. Perhaps Caligula simply resented Ptolemy, who, through Cleopatra Selene, was also a descendant of Marcus Antonius. The murder of Ptolemy provoked a revolt, which Caligula did not live long enough to suppress.

In his policy toward the Jews, Caligula was equally erratic and provocative. In Alexandria, where there was a large Jewish community, he permitted a Greek mob to sack the Jewish quarters and forcibly erect his statues in their synagogues. In 40 the Jews sent a delegation headed by the scholar Philo to Caligula but obtained no redress. Meanwhile, Caligula had instructed Petronius, his legate in Syria, to install his statue in the Temple at Jerusalem, but Caligula's death relieved Petronius of the necessity of carrying out the order.

Assassination

Caligula's brief career of extravagance, oppression, murder, and megalomania came to an abrupt end on January 24, A.D. 41, when Cassius Chaerea, a tribune of the Praetorian Guard, whom he had offended with insulting obscenities, struck him down in a secret passageway of the palace. The hand that struck was Chaerea's, but the men behind the deed were prominent members of the senate, administration, and army. Caligula had left himself no adequate basis of support anywhere.

The best thing that can be said about Caligula's reign is that it was brief. Fortunately, it had not been long enough to undo much of the good that Augustus and Tiberius had done to improve the administration and defense of Rome's vast empire. Nevertheless, it had revealed the enormous potential for unfettered despotism in the Principate. While Tiberius' personality and the paradoxical nature of the Principate itself often frustrated him, Tiberius really tried to make the senate a meaningful partner in government. Caligula, on the other hand, willfully tried to subordinate it and everything else to his own exalted self.

As a result, a significant group of senators, who still preserved the traditions of the free Republic, hoped to restore it, or some better semblance of it, upon the assassination of Caligula. The futility of such fantasies in the post-Augustan world was quickly brought home, however, by the circumstances surrounding the accession of the next Julio-Claudian.

XXVII

Claudius, Nero, and the End of the Julio-Claudians, A.D. 41–68

Claudius (A.D. 41–54) After the assassination of Caligula, members of the senate debated what to do. While they were discussing the relative merits of restoring the Republic or creating a truly elective Principate, their inability to control events was made painfully clear. Caligula's uncle Claudius, whose full name was Tiberius Claudius Nero Germanicus, had obtained the loyalty of the praetorian guardsmen by promising each one a gift of fifteen thousand sesterces. Although Tiberius and Caligula had given gifts of money to the guards after they became emperors, Claudius made clear their political power and set a dangerous precedent for the future by promising a reward for their support before he ascended to the Principate. When they demanded that the senate confirm their choice, many senators protested. Claudius rightly pointed out that with the guard behind him they had no alternative, and they yielded to the inevitable.

Suetonius depicts Claudius' accession as pure farce: While ransacking the Imperial palace after Caligula's assassination, some soldiers of the Praetorian Guard happened to see two feet sticking out from under a curtain in the balcony. They discovered that it was Claudius, the brother of Germanicus. Instead of killing him as he expected, they carried him over to their barracks where the troops tumultuously acclaimed him Emperor of Rome. That is just the way in which one would expect a man whom hostile tradition depicted as a fool to become Emperor. This story, however, probably does not give enough credit to Claudius for shrewdly seizing the opportunity that Caligula's assassination presented to make himself Emperor. Claudius was no fool, although he did have handicaps that made him an unlikely candidate for *princeps*.

Early Life All his life Claudius had had to contend with the most extreme physical and psychological handicaps: persistently poor health, physical deformity, slow mental development, social maladjustment, and timidity. A birth defect or an early attack of infantile paralysis had apparently left him with a grotesque appearance—wobbly head, spindly legs, a gawky look, and a speech impediment which made him appear simpleminded. Often his Imperial relations either felt ashamed of him and tried to keep him out of sight or else made fun of him. Caligula sometimes made him act the part of a court buffoon.

His ugliness and social awkwardness drove Claudius to drinking and gambling, which also caused embarrassment. Nevertheless, early on Augustus had realized that Claudius did possess a good intellect, and he encouraged its development by providing him with good teachers. As his mental powers developed under the tutelage of the great historian Livy and through association with Greek scientists and scholars, he became a philologist and antiquarian, and an expert on Roman law and government, and even on Etruscan and Carthaginian history, which he studied by learning Etruscan and Punic and of which he wrote multivolume accounts based on original research.

The study of law and history is not exactly poor training for a leader. Moreover, Claudius was not without some useful experience. He had been given a prominent role as a representative of the Imperial family among the *equites* and had presided over some of the major games. Under Augustus he had been made an augur and a priest of the Imperial cult; Tiberius had honored him with the consular insignia; and Caligula had made him his colleague in a joint consulship for two months. The senate had even decreed honors for him from time to time. Also, as a Julio-Claudian and brother of the once popular Germanicus, Claudius enjoyed the support of the army, the urban populace, the Italian upper class, and the people of the provinces.

The Political Philosophy and Policies of Claudius   After his accession, Claudius revealed astonishing strength of character and political acumen. From his study of Roman history and political institutions, Claudius learned that Rome owed her greatness to her willingness to devise new institutions to meet new needs. Reform, he held, lay at the very root of her tradition and would be her salvation in the noontide of her power. Like Augustus, however, whose biography he wrote, Claudius realized that reform at Rome could not move too quickly and had to be respectful to the past.

Claudius and the Senate   At the beginning of his reign, Claudius hoped to placate the sen-

atorial aristocracy by proclaiming Augustus as his model. He was no secret Republican, but he showed the senate respect and deference and earnestly desired its collaboration in the governance of the Empire. He sat between consuls or on the tribune's bench only when he had something special to propose. He religiously attended all meetings, took his seat as an ordinary senator, and expressed his opinion (*sententia*) only if and when so asked. Though proclaimed *Imperator* at least twenty-seven times for military victories won in his name, he refused the title as well as that of "Father of the Fatherland" (*Pater Patriae*). In 44 he restored to the senate the provinces of Macedonia and Achaea which Tiberius had made "imperial" in 15. He conferred upon the senate the election of curule magistrates, which Caligula, reversing the policy of Tiberius, had transferred to the people. As in the case of Tiberius' reign, however, the paradox inherent in the nature of the Principate itself strained the relations between many senators and the *princeps* and led to the continued weakening of the senate as an institution of government.

The Centralization of Government   Though truly desirous of the senate's collaboration, Claudius did not forget that he was the chief executive of an empire which could no longer be exploited as the private estate of a narrow and selfish aristocracy, as it had been under the Republic. The time had come for Rome to integrate herself with Italy and with the provinces. Good government and efficient administration must now supersede the ancient privileges of the senate.

In 47/48, Claudius revived the censorship, which had been defunct for sixty-eight years. Assuming the office himself (not even Augustus had done so), he purged the senate of some old members and added new ones. The old aristocracy were naturally affronted. A few of the new senators were his own clients, tribal chieftains of *Gallia Comata* whose families had received citizenship from Julius Caesar. They were richer than most Italian senators and controlled large and devoted clans. The admission of Gallic senators gave the Gauls political equality with the Italians and made them loyal partners in the new world state. Later emperors recognized the wisdom of such a measure and adopted it on a larger scale.

Claudius struck other blows against the Roman senatorial aristocracy. In order to reduce the possibility of being challenged by a disgruntled or ambitious senator, he weakened the senate's power over the armies and its own provinces. In the name of efficiency, he also transferred control of the Roman municipal treasury (*aerarium Saturni*) to two quaestors responsible to him and diverted revenues from several sources to the Imperial *fiscus*. Furthermore, he placed such vital services as the grain supply, aqueducts, flood control, and Italian roads, canals, and harbors under his control.

Claudius' passion for efficiency was combined with a love of equity and impartial justice that he had gained from his study of law. Therefore, the number of trials that took place in the Emperor's private court, *intra cubiculum principis,* greatly increased at the expense of the magistrates, provincial governors, and the senate. Claudius' judicial activities were popular with average citizens, but those who saw their powers diminished were naturally offended, and they probably account for some of the exaggerated stories in the ancient sources about Claudius' absent-minded, arbitrary, and even capricious behavior as a judge. Ironically, it was his earnest attempt to spare senators the indignity that they had suffered under Tiberius and Caligula in trying their own colleagues for treason that earned Claudius the most ill will. When he himself tried and condemned senators, he was suspected, sometimes with good reason, to have been influenced unjustly by his own ambitious wives and freedmen.

The Expansion of the Bureaucracy and the New Cabinet The roles of Claudius' freedmen became very important as he tried to create a more efficient, centralized administrative system for the unwieldly Empire. Centralization of government entailed an expanded bureaucracy and an enlarged privy

council, known as the "friends of Caesar" (*amici Caesaris*). Though Claudius originated neither, he took decisive steps toward the development of the later Imperial bureaucracy by his division of the executive into special bureaus or departments (*scrinia*). Each was headed by a skilled and loyal freedman, who was also a member of the privy council. Narcissus, Claudius' secretary for correspondence (*ab epistulis*), drafted all laws and decrees sent out over the Empire under the Imperial seal. Callistus headed the department which examined petitions sent to the *princeps* from the provinces (*a libellis*) and had charge of judicial investigations and trials (*a cognitionibus*). Another important official was Pallas (whom Antonia had secretly sent to report to Tiberius the conspiracy of Sejanus). As head of the treasury department (*a rationibus*), he coordinated all the provincial *fisci* and the activities of the procurators. A fourth was Claudius Polybius, keeper of the records' office and reference library (*a studiis*).

Many of the officials of the Imperial administration were freedmen of Greek or Eastern origin. They were often excellent and loyal executives, though some made use of their positions to enrich themselves. The equestrian and senatorial classes resented them because they were freedmen of foreign origin and feared their power and influence in the government. Ancient and modern writers have been too closely bound to a biased and hostile tradition when they represent Claudius as dominated by his ministers. For the most part, he was the master and they his faithful and obedient servants.

Public Works and Welfare The administrative efficiency thus achieved enabled Claudius to devote attention to public welfare and carry out a vast program of public works. He curbed some evils of moneylending by forbidding usurers to lend to teenage spendthrifts; he abolished sales taxes on food and relieved stricken communities of their tax burdens; and through his control of the Imperial mint both prevented excessive inflation

Model of an apartment block at Ostia. *(Courtesy Fratelli Alinari, Florence)*

and met the expanding needs of trade and industry, to which public works, such as aqueducts, highways, and canals, gave an added stimulus all over the Empire.

The most spectacular of these projects was the construction of an artificial harbor at Ostia, Rome's port on the mouth of the Tiber, which had become choked with silt. The new harbor allowed grain ships to dock at Ostia, whence their cargoes could be easily barged up to Rome instead of being laboriously hauled overland 138 miles from Puteoli in Campania as before. Ostia soon became a large city with a population of 100,000 from all over the Mediterranean world. Modern excavations there give a vivid picture of life in a major Imperial city.

The development of the port of Ostia raised economic problems both difficult and unforeseen. Ships using the port had to leave empty. Rome was a consumer of the world's products, not a producer. Her exports were insignificant, her imports immense—grain, fruits, fish, meats, hides, oil, and wine; minerals of every sort, marble, lumber, glass, paper, dyes, clothing, and jewelry; spices, ointments, and perfumes. No sooner had Claudius di-

verted shipping from Puteoli (the outlet of a rich exporting region of both agricultural and industrial products) than the shipowners complained of losing money because of the lack of return cargoes. To satisfy them and keep vital supplies moving into Rome, Claudius and his successors had to compensate them with special concessions, such as insurance against shipwreck, tax exemptions, the waiving of the inheritance law, and the grant of citizenship to those engaged for six years in the grain-carrying service.

Foreign Policy and Imperial Defense   Just as he dealt aggressively with internal administrative and economic matters, Claudius pursued an aggressive foreign policy, which was more like that of Julius Caesar than that of Augustus after A.D. 9 or of Tiberius and even Caligula. His motives were complex. The security of the *princeps* greatly depended on the loyalty of the provincial armies. The best way to gain their loyalty was to command them personally and lead them in conquest. Claudius had not gained any military experience or reputation and he needed to do so when he became Emperor. The danger of his situation became clear within his first year, for example, when the governor of Dalmatia, Furius Camillus Scribonianus, backed by some leading senators, persuaded his legions to revolt. Fortunately, some men remained loyal and by playing on the troops' superstitions quelled the revolt in a few days. Also, as in other matters, he was motivated by a desire to rationalize, systematize, and improve Imperial defense.

Claudius restored the peaceful provinces of Macedonia and Achaea to the senate, and in 46 annexed the turbulent kingdom of Thrace as an Imperial province. Annexation of Thrace led to Roman intervention in Dacia (modern Rumania), in the Crimean peninsula, and everywhere north of the Black Sea as far east as the Don. Claudius made the Black Sea almost a Roman lake.

In the Near East his policy was at once vigorous and cautious: he fomented internal discord and rivalry in Parthia, perennially Rome's most dangerous enemy; he reestablished the Roman protectorate over Armenia by reinstating a friendly client king, and, on the death of Herod Agrippa I, annexed Judea as a Roman province. His chief objectives were peace and Roman control over the Eastern trade routes (the Red Sea, the Indian Ocean, and the caravan route through Parthia to India and China).

Early in his reign Claudius had to suppress the revolt which Caligula had provoked in Mauretania by the murder of King Ptolemy. After crushing the revolt in two years of hard fighting, Claudius organized Mauretania into two Imperial provinces—*Mauretania Caesariensis* in the east and *Mauretania Tingitana* (Tangier) in the northwest. Though the subjugation of Mauretania was a very important and difficult military achievement, it received less fanfare than the conquest of Britain.

The Conquest of Britain, 43 The various motives that guided Claudius' military activity can be seen in his famous conquest of Britain. One powerful motive was probably his need for military glory; another undoubtedly was

the conviction that the enterprise would arouse strong national sentiment. He may have desired to protect Roman traders and to gain for Rome access to the island's reputed wealth in minerals, timber, cattle, and slaves. Nor were pretexts lacking. Claudius had received invitations to intervene from lesser British chiefs who feared the expansive power of the kingdom that Cunobelinus (the Cymbeline of Shakespeare) had established in the southeast, with its capital at Camulodunum (Colchester), northeast of London. After Cunobelinus' death (ca A.D. 40), his son Caratacus, hostile to Rome, had extended the kingdom and had stepped forward as the champion of Druidism, which Augustus and Tiberius had attempted to stamp out in Gaul because it fostered Celtic unity and resistance to Rome and practiced savage and inhuman rites. The existence of that strong British kingdom was a perpetual threat to Roman authority in Gaul.

In 43, Aulus Plautius landed an army of fifty thousand men in Kent and, after defeating the Britons in a two-day battle on the Medway, advanced to the Thames to await the arrival of Claudius, who, taking command, quickly defeated Caratacus and took his capital, Camulodonum, where he accepted the submission of eleven British kings. In tribute to the swift victory, the senate voted Claudius a triumph and the proud name of Britannicus. After the celebration of his triumph in 44, his legates had within the next eight years created a province extending from the borders of Wales in the southwest to the estuary of the Humber in the northeast near York (Eburacum).

Colonization and Urbanization in the Provinces Hand in hand with conquest and Imperial expansion went colonization, urbanization, and extension of Roman citizenship in the provinces. This process, begun by Julius Caesar, continued with restraint by Augustus, and slowed down by Tiberius, was resumed on a large scale by Claudius. It was continued by later emperors at an accelerated rate until the issuance of the *Constitutio Antoniniana* in 212 by

Caracalla, who granted citizenship to all free inhabitants of the Empire. Most of these colonies served at once as military bastions in conquered territory and islands of Roman citizenship. The conversion of rural and tribal communities into organized municipalities (*municipia*) served similar purposes. In all this work of urbanization and Romanization, Claudius paid attention, as his numerous edicts and the extant inscriptions and papyri reveal, to the smallest administrative details and exhibited an amazing knowledge of local conditions. He was hardly the old fogy depicted by biased ancient writers.

Claudius' Wives The most troublesome aspect of Claudius' reign was his marital life. In view of the loveless and lonely childhood that he had endured, it is no wonder that Claudius eagerly sought marriage. Unfortunately, his wives never loved him. His first two wives, Plautia Urgulanilla and Aelia Paetina, were merely unfaithful, and he divorced them. His third and fourth wives, however, were not only unfaithful but also ambitious so that their political impact was significant. Claudius' marriage to his third wife, Valeria Messalina, had been arranged by Caligula for political reasons. Through both of her parents, Messalina was a great-granddaughter of Augustus' sister Octavia (see p. 315). By this marriage, therefore, Caligula strengthened his branch of the Julio-Claudians for the future.

Claudius was 47 and Messalina only 15 when they were married. Claudius was enamored of her youthful beauty, but she was understandably unhappy at being forced to marry a man who was so much older than she and physically handicapped as well. While she produced two children, a daughter, Octavia, and a son, Britannicus (named in honor of Claudius' conquest of Britain), Messalina sought her pleasure elsewhere in much the same way that Augustus' daughter, Julia, had when forced to marry men whom she did not love. Also, as in the case of Julia's daughter, the younger Julia, Messalina's affairs became

linked with political conspiracies. She used her influence with Claudius to obtain the condemnation of certain senators on charges of treason, and one of her lovers, Gaius Silius, plotted with her to depose Claudius, marry her, and seize the throne himself.

When he was a consul-elect in 48 and Claudius was away at Ostia, Silius and Messalina put their plot in motion by taking public marriage vows. Claudius' freedmen Narcissus, Pallas, and Callistus, however, got word to him of the situation, and he was finally forced to take action against his treacherous wife. She, Silius, and other conspirators were swiftly executed.

Claudius did not remain a widower long. He systematically cast about for a suitable wife once more. His freedman Pallas, who had been the lover of Agrippina the Younger, Caligula's sister, successfully urged Claudius to marry her, even though she was the daughter of Claudius' own brother Germanicus. By Roman law such a marriage was incestuous. Therefore, Claudius had the law changed.

The needs of both Agrippina and Claudius were met by this marriage. From her mother, Agrippina the Elder, the younger Agrippina had received the ambition of securing the throne for the family of Germanicus, of which she and her son by her first marriage, L. Domitius Ahenobarbus, were the only survivors; Claudius, on the other hand, was already 58 years old and needed to provide the Empire with a suitable successor. His own son, Britannicus, was only five and was not yet capable of being trained for the Principate. Agrippina's son was of the right lineage and, though only 10, could begin immediately to be trained for succession. Claudius immediately betrothed his daughter, Octavia, to him and then adopted him in 50 and gave him the name Nero Claudius Caesar. Henceforth, he is known simply as Nero.

The loyalty of the Praetorian Guard to the heir apparent was secured by the appointment of Agrippina's friend Sextus Afranius Burrus as Praetorian Prefect in 51. Nero's education was entrusted to the learned philosopher Seneca the Younger. Agrippina could now face the future with considerable confidence.

She did not have to wait long. Claudius died in 54 from an undetermined cause. The story that he died as a result of eating a bowl of poisoned mushrooms served him by Agrippina comes from a hostile source (her archenemy Pliny the Elder) and should therefore be accepted with reserve. That Agrippina benefited the most immediately after his death naturally raises suspicions, but it is quite possible that Claudius, who had a reputation for overindulging in food and drink, accidentally choked to death.

Nero (A.D. 54–68) Agrippina, Seneca, and Burrus handled the succession smoothly. The inauguration of Nero was a joyous occasion. A visit to the barracks of the Praetorians (each was promised fifteen thousand sesterces), a speech carefully prepared by Seneca and delivered effectively by Nero before the senate (Nero promised to follow the policies of Augustus and respect the prerogatives and powers of the senate, keeping for himself only the command of the armies), cheers, pledges of loyalty, and other obsequious effusions highlighted the first day of Nero's reign.

The Early Years Because of what is probably a misinterpretation of a remark of the later emperor Trajan, the first five years of Nero's reign are often called the *quinquennium Neronis* ("Nero's five years") and are considered to be the best because he was guided by the able Praetorian Prefect Burrus and the philosopher Seneca. In fact, the first five years of Nero's reign do not form any recognizable unit (the influence of Burrus and Seneca lasted eight years), and Trajan was probably referring to Nero's building activities during his last five years from the time of the great fire at Rome in 64.

In the first eight years of his reign (54–62), the guidance of Seneca and Burrus certainly was beneficial in many ways. They and their collaborators in the senate seem to have found the way to make that institution a real force again. Heeding Seneca's sound advice, Nero applied the ideal of clemency extolled by the philosopher Seneca in his essay *De Clementia* by putting an end to trials *intra cubiculum principis,* which had engendered the hostility of many against Claudius. Besides respecting the privileges of the senate, Nero provided annuities to assist impoverished senatorial families.

On the impetus of the smoothly functioning administrative machinery set up by Claudius, Nero's government maintained peace and prosperity within the Empire, guarded its frontiers, kept piracy in check, and restrained the rapacity of tax collectors (*publicani*) and provincial governors by vigorous prosecution of extortion before the senate. To stimulate trade, in which the wealthy Seneca was not disinterested, oppressive taxation was mitigated, and Nero himself even proposed the total abolition of all indirect taxes and customs duties throughout the Empire. Responsible critics in the senate, however, pointed out the dire consequences of such an act to the public finances, and it was dropped. The regime also produced a respectable record of military achievement. Two of the greatest generals of the century—Gnaeus Domitius Corbulo in the East and Gaius Suetonius Paullinus in Britain—added fresh laurels to Roman arms.

Along with these positive aspects of Nero's early years, however, there were intrigue, vice, violence, and murder. Right from the start, Agrippina ruthlessly tried to establish her dominance and control the government: she directed policy; she received embassies; she had her effigy engraved on Imperial coins; and she set about eliminating family rivals. Early in the reign Agrippina contrived the murder of M. Junius Silanus, great-grandson of Augustus and proconsul of Asia, hounded Nero's aunt, Domitia Lepida, to death, and had one of Claudius' freedmen ministers, Callistus, removed from office, and another, Narcissus, summarily executed.

Seneca and Burrus intrigued to break Agrippina's influence over Nero, lest she become too powerful. Unfortunately, to do that they catered to his baser instincts. They pointed out that, as Emperor, he could now do what he wanted without his mother's interference. They encouraged him to indulge not only his taste for art, music, poetry, and chariot racing but also flattered his vanity and self-importance by pretending that all official acts were the result of his divine guidance. Everywhere thanks were offered to him with extravagantly worshipful praise. In this way they encouraged Nero to model himself on the absolute, divine Hellenistic monarchs familiar from Greek culture. Ultimately, they turned him into a creature that they could not control.

Nero Asserts Himself Nero himself, as he grew older, began to rebel more and more against his mother's domination. He was irked especially by her hypocrisy, her nagging, and her constant reminders that he owed the throne to her. His growing resentment rendered easier Seneca's attempt to circumvent, if not block, that violent and imperious woman.

The feud between Nero and Agrippina became ever more open and savage. His dismissal of her favorite, Pallas, sent her into a cascade of rage. Flinging caution aside, she threatened to depose her ungrateful son and enthrone Britannicus, the natural son and rightful heir of the divine Claudius. She would appeal to the Praetorian Guard, she ranted, and call upon the army. She attempted to arouse popular hostility against her foes by calling Nero a foul imposter, Seneca a lying sneak, and Burrus disgusting because he had a deformed hand. She warned them not to tangle with the daughter of Germanicus and great-granddaughter of Augustus.

Murder of Rivals Agrippina's tirades and wild threats aroused Nero's fear of plots against the throne. In 55 he contrived the death of Britannicus (perhaps by poison) in order to remove a possible rival. Four years later he procured the death of Agrippina because he feared her incessant intrigues against him. Then in 62 he divorced and exiled Octavia and married his mistress, the beautiful and seductive Poppaea Sabina, who had been the wife of M. Salvius Otho, one of those who eventually brought about Nero's downfall. Nero had Octavia murdered later. Poppaea's role in both assassinations evades detection.

Tigellinus After the death of Burrus in 62, Nero acquired a new favorite in Ofonius Tigellinus, a former wholesale fish merchant and horse breeder. As head of the fire and police departments and commander of the Praetorian Guard, Tigellinus took a vicious delight in tracking down plots against the throne. His organization of informers, spies, and secret agents helped him to make the latter part of Nero's principate a veritable reign of terror. His zeal was too much even for Seneca, the apologist of Nero's earlier atrocities. Loaded with wealth and honors, Seneca retired from office. He was not destined to enjoy his retirement long.

Now freed from Agrippina, Burrus, and Seneca, Nero became more and more extravagant and megalomaniacal. He spared no expense on lavish entertainments and luxuries. He appeared more and more frequently in chariot races and musical competitions, and in 64 he finally went so far as to offend the traditional Roman contempt for actors by appearing publicly in plays. Much worse, as had been the case under Caligula, wealthy men were condemned again on trumped-up charges in order to pay for the Emperor's reckless expenditures. Also, Nero's jealousy toward anyone closely related to the Julio-Claudian dynasty became murderous. Rubellius Plautus, a grandson of Tiberius, Cornelius Sulla, a son-in-law of Claudius, and D. Junius Silanus, a descendant of Augustus himself, were quickly eliminated. Naturally, the upper classes came to fear and detest this new oppressor. A famous fire soon alienated, at least temporarily, the lower classes at Rome as well.

The Great Fire of Rome, 64   In 64 there occurred a long period of hot dry weather. One sizzling night in July, a fire broke out in the slums at the east end of the Circus Maximus between the Palatine and Caelian hills. Fanned by a strong southeast wind, the flames leapt from house to house, from block to block, fed by the stores of dry wood and olive oil. The fire raged for nine days and left more than half of Rome a charred and blackened waste. Not only had acres of flimsy apartment houses and some of Rome's most venerated temples and shrines gone up in smoke, but Nero's own palace as well, with its priceless collection of books, manuscripts, and works of art.

Nero had been staying at the time at Antium (Anzio), about 35 miles south of Rome. Aroused from sleep, he swiftly sped to the scene of the conflagration. In this crisis Nero's good qualities shone. Fearing neither the assassin's dagger nor the blast of the holocaust, he gave all possible aid to the crazed and helpless victims of the fire. After a vain attempt to check the progress of the flames, he converted Mars' Field and his private gardens into shelters for the homeless and hastened the transport of grain supplies from Ostia to feed the destitute. His indefatigable energy in the alleviation of suffering, however, did not spare him from the malicious rumor that he had started the fire in order to acquire the glory of building a new and more beautiful Rome.

Rebuilding Program   While the accusation against Nero is false, it is true that he eagerly seized the opportunity to indulge his passion for esthetic enjoyment and creative activity in rebuilding Rome. Much of what he did or approved to be done was worthy of praise: Nero widened and straightened the streets and had pillared colonnades built on both sides of them to provide shade and lessen the danger of fire. The rebuilt sections of the city had many fountains and open squares. The new houses were required to have their facades and first stories built of fireproof stone and to be separated by alleys, with gardens in the rear provided with fire buckets and supplies of water.

The Golden House   The extravagance that Nero showed in rebuilding his own palace, however, helped to fuel the rumors that he was responsible for the fire. No expense was spared. Nero's new palace, the Golden House (*Domus Aurea*), probably rivaled in cost and splendor the great palace of Louis XIV at Versailles. The vestibule was lofty enough to accommodate Nero's colossal statue (120 feet high), and the hall, consisting of three pillared arcades, was almost a mile long. Together with colonnades, gardens, lakes, fields, and game parks, it occupied an area of 120 acres between the Palatine and Esquiline hills.

Nero's Persecution of the Christians   Nero's worst side, a weak and cowardly streak that sometimes resulted in infantile cruelty, is revealed in how he sought to quell the rumors against him. According to Tacitus (*Annals* 15.44, written probably as late as 120, perhaps even 123), Nero cast about for scapegoats for the fire in order to avert suspicion from himself. He found them in the Christians, the widespread prejudice against whom Tacitus expressed in the following words: "They were a detestable sect, which owed its name to Chrestus, who, in the reign of Tiberius, suffered under Pontius Pilate. Suppressed for a while, this dangerous superstition, soon revived and spread not only in Judea but even in the city of Rome, the common cesspool into which everything hateful and abominable flows like a torrent from all parts of the world. When some of these depraved and profligate wretches were induced to confess their guilt, Nero had some of them torn apart by dogs, some nailed to crosses, and others burned alive."

Reform of the Currency   The huge sums spent on the rebuilding of Rome and on Nero's Golden House soon completed the bankruptcy of the public treasury and rendered a depreciation of the currency imperative. Nero, therefore, made a virtue of necessity and carried out a currency reform; he introduced a monetary system that remained essentially unchanged until the reign of Septimius Severus (193–211). He reduced the weight of the *aureus,* the standard gold coin, by about ten percent and the silver content of the *denarius,* the standard silver coin, by a similar amount. That brought both coins into a more stable relation with each other and with a new bronze coin. The reform also brought the Roman coinage more closely in line with that of the Greek and thus promoted trade within the Empire through the adoption of a more uniform Imperial standard. The currency depreciation perhaps served another purpose: it tended to check the serious drain of gold and silver to India and southeast Asia by raising the prices for luxury imports such as spices and precious stones and thereby discouraging their purchase.

The chief disadvantage of the devaluation was that it forced prices up by about ten percent and created hardships for people dependent on savings or fixed incomes. It finally compelled Nero to extend the grain dole, formerly limited to poor citizens at Rome, to all destitute foreign and citizen residents of Rome.

Plots against the Throne   Nero's outrageous behavior, extravagance, and growing cruelty led to the formation of serious plots against him. A confused tangle of motives inspired them: some of the conspirators genuinely hoped for a restoration of the Republic; others hated Nero's increasingly vicious despotism and resented his employment of freedmen from Greece and the Near East in positions of power and influence. The most formidable attempt against the throne was the conspiracy of Gaius Calpurnius Piso in 65, which involved many *equites* as well as senators.

Nero's reprisals were savage: among his numerous victims were leading members of the senate and three of the greatest literary figures of the century—the philosopher Seneca, the poet Lucan, and the novelist and satirist Petronius, who obediently committed suicide by cutting open their own veins. One of the most eminent of Nero's victims, though perhaps not actually involved in the conspiracy, was the famous Stoic P. Clodius Paetus Thrasea, renowned for his austere conduct and high moral principles and the champion of *dignitas* and *libertas,* the traditional virtues of the old Roman aristocracy.

Nero's Concert Tour of Greece, 66 to 67   Neither fire nor conspiracy nor the arduous tasks of government interrupted Nero's musical career.

After elaborate preparations, Nero set out in the fall of 66 on a grand concert tour of Greece. He took with him many musicians, chorus singers, and a host of supernumeraries as well as officials, assistants, guardsmen, and soldiers. The tour was a personal triumph, thanks to the shrewd cooperativeness of the Greeks. He made numerous appearances as singer, tragic actor, or charioteer at Olympia, Corinth, Delphi, and many other places and came away as the winner of 1808 prizes and trophies, many of which were awarded in advance. Pleased with the flattering reception extended him by the Greeks and their appreciation of his art, he proclaimed in 67 the liberation of Greece from the governor of Macedonia in words reminiscent of the speech of Titus Quinctius Flamininus in 196 B.C. (see p. 116).

Nero's Foreign Policy   Under the able guidance of Seneca, Burrus, and their friends, Nero had maintained the peace and prosperity of the provinces; chosen, for the most part, honest and able governors, who were held strictly to account; and guarded and extended the frontiers by sending good generals to command the legions—Verginius Rufus to the

Rhineland, Suetonius Paulinus to Britain, and to the East first Corbulo, then Titus Flavius Vespasianus, the future Emperor Vespasian.

Armenia and Britain   Two danger spots remained: Armenia and Britain. Armenia, a problem since the days of Marcus Antonius, had engaged the attention of all Nero's predecessors. Rugged, mountainous, and subject to summer's heat or winter's cold, Armenia was hard to conquer, difficult to hold, and impossible to annex while Parthia remained strong and unsubdued. Neither Rome nor Parthia could allow the other to occupy it without loss of security and prestige. The only permanent solution of the Armenian problem, as Julius Caesar had foreseen, was the subjugation of Parthia.

The Armenian problem arose early in Nero's reign, when Vologeses I, the young and aggressive king of Parthia, placed his brother, Tiridates IV, upon the Armenian throne. Nero sent out to the East Cn. Domitius Corbulo, a strict disciplinarian and one of the ablest generals of the century. He placed Tigranes V, a Roman client, upon the Armenian throne. The brief period of peace and quiet in the East that ensued offered time to resume the conquest of Britain.

Military Operations in Britain, 60 to 61   To Britain, Nero sent C. Suetonius Paulinus, another able general. In 60, after he had conquered the island of Mona (Anglesey), the main center of Druidism, a dangerous rebellion broke out behind his lines among the Iceni and Trinovantes, who then dwelt between the Thames and the Wash. After the death of their king, who had willed his territory to the Roman people, Roman procurators (acting on behalf of moneylenders, such as Seneca, to whom the previous king had fallen into debt) confiscated farm lands and reduced the former owners to the level of serfs. They robbed the king's widow, Queen Boudicca (Boadicea), of her land, flogged her, and permitted the raping of her daughters. The outraged queen collected an army and captured the Roman colony of Camulodonum (Colchester). She destroyed the Roman legion sent against her and marched on Londinium (London), where she caused the massacre of seventy thousand Romans. Suetonius Paulinus defeated her army in battle by superior discipline and skill and stamped out the rebellion with ruthless efficiency. The vanquished Boadicea took her own life, and Britain thereafter remained subdued, except for a few border raids.

Armenia Again, 61 to 63   Not so Armenia. After Corbulo had pulled out his army, Tigranes V attacked Media, a powerful Parthian ally, and started a war that he could not finish. Vologeses, King of Parthia, invaded Armenia in force. In 62 he badly mauled and compelled the surrender of a Roman army that Nero had sent, at Corbulo's request, under an incompetent and cowardly commander. In 63, Corbulo again took command, outmaneuvered and defeated Vologeses, and compelled Parthia to accept Roman supremacy. In return he allowed Tiridates IV to ascend the throne of Armenia (provided that he go to Rome and receive his crown at Nero's hands).

The coronation of Tiridates was a makeshift settlement, as Nero himself clearly saw. Since the permanent solution of the Armenian problem required annexation of the country and the conquest of Parthia itself, he revived Caesar's foreign policy. To soften up Parthia for conquest, he began surrounding her with a ring of client states. In the southwest he made Aden a strong fortress, occupied Zanzibar as a naval station, and made plans for the conquest of the Somaliland and of Ethiopia by an expedition up the Nile. In the northeast he established a naval patrol on the Black Sea, liberated the Crimea from Sarmatian domination, and made preparations for a campaign against southwestern Siberia north and east of the Caspian Sea. Meanwhile, he had to deal with a revolt of the Jews.

The Jewish Revolt   Because of their unique traditions and often uncompromising monotheism, the Jewish population of the

Roman province of Judea had always hated and resisted assimilation with foreign conquerors and had often rebelled against any foreign master since the days of the Assyrian Empire. Their occasional successes, such as the revolt of the Maccabees against the Seleucid Empire, also helped to inspire further rebellions under subsequent conquerors. In 66, mob protests in Jerusalem against Roman inaction in the face of attacks by Greeks on their Jewish neighbors in the city of Caesarea quickly got out of hand when the Roman procurator, hoping to avoid further trouble, failed to crush the protests quickly. The Imperial legate of Syria, Cestus Gallus, then besieged Jerusalem with thirty thousand men. It was late in the year, however, and, not prepared for a long winter seige, Gallus suddenly retreated. The whole province then seized the chance to revolt.

Vespasian   Nero, however, gave Titus Flavius Vespasian, who had served well in Britain, a special command over an army of fifty thousand men to quell the uprising. In 67, Vespasian methodically set about retaking the countryside and drawing a tighter and tighter ring around Jerusalem. Many saw the inevitable success of this strategy and surrendered. Among them was the future historian Flavius Josephus, who had been placed in charge of the rebels in Galilee. Still, resistance was fierce, especially at Jerusalem and later Masada. Vespasian had several years of hard work ahead.

It was fortunate for him that he did. Complete success at an early date might have proven fatal to Vespasian. On the one hand, Nero had no interest in personally conducting military campaigns and visiting troops on the frontiers: he was perfectly happy to let others do that dirty work. On the other hand, he was afraid to let others have too much military success and popularity, lest they become more powerful than himself. Therefore, in 61, for example, he had recalled the successful Suetonius Paulinus from Britain and denied him due honors. In 66 and 67, even more fearful as a result of Piso's conspiracy, Nero compelled the suicides of Scribonius Rufus and Scribonius Proculus, commanders of Upper and Lower Germany, and the great general Domitius Corbulo. These actions, however, merely inspired more plots.

The Revolt of Vindex, 68   Nero had planned to tour Asia Minor and Egypt, but bad news compelled him to cancel the trip and return to Rome: C. Julius Vindex, the governor of one of the provinces of Gaul, had revolted and raised a large army. Vindex also had the support of Servius Sulpicius Galba, the governor of Nearer Spain, and of M. Salvius Otho, the governor of Lusitania (Portugal). North Africa and Rome itself were also seething with revolt.

The rebellion received a sudden check when L. Verginius Rufus, the loyal and able governor of Upper Germany, led three legions into Gaul and overwhelmed the raw and undisciplined troops of Vindex at Vesontio (Besançon). The vanquished Vindex committed suicide. Even then Nero was unsafe. The victorious legions of Rufus revolted in their turn and proclaimed their commander Emperor of Rome. Rufus rejected the acclamation and placed himself unreservedly at the disposition of the senate.

Fall of Nero, 68   The reasons for the opposition to and rebellion against Nero are not far to seek. He had antagonized the conservative upper classes (equestrian as well as senatorial), from which all provincial governors ("imperial" as well as "senatorial," and even "procuratorial"), high army officers, procurators, and other administrative officials were still recruited, by his un-Roman attitudes and activities (as Agrippina pointed out), by his seizure and confiscation of large private estates in Italy and the provinces, especially in North Africa, by his many tyrannies and executions, and by his slow but steady decline toward an absolute despotism. Not only that, but he had failed to win or hold the loyalty and affection of the legions (which was crucial).

Toward the end of his reign he allowed the pay of the troops to fall into arrears and thereby seriously undermined their loyalty and enthusiasm. Furthermore, he had neglected them. Their *Imperator* they had never seen. They did not know him. It would have been far better for him had he gone to the Rhineland to see his soldiers rather than on his triumphal tour of Greece.

Meanwhile, Galba had not been idle. He sent his agents to Rome to undermine the loyalty of the Praetorian Guard with the promise of eighty thousand sesterces to each man. The guards succumbed to the bribe, deserted Nero, and declared for Galba. Soon the armies began to renounce their allegiance. The senate proclaimed Nero a public enemy. Deserted and condemned by all and not having the courage to do himself what he had often coldly ordered others to do, he persuaded a faithful freedman to plunge a sword into his throat. Thus died Nero, the last of the Julio-Claudians. The narcissism that accounts for his obsession with the performing arts and the growing absolutism of his later years is epitomized by his purported last words, "What an artist dies in me." (*Qualis artifex pereo.*)

Sources like Tacitus, Suetonius, and Dio Cassius may have correctly conveyed the justified feelings of the upper classes toward Nero, but not that of many common people in Rome, Italy, and the provinces. To the nobles he appeared a madman and a fiend. To the masses he was often a benefactor and friend and a champion in their struggle for survival. Not until his reign had they been so well fed or so royally entertained: he had given them bread and circuses, *panem et circenses!*

The public's adoration of Nero and the flowers placed by unknown hands upon his tomb disturbed Galba and later emperors. Otho, Galba's successor, restored Nero's fallen statues and proudly took the name of "Nero"; Vitellius, who overthrew Otho, publicly praised Nero's name and even offered sacrifices to him. Years later the Emperor Domitian, who also preferred the absolutism inherent in the Principate, revered his memory and executed some of his surviving foes.

XXVIII

The Crisis of the Principate
and Recovery under the Flavians,
A.D. 69–96

Nero, last of the Julio-Claudians, had failed to learn the lessons that had enabled Augustus to establish the Principate on a solid foundation: in order to gain at least the acquiescence if not the willing cooperation of powerful aristocrats, absolute power must not be openly flaunted at the center of the Empire, and the personal loyalty of the legions around the periphery must be assiduously cultivated so that any attempt to challenge the *princeps* could be quickly crushed before it could spread. Nero's failure now threatened the stability of the Principate with the same kind of destructive competition for preeminence that had characterized the late Republic. The year 69 saw the office of *princeps* become a revolving door entered by four emperors in rapid succession through assassination and civil war. If the process had been allowed to continue, the Roman Empire would have been irreparably damaged. Titus Flavius Vespasianus, Vespasian, was able to halt it, however, and earned the reputation of being the second founder of the Principate.

Sources The most important ancient source for the events of 69 and the Flavian emperors (Vespasian, Titus, and Domitian) was Tacitus' *Histories*. Unfortunately, only the books that cover the years 69 and 70 survive. Tacitus also wrote a valuable biography of his father-in-law, Cn. Julius Agricola, who governed Britain from 77 to 84; a discussion of the state of oratory under the Principate (*Dialogue on Oratory*); and a rather fanciful ethnographic account of the Germans (*Germania*). Suetonius wrote extant biographies of the three emperors between Nero and Vespasian (Galba, Otho, and Vitellius) as well as of the three Flavians. As historical sources, they suffer from both the weaknesses of Suetonius as a scholar and the limitations of biography as a genre, but they are all the more valuable because so much of Tacitus is lost. The only connected historical narrative is provided by Byzantine epitomes of Books 65 to 77 of Cassius Dio's history of Rome. Valuable material can also be extracted from the *Natural History* of Pliny the Elder, Quintillian's *Institutes of Oratory*, Frontinus' collection of military strategems (*Strategemata*) and his treatise on Rome's aqueducts (*De Aquae Ductis*), and the poems of Statius, Martial, and Juvenal (see pp. 374–376). Numerous official and private inscriptions, works of art, buildings, public works, fortifications, coins, and artifacts also supply useful information about political, social, economic, and cultural life.

Galba (68–69) Servius Sulpicius Galba, the first to succeed Nero, reigned for only a few months. Though of an old senatorial family, he had little talent for practical politics, and since he was already in his early seventies when he came to the throne, he was too old to learn the half-conscious secrets of empire (*arcana imperii*). Before fully consolidating his power, he attempted two contradictory and impossible things: balancing the budget and winning the support of the armies. He alienated the Roman populace by cutting down the grain dole, the Praetorian Guard by his failure to pay the promised donatives, and the armies on the Rhine, already hostile and sullen, by his unwise act of recalling their beloved commander, Verginius Rufus, and replacing him with the elderly and unpopular Hordeonius Flaccus. The two armies mutinied and proclaimed one of their commanders, Aulus Vitellius, Emperor of Rome.

Even then Galba might have saved his life and throne by adopting Verginius Rufus as heir and coregent. He chose instead the aristocratic L. Calpurnius Piso Licinianus, who was very acceptable to the senate, but totally devoid of popularity or of political and military experience, and unknown to the armies. Galba's choice turned a former friend and supporter, Marcus Salvius Otho, the exhusband of Poppaea Sabina, into a jealous and dangerous enemy who hurried off to the camp of the praetorians and by liberal promises of money persuaded them to proclaim him Emperor. They promptly murdered Galba and Piso.

Otho (69) Although Otho had the support of the Praetorian Guard and the Roman populace and soon won recognition by the senate, the armies on the Rhine, who had already declared for Vitellius, marched against

him. Otho blocked the Alpine passes against them, but he was too late. Though he proved himself a fairly good strategist by defeating part of their forces at Bedriacum after a daring encircling movement, the Danubian legions on whom he chiefly depended had not all arrived on time to help him in his premature attack on superior Vitellian forces based at Cremona. Defeated after a long, hard-fought battle, he terminated his short reign by suicide. He could have regrouped and fought on, but to have done so would have devastated Italy in a protracted civil war.

Significantly, Otho was the first emperor who did not have his roots in the old Republican aristocracy. The Julio-Claudians had promoted men in Imperial service from outside traditional senatorial families in order to have a group of loyal officials to counterbalance champions of the old order in the senate. With the end of the Julio-Claudians, there were no loyalties to prevent officials of the new class from attempting the throne themselves.

Vitellius (69) The victor of Cremona was one of the most inept and helpless emperors ever to disgrace the Roman throne. During his brief reign (seven months), he reportedly spent 900 million sesterces on dinners alone. Having thus emptied the treasury, he was unable to pay his troops their promised rewards, and allowed them to make good their loss by looting and plundering Italy. Yet his reign was not entirely without significance. He was the first of Roman emperors since Tiberius not to owe elevation to the throne wholly or in part to the Praetorian Guard, whose monopoly of emperor making had now been definitely broken.

One emperor was already created by the armies of the Rhine. Now those stationed in the East were about to create another, Titus Flavius Vespasian, whom Nero had sent in 66 to Judea to suppress the uprising of the Jews. Leaving his son Titus in charge of the siege of Jerusalem, Vespasian himself hastened to

Egypt in order to prevent the shipment of grain supplies to Rome, while his adjutant, C. Licinius Mucianus, the governor of Syria, marched with twenty thousand men through Asia Minor to invade Italy.

Meanwhile the armies of the Danube had also declared for Vespasian and an army of fifty thousand men was already on the march to the Italian frontier. They seized the Alpine passes, which Vitellius had neglected to block, and without waiting for the arrival of Mucianus from Asia Minor met and routed the Vitellian forces in a bloody night battle near Cremona. They stormed the city, sacked and burnt it, and massacred its inhabitants. After that frightful outrage, they marched on Rome, where Vitellius had already begun to negotiate terms of abdication with Vespasian's elder brother Flavius Sabinus, Prefect of the City by Otho's appointment.

Vitellius' attempt to abdicate was most unacceptable to his own soldiers. They rioted, murdered Sabinus, burned down the Temple of Jupiter, and forced Vitellius to renounce his intended abdication. Whereupon the Danubian army now within sight of the city broke in, annihilated the rioting troops, killed Vitellius, and proceeded to repeat in Rome the atrocities they had committed at Cremona. Fortunately, the army of Mucianus had arrived in time to restore order and prepare for the coming of Vespasian, now proclaimed Emperor by the senate. He was able to gain permanent control and replace the dead Julio-Claudian dynasty with his own Flavian family.

Significant Trends   The change of dynasty was not the sole or the most important change in A.D. 69. Nor did its significance lie wholly in the discovery that emperors could be created elsewhere than in Rome when provincial armies proclaimed their commanders as emperors. The significance lay rather in the reinforcement and culmination of trends and tendencies that had been slowly evolving since the time of Caesar and Augustus: the progres-

sive decay of the old senatorial aristocracy;[*] the growing political importance of the frontier armies; the centralization of executive power in the hands of the emperors and their bureaucracy; the wider participation of Italy and the provinces in the government and administration of the Empire; and the evolution of a truly integrated world state through liberal grants of citizenship and privileges. For example, Galba enfranchised tribes in central Gaul, while Otho made citizens of the Lignones from eastern Gaul. Vitellius seems to have been generous with Latin Rights in Spain and North Africa. Vespasian, moreover, not only let these grants stand but also used his censorial power to add men of ability from the urbanized provinces of the West to the Roman senate itself.

Vespasian (69–79)   The accession of Vespasian ended the nightmare of 69 with its civil wars, bloodlettings, and pillage. A new day of peace and tranquillity was dawning almost as glorious and as welcome to the Roman people as the day of the Augustan victory at Actium, which had brought to an end the strife, anarchy, and civil wars of the dying Republic. Vespasian, of course, lacked the glamor and prestige of Augustus, nor was his reign quite as memorable. It did, nevertheless, usher in a new phase in the history of the Roman Empire and many of the policies typical of the second century.

Among the many problems that Vespasian had to solve were the following: the restoration of peace and the suppression of rebellions in Germany, Gaul, and Judea; the reform of the army; Imperial defense and provincial administration; the centralization of government; the expansion of the bureaucracy; the balancing of the budget and the rehabilitation of Imperial finances; and, fi-

---

* Of the four emperors, Galba alone could boast of an ancient Roman pedigree, while Otho, Vitellius, and Vespasian were all of equestrian Italian families and belonged to the newly rising aristocracy of Imperial appointees.

Bust of Vespasian. (*Courtesy New York Public Library Picture Collection*)

nally, the regulation of the succession to the throne.

Born in A.D. 9, Vespasian came from an equestrian family who lived in a small hamlet near the hilltop town of Reate in the Sabine country. His grandfather had been an auctioneer, his father an Imperial tax collector in Asia Minor and, after his retirement, a moneylender in the province of Rhaetia (southern Bavaria and eastern Switzerland). The father later returned to Italy, married into a family slightly above his own social station, and settled down on a medium-sized estate near Reate.

Young Vespasian had received a fair education and was able to make jokes not only in Latin but even in Greek, some rather corny and at times slightly obscene. His financial and military abilities had won him a number of posts under Claudius and Nero. Coming to the throne in 69 at the age of sixty, bald, wrinkled, and tough, he had behind him much administrative and military experience. He knew the needs of the Empire thoroughly for he had been, in one capacity or another, in Thrace, Spain, Gaul, Germany, Britain, Africa, Syria, and Egypt. A rugged, hard-bitten old soldier, he had the respect of the armies and could command their loyalty and obedience. They accepted his reforms without murmur or dissent. He was a tireless worker and, although he often took his time making up his mind on a specific course of action, he carried out his decisions with determination and steadfastness. Knowing from past personal experience the value of money, he gave Rome a sound fiscal policy and took endless pains in balancing the budget. Such was the man who rescued Rome from the brink of financial and political disaster and made possible more than a century of peace and prosperity.

The Restoration of Peace

German and Celtic Revolts (69 to 70)   Most urgent was the task of breaking the rebellions in Germany, Gaul, and Judea. Julius Civilis, a German tribal chieftain, had served in the Roman army and was thoroughly acquainted with Roman methods of warfare. Toward the close of the reign of Vitellius, he persuaded his tribe, the Batavi, as well as some legions, to rebel in support of Vespasian. Then, throwing off all pretense of allegiance to Rome, he proclaimed the national independence of Germany and prevailed upon other German tribes on both sides of the Rhine and the Germans serving in the Roman army to join him in creating a German national state.

Following his example, the Celtic tribes in Belgium and northeastern Gaul also rose in revolt and similarly attempted to establish a Gallic national state with a capital at Augusta Treverorum (Tréves). The Celtic uprising failed because most of the other Gallic tribes, now more or less Romanized, refused to break away from Rome.

Both the German and the Celtic national movements collapsed in the spring of 70 when there arrived in the Rhineland strong Roman reinforcements under the command of the able Quintus Petilius Cerialis.

Capture of Jerusalem (70) and Masada (73) Meanwhile, in the Jewish War, Titus, Vespasian's elder son, had stormed and captured Jerusalem. Neither side showed any mercy to the other. The slaughter was frightful, and large numbers of those Jews who survived were sold into slavery. A relief on the Arch of Titus, erected by Domitian in the Roman Forum to commemorate the capture and destruction of Jerusalem, shows a triumphal procession bearing the spoils taken from the Temple—the seven-branched candlestick, the table of the shewbread, and other spoils. Finally, to demonstrate the inevitable punishment that awaited any resistance to Rome, three legions spent three years in crushing pockets of rebels. During the final six months, they built a huge earthen ramp to reach the fanatical defenders of Masada, a sheer rock fortress 1700 feet above the Dead Sea. When the Romans finally breached their walls, the defenders set fire to their buildings, and all but two women and five children committed suicide.

To reduce the chance of organized rebellion in the future, the Jewish council of the Sanhedrin was abolished along with the office of High Priest, the Temple was destroyed, and worship there was forbidden. Furthermore, the Jews were forbidden to seek converts, and the Jewish population of the whole Empire was

Relief from the Triumphal Arch of Titus (A.D. 81), which depicts the spoils from Jerusalem. (Courtesy Fratelli Alinari, Florence)

forced to donate the tax formerly paid to the Temple at Jerusalem to Jupiter Capitolinus at Rome instead. All those born into the Jewish faith, however, were still exempted from Caesar-worship. Of the various Jewish factions only the Pharisees survived. They devoted themselves chiefly to the study of Law. With Jerusalem destroyed, the small Christian sect was further cut off from its Jewish roots and began to take on an identity more of its own, which both helped its spread among non-Jews and soon caused problems over Caesar-worship.

Reform of the Army   The part played by the provincial armies in the havoc of 69 had clearly indicated to Vespasian the urgent need for a reform of the army. First, he struck from the Roman army lists the legions that had supported the German and Celtic national movements just suppressed. Next he stopped the practice of recruiting some of the legionary and most of the auxiliary troops from the frontier regions in which they served, where they were apt to sympathize with the national aspirations of their own people. To counteract such nationalistic tendencies, he either formed new auxiliary units of mixed tribal and national origin—or transferred units to frontiers far removed from their homeland and under the command of Italian officers. Finally, in order to reduce the chances of military coups by provincial commanders and provide for tighter defense at the same time, Vespasian also tended to break up large concentrations of legions, formerly stationed in a few central camps, and space them out singly along the borders.

The popularity of military service had been steadily declining among the population of Rome and Italy as peace and prosperity increased under the emperors. To take up the slack, Vespasian extended legionary recruitment from Italy to the more cultured and educated youth of Gaul and Spain, where military academies for the training of future officers (*collegia iuvenum*) became ever more common. Thus Vespasian's military reforms not only made the army more truly the servant and defender of the Empire but went hand in hand with his broader policy of Romanizing and urbanizing the provinces.

Provincial Policy   Surpassing even Caesar, Augustus, Tiberius, and Claudius, Vespasian inaugurated a new age of municipalization in the Roman world, which lasted until about 260. Completing the work of former centuries, he made Spain an integral part of the new world state by extending Latin Rights to about 350 Spanish cities and towns. Even Dalmatia began in his reign to assume an aspect of urbanization and municipalization never before known. The Danubian provinces were the last regions in the Roman world to receive Roman citizen colonies (*coloniae deductae*) and, during Vespasian's reign, became part of a process inaugurated long before in the historic year of 338 B.C. (see p. 75).

Vespasian did more to make the Western provinces full partners in the government and administration of the Empire than to use them as recruiting gounds or to grant Roman citizenship to office-holders in the newly chartered *municipia*. He went beyond Claudius or any of his predecessors in employing the local aristocracy of Gaul and Spain in Imperial administration and in his expanded bureaucracy. He used his powers as censor to add numerous members of the municipal aristocracy of southern Gaul and of Baetica in southwestern Spain to the rolls of the Roman senate, whose ranks had become depleted by the persecution of former emperors and by the recent civil war of 69. By utilizing the talents and services of the Gallic and Spanish provincials, Vespasian had given them a stake in both the military defense of the Empire and in the maintenance of peace, order, and tranquillity in the West.

Vespasian greatly strengthened the military defenses of the northern frontiers by restoring the number of legions serving along the Rhine to eight and by his creation of two new military provinces in Upper and Lower Germany, both entirely separate from the administration of the Gallic provinces. Along the

Danubian frontier he built numerous military roads and new stone fortresses. More important still, he wiped out that dangerous salient in the defense line in what is now southwest Germany and Switzerland at the headwaters of the Rhine and the Danube by the annexation of a triangle of land called the *Agri Decumates* (now largely occupied by the Black Forest). Vespasian also sent three men of great renown to resume the conquest of Britain, which Claudius and Nero had left unfinished— Petilius Cerealis (71–74), who had vanquished Civilis in Germany, Julius Frontinus (74–77/78), who wrote the *Strategemata* and *On the Aqueducts,* and Cn. Julius Agricola (77/78–84), about whom his own son-in-law, Tacitus, wrote a famous biography, the *Agricola.*

The Near East   In the Near East, which he knew well from firsthand experience, Vespasian attempted with the limited means at his disposal to remedy some of the fundamental weaknesses in the defensive arrangements of his predeccessors. The problems on the Eastern frontier were many: the lack of natural boundaries; a long exposed frontier of some three hundred miles stretching from Syria to the Black Sea; the attempt to contain the expansionism of Parthia by placing Roman puppets on the throne of Greater Armenia and by maintaining a chain of client kingdoms to protect the long frontier extending from the Lebanon to the Black Sea; the absence of any legionary troops or camps to guard the easy crossings of the middle and upper Euphrates at Zeugma, Samosata, or Melitene; and finally, the total dependence for Eastern defense upon the slow-moving and poorly disciplined legions based in the distant province of Syria.

To rectify some of the dangerous weaknesses of Rome's position in the Near East, Vespasian attempted to maintain peaceful relations with Parthia, even to the extent of resigning control, direct or nominal, over the kingdom of Greater Armenia. His least friendly act toward the Parthians was his refusal to cooperate with them in repelling the

Alani, a Sarmatian tribe living beyond the Caucasus, who had overrun Media Atropatene and Greater Armenia and were then a threat to the very existence of the Parthian state. Instead, he only helped the king of Iberia (Soviet Georgia) to occupy the Dariel Pass and in 75 built a fortress near Tiflis.

Some of his other measures were less than pleasing to the Parthian king. First, he strengthened Roman control over the great caravan city of Palmyra and made Judea a separate procuratorial province with one full legion stationed at Jerusalem. He extended the province of Syria from the northern edge of the Lebanon to the upper reaches of the middle Euphrates by the annexation of the kingdom of Commagene, whose king he deposed, and created to the north a huge province in Anatolia by adding Cappadocia and Lesser Armenia to the former province of Galatia. There he stationed two legions, one to guard the vital Euphrates crossing at Melitene, the other the important road junction of Satala, whence roads led to Trapezus (Trebizond) and to other naval bases on the Black Sea. Thus Vespasian, except at Zeugma and Samosata, now legionary strongholds, diminished the responsibility of Syria for the Roman defense of the Near East against Parthian attempts to cross the Euphrates and created stronger bulwarks.

Vespasian's Relations with the Senate   Vespasian, like Augustus, Tiberius, and Claudius before him, and the so-called ''good'' emperors after him, treated the senate with the utmost deference and respect. He, too, extended financial assistance to impoverished but deserving members of ancient and illustrious lineage. Yet he did not treat the senate as an equal partner in the government of the Empire. Though the senate remained a sounding board of upper-class Roman and Italian opinion and therefore exerted a powerful influence upon the character of even the most autocratic Imperial regime, nevertheless it had been steadily declining as an effective organ of the government since the reign of Tiberius. The extent of its decline was marked in 73, when Vespasian, following the example of Claudius, risked offending conservative senators by assuming the censorship, which gave him the power to remove objectionable and recalcitrant senators and replace them with new men from Italy and the Western provinces, who would cooperate and obey. The new men were usually of demonstrated ability and staunch supporters of the regime. The senate had been reduced to about two hundred by the actions of Nero and the civil war of 68/69. Vespasian added eight hundred, which must have annoyed the remaining old families but increased the pool of senatorial talent that Vespasian needed to administer the Empire.

The Expansion of the Bureaucracy
The weakening of the senate resulted in a steady concentration of power and function in the Imperial executive and in the expansion of the bureaucracy, whose value as the sole means of preserving continuity of administration under rapidly changing emperors came to light more clearly than ever before in 69.

In his selection of officials, Vespasian made two important innovations: he replaced many, but not all, of the freedmen, who under Claudius and Nero had held some of the highest positions, with equestrians; and appointed more and more Italians and provincials. The reasons for these innovations are clear: the equestrians were less offensive to the senate than were freedmen, who had been offensive to the equestrians as well; also, equestrians usually had considerable business and administrative experience and, often having greater private sources of income, were somewhat less tempted than freedmen to embezzle public funds. The provincials brought with them a knowledge of local conditions that must have been most useful in the administration of a highly diversified empire.

Financial Administration
Vespasian's greatest claim to fame was his success in handling financial problems—balancing the budget and restoring the public finances, which had been thrown into chaos by Nero's extravagance and the civil wars of 69. Besides personal frugality, native shrewdness, financial experience, and an unusual ability to drive hard bargains, Vespasian had a firm control over the armies, so that he did not need to buy their loyalty or obedience by large donatives. Nor would he tolerate graft or embezzlement of public funds by government officials. Also, he vigorously imposed new and heavier taxes on the provinces and drastically cut down public expenditures.

Using his powers as censor, Vespasian had a careful census taken of the financial resources of the Empire. He discovered that the provinces after a century of peace and prosperity were able to pay much more tribute than formerly exacted from them. He assigned certain "free" cities and islands previously immune from taxation, such as Rhodes, Samos, and Byzantium, to provinces and forced them to pay taxes. He restored to the senate the province of Greece, to which Nero had granted freedom and immunity from taxes, and took back under Imperial control the richer provinces of Sardinia and Corsica. He asserted the government's claim to land seized surreptitiously by private owners or occupied illegally by squatters, took back, on behalf of the *fiscus,* many estates given by former emperors to their friends, and reorganized for revenue purposes the other Imperial estates, especially those containing mines, quarries, fisheries, and forests. In short, no source of revenue, however unorthodox or unsavory (such as a tax on public latrines), was beneath Vespasian's notice.

Despite a reputation for being tight with money, Vespasian spent freely on Imperial defense, on roads, bridges, and fortifications in the provinces, on public buildings in Rome, and on education. After repairing the damage wrought in Italy by the civil war of 69, he commemorated the end of the Jewish War by beginning construction in Rome of the Forum that bears his name (with the Temple of Peace in the center), the Arch of Titus, and the gigantic *Amphitheatrum Flavium* or Colosseum* with a seating capacity of fifty thousand spectators and built of travertine stone faced with stucco. Though used as a quarry by generations of Renaissance architects, the Colosseum of the Flavians still stands as a symbol of the might and majesty of Imperial Rome and as one of the great man-made wonders of the world. Another great architectural achievement of the reign was the completion in 71 of a new temple to Capitoline Jupiter.

As an encouragement to literature and education, Vespasian liberally subsidized poets and prose writers. From public funds he endowed schools and established a chair of literature and rhetoric, of which Marcus Fabius Quintilianus, the celebrated Spanish rhetorician, was the first incumbent (see p. 375).

The Opposition to Vespasian
Despite his conspicuous achievements and services to the Empire, Vespasian never fully escaped the opposition of Republican-minded senators and of the Stoic and Cynic philosophers. Many senators objected to his numerous consulships, by which he sought to enhance the nobility of his family, to his assumption of the censorship, his practice of admitting Italians and provincials into the senate, and his ill-concealed intention of founding a new dynasty by handing down the office of *princeps* to members of his own family. Yet, the senatorial opposition was more vocal than dangerous, and Vespasian paid little attention to it. Far more irritating were the attacks of the Stoic and especially of the Cynic philosophers, who finally nettled him into ordering their expulsion from Rome.

Vespasian's Death, 79
In the spring of 79, after a decade of hard and continuous

---

* The Colosseum owes its name, not to its own size, but to the size (125 feet high) of the statue of Nero that stood at the entrance. It was placed there by the Emperor Hadrian, who removed it from the court of Nero's Golden House.

work, Vespasian caught a fever and died, but the hour of death did not deprive him of his sense of humor. As he lay dying he muttered, ''Dear me, I think I'm becoming a god!''

Before his death Vespasian had settled the question of his successor. He had carefully prepared his elder son, also named Titus Flavius Vespasianus to succeed him by giving him army commands, the proconsular *imperium* and tribunician power, and by sharing the censorship with him for one year and the consulate for seven. He had also appointed him sole prefect of the Praetorian Guard, a wise precaution that enabled Titus to thwart immediately Aulus Caecina's grab for the throne in 79.

Titus (79–81)
After Vespasian's death, the senate at once conferred upon Titus the usual honors and titles of the Principate, though not without some qualms and misgivings. Titus was handsome, charming, genial, and generous enough, but his moral conduct had reportedly not been of the best. He had associated rather freely with the wilder elements of Roman aristocratic society, and a love affair with Julia Berenice, a sister of the Jewish king, Herod Agrippa II, revived memories of Antony and Cleopatra.

Yet once seated on the throne, Titus became the ideal *princeps,* eager to promote the welfare of his subjects and much beloved by the people. He recalled the philosophers exiled by his father and halted all treason trials. He rewarded informers with public flogging and enslavement or exile to unhealthy islands. He sent away Berenice to avoid giving offense to conservative senators, and he entertained the people with splendid games and shows to their amazement and delight.

Three catastrophes marred that brief but brilliant reign. In August of 79, Vesuvius, after centuries of quiescence (except for a severe earthquake in 63) suddenly burst forth into violent eruption. The ground quaked and heaved, the light was blotted from the sky, and tons of smoking pumice and volcanic ash rained down upon and buried the two Campanian cities of Pompeii and Herculaneum. Next, a plague, like none ever seen before, descended upon Campania. In Rome another great fire broke out and raged for three days. These disasters, occurring as they did in rapid succession, put to the severest test the energy and philanthropy of Titus.

In September of 81, after a reign of twenty-six months, Titus contracted a fever just as his father had and died at the family's home at the age of 42. The Roman people mourned the death of their beloved ruler, and the senate showered him with posthumous praises and honors. Deification followed.

Domitian (81–96)   The way was now open for Vespasian's younger son, Titus Flavius Domitianus, known as Domitian. Leaving his brother's deathbed, Domitian rode in haste to Rome. He went to the barracks of the Praetorian Guard to be acclaimed as emperor. The armies acquiesced; the senate approved. Neither had much choice, for the son of Vespasian and brother of Titus had no rival claimants to the throne. It became his, not through any special education or previous military or administrative experience, but by accident of birth. Under Vespasian and Titus he had been pushed into the background after 69, when he had acted too high-handedly at Rome before his father and Titus had arrived from the East. Rejected, neglected, ignored, he had consoled himself by writing Greek verse and studying the *Acta* or *Deeds* of Tiberius, whose reserve, grimness, and austerity he much admired and later imitated. Later gossip predictably accused Domitian of poisoning Titus, but that is unfounded.

Autocratic Behavior   Soon after taking office, Domitian incurred the senate's displeasure and hostility by his autocratic behavior. To appear before senators in the regalia of a triumphant general was an affront to their dignity. (His triumphal robes marked him as an *Imperator* with power to command. In nonmilitary attire he would have been a *princeps* seeking advice.) Also, his seventeen consulships and his exercise of the censorship for life (*censor perpetuus*) not only defied all tradition but revealed his intention of establishing an absolute monarchy. Worse still, he outdid even Caligula and Nero by permitting and encouraging poets, courtiers, and even civil servants to address him as Lord and God (*Dominus et Deus*).

He trampled underfoot the ancient prerogatives of the senate by elevating equestrians to positions of power formerly reserved to senators. He appointed equestrians to his judicial *consilium* to sit in judgment on senators and even named an *eques* proconsul of the senatorial province of Asia. Acts such as these were more intolerable than his impious pretentions to divinity. No wonder, after his death, the senate damned his memory and ordered the removal of his statues from public places.

Perhaps it is not that Domitian was essentially an evil man or a bad emperor but that he owed his reputation to his failure in public relations. Had he been a shrewder politician, like Augustus and Vespasian, and more vocally dedicated to Roman ideals like *libertas* and the *mos maiorum* with a few Ciceronian platitudes thrown in, he might easily have won over most senators without loss of real or actual power. He might even have saved his memory from the venom-dipped pens of Tacitus, the Younger Pliny, and Juvenal.

Public Benefactions, Religion, and Finance   Domitian kept the populace happy, well fed, and amused. Three times he distributed among them donations (*congiaria*) amounting to a total of 225 *denarii* a head. For their amusement he organized splendid spectacles—wild beast hunts, mock sea and land battles, gladiatorial contests in the Colosseum, and chariot races in the Circus Maximus. He built the Stadium and Odeum (Music Hall) in Mars' Field to encourage competitions in the Greek manner not only in sports but in literature. He completed the Colosseum and the Arch and Baths of Titus and restored the Pantheon and Baths of Agrippa and the fire-gutted temples of Serapis and Isis (in front of which he placed imported Egyptian obelisks). He erected a beautiful new temple to the deified Vespasian, a huge temple to Jupiter the Guardian (*Juppiter Custos*), and, most magnificent of all, a temple to Jupiter Optimus Maximus on the Capitol, with columns of Pentelic marble, gold-plated doors, and roof tiles overlaid with gold leaf.

Domitian had taken a very active interest in Roman religion at an early age, and as Emperor, he sought to revive and strengthen old practices with a view to their political usefulness. He thereby proclaimed himself a defender of *Romanitas* and the gods that had made Rome great: Jupiter, Minerva, Mars, Venus, Neptune, Vesta, Ceres, and Roma herself. It was as their champion that he advanced his claim to be one of them. Therefore, he was usually hostile to exotic foreign cults, except that of Isis, as whose acolyte he had disguised himself and escaped danger during the civil war of 69. He seems to have shown particular hostility toward Jews and Christians, which is understandable since their rigid monotheism clashed with his own desire to be recognized as a god. It was under him that treason became linked with impiety and emperor worship became a test of loyalty, which posed such problems for Christians during the next two centuries.

Domitian certainly spent sums of money worthy of a god. Not neglecting himself, he built a grand Imperial palace on the Palatine and a huge mansion on Mount Alba overlooking the placid waters of the Alban Lake. In Italy he constructed a road from Sinuessa to Cumae, and established in Britain, as well as along the Rhine and Danube, numerous fortresses and garrison camps. He raised the pay of legionary soldiers from 300 to 400 denarii per annum, and also fought several costly wars between 81 and 93.

Where he got the money for everything is a mystery. He apparently never tapped new sources of revenue nor accepted legacies from testators having five or more children. He canceled debts owed to the state for more than

five years and, unlike Vespasian, gave clear title to occupiers of public land in Italy. Unlike Nero, he never debased the coinage. To explain how he was able to pass on to his successors a fairly full treasury, it must be assumed that he had his father's financial ability and was an efficient administrator and a strict collector of provincial taxes. In addition he probably raked into the *fiscus,* now reorganized and centralized, the proceeds of considerable property confiscated from persons condemned for treason against the state, of whom there were probably not a few in the latter part of his reign.

The Rebellion of Saturninus, 89

Treason trials occurred more frequently after the rebellion of L. Antonius Saturninus, the governor of Upper Germany and commander of two legions wintering in the double camp at Moguntiacum (Mainz). On January 1, 89 he seized the army savings and payroll and used it to bribe his legions to proclaim him emperor and the Chatti, a strong German tribe dwelling east of the middle Rhine, to invade Roman territory. To crush that revolt, Domitian at once sped north with his Praetorian Guard after he ordered Trajan (the future Emperor) to bring up a legion from Spain. Both got there too late for the battle. The loyal governor of Lower Germany, aided by a sudden thaw which broke up the ice over the Rhine and prevented the Chatti from crossing to help the rebels, suppressed the rebellion and killed Saturninus. Nevertheless, Domitian did not slacken the pace of his march to the Rhine.

After his arrival, Domitian ruthlessly punished the officers and accomplices of Saturninus and expanded the Roman territory to the east of the Rhine and to the north of the river Main. He sent the severed head of Saturninus to Rome and later celebrated a double triumph, not over the Roman Saturninus, of course, but over the Chatti and the Dacians, against whom he advanced after having secured the Rhine frontier by shortened defense lines, watchtowers, and fortifications.

The Dacian Frontier, 85 to 93 The revolt of Saturninus in 89 had disrupted Domitian's conquest of Dacia (roughly equivalent to modern Rumania), which he had begun in 85, after the young and aggressive Dacian king Decebalus (85–106) had invaded the Roman province of Moesia across the Danube. A Roman army inflicted a great defeat on the Dacians in 88, but in 89 the Roman army led by Domitian himself, suffered so sharp a reverse that he gladly came to terms with Decebalus. Decebalus agreed, in 89, to surrender all Roman captives and accept the role of Roman client. In return, Domitian recognized him as the legitimate king of the Dacians, granted him an annual subsidy, and furnished him Roman engineers skilled in the art of building roads and fortresses.

The Dacian peace treaty, though dictated by expediency and considered by many senators to be an affront to Roman dignity, was of immense value to Rome. It turned Decebalus into a benevolent neutral, if not an active ally, when the Iazyges irrupted into Pannonia in 92 and attacked and cut up a Roman legion. It also helped Domitian isolate the hostile Marcomanni and Quadi by alliances with the Germanic tribes living to the north of them, with the Semnones east of the Elbe, and with the powerful Lugii of Silesia. Domitian was able to stabilize the Danubian frontier by concentrating nine or ten legions along the river in strongly fortified camps at Vindobona (Vienna), at Carnuntum (Altenburg), at Aquincum (Budapest), and at Troesmis near modern Braila. By 93, peace prevailed again along the entire Danubian frontier.

Conspiracies and Treason Trials The rebellion of Saturninus in 89 so upset Domitian that he developed a serious persecution complex and saw conspiracies forming against him everywhere. Spies and informers began to play upon his fears. In 89 he banished philosophers and astrologers from Rome but later struck out most savagely against prominent senators, some able provincial governors, and even members of the Imperial family, such as his niece Domitilla.

The Murder of Domitian, 96 When Domitia, the Emperor's wife, found out that she was going to be the next victim, she enlisted the secret aid of the two new praetorian prefects and entered into a conspiracy with a number of influential senators. They persuaded Domitian to grant audience to Domitilla's former but devoted butler, a certain Stephanus, who pretended to have secret information about an alleged conspiracy. Admitted to the Emperor's bedroom, he handed him a document. As Domitian unfolded the document, Stephanus stabbed him in the groin with a dagger concealed in an arm bandage. The wounded Domitian staggered to his bed and groped frantically under the pillow for the dagger that he kept there. The dagger was gone. Therefore, Stephanus was able to finish the deed that he had begun before Domitian's attendants burst in and killed him.

Despite Domitian's evil reputation among the senatorial nobility, all three Flavians had done great service to the Roman Empire. They had restored internal peace and prosperity, introduced greater administrative efficiency and fiscal responsibility, continued the process of integrating the status of provincials with that of the Romans and Italians (who had previously exploited them), and set a standard of personal service that inspired their successors during a century of good government.

XXIX

The Five "Good" Emperors, A.D. 96–180

The death of Domitian marked the end of the Flavian dynasty, but the stability established by the Flavians endured. No destructive period of crisis and civil war followed, as had happened upon the death of Nero. Unlike Nero, Domitian had not neglected the legions, and he had been able to crush rebellious commanders quickly. The successful conspiracy against Domitian had originated not among provincial armies but within the Imperial family and senatorial leadership at Rome. The conspirators placed a new emperor on the throne before provincial commanders had time to react. As a result, there was a fairly smooth transition of Imperial authority.

Within their own ranks the senators found a successor to Domitian, Marcus Cocceius Nerva, sixty years old and long past his prime, who posed no threat of establishing another dynasty. Generous donatives paid or promised kept both the Praetorian Guard and the provincial armies temporarily satisfied and acquiescent. Thus a peaceful transition was effected, and a new period in the history of the Principate was introduced. The emperors Nerva, Trajan, Hadrian, Antoninus Pius, and Marcus Aurelius, from A.D. 96 to 180, are often called the "five good emperors." Under

them the Roman Empire enjoyed its longest single period of stability and good government. They were benevolent rulers, whose chief concern was to promote the welfare of the Empire and the people whom they ruled.

Sources There are only two narrative sources for this period, neither of the first rank as history. The first is Cassius Dio, whose history of Rome covered the reigns involved in Books 67 to 72, which are preserved in only abbreviated form by two later Byzantine epitomes: a lengthy one now missing the reign of Antoninus Pius and the early years of Marcus Aurelius, and a shorter one based on the first. Biographies of the emperors from Hadrian to Marcus Aurelius and also of Lucius Verus and Avidius Cassius are found in a controversial collection known as the *Historia Augusta* and written probably about A.D. 395. It is generally agreed that the first four major lives in the collection are based on a fairly good source and are trustworthy for the main historical outline. The two minor lives are far less reliable and probably contain much sensationalistic fiction.

For the reigns of Nerva and Trajan, the contemporary letters of Pliny the Younger and his *Panegyric,* on Trajan, are very useful. The panegyric *To Rome* and the *Sacred Teachings* of the Greek rhetorician Aelius Aristides are useful for the period under Antoninus Pius, and the *Letters* (*Epistulae*) of Marcus Aurelius' tutor Marcus Cornelius Fronto were composed from the time of Hadrian to that of Aurelius. Of course, Aurelius' own *Meditations* provide a firsthand look into his interesting personality. Other literary and technical works and numerous Christian writings are also valuable for reconstructing the social, economic, and cultural milieu of the period (see p. 379).

Monuments, such as the triumphal arch of Trajan at Beneventum and the columns of Trajan and Marcus Aurelius, present valuable historical information, as do numerous extant coins, inscriptions, and Egyptian papyri from this era. These latter three sources, along with archaeological excavations throughout the Empire, yield interesting data on the provinces. Finally, laws preserved in the *Corpus Juris Civilis* (*Body of Civil Law*) shed light on the social and administrative developments under the ''good'' emperors.

Nerva (96–98) Though Nerva's family contained several distinguished jurists, it was not an old one and had gained social acceptance only because his maternal uncle had married a woman of Julio-Claudian birth, an ennobling but a tenuous link. Nerva himself had not won much distinction as a jurist or as a public speaker and had never governed a province or commanded an army, though he had done fairly well politically. Being a safe and innocuous man and willing to cooperate with any regime, he had had one statue erected to him in the Forum, another on the Palatine during Nero's reign. He had reached the consulship in 71 under Vespasian and again in 90 under Domitian. He also held several priesthoods. In all his past career he seems to have preferred security to fame.

The senate regarded Nerva as the ideal ruler for many reasons: his deference, his vow never to put a senator to death unless condemned by a senatorial court, his restoration to the senate of the administration of the grain dole, his suspension of the hated law of treason (*maiestas*), and his recall of senatorial exiles and suppression of informers.*

On the other hand, Nerva was unable to resist the demand for punishment of Domitian's assassins. When members of the Praetorian Guard besieged his palace and clamored for vengeance against Domitian's killers, he meekly allowed them to kill their former prefect and several other conspirators. Furthermore, despite the initially smooth transition to the new reign of Nerva, it became apparent early on that he could not hold power long without strong military backing to hold in check ambitious provincial commanders once they had a chance to reflect on the sudden turn of events with Domitian's assassination.

Therefore, the most important act of Nerva's brief rule was his adoption of Marcus Ulpius Traianus, Trajan, the very able and respected military governor of Lower Germany, as son, heir, and coregent. The choice was excellent. A year after the adoption, Nerva died before his new son had even come to Rome. But, thanks to Nerva's action, Trajan succeeded without incident.

Trajan (98–117) Trajan, the first Emperor of provincial origin, was born in Spain at Italica near Seville in the rich province of Baetica. He was proud of his father, whom Vespasian had admitted not only into the senate but into the Roman patriciate. The consulship, the Syrian command, the proconsulate of Asia, and numerous triumphal honors followed in swift succession.

Before his adoption by Nerva, Trajan too had had a long and distinguished military career under Vespasian and Domitian on the Rhine, the Danube, and the Euphrates, in Syria and in Spain. As governor of Lower Ger-

* The more agile and astute of these nevertheless managed somehow to hold positions of immense power and even serve as members of his *consilium.*

many, he had won, during Nerva's reign, the proud title of *Germanicus;* under his own auspices he would win still others: *Dacicus* and *Parthicus* (Conqueror of the Dacians and the Parthians).

After Nerva's death, two years spent in inspecting and strengthening defenses along the Rhine and the Danube preceded Trajan's long-awaited and much-acclaimed arrival in Rome. Well might both populace and senate have acclaimed such an *imperator:* the majestic figure, the rugged face, the iron-gray hair—a battle-hardened soldier in the prime of life, not a callow unpredictable youth like Caligula or Nero, nor a feeble, scraggy old man like Galba or Nerva. His very appearance commanded respect.

Trajan's Administration   Toward the senate Trajan was tactful, respectful, often gracious, even indulgent—the attitude of the ''Best Prince'' (*Optimus Princeps*), a title bestowed as early as 100, stamped on the coinage in 105, but not officially assumed till 115. Centuries later, the senate bestowed on every new emperor the supreme compliment: ''Luckier than Augustus, better than Trajan'' (*Felicior Augusto, melior Traiano*).

The senate with which Trajan had to deal was different in attitude and composition from that of the early Empire. Severely chastened by Nero and Domitian, it gladly accepted him as being at least ''better than the worst'' (*melior pessimo princeps*). Change of attitude arose out of change of composition. As inscriptions and papyri show, the senate of Claudius and even Vespasian contained only a few members of provincial origin. Under Trajan provincial senators made up slightly over forty percent of the total, more and more of whom now came from the Eastern provinces.

Enjoying, as he did, the support and affection of the senate, the people, and the provincial armies, Trajan was able to carry out his administrative program without distraction or fear. He was an energetic emperor and tried to give the Empire the best possible government. He pursued many enlightened social and eco-nomic programs and inaugurated many public works that added to both the beauty and prosperity of Rome and the provinces.

The *Alimenta:* Public Assistance for the Poor   Although it may have been instituted under Nerva, a relief program called the *alimenta* to bolster the population of Italy by supporting poor children was strongly promoted by Trajan. In the late first century A.D., Italy was declining economically because of increased competition from provincial manufacturing and agriculture, which were supplying markets formerly supplied by Italian exports, especially in the now highly Romanized provinces of Gaul and Spain (see pp. 394–395). The large landowners of Italy were able to adjust to these new circumstances without much difficulty. Land that once might have been used to grow cash crops could be given over to tenant farmers (*coloni*) in return for a fixed share of their produce, which would keep the owners supplied with foodstuffs.

The impoverishment of smaller farmers and craftsmen, however, had a serious effect on their ability to raise children. A decline in the Italian population resulted. This decline adversely affected Italian recruitment for the army, to which emperors looked not only for the loyal defense of the Empire but as a means of Romanizing the provinces and promoting Imperial unity. To alleviate this problem, Nerva or Trajan, imitating local private relief efforts by wealthy men like Pliny the Younger, set up the publicly funded *alimenta* to subsidize the care and education of poor freeborn boys and girls.

Under this plan, landowners in a given locality would pledge so much land as collateral for a loan equal to about one-eighth of its value. In return, the owners agreed to pay, apparently in perpetuity, about five percent interest a year on the amount of money received. The interest paid was put into a fund administered by Imperial officials, who then distributed it to the needy children of the local district.

It is not likely that landowners were

forced to participate in the *alimenta* or that the members of local town councils, who were large landowners, were excluded. These loans did not make sense for anyone other than the well-to-do. They would certainly not have been attractive or helpful to smaller landowners in difficulties. Such men would not have had collateral to obtain a loan of any consequence, and they would not have wished to burden their precarious finances with a permanent debt. A large landowner, however, could pledge only a part of his holdings and obtain a useable sum of money at relatively little risk and with only a small charge against future income, which he could hope to increase beyond his annual interest cost by using the principal to improve his operations or buy more land in order to increase his profits.

The measures that Trajan took to improve economic conditions in the provinces were equally impressive: roads, bridges, harbors, and aqueducts in almost every province. Unfortunately, in his efforts also to increase efficiency, Trajan introduced changes in the adminstration of cities and municipalities in Italy and the provinces that set the dangerous precedent of interference with municipal affairs and led, a century later, to the decay of local initiative in financial matters. His motives were good, however, and his intervention seemed justified at the time by the chaotic financial state of many cities.

Some cities in Italy and the Eastern provinces had become involved in financial troubles in spite of fairly large revenues— rents from suburban farms and urban real estate, fines imposed on lawbreakers, fees accompanying applications for citizenship, the sale of hunting and fishing licenses, and, in some cases, tolls and harbor dues. These revenues often failed to meet the expenditures on games, religious festivals, embassies to Rome, and ambitious building projects. The financial disabilities of some municipalities were further aggravated by the responsibility for collecting taxes for the Imperial government and making up for arrears or deficiencies.

To help the municipalities solve their financial problems, Trajan sent agents or inspectors (*curatores* or *correctores*). In 111 he sent the Younger Pliny to Bithynia. In 109 he sent a certain Maximus to Greece to investigate and regulate the affairs of Athens, Sparta, and Delphi, and an Imperial legate to the Italian Transpadana. The advice of these agents, though tendered in a polite and friendly way, was not to be ignored.

The Dacian Wars, 101 to 106 Public works and administration were not Trajan's sole employment nor his greatest interest. The army, which had been his life, continued to be his chief delight. In 101 he set out on an invasion of Dacia, with whose king, Decebalus, Domitian had concluded the treaty of 89, convenient, expedient, but galling to Roman Imperial pride.

The conquest of Dacia proved neither swift nor easy. In that land of mountain and forest defended fanatically by the fiercely independent Dacians, who were led by their wily and Roman-hating king, Trajan suffered a severe reverse at Tapae near the Iron Gates. In the spring of 102, Trajan again invaded Dacia. After several successful battles, he finally occupied the capital city of Sarmizegethusa, where he stationed a permanent garrison. Decebalus surrendered unconditionally and agreed to become once more a Roman client. Trajan then returned to Rome to celebrate his triumph and added *Dacicus* to his titulature.

In 105 Decebalus broke the peace agreement. Trajan hastened to the lower Danube with thirteen legions, crossed the stone bridge, which his architect Apollodorus had built, and broke Dacian resistance (in 106). After the suicide of Decebalus, Trajan annexed Dacia as a province and made Sarmizegethusa a colony (*Ulpia Traiana*). He settled numerous veterans and colonists from all over the Empire, ancestors of the present-day Rumanians. Fifty thousand Dacian war prisoners ended their days as slaves and gladiators in the Roman arena. Vast revenues from Dacian gold mines made possible magnificent public works in Rome, Italy, and the provinces and temporarily so disturbed the ratio between gold and silver that the Emperor slightly increased the copper content in silver coins in order, probably, to restore the balance.

The Parthian Wars, 113 to 117

After seven years of peace a war of Trajan's own making broke out with Parthia. Chosroes, the new Parthian king, provoked Trajan by deposing the king of Armenia without Rome's consent. Trajan's reaction was swift: he set sail for the East in the fall of 113.

Within two years he had extended Rome's dominion from the headwaters of the Tigris and Euphrates to the Persian Gulf. Trade routes to the far East were now within his grasp and passage to India might have been his next move. As he gazed wistfully upon the waters of the Persian Gulf and watched a ship sailing eastward, he mused resignedly: "Oh, had I been younger, I should have liked to go to India too." Instead, he went up the Euphrates to Babylon and there received disturbing news.

The Empire, which Trajan had extended to the furthest limits yet attained, was suddenly convulsed by simultaneous revolts. Seleucia, Mesopotamia, Assyria, and even Armenia all were in revolt, and powerful Parthian armies were returning to reoccupy lost territory. The Sarmatians and Roxolani along the Danube were again on the move. In Britain Roman garrisons were in retreat from the borders of Scotland.

The most serious revolts were those of the Jews in Cyrenaica, Mesopotamia, Adiabene, Cyprus, and Egypt, which were marked by savage massacre. Trajan acted with resolution and promptness; but without help of his able marshal and comrade in arms, Lusius Quietus the Moor, he would have failed to restore the rapidly deteriorating situation. Trajan himself pacified southern Mesopotamia by his capture and ruthless destruction of Seleucia on the Tigris, while his marshal reconquered northern Mesopotamia and later, as governor of Judea, stamped out all Jewish riots in Palestine. His other marshals were less successful in suppressing the revolts in Cyrenaica,

Cyprus, and Egypt. Nor was Trajan able to hold all his Parthian conquests: in 116 he surrendered the province of southern Mesopotamia to a Parthian prince, nominally a Roman client, and lost the entire province of Assyria, along with part of Greater Armenia.

The Death of Trajan, 117

Three years of hard campaigning in the desert and the strain of recent months had overtaxed Trajan's strength. He was then past sixty. On the road back from Ctesiphon he became ill and during the winter at Antioch, where he was busily preparing for another campaign in Mesopotamia in the following spring, he grew steadily worse. Reluctantly, he abandoned his plans of campaign. He set out for Rome and left Publius Aelius Hadrianus, Hadrian, the command of the Near East. He never put out to sea. At Selinus in Cilicia he suffered a stroke and died a few days later (August 9, 117).

The Effects of Trajan's War

Trajan, one of the greatest of Roman *Imperatores*, was the first to realize at least in part Caesar's plans to conquer Dacia and Parthia. Marcus Antonius had tried but never succeeded; Nero had aspired but never tried. Under Trajan the Roman Empire reached the high tide of territorial expansion; after him there was to be a slow and inexorable ebb.

The costs of Imperial expansion were high. Trajan paid the price in health; the Empire in manpower and resources. Moreover, Trajan had expanded the Empire beyond defensible limits and in the process had weakened, if not totally paralyzed, the capability of three strong buffer states—Dacia, Parthia, and Nabataean Arabia.* Rome would later have to absorb and repel the mass invasions of the Goths and other Germans, the Alans, and Iranians, who, impelled by the relentless pressure of the Huns from central Asia, would break and burst through

---

* The last had been occupied and made a province in an easy campaign of 106.

the brittle, overextended defenses of the Roman Empire on the Rhine, Danube, and Euphrates. Trajan's paralyzing of the defensive powers of the Dacians, Nabataeans, and Parthians spelled disaster for the Roman Empire of the future.

Hadrian (117—138) No sooner had news of Trajan's death reached Antioch than the armies of Syria proclaimed Hadrian, their commander-in-chief, Emperor of Rome. Several days later the senate officially confirmed the acclamation. The rumor that Hadrian owed his throne to a forged instrument of adoption carried little weight against acclamation by the army and the senate's ratification.

Hadrian's birthplace is disputed. According to the *Historia Augusta* he was born in Rome in 76, but his family on both sides belonged to Italica, the same Spanish town where Trajan was born. An orphan at the age of ten, he became a ward of Trajan, his father's cousin and closest male relative. He received an excellent education and acquired a strong and lasting love of Greek studies, Greek art and philosophy, to which interest he owed his half-contemptuous nickname of Graeculus (Greekling). He became a man of refined artistic tastes, an intellectual with a keen, penetrating intelligence.

Nor was Hadrian's training wholly academic. Healthy, well built, and strong, he liked the outdoor, strenuous life and was inordinately fond of hunting. Like Plato's philosopher king, he had a long military and official career. He had seen military service in Spain, Pannonia, Moesia, Germany, and Parthia. In the First Dacian War, he was Trajan's quaestor, in the Second, the commander of a legion. He was governor of Lower Pannonia in 107 and governor of Syria in 117. To facilitate his climb to power, however, he married Trajan's grandniece, Vibia Sabina, a strikingly beautiful but understandably frustrated woman, whom he probably would have divorced had it not been for his ambition.

Hadrian was more at home hunting or on campaign with the army or touring the provinces than at Rome. Conventional home life did not satisfy him. He seems to have had his share of mistresses in his early years, but the great passion of his life was a handsome young Bithynian Greek named Antinous, whom he met on an Eastern tour in 123. That such a relationship was most satisfying to Hadrian is understandable in light of his love of Greek art and philosophy, which were heavily imbued with the homoeroticism of aristocratic Greek culture, and much like an ancient Spartan's, his almost continuous service on active duty in the all-male society of the army.

The Early Years of Hadrian's Principate Hadrian had fallen heir to a difficult task, not rendered lighter by inevitable comparison with his illustrious predecessor, from whom he had in actual fact inherited a legacy of disturbance and revolt in Cyrenaica, Egypt, and Cyprus, in Mauretania, on the lower Danube, and in Britain. The man who helped him quell those revolts was his trusted friend, Marcius Turbo, who replaced Trajan's great Moorish marshal, Lusius Quietus.

With the new regime also came a change in foreign policy. Convinced that Trajan's wars of expansion were a drain upon the Empire's manpower and resources, at the outset of his reign Hadrian prudently abandoned all recent conquests east of the Tigris and Euphrates, allowed Greater Armenia to revert to the status of a client kingdom, and made peace with Parthia. On the other hand, rumors that he also planned to abandon Dacia were false.

If Trajan had sought to emulate, by wars of conquest, the deeds of Caesar, so Hadrian found precedent for his program of peace in the policy of Augustus, though he did not adopt the magic legend of HADRIANVS AVGVSTVS on his coins until the year 123, which happened to be the one hundred and fiftieth anniversary of the senate's conferral of the name 'Augustus' upon Octavianus.

The new "Pax Augusta" did not please everyone—especially not Lusius Quietus and three former marshals who had admired Trajan's dynamic policy and disapproved of Hadrian's new frontier policy. Mild expression of disapproval and annoyance led to overt acts of treason that finally called forth senatorial condemnation. The four were executed without Hadrian's sanction or knowledge; or so he averred. He wished his reign to be one of clemency and mercy and not stained with the blood even of trouble-making consulars.

To many high-ranking Romans his disavowals sounded evasive and hollow. Reluctantly, therefore, and under a heavy cloud he set out on his much-deferred journey to Rome. He finally arrived in Rome early in July of 118.

A day or so after his arrival, he appeared before the senate—a tall, bearded,* imposing figure—and solemnly promised the assembled dignitaries that no senator would henceforth be put to death without prior condemnation by a senatorial court.†

The senate pacified, Hadrian began to court the favor of the masses with a large distribution of gifts and a vast remission of debts and tax arrears. Day after day there hung over the Forum the smoke of burning account books as debts amounting to many millions were obliterated, an unavailing gesture of generosity that brought small comfort to him or his entourage. Hadrian's anger at the public's ingratitude was so great he left Rome again.

Hadrian's Travels The year 121 found Hadrian in Gaul and the Rhineland. The next year he went to Britain, where he inspected plans for the construction of a wall (which bears his name) from Solway Firth to the Tyne to keep marauding tribesmen of the north from raiding farmlands south of the Scottish border. On the way back from Britain he passed through Gaul and thence to Spain, where he spent the winter. In the spring he led a punitive expedition against the Moors,

who had been raiding Roman towns in Morocco. There he received news that the Parthians had again broken the peace, and he set sail for Ephesus.

His dramatic arrival in the near East, backed by impressive troop concentrations, inspired Chosroes, the Parthian King, to negotiate rather than fight. The war over, Hadrian went on to hear petitions and complaints. He punished misgovernment of the provinces, arranged for the construction of municipal temples, baths, aqueducts, and theaters, and built an enormous temple at Cyzicus.

In 128 he visited North Africa, where he inspected the Imperial estates and studied ways and means for more efficient exploitation. He spent the following winter in Athens, where he presided at games and festivals, codified laws, completed and dedicated a huge temple to Olympian Zeus, the *Olympieion,* which the tyrant Peisistratus had designed seven centuries before. In the suburbs of Athens he built a new city, named Hadrianopolis, and in it erected a pantheon, the *Stoa,* a gymnasium and a library, and another great temple, the *Panhellenion,* which he romantically dedicated to an ancient ideal—Greek unity. In the spring of 129 he again toured Asia Minor. Towns, temples, libraries, baths, and aqueducts sprang up wherever he went.

Unfortunately, he displayed a singular lack of understanding in Jerusalem. There, he insensitively resolved to found a Roman colony called Aelia Capitolina, and, on the site of the Jewish Temple, he erected a shrine to Jupiter Capitolinus. This act provoked one of the bloodiest rebellions in history.

Meanwhile, heedless of what he had done, Hadrian went to Egypt to reorganize its economic life and visit the monuments of its glorious past. While he was in Egypt, he was bereft of his beloved Antinous, who had drowned in the Nile. In his honor Hadrian founded a beautiful new city, Antinoopolis on the east bank of the Nile near where the youth had drowned. After his death, Hadrian worshipped him as divine, built shrines and

---

* The beard set a fashion for a long succession of Roman emperors.

† He kept the promise for twenty years.

Portrait relief of Antinous from Hadrian's Villa.
(Courtesy Fratelli Alinari, Florence)

temples to him, struck coins bearing his likeness, and set up busts of him all over the Empire.

The Jewish Revolt Hadrian returned to Rome to learn that the Jews had rebelled in the fall of 132 and were waging guerrilla war against the Roman army of occupation. Led by a famous guerrilla strategist, Simon Bar Kokhba (Shim'on Ben [Bar] Cosiba in the *Dead Sea Scrolls*), the Jews captured Jerusalem, slaughtered an entire Roman legion, and for a time seemed about to drive the Romans out of Palestine. Hadrian hastened back to Syria, assembled reinforcements from the other provinces, and summoned the able Julius Severus from Britain to take command. Severus began systematically isolating strongholds and inhabited places and starving out the defenders. The Romans may have slaughtered as many as half a million people and enslaved as many more. When the revolt was finally quelled in 135, stillness and desolation descended upon a ruined land.

The surviving Jewish population of Jerusalem was forcibly removed, and Jews were forbidden to enter the city except on one officially designated day each year. The name of the city was formally changed to Aelia Capitolina and remained so until the days of Constantine (324—337). The name of Judea was changed to Syria Palestina. Jews who remained there and throughout the Empire were still allowed to practice their ancestral religion and maintain their traditional schools and synagogues, but the vestiges of the national state that had been the focus of their aspirations for centuries were obliterated for 1800 years.

Frontier Defense Hadrian's renunciation of Trajan's aggressive foreign wars and his surrender of some recent conquests did not constitute a neglect of frontier defense. He was the first Emperor to erect on a large scale fixed frontier defenses such as Hadrian's Wall in Britain. He extended fortifications for 345 miles in South Germany behind continuous lines of ditches and oakwood palisades nine feet high. These fortifications, with their garrisoned forts and watchtowers, not only protected the frontier from enemy raids and even mass attacks, but marked the frontier and served as check points for the control of trade between the Roman and the barbarian world.

The Reform of the Army   Nor did Hadrian neglect the army. His reforms in discipline, recruitment, and tactics were of lasting importance. Discipline was for him almost a cult, and to secure it he personally inspected army posts all over the Empire; watched soldiers drill, march, maneuver; inspected equipment, dress, baggage, and mess kitchens; ordered fatigue marches during which, dressed as a common soldier, he marched along with the men and carried his own knapsack. To no emperor were the armies more devoted, and under none were they more disciplined and efficient.

One of Hadrian's most important army reforms was the progressive removal of distinction between the legions and the auxiliary corps (*auxilia*) with respect to training, equipment, and composition. For the first time both consisted of Roman citizens and noncitizens, recruited more and more in the frontier regions in which they were to serve. Many of the new recruits were soldiers' sons born near the permanent camps, and to them Hadrian granted the right, hitherto withheld, of inheriting their fathers' property.

In addition to the *auxilia*, which garrisoned the permanent forts strung out along the frontiers, Hadrian began to levy, especially in the German and Danubian provinces, in Britain, and in Morocco, many auxiliary units of a new type called *numeri*. These were small mobile corps, some of them light infantry, some cavalry, others mixed, while some consisted of mounted scouts known as *explora-*

tores. Though often commanded by Roman ex-centurions, the *numeri* retained their native languages, arms, and methods of fighting.

Hadrian's greatest reform in battle tactics was the introduction of an improved form of the old Macedonian *phalanx*. In offensive operations the *auxilia* would launch the initial attack while the *phalanx* of the legions advanced later to deliver the final blow. If the enemy attacked first, the *auxilia* would take the brunt of the initial assault. The legions held in reserve in camps behind the frontier forts would then advance to destroy the exhausted forces of the enemy. Hadrian's tactics were to remain standard military strategy, except for minor modifications, for over two centuries.

The Provinces   Extensive travels and detailed reports from procurators and other agents afforded Hadrian an intimate knowledge of conditions in the provinces. No detail of provincial administration, seemed too small for his personal attention, especially when it involved the defense of the weak against the strong, the poor against the rich (*humiliores contra honestiores; tenuiores contra potentiores*). Also, under Hadrian the urbanization of the Empire reached its peak, and the extension of Roman citizenship kept step with the diffusion of culture and civilization.

Hadrian frequently conferred the right of Greater Latinity (*Latium Maius*), which conferred citizenship upon all members of town councils or local senates (*decuriones*), as well as upon magistrates. This device was probably not, as commonly asserted, a sign of municipal decay, nor was it employed simply to make officeholding more attractive but to speed the growth of Roman citizenship everywhere and transform the Roman Empire into a genuine world commonwealth. It also had the very practical effect of extending the tax base and increasing the pool of citizen recruits for the army.

The Reorganization of the Imperial Bureaucracy   The growing administrative needs of the Roman world commonwealth as well as Hadrian's passion for efficiency led to further expansion and reorganization of the Imperial bureaucracy. The qualities that he demanded from civil servants were not unlike those required in most modern states. He insisted that holders of public office be able, well trained, and competent, loyal to the Emperor and devoted to the state. He paid them well and gave rewards for hard work, initiative, and efficiency.

Vespasian had reversed the policy of Claudius by employing *equites* more than freedmen in high administrative positions. Hadrian followed Vespasian's lead and appointed equestrians as directors of the four executive departments created by Claudius —imperial correspondence (*ab epistulis*), justice (*a libellis*), treasury (*a rationibus*), and the research and library service (*a studiis*). To enhance their prestige, he bestowed upon the holders of these offices such resounding titles as *vir egregius* ("outstanding man"), *vir perfectissimus* ("most perfect man"), and that of *vir eminentissimus* ("most eminent man"), held by the prefect of the Praetorian Guard. Gradations of salary also differentiated the various executive offices. Procurators, for example, received 60,000, 100,000, 200,000, or 300,000 sesterces per year, according to their rank. Four equestrian prefects commanded even higher salaries.

To these government departments Hadrian added two new ones of cabinet rank, both pointing not only to an increased centralization of government but to wider equestrian participation in government service. One of the new departments resulted from his reform of the vitally important system of the so called Imperial post and communications (*cursus publicus*), formerly a financial and administrative burden laid upon municipalities in Italy and the provinces. Hadrian lightened this burden by his reorganization of the system as a state institution controlled by a central bureau in Rome and headed by an equestrian prefect of vehicles (*praefectus vehiculorum*).

The other new department owed its origin to an overhauling of the tax-collecting system, especially that pertaining to the collection of the five percent inheritance tax (*vicesima hereditatum*), which Hadrain, in line with policies set by Caesar, Augustus, and Tiberius, transferred from tax-farming companies to a state agency presided over by an equestrian procurator. The procurator, assisted by numerous agents throughout the Empire, collected these and many other taxes, direct and indirect.

In the reorganization of the Imperial bureaucracy, Hadrian departed from the policy of Augustus by separating the civil and military careers of equestrian officials and by appointing *equites* without prior military experience to civilian posts. He probably wanted to attract into government service people of legal and philosophical interests to whom army life seemed irksome and distasteful.

In lieu of the now optional military training, Hadrian required *equites* seeking high administrative positions to begin their civilian careers by accepting such minor jobs as agents or attorneys of the treasury (*advocati fisci*), a newly created class of officials sent all over the Empire to prosecute cases of tax evasion and delinquency.

Hadrian's separation of civil and military careers was probably a poor idea since it deprived high government officials of requisite military experience and control over the army and left them helpless when confronted, as they were to be in the third century, by a formidable group of army commanders totally ignorant of civil government. In this instance Hadrian's yearning for administrative efficiency proved injurious to the future stability of the state.

The Reorganization of the Consilium

Having a mania for organization, Hadrian converted the informal conclave of palace friends and advisers, such as Augustus and his successors had consulted, into a genuine cabinet and permanent council of state (*consilium principis*). It consisted of the heads of the various departments of the government, the chief prefects, and several distinguished jurists. Besides serving as the chief policy-making body of the Empire, it also acted as a supreme court whose function was to hear cases involving senators and highranking officials and to advise and assist the Emperor in the creation and interpretation of civil and criminal law.

Legal Reforms   Of all the reforms of Hadrian, the greatest and most enduring were in the field of law. One such reform gave the unanimous opinions (*responsa*) of distinguished jurists the force of law binding upon judges trying similar cases. Only when the opinions conflicted could judges reach their own decisions. These responses later entered into the literature of Roman law and became enshrined at last into the *Digest* and *Code* of Justinian I (527–565).

More important still was the editing and codification of the *Praetorian Perpetual Edict*. Ever since early Republican times, each incoming Urban Praetor had drawn up and posted edicts setting forth the laws and court procedure that he intended to follow during his year of office. The Praetor for Aliens (*Praetor Peregrinus*) as well as the provincial governors had followed suit. Since the praetors normally retained the laws and procedure of their predecessors while adding new ones as need arose, the edicts tended to perpetuate many obsolete rules, contradictions, and obscurities, all of which seemed intolerable to Hadrian's logical and legalistic mind. He therefore commissioned Salvius Julianus to draw up a permanent edict (*edictum perpetuum*) binding upon all present and future praetors without alteration or addition unless authorized by the Emperor or by decree of the senate.

The statutes of the emperors (*constitutiones principum*) thereafter became increasingly important as sources of law. They consisted of Imperial edicts (*edicta*) issued by virtue of his *imperium*; his judicial decrees (*decreta*) or decisions; his rescripts (*rescripta*) or responses to written inquiries on specific points of law; and his mandates (*mandata*) or administrative directives issued to officials subject to his orders.

To ease the crowded calendar of the praetors' courts in Rome and expedite the administration of justice in Italy, Hadrian divided the peninsula into four judicial districts each presided over by a circuit judge of consular rank (*juridicus consularis*) to try cases of inheritance, trust, and guardianship, and probably to hear appeals from the municipal courts. Though the innovation was both salutary and necessary and not intended simply to reduce Italy to the status of a province, it evidently displeased the senate, at whose insistence Hadrian's successor, Antoninus Pius, unwisely abolished it., Marcus Aurelius had to revive it later.

Social Reforms   As the supreme source of law and justice, Hadrian exerted his authority for the protection of the weak and helpless in accordance with Stoic philosophical principles and the ideas of Seneca and the Cynics, in whose eyes even a slave was a person. Hadrian made it illegal for a master to kill, torture, or castrate slaves, or sell them as gladiators, or for any lewd or immoral purposes. He also deprived the *pater familias* of the power of life and death over his children and safeguarded the right of minors to inherit and own property.

In the field of social welfare and education, Hadrian continued Nerva's and Trajan's policy of using state funds for the maintenance and education of children of poor families in Italy and appointed a superintendent of child welfare (*praefectus alimentorum*) to administer the distribution of such funds. He also provided funds for secondary school education in many municipalities of the Empire and for pensions for retired teachers. Continuing Vespasian's policy, he endowed rhetorical, philosophical, technical, and medical schools in both Rome and the provinces.

The Last Years of Hadrian   After the Jewish War Hadrian returned to Rome (135) never to leave Italy again. He spent his last years at his beautiful villa at Tibur (Tivoli) eighteen miles up the Anio from Rome but could not enjoy himself. The man who had traveled so much and seen and done so much had lost all zest for life. Loneliness and despair had come over his mind; a wasting disease racked his body.

As his illness grew worse and death seemed at hand, he turned his attention to the problem of choosing a successor. His first choice was his friend, Lucius Ceionius Commodus Verus, and he spent large sums of money to win the support of the soldiers and the people for the adoption. The money was wasted, for Lucius Verus died early in 138. Hadrian next adopted a rich and virtuous senator, Titus Aurelius Antoninus, whom he required to adopt in turn as his sons, Marcus Annius Verus, a youth of seventeen (who later became the Emperor Marcus Aurelius) and a seven-year-old boy, Lucius Aelius Verus, the son of the late Lucius Verus. After doing that, Hadrian felt that he had followed the example of Augustus in securing the succession not just for one, but for two generations to come. His last and only wish was to die in peace.

Death came, but not soon enough for him. Maddened by pain, he longed to take his life. He begged his doctor to give him a dose of poison; the doctor took one himself. He ordered a slave to stab him in the heart; the slave ran away. Finally at Baiae near Naples on July 10th, 138, nature granted his wish. His adopted son and heir, Antoninus, had his body placed in the Mausoleum and, against the opposition of the senate, secured his deification. Another god had now entered the Roman Heaven, and Antoninus won for himself the new name of Pius.

Antoninus Pius (138—161) Despite its length (23 years), the reign of Antoninus Pius was singularly uneventful. The Empire was at peace; no major foreign wars or internal revolts disturbed the outward calm. The Emperor himself was a man of peace and the possessor of almost every known Roman virtue. According to the *Historia Augusta*, he was tall and handsome, dignified and cour-

teous, eminently talented, eloquent, scholarly, and industrious, just, honest, deeply religious, tolerant of others, a cool appraiser of himself, and withal most benevolent and serene. He had few enemies and many friends.

The life of Antoninus had always been simple, but never unpleasant; disciplined, but never strenuous; never dangerous or insecure. He was born and raised at Lanuvium, a famous old Latin town, but his family came from Nemausus (Nîmes) in southern Gaul, a rich aristocratic old family that owned numerous estates in Italy and valuable brick yards near Rome. Of all his estates the one at Lorium about ten miles west of Rome on the border of Etruria pleased him most. He spent a great deal of time there in personally managing the property. He fed his chickens, entertained his friends, hunted and fished. Rome and its palaces and Hadrian's villa held little attraction for him.

His Early Career Having held all the offices of a normal senatorial career, Antoninus intended after his second consulship in 120 to retire to his country estates and enjoy himself. Instead, Hadrian made him a district judge of Italy and, in 135/36, proconsul of Asia, where he distinguished himself as an administrator. His expert knowledge of law and his skill in administration led to further appointments, none of which were solicited by him. Hadrian made him a member of the Imperial Council and, finally his successor and colleague.

Antoninus and the Senate Antoninus' first act as Emperor was to frustrate the attempt of a number of senators to damn the memory and annul the edicts and acts (*acta*) of Hadrian, whose nonexpansionistic, philhellenic, and cosmopolitan policies they had always disliked. Pointing out that the annulment of Hadrian's acts would have meant a repudiation of his own adoption and succession to the throne, Antoninus prevailed upon the senate to decree divine honors for his predecessor. In return, he agreed to abolish the four hated judgeships of Italy and to spare the lives of senators proscribed by the dying Hadrian. Thus his relations with the senate began most harmoniously. Antoninus further improved his relations with the senate by his deferential attitude, by his attendance at meetings, by seeking its advice on policy, and by rendering financial assistance to needy senatorial families.

Public Works   Antoninus allotted to Italy a generous share of the money earmarked for public works and social welfare: harbor improvements ordered at Puteoli, Ostia, Caieta, and Terracina, baths constructed at Ostia, and an amphitheater at Capua; further endowments provided for education and child welfare and liberal distributions of food and money to the Roman populace. Last, but not least, he sponsored elaborate games and spectacles.

Nor did he entirely neglect the provinces. Under his reign of peace the upper and middle classes prospered although the masses of exploited peasants everywhere and particularly the *fellahin* of Egypt continued to be under the heel of poverty. Antoninus gave ready ear to the desires and petitions of the ruling classes of the cities of Greece and Asia Minor and some Aegean islands. He frequently reduced their taxes or canceled their debts and came to their aid when they were stricken by earthquake, fire, or flood. Furthermore, he spared them the heavy burden of the Imperial retinue by staying at home. He was content to let his power and beneficence radiate from Rome or Lorium like the peaceful glow of a late summer's afternoon.

Financial Administration   Despite his huge expenditures on charity and public works in Rome, Italy, and the provinces, Antoninus had before his death succeeded, through sound financial administration and personal frugality, in leaving behind in the treasury a surplus of 2 billion sesterces, the largest surplus since the death of Tiberius.

Legal Developments   An even prouder achievement was his contribution to Roman law. Never had a Roman emperor surrounded himself with such an array of legal talent, five jurists being members of the Imperial Council. Antoninus himself had an intimate knowledge of both the minutiae and the spirit of the law. He clarified the laws dealing with inheritance, the protection of the legal interests of minors, and the manumission of slaves. He increased penalties against masters who killed or mistreated their slaves, and imposed a severe punishment on kidnapping, hitherto a frightful scourge in Italy and the provinces. Conversely, he reduced penalties for army deserters and released captives after ten years of hard labor in the mines; he permitted Jews the right of circumcision and restricted the persecution of Christians. Of more general interest was his ruling that a man must be considered innocent until proved guilty and in cases where the opinions of the judges were evenly divided, the prisoner must receive the benefit of the doubt.

Foreign Policy   Antoninus, the living symbol of the might and majesty of the Roman state, possessed a prestige and authority far transcending the Imperial frontiers. Embassies came to him from Bactria and India. His name was heard in central Asia and China. Eastern kings sought his advice and a letter to the king of Parthia dissuaded an invasion of Armenia. He awarded thrones to some, enlarged the territories of others. Even the Quadi of Bohemia accepted a king whom he nominated for them.

Despite that, the power of Rome was waning. Its shaky foundations rested solely on Trajan's military exploits and on Hadrian's indefatigable efforts to make the Roman army an efficient, hard-hitting force. Antoninus, in his efforts to save money, allowed this force to grow soft and deteriorate, while the nations beyond the frontiers—Germans, Huns, Iranians, and Arabs—were gradually acquiring military capability by copying Roman arms and tactics. The superior equipment and training that had once made one Roman legionary a match for several Germans or Parthians was now no longer a Roman monopoly. Even such a minor uprising as that of the Moroccan tribesmen was not suppressed without considerable difficulty. Similar revolts were occurring from time to time in Britain, Germany, Dacia, Southern Russia, Asia Minor, Egypt, and Palestine.

In the only two frontier zones—Britain and Germany—where Antoninus did exhibit energy or initiative, he was simply following a policy of Hadrian's. In Scotland he pushed the frontier about 75 miles to the north and had a wall of turf and clay constructed between the firths of Forth and Clyde, a distance of some 37 miles, which was about half the length of Hadrian's Wall between the Solway and the Tyne. The purpose of the Antonine Wall, with its nineteen forts spaced two miles apart, was to overawe the natives living north and south of it and check cattle rustling or smuggling. In southwest Germany he shortened the defense line (*limes*) by pushing it forward from 20 to 30 miles, and strengthened it with new forts and watchtowers made of stone.

The Death of Antoninus The defenses that Antoninus erected in Britain and Germany stood firm to the end of his reign, but not long after. The policy of static defense and of isolationism and the failure to keep the army in top form had left the Empire poorly equipped to roll back the tide of massive assault which broke after his death. Perhaps he dimly realized his mistake as he lay dying at Lorium in March, 161. In his delirium he talked fretfully about the Empire and all the lying kings who had betrayed him.

Marcus Aurelius (161–180) After Antoninus came Marcus Aurelius, one of the most remarkable and certainly noblest of Roman emperors. He was a Stoic philosopher and a man dedicated to peace. It is one of the ironies of history that so peace-loving a man had to spend the greater part of his reign in fighting the Empire's battles against German and Parthian onslaughts upon its frontiers.

Marcus Aurelius was born in Rome in 121 of rich and illustrious Spanish parentage. He enjoyed all the educational advantages money, rank, and high favor could bestow. He was only six when Hadrian insisted that he be adopted by Lucius Commodus Verus. Later he was to be adopted by Antoninus Pius, upon whose demise he was to become Emperor of Rome.

Educational and Cultural Background Marcus had never gone to public school. He was taught by private tutors from the three R's to grammar, literature (Greek as well as Latin), science and mathematics, music, dancing, and painting. The sports that he learned included ballplaying, of which he was very fond, boxing, wrestling, hunting, and fishing.

The next stage in the education of Marcus was the study of rhetoric and Roman law, the former taught by Cornelius Fronto (ca. 100–ca.166), a famous rhetorician and advocate from Africa, the latter by the illustrious legal authority, L. Volusius Maecianus. Herodes Atticus (ca. 101–177), a Greek sophist and rhetorician of incredible wealth, came from Athens to teach him Greek oratory. Those were the most distinguished of his teachers, of whom he had altogether almost a score. But the greatest and the most beloved of all was the rhetorician, Fronto, with whom he corresponded for many years.

Philosophical Training Quite in keeping with his study of rhetoric, which, according to Fronto's ideals, should produce a person not only learned in literature and effective in speech but also of high moral character, Marcus Aurelius was greatly attracted to the philosophy of Stoicism. He studied under Junius Rusticus, who lent him a copy of the *Discourses* of Epictetus (ca. A.D. 55–135), a Phrygian slave, lame, of feeble health, and horribly treated by a freedman in Nero's court. Later freed, Epictetus taught philosophy in Rome until exiled in 90 by Domitian because of his upcompromising Stoic resistance to tyranny.

The most sublime expression of Stoicism, except possibly for the *Hymn to Zeus* by Cleanthes (ca. 310–232 B.C.), is contained in the *Meditations* of Marcus Aurelius. While encamped along the Danube during the Second Marcomannic War (169 to 175), Marcus spent his nights writing down in Greek his reflections—scattered, disjointed, and unaffected soliloquies or dialogues between himself and the Universal Power. In the *Meditations* (*Ta eis heauton*—"To Himself"), he strongly reaffirmed the traditional Stoic virtues as the basis of morality, from which the spirit is propelled into both direct communion with the divine and unapprehensive resignation to its will.

Persecution of the Christians   Like most pious pagan Romans of his time, however, Marcus Aurelius regarded the Christians as not only a depraved and superstitious sect but an illicit and subversive organization dedicated to the overthrow of the Roman way of life. The willful and obstinate refusal of the Christians to obey a magistrate's order to sacrifice to the gods of the state was regarded as opposition to the efforts of the emperors to restore the ancient Roman culture and religion as a means of strengthening the Empire against the barbarians from without and disintegration from within. The common people accused the Christians of atheism, incest, and even cannibalism and made them the scapegoats for the calamities that were falling on the state. When angry mobs, as at Lugdunum (Lyons) and Smyrna (Izmir), demanded vengeance, the officials were often sympathetic. For example, Justin Martyr (who adapted Platonic and Stoic philosophy to Jewish and Christian theology) died in Rome along with six companions; other Christians died at Scyllium in Numidia; and at Lugdunum and Vienna (Vienne) in the Transalpina numerous Christians were tortured to death at the demands of angry, bloodthirsty mobs.

Marcus Aurelius as Emperor and Soldier   Marcus Aurelius was an able administrator and commander of armies. The first two years of his reign were filled with crises: a serious Tiber flood, an earthquake in Cyzicus, a famine in Galatia, a revolt in Britain, a German crossing of the Rhine, and an invasion of Armenia and Syria by the young Parthian king, Vologeses III. Marcus' first act as Emperor was to insist on appointing Lucius Verus as his colleague, equal in honor, titulature, and power, even against the opposition of the senate, who regarded Verus as a frivolous young man addicted to pleasure and self indulgence. Verus then went to the East to deal with the Parthian threat, while Aurelius handled pressing problems in the West. This division of responsibility between two equal colleagues at the start of a reign, not merely to indicate a successor near the end of a reign, would become an increasingly attractive solution to bearing the increasing burdens of Imperial defense and administration. Eventually this practice would become formalized, and the Empire would split in two.

The Parthian War, 161 to 165   In the East, Verus cleverly combined pleasure with a thorough reorganization of the undisciplined and demoralized army of Syria and Cappadocia. He had as his subordinates two able generals. One was Statius Priscus, who invaded Armenia, captured and burnt down its capital of Artaxata; the other was the Syrian-born Avidius Cassius, a hard-bitten martinet, who whipped the Syrian army into shape, crossed the Euphrates, and invaded Mesopotamia to capture in rapid succession Edessa, Nisibis, Ctesiphon, and Seleucia, which he burnt to the ground. Both emperors jointly shared the triumph, though Aurelius, the actual author of the winning strategy, was unwilling to deprive Verus of the glory of victory.

Then suddenly two disasters struck. Soldiers returning from the fire-gutted ruins of Seleucia brought back with them a frightful plague. It forced the retreat of the victorious armies of the East, then infected Asia Minor, Egypt, Greece, and Italy, destroyed as much as a third of the population in some places, and finally decimated the armies guarding the frontiers along the Rhine and Danube.

The defenses along the Danube had already been weakened by extensive troop withdrawals for service in the East; there now burst through them a host of Germans —the Marcomanni, the Quadi, and many others, reacting at last to the slow but relentless pressure which had for centuries been building up from the vast heartland of Eurasia. Pouring through the sparsely guarded frontiers, they overran the Danubian provinces of Rhaetia, Noricum, and Pannonia, pressed down through the Julian Alps into northern Italy, and besieged Aquileia, the big seaport at the head of the Adriatic. Never since the Cimbrian and Teutonic invasions in the days of Marius was Italy in greater danger.

War on the Danube Front, 167 to 175 Ignoring an outbreak of famine in Rome, Marcus Aurelius took energetic measures. He announced to the senate that he and Verus must at once take off for the northern front. The treasury having been depleted by the expenses of the Parthian War, Marcus raised money by selling the gold vessels and art treasures of the Imperial palaces to avoid increasing taxes; drafted slaves, gladiators, and brigands into the army; hired German and Scythian tribes to harass the enemy rear; and blocked the Alpine passes and fortified towns in the danger zone. Then he hurried north to relieve Aquileia and reoccupy Noricum and Pannonia. At his approach the enemy retreated and asked for a truce. It was granted—reluctantly—only because a fresh outbreak of the plague had wrought havoc in the Roman army and almost destroyed the

garrison at Aquileia. In 169, their mission accomplished, both emperors set out for Rome. On the way, Lucius Verus, stricken with apoplexy, suddenly died.

Marcus Aurelius, now sole *princeps,* had to contend with a host of troubles: the main enemy—the Quadi, Marcomanni, and Iazyges—remained unsubdued and menacing; the Parthian king again invaded Armenia; in 169 the Chatti invaded the frontier regions of the upper Rhine, while the Chauci attacked the Belgic province; the rebellious tribesmen of Morocco harassed the shores of Africa and Spain, crossed the straits, and invaded Baetica; the herdsmen of the Nile delta rose in revolt and were subdued only by the timely intervention of Avidius Cassius; and worst of all, in 170 the Costoboci of eastern Galicia joined forces with the Sarmatians, crossed the lower Danube, broke into Moesia, overran the Balkans, and invaded Greece as far south as Attica, where they plundered the Temple of the Mysteries at Eleusis before being driven back.

In the fall of 169 Marcus Aurelius again returned to the Danubian front. He was determined to destroy the main enemy—the Marcomanni, Qaudi, and Iazyges—one by one, finally annex their lands, and bring to pass the grand strategy of Julius Caesar, which Augustus and Tiberius had abandoned. In 172 he crossed the Danube, attacked the Quadi first, then the Marcomanni, and finally the Iazyges. He forced each in turn to return all the Roman prisoners they had taken, make reparations for the damages that they had inflicted on the provinces, and evacuate a strip of territory ten miles wide running along the north bank of the Danube.

A sculptured record of this long Marcomannic War survives on the spiral frieze of Marcus Aurelius' column in the Campus Martius. Some of the 116 reliefs show Roman soldiers transporting baggage and war material, convoying booty and captives, crossing turbulent rivers, or storming German and Sarmatian strongholds. Others depict the Emperor himself, calm and self-assured, riding with his troops, consulting with his aides, receiving foreign envoys, or accepting the obsequious attentions of conquered foes.

With the subjugation of the Iazyges, the Sarmatians, and the Costoboci not yet complete, Marcus Aurelius had again to turn against the Quadi, who had already violated their treaty obligations. While thus engaged, he received disturbing news from the East.

The Usurpation of Avidius Cassius, 175   In the East Avidius Cassius, the able governor of his native Syria, but a violent and ruthless man, misled by the false rumor of the death of Marcus Aurelius, had himself proclaimed Emperor. Marcus hastily concluded peace with the still unsubdued Quadi and Iazyges, summoned his wife Faustina and young son Commodus to Sirmium (Mitrovica, Yugoslavia), and prepared to set out with them to the East. Before his departure, a legionary showed up bearing the head of Cassius, which the Emperor refused to look at but ordered reverently buried.

The death of Cassius would seem to have removed the need for Marcus to go to the East, but he went anyway, desiring perhaps to make a display of Roman power, receive expressions of loyalty, and remove disloyal officials from their posts. On his way through Asia Minor he suffered the loss of his wife, Faustina, Antoninus' daughter, a woman whom he had loved for thirty years and the mother of his thirteen children.

After traversing Asia Minor, Syria, and Egypt, greeted everywhere by acclamations of loyalty, he arrived in Rome in 176, a sad and lonely man, bereft of his wife and one of his best generals; he resolved never again to make a man governor of the province of his birth, and he at once recognized as heir and successor his son Commodus, a remarkably handsome and athletic youth but totally unlike his father in character and ideals.

In Rome, Marcus Aurelius celebrated his German and Sarmatian triumphs. In the course of the celebration he unveiled the famous equestrian statue of himself that still stands on the Roman Capitol, the prototype of most later equestrian statues, and laid the foundation stone of his column in the Campus Martius.

Return to the Danube, 178 to 180   Rumors of fresh troubles along the Danube caused the Emperor to hasten north in 178 (followed later by his son Commodus). Leading his men himself, he crossed the Danube and, after a long and strenuous campaign known as the Third Marcomannic War, crushed the resistance of the Quadi and Marcomanni. He established a new legionary camp on the Danube at Castra Regina (Regensburg in Bavaria), and proceeded to create two new provinces—Marcomannia and Sarmatia—by annexing that vast territory extending as far north as the Erzgebirge Mountains (on the border between Czechoslovakia and East Germany) as far east as the Carpathain Mountains (eastern Rumania), in order to shorten and strengthen the northern frontiers against future barbarian assaults. While engaged in this mighty task, Marcus Aurelius suddenly caught a dangerous infection (possibly the plague) and died in his camp at Vindobona (Vienna) on March 17, 180. His last words were "Go to the rising sun; my sun is setting."

The most permanent result of the Danubian campaigns consisted not in the victories of Marcus Aurelius over the Germans and Sarmatians, but in the transplantation and settlement of thousands of Germans in the war-torn and plague-devastated provinces of Dacia, Moesia, Rhaetia, Pannonia, Dalmatia, Gaul, and even Italy. This measure not only temporarily relieved the pressure on the frontiers of the Rhine and of the Danube but finally altered the entire ethnic composition of the Roman Empire.

The Problem of Succession   Those who have admired Marcus Aurelius' many fine qualities have often criticized him for designating his own unworthy son, Commodus, as his successor and abandoning the practice of adoption that had produced a series of remarkably able, dedicated, and benevolent rulers from Trajan to Aurelius himself. Such critics forget that the practice of adoption was not any kind of theoretical alternative to dynastic succession. It was not a system based upon the Stoic principle of choosing the most worthy individual regardless of birth. The practice of adoption was a reaffirmation of the dynastic principle. Roman aristocrats had always resorted to adoption to maintain their families' existence in the absence of a natural heir. Nerva and his successors until Marcus Aurelius had happened for various reasons to lack sons to succeed them. The dynastic principle was so strongly favored by the soldiers and common people, moreover, that Aurelius' four predecessors had felt it necessary to create sons where none existed. When it turned out that Aurelius had natural heirs, he had no other choice than to proclaim his eldest son as his successor. Had he not, thousands would have supported Commodus as having a superior claim to the throne, and a disastrous civil war probably would have resulted.

Problems and Trends   The second century A.D. has often been portrayed as the golden age of the Roman Empire. So it was. As with all golden ages, however, it was more plated than pure. Lurking beneath the surface there were problems and trends that had negative implications for the future. They would have to be faced during an extended crisis in the third century and beyond.

Defense   Trajan's inability to hold onto his conquests in Mesopotamia and Hadrian's decision to adopt a posture of static defense indicate that the Empire had reached the limits of its power and that its resources were becoming stretched too thin for the defensive burdens that it had to bear. That point is driven home by the great difficulty that Marcus Aurelius had in trying to defend the borders simultaneously in the East and the West. The accident of plague certainly complicated his task, but the extreme measures that he had to take to

mount his last expedition against the Germanic tribes indicate that the Empire had very little margin of safety when confronted with a major challenge on its frontiers.

Economic Weakness   Augustus had freed the Empire to realize its economic potential, and that had produced real growth in the first century, but disturbing trends appeared in the second (see pp. 394–397). The need for the *alimenta* in Italy and the bankruptcy of many Eastern cities indicate a decline of economic vigor. Trajan's conquest of Dacia and its gold mines gave the economy a welcome lift, but that only underscored the basic underlying economic weakness that would make the defense of the Empire much more difficult in the face of increased pressure on the frontiers during the third century.

Centralization of Political Power   The centralization of power in the hands of the Emperor and his bureaucratic servants accelerated as the problems of governance and defense became more complex. The very benevolence of the emperors naturally increased their power at the expense of the senate and magistrates at Rome and of the local councils (*curiae*) and officials of the provincial municipalities. The appointment of Imperial overseers to straighten out the finances of numerous provincial cities further undercut the local *curiae*. The codification of the Praetor's edict under Hadrian and the increased use of edicts, decrees, and rescripts by Trajan and his successors in an attempt to deal equitably with problems from an empirewide perspective made everyone look more and more to the Emperor as the only source of Imperial law. Even though Marcus Aurelius constantly presented laws to the senate for its action, he made his proposals so effectively and so well worked out that the senators adopted them unchanged "in accordance with the Emperor's speech," *ex oratione principis*.

The concentration of power in the hands of the Emperor undermined local initiative and tended to make everyone look to the Emperor to solve all problems. In the third century this situation rigidified the Imperial system and made it less responsive in times of crisis. Local regions came to feel remote from the central government and were willing to put regional interests above Imperial interests, which undermined the unity of the Empire.

Increasing Militarization Despite their success as civilian administrators, it was chiefly as military men on the frontiers that Trajan, Hadrian, and Marcus Aurelius made their marks. The civilian side of life was becoming subordinate to the military. The civilian senate became more and more just another municipal council, more prestigious than the others to be sure, but in reality not more powerful. After the reign of Aurelius' son, in the third and subsequent centuries, the Roman senate had little impact on affairs outside of Rome and Italy. It still formally ratified the accession of a new emperor, but the real choice increasingly lay in the hands of the provincial armies vital for the defense of a frequently besieged Empire. He who could control the soldiers could control the state; he who could not control them soon perished as the Empire of the third and fourth centuries was transformed into an absolute, regimented military monarchy.

Roman Culture and Society in the First Two Centuries A.D.

Literature The authors of the Golden Age inaugurated by Augustus had raised Latin literature to a level equal in quality, if not in quantity, to that of the Greeks. Latin literature had now Romanized all the genres of Greek. Succeeding generations of Latin writers would now look to Roman authors for their inspiration and models of excellence. Proud of their native heritage, writers of the Golden Age like Livy, Vergil, Horace, Propertius, Tibullus, and even Ovid had enshrined the values and ideals summed up in the word *Romanitas*. The works and ideals of these authors were to the educated classes of the Western provinces what Greek literature had been to earlier generations of educated Romans and Italians—the examples to emulate. Thus they absorbed the patriotic pride in the glories of Rome's past and espoused the ideals believed to have accounted for that greatness. Therefore, *Romanitas* became indelibly etched on the high culture of the Western provinces.

The Latin language and its literature was also the Western provincials' passport to the wider world of Rome itself and Imperial service, just as Greek had been the passport of earlier Romans to the wider world of Greek culture and the kingdoms of the Hellenistic East. As a result, many of the leading figures in the world of Latin letters in the first two centuries A.D. no longer came from the old Roman aristocracy or aspiring young men from the municipalities of Italy, but from the colonies and municipalities of Gaul, Spain, and North Africa. Such men were a constant source of fresh talent who gave Latin letters greater breadth and popularity than they had ever known.

Unfortunately, however, much of higher education in Italy and the West was based on training in rhetoric, which, under the Republic, had been an essential tool for success in public careers. Yet, under the emperors the scope of practical oratory was extremely restricted. Tiberius had effectively abandoned popular election to the magistracies, and the senate increasingly acted as a legislative body, so that no one had to sway public opinion in electoral campaigns and gatherings on public issues (*contiones*). Moreover, fear of or deference to the Emperor severely reduced debate in the senate itself. Debate became lifeless and perfunctory, with little chance to display one's power of argumentation and persuasion. Occasionally someone might rise to a moment of truly eloquent pleading when prosecuting or defending an important figure on trial in the senate for high crimes, but ordinary cases in the lower courts staffed by Imperial appointees were decided on technical points of law, not a vote of jurors in adversary proceedings, for which skilled oratory was essential.

Nevertheless, people were still being trained as if it were essential. Therefore, the persuasive or argumentative declamations, *suasoriae* and *controversiae,* of the rhetorical schools became increasingly artificial exercises on themes such as "Should Hannibal Have Attacked Rome?"—themes that were completely divorced from real life. As a result, rhetorical style concentrated increasingly on elaborate and exotic technique for its own sake. Style, not substance, became the goal. This constant striving for effect produced a turgid, twisted, and distorted kind of writing meant only to display one's verbal virtuosity in competition with others similarly trained.

Latin literature was not without political importance, however. Quite the opposite. *Romanitas* reflected an idealized Republican past that was basically incompatible with the autocracy that even the most restrained *princeps* found hard to mask. In the first flush of peace and "normalcy" under Augustus, this fact had been easily ignored, but as the Imperial monarchy became a permanent fixture under the Julio-Claudians, the contradictions between ideals and reality were difficult to overlook. Also, this contradiction was underlined because the educational system was designed to prepare members of the upper classes for careers as Republican statesmen, not Imperial functionaries. Many of the Latin authors of the first two centuries, therefore, look back in nostalgia or protest to the lost liberty of the Republic and take refuge in the teachings of Stoicism symbolized by the great martyr to Republican *libertas,* Cato the Younger.

Poverty of Literature under Tiberius and Caligula   The literary brilliance of the Augustan Age had already begun to fade before the end of Augustus' reign, as the confining nature of the *principate* began to be felt. No comparable writers took the places of Vergil, Horace, Propertius, Tibullus, Ovid, and Livy under the stern and intrigue-ridden reign of Tiberius or the capricious, megalomaniacal rule of Caligula. There were only three historians of note under these emperors: Aulus Cremutius Cordus (d. A.D. 25), Seneca the Elder (ca. 55 B.C.–ca. A.D. 40), and Velleius Paterculus (ca. 19 B.C.–ca. A.D. 32). Velleius, an equestrian military officer, wrote a brief history of Rome in a rhetorical style. Its importance is that it reflects the attitudes of his class and is favorable toward Tiberius, with whom he had served. Cremutius Cordus, on the other hand, wrote a history of Rome's civil wars to at least 18 B.C. and reflected the Stoic-inspired traditional aristocrats who resented the Emperor's monopoly of power and *dignitas.* Sejanus had him tried for treason, his books were burned, and he committed suicide. Seneca the Elder, Lucius (or Marcus) Annaeus Seneca (ca. 55 B.C.–ca. A.D. 40), fared better, although his history of the same period is also lost. That is unfortunate because he came from Corduba in Spain and was one of the Western provincials who were becoming prominent in early Imperial Rome. What has survived of his writings is a collection of rhetorical exercises (*controversiae* and *sausoriae*) culled from public declamations.

The only poet worthy of mention at this time was Gaius Julius Phaedrus (ca. 15 B.C.–ca. A.D. 50). He wrote poetic fables in the manner of Aesop. They were very popular in Renaissance Europe and were used as interesting yet morally edifying stories in nineteenth-century school texts. They were often thinly disguised criticisms of his own times, and Sejanus unsuccessfully tried to silence him.

The Inauguration of the Silver Age under Claudius and Nero   The death of the tyrannical Caligula and the accession of Claudius mark the beginning of renewed literary vigor at Rome. It surpassed the early years of Augustus in quantity and, with one major break, in length of sustained activity. Since its quality is generally agreed not to equal that of the Augustans, however, it is called the Silver Age. Claudius himself, of course, was a writer and historian of no small skill (see p. 328). Ironically, under the influence of Messalina early in his reign he banished Seneca the Elder's son, Lucius Annaeus Seneca (the Younger), an accomplished orator and devotee of Stoicism. This act must have cast a pall over free expression at Rome, but at the prompting of Agrippina, Claudius recalled Seneca the Younger in 49 to tutor her young son, Nero, who had artistic ambitions. From this point until Seneca's fall from power under Nero and Nero's increasing jealousy and fear, there was a great outburst of literary activity, especially among writers from Spain, many of whom were connected with Seneca's family.

Seneca the Younger (ca. 4 B.C.–A.D. 65)

L. Annaeus Seneca, the most noted literary figure of the mid-first century A.D., was born at Corduba, Spain, and came to Rome while still a boy. There he studied rhetoric and philosophy and became a lawyer. He was not only an astute politician, but he also made a fortune from banking and viticulture. Furthermore, he was one of Rome's most notable Stoic philosophers and a copious author of varied works: a spiteful burlesque on Claudius (*Apocolocyntosis*); a long treatise on natural science (*Quaestiones Naturales*); nine tragedies, typically Euripidean in plot and theme, in a highly rhetorical style striving for emotional effect more than real understanding; ten essays (misnamed *Dialogi*), containing a full exposition of Stoic philosophy, such as *De Ira* (*On Anger*), *De Vita Beata* (*On the Happy Life*), and *De Otio* (*On Leisure*); prose treatises (*De Clementia* and *De Beneficiis*); and 124 *Moral Epistles* (*Epistulae Morales*), brilliant exponents of a Stoic philosophy at once spirtual and humane.

In 65, Nero suspected Seneca of involvement with Piso in a Stoic plot against him. He ordered Seneca to commit suicide. Seneca's wife bravely insisted on dying with him. He opened his veins, which bled slowly and painfully and died with Stoic fortitude while discoursing on philosophy.

Lucan (A.D. 39–65)

M. Annaeus Lucan was Seneca's nephew. He, too, was born in Corduba, Spain, brought to Rome in infancy, and educated in a rhetorical school. His sole extant work is the *De Bello Civili* (often called *Pharsalia*), a violent and pessimistic epic poem in ten books, which narrates the war between Caesar and Pompey. It displays a strong Republican bias and a deep hostility toward Caesar. The work was never completely finished and suffers from the author's lack of maturity. Despite its irrelevant digressions, tiresome repetitions, and rhetorical exaggerations, however, it is a remarkable poem because of its forcefulness and sincerity. Also suspected of complicity in Piso's conspiracy, Lucan too committed suicide in 65.

Petronius (A.D. 66)

Nero continued his persecution of Stoic critics in 66 by condemning to death P. Clodius Paetus Thrasea. Others suspected of involvement with him were ordered to commit suicide. One of them was the novelist and satirist Titus (or Gaius) Petronius, whom Tacitus mentions as the "arbiter of social graces" (*elegantiae arbiter*) at Nero's dissolute court. His *Satyricon* is frequently described as a picaresque novel, probably in sixteen books, of which are extant only fragments of the last two.

While the *Satyricon* provides elegant wit and piquant entertainment, it also is a serious criticism of the times. Petronius portrays a world in which the old Roman values are stood on their heads. Gross materialism and sensuality are the order of the day, bad rhetoric runs riot, and everyone pretends to be what he is not. Beneath the laughter is the feeling that society has run amok.

Persius (A.D. 34–62) and Martial (ca. A.D. 40–104)

Aulus Persius Flaccus and Marcus Valerius Martialis were both satirists who escaped Nero's purges. Persius may simply have died too soon, for he was connected with the Stoic Paetus Thrasea, Seneca the Younger, and Lucan. His six surviving hexameter poems, the *Satires*, try to compress his thoughts into the fewest possible words and rely heavily on poetic allusions to express complex ideas succinctly. They are also rather academic attacks on stereotypic human failings more than attacks on the vices of anyone in particular. On the other hand, Martial, a Spaniard from Bilbilis, in the twelve books of his *Epigrams* attacks with shrewd insight the shams and vices of real people in all walks of life.

Technical Writers Another Spaniard, Columella (ca. A.D. 10–70) wrote the classic Roman handbook on farming, *De Re Rustica.* Pliny the Elder, Gaius Plinius Secundus, (c.a. A.D. 23–79) also discussed farming in his *Natural History (Historia Naturalis)*, thirty-seven books of unscientifically compiled information and misinformation on geography, anthropology, zoology, botany, and mineralogy. These two works reflect the growing popularity of handbooks and technical works during the Empire.

A new type that appeared was the learned commentary on an earlier author. The first important one was a commentary on Cicero's orations by Quintus Asconius Pedianus (9 B.C.–A.D. 76), which remains a valuable source of information for students of Cicero's time.

History Significantly, the only important historical work from Caligula to the Flavians was the *History of Alexander* by Quintus Curtius Rufus (ca. A.D. 20–80). It was more of a historical romance than serious history. Highly rhetorical, its real significance is that it furthered the romanticized tales that quickly obscured the real facts of Alexander's career after his death and were the foundation of the popular legends surrounding Alexander in the Middle Ages.

Literature under the Flavians, A.D. 69 to 96

Nero's purge wiped out a whole generation of Roman writers just as it was reaching its prime, and the political situation under the Flavians was not conducive to the emergence of a new one. Although Martial did

write most of his satires under the Flavians, he eventually left Rome and returned to Spain. Vespasian, Titus, and Domitian were not hostile to learning and literature. Far from it. Vespasian and Domitian generously endowed chairs of Greek and Latin rhetoric, and Domitian restored Rome's libraries after the disastrous fire of 79. They did not, however, encourage freedom of expression, without which great literature cannot survive. Vespasian set the tone when he banished the Stoic and Cynic philosophers from Rome and executed Helvidius Priscus.

In fairness to Vespasian, they had tried his patience sorely with carping criticism and even futile conspiracies against an emperor who understood political reality far better than they. Nevertheless, Vespasian's suppression of philosophers was bound to make any writer cautious. The situation was even worse after the rebellion of Saturninus against Domitian in 88. He banished philosophers from Rome twice, in 89 and 95, and ruthlessly employed informers to muzzle his critics. The only surviving writers who published under the Flavians were "safe" men writing on safe subjects, especially antiquarian epics of no great inspiration or political import.

Poetry Only three poets have survived. Silius Italicus (ca. A.D. 26–101) had been one of Nero's prominent informers and governor of Asia under Vespasian. He retired under Domitian to lead the life of a cultured dilettante. He wrote a technically competent but uninspired epic, the *Punica*, in seventeen books on the Punic Wars. Valerius Flaccus (ca. A.D. 70–90) had a similar career and wrote a refined but unoriginal epic, the *Argonautica,* a rehash of Jason's expedition to find the Golden Fleece. Publius Papinius Statius (ca. A.D. 45–96) is the most talented of the three. He was a professional writer patronized by Domitian. He wrote a libretto for Domitian's favorite actor and an epic on Domitian's German wars. Significantly, both are lost. Two other epics, the *Thebaid,* on the quarrel between Oedipus' sons, and the unfinished *Achil-*

leid, on Achilles, are extant. Modelled on Vergil, they have many individual passages of power and beauty but lack overall structure. Statius' best work is the *Silvae,* thirty-two individual poems, many written to friends. They reveal the warmth and genuine feelings of an affectionate and sympathetic man capable of real poetic charm.

Josephus (b. A.D. 37 or 38)   The only important historian who published under the Flavians was their Jewish client Flavius Josephus, a captured Pharisee who prophesied that Vespasian would become emperor. He wrote the *History of the Jewish War* to point out the futility of resisting Rome. Despite his pro-Roman outlook, however, he defended his people's faith and way of life to the Gentiles in his twenty-volume *Jewish Antiquities.* He also wrote *Contra Apionem* against the anti-Semitic writings of the Alexandrian Greek Apion and defended his own career in an autobiography.

Quintilian (ca. A.D. 33–ca. 100)   The central role of rhetoric in higher education resulted in a comprehensive handbook of rhetorical training by the Spaniard Marcus Fabius Quintilianus. He held Vespasian's first chair of rhetoric at Rome and tutored Domitian's heirs. His *Institutio Oratoria (Oratorical Education)* deals with all of the techniques of rhetoric and has influenced serious study of the subject ever since. It is also a source of important information on many other Greek and Latin authors.

Resurgence of Literature under the Five Good Emperors
The most important authors who came of age under the Flavians did not begin to publish their works until after the death of Domitian. His autocratic nature and constant fear of conspiracies after 86 made it dangerous to express thoughts openly on many subjects. The more relaxed atmosphere between the Five Good Emperors and the educated senatorial elite, however, was more congenial to many writers.

Tacitus (ca. A.D. 55–120) and Pliny the Younger (ca. A.D. 61–ca. 114)   The foremost author was Cornelius Tacitus, whose valuable historical works have been discussed above (see pp. 316–317, 340). He also wrote the *Dialogue on Orators,* observations on earlier orators and how the lack of free institutions in his own day produced mere striving for rhetorical effect instead of real substance in contemporary orators. Nothing underscores Tacitus' point more clearly than the *Panegyric,* a speech of the younger Pliny, Gaius Plinius Caecilius Secundus, nephew of Pliny the Elder. It is full of flattery of Trajan and only dares to offer advice indirectly by safely criticizing the dead Domitian. On the other hand, the nine books of his *Letters* are much better. In smooth artistic prose, they are addressed to Trajan and numerous other important friends. They reveal an urbane, decent individual who tried to live up to his responsibilities, avoid injustice, and do good where he could, as in endowing a school for boys and girls or refusing to accept anonymous denunciations of Christians.

Juvenal (ca. A.D. 55–ca. 130)   A far less pleasant personality is the poet Decimus Junius Juvenalis, an *eques* who may have served under Tacitus' father-in-law, Agricola, in Britain. He suffered banishment under Domitian, which seems to have embittered him permanently. Under Trajan and Hadrian he published five books of hexameters, the *Satires,* often vitriolic and sometimes offensive attacks on stereotypic vices. In his early satires he seems to express all of his pent-up rage and hatred for the conditions that had prevailed under Domitian. His vicious characterizations of women in satire 6 may reflect some romantic disappointment, and his vehement attacks on homosexuality in 2 and 9 probably show disapproval of Hadrian's proclivities. Perhaps his most original piece is satire 4, a parody of Domitian, who summons his council to discuss the momentous problem of cooking a huge fish. Juvenal was immensely popular in the Middle Ages because he titillated Christian moralists while confirming their view of pagan Roman decadence.

Suetonius (ca. A.D. 69–ca. 135)   Another writer who fascinated medieval Christians in the same way was Gaius Suetonius Tranquillus. Friend of Pliny the Younger, he served Trajan and became Hadrian's private secretary and Imperial librarian. He wrote on textual criticism, famous courtesans, illustrious men, literary figures, Greek and Roman games, and various other curious topics. Nevertheless, most of those works are lost, and his fame rests upon his major biographical work, the *Lives of the Twelve Caesars* (Julius Caesar to Domitian). These biographies, however, aim not so much at serious history as at entertainment. Therefore, although Suetonius preserves much valuable information from lost earlier sources, his portraits must be treated cautiously. Rumor, gossip, and rhetorically embellished scandal are often included so that judicious skepticism is often required on the part of the reader.

Fronto (ca. A.D. 100–ca. 170)   Suetonius' fascination with the bizarre actions of past emperors and his research on obscure topics was symptomatic of a general absorption in arcane and antiquarian subjects that became a definite literary movement, almost a cult of antiquity, under the Antonines. The man who seems to have given the most impetus to this movement was Marcus Aurelius' tutor, M. Cornelius Fronto. Significantly, Fronto had been born at Cirta in Africa, which soon replaced Spain as a provincial source of Roman writers.

Quaestor in Hadrian's reign and consul in 143, as well as Imperial tutor, Fronto moved in Rome's highest circles. He gathered around him a whole circle of literary lights, such as the famous orator Festus Postumius, the grammarian Sulpicius Apollinaris, and the philosopher Favorinus. Their major interest lay in ransacking early Latin literature for archaic and uncommon words. They wanted to expand the rather limited vocabulary of the classical writers like Cicero and Vergil and

create what Fronto called an *elocutio novella* (''new elocution'') to give greater point and variety to their expression.

Unfortunately, as Fronto's letters to Marcus Aurelius reveal, that is about as far as they went. Fronto appears as a thoroughly decent, kind, and generous man, but he discusses only how to express oneself most accurately and never seriously considers what is worth saying. His point of view was that of a professional rhetorician, not a thinker. For him history was merely an exercise in panegyric, and philosophy was positively to be avoided, a point on which Marcus Aurelius obviously disappointed his beloved tutor.

Aulus Gellius (ca. A.D. 125–ca. 175)   The danger in Fronto's approach was that arcane archaisms and recondite research would become ends in themselves without any relevance to the real world. A case in point is Fronto's cultured friend Aulus Gellius. Beginning as a student in Athens, he compiled interesting oddities culled from earlier writers and interspersed with accounts of conversations on a wide range of philological and antiquarian subjects. Called *Attic Nights* (*Noctes Atticae*) in honor of its origin, it is a very valuable work to modern scholars because it preserves much important information from now-lost earlier works. In and of itself, however, it has little value other than as an example of the pretentious rhetoric of the age and the dilettantism that passed for intellectual life then.

Apuleius (ca. A.D. 123–ca. 180)   The works of Apuleius, a poet and rhetorician born at Madauros in Africa, often exhibit the same pretentious display of archaism, florid rhetoric, and superficial learning. Eventually, he settled down as a professional rhetorician at Carthage. He paraded his knowledge in such works as *Natural Questions, On Fish, On Trees, Astronomical Phenomena, Arithmetic, On Proverbs,* and an epitome of historical works. On one topic, however, Apuleius rises above mere display and focuses his thought with really imaginative force. His *Metamorphoses* or *Golden Ass* is an original work of real genius.

Ostensibly it is a novel in the form of an old Milesian tale full of sexual escapades and dramatic reversals of fortune. In it a certain Lucius is the victim of his own experiments in sex and magic, which turn him into an ass with human senses. Numerous adventures and mishaps cause him to pass through the hands of a cruel youth, thieves, farmers, eunuch priests, a baker, a truck gardener, a cook, and finally a Corinthian circus trainer who wants to teach him to mount a woman as part of a gladiatorial show. This much seems to derive from an existing popular tale. Apuleius, however, has interspersed many additional elements from other stories, such as the beautiful story of Cupid and Psyche, to give it greater depth and in many other cases to ridicule magic and the superstition that riddled the age. In contrast, Apuleius describes the true power of pure faith in the saving grace of the goddess Isis through a moving scene of conversion at the end.

Pausanias (fl. 150) The peace and prosperity of the first two centuries A.D. and the antiquarianism of the age encouraged travel and the viewing of historical places, monuments, and museums. Therefore, travelogues and guidebooks were in great demand. Fortunately, one of the most valuable survives, the *Description of Greece* by Pausanias, a Greek geographer from Lydia in the mid-second century. Usually he outlines the history and topography of cities and their surroundings and frequently includes information on their mythological lore, religious customs, social life, and native products. He is particularly interested in historic battle sites, patriotic monuments, and famous works of art and architecture. The accuracy of his descriptions have been very helpful in locating ancient sites and reconstructing what has been recovered.

Resurgence of Greek Literature It is significant that Pausanias was a Greek writer describing great monuments and locales of ancient Greece. The first two centuries A.D. saw a renewal of cultural activity and local

pride in the Greek-speaking half of the Roman Empire. Although the Latin authors of the Augustan Age had established a body of works that were great in their own right and were highly admired by later Roman writers, Greeks could reflect with pride that upper-class Romans continued to flock to the great Greek centers of culture to complete their education just as they had done during the late Republic. The vigorous philhellenism of emperors like Nero, Hadrian, and Marcus Aurelius recalled a sense of greatness to many Greeks, a sense that the return of prosperity to Greek cities under the Imperial peace and the growing prominence of influential Greeks in Imperial administration must have reinforced. In fact, many significant Greek writers during this period were men who had successful careers in Roman government.

Plutarch (ca. A.D. 45–120) An outstanding example of such a person is Plutarch of Chaeronea in Boeotia. Under Hadrian, Plutarch was procurator of Achaea. He spent much of his time after 95 at Chaeronea, however, where he taught and wrote. A large collection of miscellaneous ethical, rhetorical, and antiquarian essays (not all genuinely Plutarch's) is entitled *Moralia*. Plutarch's most famous work is, of course, the *Parallel Lives of Noble Greeks and Romans*. The resurgence of Greek national pride is clear from the overall theme of the *Lives*: that for every important figure of Roman history, a similar and equally important character appears in Greek history. Plutarch chose his material to highlight moral character, not present an objective or critical historical analysis. He also had the instincts of a good storyteller and did not encumber his narrative with exaggerated rhetorical adornment. The subjects themselves provide all the necessary interest, which is why Plutarch remains one of the most widely read ancient authors.

Arrian (ca. A.D. 95–180) Another writer who called to mind the Greek heritage was Flavius Arrianus—Arrian—a Bithynian Greek from Nicomedia. Also a Roman citizen, he became a suffect consul in the early years of Hadrian and was governor of Cappadocia from 131 to 137. Retiring to the cultured life of Athens, he studied philosophy under Epictetus. He presented a full account of Epictetus' Stoic teachings in his *Diatribes* (*Discourses*) and a synopsis in the *Enchiridion* (*Handbook*). He even went so far as to write a treatise on hunting, *Cynegetica,* and minor biographies in imitation of Xenophon. His *Tactics* and *Voyage around the Black Sea* survive, but unfortunately his *History of Parthia* and *History* of *Bithynia* do not.

Of Arrian's extant historical works, the most important is his account of Alexander's war against Persia, the *Anabasis of Alexander,* in clear, readable prose. It is the fullest and most soundly based account of Alexander that has survived. He further imitated Xenophon by writing a sequel, *After Alexander,* whose loss makes it much more difficult to reconstruct the history of Alexander's successors.

Appian (*ca. A.D. 90-165*)   Appian, a Greek from Alexandria and Arrian's contemporary, also obtained Roman citizenship. After a successful career at Rome, he wrote a universal history in Greek like Polybius' earlier work. His universal *Roman History* (*Romaika*) in twenty-four books began with the rise of Rome in Italy and then various different ethnic groups and nations conquered by Rome. Books 13 to 17, however, form an interlude on the *Civil Wars* from the Gracchi to Actium. Appian often followed valuable, now-lost Greek and Latin sources. He too wrote in a simple, unpretentious style that is easy to read.

Lucian (*ca. A.D. 115-ca. 185*)   The best and most original writer of this period was Lucian, a Hellenized Syrian from Samosata, who held a Roman administrative post in Egypt. He was a master of the Classical Attic dialect and was deeply versed in its literature. Lucian's earlier works consist of rhetorical declamations and literary criticism, often laced with wit. His most famous works are humorous, semi-popular philosophical dialogues, such as his *Dialogues of the Dead,* which

deflate human pride, pedantic philosophers, religious charlatans, and popular superstitions. He also wrote a novel, *Lucius, or the Ass,* based on the same original as Apuleius' *Golden Ass.* He vigorously disliked all that was fatuous, foolish, or false and can still be read with pleasure today.

The Second Sophistic   The same cannot be said for the large number of Greek authors who were part of a literary movement known as the Second Sophistic. The Greek sophists of the fifth and fourth centuries B.C. had invented formal rhetoric. Hence, the professional rhetoricians of the second and third centuries A.D. were also called sophists. A number of them consciously sought to revive the vocabulary and style of earlier Greek orators, and from them the Second Sophistic takes its name. Most of them were wealthy, cultured men proud of the Greek past and eager to promote the influence of their native cities, such as Athens, Ephesus, Pergamum, Antioch, Smyrna, and Prusa, within the Roman Empire. They cultivated relations with Roman aristocrats and were often favored by emperors. Their archaizing tendencies influenced Fronto, whose *elocutio novella* represents a parallel movement in Latin.

Philostratus (ca. A.D. 170–ca. 250), a student of philosophy and patronized by Septimius Severus and Julia Domna, commemorated the leading figures of the Second Sophistic in his *Lives of the Sophists.* They included Polemon (ca. A.D. 88–ca.145), who flourished at Smyrna; Herodes Atticus (A.D. 101–177), a wealthy benefactor of Athens; and Aelius Aristides (ca. A.D. 120–189), who delivered lectures and ceremonial speeches all over the Empire. Little of Polemon and Herodes Atticus remain, but there are fifty extant works ascribed to Aristides. Aristides is by far the best stylist, but his thought is shallow and uninspiring.

Dio Chrysostom (*ca. A.D. 40-ca. 115*) The best representatives of the Second Sophistic were popular philosophical lecturers who were earnestly concerned with communicating moral lessons to a wide audience. The most noteworthy such person is Dio Chrysostom ("Golden-mouthed") from Prusa in Bithynia. His message was a mild blend of Stoicism and Cynicism that stressed honesty and the simple virtues that make civilization possible. His speeches show no great original thought, but they communicate deeply held values in a fine style that avoids the excesses of many contemporaries, who were often more interested in showing off their rhetorical skills than in their subjects.

Christian Writers   While Chrysostom was traveling the Empire and propagating what he believed were the best values of his civilization, others, although they shared with him many values of a common Greco-Roman heritage, were spreading new ideas that would eventually transform that heritage into something quite different. Because they too had something to say in which they deeply believed, some of the ablest writers of the age were Christian authors. The best known are the writers of the Four Gospels of the *New Testament*, Matthew, Mark, Luke, and John, who sought to preserve the memory and message of Christ's life and teachings, and the missionary letters of the Apostle Paul, which make up most of the remainder of the *New Testament* and form the intellectual foundation of much basic Christian theology.

Yet, there were many other Christian writers, who wrote with remarkable intellectual power and fiery zeal. The most notable were Ignatius of Antioch (A.D. 50–107), the first great ecclesiastic and the father of Christian orthodoxy; Irenaeus of Lyons (ca. A.D. 130–202), the powerful advocate of Christian unity, denunciator of heresy, and the father of systematic theology; Tatian (ca. A.D. 120–172) "the Assyrian," whose *Life of Christ,* a harmony of the Four Gospels, was read in Syrian churches for almost three centuries; and, finally, toward the end of the second century, Tertullian of Carthage (ca. A.D. 160–230?), whose vigorous Ciceronian elo-

quence, wit, and biting satire transformed Christian polemic into Latin literature and Latin into the language of Western Catholicism.

Architecture in the First Two Centuries A.D.   Probably the most creative aspect of Roman Imperial culture in the first two centuries A.D. was architecture. Augustus had used the resources of the state for building projects far more than ever before. His example was followed and enlarged upon by most succeeding emperors during this period. With the resources thus made available, architects found no end of opportunities to use their creative talents.

The possibilities of combining different structural and stylistic elements into a coherent monumental whole had been discovered by Hellenistic Greek architects and imitated in Sulla's famous Temple of Fortuna at Praeneste (see pp. 260–261). The architects of the first two centuries A.D. (many of whom were Greek) developed these possibilities to their fullest. Great complexes made up of diverse elements arranged according to an artistic design became the norm.

Imperial Palaces   Each emperor had to have his own splendid residence on the Palatine, or at least he had to add to that of his predecessor. Nero took advantage of the fire of 64 to construct a sprawling complex, the Golden House, that mirrored his own megalomania. Its size and complexity, however, made it an architectural achievement of the first order. It covered an area twice as large as that of the Vatican today and was really a complex of palaces, merely one of which had over eighty rooms. It also had its own parks, pastures, groves, and even a zoo. It had an arcaded approach a mile long and 350 feet wide. Two ponds, one fresh and one salt, were fed by aqueducts each fifteen miles long. Vespasian destroyed Nero's palace and built a smaller one on the Palatine to symbolize the beginning of a new order. Vespasian's sons, especially Domitian, continued to enlarge this

This scale model reconstructs the complex of buildings, pools, and colonnades from Hadrian's Villa at Tibur.
(Courtesy Photo Alterocca, Terni, Italy)

new palace until it too became a huge complex that destroyed or buried many older buildings beneath its foundations. Its remains are visible on the Palatine today.

The Emperor Hadrian was an innovative architect and designed a splendid villa near Tibur (Tivoli), about eighteen miles east of Rome. It far surpassed Nero's Golden House in size and complexity of design, and much remains. Covering an area 3000 feet long and 1500 wide, this villa contained eight palaces, each with a different theme or mood: a stadium, a palaestra (for wrestling), a library, a temple of Serapis (Serapeum), two pools, three dining rooms, three baths, numerous porticoes above and below ground level, and many other buildings, such as guest houses, slave quarters, and shrines. What is most striking about the whole complex is the imaginative combination of different geometric shapes— curves, octagons, rectangles, and squares— to create new visual effects.

Public Buildings Augustus' Julio-Claudian successors did not contribute greatly to the public architecture of Rome. The Flavians, on the other hand, introduced a dynamic era of public construction. They destroyed the Golden House of Nero and built the Colosseum and baths of Titus on its site. The baths, unfortunately, like many other ancient buildings were almost completely obliterated by builders who used its stones for new buildings in the Renaissance. Titus also built the arch that still stands at the eastern entrance to the Forum. It commemorates his triumph over the Jews, and its sculptures depict the sacred objects taken as spoils from the Temple at Jerusalem. Vespasian completed a temple of the Deified Claudius, and began the third Imperial Forum—the Forum of Peace (in commemoration of the end of the Jewish revolt), also called the Forum of Vespasian, east of the Forum of Augustus and just north of the original Forum.

Vespasian also probably built what is called the Temple of the Sacred City (*Templum Sacrae Urbis*) between the old Forum and his new one. It was used to house records, and on its outside north wall, which was also the inside south wall of a library in Vespasian's Forum, there was a detailed map of the whole city carved in marble. Many fragments of this Marble Plan still exist and are very useful in reconstructing the layout and monuments of ancient Rome. Domitian built a new Stadium, with seats for thirty thousand in the Campus Martius. It remained one of the city's most famous structures for centuries. The length of the arena was about 750 feet, and its shape and size are preserved by the modern Piazza Navona. Domitian also completed a Temple of Vespasian at the western end of the old Forum, just to the northwest of the Temple of Saturn and just to the southwest of the Temple of Concord. Only three large Corinthian columns still stand.

The Colosseum Vespasian began and Domitian finished the monumental task of building the Colosseum (Coliseum), or Flavian Amphitheater, as it was originally called.

It received the name Colosseum from a nearby colossal, 120-foot bronze statue of Nero, which Vespasian had reworked into a statue of the sun. The Colosseum's remains stand today as a symbol of Roman Imperial architecture, a massive structure showing a sophisticated blend of decorative styles and impressive engineering. It has an eliptical shape with a main axis of about 620 feet and a minor one of about 515, stands about 160 feet high on the outside, and could hold forty-five to fifty-five thousand spectators. The facade is a creative blend of architectural forms and styles. Three superimposed arcades of eighty arches each run around the outside of the building. Each arch is decoratively framed with engaged columns supporting an entablature. Thus the curved Roman arch and the horizontal Greek temple facade are joined together. The style of the first level is Doric, the second Ionic, and the third Corinthian. A fourth story has no arches but is decorated with a number of Corinthian pilasters in line with the rows of engaged columns of the lower stories.

Forum of Trajan Many emperors built fora to accommodate the ever-increasing of-

The Colosseum (Coliseum), or Flavian Amphitheater. (Courtesy Italian Government Travel Office)

ficial and commercial business of Rome. While Nerva's is the smallest Imperial forum, that of his successor, Trajan, is the largest. Its remains are still impressive. It was to the west of Augustus' forum, and its southern corner bordered the northern corner of Caesar's in order to complete Caesar's original plan of joining the valley of the Republican Forum with the Campus Martius. The ends of the Capitoline and Quirinal hills had to be cut back to make room for the enormous design roughly 620 feet wide and 1000 feet long. The main part of this forum consisted of an open space approximately 300 by 380 feet. The southeast, southwest, and northwest sides were surrounded by colonnades of different-colored marble. The entrance was in the mid-dle of the southeast side, through a great triumphal arch fronted by six columns and topped by a statue of Trajan driving a six-horse chariot. Behind the middle of each side colonnade was a large semicircular structure, a hemicycle. The one to the northeast is called the Market of Trajan and had two stories of shops and rooms. More levels rose on terraces behind.

The far end of the forum was closed off by the front of a great basilica, the Basilica Ulpia, raised about three feet above ground level and approached by three steps. The entrances of the basilica were flanked with columns of yellow marble and had chariots and trophies mounted above. The walls were marble-faced concrete, and there was a large

Front view of Hadrian's Pantheon, with inscription from Agrippa's earlier building.   *(Courtesy Fratelli Alinari, Florence)*

apse at each end. A double row of ninety-six marble columns surrounded the inner hall and supported an upper gallery around the nave, which was about eighty feet wide.

Behind the basilica two libraries (one Latin and one Greek, as was customary) faced each other. In the midst of the courtyard between them stood one of Rome's most remarkable monuments, the column of Trajan (see p. 387). After Trajan's death, Hadrian built a magnificent temple to the Deified Trajan and Trajan's wife, Plotina, on the open side of this courtyard so that the whole area had an architectural balance.

Hadrian's Public Buildings At Rome, Hadrian was concerned primarily with rebuilding and restoring what already existed, but he was responsible for the construction of three unique projects, which epitomize the way that Roman Imperial architecture combined disparate forms and styles into structures that are both massive and interesting. The first was the largest temple in Rome—the Temple of Venus and Rome—between the Colosseum and the northeast corner of the old Forum. It was really two temples with vaulted apses back to back. In one apse stood a statue of Venus and in the other, one of Rome. This

Artist's rendition of the interior of the Pantheon. (Courtesy New York Public Library Picture Collection)

arrangement took advantage of a convenient Latin pun: Venus is the goddess of love, *amor* in Latin, which is the name of Rome, *Roma*, spelled backward. Only its foundations remain, however.

Hadrian's most famous building is the Pantheon, Temple of All the Gods. A Christian church since 609, it is the best preserved ancient building in Rome today. It is the perfect example of the imaginative combination of shapes and forms that distinguishes Roman Imperial architecture. The front presents the columned and pedimented facade of a classical Greek temple. This facade may preserve the lines and dedicatory inscription of the original Pantheon built by Augustus' colleague Marcus Agrippa, but it and the rest are almost all Hadrian's work.

The conventional facade joins a huge domed cylinder that is the temple proper. Thus, the rectilinear is uniquely combined with the curvilinear. This theme is carried out further in the rectangular receding coffers sunk in the curved ceiling of the dome, in the marble squares and circles of the floor, and in the alternating rectangular and curved niches around the wall of the drum. Moreover, the globe and the cylinder are combined because the diameter of the drum is the same as the distance from the floor to the top of the dome, so that if the curve of the dome were extended, it would be tangent with the floor. Finally, the whole building is lighted by a round opening about thirty feet in diameter in the top of the dome. This hole is open to the weather, but because of its great height, most moisture evaporates before it reaches the floor during a rain.

The dome exemplifies how Roman engineers took advantage of the properties of concrete, whose use the Romans greatly advanced. To reduce the dome's weight, pumice was used instead of ordinary sand or gravel, and the wall was made thinner as it neared the top. The recessed coffers reduced the weight still further and created a grid of structural ribs. Once the concrete set, the dome was a solid, jointless mass of exceptional stability, as its survival for over 1850 years testifies.

Across the Tiber there arose another architectural marvel of the age—Hadrian's tomb—a colossal mausoleum, massive, solid, round, over a thousand feet in circumference. On its summit a bronze four-horse chariot stood poised for flight; inside were walls faced with Parian marble, huge columns of Eastern marble or Egyptian porphyry, mosaic floors, and numerous statues. In the Middle Ages that massive structure long served as a fortress and was known as the Castle of Sant' Angelo, a name it still bears.

Architecture in the Provinces　After Hadrian the pace of building in second-century Rome slackened considerably, but elsewhere the bustle continued. A fine example of Imperial architecture and planning in a smaller town is Thamugadi (Timgad), a colony established by Trajan for veterans in North Africa. It was laid out on a grid of broad, intersecting main streets and side streets. The main streets were colonnaded, and other amenities, including a large Greek-style theater, baths, and a well-appointed forum were provided. By A.D. 200, twelve to fifteen thousand people dwelt there in comfort and security.

Sculpture　The Roman tradition of realistic portraits and statues continued through the second century A.D., as can be seen in the busts of the various emperors. The best example is a bronze statue of Marcus Aurelius mounted on a horse. It is extraordinary only because it is the single bronze equestrian statue to survive, but it is a skillfully executed representative of a traditional type that could have been seen all over the Roman Empire. It is in the use of sculptured relief that innovations occurred. Beginning with Augustus and the Ara Pacis (see p. 303), the sculptured relief became one of the most common forms of official art. Tiberius and Claudius restated Augustan themes in famous reliefs on several altars. Titus adorned the inside of his triumphal arch with vivid scenes full of the

Bronze equestrian statue of Marcus Aurelius.   (Courtesy Art Reference Bureau, Inc.)

movement and excitement of his own victory procession. Domitian imitated the more restrained classicism of Augustus' Ara Pacis on a long relief that glorified the Flavian dynasty and, probably, his own campaign against the Chatti. At Beneventum, Trajan erected a triumphal arch that was an exact copy of Titus' arch at Rome, except that he covered every available flat surface with dense relief scenes of himself performing his duties. Moreover, these scenes were very balanced and static in the classical manner.

At Rome, however, in the courtyard behind the Basilica Ulpia, Trajan set up a completely new and extraordinary relief to commemorate his Dacian Wars. It is a column about twelve feet in diameter and exactly 100

Roman feet (about 97 English feet) high. Around this column winds a spiral relief depicting the wars themselves. The vast and complex logistical, engineering, and military aspects of the wars are portrayed in a realistically detailed narrative that leads dramatically to the death of King Decebalus. There are some twenty-five hundred separate figures, but through it all Trajan is a unifying presence appearing over fifty times. The width of the spiral and size of the figures increase as they move upward to compensate for the greater viewing distance from the ground. The top was surmounted by a bronze statue of Trajan, until it was replaced by one of St. Peter in 1588. The large pedestal on which the column rests was Trajan's mausoleum.

Arch of Trajan at Beneventum.
(Courtesy Fratelli Alinari, Florence)

Marcus Aurelius imitated Trajan's column with one of his own in the Campus Martius. Its dimensions are the same, and it has a spiral relief depicting the Marcomanic Wars. Artistically, however, this relief is very different from Trajan's. The realistic details of scenery are omitted, there is no attempt at three-dimensional spatial relationships, and there is no unified, dramatic narrative sequence. There is constant motion and striving, almost chaos. Through it all, however, Marcus Aurelius stands out. He is not merely part of the action. He repeatedly faces outward and dominates the viewer's attention to become a solid, powerful presence in the midst of all the confused action. The details of mundane reality are sacrificed to present the viewer directly with the essence of the Emperor's role

in events. This style approaches the "otherworldly" art of the late Empire and the Middle Ages.

Painting   What little is known of Roman painting in the first two centuries A.D. comes from the wall paintings found at Pompeii and Herculaneum, which were buried by the eruption of Vesuvius in 79 during Titus' reign. These frescoes are not the work of creative artists but of craftsmen copying on plaster the works of great masters or standardized decorative scenes and following the tastes of their customers. Pleasant or romantic landscapes, still lifes, and scenes from famous myths or epics abound.

Most of these works are set off by paint-

Trajan's Column. *(Courtesy Fratelli Alinari, Florence)*

ing the surrounding wall in an architectural style. From roughly 14 to 62, the Third or Egyptianizing Style was most popular. Instead of creating the illusion of depth, the painters used painted architectural forms to provide a flat frame within which the picture could be featured. After 62 the Fourth or Ornamental Style prevailed. Perspective was heavily used to give the illusion of infinite depth behind the wall. There was also great flamboyance in the design of the architectural forms. They were weighed down with intricate detail to the point of looking like baroque fantasies and probably show the influence of Nero's tastes on the trends of the time.

Mosaics, Coins, and Medallions   The numerous mosaics of the period, which are found all over the Empire, especially in the villas of North Africa, are not only very valuable documents on the social and economic life of the region, but exhibit remarkable taste and workmanship in an art destined to have a future even more brilliant. The coins and medallions of this period are

Coin of Hadrian. The obverse bears the inscription **HADRIANUS AUGUSTUS,** *and the reverse shows Roma, seated on a cuirass, holding a figure of victory and a cornucopiae. (Courtesy The American Numismatic Society, New York)*

among the finest in history. The art of medal engraving, which had its genesis in Hadrian's issue of a series of bronze medallions, reveals a love of symbolism and allegory and a skill and technique comparable to that of the most beautiful coinages in the ancient world.

Science   Abstract science was not a forte of the Romans. What scientific work that did take place in the Roman Empire was carried on by the heirs of the Greek tradition in the East. Even they did little original work. They tended to codify and systematize the discoveries of their predecessors in encyclopedic works that became standard reference works until the scientific revolution of the seventeenth and eighteenth centuries. The two major examples are the medical treatises of Galen (Claudius Galenus, ca. 130–200), a doctor from Pergamum, and those on mathematical geography and astronomy by Ptolemy (Claudius Ptolemaeus, ca. 150) of Alexandria.

Philosophy   Hellenistic Greek philosophers like Panaetius and Posidonius had adapted Stoicism to the attitudes and needs of the Romans, and the Stoics, along with their Cynic cousins, were the only philosophers to retain any vigor during the first two centuries A.D. Neither Greek nor Roman practitioners in this period broke any new ground, however. Their efforts were directed mainly at popularizing and preaching the accepted doctrines of duty, self-control, and virtue as its own reward.

Seneca expounded on numerous Stoic themes under Claudius and Nero. *De Providen-*

tia (On Providence), for example, argues that the sufferings of the good are only apparent. *De Ira (On Anger)* and *De Vita Beata (On the Happy Life)* state the case for self-control and limiting one's desires. In the 124 surviving *Epistulae Morales (Moral Letters),* Seneca addresses practical advice from the viewpoint of Stoic ethics and philosophy to a younger friend named Lucillius.

Seneca's essays did not have so wide an impact in their day as the public lectures of his contemporary Gaius Musonius Rufus (ca. A.D. 30–ca. 100). Rufus suffered banishment twice, first under Nero, after the abortive conspiracy of Piso, and again under Vespasian's crackdown on Stoic opponents. Many later Stoics were pupils of Rufus, but the most notable was the lame Greek slave Epictetus. After obtaining freedom, he began to teach at Rome but was banished by Domitian. He spent his exile teaching at Nicopolis, across the Adriatic from Italy, and attracted a large following. He did not write anything, but the historian Arrian collected his lectures, *Diatribes,* and published them along with a summary, the *Enchiridion.* He emphasized the benevolence of the Creator and the brotherhood of man. He believed that happiness depended on controlling one's own will and accepting whatever Divine Providence in its wisdom might require one to endure.

These teachings of Epictetus came into the hands of Marcus Aurelius and inspired him to exchange the study of rhetoric for that of Stoicism. The same spirit animates the *Meditations* of Aurelius. The works of Epictetus and Aurelius together have attracted sensitive readers ever since and have had a significant impact on later Western ethical thought.

Religion Nevertheless, Stoicism did not have such an impact on the first and second centuries as developments in religion. The removal of religion from the obviously cynical manipulation of late Republican politicians restored the credibility of Roman religion among all levels of society. Moreover, throughout the Empire, local cults were assimilated into parallel cults of the Roman pantheon, so that Roman paganism took on the appearance of an international religion. The emperors took their duties as *Pontifex Maximus* seriously, and the worship of the Emperor grew steadily. Many people kept shrines of the Emperor in their houses.

More significantly, at all levels of society in a centralized Imperial state that increasingly controlled temporal affairs, people sought access to divine powers in order to achieve some sense of control over their lives and destinies. Oracles, omens, and portents were eagerly sought and studied. Astrology was extremely popular. Miracle workers who claimed to have access to divine powers found eager followings. Under Nero and the Flavians, for example, the Cappadocian Apollonius of Tyana achieved great popularity as a sage and healer, so much so that Domitian banished him from Rome. After his death, he was worshipped with his own cult for a long time.

Under Antoninus Pius, another popular healer and purveyor of oracles was Alexander of Abonuteichos from Paphlagonia. He established a mystery cult that influenced a number of prominent Romans, including Fronto, the tutor of Marcus Aurelius. It too continued to exist after his death.

Mystery Cults The desires of people to connect their lives with the divine and influence their ultimate destinies can be seen in the great popularity of mystery cults whose initiates received assurances of future salvation. Dionysiac cults flourished. The initiation procedures of one such cult are vividly portrayed in a series of wall paintings at Pompeii in the Villa of the Mysteries. The cult of Demeter at Eleusis attracted initiates from all over the Empire, one of whom was the Emperor Hadrian.

Isis Alongside traditional Greco-Roman mystery cults such as these, Eastern mystery religions were growing with missionary zeal. Because of the secret nature of their mysteries and because of the complete victory of their Christian rivals later on, information about them is sketchy at best, but a few basic facts are known. One of the most popular was the cult of Isis and her male counterpart, Serapis. Originally, she had been an ancient Egyptian nature goddess, but in Hellenistic times she was transformed into a universal mother figure and savior of mankind. Apuleius celebrated her benevolence in the *Golden Ass*. Those who followed a few simple rules of conduct received promises of happiness in this world and the next. Worshippers also gained psychological satisfaction from direct participation in elaborate, emotionally charged rituals that had caused the senate to ban worship of Isis from Republican Rome. Caligula, however, finally provided a state temple for her in the Campus Martius. A major cult that had spread to every corner of the Empire could not be kept out any longer.

Mithraism Eventually, the Persian god Mithras became even more popular than Isis. The cult originated as part of Persian Zoroastrianism, in which Mithras was a god of light and truth who aided Ahura-Mazda, the power of good, in an eternal struggle with the evil power, Ahriman. He was closely associated with the sun god, an important ally of Ahura-Mazda, and he is sometimes identified as the sun. Among Mithras' divine accomplishments, the most celebrated was the capture and slaying of a sacred bull, from whose body sprang other, useful forms of life.

This death and birth are a central element in the Mithraic mysteries. The most common type of Mithraic cult statue shows Mithras sacrificing the bull. The typical

Mithraic temple, *Mithraeum,* was an artificial subterranean cave, perhaps symbolizing death and the grave. Initiates had to sacrifice a bull and were baptized with its blood after completing certain ordeals. Among them seems to have been a simulated murder. There was also a sacramental meal. All of that was conducted by a professional priesthood in impressive ceremonies and with promises of immortality. A strong moral code with injunctions to do good works also was imposed.

The worship of Mithras became popular in the Western provinces first under the Flavians, especially in military camps and seaports, where there were always many people from the Eastern provinces. The cult was restricted to men only and was particularly attractive to soldiers because of Mithras' heroic career as a fighter on the side of good. This restriction eventually, however, put Mithraism at a serious disadvantage and helps to explain why it eventually lost out to Christianity, with which it had much in common.

Christianity Christianity combined the appealing characteristics of many mystery religions: a loving, divine savior in Jesus, who overcame the forces of evil and death; a benevolent mother figure in the Virgin Mary; the promise of a blessed afterlife; a sense of belonging to a special community in an era when local values and civic institutions were losing force in the face of a distant central government. In this third aspect, however, Christianity greatly surpassed the rest. The requirements of a strict moral code and the rejection of all other gods increased the Christians' sense of specialness. Furthermore, Christ's injunction to "love one another" resulted in charitable activities within congregations that increased the feelings of fellowship and communal identity.

Strengths One of Christianity's distinctive strengths was its high degree of organization. During the first century A.D., the individual Christian communities established a local system of clergy and leaders—deacons and deaconesses (servants), presbyters (elders), and bishops (overseers)—who ministered to the needs of the congregation, established policies, and regulated activites. Later, the bishops of the early churches became the heads of groups of churches.

Like other new cults, Christianity had spread first to the major urban centers along the trade routes of the Empire. Later, missionaries, sent out from these centers and under the direction of their churches, established churches in the smaller surrounding communities. The urban bishops were the ones who coordinated this expansion and naturally came to exercise great influence and authority, so that by the end of the second century, the bishops of the major cities were recognized as the heads of whole networks of churches in their regions. Furthermore, because of the strong sense of Christian brotherhood, the bishops and various churches regularly corresponded with each other to provide mutual support in the face of difficulties. In this way they also ensured the local practices and beliefs conformed to the authoritative teachings of Christ and his disciples.

It is significant for the development of a strong interchurch organization in the first and second centuries that Christ was a recent historical person and that his immediate disciples or the Apostle Paul had founded the earliest Christian churches. These early foundations provided a direct historical link with the words and deeds of Christ himself through the apostolic succession of their bishops. Churches founded in the generation after Paul and the Disciples naturally looked to the apostolic churches for guidance and authoritative teachings when they wished to confirm that they were proceeding in accordance with the words and spirit of Christ's teachings, imperative for obtaining salvation. Therefore, the bishops of the apostolic churches, especially in the four major cities of Rome, Jerusalem, Alexandria, and Antioch, achieved great respect and authority. Accordingly, they were able to impose their will on the lesser churches, so that Christianity reached a degree of organizational and doctrinal unity matched by no other religion.

Another factor that helped the spread of early Christianity was its openness and appeal to all classes and sexes. Women were not excluded from or segregated within it. In the early Church, deacons and deaconesses shared in ministering to the congregations. The simple ceremonies and the grace-giving rites of Baptism and Communion posed no expensive obstacles to the poor. Indeed, Christ's teachings praised the poor and the humble and made their lot more bearable by encouraging the practice of charity toward them in the present and promising them a better life in the future. On the other hand, the foundation of Christianity on written works, such as the Jewish Scriptures, the Four Gospels, and the sophisticated writings of Paul, gave it an appeal to the educated upper class as well.

Converts from this class provided the trained thinkers and writers who became the early Church Fathers. In the Greek-speaking East, where training in formal philosophy had a long tradition, men like Clement and Origen, bishops of Alexandria at the end of the second century, expounded Christian theology with philosophic rigor. Others in both the East and West established a tradition of Christian apologetics aimed at counteracting popular misconceptions about Christians and official hostility toward them. Justin Martyr, who went from Flavia Neapolis (Nablus) in Palestine to establish a Christian school in Rome, addressed a defense of Christianity to Antoninus Pius and Marcus Aurelius. Tertullian of Carthage used his training as a lawyer to write a thorough defense against all of the charges frequently lodged with Roman governors against the Christians. His *Apology* is a classic of the type.

Persecution of the Christians The Christians needed to defend themselves from attack for two reasons. Their rigid monotheistic rejection of other gods and their refusal to participate in traditional activities with their pagan neighbors were an offense to those around them and bred personal hostility toward them. This hostility was fed by the normal human fear of the unfamiliar. Accordingly, people were quick to blame Christians for all manner of misfortunes that befell them individually or collectively and frequently denounced them to Roman officials for their "crimes." Moreover, Roman authorities had always been suspicious of secret societies and feared that they were plotting against the state. This fear seemed borne out in the Christians' case because they refused to propitiate the gods who protected the state and would not perform the required ceremonies before the image of the Emperor.

During the first two centuries most of the persecutions and resultant martyrdoms were the result of purely local personalities and politics, as when Jewish authorities laid accusations against Paul before Festus, the governor of Judea, or took advantage of Festus' death to execute James, leader of the church at Jerusalem. Nero's execution of Christians at Rome was a purely local act to divert the public in the aftermath of the great fire of 64. Domitian seems to have included Christians among the intellectuals whom he executed or banished as subversives, but he found no justification in the charges levelled at Jesus' relatives in Jerusalem and ordered that persecution of the Christians at Jerusalem stop.

By the beginning of the second century, however, Christianity had become widespread in the Eastern provinces, and local agitation against it was frequent. In a famous letter to Pliny the Younger, whom he had placed in charge of Bithynia-Pontus, Trajan agreed that there should be no organized hunt for Christians or acceptance of anonymous accusations. He insisted, however, that those fairly accused and convicted of being Christians be executed unless they renounced their faith and sacrificed to the gods. Hadrian demanded that accusations against Christians had to stand up under strict legal procedures or be dismissed. Although he disliked them, Marcus Aurelius himself did not actively promote the persecution of Christians, but he was too occupied with other crises to take action against governors who yielded to popular pressure and condemned Christians to torture and death.

The result of the individual martyrdoms in the first and second centuries was to strengthen the resolve of the faithful and impress thoughtful non-Christians, who were often moved to convert by the examples of heroic martyrs. Christian writers glorified and exalted the martyrs to inspire the living. As the spread of the Church proceeded apace, therefore, the third-century emperors did mount active persecutions of the Church in an attempt to appease the traditional gods and enforce unity on an increasingly chaotic Empire.

Social Developments   One of the major social trends of the first two centuries A.D. was the expansion of the Roman aristocracy to include the upper classes of Italy and the provinces. Augustus had been able to gain sole control of Rome because he had the wide support of the municipal aristocracy of Italy. Under him and his Julio-Claudian successors, numerous opportunities in military service and provincial administration were opened to them. Successful and loyal service was rewarded with offices like the consulship and membership in the Roman senate. A prime example is Vespasian, who was born to a family of the local gentry near Reate and rose through Imperial service not only to the senate but to the office of *princeps*.

The upper classes of the Romanized provinces soon followed the municipal aristocracy of Italy into Imperial service, the senate, and the office of Emperor. Descendants of the old Republican nobility had vainly opposed Claudius' appointment of senators from Gaul. Others from Gaul, Spain, and North Africa were not far behind, as the careers of Julius Vindex (revolted in Gaul in 68), Seneca, Trajan, Hadrian, and Fronto demonstrate. In fact, after the purges of Nero and Domitian, most of the old Republican noble families had disappeared, and by the end of the first century the majority of senators had their origins in the municipalities of Italy and the Western provinces. During the second century, moreover,

under the patronage of emperors like Hadrian and Marcus Aurelius, upper-class Greeks from the cities of the Eastern provinces began to enjoy Imperial careers and rose to prominence, as was the case with writers like Appian, Arrian, Cassius Dio, and Plutarch.

Upper-Class Women   In the late Republic, upper-class women had achieved considerable independence and power, which resulted in scandalous behavior and promiscuity in some extreme cases. As one might imagine, many men felt their traditional male dominance threatened, and in the early Empire there was a concerted attempt to put women back in their place. This attempt was bolstered not only by the traditional Roman ideal of the virtuous wife and mother but by widespread Roman exposure to classical Greek literature and philosophy, which tended to view women with a pathological fear, hostility, and insistence on their inherent inferiority. In Roman literature this view can be seen already in the almost universally negative attitude toward female characters in the *Aeneid* and is paramount in the sixth satire of Juvenal over a century later. Officially, it is manifest in Augustus' legislation to promote marriage and punish adultery.

This attempt to return upper-class women to their former subordination did not work, however. The popularity of Ovid's handbook for philanderers, *The Art of Love,* shows the prevailing upper-class attitude toward Augustus' moralism. Promiscuity increased, and two of the most notoriously promiscuous women of the day were the two Julias, Augustus' daughter and granddaughter.

Women of the Imperial and noble families carried on the tradition of vigorously independent aristocratic women and strove to satisfy their own ambitions. Augustus' wife Livia was a real power in his reign and was given the title Augusta in his will. More than once she annoyed Tiberius with her domineering attitude. Messalina took an active part in a plot to overthrow her husband Claudius. Agrippina the Elder was an implacable foe of Tiberius, and Agrippina the Younger maneuvered her son, Nero, to the throne by murder and intrigue, while Trajan's wife, Plotina, helped engineer the smooth succession of Hadrian. Mothers and wives of emperors were often deified or honored in order to exalt their sons and husbands. Their family connections were also advertised in dynastic propaganda as well. Wives of provincial governors were honored by inscriptions and statues for their benefactions, and numerous lesser women were honored for accomplishments as athletes, musicians, and physicians.

After Augustus, the legal status of women also improved in step with social reality. In 126, Hadrian liberalized women's right to make wills, and Marcus Aurelius made it legal for mothers, not just fathers, to inherit from children. Eventually, even the guardianship of women was abolished under Diocletian (A.D. 284–305).

The Lower Classes The lot of lower-class citizens, freedpersons, provincials, and slaves improved somewhat in the first two centuries A.D. in comparison with the first century B.C., but the poor and the powerless, male and female, in any society seldom see dramatic changes in their overall conditions. The general internal peace and prosperity of the period certainly made life a little more secure and less desperate for the great mass of people, and almost all of the emperors tried to alleviate real hardship. They made great efforts to secure a stable grain supply for Rome to sustain those who received free grain and keep the price affordable for the rest. The urban poor also benefited from the emperor's efforts to improve flood control, housing conditions, and the water supply and to upgrade public sanitation through the construction of public latrines and baths. In many of the great provincial cities, wealthy local benefactors often imitated the emperors by undertaking similar projects.

At least in Italy, the rural poor benefited from private charitable endowments and the *alimenta* of Trajan and his successors, but girls always received less per capita than boys. In the provinces the emperors' attempts to provide efficient and honest administration must have kept the peasantry from being exploited so mercilessly as they often had been, but it would be naive to think that all Imperial officials acted so scrupulously as they were supposed to.

While some well-educated Greek freedmen and slaves in the Imperial household had impressive careers, the status of the great majority had not changed. Some freedmen became very wealthy, others practiced middle-class trades and professions, others existed at the poverty level, and all remained second-class citizens despite being eligible for honorific posts such as *Augustalis*. The number of slaves seemed to have declined, but their treatment and status did not materially change. The Romans were still generous with manumissions, as the innumerable funerary inscriptions of freedpersons proves, despite Augustus' attempt to slow down the process by taxing manumissions and limiting the number of slaves that a master could free in his will. There were also attempts to restrain cruel masters, but slaves were still subject to torture as witnesses, and if a slave killed a master, all of his slaves were punished by death.

Middle-Class Prosperity Under the general peace and stability within the Empire during the first two centuries, the wealth of the Empire rose dramatically, and people of moderate means or possessed of talent and enterprise prospered to an extent never known before (and only again in recent times) as agriculture, manufacturing, and trade expanded. The provinces now shared fully in the benefits of the universal peace (*Pax Romana*). Incomes soared and gave rise to an unprecedented urge to travel which was further encouraged by the construction of a huge network of excellent roads. The provinces were urbanized and cities appeared. A traveler in Asia, Africa, Spain, or Gaul might see temples, theaters, libraries, baths, and fine homes differing only in size and splendor from those of Rome. Products of farm and shop moved freely over land and sea, and foreign commerce steadily expanded.

Economic Trends

Provincial Agriculture   While agricultural development had reached the limits of antiquity's relatively static techniques in the "advanced" parts of the Empire, the agricultural potential of the less-developed provinces was rapidly exploited. In Britain, the Yorkshire valley and the broad fields of the southeast soon produced enough grain for export. The raising of sheep for wool, much in demand for clothing the northern armies, seems to have been introduced to the Cotswolds in Gloucestershire. Another center of grain production was in the Belgic province along the Rhine. In southern Gaul, regions that are still famous for their wines became major producers and supplanted Italy in the second century as the suppliers of wine to northern Europe. They even competed in the huge market of Rome itself. Olive groves in Spain and Tunisia produced huge volumes of oil that were widely exported, also at the expense of Italian producers.

The older agricultural lands of the eastern Mediterranean also benefited from the stability and sound administration that characterized the first two centuries A.D. The valley of the Orontes in Syria reached its height as an olive-producing region, grain production flourished on the eastern side of the Jordan River, and irrigated land was increased in Egypt. Moreover, as urbanization spread and the size of cities grew, small farmers nearby found ready markets for fruits, vegetables, cheese, eggs, and poultry.

Mining and Manufacturing   The creation of stable frontiers and the construction of great roads, harbors, and canals throughout the Empire also opened up new sources of raw materials and encouraged the spread of manufacturing. The production of lead ingots and pig iron was of major importance in Britain. Tin, copper, and silver continued to be important in Spain, and the gold mines of the new province of Dacia were vigorously exploited.

In the East, the old manufacturing centers flourished. The workshops of Egypt and Syria produced papyrus, blown glass, textiles, purple dye, and leather goods. Asia Minor supplied marble, pottery, parchment, carpets, and cloth.

In the West, the Italian producers of glass, pottery, and bronze wares sent their products far and wide during the first century but went into decline as provincial centers, especially in Gaul and the Rhineland, took over their export markets during the second. In the first century, Lugdunum (Lyons) in Gaul became the center of the Western glass industry, while Colonia Agrippina (Cologne) in Germany replaced it in the second. *Terra sigillata,* the famous red dinnerware with raised decorations exported from Arretium in Italy, was successfully imitated on a vast scale for western European markets first at Graufesenque and then Lezoux in Gaul and finally at Tres Tabernae in the Rhineland. Tongres in Belgium also produced a popular black pottery, and potteries in Britain made a similar type with a gray slip. Even the famous bronze workers of Capua lost their Western markets to skilled Gallic craftsmen who set up shop at Gressnich.

Imperial Commerce   The negative social and economic impact on Italy of increased commercial agriculture and specialized manufacturing in the Western provinces has been described in the previous chapter (see pp. 354–355). The main reason that the Italians could not compete with provincial producers was the inefficiency of ancient transportation, especially by land. Despite the wonderful system of Imperial roads, transportation by wagon or cart was slow and cumbersome, not least because the ancients harnessed their horses in such a way as to choke them when straining against a load.

Once provincial farmers and craftsmen produced products comparable to those of Italy, their proximity to local markets gave them an unbeatable advantage over Italian exporters. In fact, provincial farmers near the seacoast or on waterways and enjoying easy access to more efficient water transport had a great advantage over farmers from the interior of Italy in shipping to the lucrative markets of Rome and other coastal Italian cities. For example, it was cheaper to ship an amphora of wine from Arelatae (Arles) or Narbo in southern Gaul to Rome by sea than to transport one overland to Rome from only fifty miles away in Italy.

The same factors, however, sharply limited the potential for manufacturing and commerce in the provinces beyond the points achieved by the second century A.D. Only farmers with easy access to water transport could profitably export crops. Moreover, the slowness of transportation and the lack of refrigeration or preservation techniques meant that only spoilage-resistant agricultural products like grain, olive oil, and wine could be shipped long distances. Only expensive manufactured goods whose production was limited by the geographic location of raw materials or highly specialized craftsmen could be profitably exported over significant distances. Therefore, the market for such goods was limited to the well-to-do. The mass of people either had to do without or settle for inferior imitations of local manufacture. As a result, most manufacturing tended to remain small and localized, and commerce was limited.

Foreign Commerce Because of the greater distances involved, foreign commerce was limited to luxury goods, but the increase that did occur in Imperial prosperity stimulated the demand for foreign luxuries and the exploration of foreign trade routes. Roman traders travelled north along the coast of Germany and to the Baltic islands in search of amber and furs. For example, over four thousand Roman coins have been found on the island of Gothland. During the first century, the Parthians had forced diversion of the Chinese silk trade south to India, whence it proceeded by ship to Red Sea ports. By the end of the century, however, Greek and Syrian merchants were making regular contact with silk caravans from China at Bactra (Balkh in north-central Afghanistan) and later, under Hadrian or Antoninus, a little further east at Tashkurgan (Stone Tower).

About the time of Augustus, a Greek sea captain named Hippalus discovered the princi-

ple of the Monsoons, which allowed regular seasonal sailings of merchant fleets between southern Arabia and western India for perfumes, gems, spices, and cotton cloth. By the beginning of the second century, Greek merchants had penetrated to the Punjab. In the course of the first half of the century, they had sailed around southern India and Ceylon to the east coast of India and perhaps as far as Hanoi. In 166, a group even paid court to the Chinese Emperor Huan-ti at Loyang, far up the Yellow River (Hwang-ho) to talk about setting up regular trade by sea with the West. In the long run little was accomplished, however.

There was also trade with non-Roman Africa. During the first century, merchants traded along the Somali coast for frankincense and went as far south as Zanzibar and Mozambique in search of ivory during the second. Explorers even penetrated inland to the sources of the Nile in lakes Victoria and Albert. In North Africa there was a brisk trade through Fezzan with the sub-Sahara regions for exotic animals for the innumerable games at Rome and many other cities.

Inherent Economic and Fiscal Weakness of the Roman Empire Despite the real economic growth of the first two centuries A.D., serious underlying weaknesses appear as early as the time of Nero. They limited the Empire's economic potential and contributed to a long-term decline beginning in the third century. For example, the foreign trade in luxuries had a negative impact. Much of the valuable merchandise was paid for in silver and gold, as the numerous hoards of Roman coins that help document Roman trade routes demonstrate. The elder Pliny complained that under Nero the Indian trade alone drew off sixty million sesterces a year, while the rest of the Eastern trade took another forty million. In the second century, the deficit may have been reduced by the export of some manufactured goods, such as bronze and tin goods, dinnerware, blown glass, woolen cloth, and even rewoven silk. Nevertheless, the most prized Roman products were the Empire's fine coins, and the constant drain of precious metal undermined the stablility of the monetary and financial systems.

Part of the problem lay with the nature of the monetary system itself. Except for local copper and bronze coins used for small change, the system was based upon the circulation of coins whose value was fixed by their actual content of precious metal. Credit, necessary to expand business, was severely limited by the amount of coinage in circulation. If coins were debased to sustain or increase the amount in circulation, prices rose so that no advantage was gained.

By the time of Nero, the productivity of the Spanish gold and silver mines, the main sources of supply, was falling, and that, plus the drain caused by foreign trade and his own overspending, led him to reduce the metallic content of both gold and silver coinage. A serious crisis was temporarily averted when Trajan opened up the gold mines of Dacia to Roman exploitation, but the wars of Marcus Aurelius put severe new strains on the economy.

In spite of the large surplus that Antoninus Pius had reportedly left behind in the treasury, Marcus Aurelius found himself obliged to sell the palace jewels and treasures in order to finance the Danubian campaigns and to debase the silver currency by raising its copper content to approximately thirty-four percent. To meet the crises of the third century, later emperors further debased the coinage almost to the point of total collapse, with great damage to trade commerce and economic hardship for all.

Further problems were created by the general fiscal policies of the emperors. In times of peace the revenues of the Empire barely covered expenditures. The mounting costs of government and Imperial bureaucracy, the donatives given to the troops, the vast sums spent on education and public welfare, monuments and public buildings, and relief to stricken communities normally left nothing in reserve to meet unexpected civil or military emergencies. The cancellation of arrears and reduction of taxes together with an inefficient system of tax collection kept the state perpetually on the brink of bankruptcy.

Instead of increasing the regular taxes and extending their collection to every part of the Empire, the emperors often resorted to extraordinary taxation, confiscations of capital, requisitions of money, food, and transport for the army, or compulsory labor, almost all of which fell on the agricultural sector of the economy. These disruptive levies increased dramatically during the third century and not only imposed hardship upon the municipalities and rich men made responsible for their collection, but sometimes drove peasants and tenants to strike, revolt, flee their occupations, or become brigands.

The Failure of Ancient Technology   Yet it would be erroneous to suppose that the crippling burden of taxation, the aristocratic comsumption of imported luxuries, bad financial policies, the prodigious demands of Imperial defense and government, and frequent civil wars after the second century alone provide an adequate explanation of the economic decline that can be traced from the third century onward. The root of the trouble lay rather in the persistent failure of Graeco-Roman society to transform pure science into productive technology. Although the Greeks had an impressive record of achievement in the history of theoretical science and mathematics, and in the Hellenistic period owed to Archimedes (ca. 287–212 B.C.), to Hero of Alexandria (?ca. 150 B.C.), and others the invention of many mechanical contrivances, such as the endless chain, the compound pulley, the lifting crane, the steam engine, and the reaction turbine, they never succeeded in putting these inventions to practical use to save labor, increase productive capacity, and build an industrial civilization capable of bearing the financial load of a highly centralized bureaucratic state.

The clue to the ancient failure to transform science into an industrial technology may be found not only in the slave syndrome (which had been breaking down since Augustan times) and the aristocratic leisure-class contempt for work, but also in the failure of ancient education, which reflected and perpetuated the attitudes of a class that had little to do directly with economic production. The undue emphasis upon rhetoric to the exclusion of science and practical technological training was designed to produce lawyers, administrators, and professors of rhetoric rather than scientists and industrial engineers and technicians.

The rapid disappearance of slave labor and the shortage of free labor made the need for industrial technology and for labor-saving machines particularly acute to meet the mounting crises faced by the Empire after the second century. Without them the Empire could not meet its greatly increased military needs and maintain a healthy civilian economy at the same time. Therefore, the third century began a period of serious decline.

XXXI

Crisis and Temporary Recovery under the Severi, A.D. 180 to 235

The period from the death of Marcus Aurelius in 180 to the accession of Diocletian in 285 is one of the most difficult, confusing, and misunderstood periods of Roman history. Recently, scholars have focused increasingly upon it, however, and a more detailed and reliable picture can be created than ever before. This period can be divided into two almost equal portions. The first extends from the death of Marcus Aurelius in 180 to the assassination of Severus Alexander, last of the Severi, in 235. During this time the borders of the Empire remained intact, though under pressure, and there were only two serious internal political crises: from 193 to early 197 and from 217 to 221. The second stretches from 235 to the victory of Diocletian in 285, when frequent civil wars and assassinations saw the rapid rise and fall of twenty-six emperors or pretenders, constant breakthroughs on the borders, and the near breakup of the Empire under these two stresses.

Despite the differences between the first and second halves of the century from 180 to 285, several trends can be traced throughout that give it unity. While the city of Rome itself remained of great symbolic significance, actual power shifted to more strategic locations near the borders, whose defense demanded ever more attention. The growing importance of defense and the provinces is clearly illustrated by the fact that almost all of the emperors were generals of provincial birth, many from the Danubian provinces, where the problems of defense were often acute and where many of the Empire's best soldiers were recruited.

The growing importance of the provinces and the parallel decline of Roman and Italian primacy also led to increasing regionalism, sectionalism, and disunity. Often the armies and inhabitants of one province or region would support a rival claimant to an emperor or challenger from another part of the Empire because they feared that they and their problems would be ignored while the other province or region received special attention. At times, some areas even broke away under their own emperors.

As defense and personal safety became the overriding concerns of emperors, their office increasingly lost the characteristics of a civilian magistracy that it had retained since the days of Augustus; it gradually became an absolute monarchy resting upon raw military power and the trappings of divine kingship along Near Eastern and Hellenistic lines. Also, as the emperors tried to mobilize all the state's resources to meet its defensive needs, the bulk of its people sank into the status of suffering subjects instead of satisfied citizens. While the few wealthy and influential senators and equestrians were neutralized and co-opted by grants of greater social and legal privileges and lucrative posts in the Imperial bureaucracy, the lower classes were made legally inferior and subject to even greater oppression in the name of the state, which in better times under more benevolent emperors had afforded them some measure of protection and dignity. Finally, the common people suffered increasing financial hardship as the burdens of defense, poor fiscal management, excessive taxation of agriculture, and destruction from civil wars and invasions undermined the fragile economy of the Empire.

Sources for Roman History, A.D. 180 to 285 The difficulty of understanding the complex period from 180 to 285, especially the second part, arises from the lack of reliable written accounts. Cassius Dio's later and most valuable books (except 79 and 80), which covered his own times, are preserved only in epitomes and fragments. Valuable information about the period from 180 to 238 is contained in the eight extant books of Herodian's contemporary history and the late-fourth-century *Historia Augusta,* but the biographies of emperors after 235 in the latter work are more romantic fiction than history. Minor relevant historical works from the fourth century include biographies like Aurelius Victor's *Caesares* and the anonymous *Epitome de Caesaribus* and brief histories of Rome like those of Eutropius and Festus (see p. 515). The fifth-century Greek historian Zosimus also covered the period in his history of Rome from Augustus to A.D. 410.

Christian writers became more numerous and important during the third century and have supplied much information not only on the history and doctrinal controversies of the expanding Christian Church but on secular affairs as well. Among the Latin Christian authors, the most notable in this period are Tertullian (ca. 160–ca. 230) and St. Cyprian (ca. 200–258). Tertullian was trained as a lawyer and lived at Carthage. He is the first known author to have formulated the orthodox doctrine of the Trinity. His numerous works reveal much about the social life of the period and the emerging Christian ideals of personal behavior for women. St. Cyprian counted Tertullian among his teachers and became bishop of Carthage. His works are particularly valuable for the history of the persecution of Christians that occurred in the 250s and the Donatist controversy over Christians who denied their religion during the persecution and then wanted to be accepted among the faithful afterward. Also valuable for this period are two compilations of St. Jerome (ca. 330–420): a chronicle from the Creation to 378 and a history of Christian literature.

Of the contemporary Greek Church Fathers, Clement of Alexandria (ca. 150–ca. 215) and Origen (ca. 185–ca. 255) stand out. Clement helped to impart aspects of Greek philosophy to Christian theology, and his works provided unusual glimpses into the pagan Greek mysteries that he combated. Origen, who studied under Clement, left works on many topics: textual criticism, interpretive commentaries on scripture, Church doctrine, Christian apologetics, and worship. Eusebius of Caesarea in Palestine (ca. 260–ca. 340) produced two historical works that are valuable in reconstructing the third century. His chronicle of events from Abraham to A.D. 325 is lost, but its substance is preserved in Jerome's similar work based largely on it. Fortunately, his *Ecclesiastical History* is intact and is an invaluable general account of the growth of the early Church in the Empire.

Preserved in Justinian's *Corpus Iuris Civilis* are numerous fragments of third century legal works which, together with coins, papyri, inscriptions, and archaeological material, are all excellent primary sources. Although these sources have not yet been fully explored or interpreted, they constitute the bulk of information about the third century and are constantly throwing new light upon it. Increasing interest in local archaeology throughout countries once embraced by the Roman Empire has also produced a better understanding of defensive policies and the social and economic conditions of the provinces.

Commodus (180–192) The third century A.D. in Roman history really began with the reign of Commodus, the unworthy son of Marcus Aurelius. Aurelius had no other reasonable choice than to let Commodus succeed him, but he had tried to ensure the continuation of good leadership by creating a coterie of good advisors close to the throne. For example, he married Commodus' sister Lucilla to Claudius Pompeianus, one of his own most trusted advisors. Unfortunately, the young Emperor received divided counsel upon the death of his father. Some, like Pompeianus, wanted him to finish the great war with the Quadi and Marcomanni that his father had successfully begun. Others, whether out of conviction or desire to advance in the new Emperor's favor, or both, advised him to follow the easier path of negotiating a settlement and returning to Rome.

This move seems completely irresponsible at first sight, but a negotiated settlement had much to recommend itself. The war had already placed a great strain on Imperial resources, the Roman army had been weakened by plague, and while a border based on the Elbe River and the Carpathian Mountains did have some strategic advantages over the longer Rhine-Danube line, it would greatly extend the Empire's lines of supply through territory that would take a long time and many troops to pacify adequately.

Moreover, Commodus and those to whom he listened did follow certain well-established precedents in setting terms, which the Quadi and Marcomanni readily accepted. The latter agreed to surrender Roman deserters and captives, create a demilitarized zone along the Danube, furnish troops to the Roman army, and help feed that army with annual contributions of grain. This settlement was reasonable and produced stability along

the Danube for many years. In abandoning Aurelius' scheme of conquest, Commodus also could point to the example of Hadrian, who wisely abandoned Trajan's plans despite objections from Trajan's old advisors.

Unfortunately, the young and inexperienced Commodus was no Hadrian. Instead of devoting his energies to conscientious administration, military preparedness, and internal development, Commodus headed for a life of ease. Once at Rome, he increasingly abandoned himself to physical pleasures, which are predictably exaggerated in the sources but which became more numerous, probably at the urging of those who curried favor and sought to avoid his interference by steering him along a path of self-indulgence. Though he outraged the upper-class sense of propriety by staging lion and tiger hunts in the Colosseum, he delighted the crowd by his feats. He developed such skill with the javelin that he could hit the neck of an ostrich at fifty paces, but he exhausted the treasury by his wild extravagance and mad career of dissipation. Furthermore, he delegated important responsibilities to various favorites, whom he murdered as soon as he tired of them.

As early as 182, a number of senators conspired with Commodus' sister Lucilla to assassinate the irresponsible leader whom they detested and feared to be undermining the Empire. The plot failed, however, and the Emperor naturally became fearful, suspicious, and vindictive. Under the guidance of such schemers as the Praetorian Prefect Perennis, who himself was executed for treason in 185, Commodus produced another reign of terror among the aristocracy and courtiers. The accelerating cycle of corruption, extravagance, and terror finally led to a successful plot by the Praetorian Prefect Aemilius Laetus, the chamberlain Eclectus, and Commodus' rejected mistress Marcia, who bribed his favorite wrestling partner to strangle him in his bath on the last day of 192.

Pertinax and Didius Julianus, 193 Just as Domitian's assassins had carefully arranged to provide the elderly Nerva as his successor, so Commodus' assassins had arranged for the elderly senator Pertinax, a successful *novus homo* from Africa, who was influential under Aurelius. He was quickly approved by the Praetorian Guard at Laetus' prompting and by a grateful senate and the populace, both of whom condemned Commodus' memory. Pertinax attempted to restore order and refill the treasury. He reduced taxes, granted full posssession and a ten-years remission of taxes to occupiers of war-torn and plague-depopulated land, and put up for sale the treasures that Commodus had accumulated in his palace—fine silks and costly robes and cloaks, gladiatorial paraphernalia and chariots, and most of the human resources of pleasure and vice.

Unfortunately, he made two serious mistakes. By selling off high offices to raise needed money, he alienated many senators who had been offended by the practice under Commodus. Also, like Galba after Nero, Pertinax alienated the Praetorian Guard by failing to make promised payments and by his attempt to make them submit to strict discipline. Several hundred guardsmen marched on the palace and murdered him. The guardsmen thereupon auctioned off the throne to a fabulously rich senator, M. Didius Julianus, who promised each man the sum of twenty-five thousand sesterces. Helpless, the senate confirmed the nomination.

Goaded to action by this outrageous affront to the august Imperial office, the Roman people assailed Julianus with vile names and pelted him with stones as he made his way in and out of his palace under armed escort. Then they thronged into the Circus, where they passed a resolution calling upon Pescennius Niger, the governor of Syria, to rise in arms and seize the throne. The legions of Syria saluted the governor as emperor. Simultaneously the armies of Britain and the Danube declared for their respective commanders, Clodius Albinus and Septimius Severus, and made a dash for Rome. Septimius got there first and with boldness and decision seized the throne. At first Julianus attempted to resist Severus

and then to negotiate, but deserted by the praetorians who had sold him the throne and deposed by the senate, he sought refuge in the palace, where a guardsman found him and put him to death.

The Accession of Septimius Severus

Septimius Severus, born in 146 at Leptis Magna, a town not far from Tripoli, was the second native of Africa to hold the throne, proof of the growing importance of the provinces. He had had an active career: a student of literature and philosophy in Athens, a lawyer in Rome, a tribune of the people, a praetor in Spain, and governor of Gallia Lugdunensis and finally of Pannonia. Though he spoke Latin with a Punic accent, he was well educated and loved the company of poets and philosophers. His second wife was a rich, beautiful, and intelligent Syrian woman named Julia Domna, who also had the reputation of being quite promiscuous. She bore him two sons—Caracalla and Geta.

Severus moved swiftly to consolidate his power. He seized the various treasuries, restocked the depleted granaries of the city, and avenged the murder of Pertinax, whose name he assumed. He increased the pay of his own troops to make sure of their continued loyalty and disbanded the Italian Praetorian Guard. He then replaced it with fifteen thousand of his best legionary soldiers, who had been recruited largely in Illyria and Thrace. The change in the composition of the Guard helped to remove the special privileges of Italy in the choosing of emperors and in the govenment of the Empire.

The War against Pescennius Niger, 193 to 194 Severus thereupon set about dealing with one rival at a time. He temporarily acknowledged Albinus as Caesar and adopted successor in order to secure his rear as he advanced against Niger. Niger had meanwhile won the support of Roman Asia and Egypt and had seized Byzantium as a base from which he could threaten the Danubian provinces of Severus. In a swift and savage campaign, Severus defeated Niger and captured Antioch.

Niger was overtaken and killed as he attempted to escape to the Parthians across the Euphrates.

First War against Parthia, 194 to 195
After Niger's defeat and death, Severus attacked Parthia, whose king, Vologeses IV, had not only offered assistance to Niger but had tampered with the loyalty and allegiance of the king of Osrhoene, a Roman client in western Mesopotamia. In 194/95, Severus overran Osrhoene, northern Mesopotamia, and Adiabene (the modern Azerbaijan). Here the campaign came to an abrupt end. At the other end of the Empire, Albinus had amassed an army in Britain for the conflict with Septimius.

Albinus had been growing suspicious of the Emperor's sincerity in acknowledging him as Caesar and successor. Supported by a large following in the senate, he decided to make a bid for supreme power. To enforce his claim, he crossed over into Gaul and set up headquarters at Lugdunum (Lyons). It is no coincidence that he received considerable support in Gaul, Spain, and Germany as well as Britain against Severus, who was closely tied to Africa, the Danubian provinces, and Asia Minor. Severus hastened west, and the two fought a furious battle that ended in the defeat and suicide of Albinus. Severus allowed his victorious troops to sack and burn the city of Lugdunum and carried out a ruthless extermination of the adherents of Albinus in the provinces and in the Roman senate.

New Sources of Imperial Authority and Legitimacy

Although Septimius had arrived in Rome at the head of an army in 193, he had tried to conciliate and cooperate with the senate in order to legitimize his claim to the throne against his rivals. He had already taken the name of Pertinax so that he could pose as the avenger of the previously slain senatorial appointee. In Rome he had donned civilian dress and had sworn to the senators that he would never execute a senator without a trial by his peers. He also had promised not to encourage the use of informers.

How sincere Septimius may have been is difficult to say, because the senatorial leaders gave him little chance to prove himself. Many in the senate either distrusted him or, because he had been born a provincial of only equestrian rank, disliked him. Clodius Albinus was much more acceptable to them because he was of the hereditary nobility and had served faithfully under Marcus Aurelius, a scrupulous protector of senatorial prestige. By obviously promoting the fortunes of Albinus they were bound to provoke Septimius' wrath. Therefore, after he had secured the East against Pescennius Niger and Parthia, Septimius dropped the policy of conciliation with the senate and formally relied on the army as his principal source of authority in establishing himself and his family as a new dynasty at Rome.

In the past the army had been used to force the senate to authorize an action, such as the appointment of a new emperor, because it was the recognized source of legitimate authority. Septimius, however, went a long way to making the army the recognized source of authority instead. For example, in 195 he had the army in Mesopotamia declare Albinus a public enemy in order to legitimize the war against him. In the same year he also had the army ratify his adoption into the family of Marcus Aurelius, the Antonines, and proclaim the deification of his "brother" Commodus. (Since the senate itself had condemned the memory of Commodus, he also forced it to revoke its previous action.) In 196 he had the army proclaim his elder son, Septimius Bassianus (Caracalla), as Caesar in place of Clodius Albinus and bestow the name Marcus Aurelius Antoninus upon him in order to emphasize the family's new Antonine pedigree.

This pedigree not only legitimized the claim of Septimius and his sons to the throne through dynastic succession but also allowed Septimius to claim the support of divinity for himself and his family, since he was now the "son" and "brother" of deified emperors. Along with publicizing numerous omens and portents foretelling his accession to the throne, Septimius officially reinforced his claims to divine sanction through coins, inscriptions, and the Imperial cult. In the military camps, the statues of Septimius and other members of his family were worshipped as the *domus divina* (Divine House). Septimius unofficially came to be called *dominus* (lord), a title with increasingly divine overtones. On one coin his younger son, Geta, is depicted as the sun god crowned with rays, giving a benediction, and identified as "Son of Severus the Unconquered, Pius Augustus," a designation that recalls the Unconquered Sun, an increasingly popular deity. Severus' wife, Julia Domna, is portrayed as the Great Mother Cybele on some coins and on others as seated on the throne of Juno, Mother of the Augusti, Mother of the Senate, or Mother of the Fatherland (*Mater Patriae*). Severus is also referred to in inscriptions as a *numen praesens* (present spirit), and dedications were made to him as a *numen,* clear indications of his divinity.

Systematic Reform   Having defeated Albinus and clearly established new bases of Imperial authority and legitimacy, Septimius Severus initiated the most comprehensive series of changes in the Roman government since the reign of Augustus. Up to his time, many changes had occurred, but they had been subtle and evolutionary. What Severus did was often in line with changes that had been gradually occurring, but he was the first to give them formal expression, and he was revolutionary in ruthlessly following their implications to create a clearly new system that gave an entirely different spirit to the Principate.

Major Downgrading of the Senate   With his rivals out of the way, Severus took his revenge on the senate. He revoked its right to try its own members and condemned twenty-nine of them for treason in supporting Albinus. He also appointed many new members, particularly from Africa and the East, who would be loyal to him, so that Italian senators became a minority. Moreover, he favored *equites* of military background over senators in adminis-

trative appointments. The *equites* had been making steady gains since Augustus, but with Septimius their rise became more abrupt. He appointed equestrian deputy governors in senatorial provinces and used *equites* as temporary replacements when regular senatorial governors became ill or died. When he added three new legions to the army, he put equestrian prefects instead of senatorial legates in command. He also abolished the senatorially staffed standing jury courts (*quaestiones perpetuae*) and placed cases formerly heard by them under the jurisdiction of the City Prefect (*praefectus urbi*) within a one-hundred-mile radius of Rome and the Praetorian Prefect (*praefectus praetorio*) everywhere else.

As the result of a process of evolution dating back to Augustus, the senate had become simply a sounding board of policies formulated by the *princeps* and his Imperial Council, which had now become the true successor of the old Republican senate. Since its inception the Council had grown in membership and now included not only many of the leading senators and equestrians but the best legal minds of the age—Papinian, and later, Ulpian and Paulus.

The powers of Praetorian Prefect were greatly increased: he also presided over the grain administration, was commander-in-chief of all armed forces stationed in Italy, and was vice-president of the Imperial Council, the supreme court of the Empire and its highest policy-making body. From 197 to 205 the senior praetorian prefect was C. Fulvius Plautianus, a man of extreme ambition, arrogance, and cruelty, who wielded almost autocratic power because of his overpowering personality and his influence over the Emperor. He finally fell from favor and was assassinated. The next senior prefect was the distinguished jurist, Papinian.

Financial Reforms   The confiscations of property belonging to political enemies in both East and West were so enormous that Severus created the *res privata principis* (the private property of the *princeps*), a new treasury department separate and distinct from the *fiscus,* the regular Imperial treasury, and from the *patrimonium Caesaris.* The new treasury, administered by a procurator, gave the Emperor a stronger control not only over the financial administration of the Empire but over the army, whose annual pay he probably raised from 375 to 500 denarii per man. (This increase was also necessary in order to compensate for the inflation that had raged since the reign of Commodus.) Furthermore, need for money forced Severus to reduce the silver content of the *denarius* to fifty percent. Nevertheless, his financial administration was actually sounder than that of many of his predecessors and brought about a temporary revival of economic prosperity and a fairly respectable surplus in the treasury

Legal Reforms Several legal reforms of Septimius were implicit in those of Hadrian, especially in the jurist Julianus' revision of the *Perpetual Edict.* The major Severan reform was the already mentioned abolition of the regular standing jury courts of Republican times and the transfer of their cases to the jurisdiction of the Urban Prefect and the Praetorian Prefect. Another significant Severan innovation, however, was the introduction of different scales of punishment for the two social classes into which the citizen body was now divided—the *honestiores,* consisting of senators, *equites,* all municipal magistrates, and soldiers of all ranks, and the *humiliores,* or lower orders. A privileged person might be exiled or cleanly executed, an underprivileged one sentenced to hard labor in the mines or thrown to the beasts for the same crime. Furthermore, *honestiores* had the right of appeal to the Emperor, *humiliores* had not. This change in criminal procedure continued to be reflected in the feudal society of the Middle Ages.

Provincial Administration In general, the provincial policy of Septimius Severus was a corollary of that of Hadrian and the Antonines, who had begun to raise the status of the provinces to equal that of Italy. Severus continued this policy, not out of hatred for Italy, but purely because of political and

dynastic motives. His disbanding of the Italian Praetorian Guard and his appointments of Near Eastern and African senators had been measures undertaken principally to consolidate his regime. He stationed one of his newly created legions in Italy, the other two in Mesopotamia to show that he regarded Italy as not more secure than one of the most exposed frontier provinces of the Empire. Though he spent money liberally in Rome and Italy on public works, on the feeding and amusement of the Roman populace, and on the resumption of the public alimentary and educational program (which Commodus had suspended), he spent equally vast amounts in Africa and Syria. Thus the Severan regime was the consummation of a policy begun by earlier emperors leading to a balance, equalization, and fusion of the various geographical and cultural elements of the Greco-Roman world.

As a precaution against the dangerous concentration of power in the hands of provincial governors who might prove as dangerous as Pescennius Niger and Clodius Albinus, Septimius followed the policy of Augustus, Trajan, and Hadrian and partitioned large, legion-filled provinces. He divided Syria and Britain each into two separate provinces and detached Numidia from Africa, to create smaller provinces and correspondingly weaker provincial governors.

Military Reforms Owing his power entirely to the soldiers and genuinely concerned to provide adequate defense, Septimius made significant improvements to the army, not only by increasing its size from thirty to thirty-three legions, but by making army life as attractive as possible.

Septimius made army life more attractive by allowing junior officers to organize social clubs, to which all contributed for drinks, entertainment, and financial insurance during service and after discharge. He legalized marriages between soldiers defending the Empire's frontiers and native women living near forts and encampments. Thus he abolished anomalous marriages long in existence, but not officially countenanced. The Praetorian Guard, though no longer composed solely of Italians, Western provincials, and Macedonians, continued to be an elite corps, trained in the best Roman tradition, and still remained a renowned training school for future army officers.

In his reorganization of the army, Severus began to replace senatorial commanders with *equites,* who were often excenturions promoted from the ranks. The commanders of his three new legions were no longer senatorial *legati* but equestrian prefects with the rank of *legatus,* some of them eligible for provincial governorships. Severus democratized the army by making it possible for a common soldier of ability and initiative to pass from centurion on to the rank of tribune, prefect, and *legatus,* and eventually to the high office of Praetorian Prefect, if not Emperor. Even ordinary veterans became a privileged class rewarded with good jobs in the civilian bureaucracy after discharge. Along with raising the pay of the legionaries, he also permanently leased lands from the Imperial estate to certain auxiliary units, who thus became a permanent peasant militia in their sector of the frontier.

Second Parthian War, 197 to 199 In foreign policy, Septimius adhered closely to his predecessors. He continued the historic war (interrupted under Hadrian and Antoninus Pius) against the Parthian Empire without realizing that such a policy had become untenable and even dangerous, in view of changed world conditions. He was unaware that the steppes of Central Asia had for centuries been the spawning ground for migrating Huns and other barbarian tribes who would one day descend like an avalanche upon both the Roman Empire and its neighbors. The resources and manpower of the Empire, though huge, were inadequate for waging war simultaneously against the barbarians and the Parthians.

Another dangerous consequence of the Severan resumption of war against Parthia was the further weakening of the weak and ineffectual Arsacid dynasty, which had held

sway over Parthia ever since 238 B.C., and its final overthrow in A.D. 227. As a result of Roman assaults the Arsacid dynasty eventually gave way to the more dynamic and revolutionary Sassanid dynasty and the new Persian Empire founded by Ardashir I (224–241), who was succeeded by his son, Shapur I (241–272), the most formidable opponent of Rome in the Near East since the days of Mithridates VI of Pontus. Shapur I so harassed the Romans that only after his death were they able to muster enough force to drive out the Germans who had burst in over the northern and western frontiers.

The War in Britain, 208 to 211 In the last years of his reign, Septimius, accompanied by his sons Caracalla and Geta, led an expedition into the heart of Scotland but failed in his attempt to bring the natives to battle. They resorted instead to guerrilla tactics and inflicted heavy losses upon the Roman army. Despite the losses and the apparent failure of the whole campaign, Septimius achieved important results: the display of Roman power and the thorough reconstruction of Hadrian's Wall effectively discouraged future invasions of England from the North and gave Britain almost a century of peace. Septimius, however, was not to see Rome again: he died at York in 211. According to Dio, Severus on his deathbed advised his sons, Caracalla and Geta, to "agree with each other, enrich the soldiers, and despise everyone else." Probably these words are rhetorical inventions, but they are significant in their emphasis upon favoring the military and their contrast with the failure of his heirs to work together.

Caracalla (211–217) Septimius dead, Caracalla and Geta together ascended the throne, but their attempt at joint rule proved hopeless. Each lived in mortal dread of the other until Caracalla treacherously lured Geta to their mother's apartment and there murdered him, supposedly in his mother's very arms. Afterward, he carried out a pitiless extermination of Geta's supposed friends and supporters, among them the illustrious jurist and Praetorian Prefect Papinian. To silence the murmurs of the soldiers over Geta's killing, he increased their pay from 500 to 750 denarii, an expenditure that exhausted the treasury and compelled him to raise more revenue by doubling the tax on inheritances and the manumission of slaves and by slightly deflating the currency. He issued a new coin called the *Antoninianus,* supposedly a double denarius but actually not equal in weight. He also earned the undying hatred of many nobles by continuing his father's policy of downgrading the importance of the senate while favoring the soldiers and the provincials.

Caracalla, who got his name from a long Gallic cape that he used to wear, was a fairly good soldier and strategist and had some of the instincts of the statesman. The most historic act of his reign was the extension of citizenship in 212 to all free inhabitants of the Empire, the culmination of a process initiated by Julius Caesar. By his promulgation of the famous *Constitutio Antoniniana,* Caracalla obliterated all distinction between Italians and provincials, between conquerors and conquered, between urban and rural dwellers, and between those who possessed Greco-Roman culture and those who did not. Henceforth, every free inhabitant of the Roman Empire was a Roman citizen and, of course, a Roman taxpayer.

Another manifestation of Caracalla's statesmanship was his proposal of marriage to the daughter of Artabanus V of Parthia in order to bring to pass his dream of uniting the Roman and Parthian empires. He hoped that the two great civilizing powers might present a common front to the barbarians beyond the frontiers, but it is difficult to see how either the Roman or Persian aristocracies would have tolerated such an arrangement.

German and Parthian Wars   What Caracalla had failed to achieve by diplomacy he tried to accomplish by war. In 213 he left Rome, never to return. The major part of his reign was spent in war, and Caracalla proved

himself a real soldier emperor: he ate and marched with his men and helped them dig trenches, build bridges, and fight battles.

Caracalla first proceeded to the Rhaetian *limes* to attack the Alemanni, a formidable but newly organized confederacy of mixed resident and displaced tribes that had migrated westward and settled along the right bank of the upper Rhine. After decisively defeating them on the Main, he built and restored forts, repaired roads and bridges, and extended a 105-mile stone wall from six to nine feet high and four feet thick along the Rhaetian frontier, which successfully withstood barbarian assault for the next twenty years.

After similarly strengthening the defenses in Pannonia and along the lower Danube, Caracalla proceeded to the East. He brutally suppressed an uprising in Alexandria and resumed the war against Parthia. In 216 he marched across Adiabene and invaded Media but, after sacking several fortified places, he withdrew to winter quarters at Edessa. There he made preparations to mount a more vigorous offensive the following spring, but he did not live to witness the consummation of his plans. On April 8, 217, while traveling from Edessa to Carrhae to worship at the temple of the Moon, he was stabbed to death at the instigation of the Praetorian Prefect M. Opellius Macrinus.

The most unfortunate result of Caracalla's abortive campaign against Parthia was the further weakening of an already decrepit regime and its final overthrow in 227 by the aggressive Persian dynasty of Ardashir I and Shapur I, who immediately set about recovering all the territories once ruled by the Achaemenid dynasty of ancient Persia (ca. 560–330 B.C.).

Macrinus (217–218)   M. Opellius Macrinus, the ringleader of the plot against Caracalla, secured the acclamation of the army and ascended the throne. He was a Mauretanian by birth, an *eques* in rank, and the first *princeps* without prior membership in the senate to reach the throne. To affiliate himself to the Severan dynasty he adopted the name of Severus, bestowed that of Antoninus upon his young son Diadumenianus, and even ordered the senate to proclaim Caracalla a god. Realizing that he needed some military prestige in order to hold the loyalty of the army, he embarked upon a war with Parthia, but he proved to be a poor general. After a few minor successes and two major defeats, he lost the respect of the army by his agreement to surrender to the Parthians the prisoners whom he had captured and to pay a large indemnity. This inglorious settlement, together with his unwise decision to reduce the pay for new recruits and the opposition of Severus' family, ultimately cost him his life and throne.

Impressive Syrian Queens Through his second marriage, Septimius Severus was connected with a family of remarkable Syrian women who actively sought a leading role in Imperial politics. His wife, Julia Domna, and her sister, Julia Maesa, were well educated, shrewd, and tough. Domna had enjoyed great influence at the beginning of Severus' reign but had been outmaneuvered for a time by the ambitious Praetorian Prefect Plautianus and had devoted herself to creating an intellectual circle of influential men. She was able to recover her former strength after the fall of Plautianus, to which she probably contributed through Caracalla, and she had accompanied Severus to Britain in 208. After his death she had tried to promote the interests of her more even-tempered son, Geta, but failing to prevent his murder, she had made the best of it with Caracalla. She accompanied Caracalla to Antioch on his Parthian expedition in 215 and died there soon after his assassination. Macrinus forced her sister, Maesa, to retire to Syria, and there she plotted to restore her family's Imperial fortunes.

Maesa had gone with her two daughters, Soaemias and Mamaea, to live in Emesa, a Syrian town just north of Damascus and not far from the Lebanon. Here Varius Avitus, the fourteen-year-old son of Soaemias, served as high priest of the Syrian sun god, Elagabal, and therefore received the name of Elagabalus or, more fittingly, Heliogabalus.

Heliogabalus (218–222) Knowing how the army cherished the memory of Caracalla, Maesa concocted the rumor that Varius Avitus was the natural son of Caracalla and therefore a real Severus. She presented him to the legions of Syria, who, further convinced by the offer of a large donative, saluted him as Emperor under the name of Marcus Aurelius Antoninus. Macrinus, deserted by most of his troops and defeated in battle, fled, but was later hunted down and killed.

A year later, wearing a purple silk robe, rouge on his cheeks, a necklace of pearls, and a bejeweled crown, Heliogabalus arrived in Rome. He had brought from Emesa a conical black stone—the cult image of Elagabal—which he enshrined in an ornate temple on the Palatine and worshipped with un-Roman sexual practices (which probably have been exaggerated in the retelling by hostile and sensationalistic sources) and outlandish rites to the accompaniment of drums, cymbals, and anthems sung by Syrian women. What shocked the Roman public even more than any of these strange rites was his endeavor to make the Syrian sun god, Elagabal, the supreme deity of the Roman state.

In order to devote more time to his priestly duties and debaucheries, he entrusted most of the business of government to his grandmother and appointed his favorites to the highest public offices—a professional dancer, for example, as praetorian prefect, a charioteer as head of the police and fire department, and a barber as prefect of the grain administration.

Maesa, realizing that the idiotic conduct of Heliogabalus would lead to his downfall and the ruin of the Severan family, tactfully suggested that he ought to adopt Gessius Bassianus Alexianus, her other grandson, as Caesar and heir to the throne. When Heliogabalus saw that Alexianus, whom he adopted under the name of Marcus Aurelius Severus Alexander, was preferred by the senate and the people, he regretted his decision and twice attempted to get rid of the boy.

Maesa and Mamaea appealed to the Praetorian Guards, who were happy to hunt down Heliogabalus and his mother, Soaemias. They seized the two in their hiding place: a latrine. They cut off their heads and dragged the corpses through the streets to the Aemilian bridge. There they tied weights to them and hurled them into the Tiber.

Severus Alexander (222–235) The ascension of Severus Alexander was greeted with rejoicing. Though only fourteen, he was studious, talented, and industrious. Actually, his mother, the dominating Julia Mamaea, held the reins of power. She was virtually, even to the end of his reign, the first Empress of Rome.

The reign of Alexander marked the revival of the prestige, if not the power, of the senate, whose support Mamaea sought to enlist in order to strengthen the arm of the civil government in controlling the unruly and mutinous armies. She accordingly set up a council of sixteen prominent senators to serve nominally as a regency, though actually, perhaps, only in an advisory capacity. Senators also probably held a majority in the enlarged Imperial Council. The president of both councils was the praetorian prefect, normally of equestrian rank, but now elevated while in office to senatorial status in order that he might sit as judge in trials involving senators without impairing the dignity of the defendants. At this time the praetorian prefect was the distinguished jurist, Domitius Ulpianus. Thus the new regime not only enhanced the dignity of the senate but enlarged the powers of the praetorian prefect. It also continued to weaken the old executive offices under Severus Alexander; the tribunes of the plebs and aediles ceased to be appointed.

Social and Economic Policy The government seems to have tried to win the goodwill and support of the civilian population by providing honest and efficient administration. It reduced taxes, and authorized the construction of new baths, aqueducts, libraries, and roads. It subsidized teachers and scholars and lent money without interest to enable poor people to purchase farms. One major reform was the provision of primary school education all over the Empire, even in the villages of Egypt. Another was the legalization, under government supervision and control, of all guilds or colleges (*collegia*) having to do with the supply of foodstuffs and essential services to the people of Rome. Under this category fell wine and oil merchants, bakers, and shoemakers. In return the guilds enjoyed special tax favors and exemptions and the benefit of legal counsel at public expense.

The Military Problem The fatal weakness of Alexander's regime was its failure to control the armies. In 228 the Praetorian Guard mutinied and murdered, in the Emperor's palace itself, their prefect, Domitius Ulpianus, because he seemed too strict. The Mesopotamian army mutinied and murdered their commander. Another excellent disciplinarian, the historian Dio Cassius, would have suffered the same fate, had not Alexander whisked him off to his homeland of Bithynia.

Never had the need for disciplined armies been greater than in 226/27. The new Iranian regime of Ardashir I was waging a war of aggression against Rome: he had already overrun Mesopotamia and was threatening the provinces of Syria and Cappadocia. In 232, after a futile diplomatic effort, Alexander himself had to go to the East. He planned and executed a massive three pronged attack which should have ensured a decisive victory, but, because of poor generalship and excessive caution, it resulted only in heavy losses on both sides and at best produced nothing more than a stalemate. Alexander returned to Rome to celebrate a splendid but dubious triumph.

Meanwhile, the Alemanni and other German tribes had broken through the Roman defenses and were pouring into Gaul and

Rhaetia. Accompanied by his mother, Alexander hurried north. After some early successes, he foolishly followed his mother's suggestion and bought peace from the Germans with a subsidy. His men, who would have preferred to use some of that money themselves, were disgusted. Under the leadership of the commander of the Pannonian legions, Maximinus the Thracian, they mutinied in 235 and killed both Alexander and his mother. Thus they terminated the Severan dynasty and ushered in almost a half century of civil wars that were made more intractable by such problems as Severus Alexander had faced on the borders of the Empire.

The Importance of the Severi The Severi had been responding to a number of circumstances that made necessary many of the things that they tried to do, however one may wish to criticize the manner in which they often acted. The greatest task facing any emperor by this time was the defense of the borders. Therefore, it was necessary for an effective emperor to spend much of his time with the frontier armies. To protect both himself and the Empire, he had to secure the favor and loyalty of the troops more than the senate.

Nor was it any longer practical or fair for the senatorial class and Italy to enjoy privileged positions within the Empire. The provinces now provided the bulk of Roman manpower and bore most of the expense for defending the frontier. Broadening the outlook of the senate to an Empire-wide perspective by admitting many new provincials was useful, but even that was not enough to meet Imperial needs. Despite reaching nine hundred members under the Severi, the senate was still too small to provide the large number of capable officers and administrators that an empire the size of Rome's needed. To provide more personnel it was necessary either to increase the size of the senate further by the wholesale admission of *equites* or use more *equites* directly as officers and administrators. In either case, the hereditary senators would have resented their corresponding loss of exclusivity and would have opposed any change.

Finally, with the rising importance of the provincials in the army and civilian bureaucracy, it was no longer possible to maintain Imperial unity through the figure of the Emperor as a Roman magistrate. In an Empire dominated by the Roman citizens of Italy, who had shared the political culture of the old Republic, that was a useful role for the Emperor. For the most part, however, the provincials did not share that political culture, nor was there any other secular role that would have sanctioned the Emperor's dominant position on an Empire-wide scale. The only universally acceptable sanction was the religious one of the Emperor's divinity, which could be accommodated easily in the religious outlook of all except a few extraordinary rationalists in a basically religious age and the relatively small sects of the Christians and Jews.

XXXII

The Third-Century Anarchy,
A.D. 235 to 285

The murder of Severus Alexander in 235 ushered in fifty years of unprecedented crisis for the Roman Empire. The frontiers were under repeated attack. The office of Emperor became a football tossed back and forth among a bewildering number of usurpers. Whole regions broke away under their own emperors, and the Empire seemed about to disintegrate completely. Many painful, long-term adjustments had to be made before order could be restored and the Empire preserved for the future.

Reasons for the Crisis Many interrelated factors combined to create this crisis. A number of them had existed for some time and had been the reasons for Septimius Severus' efforts to make fundamental changes in the Imperial system. Others were more recent. The combination was almost lethal.

The Failure of the Severan Dynasty One of the major factors was the failure of the Severi to produce another emperor of Septimius' stature, who could have carried out his policy of uniting the Empire on the basis of his own divine person and gained the total loyalty of the legions, so that it would have been easier to maintain unity in the face of disasters. Under increasing stresses and strains there was as yet no one person powerful enough to maintain firm control over the whole in the face of regional needs and interests. Therefore, the crisis was intensified by numerous civil wars between regionally backed rivals for the throne.

Internal Tensions Septimius Severus had grasped the essential need to eliminate the dominant position of the senate and Italy in order to create a stronger, truly united Empire in accordance with geo-political reality. Unfortunately, the integration that he had promoted had not yet been completed. Jealous in protecting their prestige and privileges, many traditionally-minded senators and Italians worked to undermine emperors of equestrian and provincial origin, whom they had had no hand in making. Since, however, they did not have the military power to protect their nominees, all that they succeeded in doing was creating more chaos.

Interregional jealousies were just as bad. The legions and inhabitants of one province or group of provinces often believed that an emperor who came from another part of the Empire was not paying enough attention to their problems. Therefore, they often rebelled and set up an emperor who would look after their needs. For example, the Pannonian legions, to whom the northern boundaries were a special concern, had mutinied against the Syrian Severus Alexander because in their eyes he had shown weakness in dealing with the invading Germans.

Defensive System and Increased Pressure on the Borders The Roman system of border defense essentially went back to Hadrian, who had formalized a policy of static defense, with units stationed in fixed camps all along the frontiers. Septimius had increased its fixed and static nature by allowing the legionary troops to marry legally and by encouraging auxiliary units to take up farming in the countryside surrounding their camps, so that they became a peasant militia. So long as the level of attacks on the borders remained relatively low or infrequent, this system could work. Local units could handle small-scale incursions, and if a major threat occured in one sector, units could be called up temporarily from others to mount a major campaign.

In the second half of the third century this system clearly was no longer effective. Not only did the level and frequency of barbarian attacks along the Rhine and the Danube increase, but Rome was faced with the active belligerence of the new Sassanid Persian dynasty on the Eastern frontier. Meeting an emergency on one front by summoning troops from another merely invited a dangerous attack on the second. Knowing that, the men who had become closely attached to their areas, because of permanent marriages and settlement, were reluctant to leave the borders entrusted to their care to fight on another. Thus, they often backed their local commanders as emperors in the hope of securing greater Imperial concern for their region.

Shortage of Manpower and Money The only way in which the system of static defense could have been made to work in the face of mounting pressure on the borders would have been to increase dramatically the size of the army, particularly in the number of well-trained and well-equipped legionary troops. As Augustus had long ago realized, however, the Imperial economy could not easily support more than twenty-eight or thirty legions, and even he had left the number at about twenty-five after the loss of Varus' three legions in A.D. 9. The number of permanent legions had not reached thirty until Marcus Aurelius, and Septimius had raised it to thirty-three. To have exceeded that number would have had a negative impact on the economy both by requiring an excessive burden of taxes and by drawing away vital manpower as well.

This problem was made even worse by a declining supply of precious metals for coinage and an imbalance in foreign trade. It was compounded by the outbreak of a devastating plague in the middle of the third century. Therefore, in order to meet the Empire's defensive needs, it would be necessary to develop either new defensive strategies or new sources of revenue and manpower or both. Such tasks would have been difficult under the best of circumstances. In light of all the other complications that the Empire faced, they were almost impossible.

Maximinus the Thracian (235–238) Having mutinied against Alexander Severus in 235, the Pannonian legions proclaimed their commander, a Thracian named Gaius Julius Maximinus, as Emperor. Although he was hardly the ignorant peasant depicted in the *Historia Augusta,* he had come from the ranks, and the soldiers under his command feared, respected, and admired him. He knew their moods and aspirations, and, after they had saluted him as Emperor, he doubled their pay. They followed him deep into Germany, defeated the Germans near Württemberg, and took thousands of prisoners and vast quantities of booty. After defeating the Sarmatians, Dacians, and perhaps even the Goths on the lower Danube, Maximinus laid plans for the total conquest of Germany.

The chief problem facing Maximinus was that of obtaining money to pay his troops.

He sent his collectors all over the Empire. They plundered all classes, especially the rich. One particularly ruthless procurator created a violent reaction in North Africa: big landowners, faced with the loss of their estates, fomented a rebellion. They killed the procurator, repudiated Maximinus, and proclaimed the extremely rich but elderly M. Antonius Gordianus as Emperor and his son of the same name as joint-Emperor. The senators, many of them Africans appointed by the Severi, who had always considered Maximinus a Thracian upstart, hailed the nomination with delight and declared Maximinus a public enemy. When the two Gordians had lost their lives, the younger by falling in battle against Maximinus' governor of Numidia, the elder by suicide, the senate then appointed two of its members, M. Pupienus Maximus and D. Calvinus Balbinus as joint emperors, and the thirteen-year-old Gordian III, a grandson of Gordian I, as Caesar. The rejuvenated senate of Alexander Severus acted with amazing resolution and speed. For a time its prestige was high.

Events in Africa and Italy forced Maximinus to set out on an immediate march on Rome. Finding his way barred at Aquileia by hostile Italian forces, he laid siege to the city but failed to take it. Finally, his own men, starving and desperate, mutinied and killed both Maximinus and his son. They acclaimed the two senatorially appointed emperors, Balbinus and Pupienus, whose arrival in Rome was hailed with delirious joy. The joy did not last. Less than two months after the death of Maximinus, the Praetorian Guard killed the two emperors and acknowledged Gordian III as the new Emperor.

Gordian III (238–244)

At the accession of the boy Emperor two powerful and dangerous enemies had begun or were about to assail the weakened frontier defenses of the Empire. The Goths were now streaming over the lower Danube and, in alliance with the Sarmatians and the Carpi, were overrunning Moesia and Thrace. In the Near East the Persians were invading the provinces of Mesopotamia and Syria. In 241 the mighty Shapur was marching toward Antioch on the Orontes.

Rome might well have suffered a disaster of unparalled magnitude had not Gordian III been able to count on the loyalty, experience, and brilliance of his own father-in-law, C. Furius Timesitheus, the praetorian prefect, who was not only a fine army commander but a superb organizer. In 242 they set out from Rome together and, after stabilizing the situation on the Danube, proceeded to Syria, where they relieved Antioch and recovered the Roman provinces. They were on the point of taking the Persian capital of Ctesiphon when Timesitheus died. Then Gordian himself died, apparently after falling from his horse in battle, although another tradition says that the new praetorian prefect, Philip, an Arab sheik from the Jordan, took advantage of a threatened food shortage and engineered a mutiny, which resulted in the death of Gordian.

Philip the Arab (244–249)

The army accepted Philip as emperor, and he made peace with Shapur. The terms were that Rome might retain the provinces of Mesopotamia and Little Armenia in exchange for waiving all interest in Greater Armenia and the payment of 500,000 denarii either as indemnity or as ransom for prisoners captured by the Persians.

Though he courted the goodwill of the senate and gave painstaking attention to the government, events were beyond his control. After a minor victory over the Dacian Carpi, he returned to Rome in 247 to make preparations for the celebration of Rome's thousandth anniversary. Even during the magnificent festival, the Goths and Carpi were thundering across the Danube. Understandably, the Danubian legions revolted and proclaimed one of their commanders emperor. Two other pretenders appeared in the East. These calamities compelled Philip to send an experienced senator, C. Decius, to the Danube. After restoring discipline in the army, Decius drove the Goths back over the Danube. Out of respect for him as a disciplinarian and general, the soldiers of the Danubian front saluted Decius as Emperor, who promptly marched into Italy against Philip. In 249 a great battle was fought near Verona, during which Philip was defeated and slain. Thus ended the principate of Philip the Arab, the last Eastern provincial to occupy the Imperial throne for many years.

Decius (249–251) Meanwhile, the Goths, led by their able king, Kniva, took advantage of the gaps that the absence of Decius and his troops left in the Danubian defenses and poured into Dacia, Lower Moesia, and Thrace. The invasion brought Decius hurrying from Rome. Though he inflicted a severe defeat on one of the Gothic armies, his forces were too weak, his marches too slow, and the support that he received from his sluggish subcommander, Trebonianus Gallus, too dubious and ineffectual to enable him to overtake and destroy the enemy. Finally, in 251, Kniva succeeded in luring Decius into a trap on boggy ground at Abrittus near Adamclisi in Dobrudja, where the Romans suffered one of the most disastrous defeats in their history. Decius and his son were slain. Gallus, proclaimed emperor by the soldiers, made a disgraceful treaty with the Goths, which permitted them to return home with all the plunder and high-ranking Roman prisoners that they had captured together with the guarantee of an annual payment of tribute by Rome.

Few emperors have aroused more controversy in ancient and modern times than Decius. Pagan Latin writers, who usually were prejudiced in favor of the senate, praised Decius highly because he was a consular senator and maintained cordial relations with the senate during his reign. In their eyes he was an admirable ruler, an excellent administrator, a brilliant general, and a man of boundless energy and iron will. Christian writers (Lactantius, for example, called him ''an execrable animal'') have condemned him because he instituted the first systematic persecution of the Christians all over the Empire. Pagan writers generally justified the persecution on the grounds that the Christians belonged to a subversive organization which refused to recognize the state religion and obstructed the defense of the Empire by preaching peace.

The next two emperors, Gallus (251–253) and Aemilianus (253), reigned only briefly. Both were assassinated by mutinous soldiers as provincial armies continued to be arbiters of the Empire's fate.

Valerian (253–260) and Gallienus (253–268) After the death of Aemilianus, Valerian was proclaimed Emperor. He named his son, Gallienus, associate Emperor and gave him full command of the West. The two reigned together until the death of Valerian in 260.

The Age of Gallienus was one of the most critical in the history of the Roman people. It witnessed the culmination of the destructive trends originating in the past and laid the groundwork for future recovery. It began in catastrophe: the barbarians were breaking through the shattered and weakly defended frontiers along the Rhine and the Danube. In the Near East the Persians had invaded the provinces of Mesopotamia, Syria, and Cappadocia. Scarcely a province escaped the havoc wrought by invasion: the widespread destruction of property, the sacking and burning of cities, and the massacre and enslavement of citizens.

Pirates infested the seas as in the days before Pompey; bands of robbers and thieves raided the countryside; earthquakes rocked both Italy and Asia Minor. At the height of the barbarian invasions a plague broke out in Egypt and infected the entire Empire, where it raged for more than fifteen years. The death toll was staggering: two-thirds of the population of Alexandria died and as many as five thousand a day in Rome alone. It created a shortage of rural and urban labor and production fell sharply. Worse still, it severly depleted the ranks of the army. The impact of all these blows occurring simultaneously or in rapid succession aggravated the problems that broke the resistance and shattered the unity of the Empire.

The breakdown of Imperial defense increased the localist spirit of the troops on the frontiers. This localist spirit, together with the constant desire for more pay as the shortage of goods drove up prices, increased the number of locally supported usurpers. During the reign of Gallienus alone, eighteen usurpers made vain attempts to seize the throne.

Foreign Affairs   Alarming reports from the Near East began to reach Rome. In 252, Shapur had engineered the assassination of the Roman client king of Armenia and replaced him with his own puppet in order to open the way for the conquest of Roman Asia Minor. He invaded Mesopotamia and Syria in 253. Shortly after that, the Goths plundered cities along the eastern and southern shores of the Black Sea and began a naval attack upon the coasts of Asia Minor.

The gravity of the situation impelled Valerian to leave Rome, probably in 256, and appear in the East, where he proved utterly incompetent. Despite a few minor skirmishes (described on his coinage as major victories), he failed to restore Roman prestige. Frustrated and depressed, he took out his resentment on the Christians and subjected them to hideous persecution. Finally, in desperation, he sent his plague-stricken army to meet the main Persian army at Edessa. The results were disastrous to both his army and himself. He fell into the hands of Shapur in 260 and ended his days in captivity, one of the most pathetic figures in Roman history.

Meanwhile Gallienus, constantly at war since 254, had been busy clearing the Alemanni and the Franks out of Gaul and the Rhineland. He beat back further attempts to cross the river, and strengthened the fortifications. Further south the Marcomanni and the Alemanni, who had been hammering away at the Danubian defenses, broke through and pushed down into Italy. The former had penetrated as far as Ravenna in 254, the latter reached Milan four years later. Gallienus first halted the Marcomanni by concluding an alliance with them and granting them land south of the Danube in Upper Pannonia, and

in 258/59 crushed the Alemanni near Milan. The next year he had to suppress two dangerous rebellions in Pannonia where the legions, irked by his continued absence on the Rhine, had thrown their support first to one pretender to the throne, then to another.

The situation in the Rhineland had rapidly deteriorated during his brief absence. The Alemanni had crossed the upper Rhine and invaded the Rhone valley and the Auvergne. The Franks had surged over the lower Rhine and overrun Gaul, Spain, and even Morocco. The Saxons and the Jutes, who dwelt along the coasts of Germany and Denmark, had begun roving the seas and raiding the shorelands of Britain and Gaul. Nor was that all. In 259 the legions on the Rhine in fear and desperation mutinied and renounced their allegiance to their absent Emperor in favor of Postumus, the general whom Gallienus had left in command of the Rhineland. The armies of Spain and Britain later followed suit.

Gallienus did not recognize the usurpation of Postumus but, hampered by the German and Gothic invasions of the Danubian provinces as well as by the rebellions of other pretenders to the throne, he could do no more than compel Postumus to confine himself to the Western provinces. Left alone, Postumus drove the Franks and the Alemanni out of Gaul, energetically defended the frontiers, issued his own coinage, and established an efficient administration. Gallienus himself could not have done better.

The Eclipse of Roman Power in the East

After their defeat and capture of Valerian in 260, the triumphant Persians plundered Antioch, occupied all of Mesopotamia, overran Cilicia and Cappadocia, and cut across Asia Minor to the Black Sea. They might have occupied all of Asia Minor permanently, had they maintained their military organization. Instead, they broke up into small looting bands cut off and isolated.

All the while Rome was preparing her counterstroke. Macrianus, one of Valerian's old generals, aided by his lieutenant Callistus, had rallied the shattered remnants of Valerian's army. Putting some of the troops aboard transports, Callistus made landings along the Cilician coast, where he surprised and defeated thousands of Persians and captured Shapur's baggage train together with his harem. That embarrassing loss impelled Shapur to evacuate Asia Minor and retreat to Ctesiphon with all his plunder and hordes of captives. On the way back, he came into conflict on the banks of the Euphrates with an unexpected enemy, Odenathus, the Roman client sheik of Palmyra. That disastrous encounter left Shapur crippled for a long time. To the end of his reign, the war-weary Shapur devoted himself to internal affairs and to his ambitious building projects, while he left the future of Asia Minor to Odenathus and Gallienus.

Palmyra   Palmyra was an oasis in the Syrian desert. It lay astride the main caravan routes from the Mediterranean to Central Asia and to the Persian Gulf. Piled high in its market place were such goods from China, India, Persia, and Arabia as textiles, spices, perfumes, jewelry, and precious stones. By the second century it had become one of the major cities of the Near East with fine wide streets and highways, shady porticoes, stately arches, and magnificent public buildings.

Since the time of Trajan, Palmyra had been an important recruiting ground for the Roman army. The famous Palmyrene cohorts of mounted archers and armored cavalry had rendered invaluable service all over the Empire. Later on, the Severi, who gave Palmyra the rank of titular colony and adlected some of its leading citizens into the senate, allowed these units, though officially part of the Roman army, to serve as a semi-independent Palmyrene army in Syria and along the Parthian frontier. That was the army with which Odenathus humbled the pride of the mighty Shapur on the western banks of the Euphrates.

The services which Odenathus had performed for Rome on his own initiative were not lost upon the shrewd and opportunistic

Gallienus, who showed his gratitude by rewarding him with flattering high-sounding titles and by making him commander of all the Roman forces in the Near East.

Macrianus, meanwhile, had broken with Gallienus and had persuaded the army to proclaim his two sons, Macrianus and Quietus, joint emperors. The long-suffering East hailed them with delight and all might have gone well had the elder Macrianus been content to limit his ambitions to the East. He resolved instead to reach out for the rest of the Empire. Leaving Quietus behind in the East, he and his elder son set out for the Danube. There they were defeated and killed by Aureolus, whom Gallienus had sent to intercept them. Then Odenathus hunted down and put to death the other pretender, along with his praetorian prefect, Callistus.

In his second campaign against Persia in 267, Odenathus turned from the siege of Ctesiphon to drive out the Goths, who had invaded Asia Minor by land and sea, had laid waste the rich cities of Chalcedon and Nicomedia, and destroyed the great temple of Dianna at Ephesus. He failed to overtake them, however, for they had already boarded ships at Heraclea Pontica with all their loot and captives. Shortly after that, an unknown assassin stabbed Odenathus to death. His widow, the beautiful, gifted, and intelligent Zenobia, assumed power in Palmyra and held it until the reign of Aurelian.

The Last Battles of Gallienus, 268
Much encouraged by their success in the previous year, the Goths began the largest invasion of the Empire of the third century. An armada of five hundred ships (some say two thousand) put to sea and a land army unbelievably reported at 320,000 men invaded the Balkans and the Aegean area, ravaged Greece, and captured the cities of Sparta, Argos, and Athens. The invaders passed north through Epirus and Macedonia and finally arrived at Naissus (modern Nish) in Moesia. There in 268 Gallienus intercepted them and, in the bloodiest battle of the third century, destroyed

thousands of them. This victory might have been the end of the Gothic peril, had not Gallienus been compelled to break off pursuit and hasten back to Italy to suppress the rebellion of Aureolus, the cavalry general to whom he had entrusted the defense of Italy against Postumus. Gallienus defeated Aureolus in battle near Milan, only to be assassinated by his own staff officers, all of them Illyrians who may have felt that Gallienus had not devoted enough energy to the defense of the Danubian lands.

The Reforms of Gallienus   Before his death, however, Gallienus laid the foundation of future recovery and prepared the way for the reforms of Diocletian and Constantine. His purpose was to strengthen the hands of the central government in restoring discipline in the armies, in preventing the rise of usurpers, and in defending the Empire against the attacks of the barbarians.

Administrative   The most radical of the reforms of Gallienus was the exclusion of senators from all high army commands and their replacement by equestrian prefects, many of whom were now coming up from the ranks. This reform was no doubt intended to prevent possible rebellions and attempts by ambitious senatorial commanders to usurp power. It also aimed at the restoration of military discipline and efficiency by providing an adequate supply of professional officers willing to endure the hardships of army life on the frontiers and capable of enforcing strict military discipline. The reform not only completed the process of democratizing the army but dealt a heavy blow to the prestige of the senate.

Equestrians also gradually replaced senatorial governors in most of the Imperial and occasionally even in the senatorial provinces. In provinces where armies were stationed, only equestrian governors held command. Senatorial governors did not. Thus in equestrian provinces there was a merger of civil and military authority, but in the senatorial provinces, a separation.

Military   The most revolutionary of the strictly military reforms of Gallienus was to supplement the fixed frontier fortifications by a system of defense in depth. Gallienus maintained the old system as the first line of defense, but behind the frontier he also fortified cities capable of absorbing and containing enemy forces after they had broken through the outer defense line.

The new strategy also called for a mobile army to be stationed at strategic points well behind the frontier lines and capable of moving at a moment's notice to the scene of greatest danger. Since the strategic points in the West were Aquileia, Verona, and especially Milan, the reform made Italy once more a center of great military importance. On the other hand, it reduced the political importance of the city of Rome and the senate because the emperors found themselves compelled to transfer to the great military centers not only the mint and arms factories but their own residences as well. Where the Emperor was, there Rome was also.

The conception of mobile defense demanded the replacement of the slow moving legion, hitherto the main offensive weapon, by a cavalry corps which was to operate independently of the infantry. The new cavalry corps consisted of Moorish bareback-riding javelin men, Dalmatian horsemen, Osrhoenian and Palmyrene mounted archers, and the heavily man-and-horse armored cavalry of the Persian type (*cataphractarii*). Gallienus regarded this cavalry corps so highly that in 263 he placed it on a par with the Praetorian Guard. Its commander soon rivaled and later eclipsed the praetorian prefect and, though only of equestrian rank, became the most powerful man in the Empire next to the Emperor. Claudius Gothicus, Aurelian, Probus, and Diocletian were later to use this command as the springboard to the Principate.

Of all his Imperial predecessors, Gallienus seems to have most closely resembled Hadrian. He had the same keen intelligence, indefatigable energy and capacity for swift decision. Gallienus shared Hadrian's love of poetry and the arts, and his admiration for

Greek culture, literature, and philosophy. He also, however, abandoned his father's persecution of Christians and established a policy of toleration that lasted for forty years.

Claudius Gothicus (268–270) Upon the assassination of Gallienus, one of his murderers, Claudius II, a member of that group of brilliant young Illyrian officers whom he had promoted from the ranks, was proclaimed Emperor. His first task as Emperor was to drive back the Alemanni, who had invaded Italy as far as Lake Garda. Then he rounded up the Goths who had escaped Gallienus, as well as those who had later invaded the Balkans. He enrolled some of the captured Goths in the Roman army; he settled others on abandoned farms in Thrace, Moesia, and Macedonia. So thoroughly had he liquidated the Gothic menace that it did not again recur on a mass scale for more than a century. For this great contribution to the Empire's reconstruction he received the richly deserved title of Claudius Gothicus.

Aurelian (270–275) When Claudius Gothicus died of the plague, the army, which now had become the major power in the state, chose as his successor another brilliant Illyrian officer, Lucius Domitius Aurelianus, whom Claudius had put in command of the cavalry corps during the Gothic war. He was a tough, skillful general whose harsh discipline earned him the nickname, *Manus ad ferrum* ("Hand on Steel"). So severe were his punishments that he seldom had to inflict them.

The tasks awaiting Aurelian were numerous and difficult. He had to secure the long Danubian frontiers from attack and Italy from invasion, restore both the Western and Eastern provinces to the Roman Empire, and solve various political and economic problems, among which was the regulation of the ruined and disorganized coinage.

The immediate task was to rescue Italy from the invasion and depredations of the Juthungi, kinsmen of the Alemanni living north of the upper Danube. At Aurelian's approach they attempted to retreat quickly with their plunder, but he caught them from ambush at the Danube and destroyed half their army. He next defeated the Asdingian Vandals, who had invaded Pannonia, and forced them to supply two thousand cavalrymen for the Roman army. Meanwhile, the Juthungi, aided by the Alemanni and the Marcomanni, invaded Italy again, besieged Milan, and occupied Piacenza. There they set an ambush for Aurelian and defeated his army, which had been wearied by the long march from the Danube. The invaders could easily have marched on and taken Rome had they kept together instead of spreading out into scattered marauding bands, which Aurelian easily destroyed. His victories on the Metaurus and near Ticinum sent the invaders scurrying back to Germany.

Reforms Aurelian, free for other tasks, returned to Rome to suppress a serious revolt of the mint officials who were aggrieved at the Emperor's efforts to check their profiteering out of debased coins. Aurelian immediately closed the mint for a time as a preliminary step toward his projected reform of the coinage. In order to protect Rome from future barbarian assault and capture, he began in 271 the construction of a brick wall around the city. The wall, which was twelve miles long, was twenty feet high and twelve feet thick. It had eighteen gates as well as many sally ports and towers for artillery. Convinced of the impossibility of permanently holding Dacia with its irreparably broken defenses, Aurelian withdrew all the garrisons and most of the civilians from the province. The withdrawal not only shortened the frontier defense line of the Empire but released troops for service elsewhere. The evacuated civilians were resettled in the ravished and depopulated provinces of Pannonia, Moesia, and Thrace, and Dacia was abandoned to the Goths.

The Reconquest of the East, 272 to 273 With Italy and the Danubian provinces temporarily safe from attack, Aurelian was free to attempt the reconquest of the East. The enemy whom he had to conquer was not the Persian King, but Zenobia, the ambitious and capable queen of Palmyra, who matched the Egyptian Cleopatra in intellect and personality and far surpassed her in beauty and virtue. Zenobia not only maintained a court of pomp and splendor but gathered about her scholars, poets, and artists. Her chief advisor was Dionysius Cassius Longinus (213?–273), the celebrated rhetorician and philosopher who probably was the author of the famous treatise *On the Sublime.*

Taking advantage of Aurelian's preoccupation in Italy and on the Danube, Zenobia seceded from the Empire and extended Palmyra's dominion over Egypt and Asia Minor as far north as Bithynia. She had concluded an alliance with the Persians but received little help from them.

Aurelian entrusted the reconquest of Egypt to Probus, and advanced through Asia Minor himself. He encountered little opposition until he reached Antioch on the Orontes, where he was engaged in battle by the Palmyrene army of mounted archers and heavy cavalry. He overcame them and proceeded to Emesa, where he engaged a large Palmyrene army. The Romans won a second resounding victory and set out under the broiling desert sun for the city of Palmyra, eighty miles away. Well prepared for a siege, Palmyra resisted long and stubbornly. It finally capitulated when the panic-stricken queen attempted to flee to Persia for help. Brought before Aurelian, the captured queen saved her life by accusing her chief adviser, Longinus, and her other advisers and friends of inspiring the aggressions. Longinus died like a true philosopher. Aurelian was most lenient with the people and city of Palmyra. He stationed a small garrison there and at once set out for Europe.

He got as far as the Danube when word came that Palmyra had risen in rebellion and massacred the garrison. Aurelian's return was swift, his vengeance terrible. Not even women or children escaped his wrath. He had Palmyra's treasures carted away, tore down the walls, and reduced the once proud and powerful city to a small desert town, which it has remained to this day.*

The Reconquest of Gaul, 273 to 274   The reconquest of Gaul was less difficult. After the murder of Postumus in 268, the Gallic succession passed first to Victorinus and then to Tetricus. Tetricus was a harmless old senator who could neither keep out the German invaders nor maintain authority over his own army officers. His opposition to Aurelian was halfhearted and ineffectual. When his subordinates finally compelled him to fight, he deserted his brave men and surrendered to Aurelian. He was forced to walk through the streets of Rome in Aurelian's triumphal parade together with a more spirited captive, the fabled Zenobia, queen of the East. After the triumph, Aurelian treated both captives with unparalled leniency and dignity. He appointed Tetricus chief inspector of Lucania. (*Corrector Lucaniae*) in southern Italy and presented Zenobia with a villa at Tivoli, where she ended her days as the wife of a Roman senator.

Upon his recovery of the lost provinces, Aurelian received the proud title of *Restitutor Orbis* ("Restorer of the World").

Economic Reforms   In 274, Aurelian grappled with another gigantic task: the restoration of internal stability. The most pressing problem was the regulation of the coinage, which had depreciated so much since 267 that people had to use *denarii* and *Antoniniani* by the sackful (3125 double *denarii* to the sack). Aurelian reduced the official valuation of the *Antoninianus* or double *denarius* from eight *sesterces* to one in order to bring it in line with the eightfold rise in the price level after 267, but whether the change actually halted inflation is debatable. He also closed down all local mints and permanently abolished the senatorial mint at Rome, a blow against municipal autonomy and the prerogative of the senate.

To relieve the distress in Rome which

---

* Soon after, he suppressed a rebellion in Alexandria with similar ruthlessness.

had resulted from the rise of food prices, Aurelian placed the bread-making industry under the direct control of the state, which sold wheat for milling to the bakers' guild and fixed the price of bread. He suspended the monthly grain dole and arranged instead for the daily distribution of two pounds of bread to all eligible citizens. For the same citizens he instituted regular distributions of pork, oil, salt, and possibly wine.

Following the example of Alexander Severus, Aurelian placed all guilds or colleges engaged in the transport and processing of food and other necessities under state control and thereby made them agencies of the government.*

Autocracy and Monotheism Two long term developments approached their culmination during the reign of Aurelian. The tendency toward absolute monarchy in government and the monotheistic trend in religion began at this time to achieve a sure dominance, and even a certain interrelation, as emperors sought religious sanctions for their authority. The rapid changing of emperors during the third century had not destroyed the monarchy; it served rather to transform the Principate into autocratic absolutism. The trend towards monotheism in religion was equally pronounced. The rise of the universal cosmopolitan state, together with the far-reaching influence of Near Eastern culture and of the westward-spreading Eastern cults, had precipitated the decline of the old national and local polytheism and the rise of a more universal and monotheistic religion. Even the Imperial cult lost its potency as a moral basis for Imperial unity and power and gave way before the twin emergence of autocracy and monotheism.

In Rome, Aurelian erected a resplendent temple to the Unconquered Sun (*Sol Invictus*) and established a college of pontiffs of senatorial rank to superintend the worship of this supreme god of the universe and divine protector of the Roman state. A single divine power was now to watch over the single earthly ruler.

Unfortunately for Aurelian, the new divinity did not save him from the fate of many other third-century emperors. A corrupt secretary, caught in a lie and fearing for his life, forged a list of the chief officers of the Guard and spread the false rumor that Aurelian planned their execution. The "condemned" officers acted swiftly; they murdered Aurelian at Caenophrurium, between Perinthus and Byzantium, in the fall of 275. When the truth finally came to light, the horror-stricken officers repented, but it was too late.

Tacitus (275–276) Contrite and dismayed, the military leaders deferred to the senate in the choice of the next Emperor. After some hesitation and delay, the senate nominated its own leader, M. Claudius Tacitus, a man in his middle seventies. In spite of a fairly successful campaign against the Goths and Alans in Asia Minor, he too fell victim to a conspiracy of his own soldiers. His six-month reign marked a fleeting resurgence of senatorial power that, meteorlike, rose, briefly flashed, and was gone forever.

Probus (276–282) After Tacitus' death, the power of making and breaking emperors reverted to the army. It soon disposed of Florianus, the late Emperor's half-brother, who had seized the throne without consulting army or senate. The army of the East had already proclaimed Emperor the mighty Probus, another great Illyrian, who was the equal of Aurelian as a general and perhaps his superior in intellect and culture. Probus continued the work of Imperial consolidation by restoring peace and order in the provinces.

The first task was the liberation of Gaul from the Franks and the Alemanni, who, after Aurelian's death, had overrun the entire province, seized some seventy cities, and laid waste

---

* This extension of bureaucratic control over economic life should not be interpreted as an anticipation of modern state socialism, for the ancient economy had never been either socialistic or capitalistic in the modern sense.

countless fertile fields. Within a year the invaders were in full retreat, with the victorious Probus in relentless pursuit, killing them by the tens of thousands and driving the rest back into the wilds of Germany. Probus built strong redoubts along the eastern bank of the Rhine opposite the Roman cities on the western bank. He also recruited sixteen thousand German soldiers for the Roman army, and assigned them in small units to the various provinces. Except for the rebellions of two disloyal and ambitious generals (which he firmly suppressed), Gaul remained quiet throughout the reign of Probus.

In 278, Probus cleared the Alemanni and Burgundians out of Rhaetia and the Vandals out of Pannonia. He settled on abandoned land in Thrace some 100,000 Scythians and Germanic Bastarnae who had been dislodged from their southern Russian homelands by the Goths. He subdued the Isaurian brigands of southern Asia Minor and established colonies of veterans there to keep the peace and breed young recruits for the Roman army. Finally he liberated Egypt from the Blemmyes who had invaded from the Sudan.

To protect his soldiers from the deteriorating effects of idleness in the barracks, he set them to work reclaiming waste and swamp lands, planting vineyards, digging drainage ditches, and building roads. That tedious work, together with the normal army discipline, which Probus never relaxed even in time of peace, aggravated the latent discontent of the men. While the soldiers were working on a drainage project near Sirmium in southern Pannonia, word came of the mutiny in Rhaetia and the proclamation as Emperor of the Praetorian Prefect, Marcus Aurelius Carus. This report fanned their discontent into open mutiny, and Probus, one of the ablest and most conscientious rulers of the century, fell victim to their hate.

Carus and his Sons, Carinus and Numerianus (282–285) Carus, the new Emperor, was another Illyrian. He too was a professional soldier and a fairly competent general. He did not even bother to seek senatorial confirmation of his position as Emperor, and upon his accession, he conferred the rank of Caesar on his two sons, Carinus and Numerianus. Leaving Carinus in charge of the defense of Italy and Gaul, he set out for the East with his other son. Early in 283, after defeating the Quadi and the Sarmatians, who had come over the Danube, he marched against the Persians. He crossed the Euphrates, and took Seleucia, then crossed the Tigris and took Ctesiphon. This series of successes came to an abrupt halt in 284 with his mysterious death attributed, by available sources, to a bolt of lightning. It is far more likely that Carus fell victim to foul play at the hands of his Praetorian Prefect, Arrius Aper, who later secretly arranged the assassination of Numerianus.

A council of war was held to pick a successor. The army of the East ignored the claims of Carinus, who was generally despised for his known addiction to vice, and nominated instead one of their own officers, Diocles. The first act of the new Emperor (who is better known as Diocletian) was to run Aper through with his sword. Carinus, who had been left in charge of Italy, refused to acknowledge Diocletian as his colleague and marched against the army of the East. The two armies clashed in Moesia in the valley of the Margus (Morava). In the fierce battle that ensued, the superior army of Carinus had almost achieved victory when Carinus himself received a dagger's thrust through the heart, by a military tribune whose wife Carinus had seduced. His victorious but leaderless army accepted Diocletian as their Emperor. Thus by a quirk of fate, the best man was found in 285 to finish the reconstruction for which Gallienus, Claudius II, Aurelian, and Probus had worked and died.*

---

* Diocletian, however, dated his reign from his initial acclamation in 284.

XXXIII

Reorganization under the Dominate of Diocletian, A.D. 284 to 305

The half century between the death of Alexander Severus and the accession of Diocletian had witnessed a series of disasters unparalleled in Roman history—many simultaneous barbarian assaults on the European and African frontiers, a disastrous war with the resurgent Sassanid kingdom of Persia, mutinies in numerous Roman armies, the secession of provinces, the violent and sudden deaths of more than a score of emperors, famine, and plague. A gigantic mobilization had rolled back the tide of invasion and checked the dissolution of the Empire, but the effect upon the Empire had been profound. The trend toward a military monarchy that had already received considerable impetus from Septimius Severus had been greatly accelerated. Under Diocletian the trend reached its culmination, and the Roman Empire emerged transformed into something socially, economically, and politically quite different from what it had been under the Principate of the first and second centuries A.D.

With Diocletian, the Principate had given way to the Dominate, a word derived from *dominus*, "lord and master," which was synonymous with absolute monarchy or autocracy and now was officially used in public documents. That was the logical outcome of developments over the previous three centuries. Drastic measures were needed to overcome chaos and preserve the existence of the Empire. Diocletian acted with boldness, determination, and even ingenuity. Some of his policies were successful. Others failed or worked at cross purposes and caused as many problems as they solved. For the short run, however, Diocletian helped the Empire to survive, although the quality of life for vast numbers of individuals was sacrificed in the process. Under the Dominate, life for many became a prison to be escaped, not a good to be enjoyed. The conditions of the late Empire began to resemble those soon to be found in Europe's Middle Ages.

Sources The sources of information for the fourth century are generally superior to those for the third. They have also enjoyed greater attention from scholars recently than ever before. Therefore, historians now have a better understanding of the events that were shaping the history of Europe for centuries to come. One of the most important sources recently investigated is Zosimus, the excellent Greek writer who, in 600 or thereabouts, published his *New History,* a narrative in six books on Roman history from 270 to 410. It was a continuation, as well as a supplement, of the *Histories* of Ammianus Marcellinus, the last great Latin historian of Rome, who, in imitation of Tacitus, wrote a reliable, penetrating, and elegant history of Rome from Nerva to Valens (378) in thirty-one books. Only the last eighteen books, which cover the period from 353 to 378, are extant.

The sources of secondary importance include the biography of Diocletian at the close of the *Historia Augusta* and several *breviaria*, brief historical surveys of Roman history, the last parts of which are of real value since they record events of the authors' own time. Of these the best are the *Caesars* of Aurelius Victor, short biographies of the emperors from Augustus to Julian the Apostate (361–363); the *Breviary* of Eutropius, which ends with the year 369; the *Breviary* of Rufius Festus, which ends with the year 371; and the anonymous *Epitome of the Caesars,* which ends with the death of Theodosius I in 395.

The works of the Christian writers are valuable sources because they contain careful verbatim citations of many documents which otherwise would have been lost—Imperial constitutions and edicts, proceedings of church councils, Imperial correspondence, and letters written by bishops and other church officials. Lactantius in his Latin tract *On the Deaths of the Persecutors,* which maintained that emperors who persecuted the Christians were doomed to a painful death, has preserved a faithful firsthand record of certain events from the accession of Diocletian to the death of Maximinus Daia in 313. Years later, St. Athanasius (ca. 296–373), the Bishop of Alexandria, wrote many document-filled tracts, the most important of which were his polemics against the adherents of the Arian heresy, which touched off a major religious conflict under Constantine that had great historical repercussions.

The most valuable Christian sources are the numerous works of Eusebius of Caesarea in Palestine. Besides those already mentioned (p. 399), his *Life of Constantine* is very important

for this period despite its obvious eulogistic bias. He also produced a valuable collection of documents and an eyewitness account of the Great Persecution under Diocletian.

The primary sources include inscriptions, papyri, coins, archaeological materials, and especially the Imperial *constitutiones** preserved in inscriptions, papyri, various juristic and literary works, in the Theodosian Code (published in 438 during the reign of Theodosius II, 408–450), and in the Justinian Code (first published in 529 during the reign of Justinian I, 527–565). The two most important inscriptional texts are Diocletian's famous *Edict on Maximum Prices,* and the great Paikuli inscription of Narses I of Persia (293–302), wherein the king recounted his triumphs and the acts of homages paid him by Roman envoys and the vassal kings of Asia.

The Rise of Diocletian   The humbleness of Diocletian's origins has been exaggerated by hostile or overly dramatic sources. One of a series of talented, well-trained officers from the Danubian provinces, he probably came from a relatively well-to-do provincial family. He had been a cavalryman under Gallienus, a *dux* or cavalry commander in Moesia, and commandant of the Imperial mounted bodyguard. His excellent military record is nevertheless overshadowed by his career as an organizer, administrator, and statesman. He was greatly aided by excellent advisors and generals, who assisted him to restore the Empire to its former greatness.

---

* The *constitutiones principum* ("Statutes of the Emperors"), which had the validity of laws, included (1) *edicta* or edicts (official proclamations of the Emperor as a Roman magistrate which were valid during his term of office for the whole Empire); (2) *decreta* or decrees (court decisions of the Emperor having the force of law); (3) *rescripta* (written responses to written inquiries on specific points of law). Although the *constitutiones* were originally valid only during the Principate of their author, they later remained in force as sources of public and private law unless revoked by a later Imperial constitution. The Emperor also became a source of law through the responses of eminent jurists to whom he had delegated the *ius respondendi* (see p. 362).

The chief problems facing Diocletian were the strengthening of the power and authority of the central government, the defense of the frontiers, the recovery of the rebellious and seceding provinces, and the removal of those conditions which favored constant attempts to seize the throne. This work, begun by Aurelian and Probus, had been halted by their assassination. Armies could again mutiny and proclaim emperors. Usurpers not only could but did arise again, and provinces seceded. The danger of secession was particularly acute in Gaul, which was suffering from repeated invasion by the Franks, Burgundians, and Alemanni and the resulting devastation and famine. Here the Bagaudae had revolted, bands of peasants driven to desperation by the triple scourge of invasion, Imperial taxation, and landlord exploitation.

Diocletian's first act was to find a loyal representative who could take over the defense of the West and permit him to concentrate his energies upon the protection of the threatened Danubian and Eastern frontiers. Such a loyal representative would convince the Western legions of his concern for Western problems and would lessen the danger of revolt. His choice fell upon Maximian, an old comrade in arms, whom he elevated to the rank of Caesar and sent to Gaul.

In Gaul Maximian quickly crushed the rebellion of the Bagaudae and, by two brilliantly executed land campaigns, drove the Germans out of Gaul into the region east of the Rhine. In recognition of these victories Diocletian raised Maximian to the rank of Augustus in 286. Maximian was to rule jointly with Diocletian and to be second only in personal prestige and authority.

Maximian had not been so successful at sea. To clear the English Channel and the North Sea of the Frankish and Saxon pirates who had been raiding the shores of Gaul and Britain, he established a naval base at Boulogne on the coast of Gaul and placed in command of the Roman fleet a certain Mausaeus Carausius. Carausius, a native of the German Lowlands and an experienced and daring sailor, overcame the pirates within a few weeks. His ambition stimulated by his naval exploits, he enlarged his fleet with captured pirate ships and men, seized Boulogne and Britain, and conferred upon himself the title of Augustus. Since Diocletian was too occupied to do more than protest, and Maximian's fleet was wrecked at sea, Carausius maintained undisturbed sway over Britain for seven years as Emperor of the North.

Diocletian himself had meanwhile not been idle. Going from province to province, he had inspected frontier defenses and repelled invasions. He had displayed the might of Rome on the Danube and Euphrates: in 289 he had defeated the Alemanni in Rhaetia, the Sarmatians and Goths in Pannonia and Moesia, and the Arabic invaders of Syria. In 291 he had defeated the Blemmyes, who had invaded Egypt from the Sudan. In 290 he had made Greater Armenia once more a client kingdom and placed upon its throne Tiridates III, a scion of the now defunct Arsacid Parthian line of kings and a Roman protégé. He also persuaded the Sassanid Persians to abandon claim to the former Roman province of Mesopotamia.

The Tetrarchy, 293–312   Diocletian was convinced that the dual *imperium* had proved itself to be a successful military and political experiment. In order to strengthen Imperial control of the armies and forestall usurpers such as Carausius, Diocletian resolved in 293 to create a four-man system, a tetrarchy. Two Caesars were to be appointed, one to serve under Diocletian in the East, the other under Maximian in the West. Diocletian selected as his Caesar, Gaius Galerius, another Danubian officer and a brilliant strategist. Maximian's choice was yet another Danubian, C. Flavius Julius Constantius, commonly called Chlorus or "Pale Face," who proved himself an excellent general, a prudent statesman, and the worthy father of the future Constantine the Great.

The tetrarchy was held together by the

personality and authority of Diocletian, and doubly strengthened by adoption and marriage, for each Caesar was the adopted heir and son-in-law of his Augustus. The tetrarchy was indivisible in operation and power; laws were promulgated in the names of all four rulers, and triumphs gained by any one of them were acclaimed in the name of all. On the other hand, each member of the tetrarchy had his own separate court and bodyguard and had the right to strike coins bearing his own image and titulature.

Each Augustus and Caesar had assigned to him those provinces and frontiers that he could conveniently and adequately defend from his own capital: Maximian protected the upper Rhine and upper Danube from Milan; Constantius shielded the middle and lower Rhine, Gaul, and later Britain from Trèves (Trier); Galerius guarded the middle and lower Danube from Sirmium on the Save; and Diocletian assumed responsibility for protecting the eastern part of the Empire from Nicomedia on the Sea of Marmara. In spite of this division of responsibility, the Empire remained a territorial and administrative whole.

Theoretically, the tetrarchy also provided for a quiet and orderly succession to the throne. On the death or abdication of an Augustus, his Caesar, also his adopted son and heir, supposedly would take his place and would, in turn, select a new Caesar. Unfortunately, the system was held together only by the dynamic personality of Diocletian. Once he was removed, his successors began struggling amongst themselves for personal dominance, and the Empire was plunged into another debilitating series of civil wars.

The Tetrarchy in Action   While he held the reins of power, however, the tetrarchy fully justified Diocletian's expectations as each of the four rulers set about restoring peace and unity in his own part of the Empire.

Constantius immediately began operations against the usurper Carausius. He captured Boulogne, and subdued the Franks and other German allies of Carausius that dwelt beside the North Sea. He transported many of the captives to eastern Gaul for peaceful farming and for future service in Roman armies. In 293, Carausius was assassinated by an ambitious and treacherous rival.

In 296, Constantius invaded Britain and reestablished Roman dominion from Land's End to Hadrian's Wall. Then he began reorganizing defenses and restoring prosperity: he provided protection for shipping in the Channel, the North Sea, and the Atlantic, and erected a series of strong and well-distributed forts to safeguard the southern and eastern shores against Saxon pirate raids. He placed all these forts, together with a powerful new fleet, under the command of a new official known as the Count of the Saxon Shore.

Constantius then returned to the Continent, where he drove the perennial German invaders back over the Rhine once more and strengthened the *limes* of the Rhineland with many redoubts and fortifications. His spectacular victory over the Alemanni near Langres in 298 brought Gaul many years of quiet and prosperity. He afterward made his capital city of Augusta Treverorum (Trèves, Trier) one of the most important and loveliest cities in the Western Empire.

Galerius and Diocletian were equally busy on the Danube and in the East and no less successful. In the years 293 to 296 Galerius had defeated the Goths, Marcomanni, Sarmatians, and Bastarnians, and had settled captured Iazyges and Carpi in depopulated Pannonia. He had built forts along the Danube, and had cleared and irrigated land for farming in the southern Danubian basin.

After helping Galerius in the defense and fortification of the lower Danube, Diocletian suppressed an uprising in Egypt where two usurpers, Achilleus and Lucius Domitius Domitianus had, in 296, proclaimed themselves respectively Corrector and Augustus. Diocletian recaptured Alexandria after eight months and put Domitianus, Achilleus, and their partisans to death.* Then he abolished

---

* There may have been some connection between these two men and the half-pagan, half-Christian sect Manichaeanism (see pp. 449–450), which Diocletian proscribed soon after their revolt.

the Alexandrian provincial mint and totally reorganized the administration of Egypt.

Taking advantage of Diocletian's preoccupation with Egypt, Narses, king of Persia, opened hostilities against Rome: he overran the kingdom of Armenia and invaded Syria. Galerius, summoned from the Danube by Diocletian in 297, rushed to the East, but at Callinicum, not far from Carrhae, he impetuously attacked the Persians with insufficient forces. He suffered a disastrous defeat which resulted in the loss of Mesopotamia. The next year, reinforced by fresh levies from the Balkans, Galerius advanced into Armenia and routed Narses at Erzerum. Galerius, whose immense booty included the king's harem, followed up his success by the reconquest of Mesopotamia, and the capture of Nisibis (a fortress of immense strategic value for maintaining Roman power in the area for the future), and the Persian capital of Ctesiphon.

The loss of his wives and children obliged Narses to accept harsh peace terms. He agreed to surrender Mesopotamia which now extended to the upper Tigris, and five small provinces beyond the Tigris. He acknowledged as Roman protectorates Greater Armenia and the kingdom of Iberia south of the Caucasus. He also agreed that merchants traveling between the Roman and Persian empires must pass through the Roman customs center of Nisibis. The victory of Galerius was so complete that the Persians did not risk war with Rome for another fifty years.

The existence of the tetrarchy had been fully justified by the victories of Constantius in the West and of Galerius in the East, by the construction of strong defenses in Britain, along the Rhine, Danube, and Euphrates, in Egypt and Mesopotamia, and by the systematic settlement of captured barbarians to repopulate and help defend lands adjacent to the frontiers. That four-headed, seemingly decentralized, but actually united power, gave Rome twenty years of stable rule, during which the defenses could be repaired and resources mobilized so that the Empire was able to survive for another two hundred years in the West and lay the foundations for the Byzantine Empire in the East.

Diocletian's Reforms   In addition to establishing the tetrarchy and consolidating the military defenses of the Empire, Diocletian carried out sweeping reforms in almost every department of the government. These reforms were not wholly without precedent, for they were not the innovations of a radical but rather the continuation and strengthening of the trend toward absolute monarchy.

Court Ceremonial   To promote stability by ensuring the personal safety of the Emperor, Diocletian surrounded himself with an aura of such power, pomp, and sanctity that an attempt to overthrow him would appear not only treasonous but sacrilegious. Diocletian assumed the title of Jovius as Jupiter's earthly representative sent to restore the Roman Empire. He bestowed upon his colleague, Maximian, the name of Herculius, the earthly Hercules and helper of Jovius. Together they demanded the reverence and adoration due to gods. Everything about them was sacred and holy—their palaces, courts, and bedchambers. Their portraits radiated a nimbus or halo, an outer illumination effluent from an inner divinity.

In order to dazzle his subjects with his power and majesty and infect them with a feeling of mystery and awe, Diocletian adopted an elaborate court ceremonial and etiquette, not unlike that prescribed at the royal court of Persia. The Emperor became less accessible and seldom appeared in public. When he did, he wore the diadem and carried the scepter. He arrayed himself in purple and gold sparkling with jewels. Those to whom he condescended to grant audience had to kneel and kiss the hem of his robe. This act of adoration was incumbent also upon members of the Imperial Council (*consilium*), which acquired the name of the Sacred Consistory (*sacrum consistorium*) from the necessity of standing while in the Imperial presence.

Provincial Reorganization and the Centralization of Imperial Power   To strengthen the central government and prevent rebellions by powerful and ambitious governors, Diocletian carried out a complete reorganization of the provinces. He divided the larger ones into smaller units, so that he increased the total number from about 50 to 100 or so. By depriving practically all the governors of their military functions, Diocletian not only reduced their power and independence and exercised closer administrative supervision of the provinces but increased the central government's control of patronage and power of appoinment, from which every government, ancient and modern, has derived its main source of strength and stability. Even more drastic but quite in line with a policy initiated by Septimius Severus was Diocletian's abolition of Italy's former privileged status. He made her subject to Imperial taxes and cut her territory up into sixteen provinces.

To enable the Imperial government to control the provincial governors more effectively, Diocletian grouped the provinces in twelve administrative districts known as dioceses. Each diocese fell under the supervision of a so-called vicar (*vicarius*), a deputy of one of the four praetorian prefects, each one of whom was in turn an administrative assistant of a member of the Imperial tetrarchy. The vicars supervised all governors within their respective dioceses (*consulares, correctores,* and *presides*), even those of senatorial rank—except the three proconsuls of Africa, Asia, and Achaea. The vicars themselves were of equestrian rank and, like all governors (except those of Mauretania and Isauria in Asia Minor), were purely civilian officials whose main function was the administration of justice.

Diocletian assigned command over the armies and garrisons stationed in the provinces to professional military men known as dukes (*duces*). To assure close supervision and the mutual restraint of ambitious impulses, he made the dukes dependent for military supplies and provisions upon the governors and other civilian officials. In some dioceses several dukes might serve under the command of a higher officer known as a count (*comes*).

Military Reforms   Despite all that Gallienus had done, military reform continued to be a pressing necessity. Throughout the third century there were never enough legions to fight major wars without a substantial withdrawal of troops from the frontier defenses. Except for the Praetorian Guard, an elite but relatively small corps, there was no mobile field army. Nor had Gallienus been able to correct the weakness of the cavalry. With characteristic energy, Diocletian set about solving these most difficult problems.

In order to strengthen the defense of the frontiers, he decreased the size of the legion from 6000 men to 1000. The number of legions was thus increased from 39 to 65 or more and the cavalry and auxiliary units correspondingly, although the increase in total armed strength was only from 400,000 to probably 500,000 men. The increased number of legions permitted a more even distribution of the troops available for frontier defense.

Diocletian also divided the army into two main and distinct branches: the *limitanei,* who served as border or frontier (*limes*) guards, and the *comitatenses* (from *comitatus,* originally "the emperor's escort," but now designating mobile field forces often commanded by the tetrarchs of their respective parts of the Empire and consisting largely of cavalry), which was stationed at strategic points well behind the frontiers and capable of moving at a moment's notice to any point of danger. The *comitatenses* had higher physical standards, better pay and food, and more privileges. Also they were required to serve only twenty years instead of twenty-five.

Another military problem, which arose from the manpower shortage, was the recruitment of soldiers. Though the old obligation of universal military service still obtained, in theory, the government actually could not afford to call too many men away from agriculture, industry, transportation, and other essential services.

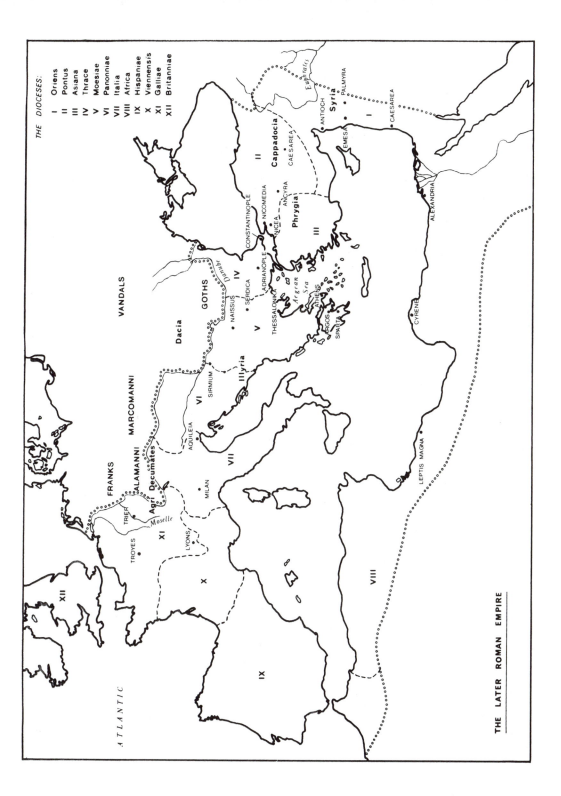

THE DIOCESES:

I   Oriens
II   Pontus
III Asiana
IV Thrace
V   Moesiae
VI Panonniae
VII Italia
VIII Africa
IX Hispaniae
X   Viennensis
XI Galliae
XII Britanniae

THE LATER ROMAN EMPIRE

ATLANTIC

FRANKS
ALAMANNI
MARCOMANNI
VANDALS
GOTHS
Dacia
Illyria
Agri Decumates

TRIER
TROYES
LYONS
MILAN
AQUILEIA
SIRMIUM
NAISSUS
SERDICA
THESSALONIKA
ADRIANOPLE
CONSTANTINOPLE
NICOMEDIA
NICEA
ANCYRA
ATHENS
ARGOS
SPARTA
Aegean Sea

Danube
Moselle

Phrygia
Cappadocia
CAESAREA
II
III
IV
V
VI
VII
VIII
IX
X
XI
XII
I

Syria
ANTIOCH
PALMYRA
EMESA
CAESAREA
ALEXANDRIA
CYRENE
LEPTIS MAGNA
Euphrates

427

Diocletian resorted to various methods to secure the required number of recruits: the draft, the enforcement of hereditary obligations, the hiring of mercenaries, and voluntary enlistment. He enforced the draft against men not engaged in essential occupations and, of course, against able-bodied beggars and tramps. He compelled the sons of German settlers to enlist in the army upon reaching the proper age, as well as the sons of veterans and even of soldiers still in active service. He enforced a modified form of the draft against landowners by requiring them to fill a legally fixed quota of recruits each year from their tenants and dependents. They might, in lieu of men, present a sum of money sufficient for the hiring of an equivalent number of mercenaries.

Voluntary enlistment was not uncommon because it frequently afforded an escape from something more unpleasant than army life or provided a means of securing legal advantages, such as immunity from municipal obligations or exemption from taxes, not enjoyed by the average civilian. A prisoner of war, for example, might enlist to escape death or enslavement and even a municipal senator or town councillor might choose army life in preference to an unbearable burden of taxes and other irksome responsibilities.

Monetary and Fiscal Reforms   One of the unfortunate results of Diocletian's military and administrative reforms was that the expansion of the army, the doubling of the number of provinces and governors, the establishment of four separate Imperial capitals, and the creation of a vast civil bureaucracy devoured enormous sums of money and put the already strained finances of the state under an even greater strain. Another source of financial stress was Diocletian's own mania for building. In addition to highways and fortifications in almost every province and the military installations (arms factories, depots, and arsenals), he embellished the four Imperial capitals with splendid palaces, basilicas, and baths. The raising of money to finance these and other ambitious projects necessitated a reorganization of the entire monetary and fiscal system.

The Reform of the Coinage, 286   By his reform of the coinage, Diocletian attempted to end the frightful monetary chaos of the third century and created a system of coinage in silver and gold, which, though not a long-term success itself, served as a model for his successors. In 286 he replaced the old *aureus* with a new gold coin at the rate of 60 to the standard gold pound of 327 grams and a new silver coin, the *argenteus,* at 96 to the pound and roughly equivalent to the *denarius* of Nero's time. To answer the need for small change, he struck silver-washed bronze coins of three weights and denominations, the heaviest often known as the *follis,* the lightest being the silver-coated *denarius,* which probably had a nominal valuation of 50,000 to the gold pound and was roughly equivalent to 20 *follis* coins.

The most enduring of the new coins was the *aureus.* After Constantine had decreased its weight in 324 from 60 to 72 to the pound, it became known as the *solidus* (and later the Byzantine *bezant*). It circulated freely throughout the Roman world and even the Persian Empire and persisted both in the Byzantine Empire and in the medieval West for more than a millennium. Its name still survives in the Italian *soldo* and the French *sou.*

Tax Reform   With his monetary reform in place, Diocletian could then proceed to tax reform. He swept away the old system of indirect taxes, provincial tribute, and testamentary bequests upon which Augustus and his successors had depended as sources of revenue. To create and maintain a steady and adequate flow of revenue into the treasury, Diocletian also abolished the irregular emergency levies and requisitions of the third century and replaced them with a regular income tax on production. Though certain traditional and local taxes continued to be payable in money, in many cases the new taxes were payable in kind, that is, in the form of agricultural products, such as grain, oil, wine, or manufactured goods, the so-called *annona,* which previous emperors had requisitioned irregularly and then only to make up for unexpected deficiencies in the regular revenues.

The main effect of Diocletian's tax reform was to convert these emergency levies, which varied in amount from region to region and from time to time, into an ordinary annual tax collectable from the entire Empire. The new tax was periodically estimated, fixed in advance, and announced by an Imperial decree or indiction (*indictio*), which specified the taxes to be collected from the Empire as a whole and from each diocese and province. Later the term "indiction" came to mean the period between two assessments, which occurred every five years between 297 and 312 but thereafter every fifteen. The cycle became so well established as a regular institution that it came to constitute an actual system of chronology.

The tax system of Diocletian introduced in 287, elaborated in 297, and perfected under his successors by 312, despite much study and research, remains obscure and perplexing. There is reason to believe that the system was not consistent in practice nor uniformly applied to every region or diocese of the Empire. Apparently, Diocletian and his administrators were flexible enough to realize that the system had to be adaptable somewhat to regional social and economic differences that would otherwise make a rigid system unworkable.

The core of Diocletian's tax reform was the system of capitation, which varied greatly from diocese to diocese within the next two centuries. Derived from *caput,* "head," it was a species of poll or personal tax, which had existed before. Diocletian's form of capitation was not an individual or personal tax but a method of assessing or evaluating for taxation purposes the totality of rural wealth and property in the Empire. It included all such concrete elements as land, labor, crops, and livestock, and the ideal unit of assessment was the *caput,* which may be defined as that quantity of labor, whether of an independent peasant owner, tenant (*colonus*), sharecropper, or hired hand, required to render parcels of land (varying in area with geographical location, climate, soil fertility, or type of crop) capable of producing crops of equivalent taxable value. A woman was rated as half a *caput,* and animals proportionately lower.

A Syriac translation of a fifth century Romano-Syrian lawbook indicates that in some provinces (Syria, for example) the unit of assessment was probably not the *caput* but a surveyor's unit of measurement called the *jugum.* In Syria at least, the *jugum* comprised an area respectively of 20, 40, and 60 Roman acres (*jugera*) of grain—planted land graded according to soil fertility; or five acres of vineyards; or level ground having on it 225 mature olive trees or mountainous terrain bearing 450. In other words, the *jugum* was that quantity of land required to produce crops having an assessable value to that of the *caput.*

In the ideal system of *jugatio-capitatio,* a *jugational* form of capitation, the two units, *caput* and *jugum,* though equivalent and even interchangeable, represented two distinct taxes. By combining the two units, the tax assessors were able to calculate all the natural physical, human and animal resources of a community, province, or diocese. Unfortunately, the perfect jugational form of capitation did not apply fully to any diocese of the Empire except possibly Asia Minor and Pontus, both of which were adjacent to Diocletian's capital of Nicomedia and therefore under his personal supervision. A less perfect and elaborate form of the system existed probably in Thrace, Illyria, and Gaul. In Egypt, land and personal taxes were kept separate until sometime between 349 and 359 in the reign of Constantius II. In North Africa, the surveyor's unit was not the *jugum,* but the *centuria* of 200 acres. Though northern Italy fell under Diocletian's system of taxation and paid the *annona* as a *regio annonaria,* the capitation tax was not assessed in conjunction with the *jugum;* in central and southern Italy (then known as *regio suburbicaria*), which supplied Rome with meat, wool, wine, wood, and lime, the unit of measurement was the *millena,* about which almost nothing is known.

The beneficial fiscal effects of Diocletian's tax reform were notable. Knowing several years in advance what the approximate tax receipts would be, the government could plan and control its expenditures and curb the excessive spending that had formerly wrought havoc with the coinage. At last the government could draft an annual budget, without which any attempt to stabilize the coinage would have been useless and absurd.

The reform also helped the taxpayers, at least in theory, by distributing the burden fairly and equitably and by announcing in advance how much they had to pay. The government was able not only to bring about a temporary stabilization of the economy but to lay the groundwork for a fiscal system that, under Rome's Byzantine successors, endured for more than a thousand years.

The Edict of Maximum Prices, 302

Diocletian's monetary reform was only a partial success. Unlike the *solidus,* the silvered bronze or billon currency underwent further depreciation, which resulted in turn in a sharp rise of prices. To combat the inflation Diocletian issued his famous *Edict of Maximum Prices* in 302. This Edict is the most important and instructive document available on Roman economic life. It has been reconstructed from numerous Greek and Latin inscriptional fragments found largely in the Eastern part of the Empire but recently also in Italy. It set a ceiling on the prices of over a thousand different items, from wheat, barley, poultry, vegetables, fruits, fish, and wines of every variety and origin, to clothing, bed linen, ink, parchment, and craftsmen's wages.

In a remarkable preamble to the law, Diocletian sharply condemned speculators and profiteers who robbed the people, soldiers, and government workers, and he invoked the death penalty against those who violated the edict. Diocletian's failure to stabilize the value of the coinage, especially the silver and copper coins used in ordinary transactions, guaranteed the failure of his attempt to fix prices. With the prices that producers could receive for goods fixed and the value of the money fall-

ing, it became unprofitable to produce goods at the official prices. Therefore, people either ceased to produce goods for the market or sold them illegally on black markets. In the face of these economic realities, the edict had to be relaxed to encourage production and distribution and was finally revoked by Constantine.

The Last Persecution of the Christians, 299 to 311

Another failure was Diocletian's persecution of the Christians, which brought his reign to a tragic and bloody close. Why he broke the forty-year religious truce proclaimed by Gallienus has been a subject of much speculation, particularly since his wife was a Christian. Some scholars have seen his persecution based on religious principle: he, the self-proclaimed representative of Jupiter, sought to restore the old Roman faith and moral code. The circumstances under which the persecution began give some support to this view, but they also show that Diocletian was politically concerned about ensuring conformity and uniformity among the population in order to strengthen the state in pursuit of security. Enemies of Christianity, like the Caesar Galerius and the Neoplatonist Hierocles, were quick to brand the Christians as subversives and evil influences on the Empire.

The persecution had begun in 299. At a public sacrifice offered to determine the will of the gods from an inspection of the entrails of the slaughtered animals, the augurs reported that the presence of hostile influences had frustrated and defeated the purpose of the sacrifice. Diocletian, suspicious and furious, gave orders that all persons in the Imperial palace—including his own wife—offer sacrifice to the traditional gods of the state or upon refusal to do so, be beaten. He next permitted Galerius to post orders that all officers and men in the army be required to offer sacrifice on pain of dismissal from the service.

In 303 he drafted an edict that ordered the destruction of the Christian churches and the surrender and burning of sacred books, prohibited Christian worship at any time or place, and restricted the rights of prosecution and defense formerly enjoyed by Christians in courts of law. One evening in the winter of 303, without having waited for the official proclamation of the above-mentioned edict, the Imperial police suddenly entered, ransacked, and demolished the Christian cathedral that stood opposite the Emperor's palace in Nicomedia. The edict was posted throughout the city the next day. An enraged Christian tore down one of the posters, was arrested, and burned at the stake.

Within the next fifteen days two fires of unknown origin broke out in the Imperial palace in Nicomedia. Numerous Christian suspects were imprisoned, tortured, and killed. At the same time, revolts ascribed to Christians in Syria and Cappadocia, though easily suppressed, led to the proclamation of two more edicts; one ordered the imprisonment of the clergy, the other sought to relieve the overcrowding of the prisons by offering liberty to all who would consent to make sacrifice to the gods of the state and condemned to death those who refused.

After his visit to Rome, where he had just celebrated the twentieth anniversary of his accession, Diocletian became very ill and ceased to attend to public affairs. According to Eusebius, Galerius seized the opportunity to draft and publish a fourth edict which required all Christians to offer the customary sacrifices under pain of death or hard labor in the mines.

None of the four edicts, except perhaps the first, was enforced everywhere with equal severity. In Gaul and Britain, Constantius limited himself to merely pulling down a few churches whereas Galerius and Maximian were far more zealous in their domains. When Diocletian abdicated, in 305, the persecution was at its height.

The Abdication   On May 1st, 305, in the presence of the assembled troops at Nicomedia, Diocletian formally abdicated. With tears in his eyes he took leave of his soldiers. He told them that he was too old and sick, probably from a stroke, to carry on the heavy tasks of government. On the same day at Milan, in fulfillment of a promise previously extracted by Diocletian, Maximian also resigned. Diocletian nominated Constantius Chlorus and Galerius as the new Augusti, with seniority for Constantius, who received as his special provinces Gaul, Britain, Spain, and Morocco. Galerius took the Balkans and most of Asia Minor. Galerius, in turn, nominated his nephew Maximinus Daia as his Caesar in the East and ruler over the provinces in the rest of Asia Minor, Syria, and Egypt, while Constantius chose Flavius Valerius Severus, who was to rule over Italy, Roman Africa, and Pannonia.

After their abdication, the two ex-Augusti went into retirement. Maximian, fuming over his enforced abdication, went to Lucania to await the first opportunity to snatch back his Empire. Diocletian retired to his enormous fortress palace at Split, where he spent the last eight years of his life.

Although all of Diocletian's reforms and policies cannot be counted as successes in the long run, his stable twenty-year reign had been crucial for preventing the immediate dissolution of the Empire. Under him the transformation of the Roman Empire into the Dominate, an absolute military monarchy ruling a highly regimented corporate state through an all-powerful, centralized bureaucracy, was essentially completed. The physical Empire known to Augustus and the Antonines was able to survive for another 200 years and the Eastern half for a millennium, but its spirit was completely altered.

XXXIV

Constantine the Great and Christianity, A.D. 305 to 337

Once just another good military officer, Diocletian had become one of the most significant Roman emperors. He had displayed the might of Rome throughout the Mediterranean world and rescued the Empire from immediate dissolution. But, despite his achievements, he lived to see the disintegration of the tetrarchy and the recognition of a religion that he himself had persecuted. He saw his own great fame fade into obscurity before the blazing light of Constantine's rising sun and died in the belief that he had worked in vain. In principle, however, after gaining control of the Empire, Constantine continued many of the social, economic, military, and administrative policies established by Diocletian.

Constantine the Great, as he came to be called, was the bastard son of Constantius Chlorus and his concubine, Helena, whom he had met in Bithynia. After living with her for some years, Constantius abandoned her in 289 in order to marry Theodora, the stepdaughter of the Emperor Maximian. Constantine grew up at Diocletian's court in Nicomedia, where he learned at first hand the secrets of empire and developed into a strong and handsome man.

Although Constantius was nominally the senior Augustus after the dual abdication of Diocletian and Maximian, Galerius was the actual master of the Empire. He still basked in the glory of his victories over Persia in 298. The two Caesars, Maximinus Daia in the East and Flavius Valerius Severus in the West, were both obligated and blindly devoted to him. Through them Galerius was able to control the major portions of the Empire. The presence of the young Constantine at his court gave him an additional advantage, both as a hostage in any future dealings with Constantius and as his spokesman and advocate with the army. The power of Galerius was now at its height.

The Rise of Constantine, 306 An invasion of England by the Scottish Picts in 306 provided Constantius a sound and plausible reason for requesting the return of his son. Unwilling to forgo Constantine's services and perhaps suspecting a coup d'etat, Galerius procrastinated as long as he could, but finally consented to let the youth go and signed the necessary travel papers. Fearing that Galerius might change his mind, Constantine stealthily disappeared one night and, after a swift journey during which—to forestall possible pursuit—he killed or lamed all the post horses he had to leave behind, he reached his father at Boulogne and with him sailed to Britain. After a swift and easy victory over the Picts, Constantius died at York (where Septimius Severus had died almost a century before). The army proclaimed Constantine Augustus in his father's place.

Constantine at once wrote Galerius to request recognition as an Augustus. Galerius did not reject this petition outright since he did not wish to risk civil war. He compromised by granting Constantine the title and rank of Caesar. The young man quietly accepted in the interests of peace and the preservation of the tetrarchy established by Diocletian, whom he still greatly respected. Nor was he much perturbed by the subsequent elevation of Severus, henchman of Galerius, to the rank of Augustus. Confident that time was on his side, Constantine kept strengthening his position by winning fresh victories over the Alemanni and the Franks, whose captured kings he cast into foul dungeons or threw to the lions in the arena at Trèves.

The Usurpation of Maxentius, 306

Maximian's son Maxentius was greatly incensed by the news of Constantine's elevation. He believed that he, the legitimate son of an ex-Augustus, had a better right to the throne. He naturally felt aggrieved to find his way blocked by Galerius, who personally detested him. In 306, he seized Rome from the unpopular Severus. Meanwhile, Maximian, chafing to recover the throne, left his estate in Lucania and set out to win over the army and help his son. He also tried, unsuccessfully, to persuade Diocletian to resume office. Finally, Maxentius induced many of Severus' soldiers to desert, and Severus surrendered to Maximian at Ravenna. When Galerius refused to grant Maxentius the title of Augustus, Maxentius assumed it himself.

In early 307, Maximian also took the title of Augustus. He went to the court of Constantine at Trèves, betrothed his teenage daughter Fausta to him, and endeavored to win his support in the coming battle against Galerius. He even recognized Constantine as an Augustus.

In September of 307, events began to follow one another with startling rapidity. Galerius marched into Italy and upon Rome. The invasion failed. Rome was too strong to be taken by storm and too well supplied with food to be starved into surrender. Some of his exhausted legions mutinied, others deserted. To escape the fate of Severus, Galerius beat a hasty retreat lest he lose the loyalty of the rest.

Maximian, however, began to resent his subordination to Maxentius. His frustration became obvious in early 308, for, after a wild, impassioned speech to the Imperial troops, he attempted in their presence to rip the purple off his son's shoulders. The soldiers sided with Maxentius and the old man again went back to Constantine's court and left Maxentius master of Rome.

Seeing the tetrarchy tottering to a fall and the impending collapse of Diocletian's grand design, Galerius, with rare statesmanship, decided to call a meeting of Augusti and Caesars at Carnuntum (Altenburg) on the Austrian Danube and persuaded Maximian and Diocletian to attend. The decisions reached at this conference appeared momentous at first. Maximian reluctantly consented to go back into retirement. Licinius, an old army man and comrade of Galerius, became Augustus in place of Severus. Maxentius, who had seized power illegally, was declared a public enemy. Constantine and Maximinus Daia, neither of whom attended the meeting, had to accept the inferior status of Caesars, both angry at the sudden elevation of the unknown Licinius. The decisions, therefore, really satisfied no one except Galerius and Licinius.

After the meeting at Carnuntum, the turbulent old Maximian again went to visit Constantine, who received him with honor and respect but did not appoint him to any important offices. Frustrated by what he regarded as shabby treatment, Maximian took advantage of Constantine's absence on a campaign against the Franks in 310 and at Arles proclaimed himself Emperor for the third and last time. Constantine, outraged at such treachery on his own territory, hurried back from the Rhine with unexpected speed and laid siege to the usurper. Maximian was forced finally to surrender at Marseilles. Later, according to official sources, he hanged himself in his own room.

Constantine's Repudiation of the Herculian Dynasty

After the death of Maximian, who had, along with Diocletian, held the title Herculius, Constantine repudiated the Herculian dynasty as the basis of his claim to rule and sought a new sanction by announcing his descent from the renowned Claudius Gothicus. In place of Hercules he adopted as his patron deity the Unconquered Sun (*Sol Invictus*), who was identified in Gaul, it seems, with Apollo. This deity had also been the protector of Claudius Gothicus and Aurelian. Constantine's claim of descent from Claudius Gothicus enabled him to assert not only his right to the throne by inheritance but his right to undivided rule over the whole Empire as well. Fortified by this new sanction, he was now ready to wage open war against Maxentius, whom he formally declared a usurper and a tyrant.

Constantine's first hostile act against Maxentius occurred in 310 with the annexation of Spain, which had been Rome's chief source of food since Africa had sided with Maximian in 308. The loss of Spain therefore created serious problems for Maxentius in Rome—famine, food riots, street fighting, and a death toll of six thousand people. The situation forced Maxentius to send an expedition for the reconquest of Africa. The success of this expedition not only solved the problem of the Roman food supply, but left Maxentius free to take up the challenge of Constantine. He charged the latter with the murder of his father Maximian and prepared for war. War was postponed only by the pressure of events taking place in other parts of the Empire.

The Edict of Religious Toleration, 311

After the abdication of Diocletian, the persecution of the Christians continued only in the dioceses of Galerius (Illyricum, Thrace, and Asia Minor) and particularly in those of Maximinus Daia (Syria and Egypt). Maximinus ordered punishments ranging from mutilations and hard labor in mines and quarries to execution for men, women, or children who refused to participate in pagan sacrifices. He also attempted to counteract the influence of the Christian Church by organizing a pagan church and priesthood with a similar hierarchy of priests, charitable institutions, and local temples subordinated to the great city temples.

Finally, in 311, while in the clutches of a mysterious disease, Galerius became convinced of the futility of the Christian persecutions. As senior Augustus he issued his famous Edict of Toleration that granted Christians all over the Empire freedom of worship and the right to reopen their churches, provided they pray for him and the state and do nothing to disturb public order. He explained his change of policy by stating that it was better for the Empire if people practiced some religion than none at all. A few days after the proclamation of this edict, Galerius died.

After the death of Galerius, the four remaining Augusti kept the Empire divided by their mutual jealousy and hate. Maximinus Daia at once overran and seized the Asiatic provinces of Galerius and threatened Licinius' control over the Balkans. In anticipation of war with Maxentius, Constantine made an alliance with Licinius and betrothed to him his sister Constantia. Meanwhile, Maximinus came to a secret understanding with Maxentius.

Constantine's Invasion of Italy, 312

Constantine launched his long awaited invasion of Italy in the spring of 312. He set out from Gaul with an army of nearly forty thousand men and crossed the Alps. Near Turin he met and defeated a large force of armored cavalry despatched by Maxentius for the defense of Upper Italy. Then, in swift succession, he captured the cities of Turin, Milan, Aquileia, and Modena and advanced against Rome. Maxentius had originally intended to defend the city behind the almost impregnable walls of Aurelian.

Had Maxentius adhered to his original strategy, which had earlier succeeded against Severus and Galerius, he might have won. Constantine's army, the smaller of the two, was too weak either to take the city by storm or to conduct a long siege. Whether through belief in religious "omens" or through fear of a popular uprising, Maxentius changed his plan and went out to meet Constantine in open battle.

The Battle of the Milvian Bridge, 312
Maxentius led out his army and crossed the Tiber over a pontoon bridge hastily constructed to replace the old Milvian Bridge, which he had ordered destroyed as a defensive measure in accordance with his earlier strategy. The pontoon bridge consisted of two sections held together by chains which could be quickly cut apart to prevent pursuit by the enemy. He advanced along the Flaminian Way as far as *Saxa Rubra* ("Red Rocks") about ten miles north of Rome. There Constantine had encamped the night before.

Lactantius says that on the night before the battle a vision appeared to Constantine and bade him place upon the shields of his soldiers the ancient symbol of victory, which was also the emblem of Christ, a monogram consisting of an X with a vertical line drawn down through it and looped at the top to represent the first two Greek letters of Christ's name, *Chi* and *Rho*. With less plausibility, Eusebius asserts that Constantine told him years later that sometime before the battle he saw in the sky across the sun a flaming cross and beneath it the Greeks words ἐν τούτῳ νίκα ("By this sign thou shalt conquer," or as handed down in the more familiar Latin form, *in hoc vince* or *in hoc signo vinces*). Constantine obeyed the omen and went forth to battle.

Constantine attacked first with the cav-

alry. The infantry followed and forced the enemy troops into a tight pocket with their backs to the rain-swollen Tiber. Unable to stand their ground, many plunged into the river, others stampeded to the shaky pontoon bridge, which parted under their weight and collapsed. Maxentius and thousands of his men fell into the swiftly running stream.

The next day Constantine entered Rome in triumph. In the forefront of the procession a soldier carried on a spear the head of Maxentius, whose body had been fished out of the river. The jubilant throng hailed Constantine as liberator. The senate damned the memory of Maxentius, declared his acts null and void, and proclaimed Constantine senior Augustus of the entire state.

Constantine and Christianity Although the senate undoubtedly hailed the elevation as the triumph of *libertas,* the true victor was the Christian Church. A victory statue of Constantine had a cross placed in his right hand, although Constantine's Arch of Triumph inscriptionally attributes the victory to the intervention of an unnamed divine power (*instinctu divinitatis*) and to his own greatness of mind (*mentis magnitudine*).

While Constantine came to ascribe his victory to the intervention of Christ, he did not become an exclusive believer in Christianity upon his victory at the Milvian Bridge. On the other hand, he clearly was a believer before his baptism at the end of his life. Exactly when his complete conversion took place cannot be said. The interaction of political considerations and personal developments made it a complex, gradual process. He was obviously too keen a statesman to attempt to impugn or suppress immediately the religious beliefs of eighty to ninety percent of his subjects, not to mention the senate, Imperial bureaucracy, and army. Also, one victory, however brilliant and decisive, could not in one day completely change his old beliefs, which only gradually were fully replaced. As Emperor, he continued to hold the ancient Roman office of *Pontifex*

Maximus. The Arch of Triumph represents the Unconquered Sun as Constantine's patron deity. A set of gold medallions struck in 313 shows the heads of Constantine and the Sun side by side. A silver medallion struck in 315 represents a blending of typical Roman and Christian symbolism: it shows the Emperor with the Christogram on his helmet, the Roman she-wolf on his shield, and a cruciform-headed scepter in his hand. Constantine continued to strike coins in honor of Mars, Jupiter, and even Hercules until 318; and coins in honor of the Sun until 323. Thus Constantine's reign was a link between the Roman Empire that was soon to pass and the Christian Empire that was to come.

As senior Augustus, Constantine ordered Maximinus Daia to discontinue his persecution of the Christians in the East. Daia obeyed. In 313, Constantine instructed his proconsul in Africa to restore to the churches all confiscated property, to furnish Caecilianus, the newly elected bishop of Carthage, funds for distribution among the orthodox bishops and clergy in Africa, Numidia, and Mauretania, and to exempt them from all municipal burdens or liturgies. That done, Constantine left Rome for Milan to attend a conference with Licinius.

The Conference of Milan, 313   At the conference of 313 in Milan, there not only took place the long-expected marriage of Licinius and Constantia, but the two emperors reached a general agreement regarding complete freedom of religion and the recognition of the Christian Church or rather of each separate local church as a legal "person."*

The publication of an actual Edict of Milan is open to some doubt, but the agreements reached included not only the Edict of Toleration of Galerius but all the Western rescripts of Constantine concerning the restitution of property and exemption from public burdens in favor of the churches. Licinius applied this Magna Carta of religion not only to

his own domains in Europe but also to the East, which was soon to be liberated from the persecutions of Maximinus Daia.

The End of Maximinus Daia, 313

Maximinus Daia, though depicted by Christian writers as a slave to vice, was undoubtedly a man of some principle, military competence, and statesmanship. Since the publication of the Edict of Galerius, he had sporadically persecuted the Christians in his dominions or subjected them to humiliating indignities. Constantine's order to desist was obeyed, but with neither alacrity nor enthusiasm.

Since becoming a Caesar, Daia had met many disappointments. Diocletian had treated him as a barbarian; he received no invitation to attend the conference at Carnuntum; Galerius had ignored or brushed aside his demand for recognition as an Augustus; Licinius had long waited for the opportunity to declare the war against him for seizing the provinces that Galerius had possessed in Asia. After the defeat and death of his ally Maxentius, Daia stood alone against the combined forces of Constantine and Licinius. Constantine's departure for Gaul to repel a Frankish invasion of the Rhineland presented Daia an excellent opportunity to attack Licinius.

In the dead of winter, Daia moved down from the snowbound highlands of Asia Minor with an army of seventy thousand men. He crossed the Bosporus and laid siege to Byzantium, which capitulated in eleven days. Licinius rushed from Milan with a smaller but better trained army. The two forces met near Adrianople. Defeated in the battle, Daia disguised himself as a slave and escaped. Licinius pursued him into Asia Minor, where he took sick and died. Licinius with the East now in his hands, granted the Christians complete religious freedom and, as he had agreed at the conference of Milan, restored to them their confiscated churches and properties.

The Empire Divided, 313 to 324

Once again the Empire was divided, as it had been in the days of Marcus Antonius and Oc-

---

* In much the same sense modern business and nonprofit corporations are legally "persons." They can own property, make contracts, and sue or be sued in court.

tavian, and had to undergo a long and bitter struggle between two rival dynasts. Neither Constantine nor Licinius liked or trusted each other. To avert or postpone the inevitable struggle, Constantine strove to create a buffer state between their two domains: he appointed Bassianus to serve as Caesar over Italy, Africa, and Pannonia. The choice of Bassianus, who was married to Constantine's stepsister Anastasia and had a brother named Senecio at the court of Licinius, seemed perfect but proved unacceptable to Licinius.

Deeply suspicious of his rival's designs, Licinius persuaded Senecio to incite Bassianus to a revolt against Constantine. The latter discovered the plot in time, had Bassianus executed, and demanded the surrender of Senecio. When Licinius rejected the demand, Constantine attacked in 316. He defeated Licinius with heavy losses in Pannonia but fought to a draw in Thrace. As neither wished the inconclusive struggle to continue, they arranged a truce in which Licinius agreed to abandon his claim to any territory in Europe but Thrace, and Constantine agreed to waive his claim to the right as senior Augustus of legislating for Licinius' part of the Empire.

The compromise peace was neither destined nor intended to last. After a few years of apparent harmony and cooperation, relations between the two emperors began slowly to deteriorate. Mutual antagonisms and rival ambitions widened the rift. Constantine did not really want peace: his claim of direct descent from Claudius Gothicus established his title to undivided rule over the Empire as a matter of manifest destiny. Licinius unintentionally helped to fulfill this destiny by his divergent religious policies. His reversal of the policies agreed upon at Milan presented Constantine a ready-made, though specious, pretext for war.

Unlike Licinius, Constantine had drawn closer to Christianity ever since the battle of the Milvian Bridge. The benefits which Constantine at this time bestowed upon the Church were to render thanks to God for the aid that he believed he had been given in battle. In turn he recognized the Christian

Church on earth and made it an effective partner of the state.

Although he had to take into account the predominance of pagans in the population, army, and bureaucracy, he authorized measures that went far beyond the Edict of Milan by granting Christians ever more privileges and immunities. An important feature of his religious policy was to permit the Pope of Rome and the orthodox clergy to determine correct doctrine and discipline within the Church and to enforce their decisions by the authority of the state. In a constitution published in 318, he recognized the legality of decisions handed down by bishops' courts. In a rescript of 321, he not only legalized bequests by Roman citizens to the Christian Church, but assigned to it the property of martyrs dying intestate. In the same year he proclaimed Sunday a public holiday and day of rest for people working in law courts and state-run manufacturing operations.* Symbolic, too, of Constantine's growing personal acceptance of Christianity was his adoption after the battle of the Milvian Bridge of the *labarum,* a standard consisting of a long-handled cross with a *Chi Rho* monogram at the top.

The Donatist Schism Constantine's personal experiences and mentors, such as Bishop Hosius of Cordoba, had convinced him of the power of the Christians' God, and he also saw the benefits that the state could derive from being united with the strong effective organization that the Christian Church had become. Therefore, Constantine took a serious view of the schism that was rending the Church in Africa and destroying unity in the state. The schism derived its name from Donatus, the fanatical leader of a radical group of dissident clergymen. This group had protested strongly against the election of Caecilianus as metropolitan bishop of Carthage on the ground that he was too ready to pardon and restore to clerical office those who

---

* The proclamation could have been interpreted either way: by a Christian as "the Lord's Day," by a pagan as "the holy day of the Sun."

had betrayed the faith during Diocletian's persecution and surrendered the Holy Scriptures for burning. Contrary to the will of the Roman Pope, the Donatists had elected as bishop of Carthage Donatus himself, who, during the persecutions, had endured six years of incarceration in a foul dungeon and had survived nine stretchings on the rack without flinching.

The African dispute rose to a crescendo of fanaticism when Constantine denied the Donatists a share in the benefactions that he had recently granted the clergy and congregations of Africa. Two church councils summoned by Constantine in 313 and 314 ruled against the Donatists. They appealed to the Emperor to judge their case himself. At last he agreed. After much deliberation, he reaffirmed the decisions of the councils and ordered the military suppression of the Donatists and confiscation of their churches. In 321, Constantine realized that persecution only heightened their fanaticism and increased the turmoil in Africa, and he ordered the persecutions to cease. He scornfully left the Donatists "to the judgment of God." His first attempt to restore peace and unity in the Church had failed dismally.

The Arian Heresy Similar religious problems confronted Licinius, but he handled them differently, yet not more successfully. At first he faithfully observed the decisions reached at Milan, but, when the Arian heresy arose in Egypt and threatened to disrupt the peace and unity of his realm, he resorted to systematic persecution of the Christians.

The seeds of the Arian heresy took root, as did those of the Donatist schism, during Diocletian's persecution. Like Donatus, Bishop Melitius of Lycopolis strongly disapproved of the readmission of wavering and renegade Christians by Peter, the Bishop of Alexandria. Melitius became the leader of a large group of dissenters, of whom a priest named Arius later became the most heretical.

The doctrine that Arius set forth in his sermons was that Christ was not "of the same substance" (*homoousios*) with the Father but of "different substance" (*heteroousios*). Since He was the Son of the Father, He must therefore have been subsequent and posterior. Though begotten before all worlds, there must have been a time when He was not.

That unorthodox doctrine, though not substantially different from occasional utterances of the three great Church Fathers of the early third century—Origen, St. Dionysius of Alexandria, and, in his old age, Tertullian —shocked and angered Peter's successor, Bishop Alexander, who held the more orthodox belief that the Son was of the same substance with the Father; and that all the three Persons of the Trinity—the Father, Son, and the Holy Spirit—were one in time, substance, and power, representing the three aspects of the Almighty Power of the Universe.

Arius, excommunicated and expelled from the diocese of Egypt, went first to Palestine to see Eusebius, the eminent church historian and Bishop of Caesarea; next to Nicomedia, the see of another Bishop Eusebius, who wielded strong influence at the court of Licinius. Arius made a powerful impression upon both bishops, as well as upon the Empress Constantia herself and upon other persons high up in affairs of church and state throughout Asia Minor.

The controversy raged throughout the East. Vitriolic letters and pamphlets went from diocese to diocese, and Arius himself composed popular songs to win the support of the common people.

Then Licinius' patience snapped. Never really sympathetic toward the Christians, he now saw in their controversies a disruptive element all the more dangerous in view of his impending power struggle with Constantine (on whose behalf he perhaps suspected that they were saying their prayers). Accordingly, in 320 he renewed the persecution of Christians.

The Defeat and Death of Licinius, 324 Although the Christian persecutions may have provided Constantine with a moral issue in his war against Licinius, he found a more immediate cause in the Gothic invasion of Moesia and Thrace in 323. To repel the invasion, Constantine had no other recourse but to trespass upon the Thracian domains of Licinius. Licinius made an angry protest; Constantine rejected it. Both sides at once mobilized.

In the middle of 324, Constantine attacked and defeated the forces of Licinius. Licinius surrendered, but an appeal by his wife, Constantia, moved Constantine to spare his life. He was exiled to Salonika. Six months later, Constantine had him put to death for treason. Constantine was now sole Emperor over an empire that became united for the first time in almost forty years. The new slogan of Empire came to be "one ruler, one world, and one creed."

The Council of Nicaea, 325 The military victory had reunited the Empire politically but did not so quickly and decisively restore the religious unity which Constantine had striven to bring about. In all his efforts to promote religious unity, Constantine labored under one distinct handicap: he failed to understand the religious importance of the controversy between Arius and the Bishop of Alexandria. Since his chief aim was to achieve harmony within the state, it made little difference to Constantine whether the Father, Son, and Holy Spirit represented one indivisible godhead or were three separate deities. Accordingly, writing to Arius and Bishop Alexander, he urged them to get down to fundamentals and abandon their battle of words over abstruse and unimportant points of theology. His letter naturally failed to end the controversy.

Still hoping for an amicable solution of the problem, Constantine summoned an ecumenical council at Nicaea, to which bishops from all over the Empire might travel at state expense and at which he himself would be present.

On May 20, 325, some three hundred bishops gathered at Nicaea in Bithynia. In his brief opening address, Constantine avowed his own devotion to God and exhorted the as-

sembled bishops to work together to restore the unity of the Church. All else, he declared, was secondary and relatively unimportant. Reserving for himself only the right to intervene from time to time to expedite debate and deliberation, he then turned the council over to them.

The Council of Nicaea defined the doctrine and completed the organization of the Catholic Church. Its decisions affected not only the problems of 325, but Christianity for all time. It formulated the Nicene Creed, which, except for some minor modifications adopted at the Council of Constantinople in 381, has remained the creed of most of the Christian Church to this day. It reaffirmed the doctrine of the indivisible Trinity, excommunicated Arius, and ordered the burning of his books. Easter was fixed to fall on the first Sunday after the first full moon following the spring equinox, and twenty canons were formulated for the regulation of church discipline and government throughout Christendom.

The historical consequences of the Council of Nicaea were momentous. First of all, it made compromise on the issue of Christ's nature more difficult and split the Church into two hostile camps for years. It also bedeviled Imperial politics since some emperors were Arian and others upheld the Nicene Creed. While enjoying official favor under Constantius II and Valens, Arians were able to spread their version of Christianity among the Germanic tribes across the Danube. They were so successful that the Vandals, Burgundians, Ostrogoths, and Visigoths were Arian Christians by the time they took over much of the Western half of the Empire, which had remained staunchly Nicene.

The irony is that relations between the Orthodox population of old Roman territory and their new Germanic overlords would have been smoother if the latter had remained pagans. Pagans could have been more easily tolerated because they merely would have been ignorant of the Faith, and one could readily have hoped to convert them. Arians, on the other hand, were, in the eyes of the Orthodox, willful heretics and, hence, more sinful, while the Arian Germans saw no need to adopt Orthodoxy. They already thought of themselves as true Christians and resented the attitude of the Orthodox. Therefore, sectarian hostility between the two groups hindered the creation of much-needed unity in the face of later invaders, who caused further destruction and cultural decline in the early Middle Ages.

The Council of Nicaea also deeply influenced future relations between Church and state during the remainder of Roman and subsequent Byzantine history. The formal role that Constantine played by convening the council reinforced the already close association between the head of state and the Church during the Donatist schism. Constantine's actions at Nicaea provided the model for the Caesropapism of later centuries, when the emperors dominated the Church and manipulated it for purposes of state. Constantine himself claimed to be *Isapostolos* ("Equal of the Apostles") and the elected servant of God.

Constantine's Secular Policies

While Constantine's religious preference was quite different from Diocletian's, the policy of centralizing religion under state control was quite similar, and he followed Diocletian's lead even more clearly in other spheres, such as monetary reform. He stabilized Diocletian's gold *solidus* at 72 to the pound, and issued a new silver coin, the *miliarense* (denoting a thousandth part of the gold pound). These constructive measures brought about a gradual revival of money economy for the next two centuries, enabled the government to collect most of Diocletian's taxes in cash, and stimulated trade not only within the Empire but far beyond the Imperial frontiers. Centuries later, it provided the Byzantine Empire with the financial stability and resources to beat back the repeated onslaughts of the Islamic Caliphate.

Military Reorganization of the Empire Constantine weakened the frontier garrisons (*limitanei*) by transferring some of the best troops to enlarge and strengthen the mobile field armies (*comitatenses*) emphasized by Diocletian, to which he added a new elite corps composed of some infantry, but mainly of cavalry, known as the Palace Guards (*palatini*). He greatly accelerated the enrollment of Germans in the Imperial armies and their appointment to high military commands and often to the highest offices in the state. He replaced the Praetorian Guard, which he had disbanded in 312, with a personal bodyguard of crack troops, most of whom were German. To this bodyguard he gave the peculiar name of "Palace Schools" (*scholae palatinae*).

Another important military development was the reorganization of the high command and the complete separation of military and civil functions. Constantine replaced the praetorian prefects with two supreme commanders knows as Master of the Infantry (*magister peditum*) and Master of the Cavalry (*magister equitum*). Similarly, he abrogated the authority of the provincial governors over the dukes and counts, who commanded the frontier garrisons.

Though stripped of their military functions, the praetorian prefects were still very powerful dignitaries. Each exercised the powers of a deputy emperor in one of the four great prefectures of Gaul, Italy, Illyricum, and the East. After 331, all judicial decisions handed down by them were final and were not subject to appeal even to the Emperor. They supervised the administration of the Imperial postal system, the erection of public buildings, the collection and storage of taxes, the control of craft and merchant guilds, the regulation of market prices, and the conduct of higher education. Even more important, their executive control over the recruiting and enrollment of soldiers, military installations, and the provision of supplies acted as a powerful brake upon ambitious army commanders.

Expansion of the Imperial Court The Master of the Infantry and the Master of the Cavalry were members of a vastly expanded Imperial Court (*comitatus*). In keeping with Diocletian's policy of surrounding the Emperor with an elaborate court ceremonial to promote an aura of sacredness, Constantine increased the number of personal attendants, many of whom, in Persian style, were eunuchs and became powerful by controlling personal access to the Emperor. The most important of them were the Chamberlain or Keeper of the Sacred Bedchamber (*praepositus sacri cubiculi*) and the Chief of the Domestic Staff (*castrensis*).

There were also many important civil officials. The minutes of the Sacred Consistory were kept by notaries (*notarii*), the chief of whom maintained the list of appointees to high office (*notitia dignitatum*). The Quaestor of the Sacred Palace (*quaestor sacri palatii*) oversaw the drafting of Imperial edicts and reviewed petitions. The Master of Offices (*magister officiorum*) was extremely powerful because he controlled the sacred secretariats (*sacra scrinia*), which handled correspondence, legal matters, and petitions, and he supervised the Imperial messenger service (*agentes in rebus*), who carried official dispatches, gathered intelligence for the central government, and controlled the movement of troops. He also oversaw the Imperial bodyguards, arsenals, and the manufacture of arms. As master of ceremonies, he even controlled appointments with the Emperor, received ambassadors, and thereby helped to direct foreign policy. The Count of the Sacred Largess (*comes sacrarum largitionum*) administered the Imperial mines and mints, and the Count of the Private Estate (*comes rei privatae*) administered the Emperor's far-flung personal properties. All of these palace officials (*palatini*) and their staffs were granted exemptions from the duties and obligations of ordinary citizens.

Final Decay of Old Offices and the Senate   Although Constantine and his successors continued to hold the office of consul on occasion, retained the title Pontifex Maximus, and still advertised their *tribunicia potestas* in the tradition of Augustus, the old magistracies continued to decline. By 300 the praetors, who had lost their judicial functions under Septimius Severus, and the quaestors, who no longer had senatorial revenues to handle after the militarization of all provinces during the third century, had been reduced to one each.

Their only duty was to conduct the games and entertainments during festivals at Rome. Two consuls continued to be appointed, one at Rome and one at Constantinople, but their office was merely honorary. The last real function of the consuls, as presidents of the senate, had already been transferred at some point to the urban prefect, whose court heard the civil suits of all senators and the criminal suits of those domiciled in Rome. All of his other functions, however, were handled by a vicar of the praetorian prefect.

The Roman senate was now, with the urban prefect, only the municipal council of Rome. It no longer ratified the appointment of emperors, and its advisory function had been taken over by the Sacred Consistory, the Imperial Council of high court officials. The Emperor now merely informed the senate of his decisions, for which courtesy he received fulsome thanks.

In keeping with a long-standing trend, Constantine finally abolished the distinction between senators and equestrians. Since the need for competent officials was great, offices previously restricted to one class or the other were now opened to both. Equites who were appointed to senatorial offices became senators, and the number of senators swelled to about twenty-five hundred. Ironically, however, this change increased the prestige of the senators as a class despite the institutional decline of the senate itself. Now senators became part of the highest strata of Imperial government, especially in the less urbanized West, where the great senatorial landowners were in a position to monopolize the highest posts. Constantine even revived the term *patrician* as an official honor for senators who had performed particularly important services.

The Founding of Constantinople, 324 to 330   Since the time of Hadrian, the city of Rome and peninsular Italy had gradually lost their earlier dominance within the Empire. Citizenship, privileges, wealth, and political power had steadily spread outward to the provincials, until they came to make up the bulk of the soldiery, the bureaucracy, and the senatorial class and finally occupied the throne itself. The city of Rome still had much symbolic value for its possessor, as its capture by Constantine in 312 demonstrated. Nevertheless, Constantine realized that Rome was no longer well placed in relation to the constantly threatened borders, and he quickly abandoned it as a working capital. (It was eventually supplanted by Milan in the West.) Moreover, to prevent anyone from seizing Rome's symbolic power to challenge the Emperor from within, Constantine had abolished once and for all the Praetorian Guard, whose control of Rome had been the key to many a usurper's success.

Like Diocletian, Constantine also realized that instead of having one capital, the Empire had to be defended and administered from capitals in both the East and the West. Also, with his conversion to Christianity, the idea of a new Rome, free from the deeply rooted pagan traditions of old Rome, appealed to him even further. Constantine's choice for an Eastern capital was the old, now-decayed Greek city of Byzantium, which was eventually renamed Constantinople in his honor.

This choice was a stroke of genius. At Constantinople (Istanbul), where the Black Sea flows through the straits leading to the Mediterranean, Europe meets Asia. Through the city passed roads linking the Near East and Asia Minor with the Balkans and Western Europe—roads with easy access to two of the main battle fronts of the Empire, the lower Danube and the Euphrates. Situated on a promontory, protected on two sides by the sea and by strong land fortifications on the third, Constantinople occupied an almost impregnable position and remained invulnerable for more than a thousand years. It also has an excellent deep-water harbor (later called the Golden Horn), the entrance to which could be quickly and easily closed against attack by sea. Ideally located for trade, it captured the commerce of the world passing east and west, north and south—furs from the North and spices from the Orient, fine wines and luxuries of every kind that added zest and elegance to life.

Beyond whatever military, strategic, and commercial possibilities Constantine may have foreseen, no place seemed more suited to become the center of the new Christian theology. Predominantly Christian, Constantinople became the first mother of churches—the Holy Peace, the Holy Wisdom (*Hagia Sophia*), and the Church of the Twelve Apostles.

In all else save religion, Constantine made the new capital an exact replica of Rome. The new capital had to have a senate. Though the Roman senate had actually become quite a superfluous institution during the dominate of Diocletian and Constantine, it was nevertheless one hallowed by an ancient and glorious past. A new senate house was therefore erected in the most exclusive part of the new city, and Constantine summoned to its meetings not only the heads of Rome's most illustrious families, but the grandees of the Eastern provinces.

The new Rome must also have a *Populus Romanus,* privileged and exempt from taxation, and, above all, a *plebs*—one, as in Rome, recipient of free entertainment, of free bread baked from the best Egyptian wheat, and of free rations of pork, bacon, oil, and even wine.

To beautify the new capital, Constantine ransacked ancient temples and shrines—even Delphi, from which he removed the Tripod and the statue of Apollo. His confiscations (amounting perhaps to sixty thousand pounds of gold) made it possible for him to build in Constantinople an enormous Imperial palace, a huge hippodrome, a university, public schools and libraries, and magnificent Christian churches.

The Death of Constantine I (The Great), 337 Domestic tragedy marred an otherwise glorious reign. In 326, Constantine had his eldest son Crispus, a youth with a brilliant military future, put to death on a trumped-up charge of raping his stepmother, the Empress Fausta (who, it appears, had engineered it to remove him as a possible rival of her own three sons—Constantine II, Constantius II, and Constans). In the same year, the Empress herself died, scalded in a hot bath after the Emperor's mother, Helen, supposedly, had revealed that Fausta had committed adultery with a slave.

In 337, while preparing to lead an army against Persia in retaliation for unprovoked aggression against the Roman protectorate of Armenia, Constantine fell ill. Feeling the relentless approach of death, he summoned Bishop Eusebius of Nicomedia, who had vigorously defended Arius against Athanasius, to administer the sacrament of baptism. (It was not uncommon to put off baptism until late in life in order to die in a blameless state.) While still arrayed in the white robes of a Christian neophyte, Constantine died. His tomb was the mausoleum connected with the Church of the Twelve Apostles.

It would be difficult to overstate the significance of Constantine's reign. By following up and skillfully modifying Diocletian's military, economic, and administrative reforms, Constantine ensured that the unity of the Roman Empire would endure for another 150 years. One can question whether such a harsh, regimented, and economically stagnant empire as resulted was worth preserving. In the midst of crisis, however, Constantine could not afford the luxury of such a question, and to the majority of his hapless subjects, for such they now were, the known evils probably were preferable to a world without Rome at all.

Constantine had also taken Christianity, a small, persecuted sect, and given it the impetus that made it eventually the religion of not only the Roman Empire but of most of the modern Western world. Nor was his impact upon it merely political. His actions greatly influenced the formulation of its most widely accepted creed and institutional structure. Finally, by his splendid choice of a new capital for his Christian Empire, Constantine laid the foundations of the Byzantine Empire, which was to last a thousand years and have an incalculable impact upon Europe and the Near East.

XXXV

Life and Culture from Commodus to Constantine, A.D. 180 to 337

The economic, social, and cultural life of the Roman Empire from Commodus to Constantine is marked by change—rapid, radical, sometimes catastrophic. The economy entered a long period of decline, which was arrested at times but from which it never really recovered. The class structure of Roman society became much more stratified and eventually rigidified as the state attempted to regiment all for the grim effort of survival. Anxiety and insecurity left their marks on all classes and are reflected in the cultural life of the time. People turned more and more to religion, magic, and superstition for reassurance; disciplined, rational thought broke down; secular literature lost its creativity; and otherworldliness and sometimes a decline of technique characterized art and architecture.

Economic Life The dominant factor in economic life after Marcus Aurelius was inflation. Given its static technology, the Roman Empire had already reached its economic potential in the early second century A.D. After Marcus Aurelius, invasions, civil wars, and plagues disrupted production and trade. The ever-increasing size of the army and the civil bureaucracy as the Emperors tried to cope with these crises demanded so much money and manpower that there was not enough left to sustain a healthy private economy, and goods became scarce. Insecurity made the situation worse, for instead of investing their money, people began to hoard it, as the numerous finds of buried caches of coins from the third century demonstrate. Consequently, business and agriculture declined even further, so that prices for scarce goods and services soared, and the coinage became worthless. For example, during the disastrous period between 267 and 274, prices had increased seven hundred percent.

The suffering that resulted was great. That is the main reason why the soldiers kept demanding more pay and donatives from Septimius Severus and succeeding emperors. They were no more greedy than anybody else. They were just in a better position to force the government to help them, while others had to protect themselves as best they could. The great landowners were strong enough to resist government tax collectors. The middle class could shift some of it tax burdens onto the poor or seek refuge by joining the bureaucracy. The poor could become dependents of the great landowners, try to find government handouts at Rome and some other favored cities, join the army, become outlaws and brigands, or flee beyond the frontiers. All of these tactics, of course, just made the economy worse.

Attempts by the Emperors to deal with the situation did not help either. Beginning with Alexander Severus, the state had assumed greater and greater control over the producers of essential goods and services through official trade guilds (*collegia*), which controlled producers by a combination of subsidies and fixed prices. Eventually Diocletian tried to fix the prices of all goods and services in the Empire. Subsidies, however, required more taxes to support them, and fixed prices did not allow the producers enough profit to survive in a period of rapid inflation. Therefore, they either ceased to produce or turned to the black market, as Diocletian soon realized. Attempts to compel people to produce also backfired, because people then fled their occupations whenever they could.

One of the main difficulties in official attempts to stabilize the value of currency was the lack of precious metals in relation to the demand for coinage. Therefore, it was difficult to effect lasting monetary reform. Both Aurelian and Diocletian failed badly. Constantine was only partially successful. He did manage to stabilize the gold coinage with his new *solidi* by minting them at seventy-two instead of sixty to the Roman pound (11 oz.) and by measures designed to release hoarded gold. He forced large taxpayers to render certain payments to the treasury in gold, required that rents on Imperial estates be paid in gold, confiscated the supplies of gold forcibly amassed by his rival Licinius, and eventually confiscated the treasures of many pagan temples.

Constantine's silver issues, however, were not very great, and his coins of copper or billon (copper with a little silver) were failures. In 334, for example, the ratio of copper *denarii* to gold was 300,000 to the pound, or between 4250 to 4500 to the *solidus*. By Constantine's death in 337, the ratio was twenty million to the pound, or 275,000 to the *solidus*.

By 357, it was 330,000,000 to the pound! Obviously, the poor did not benefit from Constantine's stabilization of the gold coinage and continued to be ravaged by inflation.

Decline of the Money Economy   The monetary chaos of the third century almost destroyed the money economy. It wiped out the public and private alimentary and educational trust funds that had been one of the finest achievements of the Principate and, in many cases, reduced trade to the level of barter. This fact is implicit in Diocletian's system of taxation, which was based on payments in kind. Diocletian's monetary reforms were aimed at reviving a money economy, and his expectations are revealed in his Edict on Maximum Prices. Constantine's stabilization of the gold currency did revive the use of money in large transactions, and he was able to commute some tax payments in kind to payment in *solidi,* but for many people, barter and payment in kind were still the only means of exchange.

Decline of Overseas Trade   Rome's own troubles and disturbances beyond the Imperial frontiers disrupted foreign trade. The disintegration of the Chinese Empire in the late second century and the rise of the hostile Sassanid Persian Empire disrupted the land routes to the Far East during the third century. The routes across the Indian Ocean seem to have been abandoned in the early third century, although trade was resumed in that area in the fourth century through native middlemen. That such trade revived at all demonstrates the wealth that was still commanded by some people in the Empire and the continued demand for luxury goods, whose high profits ensured that the demand would be met.

Decline of Agriculture   From the middle of the third century onward, agriculture went into an irreversible decline throughout much of the Roman Empire. The combination of invasions, civil wars, inflation, and excessive taxation was ruinous to many. There were exceptions. North Africa was protected from serious invasions for another 150 years and had a guaranteed outlet for its grain and olive oil in the Imperially subsidized market of Rome. As an island, Britain was also better protected from invasion, particularly under strong governors like Constantius and Constantine, and its grain also had a government supported market in the armies along the Rhine. Some areas continued to flourish because they were protected by large military encampments. For example, the lovely wine-producing valley of the Moselle was guarded by Augusta Treverorum (Trèves, Trier), an Imperial residence, and the garrison on the Rhine at Moguntiacum (Mainz).

Egypt was geographically protected and was the special concern of the Emperors. Although Egypt also suffered agricultural decline in the chaos of the mid-third century, it revived in the fourth. Under the efforts of Diocletian and Constantine, who needed grain for his new capital, order was restored, the irrigation system was repaired, and agricultural production revived. Elsewhere, however, especially in the provinces along the Rhine and the Danube, the story is one of land relentlessly abandoned by cultivators despite official attempts to keep people on the land or to resettle it with colonists of captured foes.

Increase of Great Estates   In all cases where agriculture still prospered, it tended to become the domain of great landlords residing in fortified villas. In the prosperous days of the first and second centuries A.D., the spread of *latifundia* in Italy had halted, and everywhere freehold family farms or medium-sized estates were dominant. The troubles of the third century, however, caused the rapid growth of *latifundia* once more. The hereditary senatorial magnates or powerful government officials were the only ones with the resources to buy extra land or take over what others had abandoned. Often small farmers willingly surrendered their holdings to larger neighbors and agreed to pay rent as *coloni* (tenants) in return for the protection that powerful landlords with their social connections, fortified

villas, and private retainers could provide against tax collectors, military recruiters, brigands, and barbarian raiders.

Like medieval manors, these villa estates were largely self-sufficient. They produced most of what was needed for local consumption. Tenants paid their rents in kind, which supplied the landlords with food and fiber, and resident artisans provided most of the items needed for everyday use. Only specialized products, such as iron and luxuries for the landlord, had to be bought from outside.

Collapse of Manufacturing and Commerce within the Empire   Under these conditions it is clear that large-scale manufacturing and commerce within the Empire could not have existed to the degree that they had in the past. With the purchasing power of the great majority destroyed by inflation, agriculture largely reduced to subsistence, trade routes disrupted by instability on the frontiers, and profits destroyed by taxes or forced requisitions, private business and trade were severely damaged. The large-scale glass, pottery, metalware, and cloth industries that had flourished in the Western provinces during the second century shriveled. In order to keep the armies supplied with arms and clothing, the Emperors had to set up state-run armories and cloth-making operations, which naturally reduced further the opportunities for private entrepreneurs.

Social Life

Decline of Cities   The cities of the Empire had depended on the prosperity of cultivators in the surrounding countryside and resident absentee landlords, to whom their merchants and artisans supplied goods and services. Therefore, many of them, particularly in the West, declined severely under the economic conditions that began to prevail from the third century on. Archaeologically, this trend is clear from the length of third- and fourth-century city walls, which surrounded only one-fourth or less of the ground that cities previously covered. What remained tended to be inhabited mainly by government officials, their staffs, and the few private individuals needed to supply their needs.

A few cities like Rome, Constantinople, Augusta Treverorum, Mediolanum (Milan), or Antioch flourished because of special circumstances. Rome and Constantinople grew because the Emperors directly subsidized their populations with distributions of bread, meat, wine, and olive oil in the tradition of conspicuous patronage going back to Republican times. Augusta Treverorum and Mediolanum survived as large centers because they were Imperial residences and major military bases. Even Antioch, which still carried on significant commerce, probably could not have remained such a large city if it also were not the administrative center of Syria and the location of an Imperial mint and armory.

Devastation of the Curial Class The decline of business and commerce and the shrinking of cities were accompanied by the destruction of the decurions or curial class (*curiales*): the merchants, businessmen, and medium-sized landowners who made up the *curiae* (municipal senates or councils) of their local cities or towns. The fiscal and administrative policies of the Emperors only worsened their plight. In the past, as municipal magistrates and councillors, the *curiales* not only freely spent their own money to beautify their cities and towns, but had appropriated municipal funds for public works, baths, public entertainment, and food for the indigent. They also served as collectors of Imperial taxes and provided for the feeding and bedding of troops in transit and for change of horses for the Imperial post. They performed many of these functions for the state at their own expense. Indeed, the Emperor Majorian (457–461) once called them the nerves and vital organs of the state, but this pronouncement was more descriptive of their role in the second and third centuries. By the fourth century they had already lost the power to save themselves let alone serve the state.

Every five years, if not annually, they had to pay regular taxes in money or in kind. In addition, there were special emergency taxes payable in labor or products. When Diocletian made the municipal senators responsible for the collection of taxes within their territories, he drove them into bankruptcy and ruin. They had to make up arrears and deficiencies out of their own pockets. Powerless to compel great senatorial landlords to pay their share, they attempted to shift the burden to the poorer and more helpless classes, by whom they came to be regarded as oppressors and tyrants. Their office became a cruel burden from which they sought release as soldiers, tenants on large estates, and in later times as priests or monks.

Their attempts to escape brought down upon them the heavy hand of the government, which tied them to their jobs by forcing them to belong to associations variously known as colleges, corporations, or guilds. In 314, Constantine made membership in the shipowners' corporation a compulsory and hereditary obligation. Later, he compelled other essential workers and craftsmen, such as millers, bakers, butchers, shoemakers, carpenters, and bricklayers, to stay at their jobs for life and train their sons to follow the same trade. The corporations of the late Roman Empire gave origin to the Byzantine and probably some Islamic guilds but whether to those of medieval Italy, France, and Spain is a question still much disputed.

The Urban Poor Only in Rome, Constantinople, and few other favored cities did the urban poor find any significant relief. In those cities, the poor received food and entertainment on an incongruously generous scale. In most cities, which had to depend upon local revenues to support such generosity, the poor could no longer be fed and entertained. Life became desperate, and crime, prostitution, the selling of children, military service, and flight to the countryside or barbarian lands were among the few options left.

Villa Society of the Upper Class The upper class was made up basically of two types of people, those of great hereditary wealth, mostly in land, and those who rose through the army and bureaucracy to high positions where they could enrich themselves through the exercise of power. The latter invested their gains in land, and when they retired, they imitated those of hereditary wealth by deserting the faltering cities for fortified villas and self-sufficient estates in the country. Even the Emperor Diocletian retired to a great fortified villa at *Salonae* (Spalato, Split) on the Dalmatian coast. Their wealth enabled them to enjoy the luxuries that still came by way of foreign and domestic commerce, and they maintained some of the cultural traditions of earlier centuries. More and more, however, their activities, like those of their medieval counterparts, revolved around the defense of their territories and rural pursuits, such as hunting and riding.

Enserfment of the Coloni   Labor on the *latifundia* of the third century A.D. and subsequent centuries did not depend heavily on slavery. Household slaves were still common, but the supply of cheap unskilled labor had dried up. Emperors preferred to enlist captives in the Roman army or settle them on deserted lands. Therefore, most of the agricultural labor on the great estates was performed by the increasing numbers of *coloni,* free tenants. In 322, however, Constantine greatly reduced their freedom by a law permanently binding them to the soil in order to ensure a steady supply of vital agricultural labor. He thereby created the famous *colonatus,* the perpetual and hereditary status of *colonus* or serf. Landlords were authorized to collect from *coloni* the taxes due the government, to draft their sons into the army, and to exercise over them the functions of police and judge.

Increasing Stratification and Regimentation
The creation of the legally bound colonate reflected the increased stratification and regimentation at all levels of society. Roman society had always been very conscious of status, but in the late Empire there was a proliferation of formal titles within a strictly defined hierarchy. Members of the senatorial class, which included the great palace officials,

were called *clarissimi* (sing. *clarissimus*), most excellent. The highest equestrian officials, like the praetorian prefect, were *ementissimi* (sing. *ementissimus*), most outstanding. The next level of equestrians, like the vicars, dukes, and governors, were *perfectissimi,* most accomplished. Among all of these ranks, individuals who had performed particular services that the Emperor wished to recognize were called *comites* (sing. *comes*), counts, and even they were distinguished with gradations of the first, second, or third rank (*ordinis primi, secundi,* or *tertii*). The lower classes were referred to as *humiliores* (sing. *humilior*), lower, humbler.

Quite contrary to the spirit of law in the Republic and early Principate, Diocletian and Constantine continued Septimius Severus' practice of recognizing different levels of punishment for the same crimes committed by people of the lower and upper classes. Compliance with the law was also sought by the imposition of harsher penalties for all, but in certain areas there were continued attempts to protect the defenseless. Diocletian tried to halt the increasing sale of children by destitute parents by outlawing the practice, and Constantine forbade the crucifixion and facial branding of slaves. He also restricted the power of the *paterfamilias* to inflict punishment and tried to reform prisons.

Religion, Magic, and Superstition

In an increasingly chaotic and grim world, where people had little influence over events, it is no wonder that they turned more and more to religion and the occult for comfort. In the countryside, the familiar spirits of nature received pious devotion as they always had among the peasantry and continued to do so for centuries, as witnessed by the term *pagan,* which comes from the word *paganus* (of the countryside) and which the Christians applied to nonbelievers after Christianity became dominant in the cities. In the cities and army camps of the third century, however, various mystery religions, particularly those that dealt with the very relevant subjects of the forces of evil and how to overcome them, gained in popularity over the old Greco-Roman Olympian deities. Magicians and charlatans who claimed to have supernatural powers also attracted wide followings.

Religion and the State The all-too-obvious mortality and fallibility of emperors between the Severi and Diocletian destroyed emperor worship as a serious practice, and none of them were deified after death. Therefore, various emperors tried to enlist religious support for the state by claiming the personal favor of some divinity who would protect the state. Decius, who mounted the first general persecution of the Christians (250), tried to regain the favor of the traditional anthropomorphic Olympians, to whom Rome's success in better days had been attributed. He wanted to restore what the Romans had called the *pax deorum* (Peace of the Gods), which the old public priesthoods and festivals had been supposed to preserve.

Many traditionalists in the Roman senate welcomed and participated in this movement, and pagan senators at Rome remained a bastion of the traditional state religion for at least another 150 years. Diocletian had been following the same path by taking the name Jovius and giving Herculius to Maximian to signify a special relationship with Jupiter and Hercules. Also, he and Galerius tried to suppress the new religion of Manichaeism as well as Christianity.

Other emperors were more innovative. Gallienus was deeply interested in the Neoplatonic mysticism of Plotinus (see p. 353), through which a person could attain knowledge of the divine One, who ruled the universe. Aurelian tried to promote the syncretistic, almost monotheistic cult of Sol Invictus, the Unconquered Sun, as a way of uniting the Empire under one leader. That was also the cult favored by Constantine's father and to which he himself proclaimed allegiance before his conversion to Christianity, which shared some of its symbolism.

Isism and Mithraism The mystery cult of Isis did not continue to gain strength as it had in the first and second centuries A.D. Partly it became submerged in a general syncretism of mystical Eastern cults, magic, and symbolism (pp. 452–453), and partly it failed to satisfy those seekers of religious truth for whom the question of evil in the world was a major concern. Many such people, however, continued to be inspired by Mithraism, with its savior hero Mithras on the side of light and life (Ahura Mazda) pitted against the Zoroastrian forces of darkness and death (Ahriman), which could be interpreted easily in terms of good and evil. Mithraism was favored by the Severi, and numerous shrines from the third and fourth centuries are found in cities and military camps all over the Empire.

Manichaeism One of the most potent forces in the second half of the third century and for the next two hundred years was Manichaeism, the religion of a Persian prophet named Mani. Mani was a friend of the Sassanid Persian king Shapur (Sapor) I and started preaching with his support in 242. A little over thirty years later, however, he was executed by Shapur's grandson Varanes (Vahram, Varahan, Bahram) I under the influence of a conservative religious reaction.

Because Jesus plays a central role as the agent of ultimate salvation, Manichaeism can be classed as a heretical offshoot of Christianity. It also shared many similarities with the gnostic heresies of Christianity (p. 450) and grew up in the same intellectual atmosphere. This atmosphere was a product of the Hellenistic Age, during which Greek philosophy, Persian Zoroastrianism, Babylonian astrology, and various Eastern mystery cults all interacted with each other over the vast territories of the Hellenistic empires as far east as India. Mani had even traveled to India and included Buddha along with Zoroaster and Christ as prophets.

The Zoroastrian element is clear from the fundamental starting point of Manichaean belief—the existence of the Two Principles or Roots, the Light and the Dark. They are two completely opposite, eternal, palpable physical realms. The realm of Light contained everything orderly, peaceful, intelligent, and clear; the Dark contained everything disordered, turbulent, crass, and muddy. At some time in the past, according to Mani, the Dark invaded the Light, and that was the beginning of evil. In the ensuing struggle, this world was created from the bodies of the forces of Darkness, who had swallowed part of the realm of Light. Therefore, this world and all that is in it are an admixture of particles of Light and the material of Darkness.

It was Jesus who revealed to Adam this miserable state of affairs and pointed out how he could gradually free the Divine Substance, the particles of Light, within him from its physical prison and join in the process of distilling the Light from the Darkness to restore the original perfect state. Unfortunately, the Agents of Darkness created Eve to entice Adam from his task, and through their children the particles of Light were scattered still further. Jesus, however, using the moon and the sun, set up a mechanism to distill the souls of the dead and reconstruct the Perfect Man. Eventually, Mani claimed, the world will end with Jesus' second coming, and a great fire will refine its remains for 1468 years until all heavenly material is removed and the Realm of Light is completely restored.

This blend of Zoroastrian dualism and Christian salvation was a strong rival of orthodox Christianity. It even claimed the allegiance of St. Augustine in the late fourth century before he became a true Christian. Manichaeism's major weakness in competition with orthodox Christianity, however, was its lack of personal salvation. In Manichaeism, the focus of salvation was reconstructing the realm of Light, into which the particles trapped inside the physical person were submerged. There was no survival of the individual personality, which Christianity promised and many found more appealing. Also, the Manichees never enjoyed the advantage of converting a Roman emperor and lost the support of the Persian emperors.

Judaism and Christianity Judaism maintained itself among the Jewish population dispersed throughout the Empire, but its missionary impetus was destroyed by Hadrian's ban on Jewish proselytizing, so that conversion was rare. Within that restriction, Judaism remained a protected religion. Therefore, there was no official persecution although local outbreaks of violence against Jews did occur, particularly in Greek cities like Alexandria with large Jewish communities that claimed both special status and full citizenship contrary to the whole tradition of Greek civic life.

Because Christianity had assumed an identity quite distinct from its Jewish origins, it had lost any claim to special protection when Christians refused to worship the gods of the state, and it became subject to official persecution as the third-century emperors sought unity through religious means. Persecution, however, helped Christianity by strengthening its organization and attracting publicity through the martyrs. It was during this period, moreover, that the New Testament canon of scriptures and the major theological doctrines of the Church were established, a period of tremendous ferment that resulted in the establishment of official orthodoxy at the Council of Nicea (325).

Besides the Donatist schism (pp. 437–438) and the Arian heresy (see p. 439), there were numerous other sources of contention among the thinkers of the early Church. One of the major forces in this ferment was the influence of Greek philosophy and pagan mystery cults that permeated the world in which Christianity was developing and from which it was drawing its converts. The commonest manifestation of this influence was the spread of various gnostic heresies, which paralleled the elaborate cosmologies and dualistic views of many Greek philosophers and pagan cults and saw the divine immortal soul trapped in an evil mortal body. Gnostics believed that Christ was the one who brought knowledge (*gnosis*) of these things. It was the acceptance of the truth of this knowledge that would free the soul from its mortal prison and allow it to return to the pure heavenly realm where it naturally belonged.

What prevented Christianity from becoming just another Hellenized Eastern mystery cult, however, was, first, its acceptance of the Holy Book of the Jews (the Old Testament, as it came to be called), with its completely different spirit, as the foundation for and proof of its faith in Jesus as the Messiah. Second, its unique organizational structure was based on the idea of apostolic succession, which could check the spread of beliefs and practices that diverged too radically from the spirit of the Old Testament and the early Christian writings that came to be canonized in the third century as the New Testament, written largely by men whose background was still more Jewish than Gentile. This system appears already worked out in all its major details between 180 and 190 in the works of Irenaeus, Bishop of Lyons, particularly his *Five Books against Heresies* and the *Demonstration of Apostolic Preaching*.

By 200, the Church in the West had already matured to its familiar form. Irenaeus, who was a Greek from Asia Minor, was the last major Christian writer in the West to use Greek. Latin became the standard language of the Western Church for both theology and daily use. The form and order of Sunday worship and the celebration of the Eucharist had assumed their standard outlines. By now the Bishop of Rome was recognized as having primacy over other bishops and churches and was looked up to by even the Bishop of Carthage, the second largest Western see and home of an important school of thinkers founded by Tertullian and Cyprian. (Tertullian himself, however, eventually became an adherent of the Montanist heresy (see p. 452).

In the mid-third century, disputes between Rome and Carthage arose over the question of treating apostates who wanted to return to the Church and over the validity of baptism by heretics. The Roman bishops tended to be liberal on both counts, and the Carthaginians led by Cyprian favored the more strict view of the Roman priest Novatian; but the threat of persecution from without prevented a serious breach. Eventually, of course, the issue erupted into the Donatist schism, but Carthaginian bishops generally remained loyal to Rome. Rome also rejected the Eastern practice of commemorating Christ's death on the Jewish Passover and established the observance of Easter Sunday. Complicated theories about the relationship of the divine Logos to God the Father along the lines of Greek philosophical speculation were also rejected. Eventually, this question would cause great dissension between Rome and Alexandria, but during the third century even Alexandria followed Rome and accepted the Roman New Testament as canonical.

On the whole, however, the state of the Church in the East was much more fluid than in the West during the third century. Egypt was full of gnostic heresies, and the close relationship between Rome and Alexandria was part of the effort to control them. Nevertheless, Greek-speaking Alexandria was much more open to the influence of Greek philosophical thought than the Latin-speaking West. By the end of the second century, the famous catechetical school of Alexandria was becoming a veritable Christian university. Between 180 and 200, Clement was the head of this school. Originally a pagan from Athens, he did much to impart Platonizing tendencies to the Christian theology expounded by the school. He was followed by Origen, who made logic, dialectic, natural science, geometry, and astronomy standard parts of the curriculum. With such training, the Alexandrian Church Fathers skillfully used Greek philosophy against their pagan critics and gave a greater intellectual cast to Christian thought, which gained greater respect among the pagan intellectual elite of the Empire.

It was precisely the influence of Platonic thought, however, that caused Origen to develop the heretical views that this world resulted from evil and was not a perfect creation before the Fall and that the Trinity is three separate entities, not one. On the one hand, therefore, he encouraged certain gnostic ideas, and, on the other, he set the stage for the divisive Arian heresy under Constantine.

Origen's pupils and ideas were very influential in Syria and Palestine, where speculation about the Trinity also caused controversy.

The most notable involved Paul of Samosata in Syria, who had become bishop of Antioch in the 260s. He viewed the Logos as one with the Father and the son as wholly human. The Origenist bishops condemned his views as heretical mostly on the ground of his joining the Logos with the Father in the same essence. Thus they supplied even more ammunition for the controversy that rent the Eastern Church under Constantine.

East of the Roman province of Syria, in the Mesopotamian client kingdoms and border lands, a Syriac-speaking church was founded around A.D. 170 by Tatian, a disciple of Justin Martyr. He provided a Syriac harmony (unified version) of the Four Gospels known as the *Diatesseron* (*Four-in-One*), which became its basic testament. The conversion of king Agbar of Edessa gave great impetus to the Syriac church, and it remained strong and orthodox for many centuries. It did produce one major heretic, however, Bardaisan (Bardesanes), who became a Christian about 180. He was a highly educated Aramaean trained in astronomy and astrology. He combined many of the ideas that he had picked up earlier with his new faith. This heretical synthesis of Christian and non-Christian ideas was the basis of many of the views later espoused by Mani.

In the early fourth century, Christians in Egypt and Syria became embroiled in a conflict over those who had lapsed under Galerius' persecution. Those who denied absolution to the lapsed were led by Meletius, who was condemned at the Council of Nicea in 325. His followers, however, maintained a schismatic Meletian sect for centuries.

In Asia Minor, whose churches were the earliest outside Palestine, the Christians were numerous and tended to remain on good terms with their pagan neighbors. In the mid-second century, as in North Africa, there arose an internal dispute over the question of readmitting to the Church those who had lapsed during the Decian persecution. A number of Christians in Asia Minor adopted the strict position of Novatian, whose followers had become a schismatic sect and extended to all major sins his

view on the inability of the Church to grant absolution. The Novatians, therefore, were very puritanical. They tried to lead completely sinless lives, called themselves *Cathari* (Pure Ones), and insisted on the rebaptism of converts.

In the late second century, a popular heresy had been introduced by Montanus, a convert in Phrygia. He began prophesying in the belief that the Second Coming was near and claimed inspiration by the Holy Spirit. If the validity of this prophetic movement had been granted, the doctrines of the Church would have been thrown into chaos by the constant occurrence of new revelations among those claiming divine inspiration, and the vital unity of the Church would have been destroyed before it had had a chance to consolidate its position in the Empire.

The only other controversy of note involving the churches of Asia Minor was the refusal to bow to Rome over the question of Easter.

Magic and Superstition   While Christianity was winning many converts and working out its formal theology, many people of all classes turned to various forms of magic and superstition. A collection of works under the supposed authorship of Hermes Trismegistus that dealt with astrology, alchemy, magic, and theurgy (the art of summoning and controlling divine powers) was very popular. The most famous theurge of the third century was Iamblichus of Chalcis in southern Syria. He was born about 250 and was well trained at Rome in the science and philosophy of his day, which were both very much influenced by the general religious atmosphere of the time. He returned to Syria and spent his life trying to counteract the growth of Christianity and restore paganism by creating a vast synthesis of mystery religions and pagan cults with elaborate symbolism, sacrifices, and magical spells. His followers claimed that he caused spirits to appear, glowed as he prayed, and levitated from the ground. His teachings attracted much popular interest and had a major impact later on the Emperor Julian's conversion to paganism and his attempt to restore the old religion (pp. 462–463).

Science and Philosophy   The temper of the times was not conducive to objective scientific thought. The last creative, rigorously systematic philosopher of antiquity was Plotinus (205–270), a Greek from Egypt. He had studied under a mysterious philosopher named Ammonius Saccas at Alexandria and had joined the expedition of Gordian III to Persia (243) in the hope of studying the wisdom of Persia and India. When Gordian was killed the next year, Plotinus went to Rome, where he joined a group of ascetic philosophers and set up a school.

Starting with Plato's philosophy, he propounded a systematic explanation of the universe that gave birth to a new school of thought called Neoplatonism. This system is expounded in a magnum opus known as the *Enneads* (*Groups of Nine*) in six sections of nine books each. It is heavily influenced by the mystical Pythagorean elements in Plato. For Plotinus, everything is derived from the One, a single, immaterial, impersonal, eternal force from which reality spreads out in a series of concentric circles, the utmost one of which is matter, the lowest level of reality. Each level of reality depends upon the next higher: Matter depends upon Nature, which depends upon the World-soul, which depends upon the World-mind, which depends upon the One. A person contains all of these levels of being in microcosm, and by focusing the power of the intellect can attain a level of being equal to that of the World-mind. At that point one may be able to achieve such a complete unity of self that an ecstatic union with the One itself is achieved.

Obviously, Plotinus' goal is the same as that of contemporary religion, but it is philosophical in that it is reached through pure, contemplative intellect, not through magic, ritual, or an intermediary savior. Such rigorously intellectual mysticism was far beyond most of his contemporaries, however, and Neoplatonism soon became overlaid with the magical musings of people like Iamblichus.

The *Enneads* was actually published by Plotinus' pupil and assistant Porphyry (232/33–ca. 305), teacher of Iamblichus. Porphyry was not a creative thinker, but he was quick to grasp the ideas of others and was an accurate interpreter and publicist. It was he who did the most to popularize Plotinus' ideas and saw them as the bulwark of pagan philosophy and religion against the Christians, who threatened the old ways. He wrote a massive fifteen-book defense of tradition against the Christians, which set the stage for Iamblichus' even more vehement effort to rally the forces of paganism against the Christian menace.

Literature   The works of the Church Fathers, heretics, and philosophers show that education in the arts of writing and rhetoric was still strong in the third century, at least in the major centers of the Empire. The state needed people with such training both in the army and in the civil bureaucracy. Therefore, it did not slacken in its efforts to secure them by supporting higher education through publicly salaried professorships. The system's heavy emphasis upon literature and rhetoric produced among the upper classes, who alone could afford to take advantage of the opportunity provided, innumerable people who could turn a quick hexameter or make a fine-sounding speech, and hundreds of competent but second-rate examples exist, particularly in the Greek East.

Many of the emperors were products of this system and shared the literary interests of the educated upper class. Septimius Severus was well educated in literature and law and wrote his autobiography (now lost) in Greek. His wife Julia Domna was very interested in philosophy and religion. She patronized pagan sophists and arranged a meeting with the Christian thinker Origen. Severus Alexander had an intellectual circle that included historians, orators, and jurists. Gordian I was a poet, as was Gallienus, who also took an interest in Plotinus and had plans to set up a Neoplatonic state with Plotinus as head in Campania. Carus' son Numerian was highly regarded as a poet. Diocletian could quote Vergil and appointed Lactantius to the chair of rhetoric at Nicomedia. Constantine later made him tutor of his sons at Constantinople.

Biography and History under the Severi Julia Domna's role as patroness has been exaggerated in the past to include almost every literary and intellectual figure of note in Rome at the time. The only known important member of her circle whose work has survived is Philostratus (b. ca. 170), a Greek sophist who wrote a collection of biographies of previous sophists and, at Domna's request, a biography of the first-century A.D. Cappadocian mystic and miracle worker, Apollonius of Tyana, who is presented as a pagan equivalent of Christ. Probably not long after Philostratus, another Greek biographer, Diogenes Laertius, produced a collection of biographies of ancient philosophers that is extremely useful in reconstructing the history of Greek philosophy.

Under Alexander Severus, the Greek historian Cassius Dio produced his history of Rome from its founding in 229. Although not a historian of the first rank, Dio used good sources and supplies much valuable information in the absence of other sources. A few years later Herodian produced his valuable Greek narrative of events from 180 to 238. Marius Maximus, a contemporary of Dio and Herodian, wrote a continuation of Suetonius with Latin biographies of the emperors from Nerva to Elagabalus. Their accounts often included spicy fiction with the facts but also contained much of value. Although they are now lost, they provided the basic framework for the parallel biographies in the first and best part of the notorious *Historia Augusta*.

Roman Scholarship   In the Severan and early post-Severan period, many learned treatises and commentaries were produced on classical Latin authors. Pomponius Porphryion, for example, produced an extant commentary on Horace. The tradition was continued in the early 300s by commentaries such as those of Aelius Donatus and Servius Honoratus on Terence and Vergil and by the grammatical work of Nonnius Marcellus, which also provides quotations from many lost works. Under the Severi, Claudius Aelianus preserved much curious information in moralizing compendia on animal and human life (*De Natura Animalium* and *Varia Historia*), which were highly valued in the Middle Ages.

Scholarship and History at Athens   Athens still survived as an important university town in the third century. Late in the century, Plato's Academy was headed by the rhetorician Longinus. His work *On the Sublime* is an important example of ancient literary criticism. After the Germanic Heruli raided Athens in 268, Longinus left to become an advisor to Zenobia at Palmyra and was later executed for treason by Aurelian. His place at the Academy was taken by Dexippus, a historian of considerable merit. He wrote a chronological history in twelve books down to A.D. 269/70, an account of Alexander's successors, and a history of the Gothic invasions between 238 and 270. They are all lost, but the substance of the latter is preserved in Zosimus' history (p. 515).

Scholarship and Science at Alexandria Scholarship and science continued at Alexandria in the third century, but their creative energies were spent. The best works that could be produced were repetitions or compilations of past work. The most famous is the *Deipnosophistae* (*Sophists at Dinner*) by Athenaeus. It draws on over fifteen hundred earlier works to present essays on every topic under the sun. Its chief merit is that it preserves fragments of numerous works otherwise lost. After Athenaeus, pagan scholarship at Alexandria suffered a severe blow from Zenobia's raid in 269/70, when the Museum was severely damaged.

Poetry and Greek Romances The best Latin poet of the age was Marcus Aurelius Olympicus Nemesianus in the late third century. Nemesianus was from Carthage and was close to the Emperor Carus and his son Numerian, upon whom he had hoped to write an epic. His four surviving eclogues are worthy successors to Vergil's, and his didactic poem on hunting, the *Cynegetica,* is in the tradition of the *Georgics.* In Greek the only poem of note is another didactic poem on a rural theme, the *Halieutica,* which deals with fishing and was written by Oppian at the beginning of the third century.

Much more entertaining, however, and typical of an age that sought escape from a harsh world are the Greek romances. They usually involve a virtuous heroine and steadfast hero who are separated by some mischance and experience all manner of hair-raising adventures, disasters, and narrow escapes until they are happily reunited at last. The genre originated at least as early as the first century A.D., but two of the best examples are found in the third. *Daphnis and Chloe* by Longus has remained popular down to the present. Its innocent young shepherd and shepherdess, raised as foundlings in an idyllic pastoral setting, fall in love, are separated, find their true identities in the course of various adventures, and happily find each other again. The second example is the *Aethiopica* of Heliodorus, a long tale involving a virtuous heroine separated from a devoted lover. She turns out to be the lost daughter of an Ethiopian king, and the noble lover finds and marries her in the end.

Art and Architecture

Sculpture Despite all the troubles of the age, considerable art was produced for emperors and wealthy magnates. Portraiture on coins maintained a high standard of realism as vehicles of official propaganda. Portrait sculpture also continued the vigorous Roman tradition. From the Severi to Gallienus, sculptors strove for psychological realism in order to emphasize the true character of the subject.

Under Gallienus there was a preference for the more idealized portrait in the classical Greek style, but after that, the influence of Neoplatonism caused a shift to a more schematized, geometric style that gave a transcendent quality to the subjects, a style that prefigured the Middle Ages.

Relief sculpture became a striking feature of the elaborately decorated stone sarcophagi that wealthy Christians and pagans began to use as the new religious influences of the age caused the practice of bodily burial to replace cremation. Some feature groupings of classical figures around a philosopher or poet, who symbolizes the triumph of wisdom over death. Others feature a heroic figure in the midst of a chaotic battle to symbolize the triumph of good over evil. Christians depicted the Good Shepherd or Old Testament stories of God's deliverance. Despite the unclassical lack of balance in many of these scenes, the individual figures are very skillfully carved and are thoroughly in the tradition of Greco-Roman realism.

There were not many opportunities to produce public relief sculptures throughout the difficult times of the third century. The genre revived under the more stable regimes of Diocletian and Constantine, but the spirit and quality was different. For example, reliefs such as those that were made for the Arch of Constantine rather than reused from other monuments show a stiff, frontal, stylized, hieratic quality in keeping with the otherworldly aura fostered by the Imperial Court. They are also rather hastily and crudely done, a fact that may indicate a lack of skilled sculptors.

Painting and Mosaics Painting and mosaic art, however, flourished throughout the period from the Severi to Constantine. Painting is represented mainly by murals preserved on the excavated walls of homes, public buildings, tombs, synagogues, temples, and churches from around the Empire. Excellent mosaics also adorned many of these buildings, particularly their floors. The level of technical skill remained very high, and the scenes repre-

These stylized figures at St. Mark's in Venice are thought to represent Diocletian and the other three tetrarchs.

sented are valuable in reconstructing the life of the times.

Architecture Despite the Empire's serious economic problems, the building activity under the Severi was more than had been seen for many years. At Rome the Arch of Septimius Severus still stands in the Forum. Mas-

sive new additions were made to the Imperial residence, whose foundations are visible on the Palatine. Caracalla built a huge new complex of baths and a new camp for the Imperial bodyguards, both of which are now in ruins. In North Africa, Septimius' hometown, Leptis Magna, received a whole complex of monumental buildings, whose remains today pro-

The Arch of Constantine at Rome. *Note the style of the narrow bands of relief sculpture over the side arches. (Courtesy Fratelli Alinari, Florence)*

vide a striking example of Imperial architecture and urban planning. All of these remains, moreover, show solid Roman craftsmanship.

During the anarchy between the Severi and Diocletian, there was not much opportunity for public architecture other than defensive works such as Aurelian's partially preserved twelve-mile-long wall around Rome and fortifications in the provinces. Under Diocletian and Constantine, however, public architecture enjoyed a major revival in places that received Imperial favor. At Rome, Diocletian rebuilt the senate house that still stands in the Forum and massive baths that have largely been preserved. Maxentius built a circus, which once held fifteen thousand spectators, and probably a temple that is now the Church of Saints Cosmas and Damian at the east end of the Forum. Next to this temple he also started the tremendous basilica, now mostly ruined, that Constantine finished, and Constantine himself built the great arch that still stands just to the southwest of the Colosseum. Of course, Constantine lavished great expense on fortifications, civic buildings, and churches at his new capital after 324, but they have been almost completely obliterated by the later activity of Justinian and his successors.

This fourth-century mosaic from the Sicilian villa at Piazza Amerina that may have belonged to the Emperor Maximian is from a series depicting women engaged in athletic contests. (Courtesy New York Public Library Picture Collection)

While the buildings of Diocletian and Constantine show no decline of engineering skill, the workmanship tends to be rougher and more careless than before. In all cases, however, the aim was usually massiveness, not gracefulness. The baths and palaces of the Severi, the baths of Diocletian, and the buildings of Maxentius and Constantine are grim in their determination to dwarf and overawe in the assertion of raw power. They reflect a mentality of siege, a desire to crush all into submission to the central authority, and an iron will to prevail over the forces that threatened the Empire's life.

The pressures of the third century A.D. had moved Roman social and cultural life in the direction that later Medieval Europe would follow. Barter and local self-sufficiency were becoming characteristic of economic life in many places. Large numbers of the rich had fled to their fortified villas, and the *coloni* had been turned into serfs, while the middle-class *curiales* of the frequently shrinking towns had been bankrupted. Religion and philosophy were both concerned about salvation in the next world rather than life in this one. Magic and superstition were popular everywhere, and secular letters, though far from dead, were stagnant. Physically, the Empire had taken on the look of the besieged, and so it was. Diocletian and Constantine, almost by sheer will, had pulled the Empire back from total collapse and reorganized it from top to bottom to continue the struggle against the forces of dissolution as they and their contemporaries understood them. In terms of modern ideals, there is much to criticize, but in practical terms their options were severely limited.

XXXVI

From Constantine's Dynasty to Theodosius the Great, A.D. 337 to 395

Diocletian and Constantine had helped to save the Roman Empire from the chaos that had threatened to engulf it in the last half of the third century. They had singlemindedly mobilized Rome's diminishing resources for the supreme effort of self-preservation. As a result, the Empire survived intact during the fifty-eight years between the deaths of Constantine the Great and Theodosius the Great, despite bloody feuding among Constantine's heirs, two serious military defeats, distracting struggles between Christians and pagans, and the increasing need to man the armies with Germanic recruits or mercenaries.

Sources   The general historical sources for this period are good. The best by far are the surviving books of Ammianus Marcellinus' history of Rome, written about 390. Ammianus, an experienced pagan military officer who had traveled extensively and served on major campaigns in both the East and West, was the last major Latin historian. Although he had been born in Antioch and was a native speaker of Greek, he retired to Rome, where the old aristocracy was tenaciously attempting to preserve pagan Roman culture. Similarly harking back to the past, Ammianus pro-

claimed himself the heir of Tacitus by beginning his history of Rome with the death of Domitian (where Tacitus had ended) and continuing it down to the fateful battle of Adrianople in 378. Unfortunately, the first thirteen books, covering events up to 353, are lost, but books 14 to 31 are invaluable because they cover events of which Ammianus was a contemporary.

Less valuable for the period before Adrianople but indispensible after that is the Greek *New History* of Zosimus, another pagan, who lived under Theodosius II. His theme was the decline of Rome, and the first book sketched the Empire's history from Augustus to Diocletian, while the other five books covered events in greater detail from Diocletian to Alaric's sack of Rome in 410. Although Ammianus was evenhanded in his history, Zosimus is an interesting example of the anti-Christian pagans, who ascribed Rome's troubles to the abandonment of the old faith. On the opposite side, Paulus Orosius, a friend of St. Augustine, wrote a partisan Christian account of human history from Adam to A.D. 417 in seven books. It is entitled *Against the Pagans* and attempts to show that mankind suffered even more disasters when paganism was dominant than under Christian emperors.

There are numerous minor written sources. The brief series of Imperial lives by Aurelius Victor and the anonymous *Epitome of the Caesars,* Eutropius' *Breviary* of Roman history down to 364, and St. Jerome's continuation of Eusebius' *Chronicle* all contain occasional bits of useful information. Other valuable written sources are the numerous lives of saints, the writings of the Emperor Julian, the letters and writings of Libanius of Antioch (p. 514), the orations of the late-fourth-century Greek sophist Themistius (p. 514), a collection of fourth-century Latin panegyrics, the works of Ausonius, tutor of the Emperor Gratian (p. 516), the letters of the pagan Roman noble Symmachus (p. 515), the voluminous letters, sermons, and treatises of the early Church Fathers (pp. 518–519), and the law codes of Theodosius II and Justinian, which preserve edicts and judicial decisions from this period. As always, however, these general sources must be supplemented by more specialized archaeological, numismatic, epigraphical, and papyrological research.

The Sons and Heirs of Constantine

Constantine's Christianity did not improve the character of his children or soften harsh political realities after his death. Constantine had had, besides the ill-fated Crispus, son of his first wife, three sons by Fausta—Constantine II, Constantius II, and Constans. He also had two half-brothers, Flavius Dalmatius and Julius Constantius, who themselves had several children, first cousins of his own. Since Constantine had made no clear provisions for a successor, there were numerous candidates with legitimate claims. After three and one-half months of difficult negotiations among the various claimants and powerful military officers, a settlement was reached: Constantine II received Britain, Gaul, and Spain; Constans obtained Italy, Africa, and Pannonia; Constantius II procured Asia and Egypt; one of the cousins, Dalmatius the Younger, gained Thrace and Macedonia; while another, Hannibalianus, was promised the kingship of Pontus and Armenia. Constantius II, however, a devious and ruthless man, spread false rumors that Constantine had been murdered by his half-brothers. These rumors enflamed the troops in Constantinople, and they butchered the half-brothers and their sons, with the exception of Julius Constantius' two youngest sons, the half-brothers Gallus and Julian.

Civil War Naturally, this bloodletting did not improve the situation. Constantine's three sons remained jealous and suspicious of each other. Under a new, three-way division, Constantine II received all of the Western Empire, with Constans governing Africa, Italy, and Illyricum under his supervision, while Constantius II administered the eastern half of the Empire alone. Constantine II, fearing the intentions of Constans, who refused to act like a subordinate, tried to seize his territory in 340 and was killed in the ensuing battle. To Constans, then, fell sole control of the West. While Constantius II defended the eastern boundary against the encroachments of the Persian king Shapur (Sapor) II, Constans set about restoring order in Britain and along the Rhine. Harsh with his troops and unable to relieve inflation, Constans fell victim to the conspiracy of Magnentius ten years later. Constantius II, having disengaged himself from the Persians, quickly marched west and for two years inflicted a series of defeats on Magnentius, who finally committed suicide in 353. Thus the Empire came under the rule of a single emperor once more.

Gallus Made Caesar Still, the problems of the Empire were too great for one man to manage alone. After moving west, Constantius II had soon realized that he needed a loyal subordinate to act as his personal representative in the East. Appointing such a person was always dangerous because the temptations of power and the force of events often turned the subordinate into a rival. After much hesitation, indecision, and probably some pangs of guilt, Constantius II chose as Caesar his cousin Gallus, one of the two who had been spared in the massacre of Constantine's male relatives.

It would not have been wise to choose an unrelated Caesar. On the other hand, in view of the two men's personalities, the choice of Gallus seems bound to have been unsuccessful. Gallus, only about twenty-five years old, had lived under close house arrest since the massacre of 337. He had no experience in Imperial affairs, had a hot temper, and must have had a certain dislike and distrust of Constantius II, who was responsible for the murder of his father and elder brother. Conversely, Constantius, who must have realized that and who was a naturally suspicious person, did not trust Gallus. Therefore, when he sent Gallus to Antioch to guard the eastern frontier, Constantius severely restricted his powers. He surrounded him with spies, and gave him a staff chosen more for loyalty to the Emperor than their suitability for working with Gallus.

Despite these disadvantages, Gallus handled his assignment remarkably well from his base at Antioch. Militarily, he kept the Persians from taking advantage of Rome's civil war in the West. This success alone was enough to raise Constantius' jealousy, fear and suspicion. Moreover, they were aggravated by spies and officers who sought to ingratiate themselves with him and by complaints from the Antiochene upper class, who resented Gallus' efforts to prevent them from profiteering by hoarding scarce grain. Their resistance had prompted harsh and intemperate responses (which may have been exaggerated by Ammianus, who was an upper-class Antiochene). In 354, after the death of Magnentius, Constantius felt secure enough to recall Gallus, who at first resisted and then agreed to meet him in Italy. Gallus' stop in Constantinople along the way convinced Constantius that he was aiming for the throne. When Gallus reached Italy, Constantius ordered him arrested and beheaded (354).

The Rise of Julian Constantius II soon needed a colleague again, however. While he was fighting restless tribes along the Danube, internal intrigue drove Silvanus, the valuable military commander of Gaul, into rebellion. Constantius was able to procure the speedy assassination of Silvanus, but the damage already had been done. The Germanic tribes across the Rhine had taken advantage of the confusion to seize strategic frontier forts, make deep inroads into Gaul and inflict severe damage on the region's economy. Unable to fight simultaneously on two major fronts, Constantius was forced to choose another Caesar. Despite his experience with Gallus, he was persuaded, with the advice of his wife, Eusebia, to nominate Gallus' twenty-three-year-old half-brother, Julian, the only other survivor of the massacre of 337.

The omens for success hardly seem much better in this case than they did for Gallus. Again, a totally inexperienced young man, who had spent all but his last four years under close house arrest in an atmosphere of suspicion and intrigue and having only servants, clerical tutors, and books for companions, was thrust into a position of responsibility for which he did not have the trust of Constantius. Julian, however, had the advantage of a much more congenial personality and a sharp intellect well trained in rhetoric, history, and philosophy that helped compensate for deficiencies in experience.

Quick to size up a situation, Julian was careful not to repeat Gallus' political mistakes and showed a shrewd military sense of when to act boldly without foolish risks. He soon proved invaluable against the Germans without unduly arousing Constantius' suspicions. By 357 he had achieved great popularity with the soldiers in Gaul and effective command of the army. In that year he won a smashing victory at Strasbourg over German forces several times larger than his own. Julian spent the next two years methodically restoring Roman defenses in Britain and all along the Rhine. Well-planned and bold punitive expeditions deep into German territory overawed the various tribes and made the cities and fertile lands of Gaul safe for peaceful occupation once more.

By 359, however, Julian's safety was threatened. To encourage peace and prosperity, Julian had sought to limit the abuses of Roman officials, although he had no civil authority. High officials who profited from corruption denigrated Julian at court and played on Constantius' suspicious and fearful nature. In that same year, moreover, Julian's chief advocate at court, Eusebia, died, and Constantius, moved back to the East to meet renewed threats from Persia. Constantius seized the chance to undermine Julian by summoning many of his troops to the eastern frontier. Julian's refusal to comply only increased his popularity among his troops, who did not want to leave their native region, and their friends and families, who did not want to see them go.

Finally, in February of 360, to protect themselves and their beloved commander from Constantius II, the troops proclaimed Julian Emperor, ostensibly against his will. For the next year, while Constantius was securing the eastern frontier, Julian negotiated for a peaceful settlement of the situation. Constantius adamantly refused all offers of joint rule and set out to attack Julian in 361. Julian had already seized the initiative by marching east first, but before their two armies could clash, Constantius suddenly took ill and died. Since Constantius had no son to succeed him, Julian became sole Emperor without a struggle.

The Empire Under Constantius II Although not one of history's more pleasing characters, Constantius II had not been a bad Emperor. In many ways he was a Tiberius to Constantine's Augustus. Insecure and indecisive, he was often unduly influenced by unscrupulous members of his court and resorted to deviousness to secure his ends. To the best of his limited abilities, however, he had dutifully followed the path marked out by his father. "One Empire and one Church" were the foundations of his policies, as they had been for his father. The former helps to explain his cold-blooded actions in 337, his subsequent refusal to recognize either Magnentius or Julian as coemperors, and his willingness to resort to civil war in each case.

Unlike his pleasure-loving brother Constans, Constantius II never neglected the ar-

duous duties of protecting the frontiers. Most of his reign was spent in the military camp, not the sumptuous accommodations of the new capital, and while he was not so bold a general as his father or his rival Julian, he did maintain the Empire's territorial integrity.

As an administrator, Constantius II continued the centralizing tendencies of Diocletian and Constantine. At the same time, his legislation shows an honest attempt to mitigate the abuses of bureaucratic power that the system fostered.

Finally, he zealously encouraged the union of the Christian Church and Roman state that Constantine had begun. He reaffirmed Constantine's earlier ban against pagan sacrifices and ordered the closing of all pagan temples in 356. Theologically, Constantius II espoused a moderate Arian position and promoted doctrinal unity from that perspective. In 359, he summoned two regional councils of bishops—in the West at Ariminum (Rimini) on the Adriatic coast of Italy and in the East at Seleucea on the Calycadnus in Cilicia. Both councils eventually accepted a creed that declared Christ to be "like the Father," and this creed was confirmed by a general council at Constantinople in the following year. Had Constantius lived longer and defeated Julian, he might have been able to make the compromise stick, but his death in 361 quickly threw religious matters into turmoil once more.

Julian the Apostate As had all of his relatives, Julian had been raised a Christian. His secondary education had been supervised by Bishop George of Cappadocia, and he had even taken lower orders as a lector in the Church. George, however, had a fine library of classical literature and Greek philosophy, especially Neoplatonist philosophy. Julian found the spirit of Hellenism in these works more attractive than the Christianity espoused by those who had murdered his family and forced him to endure years of lonely exile. When released from exile, Julian had gone to

Pergamum to study rhetoric and then to Athens and the study of philosophy. Some time in the course of these studies he became convinced that paganism was the path of true religion and secretly converted. Soon after he entered Constantinople in 361, however, Julian openly proclaimed his devotion to the old ways by rescinding the laws against paganism.

Officially, Julian merely proclaimed religious toleration for all; in practice, he used all the subtle powers of his office to advance paganism at the expense of the Church. While he hoped that toleration would produce the unedifying spectacle of uncompromising adherents of the Nicene Creed fighting with Arians, he worked to create a Neoplatonic syncretism of pagan cults with the sun god as the Universal One. He even tried to give this unified Neoplatonic paganism an ethical emphasis and organizational structure modeled on those of the Church that he had renounced. To the Christians Julian was a demonic agent of the Devil, an impression that was reinforced by his emphasis on magic, divination, omens, theurgy, and elaborate sacrifices, which even many of his friends thought excessive. Nevertheless, the sudden and dramatic turn that his fortunes had taken since 354 had convinced Julian that the gods were on his side, and he forged ahead.

The Persian War Convinced of his own destiny, Julian did not want to wait to prove his prowess. He quickly prepared to invade Persia in order to gain permanent security for the neighboring provinces and glory for himself as another Alexander the Great. While using Antioch as a base for preparations, Julian promoted his pagan revival among the inhabitants of this great city, one of the most staunchly Christian in the whole Empire. At best the Antiochenes ignored him; at worst they laughed at him. For the first time since his meteoric rise, Julian met failure, and it shook his self-confidence.

Confidence returned with the success of his initial invasion of Persia, and he was tempted to push on into the interior, although he had not brought the main Persian army to battle and had no clear strategic objective. He reached the Persian capital of Ctesiphon but failed to take it. Retreating in the deadly heat of summer and low on supplies, the Roman army was now constantly harassed by the main force of King Shapur II. Riding off without his breastplate to rally the troops in a sudden attack on the rear guard, Julian received a mortal spear wound in the side. Some say that it was hurled by a Christian in his own ranks. In the days following, the Persians taunted the retreating Romans with this idea to undermine morale. In the confusion of battle, however, no one had been able to tell who threw the spear, and certainty can never be attained. Julian lingered for a while and died on June 26, 363.

The death of Julian at an early date was a major turning point in Roman history. Had he enjoyed a long reign like Diocletian's or Constantine's, his policies would have had a great impact. Certainly he would not have been able to eliminate Christianity, as he fervently wished, but with official support the kind of theologically and institutionally unified paganism that he advocated could have become a strong counter force to the Christian Church and might have jeopardized the whole Empire by splitting it between two antagonistic religious camps.

On the other hand, had he been content with his initial success in Persia, he could have gained a long-term peace on the eastern frontier and continued his successful efforts against the tribes along the Rhine and Danube. Continued stability there would have fostered the growing revival of prosperity in the Western provinces, which in turn might have made possible a return to a less authoritarian government than had been necessary to save the Empire from total collapse after the disasters of the third century. Of course, no leader can single-handedly alter the course of events, but having chosen policies when faced with alternatives and given the opportunity to carry them through, he can have a profound effect.

Jovian Proclaimed Emperor (late June, 363) Julian had no heir, and like his hero Alexander, he refused to designate a successor as he talked on his deathbed with friends. Upon his death, Julian's generals, the legionary commanders, and cavalry officers met to choose a successor. Their first choice was Julian's close advisor Salustius Secundus, Praetorian Prefect of the East, a moderate pagan and a popular individual in general. Old and unambitious, however, he refused. After considerable further debate, the officers finally settled on a Christian officer ironically named Jovian.

The Romans struggled on, and after they forced a crossing to the east bank of the Tigris, Shapur, who still feared a pitched battle, offered to negotiate. Jovian, irresolute, insecure, and perhaps anxious to confirm his claim to the throne at home, accepted very disadvantageous terms. They included the surrender of Nisibis, an almost impregnable stronghold that was the anchor of Roman defenses in Mesopotamia, abandonment of Roman provinces beyond the Tigris, cessation of the Roman protectorate over Armenia, and payment of an annual subsidy to Persia to defray the expenses of defending the Caucasus. In return, Shapur granted peace for thirty years.

Jovian died after reigning only eight months. His one major act after negotiating the treaty with Shapur was to rescind Julian's anti-Christian legislation. Though pro-Christian, he did not pursue repressive policies toward pagans. Julian's pagan friends and supporters did not suffer for their earlier allegiance, and all were free to worship as they wished.

Valentinian I and Valens, 364–378

With the death of Jovian, the chief military officers and civilian officials chose as his successor Flavius Valentinianus, an experienced Christian Pannonian officer, though only of secondary rank. They also insisted that he choose a coemperor so that equal Imperial attention could be given to problems in the East

and West. Valentinian chose his brother Valens and left him in charge of the East while he oversaw the West from Milan. Julian's old Gallic legions, pagans, and many who favored the house of Constantine the Great supported Procopius, a relative of Julian's mother. He attempted to usurp the throne in late 365 but was suppressed and executed in early 366.

As military men, Valentinian and Valens energetically defended the Empire. From 365 to 375 in the West, Valentinian defeated the Germans along the Rhine, strengthened defensive works, and brought peace to Gaul. His general Theodosius pushed back the Picts and Scots in Britain and suppressed the revolt of Firmus, a Moorish chief in North Africa (374). Valentinian also strengthened the Danubian frontiers and repelled an invasion of Quadi in 375. While angrily negotiating with the Quadi, however, he suffered an apoplectic fit and died. He left his sixteen-year-old son Gratian as his successor.

In the East, Valens fought back repeated Gothic invasions in Thrace from 365 to 369. Then, in 371, he turned his attention to checking the growth of Persian power. He succeeded only in reestablising control over Armenia before he had to rush back to face a new Gothic peril.

The Battle of Adrianople (August 9, A.D. 378) Thousands of Ostrogoths and Visigoths had fled northeastern Europe before the onrushing Huns. The Visigoths and some Ostrogoths who had joined them petitioned Valens for permission to cross the Danube and settle in Thrace and Moesia. Welcoming such an addition to the Empire's manpower, Valens agreed on condition that they surrender their arms. Unfortunately, the Empire was unprepared for such a sudden mass settlement, and unscrupulous Roman officials took outrageous advantage of the unarmed Goths as they waited in crowded settlement camps. The Romans sold them bad food, even dog meat, at high prices or in exchange for other Goths, whom they sold into slavery. Abused and frustrated, the Goths rose up in mass revolt in

377, and an incompetent Roman commander lost control of the situation.

Valens arrived in the summer of 378 to take personal command. Impatient and not wanting to share the laurels of victory with his young nephew Gratian, Valens sought battle without waiting for the reinforcements sent by Gratian. In the afternoon of August 9, 378, after a morning march and no midday meal, the Romans suddenly found themselves fighting on a hot, dusty plain near Adrianople in Thrace. They did not have a chance. The slaughter was frightful. Two-thirds of the army, scores of officers, and the foolish Emperor himself perished. The Balkans were the Goths' for the taking.

Except for the disaster at Adrianople, the joint reign of Valentinian I and Valens had been militarily successful. They had strengthened the Roman army by recruiting mercenaries from the warlike tribes along Rome's borders, and they had successfully defended those borders until Valens' foolish haste at Adrianople. In civil matters, however, they had been much less successful. Men of the camp, they had little sympathy with the civilian upper class and vice versa. They tended, therefore, to choose as their civil administrators less educated and more opportunistic men of their own social class.

By their legislation the two tried to protect the poor, ensure justice, and prevent fiscal abuse. For example, Valentinian created an Empire-wide office of *defensor civitatis,* an ombudsman, whose duty was to protect citizens from arbitrary officials. Nevertheless, the good intentions of the coemperors were frequently thwarted by ruthless and rapacious officials like those who so fatefully abused the Goths. Honest officials had little chance against the influence of the corrupt. For example, when Theodosius, who had put down a revolt by Firmus in Africa, uncovered official wrongdoing in that province, powerful men at court turned the Emperor against him, and he was executed. The result of this state of affairs was economic distress again and civilian disaffection to the point where many Romans in Africa supported the rebellion of Firmus, while in other provinces people increasingly attempted to abandon their responsibilities and occupations.

On matters of religion, both emperors were tolerant of pagans and banned only sacrifices and the attendant practices of magic and divination. In the West, Valentinian was an orthodox adherent of the Nicene Creed, but he kept out of theological disputes and allowed the religious authorities to work out their own problems. He did, however, forbid unscrupulous clerics from taking advantage of widows and unmarried women to obtain lucrative gifts. In the East, Valens adhered to the official moderate Arianism established by Constantius II in 359. Unfortunately, he tried to impose it forcibly and caused clerical discontent, popular unrest, and persecution of dissenters.

Gratian and Theodosius the Great, 379–395 When Valens died, the young Gratian was at a disadvantage. He had received a good education and was guided by competent advisors, but as a young man he was in a precarious position. To ensure the loyalty of Illyricum after the debacle at Adrianople, the troops of Illyricum had proclaimed Gratian's four-year-old brother Valentinian II as coemperor. Gratian accepted their move but gave Valentinian II no further territory and left him with his mother and a Frank named Merobaudes as regents. Gratian himself recalled from exile Theodosius, the son of the Theodosius who had been unjustly executed after suppressing Firmus' revolt, and made him his colleague and brother-in-law in 379.

Theodosius' first task was to confront the Visigoths, who had been plundering the Balkans since their defeat of Valens. Theodosius pursued them for three years without inflicting a decisive defeat. Unwilling to prolong the costly conflict, Theodosius offered peace on terms reminiscent of old Republican practices. He agreed to let the Visigoths settle within the Empire as autonomous federated allies under their own kings. In return, they agreed to fight for Rome but would remain under their own national commanders. Under the circumstances, there was little else that Theodosius could have done, but his innovative settlement set a precedent that would tempt other barbarian nations to press for similar treatment later on and thus further undermine the integrity of the Empire as they remained unassimilated with the whole.

Maximus Overthrows Gratian, 383   In the West, Gratian, who had been given the finest education possible in order to receive the respect that the upper classes had denied his father, had replaced the rougher Pannonian advisors provided by his father with his own, more refined friends. He became more absorbed in the pursuit of game on royal estates than of the enemy on the frontiers. He also was intensely interested in promoting orthodox Christianity. He had issued an edict of general religious toleration upon the death of Valentinian I but had soon rescinded it, probably under the influence of the talented and zealous Bishop Ambrose of Milan. In 381, Gratian renounced the title *Pontifex Maximus,* removed the Altar of Victory from the senate house at Rome, and confiscated the endowments of the Vestal Virgins and ancient priestly colleges. The next year pagan senators petitioned for a reversal of these measures, but Pope Damasus and Ambrose helped him to keep his resolve.

Absorbed in these interests, Gratian fatally neglected his troops, whom he further insulted when he chose as his bodyguard a squadron of barbarian Alans, who were skilled huntsmen in their native land. During 383 in Britain, Magnus Maximus was proclaimed Emperor by the soldiers, moved quickly to seize Gaul, and easily captured Gratian, who was deserted by his army and was quickly executed. Unwilling to waste precious resources in a civil war and leave the East prey to the Ostrogoths and Persians, Theodosius accepted Maximus as his colleague in charge of Britain, Gaul, and Spain.

Valentinian II, under his mother Justina, received control of Italy, Dacia, and Macedonia in addition to Illyricum. In 387,

however, Maximus tried to seize control of Italy. Theodosius had just recently dealt a severe blow to the Ostrogoths and had reached a settlement of the eastern boundary with Persia in 386. Perhaps Maximus, fearing that Theodosius would now be inclined to punish him for his usurpation, sought to increase his base of power. If so, the fear became self-fulfilling, because Theodosius could now no longer let Maximus go unchallenged.

Theodosius married Galla, the sister of Valentinian II, who had fled to Thessalonica, and marched west. Maximus met him in Illyricum, was defeated twice, and retreated to Aquileia, where he was surrendered to Theodosius by his own disillusioned troops in 388. Theodosius' Frankish Master of the Soldiers, Arbogast, recovered Gaul from Maximus' son Victor, and Valentinian II was placed in charge of the West under the guidance of Arbogast.

The Revolt of Arbogast   Arbogast was one of many barbarians who reached high rank under Theodosius, who relied heavily on barbarians to make up for the chronic shortage of military manpower. Strong-willed and ambitious, Arbogast quarreled with the young Valentinian, who was eager to assert his own independence as a ruler. Arbogast had him murdered in 392 but did not dare to proclaim himself, a barbarian, as Emperor. Instead, he set up a puppet Emperor, the rhetorician Eugenius, the head of the secretarial office and probably a secret pagan. Eugenius unsuccessfully negotiated for recognition, and Theodosius reluctantly prepared to invade the West again. On September 6, 394, the two armies finally met at the Frigidus River near Aquileia. After an initial repulse, Theodosius received timely aid from a storm and the defection of some enemy troops. He defeated Eugenius and Arbogast, whereupon he became sole Emperor of the reunited Empire.

The Death of Theodosius and Division of the Empire, 395   Theodosius' health had been failing for some time, and only five

months after his victory, he died at Milan in early 395. Some say that by leaving the West to his ten-year-old son Honorius and the East to his eighteen-year-old son Arcadius, Theodosius permanently split the Empire, whose unity he had so recently preserved. Still, Theodosius was probably convinced of the strategic necessity of having an equal representative of Imperial authority in both the East and the West. It was the illegitimacy of Eugenius' rule in the West that Theodosius could not countenance, not the division of authority, which had long become an accepted principle. He had shown no predisposition to challenge the legitimate Western emperors Gratian and Valentinian II.

Much more difficult for Theodosius were the expenses of civil wars and the defense of borders. The taxes and manpower required were more than the economy and population could safely bear. They contributed to the further decline of cities, the impoverishment of the middle class, and depopulation. The situation was also made worse by Theodosius' return to an Eastern style court and the inauguration of a costly building program to increase the splendor of Constantinople. The operation of a vast bureaucracy needed to meet the increased military and fiscal burdens produced ever more problems, as numerous officials corruptly sought their own interests at the expense of everyone else.

It was primarily because of his religious activities that later, Christian ages called Theodosius "Great." A pious orthodox Christian, he increasingly supported those who accepted the Nicene Creed. In this effort he was encouraged by the zealous Ambrose of Milan. At first he applied his orthodox piety only to Christians themselves, but late in his reign edicts of 391 and 392 legally banned the outward expression of pagan worship. Theodosius did not, however, reverse the long-standing Roman policy of religious freedom for the Jews.

Paganism did not disappear in the face of Theodosius' hostility, but its adherents more and more began to resemble those who have wistfully held on to belief in other causes long after they were lost. They kept hoping that the old gods under whom Rome had risen to greatness would exact vengeance on their persecutors and restore the Empire's lost glory. That day would never come. The Christian Church and barbarian tribes were too strong for the transformation that was taking place to be stopped now.

XXXVII

The Loss of the West,
A.D. 395 to 493

The century and a quarter following the death of Theodosius the Great saw the breakup of the Roman Empire by the twin forces of internal stress and Germanic conquest. At first the Empire merely split into two separate but unequal halves: the poorer and less secure West, with its emperors living variously at Rome, Milan, or Ravenna as circumstances dictated; and the richer, more stable East, with its emperors firmly ensconced in Constantine's wealthy and impregnable city on the Bosporous. The West was rapidly transformed into separate kingdoms by Germanic tribes as the provinces of the Western emperors fell away until their power disappeared completely in A.D. 476. The East, on the other hand, survived intact, and the Imperial authority, going all the way back to Augustus, was carried on in unbroken political succession as the Eastern emperors preserved the Roman ideal of the universal state and prepared the way for its transformation into the more Hellenized and constricted Byzantine Empire of the Middle Ages.

Sources for Roman History from 395 to 518 With the notable exception of Ammianus Marcellinus and far less so of the fourth-century epitomators, the sources for the first twenty-five years of this period are much the same as for the previous chapter. After Zosimus and Orosius, whose works end in 410 and 417 respectively, however, there are no general narrative sources of even their limited breadth on which to rely. The more narrowly focused, though useful, ecclesiastical histories of Theodoret, Sozomen, and Socrates end respectively in 408, 425, and 439. Evagrius began his *Ecclesiastical History* with the Council of Ephesus (431) and carried it down to 594. Its attempt to be impartial is sometimes marred by credulity. It and the other ecclesiastical histories have one great virtue, however: they often quote official documents, a practice that secular historians usually avoided.

From 439 onward the only connected secular accounts are the very thin and often fanciful annalistic chronicles of early Byzantine writers like John Malalas, whose chronicle of the world begins with Adam and ends with Justinian. Medieval Byzantine compilers, like Photius and Constantine Pophyrogenitus, preserve many valuable fragments from lost works. For example, Porphyrogenitus' compilation of diplomatic sources preserves Priscus of Panium's fascinating look at Atilla and the Huns in his account of an embassy to

Atilla's camp. Also important for the non-Roman side of events is Jordanes, a sixth-century monk, whose history of the world included the unsettled tribes of northern Europe and whose *On the Origin and Deeds of the Goths* is based on the twelve-volume account of Cassiodorus (p. 517).

Important documentary evidence is supplied by the various compilations of Roman Law beginning with the *Code* of Theodosius II, which was published in 438 and contained many of the laws issued during the previous forty years. Subsequent collections of new laws *Novellae,* issued by Valentinian III and Theodosius II also contain valuable explanations for their issuance. Summaries of other laws issued by Theodosius II are contained in Justinian's *Code.* Another valuable document is the *Notitia Dignitatum,* an early fifth-century official list of the major civilian and military officials of the Empire. It gives important insights into the administrative structure and military dispositions of the time. Other useful contemporary writings are the poems of Claudian (p. 517), the poems and letters of Sidonius Apollinaris (p. 517), the numerous biographies of saints, churchmen, and upper-class individuals that begin to appear in this period. What they lack in breadth they make up in detail about social, economic, and cultural conditions.

The Division of East and West

The division of the Empire between two emperors in the face of its sheer size and the growing complexity of its problems had been foreshadowed by the difficulty of maintaining Imperial unity during the third century, Diocletian's creation of separate Augusti for the East and West, Constantine's decision to create an Eastern capital equal to Rome in standing, and the military officers' insistence that Valentinian appoint a coemperor. With two official capitals, permanent division probably was only a matter of time.

The time for a permanent split was hastened because Theodosius had two young sons when he died. He had already proclaimed his elder son, Arcadius, as Augustus in 383 and had left him nominally in control of the East when he marched west against Maximus in 387. In 393, Theodosius declared his younger son, Honorius, as Augustus for the West and brought him on the expedition against Arbogast and Eugenius. Upon Theodosius' death in 395, Arcadius, now seventeen or eighteen, obtained sole authority in the East, and the ten-year-old Honorius was left alone as the Western Emperor.

Child Emperors

The accessions of Arcadius and Honorius illustrate the unfortunate pattern of child heirs that weakened the whole dynasty of Theodosius in both East and West. When Arcadius died in 408, he was succeeded by his seven-year-old son, Theodosius II. Honorius was succeeded in 423 by his nephew Valentinian III, who was only six. Because of their young ages, Theodosius' sons and grandsons could not rule without the supervision of powerful ministers, upon whom they naturally became dependent and from whom they were unable to break away after reaching maturity. As ministers vied for influence and dominance at court, the general welfare was often sacrificed to private rivalries and ambitions. Interestingly, it was the women of the dynasty —Galla Placidia, half-sister of Honorius and Arcadius and mother of Valentinian III, Pulcheria, sister of Theodosius II, and his wife, Eudoxia—who were the more powerful and independent characters. Precisely because they were women, they were not subject to the dependency-inducing advice and flattery of those who guided the young, male emperors.

Under the youthful successors of Theodosius, the nominal unity of the Empire was maintained by having one of the two annual consuls nominated at Rome and the other at Constantinople. The facade of unity was reinforced by the public display of the emperors' statues together and the publication of Imperial laws with the names of both in the headings. Frequently, however, laws issued by one were not reciprocally issued by the other, and the adminstration of the East and the West went in separate ways despite instances of cooperation in times of military or dynastic crisis.

Germanic Commanders in Imperial Service

One of the outstanding features at the beginning of this period was the prominence of Germanic generals in the high Imperial commands. The trend had become significant under Gratian, and several practical reasons can explain it. The foremost probably was the sheer need for military manpower that made it attractive to recruit warlike bands of Germanic peoples for the armies, which in turn, gave able chieftains and warlords the opportunity to gain Imperial favor and advance in rank. Second, one way to turn Germanic chieftains from potential enemies into loyal allies was to offer them good positions in the Roman military, as Theodosius did by making the Visigoths federate allies. Also, it may have appeared attractive to place military power in the hands of men who had little in common with Roman civil officials, who would not likely support a barbarian in a bid for the throne. Finally, a militarily successful emperor like Theodosius the Great might have found more in common with the Germanic leaders, whose chief virtues were martial, than with his Roman subjects, who were more interested in easy, lucrative administrative posts than in hard military service.

Unfortunately, the high positions achieved by Germanic officers often aroused the jealousy and hostility of high-ranking Roman military and civilian officials. Such positions also gave their Germanic holders a chance to pursue both personal and tribal animosities in the arena of Imperial politics. This problem was exacerbated by the existence of two Imperial courts, whose generals and ministers sought to expand their influence over young and immature emperors. Accordingly, as the career of Stilicho under Honorius illustrates, all of these situations could prove dangerous to the peace and safety of the Empire, and they often explain the lack of cooperation between the Eastern and Western administrations.

Stilicho   Although Stilicho's mother may have been a Roman, his father was a Vandal who had served in the Roman army. Stilicho had followed suit by serving in the *protectores,* part of the Emperor's bodyguard and a training ground for young officers. He soon caught Theodosius' eye, and marriage to the Emperor's niece Serena soon followed. Subsequently, Stilicho quickly reached the Roman High Command as a *magister equitum,* Master of the Cavalry, in charge of one of the mobile field armies. When Theodosius came west to oppose Arbogast, Stilicho held the supreme military command as *magister utriusque militiae,* Master of Both Cavalry and Infantry. Finally, before dying, Theodosius charged Stilicho with protecting the young heirs to the throne.

As the revolt of Arbogast and Eugenius showed, if it was not possible for a Germanic general to become Emperor, it was possible for him to become the power behind the throne. Stilicho seems to have had just such ambitions and to have used his powerful position to prepare the way for his own son, Eucherius, whom he hoped to marry to Honorius' half-sister, Galla Placidia. Unfortunately, Stilicho's ambitions quickly brought him into conflict with Arcadius' corrupt and powerful praetorian prefect, Rufinus, who had maneuvered himself into a position of paramount influence in the Eastern court.

Rivalry with Rufinus   The initial struggle between Stilicho and Rufinus began in the spring of 395 over the question of who was to control the strategic Prefecture of Illyricum. In 379 Gratian had transferred Illyricum from the West to Theodosius in the East in order to help him cope with the Visigoths, who were ravaging nearby areas after the Battle of Adrianople. Stilicho claimed that it was Theodosius' wish to transfer this prefecture back to the West by assigning it to Honorius. Rufinus, however, persuaded Arcadius to reject Stilicho's claim.

Illyricum was too valuable to lose: its loss would have left Arcadius with little more than Asia Minor, the Levant, and Egypt; it dominated communications by land and sea between the two halves of the Empire; and it was one of the best recruiting grounds of valuable soldiers in either half. Claiming that he was bringing back to Constantinople those Eastern military units that Theodosius had brought west in 393, Stilicho arrived in Illyricum in the spring of 395. He had come from checking barbarian activity in Pannonia and Noricum and had a number of Western units with him too, which aroused suspicion that he hoped to seize Illyricum. The situation was complicated by an uprising of the Visigoths under a newly elected king, Alaric. The Visigoths did not think that they had been fairly treated for their services against Arbogast and ravaged Macedonia and Thrace as far as the outskirts of Constantinople. After negotiations with Rufinus, Alaric headed west, into the Prefecture of Illyricum, where he was captured by Stilicho.

Fearful that Stilicho would gain the credit for destroying the Visigothic menace and thereby strengthen his claim to Illyricum, Rufinus persuaded Arcadius to order Stilicho to send the Eastern legions immediately to Constantinople and return west. Stilicho obeyed. Perhaps he did not feel strong enough to ask the troops to disobey an order of their sovereign; perhaps he feared for his wife and children at Constantinople. He also let Alaric go free, a move that put the latter in his debt for the future and would earn Arcadius the displeasure of the defenseless Romans of the Illyrian prefecture.

The Eastern troops returned under the command of Gainas, an Ostrogoth, with whom Stilicho plotted the assassination of Rufinus. On November 27, 395, Rufinus appeared along with Arcadius to review the troops at Constantinople. Gainas and his accomplices crowded around Rufinus with friendly gestures and flattering talk. Then, with the trap closed tight, they cut him down. His severed head was mocked through the streets, and his severed right hand was shown to passers-by with requests for gifts, as a commentary on his notorious rapacity.

Alaric While Stilicho strengthened the borders of the West, Alaric and the Visigoths spent over a year plundering Greece and the Balkans without any attempt by Arcadius to stop them. But when Stilicho finally invaded Greece in the spring of 397 to oppose Alaric, Arcadius and the senate at Constantinople declared Stilicho a public enemy. They also encouraged the Moorish Count of Africa, Gildo, to rebel from Honorius. When Gildo cut off the vital flow of grain to Rome, Stilicho had no choice but to let Alaric go and hasten back home to relieve the food shortage at Rome and put down Gildo. Just as Gildo had helped crush the revolt of his brother Firmus under Theodosius, so his other brother, Mascezel, now defeated him, while Stilicho looked after Italy.

Africa was saved, but in the meantime Alaric moved north into Epirus, where he settled after obtaining the office of *magister militum,* Master of the Soldiers, from Arcadius. Stilicho strengthened himself by marrying his daughter Maria to Honorius in 398, but he was in no position to invade Illyricum. Instead, in 401, Alaric invaded Italy, when Stilicho had been called across the Alps to meet a serious invasion of Vandals, Alans, and other Germans, who were ravaging Noricum and Rhaetia under Radagaisus. After capturing a number of towns in northern Italy, Alaric was about to besiege Honorius himself in Milan when Stilicho, having defeated Radagaisus and summoned aid from Gaul and Britain, returned (February, 402). Alaric retreated from Milan and was defeated at Pollentia, where Stilicho captured his family. Negotiations ensued, and Alaric departed from Italy with his family and followers.

Both Alaric and Stilicho were buying time. Alaric reinvaded Italy in the summer of 403 and attacked Verona. Stilicho, now reinforced, defeated him again. Once more, however, Stilicho offered terms. Alaric was allowed to withdraw after agreeing to help Stilicho seize Illyricum. Unfortunately, because Stilicho had stripped the northern defenses for reinforcements, Radagaisus, now at the head of a large German force, principally Ostrogoths, crossed the Danube and drove straight into Italy. It was six months before Stilicho could defeat and kill him in August of 406.

The Downfall of Stilicho   Before Stilicho and Alaric could invade Illyricum, another crisis interfered. At the end of 406, large numbers of Vandals, Suevi, Alans, and other tribes crossed the frozen Rhine into Gaul. As had so often happened earlier, a provincial commander usurped authority in the face of the Emperor's inability to defend the borders. In Britain another Constantine was proclaimed Emperor, and he crossed over to Gaul with British units in 407 to deal with the invaders.

When Stilicho broke off the invasion of Illyricum to put down Constantine, Alaric invaded Noricum and demanded four thousand pounds of gold as a subsidy and military employment for his men. Stilicho persuaded a reluctant Roman senate to acquiesce. This action gave jealous Roman officials at court ammunition to attack him with charges of treasonable collusion with Alaric. They also rumored that he planned to set up his son as a third emperor in the Illyrian prefecture. A plot was laid by a palace official named Olympius, who turned Honorius against Stilicho and brought about his arrest and execution along with his son in August of 408.

Alaric Attacks Rome   Honorius now refused to honor the agreement with Alaric, who immediately invaded Italy and besieged Rome while Honorius cowered in the safety of Ravenna's swamps. Lacking aid from Honorius, the Roman senate negotiated with Alaric, who agreed to lift the siege in return for a huge payment. This ransom was approved on communication with Honorius, who also agreed to hand over hostages as a token of good faith. Again, however, Hono-

rius did not live up to his promises, and Alaric marched on Rome once more in late 409. Negotiations resulted in the city's being spared, and with senatorial approval, the Urban Prefect, Priscus Attalus, was made a new Emperor, who agreed to cooperate with Alaric. Alaric himself was made Master of the Soldiers (officially *magister utriusque militiae*) while his brother-in-law, Athaulf became Count of the Domestics. Other important posts were filled by friends of Attalus, all of whom belonged to the circle of powerful pagan senators that had been headed by the late Quintus Aurelius Symmachus, who had clashed with St. Ambrose about the Altar of Victory.

A terrified Honorius offered to negotiate for a joint rule, but Attalus refused. Just as Honorius was about to flee Ravenna for Constantinople, four thousand troops arrived from the East and strengthened his resolve. Differences arose between Attalus and Alaric about using barbarians to fight Romans. Alaric decided to revoke his support of Attalus and came to terms with Honorius. Sarus, a Visigothic rival of Alaric, intervened on behalf of Honorius, however, and destroyed any chance of peace. Alaric then besieged Rome again and did not spare it this time (August 24, A.D. 410). For the first time in eight hundred years, Rome was sacked by foreign invaders. For two or three days, Alaric allowed his men to plunder, loot, and burn. Although contemporary sources exaggerated the physical damage to the city, much valuable loot and many captives, including Honorius' half-sister, Galla Placidia, were carried off.

Alaric did not long enjoy what he had seized, however. After marching south to Rhegium, he died. His followers diverted the nearby Basentus River, buried him in its exposed bed, and then turned the river back into its natural course so that his final resting place could never be desecrated.

The Visigothic Migration and Settlement after Alaric   The Visigoths elected Alaric's brother-in-law, Athaulf, as their new king. After spending almost a year in raiding Italy, they crossed the Alps into Gaul in 412. At first they supported a Roman rebel named Jovius but then switched to support Honorius' efforts to regain control of the province. Honorius, who had not learned his lesson before, refused to reward them afterward. Athaulf promptly seized Narbonne, the capital of Narbonese Gaul, along with other important towns and married Honorius' captive half-sister, Galla Placidia, with her consent, in a futile attempt to gain recognition and cooperation from Honorius. Honorius sent out his Master of the Soldiers, Constantius, who had long wanted to marry Placidia, to dislodge the Visigoths. They fled to Spain, where Athaulf was assassinated (415).

After a few days of turmoil, Wallia was elected to succeed Athaulf. He failed in an attempt to lead his people to Africa, and, faced with starvation because of a Roman blockade, he negotiated with Constantius. In return for food, Wallia agreed to return the widowed Placidia and, becoming allied with Rome, to attack Vandals and Alans who had invaded other parts of Spain. His success against them frightened Constantius, who recalled the Visigoths to Gaul (where he could more easily oversee them) and settled them in southern Aquitania.

Visigoths in Gaul The Visigoths settled as federate allies governed by their own kings and bound to serve Rome militarily. Lands of Roman owners were partially divided among the Visigoths, while the Romans retained the rest of their property and remained subject to Honorius without any Visigothic control. The Visigoths wanted an independent kingdom, however, and eventually Wallia's successor, Theodoric I, forced the Romans to grant him sovereignty over Aquitania. Later, in 451, he helped the Roman Count Aetius check the Huns at the Battle of the Mauriac Plain, near Troyes, and relations between Rome and the Visigoths remained good for a time. In 466, however, an anti-Roman faction gained control and eventually seized all of southern France and part of Spain by 477, the year after

the last Roman Emperor in the West was deposed.

The Vandals, Alans, and Suevi
While Stilicho had been fighting Radagaisus and Alaric, the Vandals, Alans, and Suevi had taken advantage of the weakened defenses along the Rhine to invade Gaul. The Vandals were in two groups—the Silings from the region of the river Main in Germany and the Asdings from along the Theis River (Tiza) in Hungary. The Suevi and the Alans had come from the region of the middle Danube. On the last day of 406, these four tribes crossed the frozen Rhine. After plundering Moguntiacum (modern Mainz in West Germany), they marched west to Belgic Gaul and sacked Trèves (modern Trier, near Luxembourg). After a similarly destructive swing northward, they headed south across the Seine and the Loire to enter Aquitaine.

The Roman usurper Constantine used these calamaties to seize control of Gaul and Spain with his British legions. While mainly interested in consolidating his own power as much as possible, he did try to contain the invaders in southwestern Gaul; but in late September or early October of 409, they escaped across the Pyrenees and seized Spain. A Roman blockade of supplies, however, forced them to come to terms as Roman federates in return for land. The Asding Vandals and the Suevi settled in the northwest, the Alans received the center, and the Siling Vandals occupied the south. In 416, however, the Romans persuaded the Visigoths to rid Spain of these unwelcome guests. Under Wallia the Visigoths destroyed the Siling Vandals and decimated the Alans, whose survivors merged with the Asding Vandals, who remained free under their king, Gunderic, after the Visigoths were recalled to Gaul, and proceeded to overcome the Suevi.

Vandal Invasion of Africa In 428, Gunderic was succeeded by his able and ambitious brother Gaiseric, and in the following year, events in Roman Africa presented a golden opportunity to invade its rich agricultural lands. A dispute had arisen between Boniface, Count of Africa, and Galla Placidia, regent for Valentinian III. She had sent an army to oust him, and he called in Gaiseric, to whom he provided transportation for himself and eighty thousand men, women, and children. Too late, Boniface and Placidia had realized the folly of their actions and mended their quarrel. Once in Africa, Gaiseric overcame all opposition except for Carthage and Cirta by the end of 431.

A peace granting Gaiseric federate status in Numidia was negotiated in 435, but Gaiseric broke it in 439 by seizing Carthage. He then organized a fleet to raid Sicily and other islands. In 442, Valentinian III recognized the Vandals as an independent kingdom, and relations stabilized until 455, when Valentinian's assassination presented too tempting a chance to attack and plunder the city of Rome itself. While they spared the physical city, the Vandals carried off vast stores of movable wealth and captives, including Eudoxia, the widow of Valentinian III, and her two daughters as hostages.

Gaiseric sought to join his family to the Imperial dynasty by marrying his eldest son, Huneric, to Eudoxia's daughter Eudocia, but that did nothing to improve his relations with the Roman emperors of either the East or West. All Roman attempts to dislodge Gaiseric failed, however, and in 476, the year when the last Western Emperor was deposed, the Eastern Emperor, Zeno, acknowledged the Vandals' possession of Roman Africa, Lilybaeum in Sicily, Sadinia, Corsica, and the Balearic Isles.

The Burgundians   In the wake of the Vandals, Alans, and Suevi, the Burgundians, under King Gundahar (Gunther), crossed into Gaul from the east bank of the Rhine in 407. They settled near Worms and cooperated with the Roman usurpers Constantine and Jovinus. Subsequently, Honorius recognized them as federates. Later, Aetius, Master of the Soldiers under Valentinian III, enlisted the Huns to attack them for not supplying promised

troops to the Roman army. In 443 he settled them in Savoy, and they fought for him against the Huns in 451. After the deaths of Aetius and Valentinian III, the Burgundians extended their domain down the Rhône to the Durance. Officially their kings remained federate allies of Rome because they valued the prestige that association with the ancient Imperial throne entailed. In fact, however, they were autonomous rulers who served the Emperor at their own discretion, not his.

The Franks   Just as the Burgundians had taken advantage of the disturbed conditions in Gaul during 407 to carve out territory there for themselves, so did the Franks. There were two groups of Franks: Ripuarians and Salians. The Ripuarians had been settled along the middle Rhine on the German side for some time. They now crossed over and established themselves on the left bank as well. They too used their arms to serve Rome and helped defeat Atilla in 451.

More numerous and important, however, were the Salian Franks, who had come from the shores of the North Sea near the mouth of the Rhine. They had already crossed the lower Rhine and seized control of Toxandria, between the Meuse and the Scheldt, before 350. Julian had halted their expansion and made them federates of Rome, but they were able to take advantage of the problems in Gaul after 406 to expand southward to the Somme. As federates again, however, they aided Aetius against the Huns in 451 and remained loyal until 486, when Childeric overthrew the last vestiges of Roman power in Gaul and extended his rule to the Loire, which was the border of the Visigothic kingdom.

Angles, Saxons, and Jutes   While the Salian Franks pushed into Gaul, other German tribes along the North Sea—the Angles, Saxons, and Jutes—began to raid Britain. In 408, the Saxons made a devastating raid that undermined British loyalty to the usurper Constantine, who was in Gaul by that time.

Eventually, Roman political and military authority was reestablished, but the Western Emperors could never really spare the resources to provide adequate security. By 428, Angles, Saxons, and Jutes were making permanent settlements along the English coast. Around 442 the Roman garrison left Britain and never returned. The Germanic invaders steadily gained ground thereafter in the whole area north to the Tweed and west to the Severn.

The Huns The Germanic tribes had pressed the borders of the Roman Empire partly because of pressure from the Huns, a Mongolian people who had been driven westward from their Central Asian homelands by other people pressing on them. Short, dark, wiry, excellent horsemen, fierce fighters, and enured to hardship by a nomadic life, they terrified the more settled Germans in their path. By the time of Theodosius the Great, they had halted in the old Roman province of Dacia and exacted tribute from the Germanic tribes living in southern Russia: the Ostrogoths, Heruls, and Alans. They both raided the Roman border lands and served in the Roman armies.

Greater political unity seems to have been reached under the energetic king Rua (Ruas, Rugula, Rugila), who was able to exert greater pressure in dealing with the Romans. In 422 or 424 the Emperor Theodosius II agreed to pay a yearly subsidy of 350 pounds of gold to him to avoid attacks on the Balkans. The following year Rua sent a large army under Aetius to help the usurper John against the forces of Galla Placidia and Valentinian III. When John fell, Aetius was able to save himself in return for a promise from the Huns to quit the Pannonian province of Valeria, but in 433 and 434, Rua successfully supported Aetius in his rivalry with Boniface and Sebastian, whereupon Rua received territory in Pannonia again.

Atilla Rua was succeeded in 434 by his nephews Atilla and Bleda, who divided the kingdom. The aggressive Atilla soon eclipsed Bleda and united all the Huns under his rule after executing Bleda in 443. Atilla continued to harass the Balkans and demand increasingly larger subsidies until about 450, when he suddenly turned his attention to the West in an attempt to create a vast European empire of his own. Honoria, sister of Valentinian III, had called on Atilla to help her gain part of the West for herself, and the Vandal Gaiseric was encouraging the Huns to attack his Visigothic enemies in Gaul.

Atilla was overextended when he attacked Gaul in 451 and, failing to take Orleans, was already in retreat when Aetius, King Theoderic of the Visigoths, and other Germans fought him to a draw on the Mauriac Plain. Aetius, however, allowed the Huns, who had been very useful to him in the past, to escape. Atilla then attacked Italy to demand the hand of Honoria. The diplomacy of Pope Leo, the timely outbreak of a plague in Atilla's army, and the arrival of an army from the East induced him to withdraw in 453 without success. In 454, before he could attack again, he died while consummating a marriage with the sister of the Burgundian king. Without Atilla's forceful leadership, his empire quickly broke up under the attacks of the eastern Germanic tribes that he had dominated.

The End of the Western Emperors (408–476) By the time of Atilla's death in 454, only Italy and parts of Gaul and Spain were left to the Western Roman emperors. Intrigues of ambitious ministers and relatives at the courts of the son and grandson of Theodosius the Great had contributed to the problems that were undermining their half of the Empire, while the atmosphere of discontent and uncertainty created by the Empire's problems helped to fuel the intrigues. During the unfortunate minority of Honorius, Stilicho's attempts to play off Alaric and the Visigoths against the East in his rivalry with Rufinus over control of Illyricum had been dangerous and destructive. Nevertheless, Stilicho had been the one man who could have held Alaric in check, and Honorius had shown that he had not acquired any wisdom with adulthood when he executed Stilicho in 408.

The subsequent struggle between Olympius and Stilicho's old friend, the Praetorian Prefect Jovius, merely made relations between Alaric and Honorius worse, until Alaric first supported Attalus as a rival emperor (409) and finally sacked Rome to teach Honorius a lesson (410). The desire of the succeeding Master of Cavalry and Infantry, Constantius, for an Imperial marriage with Honorius' half-sister, Galla Placidia, helps to explain Honorius' stubborn refusal to seek good relations with the Visigothic king Athaulf after he married Placidia (414). As a result, the Visigoths had resumed devastating Roman territory. Constantius' success in finally marrying Placidia (417) and producing an heir, Theodosius' grandson Valentinian III, increased jealousy at the Eastern court. After the death of Constantius (421), Placidia and Honorius became estranged, and followers loyal to each rioted against each other. Placidia and her children took refuge with Theodosius II at Byzantium in 423. Therefore, when the childless Honorius died a few months later, no immediate successor was in the West, and a certain John was proclaimed Emperor at Ravenna.

Galla Placidia and Valentinian III   The West now had to be reconquered for the five-year-old Valentinian III with a large force suppled by Theodosius II. Instead of fighting barbarians, the Romans fought amongst themselves. Placidia, who served as regent, was also supported by Boniface, Count of Africa, while the talented Aetius supported John by raising an army of Huns, with whom he had spent his youth as a hostage. They arrived too late to save John but secured favorable terms for Aetius as Count and Master of the Cavalry to defend the Gallic provinces against the Franks and Visigoths (425). Aetius was able to force Placidia to appoint him Master of Cavalry and Infantry in 429. In the meantime Boniface had revolted in Africa and called in Gaiseric's Vandals with disastrous results. Nevertheless, Boniface became reconciled

with Placidia, and she replaced Aetius with him. Aetius called upon his old friend Rua the Hun and secured restoration to power with the rank of Patrician in 434.

The Ascendancy of Aetius   For the next twenty years, Aetius was the power behind the throne and responsible for preserving what was left of the Western Empire by skillfully playing off the Huns and Germanic tribes against each other. He was also able to betroth a son, probably Gaudentius, to Valentinian III's daughter, the younger Placidia. Understandably, however, neither the elder Placidia nor Valentinian III appreciated being dominated by the man who had once supported a usurper against them and thwarted their earlier attempts to get rid of him. It was easy, therefore, for Petronius Maximus, head of an old and powerful senatorial family at Rome, and the chamberlain Heraclius to enlist Valentinian III in a scheme to assassinate Aetius, which was successfully carried out on September 21, 454. With his own hand, the foolish Valentinian III slew the one man really capable of defending his throne. Chaos ensued.

The Death of Valentinian III and the End of Theodosius' Dynasty in the West   Valentinian now promised Placidia to Olybrius, a powerful senator. Expecting to be made Patrician in place of Aetius, Maximus was now blocked by Heraclius. Maximus then arranged with friends of Aetius to assassinate both Heraclius and Valentinian III (March 16, 455). Since Valentinian III had no male heirs, a struggle for the throne ensued. That struggle both inspired and made possible the Vandals' sack of Rome a few months later. Maximus' money obtained the support of the soldiers against Aetius' friend Maximian and Majorian, a famous senator. To strengthen his position, Maximus forced Valentinian III's widow, Eudoxia to marry him and Valentinian's daughter Eudocia to marry his son Palladius. Eudocia, however, previously had been pledged to Gaiseric's son Huneric, a match that Gaiseric wanted badly. Therefore, perhaps even with the cooperation of Eudoxia, he invaded Italy and carried both of Valentinian III's daughters back to Africa after the sack of Rome, June 3, 455. When Maximus, already hated by the populace, had tried to flee Rome a few days before, he was hit in the temple by a well-aimed rock and died.

Avitus   Once more a struggle ensued over the vacant throne. The Visigothic king, Theodoric II, supported Aetius' former subordinate Avitus, Prefect of Gaul. He was the first man to be made Emperor by non-Romans. The Visigoths proclaimed him Emperor at their capital, Toulouse, in July of 455. He was only confirmed later by a meeting of Gallo-Romans at the provincial capital of Arles. Nevertheless, he was recognized by the Eastern Emperor Marcian. He was immediately opposed by Gaiseric, and he was naturally resented by the Roman senators and soldiers, who had had no hand in his making. The latter two groups favored Majorian. He won the support also of Ricimer, whom Avitus had appointed Master of the Soldiers.

The Ascendancy of Ricimer   Ricimer was half Visigoth and half Sueve. His mother was a daughter of the former Visigothic king Wallia, and his career in Roman service had been correspondingly prestigious. As a barbarian and an Arian, however, he could never hope to be accepted as a Roman emperor himself. Therefore, he worked assiduously to be the power behind the throne for the next sixteen years. After a brief interregnum, Ricimer obtained from the Eastern Emperor Leo I confirmation of Julius Valerianus Majorianus, Majorian, as Western Emperor. He himself received the office of Patrician at the same time, April 1, 457.

Reign of Majorian (457–461)   While Ricimer protected Italy from attacks by the Ostrogoths, Alans, and Vandals, Majorian went to Gaul to check the advances of the Visigoths and the rebelliousness of the Gallo-

Romans, both of whom were resentful over the fall of their appointee, Avitus. Majorian succeeded in this effort, but when he failed in his attempt to recapture Africa from the Vandals, he lost public support, and Ricimer stripped him of office and executed him, August 21, 461.

Severus (461–465)   After three months Ricimer obtained the election of Libius Severus by the Roman senate, but he was not accepted by Leo at Constantinople. The strategic island of Sicily was overrun by the Vandals and Moors after the unsuccessful revolt there by Count Marcellinus. Leo intervened to arrange peace with Gaiseric. Gaiseric agreed to free Valentinian III's widow Eudoxia, and her daughter Placidia. On the other hand, his demand that Placidia's intended husband, Olybrius, be made Western Emperor was not acceptable to Leo. Severus died in 465, perhaps by poisoning at the instigation of Ricimer, and things remained at an impasse until 467, when Leo decided to take decisive action.

Anthemius (467–472)   Leo appointed Anthemius, who was related to the house of Theodosius by marriage, as Western Emperor and arranged a marriage between Ricimer and Anthemius' daughter. Leo then proceeded to coordinate a vast three-pronged attack on Gaiseric in 468. Unfortunately, intrigue in his own court caused the appointment of an incompetent commander, and Ricimer resented the participation of his old enemy Marcellinus, whose assassination guaranteed the expedition's failure. The result was a great waste of precious resources, and Gaiseric was left more firmly entrenched than ever.

Events in the West were beyond Anthemius' control, despite his honest and well-meaning administration. Euric, king of the Visigoths had previously seized the opportunity to extend his power in Gaul and Spain while the Romans were distracted. Anthemius and his successors were unable to keep Euric in check. In Italy, moreover, Anthemius lacked popularity because he was a Greek given over too much to philosophy and, some feared, paganism. He was, however, preferred by the senators at Rome to the barbarian Ricimer, who was based at the strategic city of Milan.

Olybrius (472)   Relations between Anthemius and Ricimer had deteriorated so badly that Italy was practically divided into separate kingdoms. Leo sent the younger Placidia's husband, Olybrius, to Rome ostensibly to arrange a reconciliation, but with secret instructions that he be murdered because of his former relations with Gaiseric. Ricimer discovered the plot and used it as an excuse to raise up Olybrius as Emperor and besiege Anthemius at Rome (472). Both Ricimer and Olybrius died before the end of the year, however, and the West was a prize for the plucking once more.

Glycerius (473–474) and Nepos (475–476)   Ricimer's nephew, the Burgundian Gundobad, succeeded him as Master of the Soldiers. After four months he arranged the accession of Glycerius, Count of the Domestics, as Emperor at Ravenna. Leo did not approve, however, and appointed Julius Nepos, a relative by marriage and nephew of Count Marcellinus. Gundobad surrendered his position to become king of the Burgundians, and Nepos easily deposed Glycerius to become the legitimate Emperor. Gundobad's place was taken by a certain Orestes, who had once been secretary to Atilla.

Romulus Augustulus (476)   Orestes immediately intrigued to replace Nepos with his own son, Romulus. Orestes had the backing of the German mercenary troops, and Nepos fled Italy to Diocletian's old palace on the Dalmatian coast. Romulus, whose name was that of Rome's legendary founder and whose nickname, Augustulus, mocked that of the first Roman Emperor, was nominally the last Western Roman Emperor. Of course, he was only Orestes' puppet and was never recognized in the East. The official Roman Emperor of the West remained Julius Nepos, who finally died an exile in 480. For all practical purposes, however, the office of the Western emperors ceased with Romulus Augustulus, whose usurpation was brought to an end by one of Orestes' German officers, Odovacer, in less than a year.

Odovacer (Odoacer, 476–493)   The Germans who had supported Orestes hoped to receive permanent lands in Italy, as the various other Germans had in the provinces. Orestes, however, tried to maintain the integrity of Italy. Under the leadership of Odovacer, they killed Orestes and sent Romulus Augustulus into forced retirement. Odovacer was proclaimed king of his German supporters, but he did not seek to become king of Roman Italy. Instead, he reached an agreement with the Eastern Emperor Zeno to govern Italy as duly appointed Patrician. In this arrangement he was supported by powerful nobles at Rome. Life in Italy went on very much as it had before, except that now Odovacer's German subjects were given a share of the Roman's lands. Supposedly, each German soldier received one-third of the estate of a corresponding Roman proprietor, but it is doubtful that Odovacer could have enjoyed senatorial support if the figure was that high in all cases.

Theodoric (the Amal) and the Ostrogoths   Zeno, the Eastern Emperor, did not trust Odovacer and feared that he had designs on Illyricum, which, being attacked by the Ostrogoths, he was preparing to invade. The Ostrogoths had been held in check on the lower Danube by the Huns, but after the death of Atilla they had forced their way into Pannonia, where the Eastern Emperor Marcian had allowed them to settle with an annual subsidy as federates. Later, Leo had refused to pay the subsidy, and they had retaliated by invading

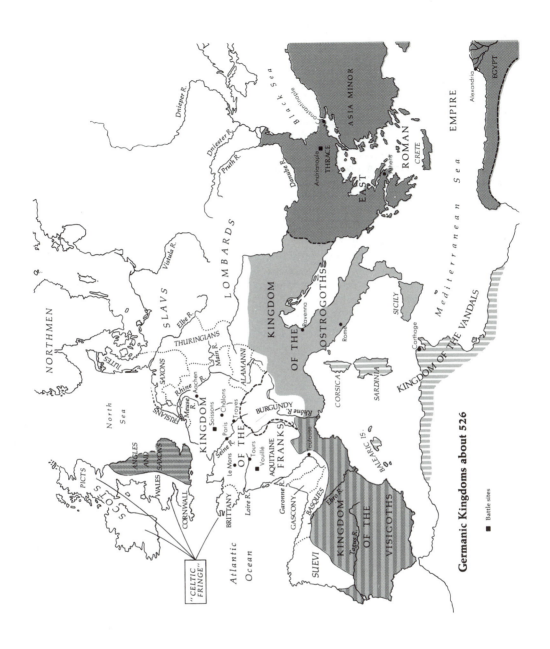

Germanic Kingdoms about 526

■ Battle sites

NORTHMEN

SLAVS

JUTES

LOMBARDS

THURINGIANS

SAXONS

FRISIANS

Vistula R.

Dnieper R.

Dniester R.

Prath R.

Danube R.

Black Sea

Constantinople

Adrianople ■ THRACE

ASIA MINOR

EAST ROMAN EMPIRE

Alexandria

EGYPT

Athens

CRETE

Mediterranean Sea

KINGDOM OF THE OSTROGOTHS

Ravenna

Rome ●

SICILY

CORSICA

SARDINIA

Carthage

KINGDOM OF THE VANDALS

BALEARIC IS.

Elbe R.

Main R.

ALAMANNI

Rhine

Aachen

Meuse R.

KINGDOM

OF THE

FRANKS

Soissons

Paris ●

Seine R.

Châlons

Troyes

BURGUNDY

Rhône R.

Toulouse

Tours ■

Le Mans

AQUITAINE

Vouillé ■

Loire R.

Garonne R.

GASCONY

BASQUES

Ebro R.

Tagus R.

KINGDOM

OF THE

VISIGOTHS

SUEVI

BRITTANY

Atlantic Ocean

North Sea

PICTS

SCOTS

ANGLES AND SAXONS

WALES

CORNWALL

"CELTIC FRINGE"

Illyricum. In 461, Leo had agreed to restore the subsidy, and Theodoric the Amal, son of the Ostrogothic king Theodemir, was sent to Constantinople as a hostage. As a gesture of friendship, Leo had allowed Theodoric to return home, and in 471 he had succeeded his father as king.

For many years Theodoric and the Ostrogoths plundered Thrace, Dacia, and Illyricum. He even marched on Constantinople in 487. In 488, however, the Eastern Emperor Zeno hit upon the idea of enlisting Theodoric to overthrow Odovacer and govern Italy as his representative. Theodoric invaded Italy in 489, and after four years Odovacer surrendered in February of 493. A few weeks later Theodoric slew Odovacer with his own hand on the pretext that Odovacer was plotting

against him. Officially, Theodoric ruled Italy as the Patrician appointed by Zeno. His position as a subordinate representative of the Eastern Emperor was confirmed and refined by the Emperor Anastasius in 497. For all practical purposes, however, Italy had now become the newest Germanic successor state of the Western Empire. The Franks had already taken the opportunity to conquer the last remaining Imperial territories in Gaul. The political transformation of the Western Empire from a unified Imperial state into a number of independent Germanic tribal kingdoms was virtually complete. The dream of the former would haunt and inspire men through the European Middle Ages and beyond, but it could never be restored.

XXXVIII

The Survival of the East, A.D. 395 to 518

While Germanic tribes had succeeded in gaining control of Italy and the Western provinces of the Empire, the Eastern provinces, under the emperors at Constantinople, had preserved their boundaries and the Empire's existence, albeit in contracted form. Without the West the Eastern half of the old Roman Empire gradually became more Greek and Near Eastern, until it was eventually transformed into the Byzantine Empire of medieval history.

That transformation was long in the making, however. For a considerable time Latin remained the official language of the army, government, and law. The emperors still thought in social, economic, political, and military terms little differently than did their predecessors during the previous two centuries. They still planned on the basis of the geographic area that the Empire had embraced at its height and hoped to recover the West. It was only the failure to realize that goal after the death of Justinian (518–565) that caused the Eastern emperors to abandon their Western dreams and become involved exclusively with preserving the unity of the East.

Arcadius (395–408) and the Germans
After the death of Theodosius the Great (395),

the East, unlike the West, avoided falling under the domination of a powerful Germanic officer like Stilicho. Luck was partly the reason. After Gainas the Ostrogoth had assassinated Arcadius' powerful Praetorian Prefect Rufinus in 395, Rufinus' dominant position at court was taken over by the chamberlain, a bald old eunuch named Eutropius. At the beginning of 400, Gainas engineered his downfall and extorted the post of Master of the Soldiers from Arcadius. Gainas clearly was aiming for the same power in the East as Stilicho enjoyed in the West. Naturally, many high officials and average citizens at Constantinople bitterly resented the power of the Germans in the army. On July 12 of 400, a major riot broke out in Constantinople, and large numbers of German soldiers were massacred. Gainas himself was driven out, and barbarian military influence sharply declined. Thereafter, Romans usually held the high military commands. Moreover, the Eastern emperors had more plentiful sources of troops within their own borders, especially from Illyricum and Asia Minor, so that they were not dependent upon Germanic mercenaries as was the West and barbarian influence could be counterbalanced by native troops.

After the fall of Eutropius, Arcadius' wife, Eudoxia (no relation to the wife of Val-

´entinian III), to whom he had originally been introduced by Eutropius, and the Praetorian Prefect Aurelian led the antibarbarian faction at court and enjoyed the greatest influence. Eudoxia gained notoriety because of her conflict with the eloquent, popular, and austere bishop of Constantinople Saint John Chrysostom ("Golden Mouth"). He publicly criticized her more than once, and she believed that his frequent sermons against luxury and immorality were aimed against her. She cooperated with his rivals and jealous detractors within the Church to depose him, first in 403 and then permanently in 404. This business caused a breach between Arcadius and Honorius, who had tried to intervene for Chrysostom. They were still unreconciled when Arcadius died in 408.

Theodosius II (408–450), Pulcheria, and Eudocia

When Arcadius died, his son, Theodosius II was only seven and his eldest daughter, Pulcheria, only nine. Someone else had to perform the real tasks of governing. This role was admirably filled by the Praetorian Prefect Anthemius. Under his direction close cooperation was reestablished between the Eastern and Western courts, Constantinople was rendered larger and impregnable by the construction of a massive western wall from the Sea of Marmara (Propontis) to the Golden Horn, a peace treaty was negotiated with Persia, the Huns were repulsed from Lower Moesia, the Danubian fleet was strengthened, and steps were taken to assure the food supply for Constantinople and provide fiscal relief for the provinces.

In 414, Pulcheria was made an Augusta and became regent after Anthemius seems to have died. Pulcheria was both religious and strong-willed. She took control of Theodosius' education to keep him from morally and politically corrupt influences. Life at court was pious, and Pulcheria prevailed upon her two sisters to follow her example in vowing perpetual virginity. Her formal regency may have ended officially with Theodosius' fifteenth

birthday, but she remained of paramount influence at court for several more years.

It was Pulcheria who chose a wife for Theodosius in 421. Her choice was excellent —Athenais, daughter of the pagan Athenian philosopher Leontius. Not only beautiful, she had received a superb education, which made her compatible with the gentle and scholarly Theodosius II. Moreover, although she converted to Christianity and took the name Eudocia, her becoming Empress must have produced a favorable impact on pagan intellectuals, who still had considerable influence among the upper classes.

Perhaps it was the learned Eudocia who helped to inspire two of Theodosius' greatest accomplishments. In 425 he created a real university at Constantinople to compete with those of Alexandria and Athens. Lecture rooms were provided in the Capitol, and ten chairs each were endowed in Greek and Latin grammar along with five in Greek rhetoric, three in Latin rhetoric, two in law, and one in philosophy. Four years later Theodosius inaugurated his most famous work, the Theodosian Code, in which all the laws issued by emperors from Constantine to himself were collected and compiled into a single work of reference. After nine years and the labor of sixteen jurists, it was jointly issued by Theodosius II and Valentinian III on February 15, 438.

It is natural that Eudocia's influence at court began to compete and conflict with Pulcheria's, but for twenty years the situation was not critical until it was exploited by the eunuch Chrysaphius, who sought to undercut them both. Shortly after 440 Pulcheria withdrew from court, and Eudocia's downfall on suspicion of infidelity followed in 444. Eudocia was allowed to retire to Jerusalem, where she spent her remaining sixteen years doing pious good works.

Persians and Huns, 408 to 450

Under Theodosius II the Eastern Empire was periodically threatened by the Persians and

Huns. Whenever the army was engaged with the Persians, the Huns would attack across the Danube. In 421 the Persian king Varanes (Vahram, Varahan, Bahram) V declared war because Theodosius was protecting Christian refugees from Persia. The Romans soundly defeated the Persians in 422, but Rua the Hun had seized the chance to raid Thrace and had to be bought off with the promise of 350 pounds of gold a year to keep peace. In 434, after troops sent to help Valentinian III fight the Vandals were defeated, Rua took advantage of their absence to make increased demands on Theodosius II. He died in the midst of negotiations, and his successor, Atilla, obtained a doubling of the subsidy to 700 pounds a year.

In 441, when another large force was sent west against the Vandals, the Persians attacked again, and Atilla made further demands. The Romans defeated the Persians in 442, but Atilla laid waste many cities and defeated the Romans when they were finally able to march against him. As a result, the Imperial treasury was saddled with an immediate payment of 6000 pounds of gold and a ruinous annual tribute of 2100. Atilla attacked and defeated the Eastern Romans again in 447 and demanded the evacuation of a strip of territory on the Roman side of the Danube, five-days journey in breadth. In 449, Chrysaphius unsuccessfully tried to procure Atilla's assassination, but instead of retaliating, Atilla set off westward in search of greater conquests.

Many wealthy senators at Constantinople resented the subsidies paid to the Huns, a significant share of which the policies of Chrysaphius made them bear. Also, no doubt, Chrysaphius' prestige was damaged by his bungled assassination attempt against Atilla. Furthermore, in the same year, he and his colleague Nomus, Master of the Offices, offended many orthodox Christians in high places by obtaining a reversal of the condemnation of the views of Eutyches, who taught the Monophysite heresy, that Christ had only one nature, the divine, which had absorbed the human. Then, shortly after Theodosius II died

without a son on July 28, 450 from injuries in a riding accident, Chrysaphius' opponents in the senate at Constantinople, in cooperation with Pulcheria and Aspar, Master of the Soldiers, elected Marcian as Theodosius II's successor. A *pro forma* marriage was arranged with Pulcheria to give him a dynastic claim. Marcian immediately overthrew Chrysaphius and Nomus and reversed both their secular and religious policies.

Marcian (450–457) First of all, Marcian refused to continue payments to Atilla, who, fortunately, was too involved in the West to retaliate before he died. The death of Atilla and the breakup of his empire also allowed Marcian to resettle the abandoned territories along the Danube with barbarian federates, particulary the Ostrogoths. Without having to pay the Huns anymore, Marcian was also able to reduce taxes, especially on the senatorial class that had supported him. He alleviated the expenses of holding offices and tried to halt the corrupt practice of selling them too. Finally, Marcian and Pulcheria, in cooperation with Pope Leo I, arranged the Fourth Council of Chalcedon to deal with the Monophysite heresy. The ideas of Eutyches and his supporters, mainly the Egyptian bishops, were condemned, a move that was to have great consequences for the unity of the Eastern Empire.

Stability Threatened With the death of Marcian in 457, the relative stability that had marked the Eastern Empire compared with the West since the death of Theodosius the Great was seriously shaken: the Ostrogoths continually disturbed the Danubian frontier, barbarian generals tried once more to become the kingmakers in Constantinople, plots for which the word Byzantine is too apt were rampant, and doctrinal conflicts released sectarian passions of the worst kind.

Leo (457–474)   When Marcian died the senate probably would have prefered to elect Anthemius, grandson of Theodosius II's identically named praetorian prefect and son-in-law of Marcian. Instead, they were constrained by Aspar, Master of the Soldiers, to elect one of his officers as Emperor Leo I. Leo, however, did not wish to be Aspar's puppet. In 466, when Tarasicodissa, an Isaurian officer produced evidence that one of Aspar's sons was conspiring with the Persians, Leo replaced the suspect with a Vandal named Jordanes. He also married his elder daughter, Ariadne, to Tarasicodissa, who took the Greek name Zeno, and made him Master of the Soldiers in Thrace. Leo's personal safety was protected by a new palace guard, probably Isaurians, called the Excubitors.

In foreign policy Leo asserted his independence by installing Anthemius as Emperor in the West and by mounting a massive joint expedition against Gaiseric the Vandal in 467. Unfortunately, Leo's general was incompetent, the expedition failed in 468, and Leo's position was weakened. Aspar seized the occasion to force a marriage between Leo's younger daughter and his second son, Patricius, and have Patricius declared Caesar. The continued intrigues of Aspar and his sons finally convinced Leo and Zeno to take desperate action. Aspar and his sons were lured into the palace and attacked by the Emperor's eunuchs. Patricius was only wounded and was allowed to live, but his father and brother died (471).

Theodoric Strabo, used Aspar's murder as an excuse to demand appointment in his place and lands in Thrace for his Ostrogoths, who now elected him their king. Leo refused, and Strabo ravaged Thrace. In 473 a compromise was reached, by which Strabo received Aspar's old post and the Ostrogoths received a subsidy of two thousand pounds of gold a year.

Leo II (473–474) and Zeno (474–491)

In 473, Leo also made Zeno's son by Ariadne, another Leo, his colleague and des-
tined successsor. Leo I died some months later in early 474. In turn, Leo II took his father, Zeno, as coemperor. He died before the end of the year and thus left Zeno in sole possession of the throne.

Soon, Zeno, whose position was weak, had to face a serious revolt led by the widow of Leo I, Verina, and the ambitious king of the Ostrogoths, Theodoric Strabo. In 476, Zeno temporarily succeeded in defeating his domestic enemies but still had to deal with Theodoric Strabo, whom he tried to fight with a rival Ostrogoth, Theodoric the Amal. Zeno adopted Theodoric the Amal, made him Master of the Soldiers, and sent him to fight Strabo in Thrace. The Amal, however, turned the tables on Zeno and tried to play Strabo off against him. More domestic plots involving the indomitable Verina followed and were not completely suppressed until 488. Meanwhile, Theodoric Strabo had died, and in 488, Zeno was also able to come to a satisfactory agreement with Theodoric the Amal, whom he authorized to overthrow Odovacer in Italy. Zeno had finally rid himself of serious foes and was free from plots for the remaining three years of his life.

Heresies and the *Henotikon*

The heresies which bedevilled the East from the time of Marcian (450–457) to the Arab conquest of Syria and Egypt two centuries later had their roots in the questions raised about the nature of Christ in the Arian heresy and in the jealousies of rival bishops (patriarchs) vying for preeminence with each other at Rome, Constantinople, Alexandria, Jerusalem, and Antioch. Nestorius, who had become patriarch of Constantinople in 427, had argued that Christ had two separate natures, human and divine, which, though found in one person, were not mixed. On the other hand, Cyril, Patriarch of Alexandria, had held that the two natures of Christ were indissolubly joined together in a personal (hypostatic) union, although they remained distinct.

As the controversy between these two

stubborn, opinionated, and jealous clerics grew, Theodosius II had tried to settle it by summoning a council at Ephesus in 431. Various maneuvers there had resulted first in the condemnation of Nestorius, next of Cyril, and then of Nestorius again. Eutyches subsequently had developed Monophysitism: Christ had only one nature (*monophysis*), the divine, which absorbed the human. This view had appealed to Dioscorus, Cyril's successor at Alexandria, but was condemned at a council in Constantinople under the patriarch Flavian in 448. That decision had been overturned a year later by a council at Ephesus under the presidency of Dioscorus, who also obtained the deposition of Flavian.

Dioscorus' victory at Ephesus had given Alexandria primacy over religious affairs in the East. The political implications of this situation had been too great for the Emperor Marcian to ignore, and in 451 he had summoned the First Ecumenical Council at Chalcedon, which had condemned Eutyches' ideas as heretical and had deposed Dioscorus. Dioscorus had been banished and troops had forcibly imposed Proterius as his successor at Alexandria.

The formula adopted at Chalcedon to define Christ's nature was based upon the views of the former patriarch of Alexandria, Cyril, and the position of Pope Leo I as set forth in *The Tome of Leo* —namely, that Christ is completely human and completely divine, one and the same Christ having two natures, without confusion or change, division or separation, each nature concurring into one person and one substance (hypostasis). This formula still prevails in the Greek Orthodox and the various Christian churches of the West, but it was widely unpopular in Syria, Palestine, and Egypt, where the Monophysites had extensive appeal.

At Alexandria, upon the death of Marcian, his nominee, the Patriarch Proterius, had been lynched in his church on Easter of 457, and Timothy Aelurus (the Cat), a Monophysite, had been installed in his place until Leo I had forcibly removed him in 460. Similar scenes had been repeated at Jeru-

salem and Antioch under Marcian and Leo. Later, the chaos in the early part of Zeno's reign had temporarily produced the restoration of the Monophysite patriarchs Timothy the Cat and Peter the Fuller at Alexandria and Antioch.

In 482, Zeno, guided by Acacius, Patriarch of Constantinople, had tried to end the disruptive religious controversy by issuing a decree of union, the *Henotikon*, which asserted the orthodoxy of the view set forth at Nicaea in 325 and Constantinople in 381, condemned the views of Nestorius and Eutyches, and anathematized anyone who had or would deviate at Chalcedon or any future council. This document had not pacified the extreme Monophysites and Chalcedonians, and Pope Felix had refused to ratify a document that ignored *The Tome of Leo*. Instead, he had excommunicated Acacius, who, along with Zeno, ignored his action.

The *Henotikon* was flexible enough that Monophysite patriarchs could assent to it and thereby hold onto their sees. As a result Alexandria, Jerusalem, and Antioch all had Monophysite patriarchs under Zeno. The problem did not really disappear, however, and continued to cause difficulties in later reigns. Eventually, the Monophysites in Egypt created their own church, the Coptic Church, which survived the Moslem conquest down to the present time.

Anastasius (491–518) The day after Zeno's death there was a public meeting of the Empress Ariadne, the various ministers, the Patriarch Euphemius, and the senate to discuss the appointment of a new Emperor. Urbicius, the Grand Chamberlain, successfully proposed that the Empress make the choice herself. She chose a well-known member of the Imperial Council, Anastasius, whose name probably had been agreed upon in advance. In religion he favored the Monophysites, and the Patriarch Euphemius refused to permit his coronation until he signed a pledge of orthodoxy. For twenty years Anastasius kept his pledge by endeavoring to uphold the

Henotikon, but his efforts were eventually brought to naught by religious extremists.

Adriadne had married Anastasius to give greater legitimacy to his accession, which was a severe disappointment to Zeno's brother Longinus and the Isaurians. On the other hand, the power of the Isaurians was bitterly resented by the Greek population at Constantinople, and a riot in the Hippodrome gave Anastasius a pretext for expelling Longinus and all other Isaurians from the capital. He forced Longinus to take holy orders, confiscated Zeno's property, and cut off the annual subsidy that Zeno had provided his countrymen. Naturally, these acts enflamed the revolt that some Isaurians had already raised, but Anastasius was determined to break Isaurian power and bring them firmly under Imperial control. It took seven years of stubborn fighting, but he succeeded. Many Isaurians were resettled in the depopulated districts of Thrace. They continued to supply valuable contingents to the army but played no further role in Imperial politics.

Wars with Persians and Bulgars   Various native peoples on the borders created the usual disturbances here and there, but the Persians and Bulgars posed major problems. In 502 the Persian king Kawad (Kavad, Kavades, Cawades, Qawad) invaded in force. He was eventually pushed back, and in 506 a seven-year truce was signed on the basis of the *status quo ante*, which remained in place even after 513. The Bulgars proved more intractable, however. They were a Mongolian tribe that had united with the remnants of Atilla's Huns after 454. They had been kept in check by the Ostrogoths, but after Theodoric's departure for Italy, they began raiding Thrace and Illyricum. Devastating raids occurred in 493, 499, and 502. Anastasius' inital response was to build the Long Wall (probably in 497), about forty miles west of Constantinople, from the Propontis to the Black Sea. After the truce with Persia in 506, however, enough troops were available to keep the Bulgars in check until 517.

Religious Conflict   By 517 the Empire had been weakened by a civil war that was related to the religious policies of Anastasius from 511 onward. For the first twenty years of his reign, Anastasius had remained relatively neutral in the dispute between the Monophysites and the orthodox Chalcedonians so long as they each supported the *Henotikon*. He had deposed the Patriarch Euphemius in 497 for intriguing against the Monophysites but had allowed him to be replaced by another Chalcedonian, Macedonius. By 511, however, the Chalcedonians had gained control of the sees of Antioch and Jerusalem as well, and Anastasius began to intervene on the side of the Monophysites by deposing Macedonius and replacing him with Timothy, a Monophysite.

Anastasius faced down an attempt to replace Timothy, but Vitalian, the Count of the Federates in Thrace, raised the standard of rebellion in Thrace and intervened on behalf of Macedonius. He marched on Constantinople in 511 and 514, but both times Anastasius was able to negotiate his withdrawal. When a promised Church council did not materialize in 515, Vitalian marched on Constantinople again, but this time he was decisively defeated by land and sea, and his revolt collapsed.

Financial Reforms   The man who led the successful attack against Vitalian was Marinus, the former Praetorian Prefect, who had helped devise financial reforms that were the most successful aspect of Anastasius' reign. In 498, Anastasius abolished the *chrysargyron*, a regressive sales tax that hurt the urban poor. Whatever revenue was lost from this measure was made up by setting aside an equivalent amount of income from the private Imperial estates. In 513 he even began to phase out the *capitatio*, which was a severe burden on the peasantry.

This latter move was probably made possible by the increased revenues that resulted from the scrupulous and systematic fiscal management that he imposed to eliminate fraud and waste. He clamped down on bureaucratic "fees" and made certain that soldiers received their proper pay. He demanded a careful accounting of military rations to prevent the theft of supplies. He also made the procurement of supplies more efficient by switching much of the land tax from payment in kind to payment in gold, so only supplies actually needed were acquired.

Anastasius further tightened the system of tax collecting by appointing *vindices* to oversee provincial officials and the municipal councillors, *curiales*. The *vindices* saw to it that the taxes were honestly collected and that the wealthy did not receive preferential treatment. Finally, Anastasius introduced a series of copper coins useful for small daily transactions. Previously, there had been nothing between the gold *solidus* and the almost worthless copper *nummus*. The new coins were denominated in units of forty, twenty, ten, and five *nummi*. Their convenience was greatly appreciated by the people, and they were profitable to the treasury because they cost less to produce than the gold *solidi*, which the treasury received in exchange.

All of these reforms increased the Imperial revenues while they actually reduced the burden of taxation. By being prudent and scrupulous in normal operations, Anastasius could afford to be generous to cities and provinces that suffered damage from war or natural disasters without straining the Imperial finances. When he died he left a surplus of 320,000 pounds of gold in the treasury, a precious legacy to his immediate successors.

Despite dynastic upheavals and divisive religious controversy in the century and a quarter since the death of Theodosius the Great, the East had survived intact, while the West had disintegrated into a number of separate Germanic kingdoms. Barbarian king-makers had been purged, the Ostrogoths had been lured off to Italy, a stable peace was in place with Persia, and the finances of the state were unusually sound. For the moment, the future of the Empire in the East appeared to offer the hope of stability if the problem of finding a successor to Anastasius could be handled quickly.

XXXIX

Justin and the Establishment of Justinian's Autocracy, A.D. 518 to 532

The death of Anastasius without a direct heir in 518 produced another crisis of succession, but most people seemed anxious to avoid a destructive struggle. Through intrigues that are not entirely clear, Justin, head of the Excubitors, the Emperor's personal bodyguard, obtained nomination from the senate and approval of the populace and chief ministers. He was an Illyrian of fairly humble origin and limited education from the region around Scupi, modern Skopje in southern Yugoslavia. Having risen to high rank, he had promoted his family's fortunes by bringing his nephews to Constantinople and obtaining for them every advantage of education and rank. Already in his sixty-sixth year, Justin groomed his favorite nephew, Justinian, for succession by closely associating him with his reign right from the start. The well-educated and energetic Justinian exercised much influence on his uncle's whole reign (518–527).

Sources for the Period of Justin and Justinian   The sources for Justin's reign are limited. In *On the Ceremonies of the Byzantine Court,* Constantine Porphyrogenitus preserves the official account of Justin's election and coronation. About twenty-five of his laws appear in Justinian's *Code,* and his letters on religious matters are extant. The principal narrative sources are the contemporary secular account of John Malalas' *Chronography* and the ecclesiastical histories of Evagrius and John of Ephesus—the former from the Chalcedonian point of view and the latter from the Monophysite.

Justinian's reign (527–565), on the other hand, is one of the best documented in ancient history. Procopius of Caesarea records, often as an eyewitness, military and diplomatic history in his *Persian War, Gothic War,* and *Vandalic War* up to 552. Writing immediately after Justinian's death, Agathias covers the events from 552 to 558 in his *Histories,* while large fragments of a continuation to 582 by Menander the Protector are preserved in the *Historical Excerpts* of Constantine Porphyrogenitus. Corippus' Latin epic, the *Johannid,* also gives a detailed picture of military action in Africa from 546 to 548.

For internal affairs, Procopius' *On Buildings* is a useful description of Justinian's extensive building program, but his *Secret History* is full of scurrilous gossip and scandalous accusations designed to present Justinian and his wife, Theodora, in the worst possible light. It does, however, give insights into the working of the bureaucracy, whose abuses are blamed on the Emperor himself. The most important sources for internal affairs are, of course, the laws preserved in Justinian's law code, the *Codex Justinianus*. The laws are quite complete up to 534, when the second edition of the code was published. Of his subsequent laws, 180, mostly from 534 to 544, are preserved in other collections. Ecclesiastical documents in great number from this period are also valuable sources of information.

The Reign of Justin (518–527)

Justin's first acts as Emperor were to secure his throne by executing his two most powerful rivals and to reverse the Monophysite policies of Anastasius. As natives of a Latin-speaking province, Justin and Justinian were both champions of Roman orthodoxy and, therefore, favored the Chalcedonians. Justin immediately convened a council of about forty bishops in Constantinople to reassert the Chalcedonian view. Provincial councils deposed the Monophysite leader Severus of Antioch and more than fifty other bishops. The imprisonments and massacres that followed failed to stamp out the heretics, however, and Timothy IV, the Monophysite Patriarch of Alexandria, was powerful enough to hold onto his own see.

To obtain the support of the orthodox Vitalian, who had revolted against Anastasius, Justin promoted him to the office of Master of the Soldiers and even made him consul in 520. That, however, was merely a ploy to disarm a man who was otherwise too powerful for comfort. Vitalian was assassinated during his consulship, and Justinian was promoted to fill his offices.

Barbarians and Persians Militarily Justin's reign was a success against barbarian tribes but not the Persians. His other nephew, Germanus, Master of the Soldiers in Thrace, defeated a major incursion of the Antae and kept them under control for almost ten years. The Tzani, a fierce tribe on the borders of Colchis and Armenia, were pacified and Chris-

tianized. Late in his reign, Justin offended the Persians on two counts and precipitated a serious war. First, when the Persians tried to impose Zoroastrianism on their Christian client kingdom of Iberia (modern Soviet Georgia), Justin intervened on behalf of the Iberians. Then, he personally insulted Kawad I, the Persian king.

Kawad wanted his third son, Chosroes (Khosroes, Khusro) I, to inherit the Persian throne, but he feared that the older sons would oppose their brother. He, therefore, sought Roman support for Chosroes by asking Justin to adopt him. Justin rejected this novel idea when it was pointed out that under Roman law Chosroes would then have a legitimate claim to the Roman throne. Stung by the rejection, Kawad and Chosroes attacked the Romans, but before any decisive battles took place, Justin fell ill and died a few months later after designating Justinian as his successor (August 1, 527).

The Accession of Justinian (527)

About forty-five years of age, Justinian ascended the Imperial throne in the prime of life. Probably no other Emperor since Marcus Aurelius had been so well educated, and probably none since the sons of Constantine the Great had had such a practical apprenticeship at the center of power. Justinian, therefore, could not only conceive far-reaching plans and reforms, but he also knew how to take effective action. As a native of a Latin-speaking province and inspired by Rome's history of great accomplishments, Justinian yearned to recover the Latin West and restore the Empire to its former power and territorial extent. As a passionate believer in orthodox Christianity as the true universal faith, Justinian also hoped to root out paganism and heresy in the united realm.

The two goals were tightly linked. On the one hand, Justinian was looking back toward the secular glories of the past; on the other, he was looking forward to the creation of a great Christian commonwealth. By championing orthodoxy, Justinian hoped to earn divine favor for his secular goals, and by his secular success, he hoped to have the opportunity to enforce the true faith on God's behalf. In the process he increased the Emperor's control over administration, defense, finance, religion, and commerce and created the model of Byzantine autocracy.

Justinian's faith was buttressed by serious theological study, which also seems to have reinforced a penchant for system, order, and fairness in secular affairs. Throughout his reign Justinian sought answers to thorny theological questions in his desire to promote orthodox uniformity of Christian doctrine. He also streamlined and reformed the legal, administrative, and fiscal systems of the Empire to promote efficiency and strengthen the state. Even his building program reflects the same love of order and system found in his other work.

This passion for order, system, and efficiency also reflects a man who wanted to be in control of everything. The difference between a conscientious and talented administrator pursuing lofty goals with systematic efficiency and an autocrat who demands uniform obedience for the good of the state in whose name he rules is not very great. Justinian's desire for religious orthodoxy led to the systematic persecution of nonbelievers and heretics. Jealous of his authority, Justinian was also reluctant to take advice from others and was too willing to listen to charges of disloyalty against those who were trying to serve him best.

Finally, he loved elaborate ceremonials and rules of etiquette designed to exalt him far above even his most distinguished subjects. Even senators had to abase themselves by prostration in the presence of either the Emperor or Empress, now called Lord and Mistress, while high officials and members of the court referred to themselves as their slaves.

Theodora Justinian's Empress was the beautiful, intelligent, and strong-willed Theodora. Her importance to Justinian's reign is difficult to overestimate. She acted with great independence, and Justinian publicly acknowledged her as a partner in counsel. He bestowed upon her the palace of Hormisdas and great estates, whose income allowed her to maintain a large number of loyal followers ready to do her bidding. She was a powerful friend, whose patronage could advance the careers of some, and a formidable foe, whose enmity could destroy those of others. She was even bold enough to act contrarily to Justinian's policies when it seemed best to her.

Theodora's power and her undeniably humble origin naturally aroused the jealousy and resentment of the senatorial aristocracy. As a result, many scandalous rumors were circulated concerning her past and her activities as Empress. Because so much about her comes from obviously hostile and biased sources, however, it is difficult to separate fact from fiction. That her birth was too humble to be acceptable for marriage to the heir to the Imperial throne probably accounts for the adamant refusal of Euphemia, Justin's wife, to agree to let Justinian marry her. Procopius, in his untrustworthy *Secret History,* tells an elaborate story of her birth as the daughter of a bearkeeper from the circus and a sordid career, first as a child actress, then as the most profligate of prostitutes.

No doubt Theodora's early life was not perfect, but much of Procopius' pornographic portrait probably was inspired by a few simple facts. She may well have been the daughter of a bearkeeper. The coincidence that Justin abrogated the law forbidding senators to marry actresses about the time that Justinian married Theodora may be the only basis for the story that she had been one. It does seem that she had borne a daughter to a lover prior to her relationship with Justinian, but that and her interest in saving impoverished young girls from the all-to-common fate of enforced prostitution may be the only facts behind the lurid tales of her youth as told by her enemies.

Protection of Women Theodora deserves much praise for her attempt to protect women from abuse and secure better rights for them. She actively worked for laws to prohibit the sale of and traffic in young girls for prostitution. She even paid her own money to free those already held captive. To provide for their refuge and rehabilitation, she converted a palace across the Bosporus into a home called *Metanoia,* Repentence. She also protected women from harsh and arbitrary divorce on charges of adultery, charges which husbands often trumped up to get rid of unwanted wives.

Religious Policies of Theodora and Justinian   Another group that benefitted from Theodora's concern was the Monophysites, whose views she favored against the orthodox Chalcedonians. Justinian, on the other hand, was a staunch Chalcedonian, and he always strove to eliminate Christian heresies. Against such heretics as the Manichees and Montanists, he employed harsh measures at the start. In the case of the more widespread Monophysite heresy, his hope was to find a theological formula that would reconcile Chalcedonians and moderate Monophysites so that extreme Monophysites could be isolated and then eliminated by harsh actions if necessary.

In 532 he convened a committee of six Chalcedonian and six moderate Monophysite bishops. They worked out a formula that condemned the views of Nestorius and Eutyches and mentioned neither a double nor single nature of Christ. It was accepted by Pope John II in 534. In 535, Timothy IV, the extreme Monophysite Patriarch of Alexandria died, and Justinian forcibly replaced him with Theodosius, a moderate. His policy seemed to be gaining ground, but Pope John II died and was succeeded by Agapetus, who was doctrinally less flexible. He rejected the compromise that John had accepted and persuaded Justinian to abandon it too. An extreme Chalcedonian patriarch, Menas, was installed at Constantinople, and he convoked a new council, which condemned the moderate Monophysites. Justinian then supported harsh persecutions of them in Syria and Egypt.

Nevertheless, Justinian still searched for a theological compromise. In 543/44 he published an edict in three chapters, each of which condemned certain Chalcedonian ideas offensive to Monophysites. Eastern Chalcedonian patriarchs accepted the edict, but Pope Vigilius alternately rejected and accepted it until forced by threats of being deposed to give it his full blessing in 554. This action merely caused a schism among the Western bishops because many refused to follow Vigilius' lead.

In the East the Three Chapters also failed to placate the Monophysites, who were rapidly developing a strong independent church under the pressure of persecution. In 564, Justinian tried a new formula for compromise by accepting the extreme Monophysite doctrine of the incorruptibility and impassibility of Christ's body, but he died without success in 565, and the Church, upon whose unity he believed the Empire's welfare to rest, was more fragmented than ever.

Justinian had also acted on many other religious matters during his long reign. With his passion for systematization and good order, he passed numerous laws regulating such internal affairs of the Church as the election of bishops, the behavior and character of the clergy, monastic discipline, and the management of Church property. He also pursued strong measures against pagans and other non-Christians. In 529 he ordered all pagans to be instructed in the Christian faith and baptized or lose their property and be exiled. He even closed the Platonic Academy in Athens and executed some prominent pagan aristocrats at Constantinople. Moreover, Justinian enacted laws against Jews and Samaritans that denied them honorable status, restricted their civil liberties, and forced them to bequeath their property to only orthodox Christians. Later, he even dictated the rules for worship in Jewish synagogues, and in 562 he persecuted pagans with renewed vigor.

Legal Reforms   Justinian's legal and administrative reforms were more praiseworthy ˙and successful than his religious policies. The disorganized mass that Roman law had become after centuries of growth and change needed rationalization and systematization. On February 13, 528 Justinian appointed a commission to collect all previous codified and uncodified Imperial edicts, update, edit, and simplify them, and codify them in a single compact work. This task was completed by Justinian's quaestor, Trebonian, and the other commissioners on April 7, 529.

In December of 530, Justinian set Trebonian to codify the legal commentaries of the classical jurists. This work was completed in three years. It was then time to update the *Code* to include the large legislative output of Justinian up to that time. This second edition, which survives today, appeared on November 16, 534. A year earlier the *Institutes* had been published as a textbook to simplify the study of law.

Administrative Reforms In the administration of the Empire, Justinian earnestly tried to eliminate corruption and increase efficiency. Although corruption and abuse in Imperial administration had never been eliminated under the Principate, the early emperors had rigorously enforced higher standards than had prevailed in the late Republic. The chaos of the third century and the tremendous growth of the bureaucracy since the reforms of Diocletian and Constantine, however, had undermined standards, increased the chances for corruption and the number of officials susceptible to it, and made it much more difficult for a conscientious emperor to oversee the system.

One of Justinian's most beneficial reforms was the elimination of *suffragia*, payments for offices, which were then recouped by graft and corruption. He also issued standard rules for provincial governors and strengthened the powers of the civic defenders, *defensors civitatis*, who were supposed to act as ombudsmen for the provincials. He streamlined provincial administration by abolishing the vicars, who had been in charge of dioceses, by combining the office of civil governor and military commander in provinces where there were no serious external threats, and by giving Christian bishops powers to oversee public officials and provide for the general welfare.

In the capital Justinian bolstered the office of police chief, *praefectus vigilum*, and gave him a new title, *praetor plebis*. He took measures to provide for the populace's security and supply food for the armies. He also created a new office, that of *quaesitor*, investigator. This official made sure that visitors to Constantinople left upon completion of their business, returned illegal immigrants to their homes, and found work for unemployed legitimate residents.

These reforms were ably carried out through Justinian's Praetorian Prefect, John the Cappadocian. As with so many reforms, however, they worked better in theory than in practice. With the abolition of the vicarates, lawless bands could escape capture by moving from one provincial jurisdiction to another. The corruption and abuse of power that thrive in large bureaucratic organizations, especially in societies where some people are viewed as superior and others as inferior, continued. In fact, with the elimination of the middle-level vicars, who, if strengthened, might more easily have checked corruption and abuses at the provincial level, the reforms probably did little more than enhance the power of John the Cappadocian.

John the Cappadocian John used his power to great advantage in the sphere of Imperial finance. Justinian's ambitious wars, diplomacy, and building projects needed vast sums of money. The surplus left by Anastasius was soon spent, and Justinian had to finance everything out of current revenues. John's success in securing those revenues made him very valuable to Justinian, but aroused the hatred of those who had to pay more taxes and the jealousy of those who resented the power and favors that he received from the Emperor. No doubt, he was ambitious, often ruthless in his methods, and eager to maximize his own financial rewards, but one must discount considerably the monstrous picture painted of him by sources like Procopius and John the Lydian. The former was a jealous courtier, and the latter reflected the views of wealthy aristocrats and officials who had evaded taxes or enjoyed profits from corruption and felt the sting of John's strong fiscal administration most severely.

The wealthy landowners must have bitterly resented John's supplementary land tax, the "air tax," which, nevertheless, they were quite able to pay and which added three thousand pounds of gold to yearly revenues. Throughout Asia Minor, the Levant, and Egypt, except on the strategic route from Constantinople to the Persian border, John also eliminated the public posting service, *cursus publicus,* an expensive service often abused by wealthy citizens and government officials. He likewise abolished four expensive *scholae,* ceremonial military units to which the wealthy sought appointment to enhance their prestige, and ordered others to the front unless their members agreed to forfeit their pay to avoid active duty. These units were a useless expense, and it was worth incurring their members' animosity to free their pay for better uses. A less wise economy, however, was the suspension of pay for border troops in the East during a period of peace with Persia, for they were demoralized and useless when war broke out again.

To check the misappropriation and mishandling of public funds, John sent out special auditors to examine records, especially municipal and military accounts. They exposed the corruption of local notables, removed absentee and unqualified soldiers from military payrolls, and stopped officers from reporting undermanned units at full strength and pocketing the difference in pay and supplies. This system was bound to anger vested interests and provoke complaints. Some auditors were themselves corrupt, but Justinian personally sought to ensure the appointment of men with integrity, and honesty was rewarded by giving them one-twelfth of the monies saved for the state.

The Fall of John the Cappadocian   Early in 532, during what is known as the Nika Revolt,

Justinian was forced to replace John with the less aggressive Phocas, a representative of aristocratic interests. In less than a year, however, when he had recovered firm control, Justinian reappointed John as Praetorian Prefect. Nevertheless, John remained the object of machinations by his enemies, particularly Theodora, who resented his influence with her husband and may honestly have thought that he had ambitions for the throne himself. Finally, in 541, with the help of Antonina, wife of Justinian's great general Belisarius, who wanted her husband to be supreme in Justinian's favor, Theodora secured his banishment and forced ordination. After Theodora's death, however, Justinian freed John and allowed him to return to Constantinople as a priest.

Administration and Finance After John   After John, Justinian adjusted the administrative system to provide a middle level of authority over groups of provinces. In the diocese of Oriens, the old *comes Orientis,* Count of the East, who had been reduced to one of the provincial governors, received authority over some of the lesser governors again (542). In 548 a *vicarius* was reappointed for the diocese of Pontus with military authority to preserve order in its provinces, and a similar official was appointed for Asia and for Thrace. Justinian also continued to issue laws designed to improve administrative procedures and control abuses.

Peter Barsymes   In the financial sphere, John's role was assumed by Peter Barsymes, first Count of the Sacred Largesse and Praetorian Prefect in 543. When he tried to increase revenues by selling off grain stored at Constantinople in 544 and then had to make compulsory purchases of grain in 545 after a bad harvest, he became very unpopular and had to be removed in 546. Nevertheless, he was soon in charge of the Sacred Largesse again and became Praetorian Prefect once more in 554 or 555.

He too is portrayed negatively by Procopius, but laws inspired by him show that he was concerned to protect both revenue and small taxpayers by fair procedures. That would not have appealed to the wealthy and powerful, who often tried to shift taxes onto the weaker citizens and exploit them. They also must have resented the innovation whereby he took advantage of the shortage of silk caused by wars with Persia to establish a state monopoly over the sale of silk at high prices and great profit to the treasury. In 552 a plan was devised by some monks to smuggle some silkworms' eggs out of China in a hollow bamboo cane, and the manufacture of raw silk was soon part of the state's monopoly. Peter also may have introduced the practice of selling monopolies in other types of business to appropriate guilds, *collegia*.

The Monetary System   Despite the financial strains caused by Justinian's programs, the coinage of the Empire remained strong and was the standard medium of exchange throughout the civilized world from Cadiz to Ceylon. The Germanic successor states in the West found it politically and economically wise to duplicate the Imperial coinage. The Merovingian kings of the Franks even put Justinian's bust on their coins with only their own initials. In Spain the Suevi continued the coin types of Honorius and Avitus, and in Italy the Ostrogothic kings merely revived the bust and legends of Anastasius rather than replace the Imperial coinage with another after Justinian attacked them.

The First Persian War   When Justinian became sole Emperor upon Justin's death in 527, he inherited the war with Persia, which was going badly. He had no desire to conquer Persian territory and hoped simply to put enough military pressure on the Persians to force them to accept a long-term peace that would free him to reconquer the West. The war seesawed back and forth until the death of the Persian king, Kawad, in September of 531, and Chosroes, who wanted to be free to meet any challenges to his succession, entered

serious negotiations with Justinian's ambassadors. Finally, in the spring of 532, a treaty of Eternal Peace was signed. The prewar boundaries were accepted by the Persians, and Justinian paid Chosroes eleven thousand pounds of gold as the price for Chosroes' agreement not to demand an annual subsidy for defending the Caucasus.

The Nika Rebellion   In the middle of the negotiations with Chosroes, Justinian almost lost his throne in an uprising involving the factions of the circus at Constantinople. The circus factions had originated during the time of the late Republic, when chariot races became the most popular spectacle at public festivals. Each race normally required four chariots. The official in charge of the games would hire the chariots and their respective drivers and horses from four different groups organized for that purpose. They came to be known as factions, and each one distinguished itself by a special color—red, white, blue, or green. Just as modern athletic teams, each one had its fiercely loyal fans, and successful charioteers earned sums as extravagant as today's multimillion-dollar professional sports stars.

The popularity of the chariot races and successful charioteers explains why all of the Roman emperors, who often relied on the good will of the masses as a counterweight to the jealousy of the senatorial aristocracy, were generous patrons of the races. Some, like Nero, Domitian, and Commodus, had even driven in the races themselves. As Roman culture spread through the Empire in the first and second centuries A.D., each provincial city of any significance had its own group of reds, whites, blues, and greens. In a society where the people had been denied any meaningful role in politics and where the urban poor led otherwise useless and frustrating lives, the excitement of the circus and the chance to obtain money by betting on the races aroused intense interest. The restless and bored, much like the members of modern motorcycle and street gangs, attached themselves to individual factions in groups called partisans. They distinguished themselves by special dress, harassed ordinary citizens, and even committed crimes. Clashes among partisans of different factions were also frequent and sometimes erupted into full-scale popular riots.

The Blues and the Greens In Constantinople by Justinian's day, the Reds and the Whites had been completely overshadowed by the Blues and the Greens. These two factions had acquired such widespread followings and organizational strength that they were a significant element in the political life of the capital. Emperors and powerful senators sought to manipulate the two factions for their own political and religious ends. The Emperor Anastasius, for example, had favored the Greens, who became associated with his Monophysite views. The orthodox Justin and Justinian, therefore, had catered to the Blues by putting some in governmental posts, supplying them with money for their activities, and protecting them from punishment for their disorders and crimes.

Once Justinian had secured his own power, however, he considered the continued disorders of both factions dangerous and tried to discipline them. On January 13, 532, when Justinian refused to commute the sentences of two men, one Blue and one Green, who had survived a bungled hanging, the two factions decided to cooperate to force their release. They adopted the word *nika* ("conquer") as their watchword, which gave the subsequent popular uprising its name.

That evening, rioters set fire to a number of public buildings, including the entrance hall of the Great Palace and the Church of the Holy Wisdom, *Hagia Sophia*. Renewal of the chariot races the next day failed to divert their attention, and they set fires at the northern end of the Hippodrome, where the races were held. The ranks of the original rioters were now swollen by those who had suffered from Justinian's fiscal policies, such as the numerous small farmers who had abandoned their land in the face of heavy taxes and had migrated to Constantinople. Encouraged by powerful senators who also resented Justinian's autocratic ways and his fiscal maneuvers, they were now demanding the removal of three key ministers: Eudaemon, Prefect of the City; Tribonian, Justinian's Quaestor; and John the Cappadocian.

Although Justinian yielded and replaced them, he still failed to quell the riots, whose powerful instigators now wanted nothing less than to depose the Emperor himself. The hope was to replace Justinian with one of Anastasius' three nephews, Probus, Pompeius, and Hypatius. They, however, seem not to have been party to the plot. Probus had fled the city to avoid being dragged in, while Pompeius and Hypatius stood by Justinian in the palace.

When Justinian realized that the rioters were bent on dethroning him, he resolved to crush them by force. The regular palace guards preferred to remain neutral and refused to attack the populace, but Justinian had others upon whom he could rely. Belisarius, who had just been recalled from the Persian War, and Mundus, who had been serving on the Danube, were present with some loyal contingents of Goths and Heruls. For two days they battled the mobs without accomplishing anything except burning more of the city.

As the situation deteriorated, Justinian became so distrustful that he dismissed everyone from the palace except his closest personal friends. He even forced Pompeius and Hypatius to leave, despite their protestations, and thereby fueled the resistance of the rioters. When he appeared in person and promised upon the most sacred oaths to grant a general amnesty and institute reforms, the people contemptuously rejected his pleas and raised the reluctant Hypatius to the throne. Justinian, therefore, decided to flee. At the crucial moment, however, the dauntless Theodora argued that the life of an exile was far less preferable than death in defense of the throne. Justinian took heart and stayed.

Justinian ordered his loyal eunuch Narses to take as much gold as he could, penetrate the crowd that was acclaiming Hypatius in the Hippodrome, sow dissension between the Blues and Greens with bribes, and arouse the jealousy of the Blues with reminders of Anastasius' former favoritism toward the Greens. In the meantime, Mundus and Belisarius positioned their men for a surprise attack on the crowded arena. When they struck, the tightly packed crowd could not resist. The few, but trained, soldiers of Mundus and Belisarius slaughtered thousands and broke the back of the revolt.

Hypatius and Pompeius were executed to prevent their being the focal point of other rebellions, and eighteen senators suspected of complicity were stripped of their property and exiled. The circus factions ceased to be a serious problem for Justinian after that, and he was able to consolidate his autocratic rule, which had provoked senatorial opposition to his policies in the first place. Theodora's toughmindedness in a desperate hour had saved Justinian's throne and won him greater freedom to act on a grand scale. It is no wonder that he was deeply devoted to her and mourned her loss when she died of cancer sixteen years later (June 28, 548).

The Rebuilding of Constantinople

Just as an earlier promoter of Imperial autocracy, Nero, had used the great fire of 64 to rebuild Rome on a magnificent scale suitable for the capital of an exalted emperor, so Justinian rebuilt Constantinople after the conflagrations of the Nika Revolt. The secular buildings that had to be restored included the Senate House, the Baths of Zeuxippus, the porticoes of the Augusteum, and parts of the Great Palace. In autocratic fashion Justinian also took the opportunity to renovate the palace entirely and decorate it with splendid mosaics glorifying his reign. He even redid the summer palace at Hêrion (Phanaraki), outside the city, in a similar vein.

In keeping with Justinian's desire for divine favor to support his rule, churches received special attention. The Church of Holy Peace, *Hagia Irene,* was rebuilt on a scale second only to that of the neighboring *Hagia Sophia,* Holy Wisdom. The earthquake-dam-

aged Church of the Holy Apostles was replaced at this time too.

Hagia Sophia was the most ambitious project and took five years to build. The best available architects, Anthemius of Tralles and Isidore of Miletus, were in charge. Anthemius, who had specialized in domed churches, conceived the novel plan of combining a domed roof with a floor plan in the shape of a Greek cross. It was about 250 by 225 feet with a dome 180 feet high above the 100-foot square where the arms intersect. To support the dome and fit its circular base over the square opening, the architects placed massive arches over each side of the square with great piers on which they rested at the corners. In each corner they constructed a pendentive, an arched and curved triangle of masonary whose apex rested on the pier, whose sides followed up the curves of each adjoining arch to its apex and whose resulting curved base formed a ninety-degree arc (one-quarter of a circle) between the apexes of the adjoining arches. For stability, half domes rested against the east and west sides of the building below the main dome, and great vertical buttresses secured the north and south. The basic structural material was brick, with the ribbed dome being built of special lightweight tiles.

The outside, as is typical of Byzantine churches, for which *Hagia Sophia* became the archetype, was plain, but the interior was richly decorated. Different-colored marbles from around the Empire were used for pillars and floors and to sheathe the walls. The domed ceiling was covered with pure gold, and huge mosaics, the greatest being a great cross on a field of stars at the top of the dome, decorated the church throughout.

The new *Hagia Sophia* was dedicated on December 26, 537. Unfortunately, however, Anthemius and Isidore had miscalculated the stresses in its innovative design, and the dome eventually collapsed in 558. Isidore the Younger built a new dome over twenty feet higher to provide more vertical thrust. It was finished in 562 and has endured to this day.

To make it a worthy monument of both Divine Wisdom and Justinian's reign, thou-

Hagia Sophia with the four minarets added by the Turks.   *(Courtesy G. E. Kidder-Smith)*

sands of pounds of gold were spent on the construction and furnishing of *Hagia Sophia*. The pulpit was covered with gold and jewels, the altar was solid gold, and the Patriarch's throne was constructed of thousands of pounds of gilded silver. One source places the total cost at 320,000 pounds of gold. Even if it is exaggerated by a factor of ten, the cost would still be staggering. Perhaps Justinian would have been wiser to put off such huge domestic expenses until he had completed his great scheme of reconquering the West. He launched this campaign right after the Nika Revolt and the signing of the peace treaty with Chosroes, and his failure to devote enough resources to operations in the West after his initial success almost ruined the whole enterprise and caused serious long-term problems in both the East and West.

XL

The Impossible Dream of Universal Empire, A.D. 532 to 565

During the previous century, the Western half of the Roman Empire had been completely lost to the Germanic successor kingdoms of the Franks, Vandals, Visigoths, and Ostrogoths. The dream of the old universal Mediterranean-European Empire of Rome lived on, however, to haunt or inspire proud generals, ambitious statesmen, idealistic philosophers, and magalomaniacal dictators down to present times. For no one did this dream seem more real than Justinian, who devoted more than thirty years in an attempt to make it come true. The task proved more difficult than he ever imagined. Opening hostilities in the West left him more vulnerable to attacks elsewhere. He was forced to spread the Empire's resources dangerously thin and thereby make the task even more difficult.

Reconquest of the North African Provinces, 533 to 534 By 532 conditions in the Vandals' kingdom of North Africa were favorable to Justinian's hopes of reconquest. The previous Vandal king, Hilderic, grandson of Valentinian III (see p. 474), had stopped persecuting the orthodox Roman Catholics in his realm and had entered into a treaty with Justinian. Unsuccessful against Moorish raiders, however, he had been deposed by his cousin Gelimer. Invoking the treaty with Hilderic, Justinian prepared to attack North Africa. His generals and advisors, recalling the disastrous human and financial losses of earlier expeditions against the Vandals, protested. Justinian rejected their advice nevertheless, and in 533 Belisarius sailed with between fifteen and twenty thousand soldiers. Commanding with Belisarius was his able and fearless wife, Antonina.

Victory was deceptively easy. Gelimer was incompetent and distracted by revolts of the Catholic Romans in Tripolitania and by his governor of Sardinia. Aided by the Ostrogoths in Sicily, Belisarius and Antonina landed on North Africa without opposition, and they were helped by the Catholic population, who resented the Arian Vandals. Within a year, by two battles that were won more because of Gelimer's astounding incompetence than the skill of Belisarius and Antonina, North Africa was reconquered. In 534 it and Sardinia were formally organized into the separate Praetorian Prefecture of Africa. Unfortunately, the unexpected ease and speed with which the African operation proceeded were a disaster in disguise. They would commit Justinian wholeheartedly to his great scheme of Western reconquests, which proved extremely difficult and costly to retain after the initial victories.

Italy　Soon after the recovery of the North African provinces, an ideal opportunity arose to restore Roman power in Italy. Theodoric had provided an enlightened regime for Italy throughout most of his reign. He greatly admired Roman culture and institutions and, though an Arian, had tried not to provoke his orthodox Catholic Roman subjects. For all classes in Italy, therefore, life had gone on much as before, and they had enjoyed relative peace and prosperity. The only major difference was that taxes were now paid to Theodoric, who held the political and military power. Unfortunately, neither the orthodox Roman aristocracy nor Theodoric's fellow Ostrogoths always appreciated his policies, but he had managed to prevail over both until his death in 526.

Theodoric was succeeded by the ten-year-old Athalaric, whose mother, Theodoric's daughter Amalasuntha, acted as regent. She continued Theodoric's policies and gave Athalaric a classical education. A powerful anti-Roman faction among the Ostrogoths, however, insisted that Athalaric be raised as a German warrior. They ultimately prevailed, and Amalasuntha entered into negotiations with Justinian for asylum. The intemperate behavior fostered by Athalaric's peers, moreover, led to his alcoholic death in 534.

Amalasuntha then offered the throne to Theodahad, with the proviso that he be guided by her. Once securely enthroned, however, Theodahad ordered her imprisoned and executed (535). The Empress Theodora may even have secretly maneuvered him into doing so in order to give Justinian the chance to act as Amalasuntha's protector.

At any rate, Theodahad's actions gave Justinian a convenient pretext to intervene. First, he seized Sicily and Illyricum and then opened negotiations with Theodahad. Ultimately, Theodahad promised to hand over Italy to Justinian in exchange for Eastern

estates with yearly revenues of twelve thousand pounds in gold. When a Gothic army momentarily recovered Illyricum, however, he reneged, and Justinian ordered Belisarius to invade Italy, while another commander, Constantian, quickly recovered Illyricum.

After a delay caused by a mutiny in Africa, Belisarius landed at Rhegium in late June of 536 with fewer than ten thousand men. Despite such small force, he made good progress because Theodahad did little to oppose him and the Catholic population of Italy usually favored him. At Naples, however, which he reached in October, there was a significant enemy garrison, and the people refused him entrance. Belisarius conducted a costly siege and was about to abandon it when he discovered that he could penetrate the walls through the channel of an aqueduct. Then, after sacking Naples, he marched on Rome.

Theodahad Replaced by Vitigis　In the meantime, the Ostrogoths deposed the faint-hearted Theodahad and crowned Vitigis, a successful commander unrelated to the royal house. Instead of marshalling his forces to defend Rome, however, Vitigis left it a garrison of only four thousand and proceeded to Ravenna. There he forcibly married Amalasuntha's daughter, Matasuntha, in order to legitimize his rule. He also sought aid from the Franks, who obliged in return for Ostrogothic territory in Gaul, and he opened last-ditch negotiations with Justinian, who seems to have rejected his offers.

At Rome, Pope Silverius, many senators, and the Catholic population in general opened the city to Belisarius. The outnumbered garrison withdrew without a fight. Vitigis finally acted by bringing back a large army to besiege Rome. Belisarius showed great resourcefulness and military leadership in keeping the city provisioned and maintaining the morale of his outnumbered forces for 374 days. He received some crucial reinforcements in November of 357 and obtained a truce for negotiations. When Vitigis violated the truce, John, nephew of Vitalian, whom Belisarius had stationed in Picenum for such an eventuality, seized Ariminum (Rimini) on the Adriatic coast near Ravenna. That maneuver forced Vitigis to abandon the siege of Rome in order to protect Ravenna (mid-March, 538).

Rival Commanders   Belisarius, however, now began to be hampered by a lack of cooperation from other commanders. First, John, who thought him too cautious, refused an order to remove his valuable cavalry from Ariminum in order not to lose its services if Vitigis besieged the city, as soon happened. Then the eunuch Narses, Keeper of the Privy Purse, who arrived in Italy with seven thousand reinforcements, refused to be subordinate to Belisarius. As a result, although John was rescued, the Ostrogoths recaptured Milan, which had willingly surrendered to Belisarius after the siege of Rome, massacred its male inhabitants, and enslaved the women (spring, 539). Justinian, therefore, recalled Narses and clearly designated Belisarius as the supreme commander.

The Capture of Ravenna (Spring, 540)   A brief invasion of Franks, who were dealing treacherously with both sides, drove the Ostrogoths from the Po, and Belisarius proceeded with his customary deliberateness to reduce the outlying Ostrogothic strongholds that protected Ravenna. While Belisarius' army received supplies by ship from Sicily and southern Italy, the Ostrogothic garrisons in the north were hard pressed for food. The war had caused such devastation in many northern districts that even many civilians were badly nourished or starving. From Ravenna, Vitigis vainly summoned the Lombards from beyond the Danube to aid their fellow Germans, and he secretly encouraged the Persian king, Chosroes, to divert the Romans by starting another war on the Eastern frontier.

Learning of the latter move, Justinian offered generous terms to Vitigis in order to avoid war on two fronts. He proposed that Vitigis surrender half of his royal treasure and cede Italy south of the Po to the Empire. In turn Justinian would recognize him as king of

Italy between the Po and the Alps. Vitigis readily agreed, but Belisarius refused to be party to such a treaty. It seemed to throw away five years of difficult warfare just as total victory was in his grasp. His refusal to sign the treaty caused the Ostrogoths to fear bad faith on Justinian's part, and a stalemate resulted.

The Ostrogoths then played into Belisarius' hands. He received a proposal that he declare himself Western Emperor and that the Ostrogoths become his loyal subjects. He pretended to accept the proposal, but when he and a body of his soldiers were received into Ravenna to consummate the agreement, he seized Vitigis and his wife, many Ostrogothic nobles, and the royal treasury (May, 540). Then he took them back to Constantinople.

Justinian was not wholly pleased by Belisarius' unauthorized actions and did not give him a triumph, as he had after the Vandalic War. Despite the superficially spectacular results, the situation in Italy was left worse than Justinian's terms would have made it. The Ostrogoths north of the Po refused to surrender to anyone after Belisarius' duplicity was revealed. Instead, they elected Ildibad, a good general, their new king. Bound by no treaty, they created the problem that Justinian had hoped to avoid—major wars on two fronts.

Troubles in North Africa   Justinian's haste to invade Italy before securing adequate control of North Africa had already produced an example of that strategic difficulty on a smaller scale. Right after Belisarius' victorious departure in 534, Moorish tribes began devastating incursions, which had taken two years to quell, and they still remained restive. No sooner had the Moors been repulsed than about two-thirds of the Roman army in North Africa mutinied for various reasons: slowness in collecting taxes in the new province caused long delays in paying the soldiers; many soldiers resented the harsh discipline of their new commander, Solomon; barbarian auxilliaries felt that they had been poorly rewarded with booty; men who had taken Vandal wives were aggrieved that the Emperor confiscated their former fathers' and husbands' estates instead of allowing their daughters and widows to inherit; and many of the Romans' barbarian allies were Arian Christians, who resented Justinian's suppression of Arianism among the conquered Vandals.

The mutineers besieged Carthage, which was rescued only when Belisarius interrupted his invasion of Italy and returned from Sicily. Belisarius soon had to return to Sicily, and Justinian placed his own capable cousin, Germanus, in charge of restoring order in North Africa. He defeated the rebels decisively in the spring of 537 and consolidated control during the next two years. In 539, Solomon returned and purged the army, exiled the troublesome Vandal women, and made sorties against the Moors. For the time being at least, these actions reduced Justinian's worries in North Africa.

The Second Persian War, 540 to 562
By 539, Justinian's biggest worry was the threat of renewed war with Persia. The situation of the eastern frontier was already unstable. In Armenia, which had always been a bone of contention between the Romans and Persians, a revolt had broken out because of Roman fiscal exactions. Unable to defeat the Romans, the rebels had appealed for help from the Persian king Chosroes. With additional encouragement from Vitigis, Chosroes opened the war in 540, and it was not officially ended until 562.

In Chosroes, the successor of Kawad, Sassanid Persia had an energetic and able leader comparable to the Roman Empire's Justinian. He continued administrative and land reforms begun by his father, he made the army more efficient, and he took great interest in literature, philosophy, and religion. In every way he hoped to increase the glory and greatness of the Sassanid Persian Empire.

Justinian's successes in Africa and Italy had aroused both fear and envy in Chosroes. He scarcely needed the pleas of either Ostrogoths or Armenians to prompt his breaking of

the Eternal Peace of 532 and renewing war on Justinian's eastern flank in 540. Fortunately for the Romans, Justinian since 532 had carefully rebuilt or strengthened frontier fortresses and the walls of cities in Mesopotamia and Syria. Chosroes' main goals, therefore, were not so much to capture Roman territory as to make a show of strength by successfully besieging some major strongholds, to obtain plunder or money from those whom he besieged or threatened, and to force Justinian to pay tribute in return for peace on the frontier. He demolished Sura, Beroea, and Antioch but had to be content with only money from Hierapolis and Edessa after failing to take them. Justinian would have agreed to pay the five thousand pounds of gold plus an annual subsidy of five hundred pounds that he demanded if Chosroes had not then unsuccessfully besieged the great fortress of Daras during negotiations.

In 541, Chosroes scored a major coup by seizing the Romans' client kingdom of Lazica, ancient Colchis, at the eastern end of the Black Sea. After garrisoning the Roman fortress city of Petra to secure his control of the kingdom, Chosroes then returned to Persian territory to face Belisarius, who had arrived to take command and had captured the Persian stronghold of Sisaurana, about thirty miles due east of Nisibis, near the upper Tigris. When Chosroes failed to take the Roman city of Sergiopolis in Syria the next year, he and Belisarius made a temporary truce (542).

Resumption of War in Italy, 541 to 543 Justinian probably was anxious to secure some kind of truce, however imperfect, in 542 because he needed the incomparable Belisarius back in Italy. The new Ostrogothic king, Ildibad, had been determined to continue the war in Italy, and Roman policies made it easy for him to do so. First, with the departure of Belisarius in 540, military command in Italy was left fragmented among his former subordinates. Second, the harsh fiscal policies of Imperial administrators were alienating both the soldiers and the very people whom Justinian claimed to be freeing from tyranny.

Starting with scarcely a thousand men, Ildibad extended Ostrogothic control over Italy north of the Po without effective opposition from the separate Roman generals. Even when Ildibad was assassinated in a private quarrel and was replaced by the incompetent Eraric, who was willing to betray northern Italy to Justinian, the Roman commanders failed to seize the advantage. Later in 541, Ostrogothic conspirators assassinated Eraric and raised up Ildibad's nephew Totila, who proved his worth.

Totila took the offensive against the divided Roman commanders in 542 and quickly recovered most of southern Italy except Naples, which fell in the spring of 543 only after a lengthy siege. He increased the ranks of his army by recruiting slaves and wisely refrained from plundering the countryside for supplies. Instead, he collected the regular taxes and rents, which provided regular income without ruining the territory. His humane treatment of captured cities and towns also advanced his cause. He did, however, demolish their fortifications because he did not have enough troops to garrison them against Roman counterattacks.

Troubles with Persia

In 542 the Romans had to battle not only the Ostrogoths and Persians, but a far more destructive enemy as well—plague. The initial outbreak was enormously destructive, and its appearance in Syria contributed to Chosroes' willingness to sign a truce. As many as 300,000 people may have died in Constantinople alone. Justinian himself fell ill but survived. Those who did survive were immune from the subsequent attacks that appeared with diminishing severity during the next twenty years, until a general immunity built up in the Empire's population.

The truce between Rome and Persia in 542 was not highly effective. Immediately afterward Chosroes demolished the Roman fortress of Callinicum (Nicephorium) on the east bank of the Euphrates, about 100 miles northwest of the junction with the Chaboras (Abrorrhas, Araxes). In 543, Chosroes' projected invasion of Roman Armenia was thwarted by an outbreak of plague and the revolt of a son. On the other hand, the Romans successfully invaded Persarmenia near the headwaters of the Euphrates. Finally, in 545, after again failing to take Edessa (544), Chosroes consented to a meaningful five-year truce. In return Justinian paid him two thousand pounds of gold, but operations in Lazica were exempted from the agreement. The truce was subsequently renewed for another five years on similar terms in 551.

Belisarius Returns to Face Totila in Italy

After the initial truce with Chosroes in 542, Justinian had reassigned Belisarius to take charge of the war against the Ostrogoths in Italy. No doubt Belisarius' preparations were hindered by the outbreak of plague at Constantinople in 543. He and his intrepid wife, Antonina, did not arrive at Ravenna until 544. Also, he desperately lacked manpower. Plague and lack of funds, because of the war with Persia and Justinian's expensive building program, probably hindered recruitment. He brought only four thousand men with him and found that many of the soldiers originally sent to Italy had deserted because they had not been paid for years. He finally persuaded Justinian to divert some troops from the East now that there was a truce with Chosroes, but they were not adequate.

In the meantime, Totila pushed into central Italy and besieged Rome in the winter of 545/46. Belisarius vainly tried to relieve the city, which finally fell through treachery. Fortunately for Belisarius, however, the Roman garrision of three thousand escaped. According to Procopius only 500 civilians were left at the end. That figure may be questioned, but starvation and flight reduced the population disastrously. Rome did not significantly revive for centuries!

Totila was not able to garrison Rome and headed south to oppose Roman forces attacking his strongholds there. Belisarius outwitted the Ostrogoths left to cover him, reoccupied Rome, and successfully withstood a siege when Totila returned. The six thousand assorted troops that Justinian sent in 548 were, however, not nearly enough to enable Belisarius to take the offensive.

Clearly, Belisarius was Justinian's best general, but even he could not successfully prosecute a war without adequate forces. Therefore, he sent the resourceful Antonina to Constantinople in the hope that she might obtain more men through her influence with Theodora. Unfortunately, Theodora had died on June 28, 548, just before Antonina arrived, and Justinian was preoccupied with finding enough men to prosecute the war in Lazica, which had been exempted from the truce with Chosroes in 545. Seeing her husband in a hopeless situation, Antonina then asked that he be recalled. It was futile to remain. He returned to Constantinople in early 549 and was reappointed Master of the Soldiers for the East, but he never actively assumed the post.

The Lazic War, 549 to 557   Chosroes was determined to preserve his unprecedented access to the Black Sea by consolidating his hold on Lazica. Justinian was just as determined to prevent Rome's ancient enemy from retaining this strategic naval advantage. The Lazi had soon begun to dislike Persian oppression even more than the Roman kind. They asked for Roman help, and Justinian sent seven thousand men to retake Lazica in 549. Petra was recaptured in 551, but the war became stalemated after that.

Peace in the East   In 557 another five-year truce was signed, and this one also included Lazica. Finally, Justinian and Chosroes worked out a fifty-year peace in 562. In return for evacuating his positions in Lazica, Chosroes received an annual subsidy of thirty thousand gold pieces. He also agreed to guard the Central Caucasus against barbarian inroads. Other provisions regulated commer-

cial, military, and diplomatic relations between the Persian and Roman empires, and rules for arbitrating personal disputes between Persians and Romans on the frontier were set up to prevent them from growing into wider conflicts. In a separate agreement, Chosroes promised to tolerate the Christians in his empire so long as they did not seek converts.

Disaster in Italy, 549 to 551   After Belisarius' departure in 549, things went from bad to worse in Italy. The ease with which Belisarius had initially reconquered both North Africa and Italy had deceived Justinian and caused him to discount the seriousness of subsequent problems in the West. Also, he needed large amounts of money to mount campaigns against Chosroes in the East or to buy him off with subsidies and to expend on buildings or art to glorify God and the Empire. Therefore, he was even more willing to believe that Belisarius and others in the West wanted more than they needed. Already undermanned, therefore, Roman armies in both Italy and North Africa suffered mutinies and betrayals by troops angry over the lack of pay.

Just such a situation caused some Isaurian soldiers to betray Rome in 550 to Totila again after Belisarius left. That finally spurred Justinian to take more vigorous action. He rejected Totila's offers to renegotiate. The latter then promptly invaded Sicily, which previously had been spared. At last Justinian placed his cousin Germanus in charge of the war. Using private as well as public money, Germanus prepared a proper expedition to recover Italy.

The Recovery of Italy, 552 to 562   Unfortunately, Germanus, who shrewdly married Amalasuntha's daughter, Matasuntha, granddaughter of Theodoric, in the hope of dividing Ostrogothic loyalties, died before he could depart for Italy. In his place Justinian appointed the popular and capable eunuch Narses. Narses arrived in Italy with at least twenty-five thousand men, almost half being

Lombards, Heruls, Gepids, and Huns. He promptly defeated Totila in a set battle (Butta Gallorum), and Totila was killed in flight.

These actions show how much Totila's earlier success was the result of Justinian's failure to commit enough resources to the war in Italy.

In the same year, Narses won another great battle against the Ostrogoths at Mons Lactarius. After that, Ostrogothic resistance was confined to a number of fortified cities, which Narses systematically reduced. On the other hand, he had to face a large army of Franks and their Alamannic subjects, who swept into Italy from the north in 553 to reap what Narses had sown. Narses kept to the fortified towns while the Franks dissipated their energies in plundering much of the rest of Italy. Finally, in 554 Narses annihilated them at a great battle outside of Capua. Italy south of the Po was free at last from warfare, but it was not until 562 that Narses finished taking Ostrogothic strongholds between the Po and the Alps.

The Pragmatic Sanction, 554 In 554, Justinian issued what is known as his *Pragmatic Sanction* to restore order and provide proper Imperial administration to Italy. It restored rights and property to prisoners and exiles, slaves to their masters, and *coloni* (tenants) to their landlords. Gothic landowners of long standing were left in enjoyment of their property, however. Justinian also forbade the kind of fiscal and administrative abuses that had caused so much discontent after the initial reconquest, and he provided for the proper provisioning of troops without undue burdens on the people.

Wars on Other Fronts, 544 to 561
While Justinian was confronting simultaneous wars or uneasy truces on the eastern frontier and in Italy, he was not free of trouble elsewhere. Remarkably, he even continued to pursue his grand scheme of reconquering other parts of the West before he had adequate control of North Africa and Italy. In 544 the

Moors revolted once more in North Africa. They were aided by the Roman general in charge of Numidia, who wished to rule Africa independently, and by troops who had not been paid. This revolt was not crushed until 547, but the Moors then remained subdued (except for a brief rebellion in 563) for the remainder of Justinian's reign.

After 550 Justinian seems to have devoted greater energy to the West. At the same time that he finally committed adequate resources to prosecute the war in Italy, he also took advantage of a dynastic struggle among the Visigoths to recapture Spain. In 551 the pretender Athanagild requested Justinian's aid against his rival, King Agila. Justinian immediately readied a fleet and army that conquered part of southern Spain along both the Atlantic and Mediterranean coasts on Athanagild's behalf. The Visigoths then accepted him as king, but the Romans refused to hand over to him what they had captured. Instead, they organized the territory, which included such important cities as New Carthage, Malaca, and Cordoba, into the province of Baetica.

In the Balkans various barbarian tribes had periodically raided Thrace and Illyricum since 529. The Bulgars hit Illyricum in 544. The Sclavenes penetrated that province all the way to Dyrrhachium (Durrazo) in 548 and ravaged Thrace, Dacia, and Dalmatia in 550 and 551. After a few years' respite, both of these tribes combined with the Cotrigur Huns in a massive invasion of 559. One group penetrated Macedonia and Greece as far south as Thermopylae, another attacked the Chersonese (Gallipoli Peninsula), and another drove through Thrace right up to the walls of Constantinople.

At Constantinople, Belisarius, who had long learned to do much with little, saved the day once more. With a makeshift army of his three hundred loyal bodyguards and some hastily recruited, poorly armed civilians, Belisarius marched out and camped at the suburb of Chettus. There he set a clever ambush for the two thousand Huns that confidently rode out to attack his small force. Without any losses his men killed four hundred Huns, who retreated in panic from Constantinople. At Thermopylae and at the entrance to the Chersonese, Roman defenses held, and the barbarians went back across the Danube after Justinian promised them an annual subsidy. A similar offer dissuaded the Avars in 561, and the Balkans remained calm for the rest of Justinian's reign.

Barbarian enemies could be persuaded to accept subsidies because it was impossible for them to remain in the Balkans for very long after an initial breakthrough. Between 540 and 549, Justinian had expended much effort on building and repairing defenses and forts at hundreds of places along the Danube and throughout the Balkan peninsula. Perhaps that is why he did not feel able also to commit adequate resources to Italy during this period. At any rate, his expenditures in the Balkans proved their worth. Although raiders could sweep through the open country, the Romans could hold the well-supplied fortified places with a few men and harass the barbarians when they scattered to plunder, or could attack them in the rear after they had exhausted available food and were returning encumbered with spoils.

Successes and Failures of Justinian's Reign

Law and Administration Justinian's policy of codifying and revising the corpus of Roman law was a great success and is what one recalls first about his reign. The elimination of outdated and contradictory laws and the systematic presentation of those retained provided a uniform and efficient body of law such as is necessary for the well-being of any large, complex state. It still provides the model for the legal systems in most European nations.

Justinian's attempt to provide more efficient and honest administration by increasing salaries, combining functions to lessen the number of officials, and centralizing authority at Constantinople was not always successful. No system is immune to corruption. Justinian remained flexible, however, corrected mistakes and abuses when he could, and definitely

improved upon what had existed before. During his reign the interests of both the ordinary person and the state as a whole were better served by Imperial administrators.

Byzantine Autocracy Both Justinian's legal and administrative reforms contributed to the creation of a fully autocratic monarchy, which was characteristic of the succeeding Byzantine Empire. The office of Emperor had grown more and more autocratic since the time of Augustus—sometimes faster, as under Caligula, Nero, Domitian, Septimius Severus, or Constantine; sometimes more slowly, as under Vespasian, Antoninus Pius, Tacitus, Probus, or Gratian. The personalities of the individual emperors had affected the pace, but in the long run the need for a powerful, efficient, central authority to deal with increasingly large and complex problems pushed the emperors in the direction of autocracy.

Justinian's policies were the culmination of that process. The Byzantine autocracy built on his model had all the unpleasant faults of any autocracy, which resulted in the pejorative meaning of the word "Byzantine" when applied to politics. Nevertheless, Justinian's successors and their ministers maintained the armies and organized the resources that preserved civilization in the East from being overwhelmed by a constant stream of barbarian attackers for centuries.

Manufacturing and Commerce For the most part, Justinian followed traditional Roman policy regarding manufacturing and commerce. Trade between the eastern and western Mediterranean had long been in the hands of Greek and Syrian merchants. The reconquest of North Africa, Italy, and part of coastal Spain must have made their trade with those areas easier and more profitable. In the East, Justinian took an active interest in the silk trade, which was monopolized by the Persians to the detriment of Roman merchants and consumers. Even worse, the profits made by the Persians increased the chronic imbalance in Roman trade with the East.

Justinian cooperated first with the Abyssinians in an unsuccessful attempt to break the Persian silk monopoly. Later, he sponsored the smuggling of silkworms out of China and the raising of silkworms within the Empire. Thus he established a whole new field of agriculture and manufacturing. The actual production of the cloth, moreover, was a highly profitable monopoly of the state.

Justinian also created a state monopoly in the manufacture of arms. His motive in this case seems to have been to keep arms out of the wrong hands rather than a desire for revenue since the state's manufacture of arms for its own needs had existed since Diocletian. Now, however, only the state could manufacture arms.

Art and Architecture   The vast building projects of Justinian were a boon to art and architecture. The distinctive Byzantine styles of architecture, mosaic decoration, and painting, as evidenced by *Hagia Sophia* and the Great Palace at Constantinople and the churches of San Vitale and San Apollinare Nuovo at Ravenna, received their basic forms under Justinian's patronage. Domed churches with unadorned exteriors, perspectiveless decorative frescoes and mosaics inside, saints shown in stiff stylized poses, and a preponderance of gold and brilliant colors remained characteristic of Byzantine architecture and churches for centuries.

Long Reign   Perhaps Justinian's greatest success was in living so long. A well-disciplined man of Spartan habits, Justinian enjoyed a sound constitution that enabled him to survive the plague that killed countless thousands. He also seems to have been safe from plots. Only two conspiracies after the Nika revolt are noteworthy, and they were revealed before he was in any serious danger.

Unfortunately, the involvement of two of Belisarius' men in one of these plots raised suspicions against him. He was forced to dismiss his armed retainers and was disgraced. Contrary to legend, however, he did not end his life as a blind beggar. Justinian restored

him to favor after less than a year, and they passed the rest of their days together. Belisarius died in March of 565, and Justinian followed a few months later on November 14, 565.

Religious Persecution   Despite notable accomplishments, on balance Justinian's reign was a failure. One of his biggest failures was in the sphere of religion. His policy of seeking divine favor by uniting the Empire under the orthodox Catholic version of Christianity as defined at Chalcedon only created deep animosities toward the Imperial government among inhabitants who espoused different faiths or other versions of Christianity. Persecution of the Jews and Monophysite Christians in Egypt and the Levant so embittered many of them that they welcomed the Moslem conquerors who seized those lands seventy-five years after Justinian's death. Similarly, the Arian Christians of North Africa resented the continued attempts to impose Catholic orthodoxy, and the resultant divisiveness made it easier for the Moslem conquerors in the mid-seventh century. Likewise, the devastating Ostrogothic rebellion after the initial reconquest of Italy was fueled by the Arian Ostrogoths' resistance to the imposition of orthodoxy.

Bankruptcy of the Empire   By the time Justinian died, the Imperial treasury had been exhausted by the expenses of his grandiose building projects, his impetuous wars, and the ruinous subsidies that he agreed to pay some enemies in order to be free to fight others. The desperate state of the treasury subsequently contributed to his successor's decision to risk war with Persia rather than continue subsidies. Ironically, that war dragged on for twenty years and weakened the Empire even further.

Mishandling of Succession   Justinian compounded problems by his poor handling of the arrangements for providing a successor. The choice of an Imperial heir lay between Justin, an able general and son of his cousin Germanus, and another Justin, a nephew whom Theodora had greatly favored. Although the latter had no conspicuous abilities, Justinian had advanced him to high rank. Nevertheless, Justinian had not clearly indicated who was to succeed. Unfortunately, the inferior Justin was well placed to seize the throne and had his rival executed when Justinian died. Justin II had pretensions that bordered on megalomania and led to disastrous foreign policies. He eventually continued disruptive religious persecutions too, and his fiscal frugality so overcompensated for Justinian's overspending that he undermined Imperial security. Finally, he became so mentally unbalanced that he could not rule and the state was thrown into debilitating confusion.

Reconquest of the West   Even Justinian's reconquest of the North African provinces, Italy, and part of Spain must be counted as a failure—his biggest. He had to weaken the defenses on other frontiers to pursue these unprovoked wars and thereby invited attacks from Persia and various barbarian tribes. The net result was to overstrain the resources of the Empire and weaken it for the future.

Furthermore, the reconquered provinces did not repay the costs of their conquest and subsequent defense. The North African provinces suffered periodic revolts and constant raids from the surrounding Moors. By the time Italy finally had been pacified, the long years of warfare had devastated its cities and permanently impaired its prosperity. The Imperial province in Spain was under constant pressure from the surrounding Visigoths, from whom it had been treacherously seized.

After all of the trouble and expense of reconquering these Western provinces, they began to be lost right after Justinian's death.

In 568 the Lombards and their allies invaded northern Italy. By 572 they held everything between the Po and the Alps. By 590 much of the rest of Italy had been lost also. About sixty years after Justinian's death, the Visigoths wrested back the territories in Spain, and after little more than a century, the Moslems had swept away Imperial power in North Africa.

Not long after Justinian, the Empire began to lose not only its newly reconquered Western provinces but also Egypt, the Levant, Thrace, and the Balkans. Furthermore, it entered a period of internal chaos aggravated by its external troubles. By the time a series of energetic emperors were able to stem the tide of disasters in the ninth century, the smaller remaining state was no longer predominantly Roman in character but had clearly become what is now called Byzantine Greek.

If Justinian had devoted his considerable talents to strengthening the defenses of the Roman Empire that he had inherited in the East instead of trying to recapture the West, and if he had not sown bitterness and discord within by his religious policies, the Roman Empire of the East would have endured much longer. Moreover, the Germanic successor states of the West would have been better able to resist the subsequent conquerors, who did more damage to Roman civilization in Europe than they had. The historical conditions that had made possible the universal Roman Empire of the first two centuries A.D. no longer existed. The resources needed to maintain it under changed circumstances had not been there to prevent the loss of the West in the first place. They were not available now. Justinian's effort to revive the dead only weakened the living.

XLI

Life and Culture in the Late Roman Empire from A.D. 337 to 565

Many of the trends seen in the third century continued after Constantine in the fourth, fifth, and sixth centuries. In some cases there were improvements in the relatively stable period immediately after Constantine, but later in the fourth and in subsequent centuries, radical changes occurred that added whole new dimensions to Imperial life. For example, the rapid spread of Christianity after Constantine made it the dominant religious force by the early fifth century, and the independent settlement of barbarian tribes within the Empire after 378 set the pattern for the transition to Germanic successor states in the West during the following century.

Economic Activity   After Constantine the economic life of the Empire became more stable while the integrity of the Imperial borders was maintained. Trade and manufacturing in the West did not recover their former prosperity, but the coastal cities of the Empire still carried on steady trade in foodstuffs, raw materials, better manufactured goods, and luxuries, many of which were still being imported from the Far East but through third parties rather than Roman merchants.

Under the Sassanids the Persians had obtained a monopoly on the silk trade with China, and until Justinian was able to obtain smuggled silkworms, the Romans had to import all of their silk through Persian customs. The trade with India and Ceylon (Sri Lanka) and the east coast of Africa was handled primarily by the Himyarites of Yemen and the Abyssinians of Ethiopia through Red Sea ports.

The barbarian invasions and Persian wars of the fifth and sixth centuries disrupted both domestic and foreign Imperial commerce but did not destroy them. Britain, for example, was increasingly isolated from other parts of the Empire in the early fifth century, and the silk-weaving industry of Tyre and Berytus (Beirut) collapsed with the loss of imported raw silk from Persia when Justinian's Second Persian War broke out in 540. All through the fifth and sixth centuries, however, Alexandria and Constantinople remained great centers of trade, and even the takeover of the West by Germanic successor states and the raids of Vandal pirates did not destroy the lucrative luxury trade in the Western Mediterranean. Greek and Syrian merchants still operated in Western ports, and for that reason Germanic kings continued to mint gold on the Imperial standard, which was universally recognized and preferred, as the finds of Roman coins from Honorius to Justinian in India attest.

The Imperial government controlled foreign trade through a few ports of entry such as Clysma (Suez), Hieron on the Bosporus, and Nisibis on the Persian frontier. Import duties were twelve and one-half percent, and the export of strategic goods like iron, bronze, and arms was forbidden. The state also continued to maintain large manufacturing operations to produce arms, armor, and uniforms for the armies and the silk cloth prized by the Emperor and upper classes.

Agriculture The agricultural life of the Empire continued the trends of the third century. Large estates continued to proliferate at the expense of small holders, who found it increasingly difficult to survive under inflation and the heavy burdens imposed by the state. Wealthy landowners often possessed numerous estates, not just in one province but in several. Absentee landlords contracted out the management of their estates to professional managers, who oversaw the *coloni* and collected rents.

Agriculture in Italy actually underwent something of a revival in the fourth and fifth centuries because wealthy inhabitants of the Western provinces considered land in Italy away from the borders a safer investment. Marginal land everywhere increasingly began to be abandoned by its owners, rich or poor, because of the increasingly heavy taxes levied on land by the Imperial government. In the sixth century, Justinian's wars of reconquest and subsequent disturbances in Africa and Italy dealt agriculture in those lands severe blows from which it never recovered.

Social Life There was no great disruption of social life during the fourth century. Stratification, with its attendant proliferation of distinguishing titles, continued. The poor also continued to sink into serfdom, the *curiales* still faced impoverishment, and the wealthy lived like kings. The immense wealth of the old, established senatorial families was truly

staggering. For example, Quintus Aurelius Symmachus, who led the fight to keep the altar of Victory in the senate house under Gratian and Theodosius, had fifteen villas in Italy alone and spent two thousand pounds of gold for his son's praetorian games at Rome. Petronius Maximus spent twice that on his games in the early fifth century.

Fifth- and Sixth-Century Changes Major changes took place in the fifth and sixth centuries, however. The Western Roman aristocracy was seriously affected by the imposition of Germanic rule. When the Visigoths and Burgundians were settled in Aquitania and Savoy in 418 and 443, the Roman inhabitants had to surrender one-third of their arable land, cattle, *coloni,* and slaves to the newcomers. Later they had to give up another third. Both the Visigoths and Burgundians governed the old Roman inhabitants under special, Roman-based codes of law. That not only tended to segregate the Romans and Germans, but made disputes between them more complicated. The Visigoths also forbade intermarriage between Romans and themselves.

In Italy, Odovacer took only one-third of the Romans' possessions for his men, and Theodoric merely assigned those thirds to his Ostrogothic followers when he took over in 493. He even allowed many landowners simply to pay one-third of their rents as taxes to the king instead of losing the land itself. Theodoric also tried to preserve the Roman administrative system intact and not segregate the old Roman inhabitants. He even allowed them to serve as military officers.

The Vandals under Gaiseric in North Africa confiscated all the property of the old Roman inhabitants and probably reduced to serfs those who did not flee. In Gaul the Franks were completely different. After their initial conquests in the north, they left the Roman inhabitants in possession of all of their property.

Understandably, the relations between the old inhabitants of the West and the newcomers were frequently strained. The Germanic tribesmen were not used to settled ways and orderly government. Germanic officials were just as corrupt as the Roman ones had been, and lawlessness and violence were common everywhere. Theodoric, for example, tried in vain to prevent his Ostrogothic warriors from plundering the country that they were supposed to protect.

Moreover, there was the added problem of the religious differences between the Arian Germans and the orthodox Catholic Romans. The old Roman upper class turned to the administration of the Church where other opportunities for leadership were restricted by their new overlords. Ethnic antagonisms and religious differences tended to become intertwined. The situation was particularly acute in the Vandal kingdom, where the kings were particularly fanatical Arians. Hunneric banished about five thousand Catholic clergy to the desert and used Catholic bishops for forced labor on Corsica.

The Burgundians, Visigoths, and Ostrogoths were more tolerant and tried to cooperate with the Catholic hierarchy. Nevertheless, Theodoric, for example, still found that orthodox clergy cooperated with his enemies. The Franks were unusual because they converted to Catholicism under the Merovingian kings at the end of the fifth century, but that did not prevent them from confiscating Church lands to reward their followers.

Urban Decline   After the fourth century, urban life declined even more precipitously in the West and was damaged considerably in the East. In the West the turmoil surrounding the Germanic conquests and settlements were particularly destructive. The Germans had little taste for urban life and generally let the cities decay. Some cities survived in severely reduced circumstances as centers of ecclesiastical administration, and a few ports, such as Arelatae (Arles), Massilia, Carthage, Naples, Ostia, and Ariminum, remained important.

The cities of Italy did not suffer so badly as elsewhere in the West during the fifth and early sixth centuries. Alaric's sack of Rome in 410 was a severe psychological shock but was not seriously destructive. Even the Vandal attack of 455 was not a devastating blow. The

wars of reconquest under Justinian, however, left most major Italian cities, even Rome, devastated and depopulated.

In the East, urban life in Thrace, Moesia, Greece and other Balkan territories suffered severely from the repeated raids of Visigoths, Huns, Ostrogoths, Bulgars, and Sclavenes during the fifth and early sixth centuries. In Greece, the only major city to escape serious attack and retain much semblance of its former self was Athens. Ironically, Athens probably suffered more from Justinian's edict of 529 in which he banned pagans from teaching. This edict effectively closed the Platonic Academy and other famous schools, which had always attracted large numbers of students and, therefore, income to Athens.

In the provinces along the Persian border, especially Syria, the wars with Sassanid Persia also severely damaged urban life. The outbreak of war with Chosroes I in 540 was particularly devastating. Not only did he strip many cities of their wealth, but utterly destroyed cities that he had to take by storm. Antioch, "Queen of the East," was among the latter. Chosroes ordered the decorations stripped from great buildings like the cathedral, deported the population, and had the city razed. It was later rebuilt. Constantinople and Alexandria remained strong.

Paganism and Christianity   Constantine made no decisive move to destroy pagan religions, which the great majority of the Imperial population still followed in his day. He officially banned animal sacrifices and withdrew state subsidies for pagan cults except for the old public cults at Rome. Otherwise, pagans were free to worship as they pleased. Such toleration, however, could be only temporary so long as the Emperors were Christian, for the whole thrust of the Old Testament and Christian beliefs derived from it demanded the exclusive worship of one god.

The contradiction between their professed faith and permitting the worship of other gods was bound to bother devout Christian emperors in the future. Moreover, in the ancient mind, religion and the welfare of the state were inextricably bound. It was the sacred duty of the ruler to secure divine favor for the state. Polytheistic pagans had no problem in seeking such favors from many sources, but the Christian deity demanded exclusive worship in return for divine blessings. Therefore, it was logically the highest civic duty of a Christian emperor to abolish the worship of other gods.

Accordingly, Constantius II decreed the closing of all temples. Such a ban, however, was impractical to enforce in the mid-fourth century. Many of the officials responsible were still pagan themselves, and sensible Christian ones realized that enforcement in heavily pagan areas would produce dangerous unrest. Many pagans protected themselves by pretending to convert to Christianity, and some even became ecclesiastical leaders in order to subvert the new power. Julian, for example, found that the bishop of Ilium (Troy) was a crypto-pagan who protected ancient shrines. Julian, of course, rescinded all antipagan legislation, and his immediate Christian successors reimposed only the ban on sacrifices.

Paganism in the Fourth Century   The ancient pagan cults, though now on the defensive against officially supported Christianity, remained important until the end of the fourth century. Constantine's removal of the Imperial court to Constantinople actually was a boon to paganism at Rome, where the traditions of the old aristocracy were closely entwined with the ancient cults under which Rome had risen to greatness. Free from the close attention of the Emperor, the old families of the Roman senate remained a bastion of traditional paganism, as witnessed by their struggle to prevent the removal of the altar of Victory from the senate and the cessation of subsidies for Rome's public cults by Gratian in 381. Theodosius' ban on pagan practices in 391 goaded them to support the revolt of Arbogast and Eugenius, who advocated the restoration of paganism and brought back the altar of Victory. Theodosius, however, removed it again after he defeated them in 394,

and he forced the senate to decree the end of pagan Roman institutions.

Elsewhere at this point, the decline of pagan rites accelerated. The Olympic Games were last held in 393. During the next few years, Theodosius systematically removed the revered statues of Zeus at Olympia, Hera at Samos, Aphrodite at Cnidos, and Athena at Lindos. In 396, Alaric's sack of Eleusis ended the Eleusinian Mysteries forever. Earlier, in 389, fanatical Christians had defiled the mysteries of Dionysus at Alexandria and destroyed the great temple of Serapis along with its valuable library. The tremendous prestige of Athens preserved its shrines for a while, but within another generation Pheidias' gold and ivory statue of Athena was removed from the Parthenon.

The Strength of Pagan Thought after the Fourth Century   Although the public cults and rituals of paganism declined rapidly under Theodosius' attack, pagan intellectualism remained strong. Theodosius had not instituted the ancient equivalent of the Inquisition. Only the outward practices of paganism, not belief itself, were attacked. Pagan books freely circulated and pagan thought dominated the schools of law, rhetoric, and philosophy. Even many high Imperial officials, who were usually trained in these schools, continued to be pagans, both openly and secretly. Athens remained a center of pagan thought for well over another century and even increased its prestige.

After the Emperor Julian's death, his friend Priscus had become head of the Academy at Athens and introduced Neoplatonism to its students. He and his successors had turned Neoplatonism into a systematic pagan theology that rivaled Christianity and perpetuated arcane magic and theurgy. Through the students who came to Athens from all over the Empire, Neoplatonism had a great impact on educated opinion everywhere. Christian leaders were rightly afraid, for speculative Christian thinkers were attracted to it also.

Alexandria had also become a major

center of Neoplatonist philosophy in the fourth and fifth centuries. In the late fourth century, the school there was headed by the noted astronomer and mathematician Theon. His daughter, Hypatia, came to be one of its most respected and popular teachers. Partisans of the Christian bishop Cyril were so afraid of her influence with the local Imperial prefect, who opposed Cyril, that they stormed her house and murdered her in 415.

Justinian's All-Out Attack on Paganism Justinian was the one who initiated what might be called an inquisition to eradicate pagan thought. He encouraged civil and ecclesiastical officials to investigate reports of continued pagan practice and forbade anyone except baptized Christians to teach. When the leaders of the schools at Athens refused to conform, Justinian confiscated the schools' endowments. Some of the scholars fled to the court of Chosroes I in Persia but soon found life uncongenial there. Chosroes did them one great service, however. In his treaty of 532 with Justinian, he stipulated that they be allowed to return to the Empire and live in peaceful retirement.

Justinian also sought to root out the paganism that had persisted among the simple folk of the countryside. He sent out aggressive officials to close out-of-the-way shrines that had escaped previous attempts at closure, and he supported wide-ranging missionary activities to enlighten the benighted. The task was made easier, however, because there had already occurred a certain synthesis of Christian and pagan practices. The former simple services of the Primitive Church had now given way to more elaborate ceremonies that included the use of incense, lights, flowers, and sacred utensils. A myriad of saints and martyrs had taken over the competing functions of many pagan deities and heroes. It is no mere coincidence, for example, that the Parthenon at Athens, home of Athena the Virgin (*Parthenos*), became a church of the Virgin Mary, that the celebration of the Nativity came to coincide with the date of Mithras' birth and the season connected with pagan celebrations

of the winter solstice, or that sleeping in a church of Saints Cosmas and Damian could now produce the cures that used to be found in the temples of Castor and Pollux. Nor would the distinction between theurgy and the celebration of the Eucharist be clear to the unsubtle mind.

Heretics and Jews Many important developments in late Imperial Christianity involved heresies and schisms, such as Arianism, Monophysitism, and the Donatist schism, which have been discussed in the chapters on the political events with which they were intimately bound because they had aroused popular passions on a large scale. Other heresies have been noted in connection with religious developments during the third century. Although it did not touch off any great popular conflict, the Pelagian heresy in the early fifth century is worthy of note because it raised fundamental questions about sin and salvation that have exercised Christian thinkers ever since.

The Church taught that saving grace could be obtained through only two sacraments, baptism and penance, which could not be repeated. Baptism would wash away the taint of Adam's original sin and any personal sins incurred in this life up to the moment of baptism, and penance could eliminate those committed thereafter. Moreover, the Church imposed rigorous moral strictures regulating sexual matters and condemned as sinful such ordinary Roman activities as going to the theater, gladiatorial contests, beast hunts, and races or performing public duties that might somehow be connected with these activities. Even worse, the Church regarded judicial executions as murder, so that any official sitting in judgment might easily become tainted with that sin too. As a result, in the fourth century, many who espoused Christianity put off baptism until the last possible moment in order to die sinless in a state of grace. After baptism in childhood or early adulthood became more common in the fifth century, penance was relied on as the means of wiping out sins committed before death. Therefore, during the greater part of their lives, many people paid little attention to the strict Christian moral code and lived lives just as sinful as non-Christians'. Indeed, there was even less need to show restraint because they knew that all could be wiped away by baptism or penance.

Among those who were troubled by this unedifying state of affairs was a Welsh layman named Morgan, later known as Pelagius, who denied the doctrine that Adam's original sin derived from his nature and was transmitted to posterity. Therefore, he argued, it was possible to gain salvation through one's own efforts in leading a righteous life. Pelagius' views were originally accepted in the East, but St. Augustine (pp. 518–519) led an attack on them in the West at a council in 416. Eventually, after numerous intervening councils, they were condemned at the Third Ecumenical Council at Ephesus in 431.

Justinian was anxious to root out heretics as much as pagans. He barred heretics from the professions of law and teaching, forbade them the right to inherit property, and would not let them bear witness in court against orthodox persons. He even instituted the death penalty for Manichees and relapsed heretics. He was just as harsh against the Samaritan offshoot of Judaism, whose synagogues he destroyed in 529. Against orthodox Jews he was only slightly less harsh. Although he did not forbid them to practice their religion, he subjected them to the same civil disabilities as heretics and Samaritans. These policies resulted in two serious revolts of Jews and Samaritans in Palestine in 529 and about 550, which produced much bloodshed and no relief for the oppressed.

Monasticism   The idea of the ascetic holy or wise man living a pure life apart from the world had a long history in the Eastern Mediterranean world. This idea became especially attractive to Christians who wished to find mystical union with God, avoid sin after baptism and penance, or earn salvation through righteous living. Numerous Christian men and women renounced the secular world and sought to live holy lives alone (*monos* in Greek) as hermits (*eremites* in Greek) in uninhabited territory (*eremos, eremia* in Greek). Their reputations for holiness soon attracted others.

One monk who became particularly famous was St. Anthony in Egypt. He fled to the edge of the Egyptian desert near Thebes in 285 and soon attracted others, who lived in makeshift cells nearby. This movement gained further momentum after Athanasius, bishop of Alexandria, wrote a popular life of St. Anthony. Therefore, Anthony is often called the founder of Christian monasticism.

Monks like St. Anthony, however, were completely autonomous. Their loose communities were called lauras and were not bound by any formal rules or institutions. Soon some monks began to live together and share a common life under fixed regulations and the direction of a leader. They came to be known as cenobites from the Greek words meaning common life (*koinos bios*), and their leaders were eventually called abbots from the Syrian word for father (*abbā*). The first known such community was founded in Egypt by St. Pachomius in 326. By the end of the fourth century, eremitic and cenobitic monasticism had been spread by pious men and women all over the East. Monasticism even reached Italy by mid-century, when Athanasius fled to Rome in the company of some monks during the Arian controversy.

Because monks were not under the control of higher civil or ecclesiastical authorities, unregulated and fanatical monks often became public nuisances and stirred up sectarian strife. Therefore, both civil and ecclesiastical pressure arose to establish stricter controls and regulations. The Emperors also worried that unregulated monasticism would encourage the flight of people from the occupations to which they were increasingly bound, and bishops were afraid that the organizational and doctrinal unity of the Church would be threatened by popular spiritual figures outside the formal structure of the Church.

The first major advance in more structured monasticism was taken in 360 by St. Basil, who founded a new monastery at Neocaesarea (Cabira, Niksar) in Pontus. His rules were more elaborate than earlier ones and prescribed more study and communal labor, rather than excessive asceticism, to keep monks occupied. Basil's rule was widely imitated and became the model for Greek monasticism. Formal action was taken by the Church at the Fourth Ecumenical Council in 451 at Chalcedon, which forbade the establishment of a monastery without permission of the bishop in its diocese and required the bishop's permission for a monk to leave the confines of a monastery.

Monasteries and convents spread less rapidly in the West than in the East. Martin of Tours pioneered the movement in Gaul at Poiteirs about 360, but only two or three more existed by 400. In the same period, St. Augustine brought monasticism to Africa, but there is no record of it in Spain. A major event in Western monasticism took place at Monte Cassino near Naples about 520 when St. Benedict founded a cenobitic monastery whose rule was based on humane common sense and stressed the value of reading and study. He thereby stimulated the collection and copying of manuscripts and helped preserve many ancient works through the Middle Ages.

Art and Architecture During the fourth, fifth, and sixth centuries, classical Greco-Roman traditions and techniques in art did not die out completely, but in an increasingly religious age the hieratic traditions of Near Eastern art became more and more prominent. This tradition deemphasized worldly naturalism and strove for a transcendent, spiritual quality. Human figures were posed in a rigidly frontal manner in order to focus on the full face. The body itself was hidden under simple drapery, and great effort was made to emphasize the spirit behind the face through the treatment of the eyes, the "windows of the soul." The use of flat, perspectiveless presentations emphasized detachment from the world by making figures

"float" on the surface of a relief, fresco, or mosaic. The importance of a figure like the Emperor or Christ was emphasized by making it bigger than surrounding figures and reducing humbler folk to smaller, schematized, even crude figures.

No significant new ground was broken in architecture until the time of Justinian. Except at Constantinople, there was little building activity beyond defensive works and churches. From the time of Constantine onward, great works of art from pagan temples were carried off to decorate the buildings of the New Rome. Many old pagan temples were used as quarries for the building of Christian churches, despite official attempts to preserve the great monuments of the past. Early Christian churches generally adopted the style of the Roman basilica, a simple rectangular building with arched windows, a semicircular apse at one end, and a pitched wooden roof, as exemplified by the early fourth-century Basilica of Trier. Eventually, side aisles were added, and then in Justinian's Church of the Holy Apostles at Constantinople, two short wings or transepts were added near one end to produce a plan in the shape of a cross. Justinian's Church of Holy Wisdom, of course, set a whole new style of church architecture (p. 496).

Secular Literature There is little secular Greek literature of note in the fourth, fifth, and sixth centuries A.D. The most significant surviving Greek authors of the fourth century are Libanius (314–395) and Themistius (d. ca. 390), sophists and professors of rhetoric who attracted large followings of pupils and were friends of the Emperors from Constantius to Theodosius. A large number of their speeches survive. They shed considerable light on politics and society in the East. A contemporary, Eunapius of Sardis, who founded a staunchly anti-Christian Neoplatonic school, wrote a number of extant biographies of other sophists and a history of his own times that survives only in fragments.

History is the primary Greek genre of note in the fifth and sixth centuries, and is represented by two important surviving authors. The earlier is Zosimus, an official of the Imperial treasury in the first half of the fifth century. His *New History* is an account of the Roman Empire from Augustus to Alaric's sack of Rome in 410. It is particularly valuable for the third and fourth centuries in the East because he used sources like Dexippus (p. 454) and Eunapius. He was outspokenly anti-Christian and constantly blames Rome's troubles on neglect of the old gods.

The outstanding figure of late Greek historiography is, of course, Procopius (ca. 500–565), who chronicled the age of Justinian as private secretary to the great Belisarius. He wrote accounts of the wars against Persia, the Vandals, and the Ostrogoths. He also recorded Justinian's massive building activities and composed the *Anecdota* or *Secret History,* in which he dredges up every imaginable scandal against Justinian and Theodora. His accounts of Justinian's wars, with many echoes of Herodotus and Thucydides, are well written, lively, and accurately based on firsthand experience. His *Secret History* is even more lively, and while the scandals that he retails probably are full of malicious gossip, they are none the less useful for revealing what the opposition was saying.

In the last half of the fourth century, pagan Latin literature enjoyed a veritable Indian summer among the senatorial upholders of ancient tradition, who steeped themselves in the works of authors like Cicero, Livy, Vergil, and Tacitus. In keeping with their outlook, many of them took a keen interest in history. This interest, however, did not reflect mere nostalgia for the past, but a sense of continuity and renewal after the near collapse of Rome in the third century.

One of the central figures in this group was Quintus Aurelius Symmachus (ca. 340–ca. 402). His family took a special interest in preserving copies of Livy's history, and he became the most famous Roman orator of his day. He held many high offices and led the fight against the removal of the altar of Victory from the senate. He published ten books of letters, which survive along with fragments of his speeches. They present a vivid picture of the life of the wealthy senatorial class in fourth-century Rome.

It was probably in this same circle that the strange biographical pastiche of fact and fancy known as the *Historia Augusta* was composed. It covers the emperors from Hadrian to the accession of Diocletian and was allegedly written by six different authors in the reigns of Diocletian and Constantine. Computerized stylistic analysis, however, confirms the theory that it was really written by one person. Perhaps it was someone who was having a good joke while playing the role of Suetonius. That such a work could be written at all, however, indicates the existence of a bold and confident spirit at the time.

Although its substance contrasts markedly with the *Historia Augusta,* the serious history of Ammianus Marcellinus (ca. 330–ca. 400) reveals a similar spirit. The last great Roman historian, Marcellinus boldly took up the mantle of Livy and Tacitus by carrying the history of Rome from where Tacitus left off in A.D. 96 to the Battle of Adrianople in 378. Born a pagan at Antioch, he was a native speaker of Greek, but he retired to Rome after a successful military career and wrote in Latin. He exercised a well-balanced judgment and used good sources. It is a shame that Books 1 to 13, covering events from 96 to A.D. 353 are lost, but Books 14 to 31 survive. He sometimes strives too hard for rhetorical effect, but he often produces a striking narrative and penetrating insights.

There was a great demand for brief summaries of Roman history among the numerous officials and emperors who came from provinces not steeped in the traditions of Rome. The African Aurelius Victor sketched the lives of the emperors through Constantius II in his *Caesares*. His advice on how an emperor should act reflects the biases of the educated upper class when he says that it is best if an emperor is both virtuous and cultured but at least he should be cultured. Shortly after the death of Theodosius (395), someone summarized Victor in the *Epitome de Caesaribus* and extended his account to 395. Another unknown writer also included Victor in a collection known as the

Tripartite History to create a complete summary of Roman history by including the *Origo Gentis Romanae* (*Origin of the Roman Race*), which covered the mythological past from Saturn to Romulus, and the *De Viris Illustribus Urbis Romanae* (*Concerning the Illustrious Men of the City of Rome*), sketches of famous men from the Alban kings to Mark Antony.

Two minor historians were members of the court of the Emperor Valens. Eutropius, who had served in Julian's Persian campaign, wrote the *Breviarium ab Urbe Condita* (*Summary from the Founding of the City*), which covered everything from Romulus to the death of Jovian (364) in ten short books. Clearly written and concise, it became very popular, was translated into Greek, and was often used in schools until recent times. Rufius Festus wrote a similar summary that competed for the attention of Valens, to whom he dedicated it. Called the *Breviarium Rerum Gestarum Populi Romani* (*Summary of the Deeds of the Roman People*), it too extended from Romulus to A.D. 364, but it gave greater stress to wars of conquest.

It was probably in this same late-fourth-century period that Julius Obsequens sought to bolster the pagan cause in the little treatise *De Prodigiis* (*On Prodigies*). He summarized the prodigies recorded by Livy from 196 to 12 B.C. and showed how the Romans avoided the calamities that they portended. He wanted to emphasize, therefore, that the old reliable rites should not be abandoned in favor of the Christianity that condemned them.

On the more literary side, the same point was made by Ambrosius Theodosius Macrobius, who rose to the office of Chamberlain under Honorius in 422. As a young man he was acquainted with the circle of Symmachus, and his major work, the *Saturnalia,* purports to be the learned conversations of Symmachus and his friends at a banquet held during the Saturnalian festival. Their discussions about the festival, Roman antiquities, grammar, and literary criticism preserve a wealth of ancient scholarship otherwise lost. Macrobius also wrote a commentary on the "Dream of Scipio" from Cicero's *Republic.* The idealized

view of the Roman statesman and the Platonized Stoicism that underlie Cicero's thought at that point were very attractive to the Neoplatonic antiquarian pagans of Macrobius' day.

Any educated man worth his salt was expected to be able to turn out a competent poem, and some produced work that, if not equal to the Golden Age, at least measured up to the Silver. The least successful of those that survive is Avianus, a friend of Macrobius. Around 400 he adapted forty of Babrius' Greek fables to Latin poetry in Ovidian meter. Sometimes his meter falls short of his model, and his echoes of Vergilian or Ovidian language are not always appropriate to the subject.

The most prolific, although not the most accomplished poet of the age was Decimus Magnus Ausonius (d. ca. 395), a professor of rhetoric at Burdigala (Bordeaux) in Gaul. He was a Christian, but he was as friendly with Symmachus as he was with Theodosius. He became the tutor of the Emperor Gratian at Augusta Treverorum and held the consulship in 399. He wrote numerous elegant trifles that are valuable chiefly for the light that they shed on the carefree villa society of late-fourth-century Gaul. His most distinguished work is the *Mosella,* a long poem that describes life in the lovely valley of the Moselle with a genuineness of feeling that raises it from a mere cultural exercise to the level of art.

Ausonius' younger contemporary and fellow Gaul, Rutilius Claudius Namatianus, wrote in the troubled period after Alaric's sack of Rome and the Visigothic invasion of Gaul. He was Master of Offices in 412 and City Prefect in 414 under Honorius. In 416 he sadly left Rome to attend to his estates in Gaul, which had been badly damaged in barbarian raids. He described his journey in the long elegaic poem *De Reditu Suo* (*On His Return*), in which he gives a moving tribute to the city of Rome, makes observations on the country through which he passes, and condemns the barbarian Stilicho, Judaism, monasticism, and all else that he saw as forces destroying paganism and the Empire. He has a real command of the elegaic meter, and his sincerity transcends mere rhetoric.

Ironically, the best Latin poet of the age, Claudian (Claudius Claudianus), was closely associated with what Namatianus hated most. He served at the court of Honorius just before Namatianus and not only was probably a Christian but also was a protégé of Stilicho. Apparently a native speaker of Greek like Ammianus Marcellinus, he had a similar command of Latin, and although he was a Christian, he skillfully used the old epic and mythological conventions. He wrote a number of panegyrics for office holders, which surprisingly manage to rise above the usual platitudes, and he has two creditable unfinished exercises on mythological subjects, the *Battle of the Giants* and the *Rape of Proserpina*. His best works, however, are those that praise the accomplishments of Stilicho and damn his enemies at the Eastern court: *Against Rufinus, Against Eutropius, The War against Gildo,* and *The Gothic War*. His passionate invective has real power, and he has keen sense for striking phrases and novel conceits.

In contrast, the poems of the Gallic bishop Sidonius Apollinaris (ca. 430–ca. 480) are uninspired commonplaces, and his letters are merely pedantic.

In the sixth century, two writers round off the history of late Latin secular literature. Boethius (ca. 480–524) was a philosopher who had enjoyed the patronage of Theodoric the Ostrogoth but was later executed on suspicion of treason. He wrote on mathematics, music, Aristotle, and Cicero and had started the monumental task of translating all of Plato and Aristotle into Latin. He also wrote defenses of the orthodox view of the Trinity. His most popular work is the *Consolation of Philosophy* written to comfort himself in jail. In it he has a dialogue with the allegorical figure of Philosophy and espouses many pagan philosophical views.

More fortunate than Boethius was Cassiodorus (487–583). Of a distinguished Italian family, he was one of the last Roman consuls,

Master of Offices, and Praetorian Prefect. During his career he published two large historical works, the *Chronica,* a world history from Adam to 519, and his *History of the Goths,* which comprised twelve books (mostly lost). Upon retirement he founded a monastery in Bruttium and promoted the study of literature. His treatise *Educational Principles of Divine and Secular Literature* was widely used in the Middle Ages.

Christianity and Classical Culture

The only reason why Justinian could bar pagans from teaching is that by the sixth century Christianity had already thoroughly absorbed pagan formal thought and literature and made them its own, as the works of Claudian, Apollinaris, Boethius, and Cassiodorus reveal. Pagans had invented the rules of formal argument and genres of literature used to communicate ideas in the Roman Empire. Christians had to learn them from the same models as their pagan rivals, usually in the same schools. The pagan Libanius, for example, was the teacher of St. Basil, founder of Greek monasticism, and St. John Chrysostom, the great Christian preacher (p. 482). The learned Symmachus, eloquent upholder of Roman paganism, was respected by numerous Christians, including St. Ambrose of Milan, who was his cousin, and the Emperor Theodosius I.

When the Emperor Julian banned Christians from teaching pagan literature, the Christian Apollinarii, a grammarian and his rhetorician son, turned the scriptures into Greek classical forms—Homeric epic for the first five books of the Old Testament, tragedy for Chronicles and Kings, and Platonic dialogue for the New Testament. They were well done, but Christian teachers eagerly returned to using the classical models themselves when the ban was lifted after Julian's death. The ecclesiastical historian Socrates explained that it was proper to do so because pagan adversaries were better defeated by their own weapons.

Moreover, while they often advocated separation from the everyday material world, most Christians were very much shoulder to shoulder with pagans in that world. Not only did they study together in the same schools, but they were often married to each other, were colleagues at work, and shared the same leisure activities in the baths, libraries, and theaters. In a thousand different ways they subtly influenced each other, and even as Christians were capturing the Empire, so they were being captured by its sophisticated culture in the same way that the conquering Romans of the Republic had been captured by the sophisticated culture of captive Greece. Indeed, many of the great Church Fathers converted to Christianity in maturity and naturally used their pagan learning in service to their new religion.

Therefore, the major ecclesiastical writers of the fourth, fifth, and sixth centuries are all indelibly stamped with classical pagan literature, philosophy, and rhetoric. Saint Jerome (ca. 348–420), for example, who had studied under the pagan grammarian Donatus and made the great Latin Vulgate translation of the Bible, yielded nothing to Juvenal in satirical invective against his theological adversaries, and his letters, rivaling Cicero's, are full of classical allusions. In fact, he was so steeped in Ciceronian Latin that the figure of Christ appeared to him in a dream one night and accused him of being not a Christian but a Ciceronian. Eusebius of Caesarea, author of the valuable *Church History* and *Life of Constantine,* worked firmly within the traditions of classical historiography and biography. Synesius of Cyrene (370–ca. 415), bishop of Ptolemais in North Africa, had studied Neoplatonism under Hypatia before his conversion, and his numerous sermons, letters, hymns, and treatises show his classical training at every turn.

The greatest example of the complex blend of pagan learning and Christian faith, at least in the West, is Saint Augustine, bishop of Hippo in North Africa (354–430). Born of a pagan father and a Christian mother, he studied rhetoric at Carthage and then went to Rome to make his mark. There he became acquainted with Symmachus and his circle. Through them he gained appointment to a professorship of rhetoric at Milan. He was greatly influenced in thought and style by Cicero, and he was a Manichee before he became an orthodox Christian at Milan through association with Saint Ambrose, who was part of an influential circle of Christian Neoplatonists.

Augustine's voluminous letters, sermons, and commentaries show the influence of pagan classical literature and philosophy everywhere. Two works stand out—his *Confessions,* which trace his intellectual and spiritual development from a callow student smitten with Cicero to a Manichee, to a Neoplatonist, and finally to a baptized Christian; and his *magnum opus,* the *City of God,* which was stimulated by Alaric's sack of Rome in 410 and the flood of upper-class pagan refugees to Africa, where their example threatened to undermine the recently won supremacy of orthodox Catholicism.

In his best Latin rhetorical style, Augustine met them on their own terms. He made a systematic critique of the ancient myths and historical views on which they based their paganism, and he presented a philosophically rigorous refutation of Neoplatonism. Even in arguing for his radically Christian view of reality, however, he argued on the basis of major shared concepts, such as Divine Providence and the quintessentially classical sociopolitical concept of the *civitas,* a community of citizens. For Augustine, the Christian is a citizen of God's perfect heavenly community and longs for it while dwelling as a resident alien in this earthly community. Yet Augustine does not reject the alien city for Christians. As part of God's creation it is good, though not perfect; and the good Christian can work to eliminate its faults while enjoying its virtues. There is no puritanical rejection of the old earthly *civitas* that pagans loved. It is simply augmented by the vision of another that is even better.

Augustine died while the Vandals were

beating on the gates of Hippo. The pagan classical world was rapidly passing. The fourth-century surge of pagan culture at Rome had already ebbed; the Olympic games had not been celebrated for a generation; the great pagan temples were being closed and stripped everywhere; in a century, Plato's Academy would be shut forever. Nevertheless, through the works of Saint Augustine and others like him, the new Christian culture had already absorbed much of the old and would preserve its influence through the Middle Ages to the Renaissance and beyond.

XLII

The Problem of Rome's Fall

Ever since the mid-eighteenth century, scholars have been vigorously debating about the fall of the Roman Empire. Each generation has offered a new cause to explain it, often in the light of current fears or intellectual fads. Some of these explanations have added new insights into the old problem; others have ended up in the dustbin of discredited ideas, or at least should have. The major fallacy in much of the work on the subject has been the attempt to find a single cause. In the last half of the twentieth century, however, historians have become much more aware of the complexity of human events and the folly of trying to find a single cause for such a phenomenon as the fall of the Roman Empire. Therefore, although the final word has in no way been spoken, a much better understanding of the problem and the outline of its solution now exist.

Before a detailed analysis can be made, two points must be emphasized. First, there was no sudden collapse of the Roman Empire, as is implied in the word *fall*. Rather, there was a long process during which a host of interacting incremental changes occurred and gradually produced a transformation of economic, social, political, and cultural life. In looking back, therefore, it is possible to say that conditions in the fifth and sixth centuries A.D. were radically different from those of the first and second, when the Empire had reached its greatest territorial extent, the general level of prosperity was at its height, and general cultural life still vigorously exhibited the traits of the classical Greco-Roman tradition. Second, the transformation was not the same everywhere. While the Western half of the Empire broke up into separate Germanic kingdoms, the Eastern half survived and underwent a much more gradual metamorphosis into the Byzantine Empire, which survived for another thousand years under the emperors at Constantinople. These two points will help to evaluate the various reasons that have been given for the so-called fall of Rome.

Untenable Causes

Race Mixture   One of the ideas that was popular in the early twentieth century is based on the discredited view of the original Romans as members of an Aryan super race who were biologically overwhelmed by the admixture of inferior races from the East. This interpretation reflected the prevalent anti-Semitism of the time and fueled Fascist propaganda about the mythical master race. It is no more morally acceptable or historically valid than they were.

First of all, the studies of race mixture were based on names taken from grave inscriptions, which are not reliable indicators of ethnic origin and whose pattern of preservation do not provide the proper distribution of data for statistically valid analysis. Second, even if a statistically valid distribution could be found, the racial concepts and stereotypes that underlie the race-mixture theory have been proven false by modern biological and anthropological research. Third, it was precisely the Eastern half of the Empire, from which the supposedly inferior races came, that survived for a thousand years after the West had disintegrated.

Lead Poisoning Another untenable explanation is the theory that members of the vital leadership class were killed off by consuming excessive amounts of lead with their water and food because they could afford to have lead pipes bring water into their homes and cook in lead utensils instead of pottery. This theory is based on the analysis of an inadequate sample of skeletons, and there is no way of telling how much lead had contaminated the bones from external sources while they were buried. Except in rare cases, it is improbable that enough lead was consumed from plumbing and cooking utensils or any other sources to have a serious effect on the upper classes. If anyone suffered from lead poisoning it is likely to have been lower-class workers in lead smelters. Historically, the lead-poisoning theory is also discredited by the survival of the Eastern half of the Empire long after the breakup of the West.

Soil Exhaustion Some have claimed that the Empire was destroyed by the decline of its vital agricultural economy through soil exhaustion. In some isolated places, soil exhaustion did occur, but it affected only a very small percentage of the total arable land and had no significant impact. If soil exhaustion had been a problem, the Romans would not have abandoned the large tracts of good soil that went out of cultivation as agriculture declined during the late Empire.

Climatic Change Others have tried to explain the decline of Imperial agriculture as a result of a drying trend in the climate, which would have diminished production. This theory, however, was based on the study of growth rings in very old California redwoods that were growing in the same latitude as Rome during late Imperial times. This research is invalid, however, because it ignores all of the particular geographic variables such as wind, ocean currents, and topography that make the climate on the coast of California different from that of other parts of the world in the same latitude. Discussions of climatic changes and their possible effects on the Roman Empire must await much more complex scientific investigation.

Class Conflict The history of modern revolutions has led some historians to explain the disintegration of the Roman Empire as the result of class conflict between the rural peasantry and the urban classes who had traditionally exploited them. According to this theory, once the Roman army became manned mostly by poor peasants, they took their vengeance by preying on the urban classes in civil wars. In fact, however, the soldiers showed no particular favoritism to one class or another and preyed on the peasantry as often as they preyed on the urban population.

Barbarization of the Roman Army Some have argued that the increased use of Germanic auxiliaries and federate allies undermined the effectiveness of Roman armies against other barbarians. Sometimes there was collusion between barbarians serving in Roman armies and barbarians who were attacking the Empire. Barbarians who returned to their native tribes beyond the borders after serving Rome also transferred valuable knowledge of Roman weapons, strategy, and tactics to barbarian foes. Nevertheless, as Aetius' defeat of the Huns in 455 showed, even Roman armies made up largely of barbarians were very effective when properly led.

It is true that the West became more and

more dependent upon barbarian armies and generals for defense, so that men like Stilicho, Alaric, Arbogast, Odovacer, and Theodoric the Ostrogoth gained increasing power until they were able to overthrow the Western emperors completely. That, however, is a result of other factors that made the West dependent upon them in the first place.

Christianity   The idea that Christianity caused the fall of the Roman Empire has been popular among many thinkers who are opposed to the irrationalism of religion or are so enamored of classical culture that they identify with the prejudices of the pagan intellectuals who dominated Roman cultural life and opposed Christianity until the fifth century A.D. They argue that Christianity fostered a dangerous pacifism that sapped the Empire's military vigor, that it drained away precious manpower into the monasteries, that it drew into the hierarchy of the Church many qualified leaders whose talents were needed to save an increasingly besieged state, and that its intolerance of other religions and its own doctrinal conflicts destroyed the internal unity necessary to preserve the state in a time of crisis. Superficially, these charges may seem valid. There are examples of Christians refusing military service on religious grounds, but the military example of Christian emperors was followed by many others, and there are even examples of Christian bishops leading the defense of their cities. Far from denying their services to the state, many talented churchmen took an active role in temporal affairs, as the legislation of Justinian makes clear. It is true that many Christians fled to monasteries, but that was not the fault of Christianity. People were fleeing from pressures that existed apart from Christianity and would have sought other refuges if there had been no monasteries. Finally, although divisive Christian doctrinal conflicts did harm the Empire, they were often symptoms of deeper socioeconomic problems that would have produced other conflicts if Christianity had not existed.

Accidental or Proximate Causes

Contingent Events and Barbarian Invasions Other explanations for Rome's fall are not wrong but alone are not sufficient for understanding such a complex phenomenon. One school has argued that there are no general causes to explain Rome's fall, only a series of contingent (accidental) events, such as the untimely death of Marcus Aurelius and Commodus' decision not to pursue his grand scheme of Germanic conquests; the Emperor Valens' foolhardy decision not to wait for reinforcements before the Battle of Adrianople in 378; the death of Theodosius the Great with only two minor heirs, who helped to split the Empire permanently; and the assassination of Stilicho, who had been able to control the Visigoths. Another school would stress the relentless barbarian invasions of the fourth and fifth centuries A.D. as the real cause of the Empire's disintegration.

Both of these explanations have some validity. The combination of both contingent events and barbarian invasions had a disastrous effect on the Empire, but concentrating on these factors merely begs the larger and more important question of why they had such a destructive effect. They are only the accidental, proximate causes of the Empire's problems. There are much more essential, ultimate causes that are linked with the very structure of the Empire and the nature of Greco-Roman civilization, which explain why the Empire could not cope with the combination of stresses and eventually broke under the strain.

Essential or Ultimate Causes

Geographic Structure of the Roman Empire The geographic structure of the Empire was an essential factor in its inability to cope with the pressure of barbarian attacks in the fourth and fifth centuries. The Empire was shaped like an elongated doughnut, with the Mediterranean Sea being a large hole in the middle. In many ways that "hole" was a great asset because it provided the ancient world's most efficient mode of transport and made it possible to link the whole Mediterranean basin together in a single empire. On the other hand, it also meant that the extent of the Empire's landward borders was very large relative to the amount of habitable land encompassed. Therefore, when those borders were seriously threatened, their defense took a large share of available human and material resources and left proportionately less for other vital activities needed to maintain a complex civilization.

That was especially true in the West. The West had longer and weaker borders than the East. The greatest number of barbarian incursions occurred across the fifteen-hundred-mile Rhine-Danube line. The West was responsible for all but the last three hundred miles of the lower Danube until the East took over the two hundred miles in Illyricum under Arcadius. Moreover, barbarians who crossed the lower Danube came up against the impregnable postion of Constantinople and often were deflected toward the hapless West. Britain required extensive protection from barbarians on the other side of Hadrian's Wall and from Anglo-Saxon sea raiders, and western North Africa had to be protected from the Moors. The East had much more secure borders in Egypt and, despite occasional wars, could usually handle the civilized Persians through diplomacy.

Shortage of Manpower   Faced with large borders to defend and increased barbarian attacks, the late Empire suffered a shortage of manpower for providing the army with soldiers and maintaining the level of economic activity necessary to support increased expenses. It is not that the population of the Empire severely declined from plague or other causes. The best available demographic research indicates that there was little or no long-term decline of the population in the late Empire, but it did not increase. Therefore, relative to the increased demand for manpower, a serious shortage of manpower developed. The West, which was far less populous than the more urbanized East and had greater defensive needs, felt this shortage even more acutely. Therefore, the West became more dependent upon the forces of powerful Germanic military leaders, who eventually were able to seize control of the West themselves.

Economic Weakness   The economic system of the Roman Empire also was not strong enough to meet the increased burdens of defense during the fourth and fifth centuries. In the past, the prosperity of the Empire had been maintained from the influx of booty taken in wars of conquest. The late Empire, however, had no profitable wars of conquest. The barbarians were poor, and the Sassanid Persian Empire was too strong. Furthermore, in modern terms, the Roman economy was basically underproductive. It was based primarily on agriculture and trade in luxury goods. Roman agriculture, with its dependence on a limited supply of human and animal labor, generated very small surpluses in proportion to the effort expended, and trade in luxury goods drained away the precious metals that were no longer being replaced through conquests.

The loss of precious metals was particularly harmful because the ancient monetary and financial system depended upon specie, coinage of full weight and value in precious metal. Such a system made it very cumbersome to finance large loans that could be used to expand business and productive economic activity. The Roman economy tended to remain static at best. As the problems of defense increased, more had to be taxed to maintain the armies and the bureaucracies that grew with them. That left less for the farmers, who starved or fled, and left fewer farmers, who had to be squeezed even harder in a vicious cycle.

The economic problems were especially serious in the less urbanized West. The drain of specie from the West was more pronounced than from the East. The luxury trade with China, Africa, and India was dominated by the inhabitants of Eastern cities. They often turned imported silk, ivory, jewels, and other precious commodities into finished products and then traded them in the West for money, part of which they kept as profit, which made up for what they had originally paid out. Therefore, the economy of the Eastern half of the Empire was more in balance. Alone, the East could support itself, but as Justinian's costly failure to restore the West shows, the East did not have the resources to preserve the weaker West too.

Low Level of Ancient Technology   Behind the Empire's relative shortage of manpower and economic weakness lay an even deeper problem—the extremely low level of ancient technology. The lack of dynamic technology meant a lack of economic growth because there was no way to increase output with a limited supply of labor. Beyond a very basic level, there was no machinery or sources of mechanical power that could make human and animal labor more productive per capita to meet the growing demand caused by increased defensive needs.

Unstable and Corrupt Political Culture   Another essential cause of the destruction of the Roman Empire was its unstable and corrupt political culture, which produced numerous civil wars and official malfeasance that aggravated its problems in the face of barbarian invasions. Precious manpower and resources were wasted in destructive struggles for the throne, which only weakened the Empire's ability to defend its borders. Imperial officials constantly abused their power to line their own pockets with money extorted from helpless subjects or with bribes from the wealthy to procure special favors. Since the rich and powerful could usually protect themselves from many fiscal burdens, the productive middle-class urban population and poor peasantry suffered the most, so that the economy of the Empire was weakened even further.

Aristocratic Value System of Ancient Society   Indissolubly linked with many of the essential causes of the late Empire's disintegra-

tion is the basic aristocratic value system of ancient society. At the heart of the aristocratic ideal was the concept of the independently wealthy large landowner who, if not engaged in war or public service, lived a life of cultured ease. This ideal had its roots in the similar origins of early Greek and Roman society, in periods when the only sources of wealth were agriculture or plundering others and only the rich could afford the armor and weapons needed to defend the community or had the leisure time to oversee public affairs.

When the cultural life of ancient Greece began to develop in contact with the older civilizations of the Near East, it was the aristocrats who had the resources to acquire higher learning and spend their time in intellectual pursuits. Therefore, aristocrats shaped and perpetuated in their thought and literature the normative values of ancient Greek society. When the Roman aristocracy came into close contact with Greek culture, they adopted and perpetuated the ideal of cultured leisure in Roman society as well.

Conditioned by the prevailing aristocratic ideals, the majority of ancients scorned the mechanical or practical occupations as unworthy. Productive labor and personally conducted trade were little valued because they were performed by ignoble people like slaves and wage earners. They were base and ignoble because they were not really free individuals in ancient terms. A slave, obviously, was someone else's property, a wage earner was dependent upon his employer for his livelihood, and a shopkeeper was dependent upon the patronage of his customers.

These attitudes were reflected and reinforced by the educational system, which stressed only training in the liberal (i.e., worthy of a free person) arts—the verbal and abstract intellectual skills that characterized the cultured aristocrat or fitted a person for the wielding of political power through rhetoric and law. As a result, ancient Greeks and Romans seldom applied abstract thought to practical, productive economic ends. They never had to worry about working and, therefore, seldom concerned themselves with making work easier and labor more productive. They simply invested their money respectably in land and large-scale financial or commercial ventures and let their slaves, freedmen, tenants, and hired managers worry about the work. Yet slaves, tenants, and poor peasants had neither the education, nor the opportunity, nor even the incentive to apply themselves to labor-saving technological innovations.

In the light of prevailing assumptions, the aristocrats benefited greatly from the lack of technological innovation because it kept the lower classes dependent upon them. One of the marks of a great aristocrat was the amount of patronage that he exercised. The more clients and dependents that a man had, the greater his status. The attitude is aptly illustrated by Vespasian, who refused to use a design for a labor-saving crane when he was building the Colosseum. When the designer asked him why he was not using it, Vespasian replied to the effect that he wanted to employ as many poor people as possible. As Emperor, Vespasian needed to demonstrate that he was the greatest patron at Rome. This same attitude explains why even in the darkest days of the Empire, emperors continued to expend huge amounts not on just feeding, but lavishly entertaining the poor in both Imperial capitals.

Similarly, the aristocratically derived concept of the city was also economically counterproductive. The ancient city was usually dominated by wealthy aristocrats who supported themselves with the profits of war, investments, and the absentee ownership of agricultural property. To them the city provided a forum for the exercise of political power, the demonstration of patronage, and the pursuit of intellectual endeavors. Therefore, they vied with each other to embellish their cities with magnificent but unproductive triumphal arches, temples, theaters, amphitheaters, circuses, and baths as monuments to their own power, status, and good taste.

The frequency of political instability and civil wars that helped to weaken the Empire was increased by the same aristocratic preoccupation with power, fame, and glory that had helped to undermine the Republic earlier. Becoming Emperor meant achieving the height of power and the fame and glory that went with it. Therefore, the temptation to seize the chance to become Emperor, even to the point of precipitating a civil war in the midst of an external crisis was always great.

On the other hand, the concentration of power in the hands of the Emperor caused many aristocrats to abdicate the public duties that had once been the focal points of their careers. Instead, they cultivated the private marks of aristocracy—great wealth, ostentatious luxury, country villas, and private armies that allowed them to ignore the central government and avoid taxes. Therefore, instead of helping to preserve the Empire, they weakened it some more.

Those who were not great aristocrats by birth aped their ideals and wanted to become like them. The only practical way in which to do that in the late Empire was through high position in the Imperial army or civilian bureaucracy. People with military and political power could use them to gain wealth through oppression and corruption. Such behavior only weakened and alienated the productive middle and lower classes, who already suffered greater burdens than they could bear. Therefore, the Empire's shortage of manpower and its economic problems were aggravated even more.

Although they have been analyzed separately, the various accidental and essential causes for the disintegration of the Mediterranean-wide Roman Empire were interrelated, and they interacted in complex ways that can never be completely unraveled. Because some of the causes operated to a greater extent in the West, it broke up into separate Germanic kingdoms that shaped the beginning of Medieval Western Europe. The more defensible, populous, and prosperous East had enough strength to preserve itself, despite sharing many other fundamental problems with the West, and it gradually evolved into the Byzantine Empire that carried on the tradition of the Caesars for almost a thousand years.

Bibliography

In the interest of economy, this bibliography has been limited to books in English, primarily of recent publication, that will be reliable guides to the subjects covered. Important journal articles and other books in all languages on these subjects will be readily available in the notes and bibliographies of the works listed here. Serious students will also consult various scholarly journals in classics and ancient history to find additional material, especially that published after the compilation of this bibliography (February, 1983). Students should also familiarize themselves with the annual publication known as *L'Année Philologique,* which lists, in the language of publication, the books and articles published each year on various topics in classics and ancient history.

I GENERAL HISTORIES AND REFERENCE WORKS

Atlas of the Classical World, ed. A. A. M. van den Heyden and H. H. Scullard. London and New York: Thomas Nelson, 1959.

Atlas of the Greek and Roman World in Antiquity, ed. N. G. L. Hammond. Park Ridge, N.J.: Noyes Press, 1981.

BICKERMAN, E. J., *Chronology of the Ancient World* (2nd ed.). London: Thames and Hudson, 1980.

The Cambridge Ancient History, vols. 7-12, ed. S. A. Cook et al. Cambridge: Cambridge University Press, 1928-1939 (new edition in preparation).

CORNELL, T. J., and J. MATTHEWS, *Atlas of the Roman World.* Oxford: Phaidon, 1982.

KAGAN, D., *Problems in Ancient History, Volume Two: The Roman World* (2nd ed.). New York: Macmillan. 1975.

LEWIS, N., and M. REINHOLD, *Roman Civilization* (sources in translation), 2 vols. New York: Harper and Row, 1966.

The Oxford Classical Dictionary (2nd ed.), ed. N. G. L. Hammond and H. H. Scullard. Oxford: Clarendon Press, 1970.

PLATNER, S. B., and T. ASHBY, *A Topographical Dictionary of Ancient Rome.* Oxford: Clarendon Press, 1929.

The Princeton Encyclopedia of Classical Sites, ed. R. Stillwell. Princeton: Princeton University Press, 1976.

SINNIGEN, W., *Rome: Sources in Western Civilization.* New York: Free Press, 1965.

Who Was Who in the Roman World, 753 B.C.–A.D. 476, ed. D. Bowder. Oxford: Phaidon, 1980.

II GEOGRAPHY

CARY, M., *The Geographic Background of Greek and Roman History.* Oxford: Clarendon Press, 1949.

GRANT, M., *The Ancient Mediterranean.* New York: Charles Scribner's Sons, 1969.

SMITH, C. D., *Western Mediterranean Europe: A Histori-*

cal Geography of Italy, Spain, and Southern France since the Neolithic. London and New York: Academic Press, 1979.

III EARLY AND NON-ROMAN ITALY

BANTI, L., *The Etruscan Cities and Their Culture*, trans. E. Bizzari. London: Oxford University Press, 1973.

BARFIELD, L., *Northern Italy before Rome*. London: Thames and Hudson, 1971.

DUNBABIN, T. J., *The Western Greeks*. Oxford: Clarendon Press, 1968.

HENCKEN, H., *Tarquinia, Villanovans, and Early Etruscans*. Cambridge, Mass.: Peabody Museum, 1968.

PALLOTTINO, M., *The Etruscans*, trans. J. Cremona, ed. D. Ridgway. London: Allen Lane, 1975.

RIDGWAY, D., and F. R. RIDGWAY, *Italy before the Romans: The Iron Age, Orientalizing, and Etruscan Periods*. London: Academic Press, 1979.

SALMON, E. T., *Samnium and the Samnites*. Cambridge: Cambridge University Press, 1967.

TRUMP, D. H., *The Prehistory of the Mediterranean*. Hammondsworth: Penguin, 1981.

IV EARLY ROME

ALFÖLDI, A., *Early Rome and the Latins*. Ann Arbor: University of Michigan Press, 1965.

BLOCH, R., *The Origins of Rome*. New York: Praeger, 1960.

HEURGON, J., *The Rise of Rome to 264 B.C.* Berkeley and Los Angeles: University of California Press, 1973.

OGILVIE, R. M., *Early Rome and the Etruscans*. London: Fontana/Collins, 1976.

SCULLARD, H. H., *A History of the Roman World, 753–146 B.C.* (4th ed.). London: Methuen, 1980.

V THE REPUBLIC

ASTIN, A. E., *Cato the Censor*. Oxford: Clarendon Press, 1978.

BADIAN, E., *Foreign Clientelae (264–70 B.C.)*. Oxford: Clarendon Press, 1958.

——, *Roman Imperialism in the Late Republic* (2nd ed.). Ithaca: Cornell University Press, 1969.

——, *Publicans and Sinners: Private Enterprise in the Service of the Roman Republic*. Ithaca: Cornell University Press, 1972.

BALSDON, J. P. V. D., *Julius Caesar: A Political Biography*. New York: Atheneum, 1967.

BERNSTEIN, A. H., *Tiberius Gracchus: Tradition and Apostasy*. Ithaca and London: Cornell University Press, 1978.

BROWN, F. E., *Cosa: The Making of a Roman Town*. Ann Arbor: University of Michigan Press, 1980.

CARNEY, T. F., *A Biography of C. Marius*. Proceedings of the African Classical Association, Supplement 1, 1962.

CLARKE, M. L., *The Noblest Roman: Marcus Brutus and His Reputation:* London: Thames and Hudson, 1981.

DUDLEY, D. R., and T. A. DOREY, *Rome against Carthage*. Garden City, N.Y.: Doubleday, 1972.

ERRINGTON, R. M., *The Dawn of Empire: Rome's Rise to World Power*. Ithaca: Cornell University Press, 1973.

GELZER, M., *Caesar: Politician and Statesman* (6th ed.), trans. P. Needham. Cambridge, Mass.: Harvard University Press, 1968.

——, *The Roman Nobility*, trans. R. Seager. Oxford: Blackwell, 1969.

GRUEN, E. S., *Roman Politics and the Criminal Courts, 149–78 B.C.* Cambridge, Mass.: Harvard University Press, 1968.

——, *The Last Generation of the Roman Republic*. Berkeley, Los Angeles, and London: University of California Press, 1974.

HARRIS, W. V., *Rome in Etruria and Umbria*. Oxford: Clarendon Press, 1971.

——, *War and Imperialism in Republican Rome, 327–70 B.C.* Oxford: Clarendon Press, 1979.

HOMO, L. P., *Roman Political Institutions*. New York: Knopf, 1962.

HOOD, D., *The Rise of Rome: How to Explain It?* Lexington, Mass.: D. C. Heath, 1969.

HUZAR, E. G., *Mark Antony: A Biography*. Minneapolis: University of Minnesota Press, 1978.

LAZENBY, J. F., *Hannibal's War: A Military History of the Second Punic War*. Warminster: Aris and Phillips, 1978.

LINTOTT, A. W., *Violence in Republican Rome*. Oxford: Clarendon Press, 1968.

MARSHALL, B. A., *Crassus: A Political Biography*. Amsterdam: Hakkert, 1976.

MITCHELL, T. N., *Cicero: The Ascending Years*. New Haven and London: Yale University Press, 1979.

RAWSON, E., *Cicero: A Portrait*. London: Allen Lane, 1975.

RIDDLE, J. M., *Tiberius Gracchus: Destroyer or Reformer?* Lexington, Mass.: D. C. Heath, 1970.

SALMON, E. T., *The Making of Roman Italy*. London: Thames and Hudson, 1982.

SCULLARD, H. H., *Scipio Africanus, Soldier and Statesman*. London: Thames and Hudson, 1970.

——, *Roman Politics, 220–150 B.C.* (2nd ed.). Oxford: Clarendon Press, 1973.

——, *From the Gracchi to Nero: A History of Rome from 133 B.C. to A.D. 68* (4th ed.). London: Methuen, 1976.

SEAGER, R. J., *The Crisis of the Roman Republic*. Cambridge: W. Heffer and Sons, 1969.

——, *Pompey: A Political Biography*. Oxford: Blackwell, 1979.

STAVELEY, E. S., *Greek and Roman Voting and Elections*. London: Thames and Hudson, 1972.

STOCKTON, D., *The Gracchi*. London: Oxford University Press, 1979.

SYME, R., *The Roman Revolution*. Oxford: Clarendon Press, 1939.

TAYLOR, L. R., *Roman Voting Assemblies: From the Hannibalic War to the Dictatorship of Caesar*. Ann Arbor: University of Michigan Press, 1966.

WARD, A. M., *Marcus Crassus and the Late Roman Republic*. Columbia and London: University of Missouri Press, 1977.

WARMINGTON, B. H., *Carthage* (2nd ed.). New York: Praeger, 1969.

WISTRAND, E., *The Policy of Brutus the Tyrranicide*. Göteborg: Universitetsbibliotek, 1981.

MILLAR, F., *The Emperor in the Roman World (31 B.C.– A.D. 337)*. London: Duckworth, 1977.

MC DERMOTT, W. C., and A. E. ORENTZEL, *Roman Portraits: The Flavian-Trajanic Period*. Columbia and London: University of Missouri Press, 1979.

MACMULLEN, R., *The Roman Government's Response to Crisis, A.D. 235–337*. New Haven and London: Yale University Press, 1976.

MOMIGLIANO, A., *Claudius, The Emperor and His Achievement* (2nd ed.). New York: Barnes and Noble, 1962.

NICOLS, J., *Vespasian and the Partes Flavianae*. Wiesbaden: Steiner, 1978.

PARKER, H. M. D., *A History of the Roman World from A.D. 138 to A.D. 337*, revised by B. H. Warmington. London: Methuen, 1958.

PEROWNE, S., *Hadrian*. London: Hodder and Stoughton, 1960.

ROWELL, H. T., *Rome in the Augustan Age*. Norman: University of Oklahoma Press, 1962.

SALMON, E. T., *A History of the Roman World from 30 B.C. to A.D. 138* (4th ed.). London: Methuen, 1963.

SEAGER, R. J., *Tiberius*. London: Methuen, 1972.

WARMINGTON, B. H., *Nero: Reality and Legend*. London: Chatto and Windus, 1981.

WELLESLEY, K., *The Long Year, A.D. 69*. London: Paul Elek, 1975.

VI THE PRINCIPATE

BIRLEY, A., *Marcus Aurelius*. London: Eyre and Spottiswoode, 1966.

——, *Septimius Severus the African Emperor*. London: Eyre and Spottiswoode, 1971.

BOWERSOCK, G. W., *Augustus and the Greek World*. London: Oxford University Press, 1965.

DE BLOIS, K., *The Policy of the Emperor Gallienus* (rev. ed.). Leiden: Brill, 1976.

EARL, D. C., *The Age of Augustus*. New York: Crown Publishers, 1968.

GARZETTI, A., *From Tiberius to the Antonines: A History of the Roman Empire, A.D. 14–192*, trans. J. R. Foster. London: Methuen, 1974.

JONES, A. H. M., *Augustus*. London: Chatto and Windus, 1970.

JONES, C. P., *The Roman World of Dio Chrysostom*. Cambridge, Mass. and London: Harvard University Press, 1978.

LEVICK, B., *Tiberius the Politician*. London: Thames and Hudson, 1976.

VII THE LATE EMPIRE

ARNHEIM, M. T. W., *The Senatorial Aristocracy in the Later Roman Empire*. Oxford: Clarendon Press, 1972.

BARKER, J. W., *Justinian and the Later Roman Empire*. Madison: University of Wisconsin Press, 1966.

BOWERSOCK, G. W., et al., *Edward Gibbon and the Decline of the Roman Empire*. Cambridge, Mass. and London: Harvard University Press, 1977.

——, *Julian the Apostate*. London: Duckworth, 1978.

BRIDGE, A. C., *Theodora: Portrait in a Byzantine Landscape*. London: Cassell, 1978.

BROWN, P., *The World of Late Antiquity: 150–750*. New York: Harcourt and Brace, 1971.

BURY, J. B., *A History of the Later Roman Empire from the Death of Theodosius I to the Death of Justinian*. London: Macmillan, 1923.

DREW, K. F., *The Barbarian Invasions.* New York: Holt, Rinehart, and Winston, 1970.

EADIE, J. W., *The Conversion of Constantine.* New York: Holt, Rinehart, and Winston, 1971.

GOFFART, W., *Barbarians and Romans, A.D. 410–584: The Techniques of Accommodation.* Princeton: Princeton University Press, 1980.

JONES, A. H. M., *The Later Roman Empire, 284–602.* Norman: University of Oklahoma Press, 1964.

KELLEY, J. N. D., *Jerome: His Life, Writings, and Controversies.* London: Duckworth, 1975.

MACMULLEN, R. *Soldier and Civilian in the Later Roman Empire.* Cambridge, Mass.: Harvard University Press, 1963.

———, *Constantine.* New York: Dial Press, 1969.

MATTHEWS, J., *Western Aristocracies and the Imperial Court, A.D. 364–475.* Oxford: Clarendon Press, 1975.

O'DONNELL, J. J., *Cassiodorus.* Berkeley, Los Angeles, and London: University of California Press, 1979.

WALBANK, F. W., *The Awful Revolution: The Decline of the Roman Empire in the West.* Toronto: University of Toronto Press, 1969.

WHITE, L. (ed.), *The Transformation of the Roman World.* Berkeley and Los Angeles: University of California Press, 1966.

VIII CITIES, PROVINCES, AND NEIGHBORS OF THE EMPIRE

BACHRACH, B. S., *A History of the Alans in the West.* Minneapolis: University of Minnesota Press, 1973.

BIRLEY, R., *Vindolanda: A Roman Frontier Post on Hadrian's Wall.* London: Thames and Hudson, 1979.

BROWNING, I., *Palmyra.* London: Chatto and Windus, 1979.

COLLEDGE, M. A. R., *The Parthians.* New York: Praeger, 1967.

DOWNEY, G., *Constantinople in the Age of Justinian.* Norman: University of Oklahoma Press, 1960.

GORDON, C. D., *The Age of Atilla.* Ann Arbor: University of Michigan Press, 1960.

LIEBESCHUETZ, J. H. W. G., *Antioch: City and Imperial Administration in the Later Roman Empire.* Oxford: Clarendon Press, 1972.

MAGIE, D., *Roman Rule in Asia Minor, to the End of the Third Century after Christ.* Princeton: Princeton University Press, 1950.

MEIGGS, R., *Roman Ostia.* Oxford: Clarendon Press, 1960.

MILLAR, F., *The Roman Empire and Its Neighbors.* New York: Delacorte Press, 1967.

SALWAY, P., *Roman Britain.* Oxford: Clarendon Press, 1981.

THOMPSON, E. A., *The Visigoths in the Time of Ulfia.* London: Oxford University Press, 1966.

IX SOCIETY AND THE ECONOMY

BALSDON, J. P. V. D., *Life and Leisure in Ancient Rome.* New York: McGraw-Hill, 1969.

BOER, W. DEN, *Private Morality in Greece and Rome: Some Historical Aspects.* Leiden: Brill, 1979.

BONNER, S. F., *Education in Ancient Rome from the Elder Cato to the Younger Pliny.* London: Methuen, 1977.

BROWN, P., *Society and the Holy in Late Antiquity.* Berkeley, Los Angeles, and London: University of California Press, 1982.

BRUNT, P. A., *Italian Manpower, 225 B.C.–A.D. 14.* Oxford: Clarendon Press, 1971.

———, *Social Conflicts in the Roman Republic.* Oxford: Blackwell, 1970.

BURFORD, A., *Craftsmen in Greek and Roman Society.* London: Thames and Hudson, 1972.

CAMERON, A. E., *Circus Factions: Blues and Greens at Rome and Byzantium.* Oxford: Clarendon Press, 1976.

CASSON, L., *Travel in the Ancient World.* London: Allen and Unwin, 1974.

D'ARMS, J. H., *Romans on the Bay of Naples: A Social and Cultural Study of the Villas and their Owners from 150 B.C. to A.D. 400.* Cambridge, Mass.: Harvard University Press, 1970.

———, and E. C. KOPFF, *The Seaborne Commerce of Ancient Rome: Studies in Archaeology and History.* Rome: American Academy in Rome, 1980.

———, *Commerce and Social Standing in Ancient Rome.* Cambridge, Mass. and London: Harvard University Press, 1981.

DUDLEY, D. R., *Roman Society.* Hammondsworth: Penguin Books, 1975.

DUNCAN-JONES, R., *The Economy of the Roman Empire: Quantitative Studies.* Cambridge: Cambridge University Press, 1974.

FINLEY, M. I. *The Ancient Economy.* London: Chatto and Windus, 1973.

———, *Ancient Slavery and Modern Ideology*. London: Chatto and Windus, 1980.

FRANK, T. *An Economic Survey of Ancient Rome,* 5 vols. and index. Baltimore: Johns Hopkins University Press, 1933–1940.

GARNSEY, P., *Social Status and Legal Privilege in the Roman Empire*. Oxford: Clarendon Press, 1970.

——— (ed.), *Non-Slave Labour in the Greco-Roman World*. Cambridge: Cambridge Philological Society, 1980.

GIACOSA, G., *Women of the Caesars: Their Lives and Portraits on Coins*. Milan: Edizioni Arte e Moneta, 1980.

GRANT, M., *The Jews in the Roman World*. London: Weidenfeld and Nicolson, 1973.

HANDS, A. R., *Charities and Social Aid in Greece and Rome*. London: Thames and Hudson, 1968.

HARRIS, H. A., *Sport in Greece and Rome*. London: Thames and Hudson, 1972.

HOLUM, K. G., *Theodosian Empresses: Women and Imperial Dominion in Late Antiquity*. Berkeley, Los Angeles, and London: University of California Press. 1982.

HOPKINS, K., *Conquerors and Slaves*. Cambridge: Cambridge University Press, 1978.

JONES, A. H. M., *The Roman Economy: Studies in Ancient Economic and Administrative History,* ed. P. A. Brunt. Oxford: Blackwell, 1974.

KING, C. E. (ed.), *Imperial Revenue, Expenditure, and Monetary Policy in the Fourth Century A.D.* Rome: American Academy in Rome, 1980.

LEFKOWITZ, M. R. and M. B. FANT, *Women in Greece and Rome*. Toronto and Sarasota: Stevens, 1977.

LIVERSIDGE, J., *Everyday Life in the Roman Empire*. London: Batsford, 1976.

MACMULLEN, R., *Roman Social Relations, 50 B.C.–A.D. 284*. New Haven and London: Yale University Press, 1974.

NICOLET, C. *The World of the Citizen in Republican Rome,* trans, P. S. Falla. London: Batsford, 1980.

POMEROY, S. B., *Goddesses, Whores, Wives, and Slaves: Women in Classical Antiquity*. New York: Schocken Books, 1976.

RICKMAN, G., *The Corn Supply of Ancient Rome*. Oxford, Clarendon Press, 1980.

ROSTOVTZEFF, M. I., *Social and Economic History of the Roman Empire* (2nd ed.), revised by P. M. Frazer. Oxford: Clarendon Press, 1957.

SALLER, R. P., *Personal Patronage under the Early Empire*. Cambridge: Cambridge University Press, 1981.

SHERWIN-WHITE, A. N., *The Roman Citizenship* (2nd ed.). Oxford: Clarendon Press, 1973.

STRONG, D., and D. BROWN (eds.), *Roman Crafts*. London: Duckworth, 1976.

TAYLOR, D., *Work in Ancient Greece and Rome*. London: Allen and Unwin, 1975.

TREGGIARI, S., *Roman Freedmen during the Late Republic*. Oxford: Clarendon Press, 1969.

VOGT, J., *Ancient Slavery and the Ideal of Man,* trans. T. Wiedemann. Oxford: Blackwell, 1975.

WHITE, K. D., *Roman Farming*. Ithaca: Cornell University Press, 1971.

WIEDEMANN, T., *Slaves in Greece and Rome*. Baltimore: Johns Hopkins University Press, 1981.

X LITERATURE AND RHETORIC

BINNS, J. W. (ed.), *Latin Literature of the Fourth Century*. London and Boston: Routledge and Kegan Paul, 1974.

Cambridge History of Classical Literature, ed. P. E. Easterling and E. J. Kenney. Vol. 2: Latin Literature. Cambridge: Cambridge University Press. 1982.

CLARK, D. L., *Rhetoric in Greco-Roman Education*. New York: Columbia University Press, 1957.

DOVER, K. J., et al., *Ancient Greek Literature* (covers Roman Imperial writers). London: Oxford University Press, 1980.

GOLD, B. (ed.), *Literary and Artistic Patronage in Ancient Rome*. Austin: University of Texas Press, 1982.

HÄGG, T., *The Novel in Antiquity*. Princeton: Princeton University Press, 1983.

KENNEDY, G. A., *The Art of Rhetoric in the Roman World, 300 B.C.–A.D. 300*. Princeton: Princeton University Press, 1972.

———, *Greek Rhetoric under Christian Emperors*. Princeton: Princeton University Press, 1983.

OGILVIE, R. M., *Roman Literature and Society*. New York: Barnes and Noble, 1980.

QUINN, K., *Texts and Contexts: The Roman Writers and their Audiences*. London and Boston: Routledge and Kegan Paul, 1979.

RAMAGE, E. S., *Roman Satirists and Their Satire: Fine Art of Criticism in Ancient Rome*. Park Ridge: Noyes Press, 1980.

REYNOLDS, L. D., and N. G. WILSON, *Scribes and Scholars: A Guide to the Transmission of Greek and Latin Literature*. London: Oxford University Press, 1974.

WEST, D., and A. J. WOODMAN (eds.), *Creative Imagination in Latin Literature.* Cambridge: Cambridge University Press, 1979.

XI ART AND ARCHITECTURE

ANDREAE, B., *The Art of Rome.* London: New English Library, 1978.

BRENDEL, O. J., *Prolegomena to the Study of Roman Art.* New Haven and London: Yale University Press, 1979.

CUNLIFFE, B., *Rome and Her Empire.* London: Bodley Head, 1978.

DUNBABIN, K. M. D., *The Mosaics of Roman North Africa.* Oxford: Clarendon Press, 1978.

MAC CORMACK, S. G., *Art and Ceremony in Late Antiquity.* Berkeley, Los Angeles, and London: University of California Press, 1981.

TOYNBEE, J. M. C., *Roman Historical Portraits.* London: Thames and Hudson, 1978.

WARD-PERKINS, J. B., *Roman Architecture.* London: Academy Editions, 1979.

XII RELIGION

BREGMAN, J., *Synesius of Cyrene, Philosopher Bishop.* Berkeley, Los Angeles, and London: University of California Press, 1982.

DE LABRIOLLE, P., *History and Literature of Christianity from Tertullian to Boethius.* New York: Barnes and Noble, 1968.

FERGUSON, J., *Greek and Roman Religion: A Source Book.* Park Ridge: Noyes Press, 1980.

GRANT, R. M., *Augustus to Constantine: The Thrust of the Christian Movement into the Roman World.* New York: Harper and Row, 1970.

LIEBESCHUETZ, J. H. W. G., *Continuity and Change in Roman Religion.* London: Oxford University Press, 1979.

LITLIA, S. R. C., *Clement of Alexandria: A Study in Christian Platonism and Gnosticism.* Oxford: Clarendon Press, 1971.

MACMULLEN, R., *Paganism in the Roman Empire.* New Haven and London: Yale University Press, 1981.

REITZENSTEIN, R., *Hellenistic Mystery Religions.* Edinburgh: T. and T. Clark, 1979.

SCULLARD, H. H., *Festivals and Ceremonies of the Roman Republic.* London: Thames and Hudson, 1981.

SOLMSEN, F., *Isis among the Greeks and Romans.* Cambridge, Mass. and London: Harvard University Press, 1980.

TAYLOR, L. R. *The Divinity of the Roman Emperor.* Middletown, Conn.: American Philological Association, 1931.

XIII PHILOSOPHY AND THE WORLD OF IDEAS

ADCOCK, F. E., *Roman Political Ideas and Practice.* Ann Arbor: University of Michigan Press, 1959.

ATHANASSIADI-FOWDEN, P., *Julian and Hellenism: An Intellectual Biography.* Oxford: Clarendon Press, 1981.

CHADWICK, H., *Boethius: The Consolations of Music, Logic, Theology, and Philosophy.* Oxford: Clarendon Press, 1981.

CLARKE, M. L., *History of Thought from Cicero to Marcus Aurelius.* New York: W. W. Norton, 1968.

EARL, D. C., *The Moral and Political Tradition of Rome.* London: Thames and Hudson, 1967.

GIBSON, M. (ed.), *Boethius: His Life, Thought, and Influence.* Oxford: Blackwell, 1981.

HARRIS, R. B. (ed.), *The Significance of Neoplatonism.* Albany: State University of New York Press, 1976.

LEWIS, N., *The Interpretation of Dreams and Portents.* Toronto and Sarasota: Samuel Stevens, Hakkert and Co., 1976.

NORTH, H. F., *From Myth to Icon: Reflections of Greek Ethical Doctrine in Literature and Art.* Ithaca and London: Cornell University Press, 1979.

WALLIS, R. T., *Neoplatonism.* London: Duckworth, 1972.

WIRSZUBSKI, C., *Libertas as a Political Idea at Rome during the Late Republic and Early Principate.* Cambridge: Cambridge University Press, 1950.

XIV SCIENCE AND ENGINEERING

HAMEY, L. A., and J. A. HAMEY, *The Roman Engineers.* Cambridge: Cambridge University Press, 1981.

HEALY, J. F., *Mining and Metallurgy in the Greek and Roman World.* London: Thames and Hudson, 1978.

HODSON, F. R. (ed.), *The Place of Astronomy in the Ancient World: A Joint Symposium of the Royal Society of the British Academy.* London: Oxford University Press, 1974.

LANDELS, J. G., *Engineering in the Ancient World*. London: Chatto and Windus, 1978.

SCARBOROUGH, J., *Roman Medicine*. London: Thames and Hudson, 1969.

STAHL, W. H., *Roman Science: Origins, Development, and Influence to the Late Middle Ages*. Madison: University of Wisconsin Press, 1962.

XV LAW

CROOK, J., *Law and Life of Rome*. Ithaca: Cornell University Press, 1967.

HONORÉ, T., *Emperors and Lawyers*. London: Duckworth, 1980.

JOLOWICZ, H. F., and B. NICHOLAS, *Historical Introduction to the Study of Roman Law* (3rd ed.). Cambridge: Cambridge University Press, 1972.

JONES, A. H. M., *The Criminal Courts of the Roman Republic and Principate*, ed. J. Crook. Oxford: Blackwell, 1972.

KUNKEL, W., *An Introduction to Roman Legal and Constitutional History* (2nd ed.), trans. J. M. Kelley. Oxford: Clarendon Press, 1973.

WATSON, A., *Law Making in the Later Roman Republic*. Oxford: Clarendon Press, 1974.

————, *The Making of the Civil Law*. Cambridge, Mass. and London: Harvard University Press, 1981.

XVI COINAGE

CARSON, R. A. G., *Principal Coins of the Romans* (3 vols.). London: British Museum Publications, 1978–1981.

CRAWFORD, M. H., *Roman Republican Coinage*. Cambridge: Cambridge University Press, 1974.

KENT, J. P. C., *Roman Coins*. London: Thames and Hudson, 1978.

SUTHERLAND, C. H. V., *Roman Coins*. London: Barrie and Jenkins, 1974.

XVII MILITARY AND NAVAL AFFAIRS

CASSON, L., *Ships and Seamanship in the Ancient World*. Princeton: Princeton University Press, 1971.

CONNOLLY, P. *Greece and Rome at War*. London: Macdonald Phoebus, 1981.

GABBA, E., *Republican Rome, the Army and Allies*, trans. P. J. Cuff. Oxford: Blackwell, 1977.

GARLAN, Y., *War in the Ancient World: A Social History*. London: Chatto and Windus, 1975.

LUTTWACK, E. N., *The Grand Strategy of the Roman Empire from the First Century A.D. to the Third*. Baltimore and London: Johns Hopkins University Press, 1976.

MAXFIELD, V. A., *The Military Decorations of the Roman Army*. Berkeley, Los Angeles, and London: University of California Press, 1981.

STARR, C. G., *The Roman Imperial Navy* (2nd ed.). New York: Barnes and Noble, 1959.

WARRY, J., *Warfare in the Classical World*. London: Salamander, 1980.

WATSON, G. R., *The Roman Soldier*. London: Thames and Hudson, 1969.

WEBSTER, G., *The Roman Imperial Army* (2nd ed.). London: A. and C. Black, 1979.

Index